# COMPUTERS in BUSINESS

Photo by Marty Chamberlain.

## ABOUT THE AUTHOR

Dr. Larry Long, a partner at Long and Associates, is a lecturer, author, columnist, consultant, and educator in the computer and information services fields. His many books cover a broad spectrum of MIS related topics from programming to MIS strategic planning. Dr. Long addresses a breadth of management, computer, and MIS issues in "Turnaround Time," a column that appears in *Computerworld* and sister affiliates throughout the world. He presents seminars to top corporate executives and to MIS personnel both in the United States and abroad and is a frequent lecturer at professional conferences. His consulting practice has enabled him to interact with all levels of management in virtually every major type of industry. Dr. Long has over a decade of classroom experience at the University of Oklahoma and at Lehigh University, where he continues to be an active lecturer. The author received his Ph.D., M.S., and B.S. degrees in Industrial Engineering at the University of Oklahoma and holds certification as a C.D.P. and a Professional Engineer.

# COMPUTERS
## in
# BUSINESS

## Larry Long

PRENTICE-HALL, INC., Englewood Cliffs, N.J. 07632

LIBRARY OF CONGRESS CATALOGING-IN-PUBLICATION DATA

Long, Larry E.
    Computers in business.

    Bibliography.
    Includes index.
        1. Business—Data processing.   2. BASIC
(Computer program language)   3. Information storage
and retrieval systems—Business.   4. Microcomputers.
5. Business—Computer-assisted instruction.   I. Title.
HF5548.2.L586     1987          650'.028'5          86–30412
ISBN   0–13–164294–4

Editorial/production supervision by Margaret Rizzi
Interior design and Cover design by Janet Schmid
Cover photograph: © Michael Furman Photographer, 1984
Interior Illustrations: Fine Line
Page layout by Gail Cocker
Manufacturing buyer: Ed O'Dougherty

Printed in the United States of America

10   9   8   7   6   5   4   3   2

ISBN   0-13-164294-4          025

Prentice-Hall International (UK) Limited, *London*
Prentice-Hall of Australia Pty. Limited, *Sydney*
Prentice-Hall Canada Inc., *Toronto*
Prentice-Hall Hispanoamericana, S.A., *Mexico*
Prentice-Hall of India Private Limited, *New Delhi*
Prentice-Hall of Japan, Inc., *Tokyo*
Prentice-Hall of Southeast Asia Pte. Ltd., *Singapore*
Editora Prentice-Hall do Brasil, Ltda., *Rio de Janeiro*

# OVERVIEW

# CONTENTS

# PART II

## INFORMATION SYSTEMS

# PART III

## HARDWARE AND COMMUNICATIONS

# PART IV

## SOFTWARE AND DATA MANAGEMENT

# PART V

## INFORMATION SYSTEMS DEVELOPMENT

# PART VI

## OPPORTUNITY
## AND CHALLENGE

## MICROCOMPUTER PRODUCTIVITY SOFTWARE 392

## BASIC PROGRAMMING 462

### LEARNING MODULE I BASIC Basics 464

### LEARNING MODULE II Getting Started in BASIC 474

# PREFACE TO THE STUDENT

The computer revolution is upon us and computers are now an integral part of doing business. The material in this text offers an overview of this exciting and challenging field. Once you have read and understood its content, you will be poised to play an active role in this revolution.

## Getting the Most from This Text

Every sentence, every piece of art, and every photo in the conceptual material in the chapters, the case studies, and the special skills sections on microcomputer productivity software and BASIC programming were selected with you in mind. The layout and organization of the text and its content are designed to be interesting; to present concepts in a logical and informative manner; and to provide a reference for the reinforcement of classroom lectures.

Reading a Chapter.   A good way to approach each chapter is to:

1. Look over the Student Learning Objectives, Focus of the Zimco Case Study, and the executive perspective in the chapter opener.
2. Turn to the back of the chapter and read the Summary and Important Terms.
3. Read over the major headings and subheadings and think how they are related.
4. Read the chapter and note the important terms that are in **boldface** type and in *italic* type.
5. Relate photos and photo captions to the textual material (a picture is worth a thousand words).
6. Go over the Summary Outline and Important Terms again, paying particular attention to the boldface terms.
7. Take the Self-Test. Reread those sections that you do not fully understand.
8. Answer the questions in the Review Exercises.
9. Read the Zimco Enterprises case study at the end of the chapter.
10. Relate the typical business circumstances and scenarios portrayed in the Zimco case study to the conceptual material presented in the chapters.

**11.** Answer the Discussion Questions at the end of the Zimco case study.

**The Case Study Approach.**  Throughout this text, computer, information processing, and business systems concepts are illustrated within the context of a running *case study* of a fictional company—*Zimco Enterprises.* The Zimco case study is intended to help you make the association between concept and practice. Each case study focuses on some facet of how computers are used at Zimco. The Zimco case study is presented in 13 topical segments, one for each of the 13 chapters of this book.

**The Rainbow.**  Color is used throughout the book to add another dimension to the learning process. There are many instances where concepts can be reinforced and made easier to understand with a spectrum of colors. I call this the *functional use of color.* For example, the spectrum of discussion items often runs: slow to fast, first to last, small to large, low to high, general to specific, and near to far.

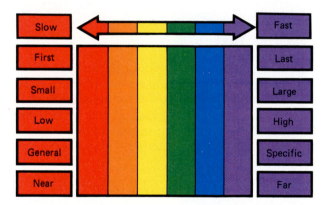

These spectrums are visually represented in the book by the spectrum of prismatic colors in the *rainbow.* Red, the first color in the rainbow, would represent such concepts as the first step, the smallest portion, or the general concept. Each increment in a conceptual spectrum is represented by the subsequent colors of the rainbow: orange, yellow, green, blue, and violet. The functional use of color is designed to help you relate the textual material to the illustrations.

**Learning Supplements.**  The text is supported by an optional *Study Guide/Lab Manual, software supplements,* and *videotapes.* Ask your instructor about the availability of these learning supplements.

## You, Computers, and the Future

Whether you are pursuing a career as an economist, an attorney, a financial advisor, an accountant, a computer specialist, a sales manager, a market analyst, or virtually any other career from shop supervisor to politician, the knowledge you gain from this course will ultimately prove beneficial. Keep your course notes and this book because they will provide valuable reference material in other courses and in your career. The chapter material addresses a broad range of computer concepts that pop up frequently in other classes, at work, and even at home. The skills sections on *Microcomputer Productivity Software* and *BASIC Programming* will prove valuable if you anticipate working with electronic spreadsheet, word processing, or data base software, or if you anticipate writing programs.

The career opportunities are there for those with an understanding and a working knowledge of computers. Less than 5% of the population is computer literate, yet employers of virtually every discipline are seeking to hire people who can take advantage of the computer revolution.

The use of computers for information processing is in its infancy. By taking this course, you are getting in on the ground floor. Each class you attend and each page you turn will present a learning experience that will let you advance one step closer to an understanding of how computers are making the world a better place in which to live and work. Most importantly, you will be gaining the knowledge necessary to become an active participant in what is the most exciting decade of technological innovation and change in recorded history.

# PREFACE TO THE INSTRUCTOR

As a business tool, most would agree that the computer has no equal. Only a few years ago, access to computers was limited to computer specialists—now, computers are commonplace in every business endeavor, from materials management on the shop-room floor to strategic planning in the board room. By 1990, virtually all office workers, from the clerical level to the strategic level, and many blue-collar workers will routinely interact with computer-based systems. To make the most effective use of this valuable business tool, these people will need a solid foundation of computer understanding. This book is about computers and their application within the context of the business environment.

*Computers in Business* is designed to enhance the learning experience by relating *concept* to *business practice*. Each of the thirteen chapters is followed by a case study. The running case study places the concepts that students have learned into a business perspective.

Two special skills sections provide students with support material for hands-on study in *microcomputer productivity software* (word processing, electronic spreadsheet, data base, graphics, idea processor, and communications) and *BASIC programming*.

## Intended Audience

*Computers in Business* and its comprehensive supplements package are designed to be used in support of an introductory computer course that is aimed primarily at business students. The syllabus of the "intro" course using this text could include one or more of the following areas of study: fundamental computer concepts, MIS topics, micro software (electronic spreadsheet, word processing, and so on), and/or structured BASIC Programming.

## Features

- Business-orientation. The focus of the text is "computers in business"—this is reflected in the design of the text and in all examples, including those in the skills sections on micro software and BASIC.
- Case Study. A comprehensive 13-part running case study helps students put what they have learned into a business perspective.

- **Executive Perspectives on Computers.** Chief executive officers and presidents of major corporations from a wide range of industry types offer their perspectives on computers, information processing, and the business endeavor.

- **Micro Software Tutorials.** A comprehensive skills section, "Microcomputer Productivity Software," contains business-oriented tutorials on word processing, electronic spreadsheet, data management, graphics, idea processor, and communications software packages.

- **Structured BASIC Programming.** A comprehensive skills section, "BASIC Programming," emphasizes structured programming techniques and business applications from the first example to the last.

- **Comprehensive Teaching/Learning Package.** *Computers in Business* is the cornerstone of a comprehensive teaching/learning package.

- **Presentation Style.** The entire book and all supplements project the excitement and potential of the field of computers in a manner that encourages the student to adopt a positive and aggressive attitude toward learning the material.

- **Functional Use of Color.** A "rainbow" of colors adds another dimension to the teaching and learning process. Color is used functionally to relate ideas to one another and to illustrate the textual material.

- **Readability.** All elements (case study, photos, art, and so on) are integrated with the textual material to create a reading and study rhythm that complements and reinforces learning.

- **Currency Plus.** The material is more than current, it's "current plus," anticipating the emergence and implementation of computer technology.

- **Flexibility.** The text is organized to permit maximum flexibility in the selection and assignment of material from the three business-oriented areas of computer study: computer/MIS concepts (Chapters 1–13), practical application (Zimco case study), and hands-on skills (micro software and BASIC programming skills sections).

## The Support Package

The components of the comprehensive teaching/learning package that accompanies *Computers in Business* are discussed briefly below.

**Instructor's Resource Manual with Test Item File.** The *Instructor's Resource Manual* contains (for each chapter): Student Learning Objectives, Teaching Hints (including the use of support software and the videotapes), Lecture Notes, Supplementary Material, Answers to End-Of-Chapter Review Exercises, and Exercises and Project Assignments. The lecture notes are in an outline format. Boldface terms, in-class discussion questions, and references to appropriate transparencies are embedded in the outline.

**Computer-based Test Generation.** The Hard copy of the *Test Item File* is included in the *Instructor's Resource Manual*. The test item file is organized by numbered section heads within each chapter to facilitate question selection and uniform coverage of the material. Three types of questions (true/fasle, multiple choice, and essay) are provided for each chapter and for the special skills sections. A computerized version of the *Test Item File* is available on *diskettes* for popular microcomputers. Instructors can select specific questions or request that the exams be generated randomly. Instructors can also edit test item file questions and add questions of their own. When printed, the exam is ready for duplication. An answer sheet is also produced.

**Study Guide and Lab Manual.** The student *Study Guide and Lab Manual* is organized to support the student learning objectives. Each chapter contains: Student Learning Objectives, Important Terms, Chapter Checkups and a Self-Test (by numbered section head and case study). It also has Checkups and Self-Tests on "Microcomputer Productivity Software" and "BASIC Programming." Each chapter makes reference to the "guide to the Videotape Series" that is included in the *Study Guide and Lab Manual.*

Each chapter and the special skills sections reference the Software Activities section of the *Study Guide and Lab Manual.* This section contains lab activities and questions to be used with SuperSoftware and The OUTLINER, two of the software supplements.

**Software Supplements.** Several *Software Supplements* accompany the text.

*For IBM PC and Compatibles.*

- SuperSoftware (*Computers in Business* version)
- The OUTLINER (fully-functional idea processor)
- Test Generator (exam preparation software distributed with test item file)
- Availability of other commercial software packages to be announced

*For the Apple IIe and IIc.*

- SuperSoftware (*Computers in Business* version)
- Test Generator (exam preparation software distributed with test item file)
- Availability of other commercial software packages to be announced

*Commercial Software Packages Available to Adopters.* A full range of productivity software, including popular packages like *dBASE III+* (Ashton-Tate) and *The OUTLINER*, will be available to adopters of *Computers in Business* as educational needs evolve. Your Prentice-Hall representative will have an up-to-date list of all productivity software that accompanies *Computers in Business*. Comprehensive keystroke-by-keystroke tutorials of these and other packages are contained in the *Study Guide/Lab Manual.*

*SuperSoftware.*  SuperSoftware, which contains 50-plus hours of hands-on lab activity for the IBM PC version (25-plus hours for the Apple version), is designed to instruct, intrigue, and motivate. The design philosophy of this supplement is to actively involve students through interactive communication with the computer. Graphic images and icons enhance the software's "user friendliness." The *Study Guide/Lab Manual* contains specific hands-on activities and exercises.

Scores of interesting and graphic programs, such as "Introduction to the PC," encourage students to become familiar with the computer. There are many business applications, such as airline reservation systems and home banking.

SuperSoftware interactively demonstrates micro software (word processing, data base, and so on) concepts through imaginative simulations.

The BASIC programming activities in SuperSoftware are organized by learning module. For each learning module, the software demonstrates the BASIC concepts introduced in that module, has debugging exercises, and contains the example programs in the book.

SuperSoftware is available for the IBM PC (and IBM PC compatibles). A substantial subset is available for the Apple IIe and IIc. Any institution adopting this book for educational use will be awarded a site license to use SuperSoftware.

Videotapes.  A *Videotape Series,* entitled "Computers and Information Processing," is comprised of eight videotapes that set the text in motion. Each video addresses a particular facet of the use and application of computers in business.

Transparencies (color acetates and black-line masters).  Seventy *Color Transparency Acetates* and 150 black-line *Transparency Masters,* which support material in the text and the *Instructor's Resource Manual,* are provided to facilitate in-class explanation.

Author "Hotline".  Professors and administrators of colleges adopting *Computers in Business* are encouraged to call Larry Long (215-866-5002) to discuss specific questions relating to the use of the text and its support package or to discuss more general questions relating to course organization or curricula planning.

## Organization: Computer/MIS Concepts, Practical Application, and Hands-on Skills

*Computers in Business* is organized to strike a balance between computer/MIS concepts, the practical application of these concepts, and hands-on skills. Most will agree that someone aspiring to employment in the business world must have a grasp of certain computer concepts, but those same people would insist that the student be able to put these concepts into a business perspective. The thirteen chapters and their accompanying case studies focus on the concepts and their application in the business environment. The special skills sections on *Microcomputer Productivity Software and BASIC Programming* enable the student to learn a computer skill. Acquiring a computer skill is important because it helps students gain confidence in computers and in their ability to effectively use them.

## Chapters and Case Studies

*Computer/MIS Concepts.*    The concepts portion of the text is presented in thirteen chapters and is divided into six parts.

- *Part I—The Computer Revolution* presents background information to help clarify the student's perspective on computers. Trends, fundamental concepts of a computer system, categories of computer usage, an overview of computer applications, and the history of computers are discussed.
- *Part II—Information Systems* expands on MIS concepts and applications of the computer by examining how computers are used in business and government.
- *Part III—Hardware and Communications* presents an overview of a variety of computer systems (micros, minis, mainframes), an operational description of computers and computer peripheral devices, and an introduction to data communications.
- *Part IV—Software and Data Management* presents a survey of programming languages, software concepts, and approaches to data manipulation and information retrieval.
- *Part V—Information Systems Development* includes a discussion of a systematic procedure by which information systems are conceived, designed, developed, implemented, and evaluated. The concepts and activity of programming are introduced in some detail.
- *Part VI—Opportunity and Challenge* presents the student with the breadth of career opportunities awaiting those with an interest in pursuing a computer-related career and for those with a computer knowledge who pursue other careers. A perspective is given on how computers will be used and how they will impact society in the future.

*The Zimco Enterprises Case Study.*    Computer and MIS concepts are illustrated within the context of a running case study of the fictional company—Zimco Enterprises. The Zimco case study is intended to help students make the association between concept and practice, and to provide you with a backdrop for discussing "real-life" applications of computer concepts. Each of the thirteen Zimco case studies (one for each chapter) focuses on some facet of how computers are used at Zimco.

The first case study provides background information on Zimco and introduces the concept of a business system. Five of the case studies are devoted to discussing and illustrating the data and information flow in and between the four components of Zimco's MIS (i.e., finance and accounting, personnel, operations, and sales and marketing). Other case studies present typical computer/MIS-related business scenarios:

micro acquisition policy, the computer network, MIS strategic planning, and so on.

To help the student get a better feel for computers in business, the case studies are written such that a *business need is articulated and a description of a computer-based solution* follows.

The Zimco case study, which is an integral part of the pedagogy of this text, makes it possible to use business examples to reinforce the concepts introduced in the chapter material and to introduce new concepts within the context of a business environment.

**The Hands-on Skills Sections.**    The *Microcomputer Productivity Software and BASIC Programming* sections are positioned at the end of the text so that these hands-on skills can be introduced at any point in the course.

*Microcomputer Productivity Software.*    The section on micro software provides generic yet detailed coverage of word processing, electronic spreadsheet (oriented to Lotus 1–2–3), data management (oriented to dBASE III), graphics, idea processor, and communications software. Once the student has read and understood the principles, the student can easily relate what has been learned to the specifics of your hardware/software environment. With a little practice, the student has a computer skill.

When used in conjunction with hands-on exposure to specific operational software packages, there is sufficient material and exercises in the *Microcomputer Productivity Software* section, Chapter 5 (Computer Systems—Micros, Minis, and Mainframes), Chapter 6 (Inside the Computer), Chapter 7 (Peripheral Devices— I/O and Data Storage), and the *software supplements* to support a complete course in the use and application of common business-oriented microcomputer software packages.

*BASIC Programming.*    The *BASIC Programming* section is divided into nine learning modules so that the student can systematically progress through increasingly sophisticated levels of understanding. If you only wish to expose the student to BASIC and assign a few simple programs, then Modules I, II, and III will suffice. Modules IV, V, and VI take the student up to an intermediate skill level. Modules VII and VIII introduce advanced features and techniques, and Module IX presents an overview and examples of the 1985 ANS BASIC.

The material and exercises in the BASIC Programming section, Chapter 12 (Programming Concepts), and SuperSoftware are sufficient to support a complete course in BASIC.

## Pedagogy

**Functional Use of Color.**    The design of this book is integral to its pedagogy. Rather than simply use color for splash, the four-color design was employed to add another dimension to the presentation of the material—the *functional use of color*. Throughout the book a "spectrum" of ideas is related to a spectrum of prismatic colors so that the student can more easily relate the ideas to one another and to illustrations and textual material. The functional use of color is explained and illustrated in more detail in the "Preface to the Student."

**Level of Detail.** Content material is presented at a *consistent level of detail*. Considerable thought was given by me and by your colleagues as to whether a topic should be covered and at what level it should be covered. Also, the reading level was carefully monitored to avoid the problems associated with inappropriate levels of presentation.

**Chapter Features.** Chapter organization is consistent throughout the text. The *chapter body* is prefaced by *Student Learning Objectives* and a *perspective on computers* contributed by some of the nation's top corporate executives. These quotes were prepared especially for this book and for the benefit of your students.

In the body of the chapter, all major headings are numbered (i.e., 1–1, 1–2, and so on) to facilitate selective assignment and to provide an easy cross reference to all related material in the supplements. Important terms and phrases are highlighted in **boldface** print. Words and phrases to be emphasized appear in *italics*. Informative photos, "Memory Bits" (outlines of key points), and cartoons are interspersed throughout each chapter.

Each chapter concludes with a *Summary Outline and Important Terms, Review Exercises* (concepts and discussion), and a *Self-Test*. A thematic business *Case Study* with *Discussion Questions* follows each chapter.

**Photos.** The *photographs* are an integral part of the text and the learning experience. Computers and the people who use them are more than words and diagrams—they are dynamic and alive. I wanted to proejct this energy to the student and one way to do this is through photos and their captions. Carefully selected photos with informative captions enhance the understanding of the core material and create a visually stimulating text. Photo placement is key to the design of the book. When I talk about an application, a situation, a computing device, or perhaps a person, there is usually a support photo and descriptive caption on the same page.

## Adherence to Curriculum Guidelines

**DPMA.** In accordance with the guidelines for the first course in the Data Processing Management Association (DPMA) Model Curriculum for Undergraduate Computer Information Systems, the material presented in this text provides "an introductory survey of the needs for and roles of computer information systems in business organizations." All subject areas listed in the DPMA curriculum guidelines for CS/86–1, "Introduction to Computer Information Systems," are covered in this book.

ACM.  The textual material provides a business-oriented survey of all major topics introduced in the Association for Computing Machinery (ACM) curricula recommendations for undergraduate and graduate programs in information systems.

AACSB.  The pedagogical objectives of this book are consistent with the guidelines set forth by the American Assembly of Collegiate Schools of Business (AACSB) for study in the computer field. The business student who studies the topics in this book will have a solid base of MIS and computer understanding that can be readily applied in the business environment.

## Acknowledgements

A book like *Computers in Business* is not merely written, it evolves as a product of need and as a reflection of the collective thinking of my colleagues in the academic and business communities. I would like to extend a special thank you for the valuable contribution made by those professors who reviewed a draft of the manuscript:

- Howard Aucoin, Suffolk University
- Bonnie Bailey, Morehead State University
- Greg Baur, Western Illinois University
- Chris Carter, Indiana Vocational Technical College
- William H. Charlton, Villanova University
- Bernadine Kolbert Esposito, University of Baltimore
- Marcia Frank, Owens Technical College
- William B. Jones, St. Clair College of Applied Arts and Technology
- Leo Kerklaan, McGill University
- William Knauth, Heald College
- Kenneth E. Martin, University of North Florida
- Jeff Mock, Diablo Valley College
- Malik Nazir, Illinois State University
- Beverly Oswalt, University of Central Arkansas
- Frank Relotto, DeVry Institute of Technology, Woodbridge
- Bob Roberts, University of Oklahoma
- Al Schroeder, Richland Community College.

The "perspectives" of fourteen of the nation's top executives open each chapter. I would like to thank them for their time, their "computers-in-business" insight, and for their commitment to the academic ideal:

- Mary Kay Ash, Chairman of the Board, Mary Kay Cosmetics, Inc.
- B. C. Bartlett, President, Deere & Company
- Glenn A. Cox, President and Chief Operating Officer, Phillips Petroleum Company
- John J. Cullinane, Chairman of the Board, Cullinet Software, Inc.
- R. W. Fleming, Chairman, Department of Administration, Mayo Clinic

- Irwin Greenberg, President and CEO, Hess's Department Stores, Inc.
- Gerald Greenwald, Chairman of Chrysler Motors, Chrysler Corporation
- John H. Johnson, Editor and Publisher, Johnson Publishing Company, Inc.
- Robert F. McDermott, Chairman, USAA
- John S. Scott, President and CEO, Richardson-Vicks Inc.
- Peter Scanlon, Chairman, Coopers & Lybrand
- Frederick W. Smith, Chairman, President and CEO, Federal Express Corporation
- Richard E. Snyder, Chairman and CEO, Simon & Schuster, Inc.

To the Prentice-Hall team, I wish to extend my heartfelt gratitude for their friendship and for their consistently superior support. My editor, Marcia Horton, is living proof that the 5 P's of programming can be applied to publishers as well, for she is delightfully *perceptive, patient, persistent, picky,* and *productive.* Jim Fegen, Executive Editor, is to be lauded for his always-available cache of publishing wisdom. Margaret Rizzi deserves a chorus of bravas for her artful coordination of the editorial and production process. Janet Schmid's innovative design and art program seems to set my lyrics to music. Dozens of Prentice-Hall professionals have made significant contributions to this project. A few of the many include Gail Cocker, Ed O'Dougherty, Carole Brown, Maureen Lopez, Jim Borghoff, Diana Ullman, Seth Reichlin, and Diane Penha.

A round of applause is also in order for the sales and marketing arms of Prentice-Hall. Several hundred sales managers and field reps throughout the world have proven time and again that they are enthusiastic and knowledgeable proponents of their products. The feedback that I receive from the field has had a profound impact on the content and pedagogy of this book. Marketing manager Niels Nielsen and his team created an informative and innovative campaign.

Literally hundreds of companies have in some way participated in the compilation of this book and its support package. A grateful academic community would like to thank them, one and all, for their ongoing commitment to education.

Marty Chamberlain, co-author of the *Study Guide/Lab Manual,* has etched his flair for the extraoridinarie throughout the teaching/learning package.

Besides co-authoring the *Study Guide/Lab Manual,* my wife Nancy has added her Midas touch to virtually every facet of this project. I am indeed fortunate to share my life and my work with this beautiful person.

## Dedication

For their commitment to and pursuit of publishing excellence, I am honored to dedicate this book to the professionals at Prentice-Hall.

Larry Long, Ph.D.

# COMPUTERS
## in
# BUSINESS

# PART 1 THE COMPUTER REVOLUTION

At this moment, some 2000 computers—from IBM PCs to the mammoth Cray-1M—are meeting Phillips' every business need from word processing to worldwide inventory control. Here's a glimpse of what computers are doing for us at some 250 locations worldwide:

Offshore California computers are helping us find new oil and gas reserves by giving us a three-dimensional look at rock formations beneath the ocean floor.

In St. Louis, Dallas, and other major metropolitan areas, computers are enabling motorists to pay quickly and conveniently for Phillips gasoline purchases with credit card and cash acceptors located at the pumps.

And at our headquarters in Bartlesville, Oklahoma, computers are helping us keep track of millions of pieces of equipment—from crude oil tankers in the North Sea to pipe wrenches in Odessa, Texas.

Phillips may not be in the computer business, but there's no doubt in my mind that without computers, we'd have a difficult time doing business at all.

Glenn A. Cox
President and Chief Operating Officer
Phillips Petroleum Company

# The World of Computers

CHAPTER

1

## STUDENT LEARNING OBJECTIVES

- To grasp the scope of computer understanding needed by someone in the business community.
- To distinguish between data and information.
- To contrast the function and purpose of an information services department to that of an information center.
- To understand the relationship between the levels of the hierarchy of data organization.
- To describe the fundamental components and the operational capabilities of a computer system.
- To identify and describe uses of the computer.
- To describe the general function and purpose of the microcomputer productivity tools: word processing, electronic spreadsheet, data management, graphics, idea processors, and communications.

## FOCUS OF ZIMCO CASE STUDY

- Zimco's background, function, and organization.

**THE INFORMATION SOCIETY** _____

**From Dirt to Data.** Two centuries ago, 90 of every 100 people worked to produce food. As people became more efficient in the production of food, an _agrarian society_ gave way to the growth of an _industrial society_. Our transition to an industrial society was slow and marked with social strife. Each new technological innovation had a profound impact. For example, the steam shovel did the work of 100 men.

We know now that the industrial revolution shortened the work-week, provided greater opportunities for employment, and generally improved the quality of life for all. But at the time, no argument could convince any of the 100 men who lost their jobs to a steam shovel that the industrial revolution would eventually improve their plight in life.

Today, two people produce enough food for the other 98 and we are in the middle of a transition from an _industrial society_ to an _information society_. The trend in today's offices and factories is paralleling that of the farm 200 years earlier. If history repeats itself—and most experts believe that it will—automation will continue to reduce the number of workers needed to accomplish unskilled and semiskilled tasks. Also, automation will provide workers with valuable information that will help them to better do their jobs.

Computers have become as much a part of the office as the telephone. This company conducts opinion surveys on everything from product recognition to political preference. These pollsters rely on computers to help collect, store, and analyze the data.
(Courtesy Burroughs Corporation)

In the information society, workers will focus their energies on providing a myriad of information services. Today, it is a bit difficult to imagine a society that may become desperately dependent on certain information services. But let's put this concern into its proper perspective. Can you imagine our nineteenth-century forefathers becoming desperately dependent on the speed of air travel or hair dryers? Who among us would give up our hair dryer!

**The Computer Revolution.** The driving force behind our transition to an information society is the *computer*. The computer and the emerging information society are having a profound impact on the business community. Retailers are making it possible for us to do more shopping from the comfort of our own homes. Financial analysts are consulting their computer "partner" before advising a client on the best investment strategy. Some factories have no windows or lights—computer-controlled robots don't need to see!

The *computer revolution* is upon us. This unprecedented technical revolution has made computers a *part of life*. With the rapid growth in the number and variety of computer applications, they are rapidly becoming a *way of life*.

In our private lives, computers may speed the checkout process at supermarkets, enable 24-hour banking, provide up-to-the-minute weather information, and, of course, entertain us with video games. And if that is not enough, computers are the culprits behind our "conversations" with elevators, automobiles, and vending machines.

In our professional lives, the computer is an integral tool in the performance of many jobs. Retailers query their computer systems to determine which products are selling and which are not. Managers

Color computer graphics are used by architects to produce realistic interior and exterior models. This graphic three-dimensional model of an office building's lobby even depicts shadows.
(Intergraph Corporation)

The precise, untiring movement of computer-controlled industrial robots helps assure quality in the assembly of everything from electrical components to automobiles. Here, a robot applies spot welds.
(TRW Inc.)

With a personal computer, you are the boss! Computing capabilities similar to those of much larger computers are within an arm's reach. This commercial real estate executive uses his personal computer to investigate alternative methods of financing.
(Copyright 1984 GTE Telenet Communications Corporation)

use word processing systems to compose memos and to check spelling, grammar, and style. Geologists rely on an "expert" computer system for guidance in the quest for minerals. Bankers examine up-to-the-minute securities information from their computer terminals.

The overwhelming majority of people believe that computers enhance the quality of life. The people of the world have become committed to a better way of life through computers, and it is unlikely that the momentum toward this goal will change. It is our responsibility to ensure that this inevitable evolution of computer technology is directed to the benefit of society.

## 1-2   LEARNING ABOUT COMPUTERS

**Cyberphobia.**   Computers are synonymous with change, and any type of change is usually met with some resistance. We can attribute much of this resistance to a lack of knowledge about computers and, perhaps, to a fear of the unknown. People seem to perceive computers as mystical. It is human nature to fear that which we don't understand, be it the Extra Terrestrial or computers. Less than 5 percent of the population is comfortable enough with computers to deem themselves "computer literate." Society will remain "in transition" from an industrial to an information society until the majority of workers are computer literate. That may not happen until the mid-1990s.

Fear of the computer is so widespread that psychologists have created a name for it: **cyberphobia.** Cyberphobia is the irrational fear of, and aversion to, computers. In truth, computers are merely machines and don't merit being the focus of such fear. If you are a cyberphobic, you will soon see that your fears are unfounded.

**The Computer Adventure.**   A decade ago, anyone pursuing a career in business was content to leave computers to computer professionals. Either you were a computer professional who had dedicated years of study to computers, or you were not. Well, things have changed. Computers are now an integral part of the learning experience of anyone pursuing a career in business. By the time you complete this course, you will have an understanding of computers that will enable you to be an active and effective participant in a business community that is undergoing a rapid transition to an information society. You should

1. Feel comfortable in the use and operation of a computer system
2. Be able to make the computer work for you through judicious development *or* use of **software** ("Software" refers collectively to a set of machine-readable instructions, called **programs,** that cause the computer to perform desired functions.)
3. Be able to interact with the computer—that is, generate input to the computer and interpret output from the computer
4. Understand the impact of computers on society, now and in the future
5. Be an intelligent consumer of computer-related products and services

While on the road, this accounting manager composed a memo on his portable personal computer, then he transmitted it to the headquarters office for immediate distribution to his staff. (Photo supplied courtesy of Epson America)

You are about to embark on an emotional and intellectual *journey* that will stimulate your imagination, challenge your every resource from physical dexterity to intellect, and perhaps, alter your sense of perspective. Learning about computers is more than just education—it's an adventure. Enjoy your journey into the world of computers!

## 1–3   COMPUTERS ARE FOR EVERYONE

**Business Computer Systems in "The Old Days."**   In "the old days," that is, during the 1950s, 1960s, and even into the 1970s, business computer systems were designed such that a computer professional served as a middleperson between the **end user** and the computer system. End users, or simply **users,** are blue- and white-collar workers who use the computer to do their jobs better. In the past, plant supervisors, financial directors, and marketing managers would relate their information needs to computer professionals, such as programmers or systems analysts, who would then work with the computer system to generate the needed information.

In "the old days," the **turnaround time,** or elapsed time between the submission of a request for information and the distribution of the results, could be at least a week or as much as a month. The resulting information was often obsolete or of little value by the time it reached the manager.

Two centuries ago, our agrarian society began to evolve into an industrial society. Today, we are rapidly transitioning to an information society where "knowledge" workers depend on computer-generated information to accomplish their jobs. (AT&T Information Systems)

As oil companies automate the distribution of gasoline and the handling of credit transactions, service station owners, attendants, and customers are learning to use computers.
(Phillips Petroleum Company)

**Business Computer Systems Today.** The *timeliness of information* is critical in today's fast-paced business world. Managers can't wait for the information that they need. They want it now, not next week or next month. In response to managers' requests for more timely information, computer systems are now designed to be *interactive*. **Interactive computer systems** eliminate the need to interact directly with a middleperson (the computer professional) and permit users to communicate directly with the computer system. This interactive mode of operation gives managers the flexibility to analyze the results of one query, then make subsequent queries based on more information.

Today, computers and software are being designed to be **user friendly.** Being user friendly means that someone with a fundamental knowledge of and exposure to computers can make effective use of the computer and its software. Ten years ago, such was not the case. If you didn't have a computer science degree and the mental agility of a wizard, you were out of luck.

**Users, Professionals, and Hackers.** By the early 1990s, the average white-collar worker will spend 50 percent of each working day interacting with a computer system. Many blue-collar workers will spend up to 100 percent of their day interacting with some kind of computer-based system. Recognizing the inevitable emergence of the information society, more and more users are taking a keen interest in computers and are educating themselves so that they will be able to write their own programs and/or feel comfortable with user-friendly software.

Many of these users are **hackers,** a name given to computer enthusiasts who use the computer as a source of enjoyment as well as a business tool. Hackers all over the country have formed clubs and associations to share interesting computer discoveries. Hackers are old and young, manager and laborer, ecologist and geologist, all sharing a commond bond: to explore the seemingly infinite capabilities of their computers. On occasion, hackers have carried their enthusiasm for computers beyond the limits of the law. It is perfectly legal for willing hackers to share ideas and public-domain data files, but it is not legal for hackers to use their computers to tap into sensitive business and government data bases. Unauthorized access to data bases is discussed in more detail in Chapter 3, "Management Information Systems."

## 1–4　SUPPORTING A COMPANY'S INFORMATION NEEDS

### The Information Services Department

Most companies have a computer center and the personnel to support their **information systems.** An information system is a computer-based system that provides data processing capability and information for making decisions. This combination of computing equipment (called **hardware**), the software that instructs the computers what to do, and the people who run the computers and develop the software is often

These programmers and systems analysts work in an information systems
department for a medical instruments manufacturer. Their current project is a
human resources information system that will help managers more effectively
use the skills of their workers.
(Microdata Corporation)

referred to as the *information services department* or the *data processing (DP) department*.

The information services department handles the organization's
information needs in the same way that the finance department handles
the organization's money needs. The department provides data processing and information-related services to virtually every business area.
For example, programmers and systems analysts might work with plant
managers and engineers to develop a computer-based production and
inventory-control system. Jobs and employment opportunities in an
information services department are discussed in the case study following Chapter 2.

## The Information Center

An **information center** is a "hands-on" facility in which computing resources are made available to various user groups. Users come to an
information center because they know that they can find the computing
resources and technical support that they need to help with their personal short-term business information and computing needs. The computing resources might include:

- *Workstations* that enable users to interact directly with the busi-
  ness's central computer system
- *Microcomputers* for "personal" or stand-alone computing
- *Printers* for **hard copy,** or printed output
- *Plotters* for preparation of presentation graphics

The information center would also have a variety of software packages available for use, such as electronic spreadsheet, word processing, data management, and graphics. The center might also provide decision support software and the capability to write programs. All of these hardware and software tools are discussed in detail in later chapters.

Perhaps the most important component of an information center is the people who assist users. These people, called **information center specialists,** conduct training sessions, answer questions, and generally *help users to help themselves*.

## 1–5   DATA MANAGEMENT: A PREVIEW

### Data versus Information

Up to now we have talked quite a bit about information, but little about the origin of information—data. **Data** (the plural of *datum*) are the raw material from which information is derived. **Information** is comprised of data that have been collected and processed into a meaningful form.

We routinely deal with the concepts of data and information in our everyday experiences. We use data to produce information that will help us make decisions. For example, when we wake up in the morning we collect two pieces of data. We look at the time, then recall from our memory the time when our first class begins, or when we are to be at work. Then we subtract the current time from the starting time of the class (or work). This mental computation provides information on how much time we have to get ready and go. Based on this information, we make a decision to hurry up or to relax and take it easy.

We produce information from data to help us to make decisions for thousands of situations each day. In many ways, the contents of this book are just an extension of concepts with which you are already familiar.

### The Hierarchy of Data Organization: An Overview

So that you can better appreciate discussions of hardware and information systems, you will need a fundamental understanding of how data are organized in a computer system. This section contains a *brief overview* of the *hierarchy of data organization* (see Figure 1–1). An in-depth treatment of the topic is provided in Chapter 10, "Data Organization and File Processing." Although you may not be familiar with this terminology, you are probably familiar with the concept of the hierarchy of data organization.

In Chapter 6, "Inside the Computer," we introduce how computers store data as 1s and 0s, or binary digits, called **bits.** But for now it is enough to say that the bit is the lowest level of the hierarchy of data organization. A series of *bits* can be configured to represent a *character*. For example, the bit configurations of 01000001 and 01000010 represent the characters A and B inside a computer (see Figure 1–1).

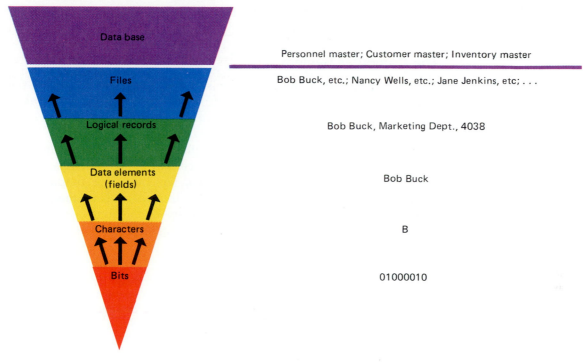

FIGURE 1–1
The Hierarchy of Data Organization

At the next level of the hierarchy, characters are combined to represent the value of a **data element.** The data element, sometimes called a **field,** is the smallest logical unit of data. Some examples are name, employee number, and marital status. Related data elements are then grouped to form **logical records,** or simply **records.** In Figure 1–1, for example, the data elements of name, department, and telephone extension number are grouped to form the employee record.

At the fourth level of the hierarchy, records with the same data elements are combined to form a **file.** In Figure 1–1, the file contains the name, department, telephone extension number, and other employee data for all employees in the company. This permanent source of employee data is called a **master file. A transaction file** might contain the data elements of name and a *new* telephone extension number. Compare the personnel master file to a transaction file that is used to periodically update the data on a master file.

A **data base,** the next level in the hierarchy, contains several different record types and defines their relationships. We will wait until Chapter 10, "Data Organization and File Processing," to discuss more about data base concepts. At that time you will have a better understanding of hardware, software, and uses of data. For now, just keep in mind that a data base is an organization's data resource for all computer-based information.

Supervisors at this plant rely on computers to help them schedule the maintenance and repair of diesel engines. The system lets supervisors make inquiries to a data base about the status of any diesel engine at the plant.
(Santa Fe Industries)

## 1–6   UNCOVERING THE "MYSTERY" OF COMPUTERS

### The Computer System

Technically speaking, the computer is any counting device. But in the context of modern technology, we'll define the **computer** as *an electronic device capable of interpreting and executing programmed commands for input, output, computation,* and *logic operations*.

Computers may be technically complex, but they are conceptually simple. The computer, also called a **processor,** is the "intelligence" of a **computer system.** A computer system has only four fundamental components—*input*, *processing*, *output*, and *storage*. Note that a computer system (not a computer) is made up of the four components. The actual computer is the processing component and is combined

**FIGURE 1–2**
**The Four Fundamental Components of a Microcomputer System**
In a microcomputer system, the storage and processing components are often contained in the same physical unit. In the illustration, the diskette storage medium is inserted into the unit that contains the processor.

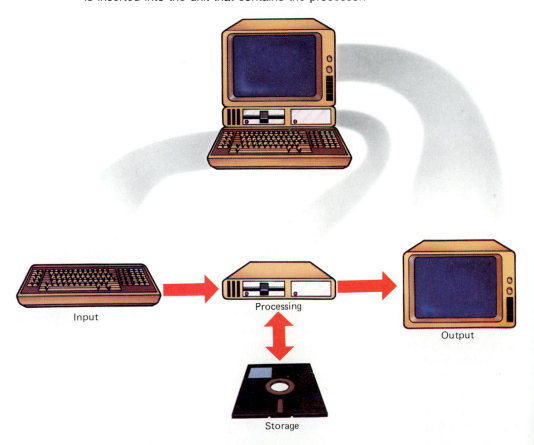

Input

Processing

Output

Storage

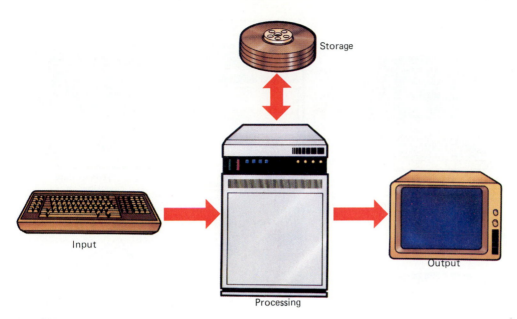

**FIGURE 1–3**
**The Four Fundamental Components of a Computer System**
In larger computer systems, each of the four components is contained in a
separate physical unit.

with the other three to form a *computer system* (see Figures 1–2 and
1–3).

The relationship of data to a computer system is best explained
by an analogy to gasoline and an automobile. Data are to a computer
system as gas is to a car. Data provide the fuel for a computer system.
A computer system without data is like a car with an empty gas tank:
no gas, no go; no data, no information.

## How a Business Computer System Works

The payroll system in Figure 1–4 illustrates how data are entered and
how the four computer system components interact to produce information (a "year-to-date overtime report") and the payroll checks. The
hours-worked data are *input* to the system and are *stored* on the personnel master file. Remember, the storage component of a computer
system stores data, not information!

The payroll checks are produced when the *processing* component,
or the computer, executes a program. In this example, the employee
record is recalled from storage, and the pay amount is calculated. The
*output* is the printed payroll checks. Other programs extract data from
the personnel master file to produce a year-to-date overtime report
and any other information that might help in the management decision-
making process.

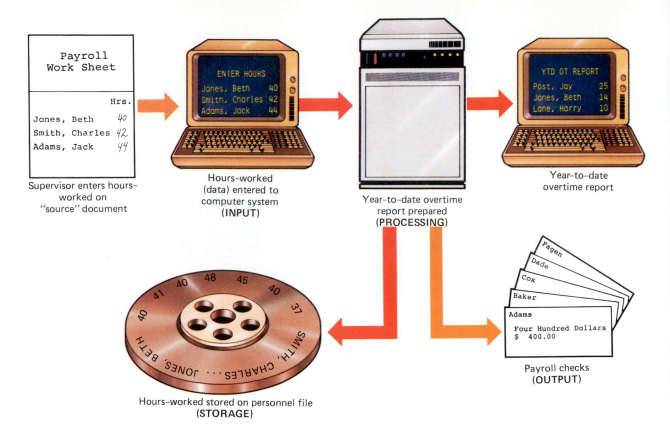

**FIGURE 1–4**
**Payroll System**
This payroll system illustrates input, storage, processing,
and output.

## The Hardware

In the payroll example, data are entered (input) on a **video display terminal** (VDT). A video display terminal, also called a **workstation,** is a device with a typewriterlike **keyboard** for input and a televisionlike (video) screen, called a **monitor,** for output. The payroll checks are then output on a device called a **printer.** Data are stored for later recall on **magnetic disk.** There are a wide variety of input/output (I/O) and storage devices. The variety of hardware devices that make up a computer system are discussed in detail in Part II, "Hardware and Communications."

The principles discussed above apply equally to **microcomputers** (Figure 1–2), also called **personal computers,** and **mainframe computers** (Figures 1–3 and 1–4). Each has the four components and each uses data to produce information in a similar manner. The difference is that personal computers are more limited in their capabilities and are designed primarily for use by *one person* at a time. Mainframe computers can service *many users*, perhaps every manager in the company, all at once. In Chapter 5 we discuss microcomputers and mainframe computers in detail.

## What Can a Computer Do?

Remember from our previous discussion that the *input/output* and *data storage* hardware components are "configured" with the *processing* component (the computer) to make up a computer system (see Figures 1–2 and 1–3). Let's discuss the operational capabilities of a computer system just a bit further.

Input/Output Operations.   The computer *reads* from input and storage devices. The computer *writes* to output and storage devices. Before data can be processed, they must be "read" from an input device or data storage device. Input data are usually entered by an operator on a video display terminal (VDT) or retrieved from a data storage device, such as a magnetic disk drive. Once data have been processed, they are "written" to an output device, such as a printer, or to a data storage device.

Input/output (I/O) operations are illustrated in the payroll system example in Figure 1–4. Hours-worked data are entered and "read" into the computer system. These data are "written" to magnetic disk storage for recall at a later date.

Processing Operations.   The computer is totally objective. That is, any two computers instructed to perform the same operation will arrive at the same result. This is because the computer can perform only *computation* and *logic operations.*

The computational capabilities of the computer include adding, subtracting, multiplying, and dividing. Logic capability permits the computer to make comparisons between numbers and between words, then, based on the result of the comparison, perform appropriate functions. In the payroll system example of (Figure 1–4), the computer calculates the gross pay in a computation operation (e.g., 40 hours at $15/hour = $600). In a logic operation, the computer compares the number of hours worked to 40 to determine the number of "overtime" hours that an employee works during a given week. If the hours-worked figure is greater than or equal to 40, say 42, the difference (2 hours) is credited as overtime and paid at "time and a half."

## Computer System Capabilities

In a nutshell, computers are fast, accurate, and reliable; they don't forget anything; and they don't complain. Now for the details.

Speed.   The smallest unit of time in the human experience is, realistically, the second. With the second as the only means of comparison, it is difficult for us to comprehend the time scale of computers. Even the operations (the execution of an instruction) for personal computers are measured in thousandths of a second, or **milliseconds.** Operations

With computers handling more and more routine tasks, we have more time to be creative. For this product marketing manager, time-consuming calculations are handled by the computer, thereby giving her more time to create the most effective promotional campaign. Her personal computer has a keyboard for input and both a video display terminal and a printer for output.
(Honeywell, Inc.)

| MEMORY BITS |
| --- |
| **COMPUTER OPERATIONS** |
| ■ Input/output<br>　　Read<br>　　Write |
| ■ Processing<br>　　Computation<br>　　Logic |

A computer's speed is measured in millions of instructions per second, or MIPS. An instruction may be to add two numbers or to compare two numbers. The computer in this public works consulting firm can execute more instructions in one second than an average person will take steps in a lifetime.
(Control Data Corporation)

for larger processors are measured in **microseconds, nanoseconds,** and **picoseconds** (one millionth, one billionth, and one trillionth of a second, respectively). To give you a feeling for the speed of processors, a beam of light travels down the length of this page in about 1 nanosecond!

Accuracy.   You may work for years before experiencing a system error, such as an updating of the wrong record or an incorrect addition. Errors do occur in computer-based information systems, but precious few can be directly attributed to the computer system. The vast majority of these errors can be traced to a program logic error, a procedural error, or erroneous data. These are *human errors*. Hardware errors are usually detected and corrected by the computer system itself.

Reliability.   Computer systems are particularly adept at repetitive tasks. They don't take sick days and coffee breaks, and they seldom complain. Anything below 99.9 percent *uptime* is usually unacceptable. Unfortunately, *downtime* sometimes occurs at the most inconvenient times. For some companies, any downtime is unacceptable. For example, automobile manufacturers must have their computers operational at all times. If the computers fail in an automobile assembly plant, the line is shut down and thousands of people become idle. These companies provide *backup* computers that take over if the main computers fail.

Memory Capability.   Computer systems have total and instant recall of data and an almost unlimited capacity to store these data. A typical mainframe computer system will have many billions of characters, and perhaps thousands of graphic images, stored and available for instant recall. To give you a benchmark for comparison, this book contains approximately 1,500,000 characters.

## 1–7   HOW DO WE USE COMPUTERS?

For the purpose of this discussion, we will classify the uses of computers into six general categories: *information systems/data processing, personal computing, science and research, process control, education,* and *artificial intelligence.* Figure 1–5 shows how the sum total of existing computer capacity is apportioned to each of these general categories. In the years ahead, look for personal computing, process control, education, and artificial intelligence to grow rapidly and become larger shares of the computer "pie."

**FIGURE 1–5**
**The Way We Use Computers**
This pie chart is an estimate of how existing computer capacity is distributed among the general categories of computer usage.

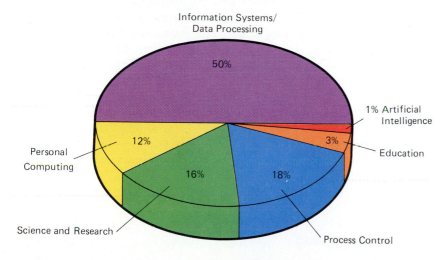

Information Systems/
Data Processing

50%

1% Artificial
Intelligence

3%

Education

Personal
Computing

12%

16%

18%

Science and Research

Process Control

While meeting with a customer, this pharmaceutical field sales representative uses a workstation that is linked to the company's central computer center to request up-to-the-minute pricing information and to enter orders. The customer is even given a copy of the order before the representative leaves.
(Copyright 1984 GTE Telenet Communications Corporation)

## Information Systems/Data Processing

The bulk of existing computer power is dedicated to *information systems* and *data processing*. This category includes all uses of computers for business purposes. Example applications include payroll systems, airline reservation systems, student registration systems, hospital patient billing systems, and countless others.

To give you a feeling for how computers help to meet the data processing and information needs in a typical manufacturing company, each chapter in this text is followed by a case study of a fictional company—*Zimco Enterprises*. Each case study focuses on some facet of how computers are used at Zimco. In Zimco's *Finance and Accounting Division*, all financial and accounting systems are computerized. Zimco's *Operations Division* uses information systems for such applications as inventory control and production scheduling. As competition becomes keener, Zimco's *Sales and Marketing Division* has turned to Zimco's *Computer and Information Services Division* for assistance in fine tuning the marketing effort. The *Personnel Division* has automated the basic personnel functions of employment history and career planning. Zimco's *headquarters staff* and top management routinely make "what if" inquiries, such as "What *if* the advertising budget were increased by 20 percent, how might sales be affected?"

The Zimco case study following Chapter 2 contains an overview of Zimco's business systems. Specific information systems are discussed in subsequent chapters. The influence of computer information systems is just as pervasive in hospitals, government agencies, or colleges. A wide variety of information systems for virtually every industry are described and discussed throughout the book.

## Personal Computing

Individuals and companies are purchasing small, inexpensive microcomputers, also called personal computers, for a variety of business and domestic applications. A microcomputer system, or a **micro** for short, easily sits on a desktop and can be controlled by one person. The growth of this general area, called **personal computing,** has surpassed even the most adventurous forecasts of the mid-1970s. By 1990, personal computers will be as commonplace as telephones are now, both at home and at work. Even now, personal computers actually outnumber mainframe computers. But, of course, a single mainframe computer may have the processing capacity of 1000 personal computers.

Microcomputers have become part of the scenery in every medical clinic. This clinic's business manager is using a microcomputer to graphically highlight revenues generated from various testing procedures.
(Texas Instruments, Inc.)

**Domestic Applications for Personal Computing.** A variety of domestic and business applications form the foundation of personal computing. Domestic applications include some of the following: maintaining an up-to-date asset inventory of household items; storing names and addresses for a personal mailing list; maintaining records for, preparing, and sending income tax returns; creating and monitoring a household budget; keeping an appointment and social calendar; handling household finances (e.g., checkbook balancing, paying of bills, coupon refunding); writing letters; education; and of course, entertainment. You can purchase software for all of these applications, and you can probably obtain software for your special interest, whether it be astrology, charting biorhythms, composing music, or dieting.

**Business Applications for Personal Computing.** Of course, virtually any business application (e.g., payroll, sales analysis) discussed in this book is supported on a personal computer, but the most popular business use of personal computers is with *"productivity" software*. Microcomputer-based productivity software is a series of commercially available programs that can help people in the business community to save time and obtain information they need to make more informed decisions. These programs, collectively known as *productivity software*, are the foundation of personal computing in the business world. These applications include *word processing*, *electronic spreadsheets*, *data management*, *graphics*, *idea processing*, and *communications*. The *function* of each of these applications is described below. The *concepts* and *use* of these productivity tools are described in considerable detail in a special skills section, called *Microcomputer Productivity Software*, that follows Chapter 13.

*Word Processing.* **Word processing** is using the computer to enter text, to store it on magnetic storage media, to manipulate it in preparation for output, and to produce a hard copy. Numerous applications involve written communications: letters, reports, memos, and so on. As well as being one of the microcomputer productivity tools, word processing is also part of a set of applications collectively referred to as *office automation*. Office automation applications are discussed in detail in the Zimco case study following Chapter 4.

If you use word processing to prepare your reports, you will only have to key in the initial draft. Revisions and corrections can be made on the disk before the report is printed in final form. If you forgot a word or need to add a paragraph, you do not have to retype a page or, in the worst case, the whole report. For example, the original text for this book was keyed in only once on a microcomputer. Editorial changes (all 418,602 of them) were then entered by the author on a keyboard before the final manuscript was submitted to the publisher.

*Electronic Spreadsheet.* A popular microcomputer application is the **electronic spreadsheet.** The spreadsheet contains a tabular structure of rows and columns. The user, instead of writing the entries manually in the rows and columns of a worksheet, has them stored in an "electronic" data base, which can contain thousands of entries. Obviously, all entries in a large matrix cannot be displayed at the same time, so

With word processing systems, changes to reports and letters can be made quickly and easily.
(Photo courtesy of Hewlett-Packard Company)

A buyer for a furniture store tracks actual versus planned sales for various classes of furniture with an electronic spreadsheet. This microcomputer permits voice, as well as keyboard, input. (Texas Instruments, Inc.)

the data are displayed in **windows,** or parts of the total matrix. The user can display one or several windows on the screen at one time.

The applications of electronic spreadsheets are endless. Think of anything that has rows and columns. For example, spreadsheet software is often used to work with profit and loss statements, sales forecasts, and budget summaries.

The intersection of a row and column is called a *cell* and is referenced by its position within the matrix. In a profit and loss statement, for example, the entry in cell A4 (the first or A column, row 4) might be "Cost of Goods Sold," and the entry in cell B4 might be "$30,780." Columns are lettered and rows numbered. Cell entries can be either words or numbers.

Once the data are entered for a profit and loss statement, an electronic spreadsheet permits the user to manipulate and analyze the data. For example, the user can "electronically" increase sales by 20 percent per year and the cost of goods sold by 10 percent per year, then see how these changes affect profit over the next three years.

*Data Management.* *Data management* software, also called *database* software, permits the user to create and maintain a data base, and also to extract information from the data base. "Database," as one word, is an alternative terminology for data management software. "Data base," as two words, refers to the highest level of the hierarchy of data organization (see Figure 1–1). To minimize confusion, we will use data management instead of data base for references to the software. With data management software, the user first identifies the format of the data, then designs a display screen format that will permit interactive entry and revision of the data. Once it is part of the data base, a record can be deleted or changed. The user can also retrieve and summarize data, based on certain criteria (e.g., list all salespersons over quota for July). Also, data can be sorted for display in a variety of formats (e.g., listing salespersons by total sales, or listing them alphabetically).

*Graphics.*   *Graphics* software enables you to create a variety of presentation graphics based on data in a data base or a spreadsheet. These graphics take the form of bar charts, pie charts, and line charts.

   A pie chart is easily produced from a spreadsheet containing regional sales data. Each slice of the "pie" might depict the sales for each region as a percentage of total sales. The slices are in proportion. For example, if sales in the northeast region are $10 million and sales in the southwest region $5 million, the northeast region slice is shown twice the size of that of the southwest region.

*Idea Processors.*   An idea processor is a productivity tool that allows you to organize your thoughts and ideas. Such software can be used for brainstorming, outlining project activities, developing speeches and presentations, compiling notes for meetings and seminars, and a myriad of other uses. Idea processors let you work with one idea at a time within a hierarchy of other ideas such that you can easily organize and reorganize your ideas. When you use an idea processor, you can focus your attention on the thought process by letting the computer help with the task of documenting your ideas.

*Communications.*   *Communications* software is available for micros that, in essence, makes the micro a video display terminal. But a micro can do more than a terminal can. It not only can transmit and receive data from a remote computer, it can process and store data as well. Communications software automatically "dials-up" the desired remote computer, perhaps your company's central computer system, then it "logs-on" (establishes a communications link with the remote computer, usually via a telephone line). Once on-line, you can communicate with the remote computer or request that certain data be transmitted to your micro so that you can work with the data using the micro as a stand-alone computer.

*Productivity Software Summary.*   One of the beauties of productivity software is that data can be passed between each of the tools. For example, you can move easily between entering data with data management software and manipulating the data with electronic spreadsheet software. Data can be passed freely between the various pieces of software. For example, a spreadsheet can be created from a data base. The data can be analyzed by the spreadsheet software and displayed as a bar chart with the graphics software. A paragraph of explanation can be added using word processing. Then both the chart and the explanation can be transmitted with the communications software to a mainframe computer for distribution to other departments. This type of transmission (micro-to-another-computer) is called **uploading.** The reverse is called **downloading.**

Information Services.   Personal computers, or **PCs,** are normally used as stand-alone computer systems, but as we have seen from earlier discussions, they can also double as remote terminals. This dual-function capability provides you with the flexibility to work with the PC as a stand-alone system or to link with a larger computer and take advantage of its increased capacity. With a PC, you have a world of

| MEMORY BITS |
|---|
| **PRODUCTIVITY SOFTWARE** |
| ■ Word processing |
| ■ Electronic spreadsheet |
| ■ Data management |
| ■ Graphics |
| ■ Idea processor |
| ■ Communications |

An information network includes such services as news and electronic shopping.
(Copyright Viewdata Corporation of America 1984)

information at your fingertips. The personal computer can be used in conjunction with the telephone system to transmit data to and receive data from an **information network.**

A growing trend among personal computer enthusiasts is to subscribe to the services of an information network. These information networks have one or several large computer systems that offer a variety of information services, from hotel reservations to daily horoscopes. Besides a micro, all you would need in order to take advantage of these information networks is a **modem** (the interface between the telephone line and a micro), a telephone line, and a few dollars. You would normally pay a one-time fee. For the fee, you get an account number that will permit you to establish a link with the network. You are then billed based on your usage of the information network.

The following list summarizes the types of entertainment, information, and services available through information networks.

*Home Banking.*   Check your account balances, transfer money, and pay bills in the comfort of your home or office.

*News*, *Weather*, *Sports*.   Get the latest releases directly from the wire services.

*Games.*   Hundreds of single and multiplayer games are available. You can even play games with friends in other states!

*Financial Information.*   Get up-to-the-minute quotes on stocks, securities, bonds, options, and commodities.

*Bulletin Boards.*   Special-interest bulletin boards offer users a forum for the exchange of ideas and information. Besides those offered by information networks, thousands of bulletin board systems (BBSs) are made available free of charge by individuals and computer clubs.

*Electronic Mail.*   Send and receive mail to and from other network users. Each network subscriber is assigned an ID and an electronic mailbox. To retrieve mail, a subscriber must enter a secret password.

*Shop at Home.*   Select what you want from a list of thousands of items offered at discount prices. Payment is made via electronic funds transfer (EFT) and your order is delivered to your doorstep.

*Reference.*   Look up items of interest in an electronic encyclopedia. Scan through various government publications. Recall articles on a particular subject.

*Education.*   Choose from a variety of educational packages, from learning arithmetic to preparing for the Scholastic Aptitude Test (SAT). You can even determine your own IQ!

*Real Estate.*   Moving? Check out available real estate by scanning the listings for the city to which you are moving.

*Travel.*   Plan your own vacation or business trip. You can check airline schedules and make your own reservations. You can even charter a yacht in the Caribbean or rent a lodge in the Rockies.

The computer's ability to analyze large volumes of data is enabling research and development scientists to investigate the perimeters of knowledge. These chemists are working on a solar cell that uses silicon to absorb the sun's light and create electricity.
(Phillips Petroleum Company)

These and many other timesaving applications should eventually make personal computers a "must-have" item in every home and business. Some PCs are already priced lower than a good pair of running shoes!

## Science and Research

Engineers and scientists routinely use the computer as a tool in experimentation and design. Mechanical engineers use computers to simulate the effects of a wind tunnel to analyze the aerodynamics of an automobile prototype. Political scientists collect and analyze demographic data, such as median income and housing starts, to predict voting trends. Chemists use computer graphics to create three-dimensional views of an experimental molecule. There are at least as many science and research applications for the computer as there are scientists and engineers.

## Process Control

Computers used for **process control** accept data in a continuous *feedback loop*. In a feedback loop, the process generates data that become input to the computer. As the data are received and interpreted by the computer, the computer initiates action to control the ongoing process. For example, process-control computers monitor and control the environment (temperature, humidity, lighting, security) within skyscrapers (see Figure 1–6). These computer-controlled skyscrapers are often referred to as "smart" buildings.

Tiny "computers on a chip" are being embedded in artificial hearts and other organs. Once the organs are implanted in the body, the com-

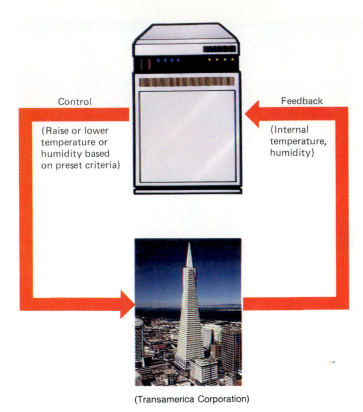

Control

(Raise or lower
temperature or
humidity based
on preset criteria)

Feedback

(Internal
temperature,
humidity)

**FIGURE 1–6**
**Process-Control Feedback**
**Loop**
Computer-based environmental
control systems monitor and
control the temperature and
humidity in thousands of
buildings.

(Transamerica Corporation)

puter monitors critical inputs, such as blood pressure and flow, then takes corrective action to ensure stability of operation in a continuous feedback loop.

## Education

Computers can interact with students to enhance the learning process. Relatively inexpensive hardware that is capable of multidimensional communication (sound, print, graphics, and color) has resulted in a phenomenal growth of the computer as an educational tool in the home, the classroom, and in business. Computer-based education will not replace teachers and books, but educators are in agreement that *computer-assisted instruction* (CAI) is having a profound impact on traditional modes of education.

Computers have been used for drill and practice for over a decade. Only recently has sophisticated CAI been economically feasible. Now, powerful personal computers have added a dimension that is not possible with books and the traditional classroom lecture. The student controls the pace of learning and can interact directly with the computer system. Through interactive computer graphics, a CAI system can demonstrate certain concepts more effectively than can books or even teachers. The teacher-book-CAI approach has spawned a new era in education. The software supplement to this text provides many examples of sophisticated CAI.

## Artificial Intelligence

**Human Beings Are Born, Not Manufactured.**   Today's computer's can simulate many human capabilities, such as reaching, grasping, calculating, speaking, remembering, comparing numbers, and drawing. Researchers are working to expand these capabilities and, therefore, the power of computers to include the ability to reason, to learn or "accumulate knowledge," to strive for self-improvement, and to simulate human sensory capabilities. This general area of research is known as **artificial intelligence (AI).**

"Artificial intelligence?" To some, the mere mention of artificial intelligence creates visions of electromechanical automatons replacing human beings. But, as anyone involved in the area of artificial intelligence will tell you, there is, and will always be, a distinct difference between human beings and machines. Computers will never be capable of simulating the distinctly human qualities of creativity, humor, and emotions!

**Computer Simulation of Human Capabilities.**   Computer systems with artificial intelligence can see, smell, feel, write, speak, and interpret spoken words. To varying degrees, these artificial intelligence capabilities are possible with current technology.

The simulation of human sensory capabilities is extremely complex. For example, a computer does not actually see and interpret an image the way a human being does. The image is first detected by a camera and is **digitized**—that is, translated to a form that computers can interpret. The digitized image is then compared to other digitized images stored in the computer's data base. Through a matching process, the computer interprets the image.

Voice inflections, grammatical exceptions, and words that have several meanings have combined to make speech interpretation and voice synthesis difficult, but not impossible. For example, "I'm OK!" differs from "I'm OK?". For human beings, distinguishing these subtle differences is second nature. For machines, these subtleties must be programmed and made part of the permanent data base.

**Expert Systems.**   One area of artificial intelligence research that holds great promise for the business community is **expert systems.** Expert

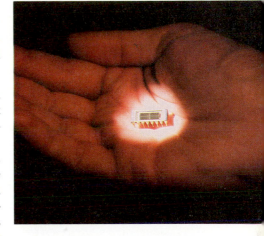

This tiny silicon chip, sometimes called a "computer on a chip," contains one million electronic circuits. The human brain has 10 trillion circuit elements, about 10 million times as many as this state-of-the-art silicon chip. (AT&T Technologies)

Locomotive mechanics get troubleshooting help with this computer-based expert system. The mechanic simply keys in responses to questions asked by the "expert" about the malfunction. Through interactive questioning, the expert system eventually identifies the cause of the malfunction and demonstrates repair procedures on the video monitor (screen at left). (General Electric Company)

systems are computer-based systems that help managers resolve a solution to a problem or to make better decisions. An expert system is an interactive computer-based system that responds to questions, asks for clarification, makes recommendations, and generally aids in the decision-making process. Expert systems are discussed in more detail in Chapter 4, "Computers and Information Systems in Business and Government."

## 1–8   COMPUTERS AND OPPORTUNITY _____

Computers provide many opportunities for us to improve the quality of both our private and professional lives. The challenge is to take advantage of the opportunities afforded by the computer revolution and our emergence to an information society. People, like you, who are willing to put forth the effort and accept the challenge will be the ones who benefit the most.

Your marketability for employment is improved. You have an advantage over those of your peers who are uncomfortable with computers. If you are or will become a self-employed professional, such as an attorney or an accountant, an introductory computer education will provide you with the prerequisite knowledge that you will need to maintain a competitive edge. Moreover, the rate at which you can learn more about computers is accelerated. Your base of knowledge will grow so that you will be better equipped to keep pace with a rapidly changing technology.

For some, this course will be a stepping-stone to more advanced topics and, perhaps, a career in information systems or computer science. For others, this course will provide a solid foundation that will prove helpful in the pursuit of virtually any business career. In either case, you will be prepared to play an active role in the age of information.

## SUMMARY OUTLINE AND IMPORTANT TERMS _____

**1–1**   THE INFORMATION SOCIETY.   After existing for millennia as an agrarian society, the people of the world progressed to an industrial society. Today, what is emerging is an information society. Each year, computers, both in general and at a more personal level, are having a greater influence on our lives. It is our responsibility to direct the application of computers to the benefit of society.

**1–2**   LEARNING ABOUT COMPUTERS.   **Cyberphobia,** the irrational fear of, and aversion to, computers, is a result of people's fear of the unknown. People overcome cyberphobia by learning about computers. Computer-literate people know how to purchase, use, and operate a computer system and to make it work for them. The computer-literate person is also aware of the computer's impact on society.

**1-3** COMPUTERS ARE FOR EVERYONE.   During the 1950s, 1960s, and 1970s, **end users,** or simply **users,** would relate their information needs to computer professionals, such as programmers or systems analysts, who would then work with the computer system to generate the needed information. In "the old days," the **turnaround time** was so long that the resulting information was often obsolete or of little value by the time it reached the manager. In response to managers' requests for more timely information, **interactive computer systems** permit users to communicate directly with the computer system via **user-friendly** software.

   Both white-collar and blue-collar workers will begin to spend more and more of each working day interacting with some kind of computer-based system. Already, **hackers** everywhere use the computer as a source of enjoyment as well as a business tool.

**1-4** SUPPORTING A COMPANY'S INFORMATION NEEDS.   Companies depend on **information systems** and the capabilities of computing **hardware** for their data processing and information needs. The organizational entity charged with supporting these needs is called the information services department or data processing department. An **information center** is a facility that includes a variety of computing resources: workstations, microcomputers, printers for **hard copy,** plotters, a variety of user-oriented software packages, and **information center specialists** who help users to help themselves.

**1-5** DATA MANAGEMENT: A PREVIEW.   **Data** are the raw material from which information is derived. **Information** is comprised of data that have been collected and processed into a meaningful form. A string of **bits** is combined to form a character. Characters are combined to represent the values of **data elements,** also called **fields.** Related data elements are grouped to form **records.** Records with the same data elements combine to become a file. A **data base** contains several different record types and defines their relationships.

**1-6** UNCOVERING THE "MYSTERY" OF COMPUTERS.   The **computer,** or **processor,** is an electronic device capable of interpreting and executing programmed commands for input, output, computation, and logic operations. Computer system capabilities are defined as either input/output or processing. Processing capabilities are subdivided into computation and logic operations. A **computer system** is not as complex as we are sometimes led to believe. Personal computers, also called **microcomputers,** and **mainframe computers** are all computer systems, and each has only four fundamental components: **input** (e.g., the keyboard of a **video display terminal (VDT** or **workstation),** processing (executing a program), **output** (e.g., a **monitor** or a **printer**), and storage. The computer is fast, accurate, reliable, and has an enormous memory capacity.

1–7   HOW DO WE USE COMPUTERS?   The uses of computers can be classified into six general categories:

- *Information systems/data processing*. The computer is used to process data and produce business information.
- *Personal computing*. The computer is used for a variety of business and domestic "personal" applications, including the use of such productivity software tools as **word processing, electronic spreadsheet,** *data management*, *graphics*, *idea processing*, and *communications*. Personal computers, or **PCs,** can be used in conjunction with the telephone system to transmit data to and receive data from an **information network.**
- *Science and research*. The computer is used as a tool in experimentation and design.
- *Process control*. The computer is used to control a process by accepting and evaluating data in a continuous feedback loop.
- *Education*. The computer is used to communicate with a student for the purpose of enhancing the learning process.
- *Artificial intelligence*. The computer is used in applications that simulate such human capabilities as reaching, speaking, drawing, smelling, and the abilities to reason, learn, and strive for self-improvement. **Expert systems** are computer-based systems that help managers resolve a solution to a problem or to make better decisions.

1–8   COMPUTERS AND OPPORTUNITY.   A knowledge of computers is the door to opportunity in many professions.

## REVIEW EXERCISES

### Concepts

1. What are the four fundamental components of a computer system?
2. Which component of a computer system executes the program?
3. Name and give an example for each level of the hierarchy of data organization.
4. Associate the following with the appropriate category of computer usage: continuous feedback loop, experimentation, home use, CAI, synthesized speech, and business systems.
5. Light travels at 186,000 miles per second. How many milliseconds does it take for a beam of light to travel across the United States, a distance of about 3000 miles?
6. Compare the information processing capabilities of human beings to that of computers with respect to speed, accuracy, reliability, and memory.

7.  What are the primary functions of an organization's information services department?

8.  Suppose that you are the president of a company. Give examples of "what if" questions that you would like to submit to the company's accounting and financial information system. One example might be, "What if we made a $5,000,000 capital expenditure; how would that effect the company's tax liability over the next five years?"

9.  Describe the relationship between data and information.

10. In computerese, what is meant by "read" and "write"?

11. Name and briefly describe the six microcomputer tools that are collectively referred to as productivity software.

12. Which of the six microcomputer productivity tools would be most helpful in writing a term paper? Explain.

13. What is the software capability that enables viewing of electronic spreadsheet data and a bar graph at the same time?

14. List at least six information network services.

15. What type of hardware and software would be appropriate for an information center?

## Discussion

16. The computer has had far-reaching effects on our lives. How has the computer affected your life?

17. What is your concept of computer literacy? In what ways do you think achieving computer literacy will affect your domestic life? Business life?

18. Discuss how the complexion of jobs will change as we evolve from an industrial society to an information society. Give several examples.

19. The use of computers tends to stifle creativity. Argue for or against this statement.

## SELF-TEST (by section)

1–1. To be computer literate, you must be able to write computer programs. (T/F)

1–2. The irrational fear of, or aversion to, computers is called _____ .

1–3. A computer enthusiast is: (a) user friendly, (b) a hacker, or (c) a computerist.

1–4. The information center is a company's primary resource for the development of full-scale information systems. (T/F)

1–5. (a)  _____ are the raw material from which _____ is derived.

    (b)  Related data elements are grouped to form _____ .

**1-6.** **(a)** A printer is an example of which of the four computer system components?

**1-6.** **(a)** Related data elements are grouped to form _____ .

**(b)** The two types of processing operations performed by computers are _____ and _____ .

**(c)** A microsecond is 1000 times longer than a nanosecond. (T/F)

**1-7.** **(a)** The greatest amount of available computing capacity is dedicated to the information systems/data processing category of computer usage. (T/F)

**(b)** The transmission of data from a microcomputer to a mainframe computer is called uploading. (T/F)

**(c)** The microcomputer productivity tool that manipulates data that are organized in a tabular structure of rows and columns is called an _____ .

**(d)** Artificial intelligence is that area of research that deals with using computers to simulate human capabilities. (T/F)

**1-8.** The rate at which you can learn more about computers is accelerated once you gain a basic understanding of computers. (T/F)

*Self-Test answers.*   1–1, F; 1–2, cyberphobia; 1–3, b; 1–4, F; 1–5 (a), data, information; (b), records; 1–6 (a), output; (b), computation, logic; (c), F; 1–7 (a), T; (b), T; (c), electronic spreadsheet; (d), T; 1–8, T.

# Zimco Enterprises

## THE CASE STUDY APPROACH

Throughout this text, computer, information processing, and business systems concepts are illustrated within the context of a "running" case study. The case study, which is an integral part of the pedagogy of this text, makes it possible to use business examples to reinforce the concepts introduced in the chapter material and to introduce new concepts within the context of a business environment.

The case study focuses on Zimco Enterprises, a fictitious medium-sized manufacturer of handy consumer products. The Zimco case study is presented in 13 topical segments, one for each of the 13 chapters of this book. There are also occasional references in the chapter material to the case study. The Zimco Enterprises case study is designed to make effective use of your study time by presenting only those facets of Zimco's operation that are pertinent to immediate discussions.

By the time you finish this book, you will probably feel some affection for Zimco and may even come to know its employees as your friends. Zimco is, of course, a fictional company, but it is very real in that its people, systems, methods, and planning mirror that of other successful businesses. In fact, the company as well as its people are composites of real companies and real people.

The case study material that follows and that in Chapter 2 is designed to familiarize you with Zimco's background, product line, management philosophy, organization, and people. As you begin to "know" Zimco, making the association between concept and practice will be a breeze.

The fictional nature of Zimco leaves the door open for a little tongue-in-cheek pedagogy. After all, there is no law that says that learning can't be fun.

## BACKGROUND, FUNCTION, AND ORGANIZATION OF ZIMCO ENTERPRISES

### BACKGROUND SUMMARY

Zimco was founded in 1876 during the post–Civil War era by Ezekiel "Zeke" F. Zimmers. Zeke, an immigrant from Europe, was an upholsterer by trade. Much of his day was spent stretching fabric over wooden furniture frames. He secured the fabric to the frame with small tacks. Over the years, these menacing little tacks caused Zeke a lot of pain. He and other upholsterers had trouble holding the tightly stretched fabric and hammering in the tack at the same time.

Zeke and his upholstery friends were constantly complaining to their wives about smashed thumbs.

Zeke's wife, Bertha, sympathized with him, but she had no desire to spend the rest of her life hearing complaints about black-and-blue fingers. So she did something about it. She converted a small magnet, which she had been using to hold her sewing needles, into a combination tack and fabric holder. First, she notched the magnet with a small "V," then she placed a glue-and-sand mixture on the bottom of the magnet. Then she affixed a small eight-inch handle to the magnet and *voilá*, a new industry was born.

One year later, Zeke perfected the tool, named it the *Stib* (see Figure Z1–1), founded Zimco Enterprises, and created the now famous slogan, "Don't be dumb and hit your thumb, buy a Stib." The Stib was an instant success.

Fascinated with cowboys and the "wild west," Zeke moved his small but growing business to Dallas, Texas, in 1890. Zimco is still headquartered in Dallas. Ezekiel F. Zimmers, Jr. became president in 1900 upon his father's retirement. Under Zeke, Jr., Zimco continued to thrive in an economy that relied more and more on tacks and, therefore, the need for Stibs. In 1935, Ezekiel F. Zimmers III inherited Zimco Enterprises, but he was simply not cut out for management. He wanted the money, not the responsibility of a company. In 1936, Zimco Enterprises went public and is now owned by shareholders from every walk of life.

Oldtimers at Zimco still tell stories about Ezekiel III. For several decades he was a mainstay with the jet set and was often photographed with budding starlets. Eventually, the money ran out and he returned to the trade of his grandfather—he became a master upholsterer.

## THE MODERN ERA

Zimco's new management continued to focus on the sale of Stibs to the upholstery industry until the late 1950s and the introduction of staple guns. The upholsterers embraced the staple gun with the same fervor that they had embraced the Stib 75 years earlier. Many industry analysts thought that the staple gun would be the "death nail" (or "tack") to the Stib. Such was not the case. Aggressive Zimco managers were among the first to recognize the beginning of the "do it yourself" era. They knew that eventually just about every handy man and handy woman would smash a thumb in an attempt to hammer in a tack, so they initiated an aggressive marketing campaign to let consumers know that they had a product that would eliminate black-and-blue thumbs.

Before staple guns, Zimco didn't even have a marketing department. The product sold itself in the upholstery industry. In the 1950s, the consumer public had never heard of a Stib—but they certainly have now. Via every medium, including billboards, newspapers, and television, consumers read or heard "Don't be dumb and hit your thumb, buy a Stib." Frustrated tack-hammering consumers rushed to buy Stibs, and the rest is business history.

## ZIMCO MANAGEMENT PHILOSOPHY

Zimco management adopted a simple entrepreneurial philosophy: Produce a limited line of high-quality consumer products that are innovative and for which there is relatively little (or no) competition. Management figured that if they could identify a need early and produce the right product at the right price, they could corner the market, just as founder Zeke Zimmers did with Stibs 75 years earlier.

## THE ZIMCO PRODUCT LINE TODAY

Today, Zimco produces and sells four very successful consumer products. These are the Stib, Farkle, Tegler, and Qwert.

- *Stib*. Even after 100 years, the Stib (see Figure Z1–1) is relatively unchanged. It still holds tacks and saves thumbs. The slogan remains the same, "Don't be dumb and hit your thumb, buy a Stib."
- *Farkle*. Like the Stib, the Farkle (see Figure Z1–2) was born of need. Commuters wanted relief from the hard plastic seats in buses and subways on their journeys to and from work. Zimco researchers produced a portable inflatable cushion that could be blown up with a few breaths of air, then collapsed to the size of a pocket calendar for ease of carrying. Millions of commuters are now believers in Farkle comfort. Commuters often tout the wonders of the Farkle to non-Farkle users by repeating its slogan: "Farkles add sparkle."

**FIGURE Z1–1**
**Stib**
Zimco Enterprises' Stib, a tack holder.

**FIGURE Z1–2**
**Farkle**
Zimco Enterprises' Farkle, an inflatable commuter cushion.

**FIGURE Z1–3**
**Tegler**
Zimco Enterprises' Tegler, a flavored pen cap.

**FIGURE Z1–4**
**Qwert**
Zimco Enterprises' Qwert, a watchlike biofeedback mechanism.

■ *Tegler*. Teachers, parents, friends, and colleagues have cautioned others that chewing on ball-point pen caps is unsightly and socially unacceptable. Nevertheless, millions of "closet" chewers unconsciously nibble on these caps at every opportunity. Pen-cap addicts are found from grammar school classrooms to corporate boardrooms. Zimco's market research identified the need and Zimco's research department developed a product.

In 1978, Teglers hit the market with a bang. Teglers (see Figure Z1–3) are flavored pen caps that add a little zip to the enjoyment of habitual pen-cap chewers. The one-size-fits-all Teglers are sold everywhere in packages of five: licorice, peppermint, cherry, lemon, and avocado. The beauty of Teglers is that the flavor comes through without leaving telltale teeth marks on the caps. As the slogan says, "Any time is Tegler time."

■ *Qwert*. The Qwert, introduced in 1987, is Zimco's most recent product. After five years of intense research and development, Zimco became a high-tech company with the introduction of the Qwert (Figure Z1–4), a watchlike biofeedback mechanism. When placed around the wrist, the Qwert measures the variations in galvanic skin response and heart rate. A tiny computer in the Qwert (which doubles as a digital watch), continuously collects and analyzes the galvanic and heart rate data. These data are analyzed by the computer, then a digital readout of a person's physical and, to some extent, emotional well-being, is displayed.

The readout varies from 1 to 10, with 1 being extreme lethargy and 10 being extreme anxiety. With a little practice and the Qwert providing the biofeedback, Qwert users can learn to adjust their body chemistry to optimize their mental acuity and reduce stress and tension (readouts of 4, 5, or 6). As the saying goes, "Do smart work with a Qwert."

## ZIMCO'S SIZE AND ORGANIZATIONAL STRUCTURE

Zimco is a $150 million (annual sales) company with about 1500 employees nationwide. Except for 100 field representatives, all employees work out of the Dallas, Texas, headquarters office or one of the four regional plants, located at Dallas, Becker (Minnesota), Eugene (Oregon), and Reston (Virginia). Stibs are manufactured at Dallas, Farkles at Becker, Qwerts at Eugene, and Teglers at Reston. Each of the four plant sites is also a *regional distribution center* and a *regional sales office* for all Zimco products (Figure Z1–5).

Figure Z1–6 illustrates the basic structural organization of Zimco. It is classically organized into four *line* divisions and one *staff* division. The line divisions are the Finance and Accounting Division, Sales and Marketing Division, Personnel Division, and Operations Division [which includes manufacturing, distribution, research and development (R and D), and purchasing.] The Computer and Information Services Division, which is commonly abbreviated CIS, provides services to all areas of corporate operation. All division heads are vice-presidents and report directly to the president, *Preston Smith*. The corporate staff, which includes legal affairs, public re-

lations, and other support groups, also reports to the president.

The function and operation of each of the divisions is described briefly below. Details of how these divisions interact with one another via integrated computer systems (e.g., information flow) are illustrated and discussed in later segments of the Zimco case study.

## Computer and Information Services Division (CIS)

The VP of the Computer and Information Services (CIS) Division, *Conrad Innis*, is charged with the support of all Zimco Enterprises information processing requirements that are consistent with corporate objectives. Specific responsibilities include:

■ The development, ongoing operation, and maintenance of information systems
■ Serving as a catalyst for the development of new information systems
■ Coordinating systems integration
■ Evaluating and selecting hardware and software
■ Setting of standards and policy relating to computers and information processing

**FIGURE Z1–5**
**Zimco Headquarters and Plant Sites**

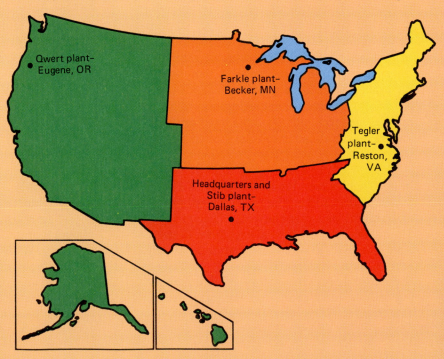

Qwert plant–
Eugene, OR

Farkle plant–
Becker, MN

Tegler plant–
Reston, VA

Headquarters and
Stib plant–
Dallas, TX

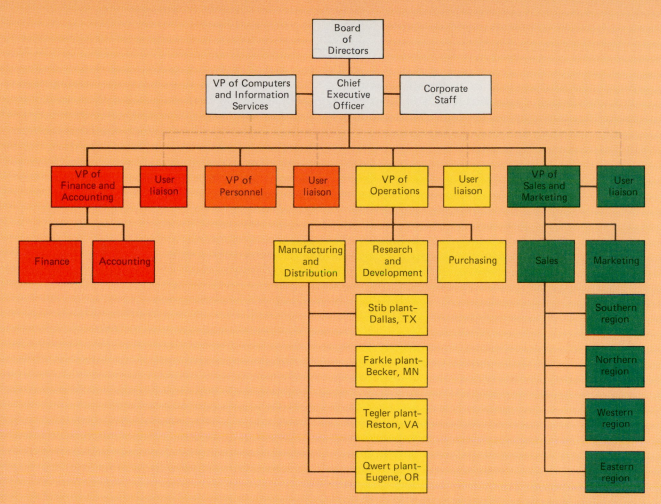

**FIGURE Z1–6**
**Zimco Organizational Chart**

## Finance and Accounting Division

The head of the Finance and Accounting Division, *Monroe Green*, oversees the Finance and Accounting Departments. The Accounting Department collects and manipulates monetary data to provide information that reflects Zimco's monetary activity. For example, accounting systems generate the profit and loss statements, allocate expenses to various accounts, and reflect the value of finished goods inventory. The Finance Department seeks to optimize Zimco's cash flow. They make sure that Zimco is liquid enough to meet short-term financial obligations while investing extra funds until they are needed.

## Sales and Marketing Division

*Sally Marcio*, the VP of the Sales and Marketing Division, is responsible for the activities of the Sales and Marketing Departments. Zimco relies exclusively on field sales representatives to sell their products. The Sales Department field reps work out of the four regional sales offices (southern, northern, western, eastern) and call on thousands of retailers and wholesalers throughout the country. Over 95 percent of the Zimco products are sold to drugstores, supermarkets, hardware stores, specialty stores, department stores, and mail-order companies. The Marketing Department is concerned primarily with making consumers aware of the spectacular products that Zimco has to offer.

## Personnel Division

The VP of the Personnel Division, *Peggy Peoples*, has the responsibility for all personnel accounting functions. Peggy's division hires people to meet work force requirements, then provides services to individuals and departments regarding personnel benefits, compensation, and other personnel matters. The department also maintains a skills inventory and does the background work for internal training sessions.

## Operations Division

*Otto Manning*, VP for the Operations Division, sees that the products are made and delivered to customers. The plant managers in Dallas, Eugene, Becker, and Reston report to the manager of Manufacturing and Distribution, who, in turn, reports to Otto Manning. Associated with each plant is a regional distribution center for all Zimco products. Managers of the Research and Development Department and the Purchasing Department also report to Otto.

## User Liaisons

The intensity of computer and information processing activity is very heavy in companies that seek to take full advantage of the potential of automation. Zimco, being one of these companies, has assigned a user liaison to work directly with each of the four "functional area" vice-presidents. The user liaison is a "live-in" computer specialist who coordinates all computer-related activities within a particular division. The user liaison is intimately familiar with the functional area (e.g., marketing, accounting, etc.) as well as the technical end of computers and information processing. The user liaison is the catalyst for new system development and coordinates system conversions.

## THE BUSINESS SYSTEM

The focus of this running case study is to describe how Zimco Enterprises uses available computing and information resources. So that you can better understand future discussions of Zimco operations, let's look at Zimco as a business system. Figure Z1–7 graphically illustrates how some of the pieces fit together.

The heart of any company is its people (the pyramid in Figure Z1–7). Like most medium-sized and large companies, Zimco has three levels of management: operational, tactical, and strategic.

Managers at each level have an ongoing need for information that will enable them to better use the resources at their disposal to meet corporate objectives and to perform the management functions of *planning*, *staffing*, *organizing*, *directing*, and *controlling*. These resources are *money*, *materials* (to include facilities and equipment), *people*, and *information*. As illustrated in Figure Z1–7, these resources become "input" to the various functional units of Zimco (operations, sales, etc.). The people at Zimco use their talent and knowledge, together with these resources, to produce the Zimco products (Stibs, Farkles, Teglers, and Qwerts).

The business system acts in concert with several *entities*. An entity is the source or destination of information flow, or an entity can be the source or destination of materials or product flow. For example, suppliers are both a source of information and materials. They are also the destination of payments for materials. The customer entity is the destination of products and the source of orders. *Flow diagrams* in later chapters detail direct interaction between all departments and entities in the business system.

## DISCUSSION QUESTIONS

1. What special challenges faced Zimco management when Zimco transitioned from a privately held to a public corporation in 1936? How did this transition affect the need for data processing and information for management decision making?

2. In the current Zimco organization, the VP of CIS reports to the president, Preston Smith, in a staff capacity, where the other VPs report to him in a line capacity. Discuss the advantages of such an organization.

3. One of the stated responsibilities of the Computer and Information Services Division is "serving as a catalyst for the development of new information systems." How might the VP of the Operations Division interpret this charge?

4. Zimco Enterprises manufactures and sells three relatively low-tech products and one very high-tech product. Discuss the effects, if any, that the mixing of low- and high-tech

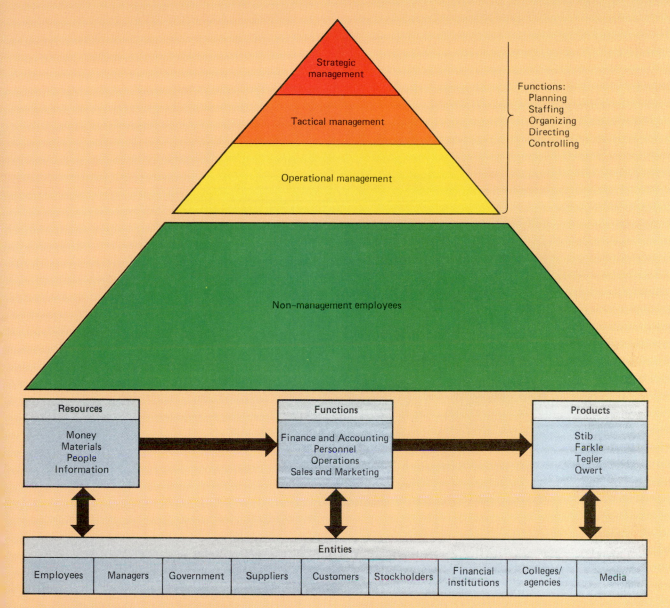

**FIGURE Z1–7**
**A Business System Model for Zimco Enterprises**

products might have on the design of basic information systems such as an accounting system or an inventory control system.

5. Zimco's Sales and Marketing Division is a heavy user of CIS services. Speculate on how the field sales representatives might use Zimco's corporate data base at Dallas.

6. Discuss the advantages and disadvantages of having user liaisons in each of Zimco's four functional divisions.

7. For each of the three levels of management illustrated in the business system model in Figure Z1–7, what would be the horizon (time span) for planning decisions? Explain.

8. Top managers at Zimco have always treated money, materials, and people as valuable resources, but only recently have they recognized that information is also a valuable resource. Why do you think they waited so long?

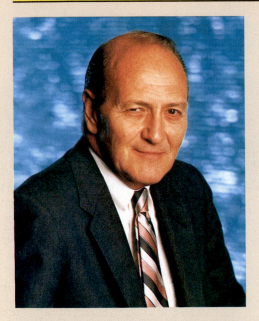

Traditionally, we have used computers at Richardson-Vicks Inc. in an operational sense. They have helped us to keep our records accurate and greatly speed up the flow of detailed information.

We recognize that we should exploit the technology to achieve competitive advantage. We are investigating several opportunities and have begun pilot programs that, when fully implemented, will position Richardson-Vicks Inc. in front of competition. Specifically, we expect our experiments in electronic data interchange (EDI) with our customers will yield such advantage.

We further recognize that this is a moving target. Success in technological advantage may last only a limited period of time. We plan to press on with other opportunities to maintain a competitive advantage.

John S. Scott
President and CEO
Richardson-Vicks Inc.

# Computers—Yesterday and Today

## STUDENT LEARNING OBJECTIVES

■ To put the technological development of computers into historical perspective.

■ To identify and describe the feats of computer pioneers.

■ To acquire a frame of reference for the computer innovations of the future.

■ To appreciate the scope, influence, and potential of computers in business.

■ To put society's dependence on computers in perspective.

## FOCUS OF ZIMCO CASE STUDY

■ Zimco's Computer and Information Services Division.

## 2–1 THE HISTORY OF COMPUTING: FROM THE ABACUS TO PUNCHED CARDS_____

### Historical Perspective

The history of computers is of special significance to us, because many of its most important events have occurred within our lifetime. The last two decades have been the most exciting part of the short but event-filled history of the electronic computer. In terms of the way people live and work, John V. Atanasoff's invention of the computer (1942) can be considered one of the most significant events in history. The overview of the history of computers that follows will provide you with a historical perspective and a feeling for the "roots" of the modern computer.

**The Abacus.**  The abacus was probably the original mechanical counting device. It has been traced back at least 5000 years, and its effectiveness has withstood the test of time. It is still used to illustrate the principles of counting to school children.

**The Pascaline.**  Inventor and painter Leonardo da Vinci (1452–1519) sketched ideas for a mechanical adding machine. A century and a half later, the French philosopher and mathematician Blaise Pascal (1623–1662) finally invented and built the first mechanical adding machine. It was called the Pascaline and used gear-driven counting wheels to do addition. Although Pascal was praised throughout Europe for his accomplishments, the Pascaline was a dismal financial failure. At that time, the Pascaline was more expensive than human labor for arithmetic calculations.

Blaise Pascal's early work on mechanical calculators is recognized today in the popular computer programming language that bears his name.
(Courtesy of International Business Machines Corporation)

Pascal built the Pascaline to help his father, a tax collector, calculate tax revenues. The numbers for each digit position were arranged on wheels so that a single revolution of one wheel resulted in one-tenth of a revolution of the wheel to its immediate left.
(Courtesy of International Business Machines Corporation)

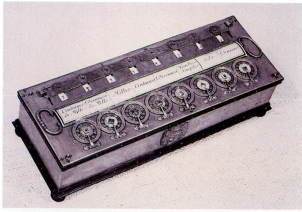

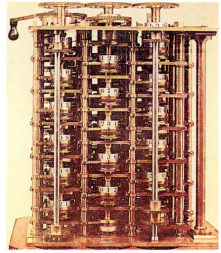

Concepts used in today's general-purpose computer were introduced over 100 years ago by Charles Babbage.
(Courtesy of International Business Machines Corporation)

Babbage's Difference Engine was the first practical mechanical calculator.
(New York Public Library Picture Collection)

**Babbage's Folly.** Charles Babbage (1793–1871), an English visionary and Cambridge professor, might have hastened the development of computers had he and his inventive mind been born 100 years later. He advanced the state of computational hardware by inventing a "difference engine," capable of computing mathematical tables.

In 1834, while working on advances to the difference engine, Babbage conceived the idea of an "analytical engine." In essence, this was a general-purpose computer. As designed, his analytical engine would add, subtract, multiply, and divide in automatic sequence at a rate of 60 additions per minute. The design called for thousands of gears and drives that would cover the area of a football field and be powered by a locomotive engine. Skeptics nicknamed his machine "Babbage's Folly." Babbage worked on his analytical engine until his death.

Babbage's detailed drawings described the characteristics embodied in the modern electronic computer. Had Babbage lived in the era of electronic technology and precision parts, he might have advanced the birth of the electronic computer by several decades. Ironically, his work was forgotten to the extent that some pioneers in the development of the electronic computer were completely unaware of his ideas on memory, printers, punched cards, and sequential program control.

## Two Centuries of Punching Holes in Cards

**The First Punched Card.**   The Jacquard weaving loom, invented in 1801 by the Frenchman Joseph-Marie Jacquard (1753–1834) and still in use today, is controlled by **punched cards.** In the operation of Jacquard's loom, holes are strategically punched in cards and the cards are sequenced to indicate a particular weaving design.

Charles Babbage wanted to use the punched-card concept of the Jacquard loom for his analytical engine. In 1843, Lady Ada Augusta Lovelace suggested that cards could be prepared that would instruct Babbage's engine to repeat certain operations. Because of her suggestion, some people call Lady Lovelace the first programmer.

**The Emergence of Automated Data Processing.**   The U.S. Bureau of the Census did not complete the 1880 census until almost 1888. Bureau management concluded that before long the 10-year census would take more than 10 years to complete! The Census Bureau commissioned Herman Hollerith, a statistician, to apply his expertise in the use of punched cards to take the 1890 census. With punched-card processing and Hollerith's punched-card tabulating machine, the census was completed in just three years and saved the bureau over $5,000,000. Thus

Herman Hollerith was awarded an honorary doctorate from Columbia University for his invention of the punched-card tabulating machine. Workers at the Bureau of the Census were not as excited about his invention. Fearing that it would replace them, they turned it off whenever the supervisor was not looking.
(Courtesy of International Business Machines Corporation)

Dr. Hollerith's punched-card tabulating machine had three parts. Clerks at the Bureau of the Census entered data into the cards with a hand punch. Cards were read and sorted by a 24-bin sorter box. The tabulator, which was electrically connected to the sorter box, summarized the totals on its numbered dials.
(Courtesy of International Business Machines Corporation)

began the emergence of automated data processing. Dr. Hollerith's work proved once again that "necessity is the mother of invention."

Hollerith's idea for the punched card came not from Jacquard or Babbage, but from "punch photography." Railroads of the day issued tickets with physical descriptions of the passengers. Conductors punched holes in tickets that noted a passenger's hair and eye color and the nose shape. Hollerith's daughter later said that "This gave him the idea for making a punch photograph of every person to be tabulated."

Hollerith founded the Tabulating Machine Company and marketed his products all over the world. The demand for his machines spread even to Russia. Russia's first census, taken in 1897, was recorded with Hollerith's tabulating machine. In 1911, the Tabulating Machine Company merged with several other companies to form the Computing-Tabulating-Recording Company.

**Electromechanical Accounting Machines.**   Tabulating-machine results had to be posted by hand until 1919, when the Computing-Tabulating-Recording Company announced the printer/lister. The printer/lister revolutionized the way companies did business. To better reflect the scope of their business interests, in 1924 the company was renamed the International Business Machines Corporation (IBM).

For decades, through the mid-1950s, punched-card technology improved with the addition of more punched-card devices and more sophisticated capabilities. Since each card usually contained a record (e.g., an employee's name and address), punched-card processing also became known as **unit-record processing** (one card equals one record).

The **electromechanical accounting machine (EAM)** family of punched-card devices includes the *card punch*, *verifier*, *reproducer*,

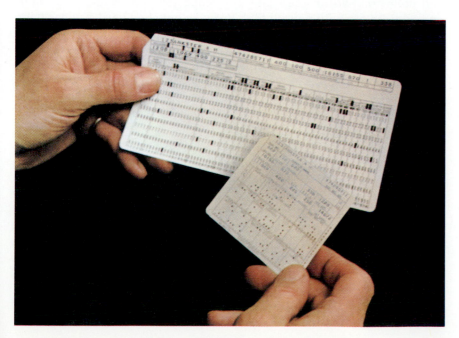

The 80-column card was the standard for punched-card data processing for over 50 years. The smaller 96-column card was introduced by IBM in the late 1960s for use with their small business computers.
(Courtesy of International Business Machines Corporation)

Electromechanical accounting machine (EAM) installations handled data processing activities during the 1940s and 1950s.
(Courtesy of International Business Machines Corporation)

*summary punch*, *interpreter*, *sorter*, *collator*, *calculator*, and the *accounting machine*.

Most of these devices were "programmed" to perform a particular operation by the insertion of a prewired control panel. A different panel was "wired" for each type of operation to be performed.

**Punched-Card Processing.** A machine-room operator in a punched-card installation had a physically demanding job. Some machine rooms resembled a factory. Punched cards and printed output were moved from one device to the next on hand trucks. The noise was no less intense than that in an automobile assembly plant. Today's machine-room operators use their brains rather than their backs.

To prepare punched-card files for processing, the cards had to be **sorted** (sequenced by employee last name, part number, and so on) and **collated** (two or more files combined for processing—e.g., name and address file with payroll file). Because punched-card devices operate independently, several steps, called **machine runs,** are required to produce a given output. In a run, each file is "read" one card at a time. In most modern information systems, only that portion of the data base that is needed is processed, usually in one run.

## 2-2  COMPUTER PIONEERS

**Atanasoff and Berry.** An early patent on a device that most people thought to be the first electronic digital computer was invalidated in 1973 by a federal court ruling, and Dr. John V. Atanasoff was officially credited with the invention of the electronic digital computer. Dr. Atanasoff, a professor at Iowa State University, developed the first electronic digital computer during the years 1937 to 1942. He called his invention the Atanasoff-Berry Computer or, simply, the *ABC*. A graduate student, Clifford Berry, was instrumental in helping Dr. Atanasoff build the ABC computer.

The ABC was born of frustration. Dr. Atanasoff later explained

This is the ABC computer. These words appear on a plaque in the old physics building at Iowa State University: "The world's first automatic electronic digital computer was constructed in this building in 1939 by John Vincent Atanasoff, a mathematician and physicist on the Iowa State faculty, who conceived the idea, and by Clifford Edward Berry, a physics graduate student."
(Courtesy of Iowa State University)

that one night in the winter of 1937, "nothing was happening" with respect to creating an electronic device that could help solve physics problems. His "despair grew," so he got in his car and drove for several hours across the state of Iowa and the Mississippi River. Finally, he stopped at an Illinois roadhouse for a drink. It was in this roadhouse that Dr. Atanasoff overcame his creative block and conceived ideas that would lay the foundation for the evolution of the modern computer.

**Mauchly and Eckert.**   After talking with Dr. Atanasoff, reading notes describing the principles of the ABC, and seeing the ABC, Dr. John W. Mauchly collaborated with J. Presper Eckert, Jr., to develop a machine that would compute trajectory tables for the U.S. Army. The end product, a large-scale fully operational electronic computer, was completed in 1946 and called the *ENIAC* (*E*lectronic *N*umerical *I*ntegrator *A*nd *C*omputer). The ENIAC, built for World War II applications, was completed in 30 months by a team of scientists working around the clock.

A thousand times faster than its electromechanical predecessors, the ENIAC was a major breakthrough in computer technology. It could do 5000 additions per minute and 500 multiplications per minute. It weighed 30 tons and occupied 1500 square feet of floor space. Unlike computers of today that operate in binary (0, 1), the ENIAC operated in decimal (0, 1, 2, . . . , 9) and required 10 vacuum tubes to represent one decimal digit. With over 18,000 vacuum tubes, the ENIAC needed a great amount of electricity. Legend has it that the ENIAC, built at the University of Pennsylvania, dimmed the lights of Philadelphia whenever it was activated. The imposing scale and general applicability of the ENIAC signaled the beginning of the first generation of computers.

Dr. John V. Atanasoff, inventor of the electronic digital computer, is seen at a banquet given in his honor by Iowa State University. A binary memory drum, the only major piece of the ABC that remains, can be seen in the foreground.
(Courtesy of Iowa State University)

THE ENIAC, recognized as the first all-electronic general-purpose digital computer, signaled the beginning of the first generation of computers. The ENIAC could perform calculations 1,000 times faster than its electromechanical predecessors. The two men in the foreground are its inventors, J. Presper Eckert and Dr. John W. Mauchly.
(United Press International Photo)

## 2–3   COMPUTER GENERATIONS

### The First Generation of Computers (1946 through 1959)

**The UNIVAC I.**   The **first generation of computers** was characterized by the most prominent feature of the ENIAC—*vacuum tubes*. Through 1950, several other notable computers were built, each contributing significant advancements, such as binary arithmetic, random access, and the concept of stored programs. These computer concepts, which are common in today's computers, are discussed later in the book.

They say that history repeats itself, and so it did with the installation of the first commercial computer in the U.S. Bureau of the Census in 1951. The computer, called the Universal Automatic Computer (*UNIVAC I* for short), was developed by Mauchly and Eckert for the Remington-Rand Corporation. This put the Sperry UNIVAC Division of what became the Sperry Corporation years ahead of the competition. The federal government got their money's worth out of the UNIVAC I: The Census Bureau used it for 12 years!

Today we take for granted that computers can be used to predict winners in national elections. Predictions are often made on the national returns before the polls close in the west coast states. In late 1951, CBS News became a believer when the UNIVAC I correctly predicted Dwight Eisenhower's victory over Adlai Stevenson in the presidential election with only 5 percent of the votes counted. Today, sophisticated information systems are essential tools for comprehensive television election coverage.

By 1951, other manufacturers, primarily in the punched-card and electronics industries, were beginning to enter the commercial computer market. This group included Burroughs, Honeywell, International Business Machines (IBM), and Radio Corporation of America (RCA).

Mr. Eckert instructs newsman Walter Cronkite in the use of the UNIVAC I computer prior to the 1952 presidential election. After the election, *The New York Times* referred to the Univac I as a ". . . super-duper electronic brain . . ." that was ". . . more of a nuisance than a help." (Sperry Corporation)

IBM Enters the Computer Market.   The first electromechanical computer, called the *Mark I*, was the result of IBM-sponsored research. Howard Aiken, a Harvard University professor, completed the Mark I in 1944. The Mark I was essentially a serial collection of electronic calculators and had many similarities to Babbage's analytical engine. Three years after completing the Mark I, Aiken became aware of Babbage's work and remarked, "If Babbage had lived 75 years later, I would have been out of a job."

The Mark I was a significant improvement in the state of the art, and several years later the ENIAC was offered to IBM, but IBM's management still felt that computers would not replace punched-card equipment. At the time, IBM held a virtual monopoly on punched-card data processing equipment and was doing quite well with meat slicers and scales for delicatessens, time clocks, and other products. Not until the success of the UNIVAC I did IBM make the decision and the commitment to develop and market computers.

IBM's first entry into the commercial computer market was the *IBM 701* in 1953. IBM introduced the IBM 701 with a bang—literally. It blew up during the demonstration for the press! After a slow but exciting beginning, the IBM 701 became a commercially feasible product. However, the *IBM 650*, introduced in 1954, is probably the reason that IBM enjoys such a healthy share of today's computer market. Unlike some of its competitors, the IBM 650 was designed as a logical upgrade to existing punched-card machines. IBM management went out on a limb and estimated sales of 50. This figure was greater than the number of installed computers in the United States at that time. IBM actually installed more than 1000. The rest is history.

The Computer Industry Comes of Age.   By the late 1950s a number of other manufacturers, including Control Data Corporation (CDC), General Electric (GE), and National Cash Register (NCR), had decided to commit their resources to computers and test the water. Each new entrant to the computer business made significant contributions to the state of the art of computer technology.

## The Second Generation of Computers
## (1959 through 1964)

To most people, the invention of the *transistor* meant small portable radios. To those in the data processing business, it signaled the start of the **second generation of computers.** The transistor meant more powerful, more reliable, and less expensive computers that would occupy less space and give off less heat than did vacuum-tube-powered computers.

The expense item should be emphasized. The cost of a computer during the first, second, and part of the third generation represented a significant portion of a company's budget. Computers were expensive. Cost per instruction executed can be used to compare the cost of computers over the last three decades. Significant innovations, spurred by intense competition, have resulted in enormous increases in computer performance and substantial reductions in price. This trend, established with the introduction of second-generation computers, continues today. Getting "more bang for the buck" has become a tradition in the computer industry; today it is not only anticipated, it is expected. If the automobile industry had realized the price/performance improvements of the computer industry (see Figure 2–1), we would all have a Rolls-Royce as a second car.

The dominant characteristics of the second generation were:

1. The transistor.
2. Limited **compatibility**. Programs written for one computer usually required modification before they could be run on a different computer.
3. Continued orientation to tape sequential processing (discussed in Chapter 10, "Data Organization and File Processing").
4. Low-level, symbolic programming languages (discussed in Chapter 9, "Programming Languages and Software Concepts").

Honeywell established itself as a major competitor during the second generation of computers. Burroughs, Univac, NCR, CDC, and Honeywell, IBM's biggest competitors during the 1960s and early 1970s, became known as the BUNCH (the first initial of each name).
(Honeywell, Inc.)

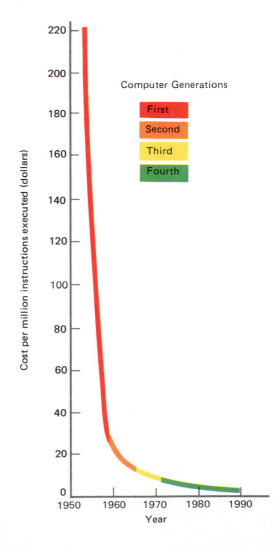

**FIGURE 2–1**
**The Cost of Computers**
Advancing computer technology makes it possible for more instructions to be executed at less cost each year.

## The Third Generation of Computers (1964 through 1971)

Characteristics.   What some computer historians consider to be the single most important event in the history of computers occurred when IBM announced their *System 360* line of computers on April 7, 1964. The System 360 ushered in the **third generation of computers.** *Integrated circuits* did for the third generation what transistors did for the second generation. The System 360s and the third-generation computers of Honeywell, NCR, CDC, UNIVAC, Burroughs, GE, and other manufacturers made all previously installed computers obsolete.

The compatibility problems of second-generation computers were almost eliminated in third-generation computers. However, third-generation computers differed radically from second-generation computers. The change was revolutionary, not evolutionary, and caused conversion nightmares for thousands of computer users. In time, the conversion of information systems from second-generation to third-generation hardware was written off as the price of progress.

By the mid-1960s, it became apparent that almost every computer installation could expect rapid growth. An important characteristic of third-generation computers was **upward compatibility,** which meant that a company could buy a computer from a particular vendor and then upgrade to a more powerful computer without having to redesign and reprogram existing information systems.

Third-generation computers work so quickly that they provide the capability to run more than one program concurrently **(multiprogramming).** For example, at any given time the computer might be printing payroll checks, accepting orders, and testing programs. Although third-generation computers continued to provide tape-processing capabilities, the computer systems were developed to encourage the use of random processing and rotating magnetic disks.

The Minicomputer.   The demand for small computers in business and for scientific applications was so great that several companies manufactured only small computers. These became known as **minicomputers.** Digital Equipment Corporation (DEC) and Data General Corporation took an early lead in the sale and manufacturer of "minis."

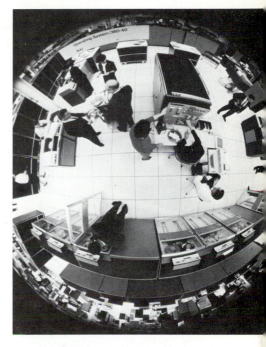

Business Week reported IBM's announcement of their System 360 line of computers saying that, "In the annals of major product changes, it is like Ford's switch from the Model T to the Model A." This fish eye view of the System 360 captures the essence of its "360" name.
(Courtesy of International Business Machines Corporation)

## The Fourth Generation of Computers

Most computer vendors classify their computers as being in the **fourth generation of computers,** and a few call theirs the "fifth generation." The first three generations were characterized by significant technological breakthroughs in electronics—the use of vacuum tubes, then transistors, and then integrated circuits. Some people prefer to pinpoint the start of the fourth generation as 1971, with the introduction of *large-scale integration* (more circuits per unit space) of electronic circuitry. However, other computer designers argue that if we accept this premise, there would probably have been a fifth, a sixth, and maybe a seventh generation since 1971.

The microcomputer was a product of the fourth generation of computers. A manager of a dry cleaning shop uses his microcomputer to examine monthly revenues for each of the various articles of clothing (e.g., shirts, pants, coats).
(Texas Instruments, Inc.)

The base technology of today's computers is still the integrated circuit. This is not to say that two decades have passed without any significant innovations. In truth, the computer industry has experienced a mind-boggling succession of advances in the further miniaturization of circuitry, data communications, the design of computer hardware and software, and input/output devices.

The Microprocessor.   One of the most significant contributions to the emergence of the fourth generation of computers is the **microprocessor.** The microprocessor, which can be contained on a single silicon chip, is a product of the microminiaturization of electronic circuitry. The first fully operational microprocessor, sometimes called a "computer on a chip," was invented in 1971. Today, there are more microprocessors on Earth than there are people. This device costs less than a soft drink and can be found in everything from elevators to satellites.

The Microcomputer.   The microprocessor is the processing component of the small, relatively inexpensive, but powerful *microcomputer.* the microcomputer, also called the *personal computer,* has made it possible for small businesses and individuals to own computers.

## Generationless Computers

We may have defined our last generation of computers and begun the era of **generationless computers.** Even though computer manufacturers talk of "fifth"- and "sixth"-generation computers, this talk is more a marketing ploy than a reflection of reality. Advocates of the concept of generationless computers say that even though technological innovations are coming in rapid succession, no single innovation is, or will be, significant enough to characterize another generation of computers.

Someone being exposed today to computer systems and information processing for the first time might look back on the short but interesting history of computers and wish that he or she had been in on the ground floor (see the chronological perspective, Figure 2–2). In the history of computers, however, *now* is the ground floor.

The concept of a "computer on a chip" is changing every day. These "superchips" are paving the way for hand-held computers that will have capabilities equal to that of today's desk-size mainframe computers.
(General Electric Company)

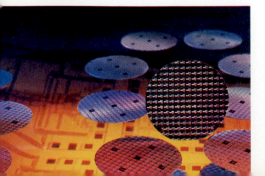

**FIGURE 2–2**

| Year | Historic Event | Processing | Input | Output | Storage (secondary) | Software | Systems Concepts | Information Systems Organization | Information Systems Personnel |
|---|---|---|---|---|---|---|---|---|---|
| 1940 | World War II begins | Electro-mechanical accounting machines; ABC computer | Punched card; Paper tape; Mark sense | Punched card; Paper tape; Printer | Punched card; Paper tape | Wired panels; Switches | Data processing (DP) | Centralized punched card departments | |
| | And ends | 1st generation (vacuum tubes); ENIAC | | | | Machine language; Stored program | | | Programmer |
| 1950 | | UNIVAC I (1st commercial) | | | | Assembler language | | | |
| | Ike elected President | IBM 650 | | | Magnetic tape | Compilers | | | Operator; Data entry; Systems analyst |
| | Sputnik launched | 2nd generation (transistors) | Magnetic ink character recognition (MICR) | Plotters; MICR | Magnetic disk | FORTRAN | | | |
| 1960 | | | | | | COBOL; LISP | | Trend to large centralized information systems departments | Librarian; Programmer (systems and applications) |
| | JF Kennedy assassinated | Minicomputer; 3rd generation (integrated circuits); IBM 360 family | Optical character recognition (OCR) | OCR | Mass storage devices | Multiprogramming; RPG; PL/I; BASIC | Management information systems (MIS) | | Control clerk |
| | | Computer networks | Keyboard (on-line); Light pen | Voice (recorded); Soft copy (VDT) | | APL; LOGO | | | |
| 1970 | Apollo II lands on moon | 4th generation (large-scale integration); Microprocessors; Microcomputers | | Computer output microfilm (COM); Graphics (VDT) | IK RAM chip; Floppy disk | Pascal; Word processing | | | Data base administrator; Project leader |
| | Watergate burglary | | Mouse; Hand print | Color graphics | | Query languages; UNIX operating system; Application generators | Information resource management (IRM); Decision support systems (DDS) | Trend to decentralization and distributed processing | Education coordinator; Documentalist; Office automation specialist |
| | USA's 200th birthday | Personal computers; Word processors | Voice; Vision input systems | High-speed laser printers; Voice (synthesized) | Video disk | Electronic spreadsheet; Ada | | | MIS long-range planner |
| 1980 | Mt. St. Helens erupts | Distributed processing | | | Optical laser disk | Integrated micro software | | Information centers | User-analyst; Information center specialist |
| | E.T. lands | Pocket computers; multiuser micros | | | | | | | User liaison |
| | Reagan begins second term | | | | | | Expert systems | | Microcomputer specialist |
| | XXII Olympiad | | | | 1 megabit RAM chip | | | | |
| 1990 | | | | | | | | | |

**Chronology of Computer History**
This chart includes events that are discussed in this chapter and throughout the book.

## 2-4   COMPUTERS TODAY: THE SKY'S THE LIMIT

The door is now open for applications of the computer that were only dreams or fantasies two decades ago. The number and the type of applications for the computer are limited only by our imaginations. This section contains a brief overview of a variety of familiar business applications for the computer. You have probably had occasion to use, either directly or indirectly, each of these information systems at one time or another. Other applications will be presented throughout the book in the textual material, in photo captions, and in the Zimco case study.

### Airlines

An airline reservation system is a classic example of an information system that reflects an up-to-the-minute status. An airline reservations agent communicates with a centralized computer via a remote terminal to update the data base the moment a seat on any flight is filled or becomes available.

An airline reservation system does much more than keep track of flight reservations. Departure and arrival times are closely monitored so that ground crew activities can be coordinated. The system offers many kinds of management information needs: the number of passenger-miles flown, profit per passenger on a particular flight, percent of arrivals on time, average number of empty seats on each flight for each day of the week, and so on.

It is interesting that airlines overbook almost every flight; that is, they book seats they do not have. The number of extra seats sold is based on historical no-show statistics that are compiled from the reservation system data base. Although these statistics provide good guidelines, occasionally everyone does show up!

Before each flight, the pilot and copilot get a weather briefing and pick up a "computer" flight plan. Just as cars travel on highways, airplanes travel on airways. Based on wind speed and direction, the computer selects the best airway route and projects a flying time for each leg. The flight plan also suggests flying altitudes that minimize fuel consumption.
(AT&T Technologies)

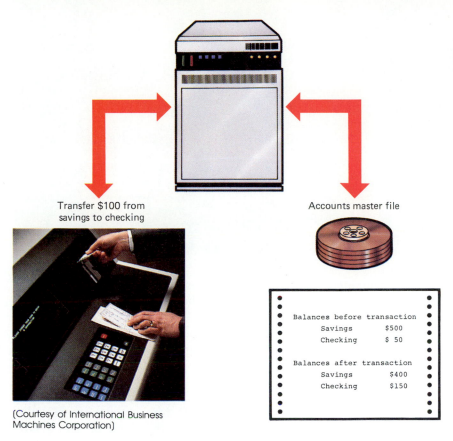

Transfer $100 from
savings to checking

Accounts master file

```
Balances before transaction
     Savings        $500
     Checking       $ 50

Balances after  transaction
     Savings        $400
     Checking       $150
```

(Courtesy of International Business
Machines Corporation)

**FIGURE 2–3**
**Banking Transactions at an
Automatic Teller Machine**
The electronic funds transfer
(EFT) of $100 from savings to
checking causes the accounts
master file to be updated.

## Banking

The use of the ever-present **automatic teller machine (ATM)** is an application of **electronic funds transfer (EFT).** ATMs are strategically placed
throughout the city and linked to a central computer. ATMs enable
bank customers to deposit, withdraw, and transfer funds from or to
their various accounts. As each money transaction is completed, the
customer's record is updated and the customer is provided with a
printed receipt (see Figure 2–3). The widespread acceptance of the
convenience afforded by ATMs has prompted the banking industry
to expand the scope of this service. Recognizing that our society is
becoming increasingly mobile, participating banks are linking their
computers so that customers can complete banking transactions on
ATMs anywhere in the country.

## Municipal Government

Have you ever driven an automobile through a city with an automated
traffic-control system? If so, you would soon notice how the traffic
signals are coordinated to minimize delays and optimize traffic flow.
Traffic sensors are strategically placed throughout the city to feed data
continuously to the computer on the volume and direction of traffic
flow.

The city of Chicago's automated traffic control system is one example of how a municipal government uses computers for process control applications. Other process control uses include control of the water distribution system and temperature control of city buildings. Many of these office buildings have process control computers that monitor fire alarm and security systems.
(Commonwealth Edison)

The computer system that activates the traffic signals is programmed to "plan ahead." That is, if the sensors locate a group of cars traveling together, then traffic signals are timed accordingly. An automated traffic-control system is a good example of the continuous feedback loop in a computerized process-control system.

## Retail Sales

In the retail sales industry (see Figure 2–4), transactions are recorded on cash-register-like computer terminals at the **point of sale (POS)**. Each point-of-sale terminal is linked to a central computer and a shelf-item master file. To record a sale, the salesclerk enters only the item number. The current price and item description are retrieved from the

**FIGURE 2–4**
**Point-of-Sale (POS) System**
POS systems permit retailers to check a customer's line of credit, update inventory, and record each sale on the customer master file.

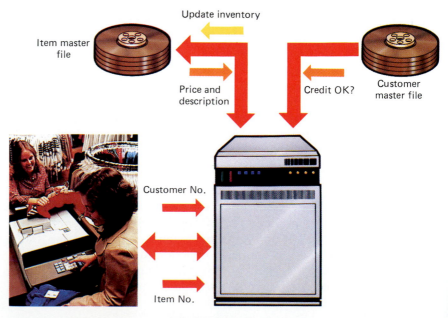

Update inventory

Item master file

Price and description

Credit OK?

Customer master file

Customer No.

Item No.

(Courtesy of International Business Machines Corporation)

Competition demands that these buyers at a California-based department store chain tap into the corporate data base to monitor and evaluate consumer buying trends. Consumer sales data are gathered from 17,000 point-of-sales workstations located in 300 locations.
(Courtesy of International Business Machines Corporation)

item master file. A sales ticket and customer receipt are printed automatically. The item master file is always up to date because the file is updated each time an item is sold. Without taking a physical inventory, managers know which items are moving, which are not, and when to order and restock an item.

Some point-of-sale systems go one step further than this; they also handle credit transactions. When a customer purchases an item on credit, the salesclerk enters the customer number. The point-of-sale system automatically checks the amount of the purchase against the customer's credit limit. An "OK" light on the terminal is a signal to the salesclerk that the transaction can be completed.

## 2–5 COMPUTERS: DO WE REALLY NEED THEM?

**Reaching the Point of No Return.**   Computers and information systems, such as those discussed in the preceding section, have enhanced our life-styles to the point that most of us take the computer for granted. There is nothing wrong with this attitude, but we must recognize that society has made a very real commitment to computers. You might say that we have passed the point of no return. The dependence of industry and government on computers cannot be overlooked. Turn off the computer system for a day in almost any organization and observe the consequences. Most organizations would cease to function.

Albert Einstein said that "concern for man himself and his fate must always form the chief interest of all technical endeavors." There are those who believe that a rapidly advancing computer technology exhibits little regard for "man himself and his fate." They contend that computers are overused, misused, and generally detrimental to society. This group argues that the computer is dehumanizing and is slowly forcing society into a pattern of mass conformity. To be sure, the "computer revolution" is presenting society with difficult and complex problems, but they can be overcome.

Whether it is good or bad, society is very dependent on computers. In the business community, stiff competition demands a continued and growing use of computers. On a more personal level, we are reluctant to forfeit the everyday conveniences made possible by computers. More and more of us find that our personal computers are an integral part of our daily activities.

Give Up My Computer? Never!   Ask a secretary to trade a word processing system for a typewriter. Ask a marketing manager to return to manual analysis of market research data. Ask airline executives how long they could continue to operate without their on-line reservations system. Ask yourself if you would give up the convenience of remote banking at automatic teller machines.

Our dependence on food has evolved into the joy of gourmet eating, and so it is, or can be, with computers. Dependence is not necessarily bad as long as we keep it in perspective. We can't passively assume that computers will continue to enhance the quality of our lives. It's our obligation to learn to understand computers so that we can better direct their application to society's benefit.

## SUMMARY OUTLINE AND IMPORTANT TERMS

**2-1**   THE HISTORY OF COMPUTING: FROM THE ABACUS TO PUNCHED CARDS.   The most exciting part of the modern computer's brief history has transpired during our own lifetime. An appreciation of this history provides a frame of reference for future events.

Early mechanical computers include the abacus, the Pascaline, and Charles Babbage's difference engine. Babbage later invented an analytical machine with design characteristics similar to those of the modern electronic computer.

Some computer historians believe that Lady Ada Lovelace became the first programmer when she suggested that punched cards, fashioned after those used on the Jacquard loom, be used to represent repetitive operations on Babbage's analytical machine.

Herman Hollerith and the U.S. Bureau of the Census collaborated and used **punched-card** technology to introduce automated data processing to the business world. Punched-card technology and **electromechanical accounting machines (EAMs)** were used for routine data processing tasks for half a century. Punched-card processing, or **unit-record processing,** required cards to be **sorted** and **collated** before **machine runs.**

**2-2**   COMPUTER PIONEERS.   Dr. John V. Atanasoff and Clifford Berry developed the first electronic computer between 1937 and 1942. They called it the ABC. Dr. John W. Mauchly and J. Presper Eckert, Jr., expanded on Dr. Atanasoff's basic design concepts to produce the first full-scale computer. It was called the ENIAC.

**2–3**   COMPUTER GENERATIONS.   Vacuum-tube technology characterized the **first generation of computers.** IBM started late, but passed the early front-runner, UNIVAC, to secure the dominant position in the computer industry. Early first-generation computers were punched-card oriented, with later versions relying more on magnetic tape.

Second-generation computers used transistor technology, which made computers less expensive and, therefore, more available to more organizations. These tape-oriented computers had limited compatibility and used low-level programming languages.

Integrated circuits replaced transistors in **third-generation computers.** Computer manufacturers provided disk-oriented systems with **upward compatibility** and **multiprogramming** capability. Data communications and on-line systems are also products of the third-generation.

**Fourth-generation computers** are associated with the large-scale integration of electronic circuitry. A product of this technology is the **microprocessor.** This "computer on a chip" made it economically feasible for individuals to own personal computers.

Computer technology is advancing at such a rapid pace that we may have begun the era of the **generationless computer.**

**2–4**   COMPUTERS TODAY: THE SKY'S THE LIMIT.   The door has been opened for computer applications that were only dreams or fantasies two decades ago. Computer-based information systems can be found in diverse business and government environments, including airlines, banking (e.g., **ATM** and **EFT**), municipal government, and retail sales (e.g., **POS**).

**2–5**   COMPUTERS: DO WE REALLY NEED THEM?   Society has reached a point of no return with regard to dependence on computers. Business competition demands the use of computers. We are also reluctant to give up those personal conveniences made possible by the computer. Only through understanding can we control the misuse or abuse of computer technology.

# REVIEW EXERCISES

## Concepts

1.   What is considered the original mechanical accounting device?
2.   A computer can be placed on a single silicon chip no larger than a fingernail. What is this computer called?
3.   What is the equipment called that was used for data processing prior to computers? What medium did these devices use for data storage?

4.  What electrical components are usually associated with each of the first three generations of computers?

5.  Briefly describe the major achievements of the following pioneers in computers and automation: Babbage, Mauchly and Eckert, Lovelace, Hollerith, Atanasoff, and Pascal.

6.  Group the following items by generation of computers: multiprogramming, UNIVAC I, transistor, minicomputer, microprocessor, integrated circuits, and ENIAC.

7.  The use of automatic teller machines (ATMs) is an example of what computer application?

## Discussion

8.  Of those computer-manufacturing companies mentioned in this chapter, which still manufacture computers? Can you name five more manufacturers of computers?

9.  Compare the history of computers with the history of aviation. Use the history of aviation to draw conclusions about the future of computers.

10. According to the author, we may have entered the era of generationless computers. Support or discredit the author's premise.

11. What do you think the computer historians of the year 2000 will say about computer advances during the 1980s?

12. The first computer predictions for a presidential election occurred in 1951. Since then, accurate predictions are often made before the polls close. Discuss the advantages and disadvantages of such predictions.

13. Banks are offering their customers money and prizes just to try automatic teller machines, yet only a handful of banks have more than 30 percent of their customer base using ATMs. Why are bankers so anxious for their customers to use ATMs, and why are so many people avoiding them?

14. Describe what yesterday would have been like if you did not use the capabilities of computers. Keep in mind that businesses with which you deal rely on computers and that many of your applicances are computer-based.

## SELF-TEST (by section)

2–1. **(a)** John V. Atanasoff's invention of the computer in 1933 is considered one of the significant events in history. (T/F)

**(b)** _____ 's detailed drawings of his analytical engine described the characteristics embodied in the modern electronic computer.

**(c)** Herman Hollerith first used his tabulating machine for automated data processing at the U.S. Bureau of the Census. (T/F)

**2–2.** **(a)** The first patent for an electronic digital computer was awarded to John V. Atanasoff for the ABC computer. (T/F)

**(b)** The ENIAC was developed to compute trajectory tables for the U.S. Army. (T/F)

**2–3.** **(a)** The Mark I was IBM's first electronic digital computer. (T/F)

**(b)** Multiprogramming and upward _____ were characteristics of the third generation of computers.

**(c)** The _____ is the processing component of a microcomputer.

**2–4.** In the retail industry, _____ terminals are linked to a central computer to record sales transactions.

**2–5.** If the number of computer applications continues to grow at the present rate, our computer-independent society will be dependent on computers by the year 2000. (T/F)

*Self-Test answers.*   2–1 (a), F; (b), Babbage; (c), T; 2–2 (a), F; (b), T; 2–3 (a), F; (b), compatibility; (c), microprocessor; 2–4; point-of-sale (POS); 2–5, F.

# Zimco Enterprises

## ZIMCO'S COMPUTER AND INFORMATION SERVICES DIVISION

### HISTORY

Ever since Zimco went public in 1936, Zimco management has taken pride in the fact that they have always kept pace with the technology. Zimco relied on various types of punched-card-oriented accounting machines until 1959. During the period 1936 to 1945, the entire data processing, or DP, staff consisted of one manager and one combination keypunch/machine operator. Together, they wired the control panels for the various punch-card machines and maintained automated payroll, accounts receivable, and general ledger systems. In 1945, they added an accounts payable and an inventory control system, and one more keypunch/machine operator. The DP department stayed at three people until 1959, even though Zimco grew from 200 employees in 1945 to 450 in 1959.

In 1959, electronic accounting machines were commonplace, even in small companies, but expensive computers were used almost exclusively by very large companies. Zimco was one of the first relatively small companies to purchase an electronic computer. It was even written up in the *Business Weekly* and called "one of the country's most aggressive users of emerging computer technology." During the second generation of computers, most of the medium-sized companies adopted a "wait and see" attitude toward computers—but not Zimco.

Zimco ordered a small third-generation computer the day they were announced and took delivery 20 months later in December 1965. Early third-generation computers were made to order and they were in great demand. It was not uncommon for a company to wait more than a year to receive a computer! Each computer manufac-

tured had a customer's name on it. Zimco's president at the time visited the factory and spent a couple of hours watching "his" computer being built.

### The Computer Arrives

The 20 months following the order were busy times for the DP department. Management was confident that this new generation of computers would make life a breeze for the people in the DP department. But as Conrad Innis, the current VP of CIS, often says, "Confidence is that feeling you get before you fully understand the situation." Eventually, life would be easier with third-generation computers, but for the present, the conversion from second- to third-generation computers involved more than replacing one computer with a faster one.

Since existing programs did not run on the new generation of computers, all systems had to be redesigned and the programs rewritten—all 243 of them! The situation was further complicated by the fact that the people in the DP department had to learn a new programming language called COBOL. The DP manager hired two new programmers to help with the conversion and an expected increased demand for services from nonfinancial departments.

### The DP Department Comes of Age

By 1972, Zimco had taken delivery on a fourth-generation computer, increased their staff to 10, and was providing computing support for all of Zimco's departments. In 1976, the DP manager, who reported to the VP of Finance, was promoted and the "data processing" function was made a division. The new vice-president of the Computer and Information Services (CIS) Division reported directly to the president in a staff position. The name was changed to better reflect the role that CIS played in the overall operation of Zimco Enterprises.

The CIS staff, which now numbered 30, was constantly involved in developing systems to support all aspects of a rapidly expanding and very successful company.

## The Integration of Zimco's Information Systems

The demand for CIS services was so great that the division seemed to be growing out of control. In 1981, a new VP of CIS was hired to put some semblance of order back into CIS operation. The new VP, Conrad Innis, later observed that the "chaos in CIS was a result of an understaffed organization trying desperately to meet the seemingly endless information needs of the user departments." Conrad was a firm believer in order. He believed that each step forward should be well planned and cost justified.

Before Conrad arrived, systems were developed and files were created to meet a specific need. The result was dozens of autonomous information systems and a lot of data redundancy. Conrad shifted the emphasis from *autonomous* systems to *integrated* information systems. Before the movement to integrated information systems, CIS maintained autonomous systems for accounting, sales, marketing, and manufacturing, each of which had at least one computer-based file containing order information. Now order information is available to accounting, sales, marketing, manufacturing, or any other part of the company via a *centralized* integrated data base. Today, the VP of CIS has a staff of 51 in Dallas, and five at each of the three plant sites.

## ROLES AND RESPONSIBILITIES

When Conrad Innis arrived at Zimco in 1981, the first thing he noticed was that CIS had no well-defined direction or purpose. Programmers and systems analysts "barely had time to catch their breath, much less know where they are heading and what they are supposed to be do-

ing." Being a man of order, Conrad established a CIS charter that clarified *roles* and *responsibilities* of the CIS Department. The following charter was approved by the president, Preston Smith, in July 1982.

CIS is charged with the support of those information processing requirements that are consistent with corporate objectives. CIS responsibilities complementary to this charge include:

1. Development, ongoing operation, and maintenance of production information systems
2. Acting as an advisor to users throughout Zimco on computer-related matters
3. Serving as a catalyst for improving operations through system enhancements or new systems development
4. Coordinating data and systems integration throughout Zimco
5. Establishing standards, policy, and procedures relating to computers and information processing
6. Evaluating and selecting hardware and software
7. Conducting end-user education programs

With the CIS charter in place, there is seldom any question about who does what. This is often a problem in other companies.

## ORGANIZATION

Background.   In most businesses, the information services departments evolved as part of the accounting/finance function, and so it was with Zimco. As accounting systems, such as payroll and accounts receivable, proved the worth of the computer, other Zimco departments, such as personnel and marketing, began to request that systems be developed for them. From the beginning, Zimco's DP department was centralized to take advantage of the economies of scale. But rapid growth caused some information services departments, including Zimco's CIS, to become cumbersome and unnecessarily complex.

By the early 1980s, a *lack of responsiveness* to the regional plants and the *availability of small, cost-effective computers* was beginning to reverse Zimco's trend toward centralization.

In order to be more responsive to user information requirements, Conrad Innis decentralized parts of the information services function through *distributed processing*. However, he remained committed to a centralized CIS so that he could effectively coordinate all the activities involving information resources, such as hardware acquisition, information planning, and so on.

In effect, distributed processing is moving hardware, software, data, and computer specialists closer to where they are needed—the user areas. For example, each of the three plants outside of Dallas (Reston, Eugene, and Becker) has their own computer systems and computer specialists. These "distributed" computer systems are linked to Zimco's centralized computer system in Dallas.

Current CIS Organization.   CIS is the data and information "nerve center" of Zimco. The *data* are supplied by the various user groups. In return, the Computer and Information Services Division provides the software and operational support needed to produce *information*. Recognizing how important it is to be responsive to the company's information processing needs, Conrad Innis iden-

tified two basic objectives when he set out to reorganize the CIS Department in 1986. His first objective was to be responsive to the information needs of CIS users. The other objective was to have an organization that could operate efficiently to accomplish the responsibilities set forth in the CIS charter. The resultant organization is shown in Figure Z2–1.

Notice that CIS is divided into six groups, each with a manager. These groups are *systems analysis*, *programming*, *technical support*, *data communications*, *operations*, and *education*. The managers of the three regional computer centers at Eugene, Becker, and Reston also report to the VP of CIS. Conrad Innis also has "dotted line" responsibility for the user liaisons in each of the four functional divisions: finance and accounting, sales and marketing, personnel, and operations. The role of the VP of CIS and each of the six departments in CIS and the regional computing centers is described below.

## The Role of the Vice-President of CIS

*Conrad Innis*, the VP of CIS, is the chief information officer (CIO) and has responsibility for all

**FIGURE Z2–1**
**Organization Chart for Zimco's**
**Computer and Information**
**Services Division**

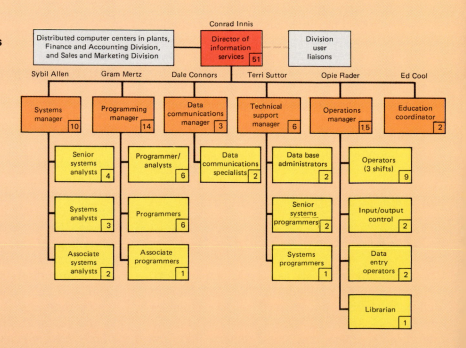

Systems analysts at Zimco work with users to ensure that they get the information they need in a format that they can easily understand. This analyst recommended presenting productivity data in the form of a color-coded pie chart.
(Dataproducts Corporation)

computer and information systems activity at Zimco. At least half of his time is spent interacting with user managers and executives. In this capacity, Conrad coordinates the integration of data and information systems and serves as the catalyst for new systems development. The remainder of his time is devoted to managing the Computer and Information Services Division.

## Systems Analysis Department

*Sybil Allen* heads the Systems Analysis group and has a staff of nine **systems analysts** working for her. The systems analysts, or simply "analysts," do the analysis, design, and implementation of information systems. The analysts work closely with people in the four user areas to design information systems that meet their data processing and information needs. These "problem solvers" are assigned a variety of tasks, which might include feasibility studies, system reviews, security assessments, long-range planning, and hardware/software selection.

The role of these "problem solvers" is expanding with the technology. For example, with recent innovations in programming languages (see Chapter 9), users and analysts can work together at a workstation to design *and* implement certain information systems—without programmer involvement!

## Programming Department

*Gram Mertz* manages the Programming Department. The **applications programmers** in his group, or simply **programmers,** translate analyst-prepared system and input/output specifications into programs. Programmers design the logic, then code, debug, test, and document the programs. Gram's people write programs for a certain application, such as market analysis or inventory management.

Sometimes called "implementers" or "miracle workers," programmers are charged with turning system specifications into an information system. To do this, they must exhibit logical thinking and overlook nothing. Gram characterizes a good programmer as *perceptive*, *patient*, *persistent*, *picky*, and *productive*: the five Ps of programming."

Some companies distinguish between *development* and *maintenance* programmers. Development programmers create *new* systems. Maintenance programmers enhance existing systems by *modifying* programs to meet changing needs. At Zimco, all programmers do both. About 50 percent of the applications programming tasks are related to maintenance and 50 percent to new development.

A person holding a **programmer/analyst** position performs the functions of both a programmer and a systems analyst. At Zimco, the more senior people in the Programming Department are programmer/analysts.

## Data Communications Department

The **data communications specialists,** managed by *Dale Conners*, design and maintain computer networks that link computers and workstations for data communications. This involves selecting and installing appropriate hardware, such as modems, data PBXs, and front-end processors, as well as selecting the transmission media. These concepts are discussed in detail in Chapter 8, "Data Communications." Data communications specialists also develop and implement the software that controls the flow of data between computing devices.

## Technical Support Department

The Technical Support Department, managed by *Terri Suttor*, designs, develops, maintains, and implements *systems software*. Systems software is fundamental to the general operation of the computer; that is, it does not address a specific business or scientific problem.

The types of positions that report to Terri are systems programmers and the data base administrator. **Systems programmers** develop and maintain systems software. The **data base administrator (DBA)** position evolved with the need to integrate information systems. The data base administrator designs, creates, and maintains Zimco's integrated data base. The DBA coordinates discussions between user groups to determine the content and format of the data base so that data redundancy is kept to a minimum. Accuracy and security of the data base are also responsibilities of the data base administrator.

## Operations Department

*Opie Rader* is the manager of the Operations Department and of people who perform a variety of jobs, each of which is described in the following paragraphs.

*Computer Operator.* The **computer operators** at Zimco perform those hardware-based activities that are needed to keep production information systems operational. An operator works in the machine room, initiating software routines and mounting the appropriate magnetic tapes, disks, and preprinted forms. The operator is in constant communication with the computer while monitoring the progress of a number of simultaneous production runs, initiating one-time jobs, and troubleshooting. If the computer system fails, the operator initiates restart procedures to "bring the system up."

*Control Clerk.* The **control clerk** accounts for all input to and output from the computer center. Control clerks follow standard procedures to validate the accuracy of the output before it is distributed to the user department.

*Data Entry Operator.* **Data entry operators,** sometimes called key operators, use key entry devices to transcribe data into machine-readable format. At Zimco, only a small data entry group is attached to CIS because the majority of the data entry operators are "distributed" to the user areas.

*Librarian.* The **librarian** selects the appropriate interchangeable magnetic tapes and disks and delivers them to the operator. The operator mounts the tapes and disks on the storage devices for processing, then returns them to the librarian for storage. The librarian maintains a status log on each tape and disk. Zimco, like other companies its size, has hundreds of tapes and disks.

The librarian is also charged with maintaining a reference library filled with computer books, periodicals, and manuals, as well as internal system and program documentation (i.e., logic diagrams, program listings).

## Education Department

*Ed Cool* is the **education coordinator** at Zimco. He and his assistant coordinate all computer-related educational activities. Ed says that "anyone who works with computers or selects a computer-related career automatically adopts a life of continuing education. Computer technology is changing rapidly and you have to run pretty fast just to stand still!" He schedules users and computer specialists for technical update seminars, video training programs, computer-assisted instruction, and others, as needed. Ed often conducts the training sessions himself.

## "Distributed" Computer Centers

It's not unusual for people working in small computer centers and distributed computer centers, such as those in Reston, Eugene, and Becker, to be accomplished at a variety of jobs. Both small

and large "shops" (a slang term for information services departments) must accomplish the functions of systems analysis, programming, technical support, data communications, operations, and education. In larger shops, such as Zimco's CIS in Dallas, the people are highly specialized; but in the small distributed shops, each person must be a generalist, capable of doing whatever needs to be done. The three people in each of the distributed centers at the remote plants double-up on duties. For example, one person who does primarily applications programming is also the data base administrator at the Reston plant.

## HIRING PRACTICES

Zimco has had great success hiring recent college graduates. New hires go through an 18-month training program. Most people with associate or bachelor's degrees begin work as programmers. Technical school graduates and some associate-degree holders begin working as operators, control clerks, librarians, and data entry operators, depending on their qualifications. After gaining operations experience, those with associate de-

Zimco has six distributed computer centers which are linked to the central computer center in Dallas. Because only a few people work at each of the distributed computer centers, each must acquire skills in a variety of computer specialists positions, from operations to data communications.
(Honeywell, Inc.)

grees and programming education often are promoted to programming positions.

Like most companies, Zimco doesn't recruit recent graduates to fill *systems analyst* positions. They prefer their analysts to have programming experience. Occasionally, CIS hires a *programmer/analyst*, but assignments for a rookie programmer/analyst are usually programming tasks for the first couple of years.

Zimco's rationale behind starting people as programmers is well founded. Gram Mertz explained their policy. "Programming not only develops logic and design skills, but it also provides real-world insight into the capabilities and limitations of a computer system. We want our computer specialists to know what a computer system can and cannot do and programming is about the best way for them to acquire this knowledge."

Once a Zimco employee has a solid foundation in programming (18 months to three years), he or she can pursue a career as a programmer or branch out into other information services careers. There is no traditional career path at Zimco; two people rarely advance through the ranks in the same manner. Most are faced with the luxury of having several promotion alternatives at each level.

## SUMMARY OF ZIMCO'S CIS ORGANIZATION

The central focus of the Computer and Information Services Division is the development and ongoing operation of information systems. Figure Z2–2 graphically summarizes the relationship between the positions that have been described and the development and operation of an information system. A *user* request for a computer-related service, called a **service request,** is compiled and submitted to the CIS department. Because resources are limited, the VP of CIS, Conrad Innis, approves those requests that appear to offer the greatest benefits to the organization.

A project team made up of *systems analysts*, *programmers*, *user liaisons*, and possibly the *data base administrator* is formed to develop and implement the information system. *Systems programmers* and *data communications specialists* make changes to the hardware configuration, data communications network, and systems software, as required. The *education coordinator* schedules needed training sessions for both computer specialists and users. Once the system is implemented and becomes operational, operations people handle the routine input, processing,

**FIGURE Z2–2**
**Position Functions and Information Systems at Zimco**
This chart summarizes the relationship between the various positions in the Computer and Information Services Division and user personnel in the development and operation of an information system.

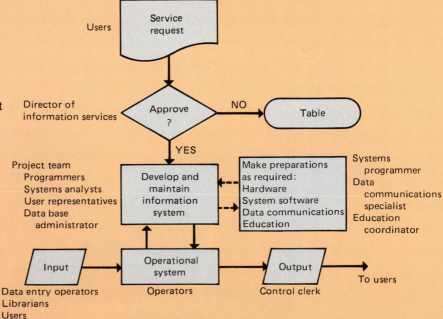

and output activities. *Data entry operators* transcribe the raw data to machine-readable format. The *librarian* readies magnetic storage media for processing. *Operators* initiate and monitor computer runs and distribute the output to *control clerks*, who then check the output for accuracy before delivering it to the *users*.

## DISCUSSION QUESTIONS

1. Zimco's Data Processing Department consisted of three people from 1945 to 1959, even though the company grew from 200 to 450 people. Why did all departments, except DP, expand markedly during this period?

2. Why do you think Zimco skipped the first and second generations of computers?

3. The people in the DP Department had a 20-month lead time prior to the delivery of their first computer in 1965. What did they do in preparation for its arrival?

4. In 1981, why did Conrad Innis want to shift the emphasis from autonomous information systems to an integrated information system?

5. During the formation of the CIS charter, several items in the charter were debated heavily. Which charter items do you think are the most controversial, and why?

6. What prompted Conrad Innis to decentralize certain operations through distributed processing?

7. Sybil Allen has suggested on several occasions to Conrad Innis that both programmers and systems analysts should report to a single manager. Discuss the pros and cons of her suggestion.

8. Gram Mertz uses the "five Ps of programming" to describe a "good programmer." Discuss desirable characteristics of a good systems analyst.

9. Zimco encourages the hiring of recent college graduates. Other companies prefer hiring those with experience. Discuss the advantages and disadvantages of each approach.

# PART 2 INFORMATION SYSTEMS

In the 1960s many of our larger clients began to extensively use the computer to process accounting records. They called on Coopers and Lybrand to help them understand the control issues involved and to advise them on effective system development.

Today, twenty years later, a revolution has taken place. The computer has far outstripped its role as an assembler of data and an efficient calculator. Companies of every size have captured almost all their accounting and financial data on computer systems—systems closely linked to both business support and operational management. Most companies also employ data base technology and data communications.

Over the course of their business careers, today's students will have opportunities to use computers in ways we're only just beginning to anticipate. Full portability of equipment, voice activation, optical transfer, expert systems—these and other innovations will make computer power economical and readily available, to anyone at any time in any place.

We need a generation of business people who neither fears the computer nor stands in awe of it, people who have the imagination and creativity to harness the computer's potential and use it to rethink and improve the management strategies of the future.

Peter Scanlon
Chairman
Coopers & Lybrand

# Management Information Systems

## CHAPTER 3

## STUDENT LEARNING OBJECTIVES

- To identify the elements and scope of a management information system.
- To describe how information needs vary at each level of organizational activity.
- To explain the concept of user-friendly systems.
- To contrast the concepts of on-line and off-line.
- To describe the circumstances appropriate for batch and transaction-oriented data entry.
- To identify points of security vulnerability for the computer center and for information systems.
- To present benefits and costs associated with justifying the implementation of computer technology.

## FOCUS OF ZIMCO CASE STUDY

- Management information systems at Zimco.

## 3

### 3–1  MANAGEMENT'S CHALLENGE

Management in every area of business endeavor is being challenged to increase productivity and, thereby, profitability. In the past, management has relied heavily on work-simplification techniques and employee motivation to achieve enhancements in productivity. These approaches have proven successful, but they alone are not enough for a company to remain competitive in a "world" market. In an all-out effort to meet the "productivity" challenge, managers are looking to the information resource.

Managers have become very adept at taking full advantage of the resources of *money*, *materials*, and *people*; but only recently have managers begun to make effective use of the fourth major resource—*information*. In fact, corporate management everywhere is adopting a new attitude called **information resource management (IRM).** Information resource management is a concept advocating that information is a valuable resource and should be managed accordingly, just like money, materials, and people. The IRM attitude has whetted every manager's appetite for more and better information and in so doing, managers have demonstrated a desire to learn more about tools of information—computers.

An automobile manufacturer has lowered the cost of producing automobiles while retaining maximum flexibility in what is made. To do this, a computer system was installed to control the assembly line and enable the communication and implementation of last-minute order changes.
(Courtesy of International Business Machines Corporation)

## 3–2   MANAGEMENT'S THIRST FOR INFORMATION

### Information Systems

We combine *hardware*, *software*, *people*, *procedures*, and *data* to create an **information system.** A computer-based information system provides a manager's department with *data processing* capabilities and managers with the *information* they need to make better, more informed decisions. The data processing capability, or the handling and processing of data, is only one facet of an information system. A complete information system provides decision makers with on-demand reports and inquiry capabilites, as well as routine periodic reports. Because an information system aids management in making business decisions, it is sometimes called a **management information system (MIS).** In practice, the terms "information system," "management information system," and "MIS" are used interchangeably.

Until recently, most payroll systems were data processing systems that did little more than process time sheets, print payroll checks, and keep running totals of annual wages and deductions. Managers began to demand more and better information on their personnel. As a result, payroll *data processing systems* evolved to human resource *information systems*. These systems are capable of predicting the average number of worker sick days, monitoring salary equality between minority groups, making more effective use of available skills, and much more.

### Decision Support Systems

**Decision support systems (DSSs)** generally reference user-friendly software that produces and presents information that is targeted to support management in the decision-making process. DSS software often involves the latest technological innovations (e.g., color graphics, database management systems), planning and forecasting models, user-oriented query languages (discussed in Chapter 9), and expert systems. Managers spend much of their day requesting and analyzing information before making a decision. Decision support systems help close the information gap so that managers can improve the quality of their decisions.

Decision support systems provide these land developers with direct access to the information they need to make critical decisions about the ecological and economic consequences of developing certain parcels of land. A DSS can supply the information when they want it and in the form they want it.
(Cullinet Software, Inc.)

Decision support systems help to remove the tedium of gathering and analyzing data. No longer are managers strapped with such laborious tasks as manually entering and extending numbers (summing rows and columns of numbers) on spreadsheet paper. Graphics software enables managers to generate in minutes illustrative bar and pie charts. And now, with the availability of a variety of DSSs, managers can get the information they need without having to depend on direct technical assistance from an MIS professional.

Some people attempt to draw a line between an MIS and a DSS. They limit an MIS to providing periodic, preprogrammed reports, such as a weekly regional sales summary. On the other hand, they say that a DSS is less structured and provides managers with the flexibility to look into the future and ask "what if" questions. In practice, well-designed management information systems embody the capabilities of a decision support system.

## User-Developed Information Systems

The information demands in a typical business are almost endless. To give you an idea of management's demand for decision support information, the average information services department carries a $3\frac{1}{2}$-year backlog of service requests. We have heard that "time is money"; it is also true that "information is money." Users cannot wait three or four years for the information they need. Most can't wait a week, so many users are taking matters into their own hands. With the help of user-friendly software tools, such as query languages, electronic spreadsheets, and decision support systems, they are developing their own information systems.

The combination of distributed processing, powerful micros, and user-friendly software has resulted in rapidly expanding the base of computer-wise users. These users have the tools and knowledge to meet many of their own information processing needs. In fact, a greater percentage of an organization's ever-growing information processing needs are being met with little or no involvement on the part of the professional programmers in an information services department. This trend is illustrated in Figure 3–1. Notice that each year a growing percentage of a company's information processing needs are being met by the user community.

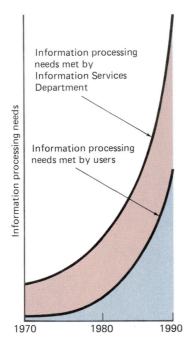

Information processing needs met by Information Services Department

Information processing needs met by users

Information processing needs

1970        1980        1990

**FIGURE 3–1**
**Meeting Information Processing Needs**
Each year a greater percentage of a company's total information processing needs are being met by the user community.

In the construction business, the accuracy of cost estimates may mean the difference between making or losing money. This engineer developed an information system that uses historical data and updated cost data to produce reliable estimates of project costs.
(Courtesy of Apple Computer, Inc.)

User-developed information systems are limited in scope and sophistication, and they are usually *function based*; that is, they are designed to support an individual's or a department's information needs. In contrast, information systems developed by the information services department usually are *integrated* and are designed to support several departments, or the company as a whole.

## Systems Ripe for Computerization

A manual system has the same components as a computer-based system—input, processing, output, and storage. If we were to talk in terms of numbers of systems, the overwhelming majority in both business and government are still manual. This is true of large companies with complex computer networks as well as of small companies without computers. Tens of thousands of manual systems have been approved to be upgraded to computer-based information systems. Ten times that many are awaiting tomorrow's talented and creative people—perhaps you—to identify their potential for computerization.

As in a computer-based system, a manual system has an established pattern for work and data flow. For example, a payroll clerk receives the time sheets from supervisors; the individual employee's records are retrieved from folders stored alphabetically in a file cabinet; the payroll clerk uses a calculator to compute gross and net pay, then manually types the payroll check and stub. Finally, the payroll register, a listing of the amount paid, and the deductions for each employee is compiled on a tally sheet with column totals. About the only way to obtain information in a manual system is painstakingly to thumb through employee folders to find and extract what we need.

Today, most payroll systems have been automated. But look in any office in almost any company and you will find rooms full of filing cabinets, tabbed three-ring binders, and drawers filled with 3- by 5-inch name-and-address cards. These manual files are symbols of opportunities to improve a company's profitability and productivity through computerization—a type of automation intended to *improve* jobs, *not to eliminate* jobs.

## Computerization Means Change

The development and implementation of virtually any MIS involves change; therefore, *change management* comes into play. To achieve an orderly transition from a manual system to a computer-based information system or to an enhancement of an existing information system, managers must pay particular attention to the effects of change. A good manager is proactive and does not react to the problems of change. The proactive manager keeps everyone informed, thereby silencing the "rumor mill." Inevitably, the implementation of a new information system will result in some shifts in responsibilities. The implementation of an integrated MIS often prompts a major reorganization.

Perhaps the most important managerial concern is the attitude of the subordinates toward the changes brought about because of computerization. To combat negative attitudes, the manager must demon-

MEMORY BITS

| Hardware Software People Procedures Data | are combined to create: | *Information systems* | that provide: | Data processing Information |

strate to subordinates how the proposed MIS will help them to do their jobs better and how it will provide greater career opportunities. Workers who understand the benefits of an MIS are much more willing to participate in the conversion.

## 3–3  LEVELS OF ORGANIZATIONAL ACTIVITY: WHO GETS WHAT INFORMATION

A company has four levels of activity—*clerical*, *operational*, *tactical*, and *strategic*. Information systems process data at the clerical level and provide information for managerial decision making at the other three levels. The top three levels of activity were discussed briefly as part of the business system model (Figure Z1–7) in the Zimco case study following Chapter 1.

The quality of an information system is judged by its output. A system that generates the same 20-page report for personnel at both the clerical and strategic levels is defeating the purpose of an information system. The information needs at these two levels of activity are substantially different: a secretary has no need, or desire, for such a comprehensive report; the president of the company would never use the report because it would take too long to extract the few pieces of important information.

Programmers, systems analysts, and users must determine the specific informational needs at each level of organizational activity during the system design process. The key to developing quality information systems is to "filter" information so that people at the various levels of activity receive the information they need to accomplish their job function—no more, no less. The quality of an information system depends very much on getting the *right information* to the *right people* at the *right time*.

Clerical Level.  Clerical-level personnel, those involved in repetitive tasks, are concerned primarily with transaction handling. You might say that they process data. For example, in a sales information system, order entry clerks key in customer orders from their workstations.

Operational Level.  Personnel at the operational level have well-defined tasks that might span a day, a week, or as much as three months, but their tasks are essentially short-term. Their information requirements are directed at operational feedback. In the sales information system, for example, the manager of the Eastern Region Sales Department might want an end-of-quarter "Sales Summary" report. The report, illustrated in Figure 3–2, shows dollar volume sales by

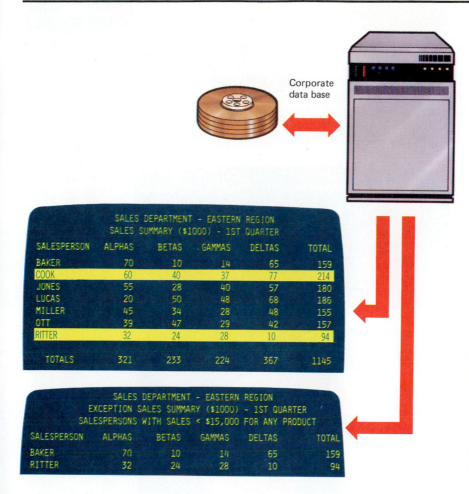

SALES DEPARTMENT - EASTERN REGION
SALES SUMMARY ($1000) - 1ST QUARTER

| SALESPERSON | ALPHAS | BETAS | GAMMAS | DELTAS | TOTAL |
|---|---|---|---|---|---|
| BAKER | 70 | 10 | 14 | 65 | 159 |
| COOK | 60 | 40 | 37 | 77 | 214 |
| JONES | 55 | 28 | 40 | 57 | 180 |
| LUCAS | 20 | 50 | 48 | 68 | 186 |
| MILLER | 45 | 34 | 28 | 48 | 155 |
| OTT | 39 | 47 | 29 | 42 | 157 |
| RITTER | 32 | 24 | 28 | 10 | 94 |
| TOTALS | 321 | 233 | 224 | 367 | 1145 |

SALES DEPARTMENT - EASTERN REGION
EXCEPTION SALES SUMMARY ($1000) - 1ST QUARTER
SALESPERSONS WITH SALES < $15,000 FOR ANY PRODUCT

| SALESPERSON | ALPHAS | BETAS | GAMMAS | DELTAS | TOTAL |
|---|---|---|---|---|---|
| BAKER | 70 | 10 | 14 | 65 | 159 |
| RITTER | 32 | 24 | 28 | 10 | 94 |

**FIGURE 3–2**
**An Operational-Level Sales-Summary and Exception Report**
These sales reports are prepared in response to inquiries from an operational-level manager. Contrast the reports in this figure with those in Figures 3–3 and 3–4.

salesperson for each of the company's four products: Alphas, Betas, Gammas, and Deltas. In the report, the sales records of the top (Cook) and bottom (Ritter) performers are highlighted so that managers can use this range as a basis for comparing the performance of the other salespersons.

Managers at the operational, tactical, and stragetic levels often request **exception reports** that highlight critical information. Such requests can be made to the information services department, or managers can make inquiries directly to the system using a query language. For example, the eastern regional sales manager used a query language

This regional sales staff works primarily at the operational level of activity. Their information horizon is normally less than three months: If they can't get their product to their customer in this time span, a competitor will.
(Bethlehem Steel Corporation)

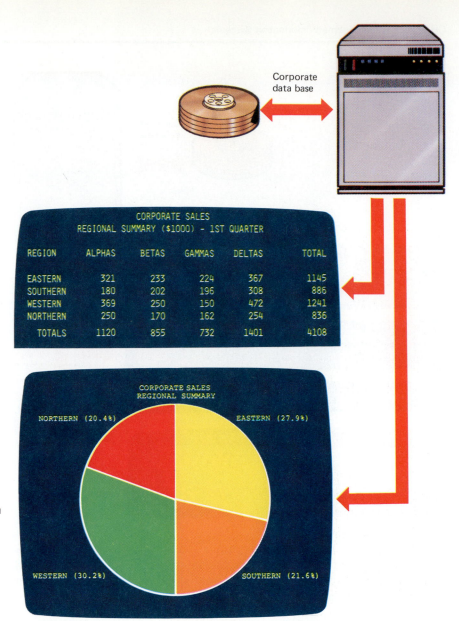

**FIGURE 3–3**
**A Tactical-Level**
**Sales-Summary Report Shown**
**in Tabular and Graphic Form**
The sales summary report and
pie chart are prepared in
response to inquiries from a
tactical-level manager. Contrast
the reports in this figure with
those in Figures 3–2 and 3–4.

(discussed further in Chapter 9, "Programming Languages and Software Concepts") to generate the exception report of Figure 3–2. The manager's request was: "Display a list of all eastern region salespersons who had sales of less than $15,000 for any product for this quarter." The report highlights the subpar performances of Baker and Ritter.

Tactical Level.   At the tactical level, managers concentrate on achieving that series of goals required to meet the objectives set at the strategic level. The information requirements are usually periodic, but on occasion, managers require "what if" reports. Tactical managers are concerned primarily with operations and budgets from year to year. In the sales information system, the national sales manager, who is at the tactical level, might want the "Corporate Sales" report of Figure 3–3. The report presents dollar volume sales by sales region for each of the company's four products. To get a better feeling for the relative sales contribution of each of the four regional offices during the first quarter, the national sales manager requested that the total sales for each region be presented graphically in a pie chart (see Figure 3–3).

Strategic Level.    Managers at the strategic level are objective minded. Their information system requirements are often one-time reports, "what if" reports, and trend analyses. For example, the president of the company might ask for a report that shows the four-year sales trend for each of the company's four products and overall (Figure 3–4). Knowing that it is easier to detect trends in a graphic format than in a tabular listing, the president requested that the trends be summarized in a bar graph (Figure 3–4). From the bar graph, the president can easily see that the sales of Alphas and Gammas are experiencing modest growth while the sales of Betas and Deltas are more to his liking.

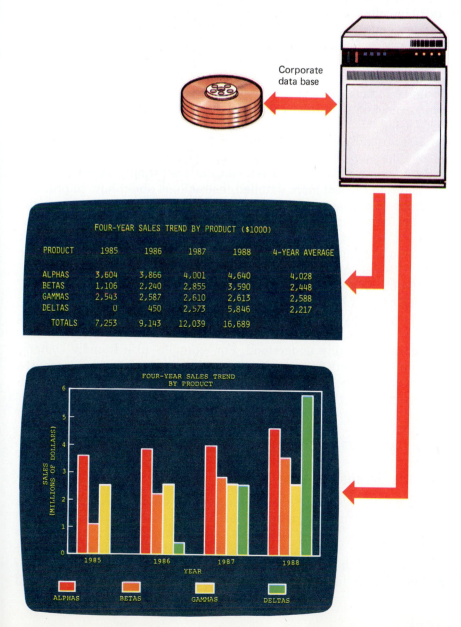

Corporate data base

**FIGURE 3–4**
**A Strategic-Level Sales-Trend-by-Product Report Shown in Tabular and Graphic Form**
The sales-trend report and bar chart are prepared in response to inquiries from a strategic-level manager. Contrast the reports in this figure with those in Figures 3–2 and 3–3.

FOUR-YEAR SALES TREND BY PRODUCT ($1000)

| PRODUCT | 1985 | 1986 | 1987 | 1988 | 4-YEAR AVERAGE |
|---|---|---|---|---|---|
| ALPHAS | 3,604 | 3,866 | 4,001 | 4,640 | 4,028 |
| BETAS | 1,106 | 2,240 | 2,855 | 3,590 | 2,448 |
| GAMMAS | 2,543 | 2,587 | 2,610 | 2,613 | 2,588 |
| DELTAS | 0 | 450 | 2,573 | 5,846 | 2,217 |
| TOTALS | 7,253 | 9,143 | 12,039 | 16,689 | |

MEMORY BITS

### INFORMATION REQUIREMENTS

| | | |
|---|---|---|
| ■ Clerical level | → | Primarily transaction handling |
| ■ Operational level | → | Short-term operational feedback |
| ■ Tactical level | → | Long-term operational feedback |
| ■ Strategic level | → | "What if" and trend analysis |

## 3–4　USER-FRIENDLY INFORMATION SYSTEMS

Within a few years the majority of professional people, and virtually all office workers, will spend some portion of their day interacting with a computer system. In a few more years almost everybody, including blue-collar workers, will use the computer regularly. Interacting with workstations will become part of the daily routine of accountants, lawyers, shop foremen, architects, clerks, plant managers, and virtually everyone else in the business community. In anticipation of this upswing in the number and variety of computer users, systems are being designed to be more *user friendly*. A system is said to be user friendly when someone with relatively little computer experience has no difficulty using it.

User-friendly systems simplify user interaction by communicating easily understood words, phrases, and even pictographs, called *icons*, to the end user. If confusion arises, the end user simply issues a "HELP" command to request more detailed instructions about how to proceed. Programmers occasionally insert humor into system responses to maintain the "user-friendly" philosophy and to break the monotony. For example, instead of responding "TRANSACTION COMPLETE," one programmer designed the information system to respond randomly with one of 20 responses, such as "LOOKING GOOD," "NICE GOING," or "JOLLY GOOD SHOW." An input error resulted in "WHOOPS" or "YOU GOTTA BE KIDDING!"

User-friendly systems not only assist the user while interacting with the system, but they also present information in a format that can be more readily understood. For example, user-friendly systems provide the facility to present tabular data as bar charts, pie charts, and line drawings. Most of us can absorb a graphic summary of information more quickly than a screen full of numbers.

## 3–5　MIS CONCEPTS

### On-Line versus Off-Line

In a computer system, the input, output, and data storage components receive data from, and transmit data to, the processor over electrical cables or "lines." These hardware components are said to be **on-line** to the processor. Hardware devices that are not accessible to, or under the control of, a processor are said to be **off-line.** The concepts of on-line and off-line apply also to data. Data are said to be *on-line* if

This portable computer has more power than some mainframes of a decade ago. These supervisors are entering data that reflect the receipt of certain building materials. The data are entered off-line at the work site. Later, the data are "downloaded" or sent on-line to the company's mainframe computer system as input to the accounts payable system.
(Courtesy of International Business Machines Corporation)

they can be accessed and manipulated by the processor. All other data are *off-line*.

"On-line" and "off-line" are important MIS concepts. Consider the payroll example in Figure 3–5. In an *off-line* operation, all supervisors complete the weekly time sheets. The time sheets are then collected and *batched* for input to the computer system. When transactions are grouped together for processing, it is called **batch processing.**

Before the data can be entered and the payroll checks printed, the payroll master file must be placed on-line. To do this, the master file is retrieved manually from a library of disk files and "loaded" to a storage component called a disk drive. Once loaded, the payroll master file is on-line. The process is analogous to selecting the phonograph record that you wish to play and mounting it on the turntable.

**FIGURE 3–5**
**On-Line and Off-Line Operations**
Those processing activities, hardware, and files that are not controlled by, or accessible to, the computer are referred to as off-line.

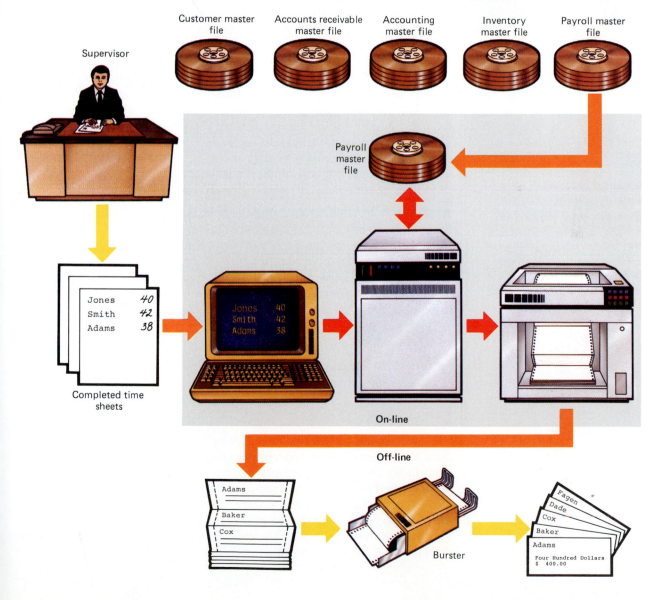

An operator at a workstation enters the data contained on the time sheets directly into the computer system in an *on-line* operation. Employee data, such as name, social security number, pay rate, and deductions, are retrieved from the payroll master file and combined with the number of hours worked to produce the payroll checks. The payroll checks are produced on a printer, which is an output device.

Since the payroll checks are printed on continuous preprinted forms, they must be separated before they can be distributed to the employees. In an *off-line* operation, a machine called a burster separates and stacks the payroll checks.

## Data Entry

Each day, this government office receives hundreds of applications for aid to small businesses. The applications (the source documents) are batched and the data from these source documents are entered and verified at these workstations.
(National Computer Systems)

Source Data.   Most data do not exist in a form that can be "read" by the computer. In the example of Figure 3–5, the supervisor uses a pencil and paper to manually record the hours worked by the staff on the time sheet. Before the payroll checks can be computed and printed, the data on these time sheets must be *transcribed* (converted) into a *machine-readable format* that can be interpreted by a computer. This is done in an *on-line* operation by someone at a workstation. The time sheet is known as the **source document,** and, as you might expect, the data on the time sheet are the **source data.**

Not all source data have to be transcribed. For example, the numbers imprinted on the bottom of your bank checks indicate your individual account number and bank. These numbers are already machine readable, so they can be "read" directly by an input device.

Approaches to Data Entry.   The term **data entry** is used to describe the process of entering data into a computer-based information system. Information systems are designed to provide users with display-screen "prompts" to make on-line data entry easier. The display on the operator's screen, for example, may be the image of the source document (such as a time sheet). A **prompt** is a brief message to the operator that describes what should be entered (e.g., "INPUT HOURS WORKED _____ ").

Data can be entered on a workstation in the following ways:

- *Batch*. Transactions are grouped, or *batched*, and entered consecutively, one after the other.
- *Transaction-oriented*. Transactions are recorded and entered as they occur.

To illustrate the difference between batch and transaction-oriented data entry, consider an order processing system for a mail-order merchandiser. The system accepts orders by both mail and phone. The orders received by mail are accumulated, or batched, for data entry—usually at night. For phone orders there are no handwritten source documents; persons taking the phone orders interact with the computer via workstations to enter the order data on-line while talking with the customer (see Figure 3–6).

All airline reservation systems are transaction-oriented systems. The workstations at ticketing counters in airports are on-line to a centralized computer facility. Each time an agent writes a ticket and assigns a passenger a seat, the master record for that flight is immediately updated to reflect the addition of one more passenger.
(Long and Associates)

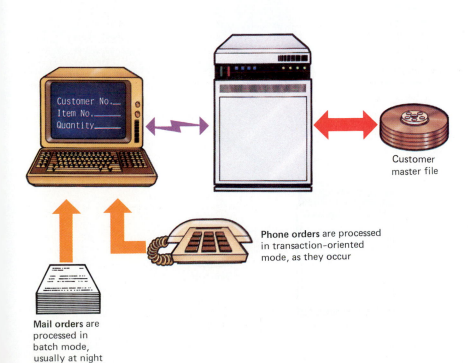

Customer master file

Phone orders are processed in transaction-oriented mode, as they occur

Mail orders are processed in batch mode, usually at night

**FIGURE 3–6**
**Batch and Transaction-Oriented Data Entry**
Mail order merchandisers accept orders by mail and by phone.

On-Line Data Entry.   Most data entry to mainframe computer systems, both batch and transaction-oriented, is done on-line. Workstation operators enter data *directly* to the host computer system for processing, as shown in Figure 3–7. The primary advantage of transaction-oriented data entry is that records on the data base are updated immediately, as the transaction occurs. This is quite different from batch data entry, where records are batched periodically. Another advantage of transaction-oriented data entry is that operators can make inquiries to the system. In the example of Figure 3–6, a salesperson can check the availability of an item and tell the customer when to expect delivery.

On-line data entry is critical to companies whose data base must be current every minute of the day. Hotel reservation systems provide excellent examples of on-line data entry. All the major hotel chains have similar reservation systems. Someone wishing to make a reservation may do so at any hotel or by calling a toll-free reservation number.

**FIGURE 3–7**
**On-Line Data Entry Process**
Operators enter data directly to the host computer system for processing. Information systems that rely on up-to-the-minute accuracy of the data base are designed for on-line data entry.

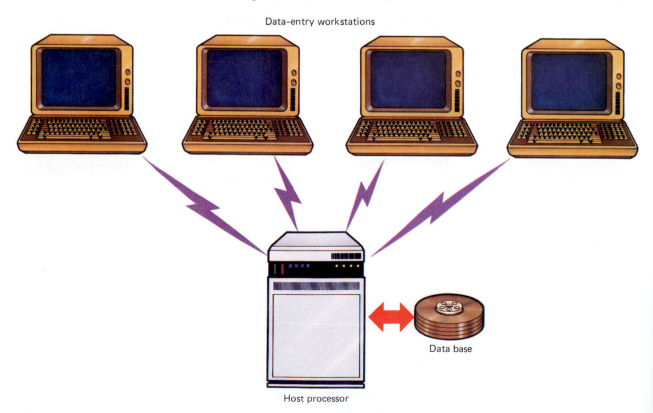

Data–entry workstations

Data base

Host processor

The following is representative of the data entered by a hotel reservations clerk.

1. Name of guest
2. Location (city and particular hotel)
3. Date of reservation
4. Type of room desired
5. Number of nights
6. Number of persons
7. Credit card number and type
8. Phone number of guest

On-line data entry is critical to the routine operation of all hotel chains. Since each hotel has a limited number of rooms, once they are all taken for a particular night, no more reservations can be accepted. So as soon as an operator receives a call for a room reservation, the operator checks the data base to make sure that rooms are still available. As the reservation is made, the central data base is updated to reflect that one less room is available on certain nights at a particular hotel.

## 3–6   MIS SECURITY

Certainly, one of the most important considerations in the development and ongoing operation of a management information system is security. As more and more systems go on-line, more people have access to the system. A company must be extremely careful not to compromise the integrity of the system. The company must be equally careful with the "engine" for the information system—the computer.

An MIS has many points of vulnerability and too much is at stake to overlook the threats to the security of an information system and a computer center. These threats take many forms: white-collar crime, natural disasters (e.g., earthquakes, floods), vandalism, and carelessness.

White-collar crime is real and exists undetected in some of the most unlikely places. It is sophisticated crime with sophisticated criminals. And it is more widespread than estimates would lead us to believe. Most computer crimes are undetected; others are unreported. A bank may prefer to write off a $100,000 embezzlement rather than publicly announce to its depositors that its computer system is vulnerable.

This section is devoted to discussing the security measures needed to neutralize security threats to an information system or to a computer center (see Figure 3–8).

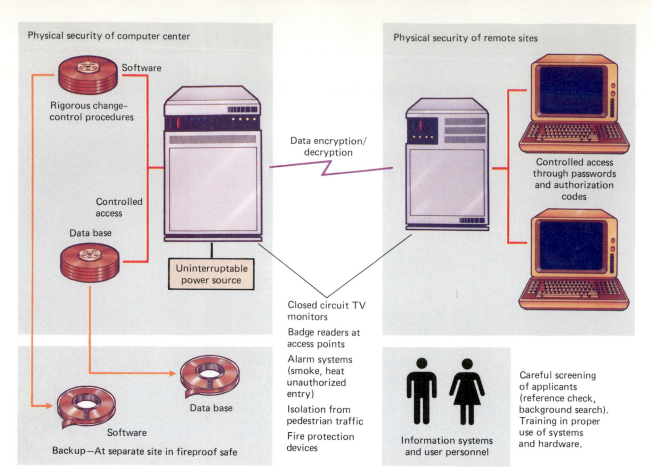

Physical security of computer center

Software

Rigorous change-control procedures

Controlled access

Data base

Backup—At separate site in fireproof safe

Software

Data base

Uninterruptable power source

Data encryption/decryption

Closed circuit TV monitors

Badge readers at access points

Alarm systems (smoke, heat unauthorized entry)

Isolation from pedestrian traffic

Fire protection devices

Information systems and user personnel

Physical security of remote sites

Controlled access through passwords and authorization codes

Careful screening of applicants (reference check, background search). Training in proper use of systems and hardware.

Biometric identification systems are beginning to replace systems that use the plastic card (badge) as a "key" for entry to secured areas, such as computer centers. One such system asks users for their signature before permitting entry to a secured area or access to a sensitive data base. If the digitized image of the signature does not match that of the authorized signature, then entry or access is denied.
(Courtesy of International Business Machines Corporation)

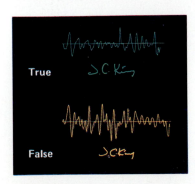

**FIGURE 3–8**
**Security Precautions**
Some, or all, of the security measures noted in the figure are implemented in most computer centers. Each precaution helps to minimize the risk of an MIS's or a computer system's vulnerability to crime, disasters, and failure.

## Computer-Center Security

A company's computer center has a number of points of vulnerability; these are *hardware*, *software*, *files/data bases*, *data communications*, and *personnel*. Each is discussed separately below.

**Hardware.**   If the hardware fails, the MIS fails. The threat of failure can be minimized by implementing security precautions that prevent access by unauthorized personnel and by taking steps to keep all hardware operational.

Common approaches to securing the premises from unauthorized entry include closed-circuit TV monitors, alarm systems, and computer-controlled devices that check employee badges, fingerprints, or voice prints before unlocking doors at access points. Also, computer centers should be isolated from pedestrian traffic. Machine-room fires are extinguished by a special chemical that douses the fire but does not destroy the files or equipment.

Computers, especially mainframe computers, must have a "clean," continuous source of power. To minimize the effects of "dirty" power or power outages, many computer centers have installed an **uninterruptible power source (UPS).** Dirty power, such as sags and surges in power output or brownouts (low power), causes data transmission errors and program execution errors. An UPS system serves as a control buffer between the external power source and the computer system. In an UPS system, the computer is powered by batteries (which deliver clean power), which in turn are regenerated by an external power source. If the external power source fails, the UPS system permits operation to continue for a period of time after an outage. This allows operators to either "power-down" normally or switch to a backup power source, normally a diesel generator.

**Software.** Unless properly controlled, the software for an MIS can be modified for personal gain. Thus close control over software development and the documentation of an MIS is needed to minimize the opportunity for computer crime. Operational control procedures that are built into the design of an MIS will constantly monitor processing accuracy. These controls are discussed in Chapter 11, "The Systems Development Process." Unfortunately, cagey programmers have been known to get around some of these controls. Perhaps the best way to safeguard programs from unlawful tampering is to use rigorous change-control procedures. Such procedures make it difficult to modify a program for purposes of personal gain.

This is one of ten aisles in a large magnetic tape library. The entire library is secured in a fire-proof vault to protect the data stored on the tapes from theft and environmental disasters.
(Phillips Petroleum Company)

Bank programmers certainly have opportunities for personal gain. In one case, a couple of programmers modified a savings system to make small deposits from other accounts to their own accounts. Here's how it worked: The interest for each savings account was compounded and credited daily; the calculated interest was rounded to the nearest penny before being credited to the savings account; programs were modified to round down on all interest calculations and put the "extra" penny in one of the programmer's savings accounts. It may not seem like much, but a penny a day from thousands of accounts adds up to big bucks. The "beauty" of the system was that the books balanced and depositors did not miss the 15 cents (an average of $\frac{1}{2}$ cent per day for 30 days) that was judiciously taken from each account each month. Even the auditors have difficulty detecting this crime because the total interest paid out for all accounts is correct. However, the culprits got greedy and were apprehended when someone noticed that they repeatedly withdrew inordinately large sums of money.

Unfortunately, other enterprising programmers in other industries have been equally imaginative.

**Files/Data Bases.** The data base contains the raw material for information. In some cases, the files/data bases are the life blood of a company. For example, how many companies can afford to lose their accounts receivable file, which documents who owes what? Having several *generations of backups* (backups to backups) to all files is not sufficient insurance against loss of files/data bases. The backup and master files should be stored in fireproof safes in separate rooms, preferably in separate buildings.

**Data Communications.** The mere existence of **data communications** capabilities, where data are transmitted via communications links from one computer to another, poses a threat to security. A knowledgeable criminal can tap into the system from a remote location and use the system for personal gain. In a well-designed system, this is not an easy task. But it can be and has been done! When one criminal broke a company's security code and tapped into the network of computers, he was able to order certain products without being billed. He filled a warehouse before eventually being caught. Another tapped into an international banking exchange system to "reroute" funds to an account of his own in a Swiss bank. In another case, an oil company was able to consistently outbid a competitor by "listening in" on their data transmissions. On several occasions, overzealous young "hackers" have tapped into sensitive defense computer systems; fortunately, no harm was done.

Some companies use *cryptography* to scramble messages sent over data communications channels. Someone who unlawfully intercepts such a message would find meaningless strings of characters. Cryptography is analogous to the "code book" used by intelligence people during the cloak-and-dagger days. Instead of a code book, however, a "key" is used in conjunction with *encryption/decryption* hardware to unscramble the message. Both sender and receiver must have the key, which is actually an algorithm that rearranges the bit structure of a message. Companies that routinely transmit sensitive data over communications channels are moving to data encryption as a means to limit access to their MISs and their data bases.

**Personnel.**   Managers are paying close attention to who gets hired for positions that permit access to computer-based information systems and sensitive data. Someone who is grossly incompetent can cause just as much harm as someone who is inherently dishonest.

## Information Systems Security

Information systems security is classified as physical or logical. *Physical security* refers to hardware, facilities, magnetic disks, and other things that could be illegally accessed, stolen, or destroyed.

*Logical security* is built into the software by permitting only authorized persons to access and use the system. Logical security for on-line systems is achieved primarily by **passwords** and **authorization codes.** Only those persons with a "need to know" are told the password and given authorization codes. On occasion, however, these security codes fall into the wrong hands. When this happens, an unauthorized person can gain access to programs and sensitive files by simply dialing up the computer and entering the codes.

Keeping passwords and authorization codes from the computer criminal is not easy. One computer criminal took advantage of the fact that a bank's automatic teller machine (ATM) did not "time out" for several minutes. That is, the authorization code could be entered without reinserting the card to initiate another transaction. Using high-powered binoculars, he watched from across the street as the numeric code was being entered. He then ran over to the ATM and was waiting when the customer left. He quickly entered the code and made with-

This programmer/analyst works for a computer services company. He must enter his password and authorization code before he can gain access to the computer system and its data base. The nature of the work and the availability of specially designed workstations has made careers that involve working with computers particularly inviting to the physically challenged.
(Boeing Computer Services)

drawals before the machine timed out. Needless to say, this design flaw has been eliminated in existing ATM systems.

## Level of Risk

No amount of security measures will completely remove the vulnerability of a computer center or an information system. Security systems are implemented in degrees. That is, an information system can be made marginally secure or very secure, but never totally secure. Each company must determine the level of risk that it is willing to accept. Unfortunately, some corporations are willing to accept an enormous risk and hope that these rare instances of crime and disaster do not occur. Some corporations have found out too late that *rarely* is not the same as *never*!

## 3-7   JUSTIFYING A MANAGEMENT INFORMATION SYSTEM

Whether in business or government, you don't decide to use the computer just because it sounds like a good idea or it might be fun. An information system, robotics, CAI, or any other use of the computer is like any other investment opportunity—it must be justified. In the final analysis, uses of the computer are normally approved if, and only if, *the benefits are greater than the costs*.

Benefits.   The benefits of a computer system are either *tangible* or *intangible*. The tangible benefits result in monetary savings or earnings. For example, a plant production scheduling system saves a company money by providing information that helps its managers use resources more efficiently than they might without one.

Intangible benefits are difficult to quantify, but they are a major consideration when justifying expenditures for computing hardware and software. For example, the prestige and convenience associated with a bank's automatic teller machines may lure customers from other banks. As another example, a sales analysis system may help salespeople to better identify sales prospects, but the system doesn't make the sale. Intangible benefits cannot be readily translated into earnings or savings, but they are real benefits, so they must be considered when making a decision to automate.

Costs.   The two types of costs associated with computers and information systems are *one-time* costs and *recurring* costs. The one-time costs include all expenses associated with the development and implementation of a particular use of computer technology. The largest share of the one-time costs are usually personnel, hardware, and software.

Sometimes in our evaluation we overlook the recurring costs. These are costs that are incurred after implementation. Depending on the system being evaluated, recurring costs could include the programmers' time for systems maintenance, data entry, computer time and data storage, paper and other consumable materials, hardware upgrades,

The intangible benefits were an important consideration when evaluating the implementation of this PC- and laser-based system to verify blood types. The system has little economic value, but it helps to minimize the risk of mismarking the blood or administering the wrong blood type.
(Courtesy of International Business Machines Corporation)

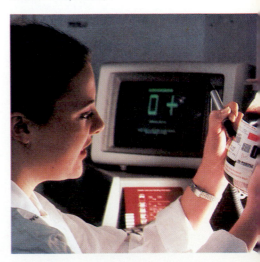

| MEMORY BITS |
|---|
| **BENEFIT/COST ANALYSIS** |
| IF    $\dfrac{\text{Benefits}}{\text{Costs}} > 1$ |
| THEN    Approve proposal for new system |
| ELSE    Reject proposal |

and charges for data communications services (e.g., telephone line charges).

**Benefit/Cost Analysis.**   Managers weigh benefits against costs by using what is called **benefit/cost analysis.** Simply stated, if the tangible benefits outweigh the cost, the system is normally approved.

You might be faced with evaluating a proposal where the estimated costs are greater than the estimated savings. In these cases, you must subjectively weigh the anticipated loss against the intangible benefits. If the intangible benefits appear to be greater than the loss, the system is usually given the go-ahead.

## 3–8   MIS SUMMARY

A *good* management information system has several very noticeable qualities.

- It is integrated such that it supports a variety of functional areas.
- It is flexible and can be readily adapted to meet changing information needs.
- It provides the right information to the right people at the right time.
- It can grow with the company.
- It provides authorized users with easy access to information.
- It provides an envelope of system security that limits access only to authorized personnel.
- Its existence yields a net benefit to the company.

The word "good" is highlighted in the first sentence of this section because not all information systems possess these very desirable qualities. Some are not well thought out and are cumbersome to use. Some provide too much information to managers, sometimes called "information overload." Others are vulnerable to tampering from persons outside the company. Others require major modifications to accommodate small changes in a company's information needs. These MISs are expensive and of questionable benefit to their respective companies.

The key to successful implementation of an MIS is to *do it right the first time*. System designers must be deliberate in their analysis and involve all people who will be affected by the system. A conscientious project team that invites user feedback each step of the way will invariably end up with a workable management information system that will *increase corporate productivity* and *aid in decision making*.

## SUMMARY OUTLINE AND IMPORTANT TERMS

**3–1**   MANAGEMENT'S CHALLENGE.   The attitude of management toward the use of computers has evolved from basic data processing to **information resource management (IRM).** The need for more timely and meaningful information prompted this change of attitude.

**3-2**   MANAGEMENT'S THIRST FOR INFORMATION.   An **information system** is a computer-based system that provides both a data processing capability and information to help managers make decisions. An information system is also called a **management information system (MIS)** because of its orientation to management. A **decision support system** is user-friendly software that makes use of the latest hardware and software technologies to provide better, more timely information to support the decision making process.

Each year, a growing percentage of a company's information processing needs are being met by the user community.

Thousands of manual and dated computer-based systems offer opportunities to enhance profitability and productivity. However, any upgrade to an existing system should involve careful attention to the principles of change management.

**3-3**   LEVELS OF ORGANIZATIONAL ACTIVITY: WHO GETS WHAT INFORMATION.   The four levels of organizational activity are strategic, tactical, operational, and clerical. Information must be filtered at the various levels of activity to ensure that the intended end user receives that information necessary to accomplish his or her job function. Too much information will be confusing, and too little information will not allow end users to accomplish their jobs effectively.

Managers at the operational, tactical, and strategic levels often request **exception reports** that highlight critical information.

**3-4**   USER-FRIENDLY INFORMATION SYSTEMS.   User-friendly systems permit end users who have very little computer experience to interact easily with a computer system. Icons and "HELP" commands contribute to a system's user friendliness.

**3-5**   MIS CONCEPTS.   Data or hardware devices are said to be **on-line** if they are directly accessible to, and under the control of, the computer. Other data and hardware are said to be **off-line**. In **batch processing**, transactions are grouped before they are processed.

**Source data** are transcribed to a machine-readable format or read directly by data entry devices. In batch **data entry**, source data are entered consecutively as a group. In transaction-oriented data entry, the operator interacts directly with the data base and updates the data base as the transaction occurs. The trend in data entry is to minimize the number of transcription steps by entering data on-line, at the source.

**3-6**   MIS SECURITY.   The threats to the security of computer centers and information systems call for precautionary measures. A computer center can be vulnerable in its hardware, software, files/data bases, data communications, and personnel. Information systems security is classified as physical security or logical security. Security systems are implemented in degrees, and no system or computer center can be made totally secure.

**3–7**   JUSTIFYING A MANAGEMENT INFORMATION SYSTEM.   An information system is just like any other investment opportunity in that it must be cost justified. When weighing the results of a **benefit/cost analysis,** the benefits, both tangible and intangible, should be greater than the cost of a proposed system.

**3–8**   MIS SUMMARY.   A "good" management information system is integrated and flexible, provides timely information, can grow, provides logical and physical security, and benefits the company. The key to successful **MIS** implementation is to do it right the first time.

## REVIEW EXERCISES

### Concepts

1. What elements are combined to create an information system?
2. What is IRM, and how does it relate to money, materials, and people?
3. What differentiates a decision support system from an information system?
4. List and briefly describe three manual systems, either personal or professional, with which you are familiar and that you feel are prime candidates for computerization.
5. What are the levels of organizational activity, from specific to general?
6. Distinguish between on-line operation and off-line operation.
7. What advantages does transaction-oriented data entry have over batch data entry?
8. What is the purpose of a "key" in cryptography?
9. What precautions can be taken to minimize the effects of hardware failure?
10. The mere fact that a system uses data communications poses a threat to security. Why so?
11. Identify the recurring costs of an on-line sales information system.

### Discussion

12. It is often said that "time is money." Would you say that "information is money"? Discuss.
13. Suppose that the company you work for batches all sales data for data entry each night. You have been asked to present a convincing argument to top management on why funds should be allocated to convert the current system to transaction-oriented data entry. What would you say?
14. Why is change management so important when converting from a manual system to a computer-based information system?
15. Give examples of reports that might be requested by an operational-level manager in an insurance company. A tactical-level manager. A strategic-level manager.

**16.** A company retained a computer consultant to determine if they should computerize certain aspects of corporate operation. The consultant's response was, "You can't afford not to." What is the implication of the consultant's assessment?

**17.** In a federal agency, passwords are given to people who need access to confidential information. A new set of passwords is issued every other month. Is this extra work of issuing new passwords really necessary? Discuss.

**18.** Evaluate your college's (or your company's) computer center with respect to security. Identify areas where you think it is vulnerable and discuss ways to improve its security.

**19.** Discuss the short- and long-term benefits of designing an information system to be user friendly.

**20.** Why would a bank officer elect not to report a computer crime?

## SELF-TEST (by section)

**3–1.** The four major corporate resources are money, materials, information, and _____ .

**3–2.** **(a)** We combine hardware, software, people, procedures, and data to create an _____ .

**(b)** A manual system has the same components as a computer-based system. (T/F)

**3–3.** **(a)** Operational-level personnel are concerned primarily with transaction handling. (T/F)

**(b)** Exception reports are produced for managers at the operational, tactical, and strategic levels. (T/F)

**3–4.** **(a)** Pictographs, called _____ , help systems to be more user friendly.

**(b)** Trends are more easily recognized when data are presented in tabular rather than graphic format. (T/F)

**3–5.** **(a)** A device is said to be _____ when it is accessible to, or under the control of, the processor.

**(b)** A _____ is a brief message to an operator that describes what data are to be entered.

**3–6.** **(a)** Logical security for on-line systems is achieved primarily by _____ and authorization codes.

**(b)** Cryptography is the study of the assignment of security codes. (T/F)

**3–7.** A proposed system is normally given the go-ahead if the intangible benefits are greater than the cost. (T/F)

**3–8.** Two desirable qualities of a good management information system are flexibility and ability to grow with the company. (T/F)

*Self-Test answers.*   3–1, people; 3–2 (a), information system; (b), T; 3–3 (a), F; (b), T; 3–4 (a), icons; (b), F; 3–5 (a), on-line; (b), prompt; 3–6 (a), passwords; (b), F; 3–7, F; 3–8, T.

# Zimco Enterprises

## MANAGEMENT INFORMATION SYSTEMS AT ZIMCO

### DOCUMENTING INFORMATION AND WORK FLOW

The four functional divisions at Zimco Enterprises (Finance and Accounting, Sales and Marketing, Operations, and Personnel) work together as a unit to accomplish the goals of the corporation. Each division is very much dependent on information derived from the others. In this Zimco case study, we'll take a *top-down* view of Zimco's overall management information system. To do this, we'll start at the "top" (general overview) and examine a diagram that illustrates the basic information flow between the four divisions. In subsequent extensions of the Zimco case study, we'll move "down" the ladder and take a closer look (greater detail) at the information flow within each of the four divisions. The design tool that Zimco uses to graphically illustrate the flow of information, at both the overview and detailed levels, is the **data flow diagram.**

There are a number of techniques that aid systems analysts and programmers in the design and documentation of an information system, but Sybil Allen, the manager of the Systems Analysis Department, feels that data flow diagrams, or **DFDs**, are perfect for Zimco. Sybil says, "DFDs are particularly well suited to our purposes because we encourage top-down design and they can be easily understood by management at all levels." DFDs enable an MIS to be portrayed graphically at several levels of generality.

Only four symbols are needed for data flow diagrams: *entity, process, flow line,* and *data store.* The symbols are summarized in Figure Z3–1 and their use is illustrated in Figure Z3–2. The entity symbol ⬜, a square with a darkened border on the top and left sides, is the source or destination of data or information flow. An entity can be a person, a group of persons (e.g., customers or employees), a department, or even a place (e.g., First National Bank). Each process symbol ⬭, a rectangle with rounded corners, contains a description of a function to be performed. Sybil says that "we use the process symbol to show processes associated with data entry, verification, calculation, storage, creation, and production." Process symbol identification numbers are assigned in levels. The first-level processes are labeled 1, 2, 3, and so on. Second-level processes that are subordinate to process 1 are labeled 1.1, 1.2, 1.3, and so on. The flow lines → indicate the flow and direction of data or information. Data storage symbols ▭, open-ended rectangles, identify storage locations for data. A storage location could be a file drawer, a shelf, a data base on magnetic disk, and so on.

A diagonal line in the lower right corner of the entity symbols indicates that the entity is repeated elsewhere on the same diagram. When the same data store is repeated on the same chart, the left end of the data store symbol is drawn to be diagonal rather than vertical.

**FIGURE Z3–1**
**Data Flow Diagram Symbols**

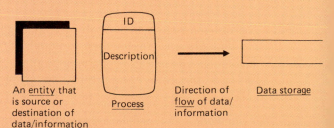

An entity that is source or destination of data/information

Process

Direction of flow of data/ information

Data storage

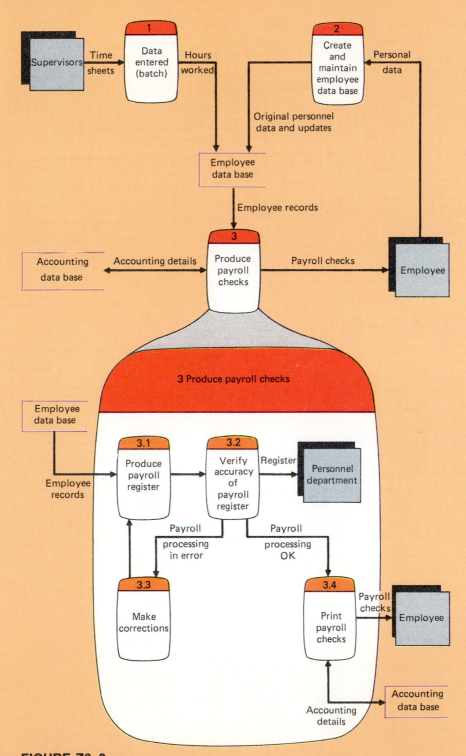

**FIGURE Z3–2**
**Data Flow Diagram**
In the example data flow diagram of a payroll system, process 3 is exploded to show greater detail.

"At Zimco, DFDs were our primary documentation tool even during the days of autonomous, function-based systems," says Sybil Allen. Zimco's "old" (i.e., before implementation of their current MIS) systems are easy to understand and provide good examples of the principles of data flow diagrams. For example, Figure Z3–2 shows that portion of a payroll system that produces payroll checks. Processes 1 and 2 deal with the employee data base, but in Process 3 the actual payroll checks are produced. In the bottom portion of Figure Z3–2, Process 3 is *exploded* to show greater detail. Notice that the *second-level* processes within the explosion of Process 3 are numbered 3.1, 3.2, 3.3, and 3.4. Process 3.1 could be exploded to a third level of processes to show even greater detail (e.g., 3.1.1, 3.1.2, etc.).

## STRATEGIC-LEVEL INFORMATION FLOW

Conrad Innis, VP of CIS, with help from Sybil Allen, compiled the "MIS overview" of Figure Z3–3 to provide top management with a strategic overview of the information flow within Zimco Enterprises. Conrad had another reason. People in CIS are always enhancing existing systems or developing new systems, so he wanted to document Zimco's information systems. Conrad has a saying: "If you don't know where you are, how can you know where you're going?"

In the "business system" model (Figure Z1–7) presented in the Zimco case study following Chapter 1, the corporate resources (money, material, people, and information), the corporate functions, and the products are shown to interact with a variety of "entities," both within and outside of Zimco. These interactions, as well as the basic information flow between the four functional areas, are graphically portrayed in the overview data flow diagram of Figure Z3–3. These interactions are further expanded, or "exploded," in tactical- and operational-level DFDs in the "Information Systems at Zimco" case studies following these chapters:

- Chapter 7 (Finance and Accounting)
- Chapter 9 (Personnel)
- Chapter 10 (Operations)

- Chapter 11 (Sales and Marketing)

The function of the CIS Division is to facilitate the flow of information within Zimco Enterprises. Since all computer-based information at one time or another passes through the CIS division (or its computers), you might say that CIS is the nucleus of information flow within Zimco. However, to simplify things, the intermediate flow of information through CIS is omitted in the overview data flow diagram of Figure Z3–3 such that information is shown to flow directly from one functional division to the next.

The MIS overview (Figure Z3–3) highlights the interdependence between the four line divisions at Zimco. For example, the Finance and Accounting Division receives purchase orders from the Operations Division, accounts receivable data from the Sales and Marketing Division, and pay and benefits data from the Personnel Division. In turn, the Finance and Accounting Division provides cost information to the Operations Division, gross sales information to Sales and Marketing Division, and information regarding the division's work force requirements to the Personnel Division. Information flows to and from the other three divisions are illustrated in Figure Z3–3.

The two entities internal to Zimco are *employees* and *managers*. The employees entity encompasses all employees, including managers. The mangers entity includes managers at the operational, tactical, and strategic levels. The interaction between Zimco's integrated MIS and the employees entity generally falls into the areas of pay, benefits, and training. The interaction between the MIS and managers entity is primarily in the areas of management inquiries, reports, and directives. For example, in the Sales and Marketing Division, management routinely makes inquiries regarding the progress of sales of certain products. The system also supplies forecasts of potential sales. These forecasts eventually become input to the Operations Division.

There are many external entities from which the Zimco MIS receives input and to which it must provide output. These external entities include the *government* (all levels), *suppliers*, *customers*, *stockholders*, *financial institutions*, *colleges/agencies*, and the *media*.

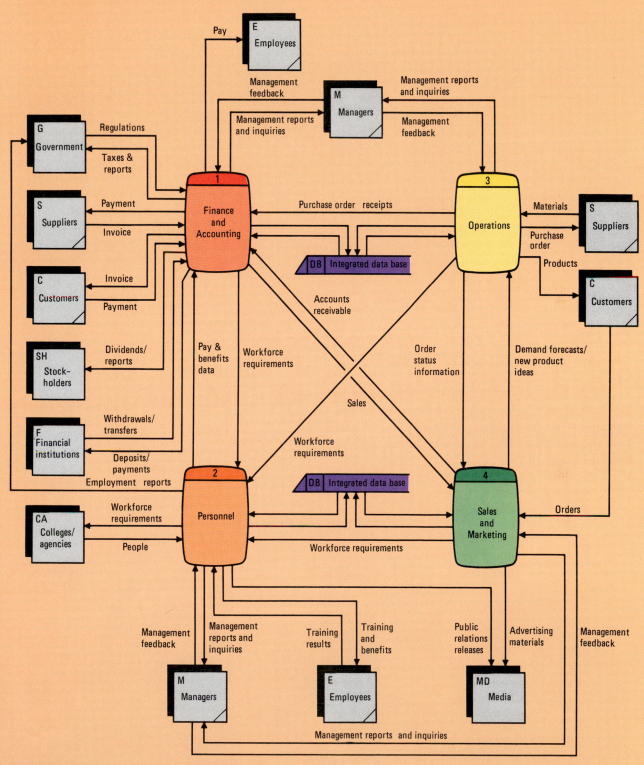

**FIGURE Z3–3**
**MIS Overview for Zimco Enterprises**

Zimco's primary interaction with the government is in the area of taxes. Payment is made to suppliers for the materials that they provide. Zimco's customers, who are primarily retailers and wholesalers, are the primary source of revenue (and "headaches," so says Cullen Certain, manager of the Customer Service Department). The stockholders own Zimco and therefore are interested in its ongoing well-being and its dividends. The financial institutions service Zimco in much the same way that they service individuals; that is, Zimco deposits, withdraws, transfers, and invests money as needed to meet the company's liquidity requirements. Colleges and employment agencies are the primary source of Zimco's people resources. Zimco routinely uses the media, primarily newspapers, magazines, radio, and television, to advertise their products. Also, promotions and Zimco news items are released to local newspapers.

## THE INTEGRATED DATA BASE

The only data store (the open-ended boxes) in Figure Z3–3 is Zimco's integrated data base. The data base symbol is repeated to simplify the presentation of the DFD. The diagonal line on the left end of the data-store symbols indicates that the data store is repeated elsewhere in the DFD.

To explain the concept of an integrated data base, we need to back up a few years and discuss Zimco's data base as it was prior to 1980. At that time, Zimco had several dozen files, each designed to meet a specific user group's requirements. When a file was designed and created, very little thought was given to how it would benefit Zimco as a whole. As a result, many very similar, but different files were created. For example, basic customer data were collected and maintained in separate files for the headquarters sales office, for the Distribution Department, for the Accounting Department, and for the Customer Service Department. Imagine, when customer data changed (e.g., the name of the purchasing agent), each file would have to be updated separately!

Conrad Innis recognized that *data redundancy* is costly. When he joined Zimco, he said, "data redundancy can be minimized by designing an *integrated data base* to serve Zimco as a whole, not a single department. To do this we'll need **database management system (DBMS)** software." DBMS software is discussed in more detail in Chapter 10, "File Processing and Data Organization."

Zimco first installed DBMS software in 1981 and has upgraded it several times since. The four categories of data included as part of Zimco's integrated data base are: *manufacturing/inven-*

Over 300 workstations throughout Zimco Enterprises provide authorized persons with ready access to the integrated data base.
(Honeywell, Inc.)

*tory*, *customer/sales*, *personnel*, and *general accounting*. The Technical Support Department, managed by Terri Suttor, is responsible for maintaining the integrated data base. Terri says, "Zimco employees are authorized access to all or part of the data base, depending on their need to know."

Zimco's integrated data base provides its managers with enormous flexibility in the types of reports that can be generated and the types of on-line inquires that can be made. Otto Manning, VP of Operations, said recently that "the greater access to information provided by Zimco's integrated data base enables me to make better decisions. As a result, we are able to produce a quality product at less cost than our competitors."

## DISCUSSION QUESTIONS

1. Identify the data elements that would provide the links between the four categories of data in Zimco's integrated data base (*manufacturing/inventory*, *customer/sales*, *personnel*, *and general accounting*). For example, the customer account number data element is common to all data categories except personnel.

2. Describe the information flow between Zimco Enterprises and all levels of government, and between its suppliers, customers, and stockholders.

3. Describe the information flow between Zimco Enterprises and those financial institutions, colleges/agencies, and media organizations with whom they have business relations.

4. In the example of Figure Z3–2, identify and describe processes that would be subordinate to Process 2, "Create and Maintain Employee Data Base."

5. Conrad Innis and Sybil Allen created the MIS overview in Figure Z3–3 while using a software package that enabled them to interactively create a data flow diagram directly on the workstation display. Discuss the advantages of using an automated design tool versus pencils, templates, and paper to create the DFD.

6. Prior to the implementation of Zimco's integrated data base in 1981, CIS maintained 113 separate computer-based files. Most of these files supported autonomous, departmental information systems and had numerous instances of redundant data. Discuss the impact that redundant data have on the integrity or accuracy of data.

7. Would it be possible for Zimco Enterprises to maintain a skeleton information services department of about 10 people and use commercially available packaged software for all their computer application needs? Explain.

8. In Figure Z3–3, Zimco's MIS is logically organized into four major processes. Discuss an alternative organization that would involve five, six, or seven major processes. Discuss the advantages of such an organization.

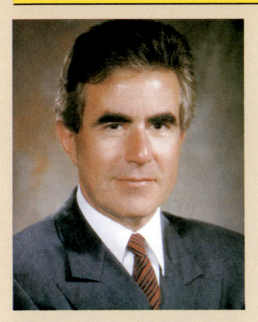

The American automobile industry has been working overtime in the past few years to scrub off that big rust-colored "S" from its chest—the one that stands for "smokestack" industry. And playing a key role in this effort has been that best-known symbol of high technology: the computer.

At Chrysler, from the wheels up, our cars are the products of computers. Using the most sophisticated CAD/CAM system in the industry, Chrysler engineers have automated two-thirds of our design and drawing work, giving us as much as 70-to-1 productivity gains in some area. And under the hood, computers are a driver's built-in mechanic. Our new cars today carry up to seven on-board microprocessors, and they do it all: calculate gas mileage, regulate exhaust, adjust spark time, control the air conditioner, and even tune the radio.

Computers are also the nerve center of our plants. Through a state-of-the art process known as In-line Sequencing, computers schedule and monitor every step of the production process—from the start of assembly, until the car rolls off the line two days later and several miles down the conveyor.

And as computer-sophisticated as automobiles are today, it's predicted that by 1992 your new car will contain four times the electronics (in terms of dollar value) as a 1985 model. On the horizon are new features unheard of just a few years back—like satellite-fed in-dash electronic maps that will quite literally tell you where on earth you are, give or take a hundred feet. Or remote-control starting systems that will allow you to "warm up" your car in the morning without even leaving your bacon and eggs.

The modern computer is giving Chrysler and the rest of the American auto industry the ability to build quality cars and trucks with control, precision, and speed. But more important, computers help us give customers what they really want: products that better serve their needs.

Gerald Greenwald
Chairman of Chrysler Motors and
Member of the Executive Committee
of Chrysler Corporation

# Computers and Information Systems in Business and Government

## STUDENT LEARNING OBJECTIVES

- To discuss a variety of computer-based applications in business and government.
- To discuss the principles and use of expert systems.
- To describe applications of special-purpose computer systems.

## FOCUS OF ZIMCO CASE STUDY

- Office automation at Zimco.

## 4

## 4–1 BUSINESS APPLICATIONS OF COMPUTER TECHNOLOGY

Computers and information systems are part of the everyday routine in every *functional area* in every *type of business*. Application areas that are normally computerized within the various industry groups are listed in Figure 4–1 and briefly discussed in the following sections. Each of these application areas can be, and usually is, integrated (i.e., it shares a data base) to some extent.

Certain computer applications and information systems are universal and are equally appropriate at a manufacturing company, an airline, a hospital, or even a **cottage industry** (people working out of their home). These applications normally involve *personnel* and *monetary* accounting (e.g., personnel system, accounts receivable system), but they also include several other common application areas, such as inventory control and office automation. These "common" applications are presented in the context of the Zimco Enterprises case study. Office automation is presented in the Zimco case study following this chapter.

The following industry-by-industry discussion is not an exhaustive treatment of computer applications in business—such a discussion

**FIGURE 4–1**
**Summary of Computer Applications by Industry**
These are but a few of the many computer applications for selected industries and for all levels of government.

---

**GENERAL**
Payroll
Accounts receivable
Accounts payable
General ledger
Inventory management and control
Human resource development
Budgeting
Office automation
   Word processing
   Data entry
   Electronic mail
   Image Processing
   Office information systems

**MANUFACTURING**
Order-entry and processing
Production scheduling
Market analysis
Project management and control
Standard costing
Manufacturing resource planning (MRP)
CAD/CAM
Robotics

**FINANCIAL SERVICES**
Electronic funds transfer (EFT)
Automatic teller machines (ATM)
Home banking
Financial planning

**RETAIL SALES**
Point of sale (POS)
Intercompany networking

**PUBLISHING**
Word processing
Typesetting
Graphics design
Page formatting
Educational support software
Customized printing on demand
Magazines on a disk

**TRANSPORTATION**
Reservations
Fleet maintenance
Satellite monitoring systems

**INSURANCE**
Policy administration
Claims processing
Actuarial accounting

**ENTERTAINMENT**
Professional sports systems
Film industry
   Special effects
   Animation
   Colorization
Theater

**HEALTH CARE**
Hospitals
   Room census
   Patient accounting
   On-line patient information
   Operating room
   Intensive care unit
   Physicians accounting
Private practice
Medical research

**GOVERNMENT**
Local
   Utility billing
   Tax collection
   Police systems
   Fire incident reporting
   Census and urban planning
   Election reporting
   License and permit administration
   Traffic control
   Parking meter systems
State
   Welfare
   Employment security
   Highway patrol
   Revenue
   Education
   Lottery
   Crime bureau
Federal
   National crime information system
   Grant administration
   Filing of taxes
   National defense systems
   Congressional computer network
   Space programs (NASA)

would take the rest of this book and many others. These applications are presented to illustrate and acquaint you with some of the ways computers and information systems are used in a variety of industries. How computers and information systems are used in government is discussed in Section 4–2.

## Manufacturing

In a manufacturing company, the *order entry and processing* system accepts and processes customer orders. The system then feeds data to the warehouse or plant, depending on whether the order is for stock items or special order, and to the *accounts receivable system* for billing. The system also tracks orders and provides order status information from the time the order is received until it is delivered to the customer.

*Production scheduling* systems allocate manufacturing resources in an optimal manner. A well-designed system will minimize idle time for both workers and machines and ensure that needed materials are at the right place at the right time.

*Market analysis* systems rely on historical and current data to identify fast- and slow-moving products, to pinpoint areas with high sales potential, to make forecasts of production requirements, and to plan marketing strategy. For example, in Figure 4–2, the scatter plot of regional sales over the last four quarters demonstrates clearly that fourth-quarter sales in the northeast region did not keep pace. Based on this finding, management might elect to focus more attention on the northeast region during the coming quarter.

*Project management and control* systems provide management with the information necessary to keep projects within budget and on time. Periodic reports would present actual versus anticipated project costs and the number of days ahead or behind schedule.

Other information systems commonly found in manufacturing companies include *standard costing*, *manufacturing resource planning* (*MRP*), and *CAD/CAM* (computer-aided design/computer-aided manufacturing). *Robotics* is also an application of computers in manufacturing. CAD/CAM and robotics are discussed in more detail in Section 4–3.

This shop supervisor relies on a production scheduling system to help him make the best possible use of expensive computer-controlled machine tools.
(Sperry Corporation)

With the prospect of increased productivity, manufacturing companies have been rushing to install more and more applications of computer-aided design (CAD) and robotics. In the photo, an industrial robot positions materials for assembly in a "pick and place" application.
(Calma Company)

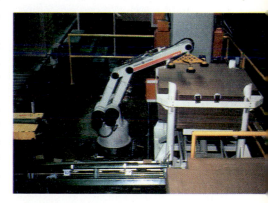

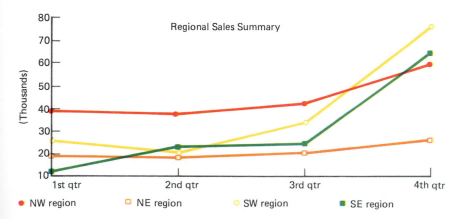

**FIGURE 4–2**
**Scatter Plot of Regional Sales**
Quarterly sales figures from four regions are plotted to aid in market analysis.

## Financial Services

The financial services industries, which include banking, savings and loan, and brokerage firms, are entering an exciting era. The computer is the impetus behind some radical and progressive changes in the way these money brokers do business. For example, financial services organizations serve as a money "buffer" between buyer and seller. The traditional approach to money exchange has been for the seller to bill the buyer, the buyer to write a check for the amount of the bill, the seller to deposit the check, and the bank to transfer the funds from the buyer's to the seller's account. This approach is not only time consuming, but it is expensive for all concerned. Throughout the remainder of the 1980s we can expect to see this traditional approach give way to more and more EFT.

In electronic funds transfer, the amount owed is transferred "electronically" from one account to another (in a bank, savings and loan, or brokerage firm). For example, rather than sending out thousands of statements that require each customer to pay the bill in his or her own way, some utility companies are cooperating with customers and banks so that payments are transferred electronically at the end of each billing period. As another example, some employers are bypassing the printing of payroll checks. Based on data supplied to the banks, pay is electronically transferred from employer to employee accounts.

*Automatic teller machines* (*ATMs*) are the most visible symbol of EFT. In over 100 banks, however, EFT has been extended to the home in the form of *home banking* systems. Subscribers to a home banking service use their personal computers as workstations to pay bills, transfer funds, and inquire about account status. Some systems also provide subscribers with other services, such as "electronic" shopping, electronic mail, and up-to-the-minute stock market quotations. Other financial services organizations offer similar systems. For example, several brokerage firms permit clients to use their PCs to tap into a data base that contains their account data as well as timely information about the securities market.

All financial institutions offer *financial planning* services. Part of the service involves a computer-based analysis of a customer's investment portfolio. Input to the system includes current and anticipated income, amount and type of investments, assets and liabilities, and financial objectives (e.g., minimize taxes, pension level at age 65). The output from the analysis consists of recommendations aimed at optimizing the effectiveness of a particular person's investment portfolio.

Futurists are predicting that the current system of currency exchange will gradually be replaced by EFT. By the end of the decade, the corner drugstore will probably have a point-of-sale workstation that will allow you to buy even a candy bar through EFT. The transaction will be faster than reaching for your billfold. All that you will have to do is enter your security code, probably a voice print and/or fingerprint, then enter the amount to be transferred via a keyboard. The rest will be automatic.

The banking industry would prefer that their customers use ATMs for banking transactions rather than tellers. The average ATM transaction takes less time, but most importantly, it costs less than half that of a teller transaction. We can expect the cost of banking services to drop as more and more people use ATMs.
(Honeywell, Inc.)

Point-of-sale workstations are a convenience to both customers and retailers. This grocery store has the capability to operate without cash transfers. The customer swipes her bank card (containing account number and authorization data) through a badge reader and enters a personal identification number on the keyboard, both of which are connected to a network of banking computers. The customer then enters the amount of the purchase. This amount is deducted from her bank account and credited to that of the grocery store.
(Diebold, Incorporated)

## Retail Sales

The most prominent system in the retail sales industry is the *point-of-sale* (*POS*) system. The cash-register-like POS workstation logs the transaction of the sale (see the example and illustration in Chapter 2, Figure 2–4), and the sale also updates the inventory status of the item sold. This immediate feedback is valuable input to marketing strategy. For example, a department store chain relies on its POS system to identify fast-selling items so that they can be reordered before the stock is depleted. This system also identifies slow-moving items so that management can reduce the price accordingly.

Traditionally, orders for shelf items are computer generated in hard-copy format, then sent by mail to wholesale distributors. It is not unusual for a single order from a department store chain to list thousands of items. When the wholesaler receives the order, key entry operators enter the orders. The trend today is to use *intercompany networking* (linking of the computers of different companies, e.g., buyer and seller). The orders are sent from the retailer to the distributor via data communications, thereby eliminating the need for hard-copy orders and redundant key data entry.

More and more point-of-sale systems are being integrated with EFT (electronic funds transfer) systems, so that what is now a *credit* transaction will be a *cash-transfer* transaction. That is, when a customer purchases an item, the amount of the sale is debited, via EFT, from the customer's checking account and credited to the account of the retail store. No further funds transfer is needed. Of course, the option to make a credit purchase will remain.

## Publishing

*Word processing*, computerized *typesetting*, computer-aided *graphics design*, and *page formatting* have revolutionized the way newspapers, books, and magazines are produced. Reporters and writers

An information system at this newspaper handles news editing, classified advertising, page formatting, and numerous other related tasks.
(Courtesy of International Business Machines Corporation)

enter and edit their stories on their portable micros or on-line workstations. Once all copy is on-line, pages are automatically formatted according to type and spacing specifications. Traditionally, a manually produced document, prepared with pencils, paper, and typewriters, went on to editing, retyping, composing, proofreading, cutting, pasting, and photographing of the final page format before plates could be made for the presswork.

Publishers of books have traditionally produced hard-copy products, but more and more they will also be involved in the production of *educational support software*. For example, within a few years, most introductory textbooks will be accompanied by educational software (e.g., this book has a software supplement). The interactive nature of software adds a new dimension to the learning process.

Eventually, *customized printing on demand* will be available at bookstores. Instead of making a selection from available books, you will make a selection from a list of virtually any current book. The book will then be printed (figures and all) and bound while you wait. This approach will provide a greater selection for the customer and vastly reduce costly inventory for both bookstore and publisher.

Although customized printing on demand is a few years away, *magazines on a disk* are here today. These magazines are distributed in diskette format for display on home PCs. In the same vein, dictionaries and encyclopedias are already being sold in the form of high-density laser disks.

## Transportation

Airline *reservation* systems, discussed briefly in Chapter 2, are among the most sophisticated of information systems. Airline and travel agents have workstations on which they can make reservations for any U.S.-based airline. The tickets are even printed at the travel agents' workstations. The same is true for rail and bus services and for auto rentals.

A major concern of airlines, railroads, and bus lines is the periodic upkeep of their fleet of transport vehicles. With hundreds, and even thousands, of vehicles, it is difficult for maintenance crews to keep track of when to change the oil, when to replace a particular part, and many other routine preventive maintenance tasks. A *fleet maintenance* system (see Figure 4–3) periodically prompts maintenance personnel to perform these routine tasks, vehicle by vehicle.

**FIGURE 4–3**
**Fleet Maintenance Report**
This report is produced periodically to alert maintenance personnel to fleet maintenance requirements.

MAY MAINTENANCE SCHEDULE - - FIRST WEEK

| VEHICLE NO. | DESCRIPTION | MAINTENANCE ACTIVITY |
|---|---|---|
| 7 | EXECUTIVE LIMO | SEMI-ANNUAL PM |
| 12 | 1-TON TRUCK | OIL CHANGE AND FILTER LUBE |
| 22 | 1-TON TRUCK | ROTATE TIRES |
| 33 | 9-PASSENGER VAN | REPLACE TIRES REPLACE WATER HOSES |

A *satellite monitoring system* uses satellite communications to monitor the status of trucks. The system detects when a truck is idle or moving, the weight of the truck's contents, the speed of the truck, and its location. As anticipated, truckers are resisting the implementation of this "spy in the sky."

## Insurance

The information systems of an insurance company have more external interaction, or communication with people outside the company, than do most other businesses. Most of the external communication is with customers. The volume of transactions makes computer-based *policy administration* and *claims processing* systems a necessity. Insurance agents hook up to headquarters computers so that they can quote, write, and deliver insurance policies while customers wait.

An insurance company makes or loses money on the basis of the accuracy of its *actuarial accounting* system. This system maintains countless statistics that serve as the basis for the rate structure. An actuarial system provides the following kinds of information: the probability that a 20-year-old Kansas City resident with no automobile accident history will have an accident; or the life expectancy of a 68-year-old female whose parents died of natural causes.

As each truck departs, this dispatcher updates the data base to reflect the status of the load and sends a departure message to the destination depot.
(Santa Fe Industries)

## Entertainment

The computer is now an integral part of the entertainment industry. *Pro football* coaches rely heavily on feedback from their computer systems to call plays and set defenses during a game. The system predicts what the opposing team is expected to do based on statistics of what they have done in the past. In fact, the computer is becoming the deciding factor between evenly matched opponents in many sports. In *professional tennis*, specially designed portable computers are used to keep statistics on stroke effectiveness and strategies. Pro tennis players analyze the results; then, during play, they emphasize their strengths and attack an opponent's weaknesses.

Computers have had quite an impact on the *film industry*. Many *special effects* and even the sets for some movies are generated with computer graphics. *Animation*, for cartoons and movies, is no longer drawn one frame at a time. The scenes and characters are drawn, by hand or with a computer, then manipulated with computer graphics to create the illusion of motion.

Computer graphics has even made it possible to revive old black-and-white movies—in color! Imagine Laurel and Hardy in living color! Now, through an innovative use of computer technology, called *color-ization*, it is possible to change the old black-and-white films to color. This colorizing process uses an electronic scanner that breaks each frame of the film into an array of 525,000 separate dots. Each dot is stored and manipulated by the computer. An art director reviews the frames at the beginning, middle, and end of a scene and selects a specific color for every object in the scene (e.g., a coat, a chair, etc.).

Coaches in many sports, including swimming, have turned to computers to help provide them with better information about the performance of their athletes.
(Courtesy of International Business Machines Corporation)

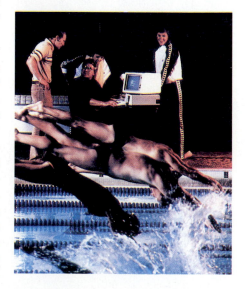

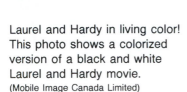

Laurel and Hardy in living color!
This photo shows a colorized
version of a black and white
Laurel and Hardy movie.
(Mobile Image Canada Limited)

The nurse's station is the hub of
hospital activity and the source
of information for both nurses
and doctors. They use the
terminals at the nurse's station
to retrieve information from the
hospital's information system.
(Texas Instruments, Inc.)

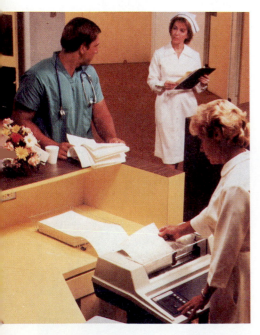

The computer operator, with a digital graphics tablet and electronic palette as tools, "hand paints" the images according to the art director's color specifications, much like paint-by-the-numbers. Then a specially designed, high-speed computer colors the remainder of the frames in a scene by comparing every new frame with the preceding one. Since the colors of less than 4 percent of the dots will change from frame to frame, the computer is able to keep track of moving objects.

In the *theater*, playwrights use word processing systems that are especially designed for the theater environment. Besides the obvious benefits of word processing, there are side benefits to having the script "on-line." Actors can learn their lines while interacting with a computer that "reads" the lines of other actors; that is, only the lines of other actors are displayed on the screen, unless the actor requests that all lines be displayed. Using computer graphics, set designers lay out the backdrops and props before they are built. Again, there are side benefits to having the set design "on-line." The director can work out and document the stage movements of all actors before the start of rehearsals.

## Health Care

Hospitals.   In health care, the computer is a constant companion to both patients and medical personnel. This is especially so in hospitals, where at the beginning of each day the status of each room is updated in the *room census* data base (see Figure 4–4). The *patient accounting* system updates patient records to reflect lab tests, drugs administered, and visits by a physician. This system also handles patient billing.

In the *operating room*, surgeons have on-line access to the patient's medical records. Some of these interactive systems are even voice activated to free the surgeon's hands for more critical tasks. Computers have taken some of the risk out of complex surgical procedures by warning surgeons of life-threatening situations. For example, during brain surgery, a computer monitors the patient's blood flow to the brain.

```
              ROOM CENSUS REPORT (BY ROOM NUMBER)
                          FIRST FLOOR

ROOM NO.          PATIENT NAMES
             BED 1                       BED 2

  101S    MARK MILLS
  102D    JAMES FLOYD              LARRY SMITH
  103D    ELLEN MOREL             -----------
  104W4   JANE WEAR               SALLY ABLE
          NANCY YOUNG             ----------
  105S    FRED KENT
  106S    ----------
  107D    MATT KENNEDY            HANK OREM

   S-SINGLE      D-DOUBLE    W-WARD (NO. OF BEDS)
```

```
              ROOM CENSUS REPORT (BY LAST NAME)
                        FIRST FLOOR


    PATIENT NAME                          ROOM NO.

    SALLY ABLE                              104
    JAMES FLOYD                             102
    MATT KENNEDY                            107
    FRED KENT                               105
    MARK MILLS                              101
    ELLEN MOREL                             103
    HANK OREM                               107
    LARRY SMITH                             102
    JANE WEAR                               104
    NANCY YOUNG                             104
```

**FIGURE 4–4**
**Hospital Room Census Reports**
Room census reports are compiled by room number (soft copy) and patient name (hard copy).

Once discharged to an *intensive care unit*, computers continue to monitor a patient's vital signs and alert attending personnel of danger situations. Most life-support systems (e.g., artificial lungs) are also computer controlled.

In recent years the cost of the hospital room has soared, and still some hospitals operate in the red. To get back in the black, hospitals are implementing procedures to better control costs. For the first time, they are implementing systems that optimize the use of their resources, while maximizing revenue. A *physician's accounting* system provides hospital administrators with information about how each physician is using hospital facilities. For example, such systems identify physicians who tend to admit patients who could just as well be treated as outpatients. These patients typically generate less revenue for the

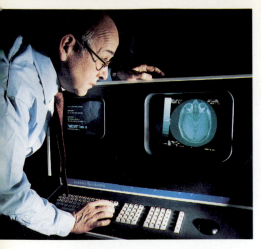

Data obtained during scanning by magnetic resonance (MR) diagnostic equipment are computer-reconstructed to form cross-sectional images of the body's tissues and organs. This technology enables doctors to distinguish between benign and malignant tumors, and to detect conditions that could lead to heart attacks.
(General Electric Company)

Paraplegic Nan Davis demonstrates an experimental outdoor tricycle which uses a computerized electrical stimulation-feedback system to stimulate paralyzed muscles to pedal the tricycle.
(Wright State University, Dayton, Ohio)

hospital and take up a bed that could best be used by a seriously ill patient.

**Private Practice.** Why does a physician or dentist need a computer in *private practice*? That answer is simple—private practice is a business that necessitates the handling of many administrative functions, such as patient record keeping, billing and collections, appointment scheduling, and insurance processing. Of course, physicians can also use computers to improve their delivery of patient care. Doctors can tap into a variety of medical information services from their office workstations: medical diagnosis systems, medical data bases (for researching an illness), prescription data bases, and drug-interaction data bases. A physician can even link to a hospital's mainframe computer system to check patient status.

**Medical Research.** The microprocessor has opened new vistas for *medical research*. Our body is an electrical system that is very compatible with these tiny computers. Researchers have made it possible for paraplegics to pedal bicycles and take crude steps under the control of external computers. In the system, various muscle groups in the legs are excited electronically to cause the legs to perform a walking motion. The system has given new hope to paraplegics who were told they would never walk again. To be sure, much remains to be done, but researchers insist that someday, computer implants will enable paraplegics to walk.

## 4-2 GOVERNMENT APPLICATIONS OF COMPUTER TECHNOLOGY

### Local Government

Local governments use a wide variety of information systems (see Figure 4–1). Most cities supply and bill citizens for at least one of the three major utility services: water, refuse, and electricity. Besides these *utility billing* systems, a *tax collection* system periodically assesses citizens for income, school, and real estate tax.

Cities also have *police systems* which are used for incident reporting, inquiry, and dispatching. Many police departments even have workstations mounted in their cruisers. From these workstations, officers can view the arrest record of an individual, request a "rundown" on an auto's license number, or check out what other officers are doing. Police detectives can search data bases for suspects by matching modus operandi, nicknames, body marks, physical deformities, locations, time of day, and even footwear.

Some fire departments are electronically informed of the location of a fire by a *fire incident reporting* system. Here's how it works. Someone at the site of the fire calls a three-digit "fire reporting" number. In a split second, a computer system searches its data base for the address of the calling phone (therefore, the location of the fire), then automatically dispatches vehicles from the nearest fire station.

Other systems that are typically supported by local governments include *census and urban planning*, *election reporting*, *license and permit administration*, *traffic control*, and even *parking meter systems*.

## State Government

At the state level of government, each major agency has its own information services department. *Welfare*, *employment security*, *highway patrol*, *revenue*, and *education* are only a few of the many state agencies that have information services departments. In some states, one of the most visible systems is the *lottery* agency. A bet is registered immediately at any of thousands of on-line workstations located in stores and restaurants throughout the state. The on-line lottery systems have made it possible for people to be "instant" winners (or losers).

Several state *crime bureaus* are using computers for fingerprint identification. Once the millions of fingerprints have been converted to digital data and stored on magnetic disk, the system can check up to 650 prints per second. In a manual search, an investigator would take hours to do what a computer can do in a single second. This new technology doesn't give criminals much of a head start!

## Federal Government

The federal government has thousands of computer systems scattered throughout the world. The Federal Bureau of Investigation (FBI) has its *national crime information system* (*NCIS*) to help track down criminals. The National Science Foundation (NSF) has a *grant administration* system that enables it to monitor the progress and budgets for research projects. The Internal Revenue Service (IRS) now permits on-line *filing of tax returns* from home PCs. This service saves us and the IRS a lot of time and money. For us, the on-line system performs all of the necessary table searches and computations, and it even cross-checks the accuracy and consistency of the input data. For the IRS, no further data entry or personal assistance is required.

*National defense systems* are becoming more "high tech." Missiles use computer-controlled guidance systems to travel thousands of miles and land on or within feet of their targets. Some aircraft are equipped with sophisticated computer-controlled autopilots that can be activated to actually land an aircraft, even on moving aircraft carriers. Intelligence photos, taken at high altitudes, can be computer enhanced to show incredible detail—would you believe the headlines of a newspaper? The Aegis System can track hundreds of approaching missiles and aircraft and, based on system input, determine the best defense strategy, then select and activate defensive weapons systems. Controversial proposals for so-called "star wars" systems are based on sophisticated computer technology.

Computer technology has caused Congress to take on a new look. Senators and representatives have workstations in their offices that permit them to scan proposed legislation, send electronic mail, vote on legislation from their offices, do research, and correspond with constituents. The system also allows lobbyists, reporters, and other inter-

The local fire and police departments fight crime and fires and attend to other emergencies with the help of an information system. In seconds, dispatchers can select which squad car or fire station would be the most responsive to a given emergency.
(Courtesy of International Business Machines Corporation)

In the past, a manual search through a fingerprint file could take a detective months—often without success. Today, computers take only a few minutes to check fingerprints from the scene of a crime against a large data base of fingerprints—often with great success.
(Courtesy of NEC Information Systems, Inc.)

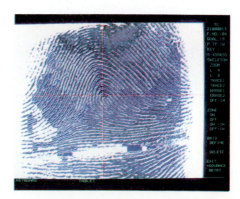

Offices in the legislative branch of government are interconnected by a computer system that integrates voice, data, and video communication. A computer-based information system records each vote registered by a senator or congressperson. Legislators make inquiries to this data base to determine which of their colleagues are sympathetic to their special interests. Lobbyists also take advantage of this information.
(AT&T Technologies)

ested persons to monitor voting records, session attendance, and other matters of public interest. Another benefit of the *congressional computer network* is that it lets congressional committees poll members of congress for their feedback while legislation is still in draft form, instead of waiting until the legislation is put to a vote.

The most sophisticated government computer systems are associated with *NASA* and the space program. A mind-boggling network of ground and on-board computers must work together, without malfunction, to take people to the moon and shuttle people between the earth and orbit about the earth.

## 4–3   EXPERT SYSTEMS

Perhaps the ultimate decision support system is the **expert system.** Expert systems, which were mentioned briefly in Chapter 1, are part of the general area of research known as *artificial intelligence* (AI). Expert systems provide "expert" advice and guidance in a wide range of activities, from locomotive maintenance to surgery. An expert system is an interactive system that responds to questions, asks for clarification, makes recommendations, and generally aids in the decision-making process. At the heart of an expert system is a **knowledge base.**

A knowledge base is *not* a data base. The traditional data base environment, as illustrated in the example of Figure 1–4 in Chapter 1, deals with data that have a static relationship between the elements. That is, the employee name and pay rate fields have a fixed relationship with the employee record. A knowledge base is created by *knowledge engineers*, who translate the knowledge of real, live human experts into rules and strategies. A knowledge base is heuristic; that is, it provides the expert system with the capability to recommend directions

These financial analysts rely on historical and predictive data as well as up-to-the-second stock trading information to advise their clients. They sometimes request a second opinion from an expert system before advising their clients.
(Quotron Systems, Inc.)

for user inquiry. It also encourages further investigation into areas that may be important to a certain line of questioning, but not apparent to the user. Moreover, a knowledge base grows because it "learns" from user feedback. An expert system learns by "remembering"; that is, it stores occurrences of the past in its knowledge base. For example, a recommendation that sends a user on a "wild goose chase" is thereafter deleted as a workable strategy for similar future inquiries.

In effect, expert systems simulate the human thought process. To varying degrees, they can reason, draw inferences, and make judgments. Here is how an expert system works. Let's use a medical diagnosis system as an example. Upon examination of a patient, a physician might interact with an expert diagnosis system to get help in diagnosing the patient's illness or, perhaps, to get a "second" opinion. First, the doctor would relate the symptoms to the expert system: male, age 10, temperature of 103°, and swollen glands about the neck. Needing more information, the expert system might ask the doctor to examine the parotid gland for swelling. Receiving an affirmative answer, the system might ask a few more questions and perhaps even for lab reports before giving a diagnosis. A final question put to the physician might be whether the patient had been previously afflicted with or immunized for parotitis. If not, the expert system diagnoses the illness as parotitis, otherwise known as the mumps.

Computer-based expert systems have fared well against real expert physicians in effectiveness of diagnosis of illnesses. Other expert systems help crews to repair telephone lines, financial analysts to counsel their clients, computer vendors to configure computer systems, and geologists to explore for minerals.

Some computer industry observers believe that expert systems are the wave of the future and that each of us in the business community will have "expert" help and guidance in our respective professions. Others say "no way." Time will tell!

## 4-4   APPLICATIONS OF SPECIAL-PURPOSE COMPUTER SYSTEMS

So far, our discussions have centered around computer systems with the flexibility to do a variety of tasks, such as computer-assisted instruction, patient accounting, and home banking. These are called **general-purpose computers.** Now let's turn our attention to those computers that are designed for a specific application. There are called **special-purpose computers.**

A special-purpose computer is just another micro or mainframe computer system, but it is *dedicated* to a single application and may have special requirements for input/output connections. Special-purpose computers are installed in aircraft to aid in navigation and in general flight control. They are the violins, clarinets, and drums of music synthesizers. They are also used for materials handling in warehouses to select and move containers without human intervention. Sev-

In the textile industry, computer-aided design (CAD) allows manufacturers to create and view cloth patterns in a fraction of the time it would have taken to prepare a preproduction sample for customer inspection.
(Courtesy of International Business Machines Corporation)

eral common applications for special-purpose computers in business are described below.

## Computer-Aided Design

**Computer-aided design (CAD)** has revolutionized the way in which engineers and scientists design, draft, and document a product. A CAD computer system includes a graphics workstation, disk storage, and a plotter. An engineer can design a part at the workstation and produce the blueprint automatically on a plotter. By working in two or three dimensions, an engineer can manipulate the design to the desired specifications. Many CAD systems provide the added benefit of color graphics.

With CAD, most of the bugs can be worked out of a design before a prototype is built. Take as an example the design of an automobile. At the stage where it is no more than an idea in an "electronic data base," an automobile design can be put through the paces in a simulated wind tunnel and on a simulated test track. It can even be crashed into a brick wall. It's a lot less expensive to crash an electronic image than the real thing! All of this is made possible with computer-aided design computers.

A CAD system is both a design tool and a laboratory. Just as the automobile design is created electronically, a wind tunnel can be created that simulates the effects of an actual wind tunnel. As an engineer alters the speed and direction of the "wind," the CAD system provides continuous feedback on drag and stability. Based on this feedback, an engineer might wish to alter the design and run the test again.

## Robotics

Rudimentary Robotics.    Special-purpose computers control industrial **robots.** The integration of computers and industrial robots is called **robotics.** Contrary to what some might believe, robots are quite different

Robots apply spotwelds to car bodies in this automobile assembly plant. They then paint every nook and crevice of the body.
(GM Assembly Division, Warren, Michigan)

in appearance and function from R2/D2 and C-3PO of *Star Wars*. The most common industrial robot is a single mechanical arm that is controlled by a computer. The arm, called a manipulator, is capable of performing the motions of a human arm. The manipulator is fitted with a "hand" that is designed for each specific task, such as painting, welding, moving parts, and so on.

A computer program is written to control the robot just as a program is written to print payroll checks. The program includes such commands as when to reach, in which direction to reach, how far to reach, when to grasp, and so on. Once programmed, robots don't need much attention. One plant manufactures vacuum cleaners 24 hours a day, seven days a week, *in total darkness*! Since the entire work force is robots, there is no need to turn on the lights and run up the electricity bill.

An industrial robot is best at repetitive tasks, moving heavy loads, and working in hazardous areas. These types of tasks exist in virtually every kind of industry, from hospitals to cannery row. During the next decade we can anticipate that many less-desirable jobs will be relegated to robots. This concerns and affects a great many people.

**Robots in the Future.**   It will be a very long time before our companions and workmates are robots. Before that happens, scientists must overcome several formidable technological hurdles. The first of these is "vision." In the present state of the art of vision systems, distinguishing between a scalpel and a Band-Aid would be a real challenge for a robot. Most robots are programmed to reach to a particular location and find a particular item, then place it somewhere else. This application of robotics is called "pick and place." If robots could "see," there would be greater flexibility in the tasks they could be programmed to do.

Once robots achieve some vision capabilities, researchers will begin working on "navigation." Most robots are stationary, and those that aren't can detect the presence only of an object in their path, or

This computer-controlled materials distribution system is an example application of computer-aided manufacturing. The system helps in the handling and transportation of parts to production sites. Data gathered from this system are transmitted to another computer that monitors all manufacturing processes.
(Courtesy of International Business Machines Corporation)

they are programmed to operate within a well-defined work area where the position of all obstacles is known.

## Computer-Aided Manufacturing

**Computer-aided manufacturing (CAM)** is a term that was coined to highlight the use of computers in the manufacturing process. There are literally thousands of uses for special-purpose computers in the manufacturing environment. Robots and computer-aided design are typical CAM applications. The movements of machine tools, such as lathes and milling machines, are also controlled by special-purpose computers. Other CAM applications for special-purpose computer systems include automated materials handling and assembly-line control.

The integration of the computer with manufacturing is called **integrated CAD/CAM** or **computer-integrated manufacturing.** In **computer-integrated manufacturing (CIM)** the computer is used at every stage of the manufacturing process, from the time a part is conceived until it is shipped. The various computer systems are linked together via data communications and feed data to one another. An engineer uses a CAD system to design the part. Then the design specifications are produced and stored on a magnetic disk. The specifications, now in an "electronic data base," become input to another computer system that generates programs to control the robots and machine tools that handle and make the part. The special-purpose process-control computers are even linked to the company's general-purpose MIS computers to provide data for order processing, inventory management, shop floor scheduling, and general accounting.

The scope of applications of computer technology in business and government is limited only by our imagination. In this chapter we have barely touched the tip of the proverbial iceberg. There are literally thousands of yet untapped opportunities for computerization. Applications not dreamed of today will be commonplace in the not-to-distant future.

## SUMMARY OUTLINE AND IMPORTANT TERMS

**4-1**  BUSINESS APPLICATIONS OF COMPUTER TECHNOLOGY. Certain computer applications and information systems are universal and are equally appropriate in any business environment. These applications normally involve personnel and monetary accounting, but they also include several other common application areas, such as inventory control and office automation.

Some computer applications are unique to a particular type of business, such as production scheduling (manufacturing), electronic funds transfer (financial services), point-of-sale (retail), typesetting (publishing), reservations (transportation), actuarial accounting (insurance), special effects (entertainment), and on-line scripts (the theater).

In health care, computers help hospital administrative personnel with billing and help doctors to diagnose illnesses. The computer has enabled medical research to advance in leaps and bounds.

**4–2**  GOVERNMENT APPLICATIONS OF COMPUTER TECHNOLOGY.   Some of the computer applications found in local government include utility billing, tax collection, police and fire incident reporting, and urban planning. State governments use computers for everything from fingerprint analysis to running statewide lotteries. The federal government has thousands of computer systems throughout the world that are used in a wide variety of computer applications.

**4–3**  EXPERT SYSTEMS.   **Expert systems** are part of the general area of research known as artificial intelligence. An expert system is an interactive system that responds to questions, asks for clarification, makes recommendations, and generally aids in the decision-making process. At the heart of an expert system is a **knowledge base.** In effect, expert systems simulate the human thought process.

**4–4**  APPLICATIONS OF SPECIAL-PURPOSE COMPUTER SYSTEMS.   In contrast to **general-purpose computers, special-purpose computers** are designed for and usually dedicated to a specific application. **Computer-aided design (CAD), robotics** (the integration of computers and **robots**), **computer-aided manufacturing (CAM),** and **computer-integrated manufacturing (CIM)** are a few of the hundreds of applications for special-purpose computers.

# REVIEW EXERCISES

## Concepts

1. Electronic funds transfer is associated with what industry?

2. Information systems that are common to most businesses usually involve accounting for what two corporate resources?

3. How do computers help surgeons in an operating room?

4. Name four applications of the computer in a municipal government.

5. CAD/CAM and robotics are usually associated with what industry?

6. What term is used to describe the linking of computers of different companies?

7. Name two medical information services that are available to physicians in private practice.

8. What computer-based applications are unique to hospitals?

9. What is the basic difference between an expert system's knowledge base and a data base?

10. In the field of robotics, to what does "navigation" refer?

11. How do computers help professional tennis players?

12. Contrast general-purpose computer systems to special-purpose computer systems.

## Discussion

13. Would you buy a "magazine on a disk"? Why or why not?

14. Movie purists abhor the thought of great black-and-white classics, such as *Casablanca*, being changed to color with the aid of computer technology. What do you think?

15. Why do you suppose truckers are resisting the implementation of satellite monitoring systems when they know that such a system will provide management with better control information?

16. Has the application of computer technology in the theater in any way stifled artistic creativity? Has it enhanced creativity? Explain.

17. Identify the routine periodic outputs generated by a point-of-sale system in a department store chain.

18. Discuss the emerging role of personal computers in electronic funds transfer.

19. Home banking services are available only to those who have home computers with communications capabilities. To encourage customer participation, some banks offer this service at a price that is below their cost. Excess cost is then passed on to all customers. Is this fair? Explain.

20. Physician's accounting systems have been implemented under a cloud of controversy. Why?

21. Identify the tangible and intangible benefits of an automated traffic control system.

22. Research in artificial intelligence is accelerating much faster than anyone would have imagined in 1980. Perhaps this increase in research can be attributed to AI's potential for increasing productivity in the plant and improving decision making. Is this the case, or will it mean fewer paychecks? Discuss.

23. Management, labor, and government are cooperating to develop robots that will surely eliminate some jobs. Why are they doing this?

24. Identify the routine periodic outputs generated by a market analysis system in a consumer goods manufacturing company.

## SELF-TEST (by section)

4-1. **(a)** Automatic teller machines are an implementation of EFT. (T/F)

**(b)** Actuarial accounting systems are associated with the _____ industry.

**(c)** The primary use of computers in hospital intensive care units is to collect patient billing information. (T/F)

**(d)** The most prominent system in the retail sales industry is the _____ system.

**(e)** Among financial institutions, only brokerage firms offer computer-based financial planning services. (T/F)

4-2. **(a)** Computer-based traffic control systems are implemented at the _____ level of government.

**(b)** The Internal Revenue Service is investigating the feasibility of allowing people to file tax returns from their personal computers, but such a service is not yet available. (T/F)

**(c)** Senators can use the congressional computer network to vote on legislation while sitting in their offices. (T/F)

4-3. **(a)** Expert systems are part of the general area of research known as _____ .

**(b)** All management information systems rely on the availability of a knowledge base to generate routine management reports. (T/F)

4-4. **(a)** A _____ -purpose computer is designed for a specific application.

**(b)** The integration of the computer with manufacturing is called CIM or _____ .

**(c)** Industrial robots are programmed to perform a particular function. (T/F)

*Self-Test answers.*   4-1 (a), T; (b), insurance; (c), F; (d), point-of-sale (POS); (e), F; 4-2 (a), local; (b), F; (c), T; 4-3 (a), artificial intelligence (AI); (b), F; 4-4 (a), special; (b), computer-integrated manufacturing; (c), T.

# Zimco Enterprises

## OFFICE AUTOMATION AT ZIMCO

### THE AUTOMATED OFFICE

One Monday morning last April, Sally Marcio, Zimco's VP of Sales and Marketing, came to work as usual in the Dallas office and greeted her assistant, Lynn Lester. "Good morning. Did you have a nice weekend?"

Lynn responded, "Very nice, thank you."

"Lynn, have you finished that report for the Burpo account? I'd like to make a few quick changes."

"Sure have. You can call it up on your workstation."

Sally was obviously happy that the report was ready. She replied, "I'll make those changes and route it via electronic mail to Burpo headquarters in St. Paul. If we don't have it to them by noon today, we may lose their business."

"Oh, by the way Sally, this new ad piece for the Qwert just arrived from the Art Department."

Seeing the finished product, Sally voiced her personal approval. "Wow! That new presentation graphics equipment has certainly improved the quality of work coming out of the Art Department. Before we send this to the Printing Department, we need to get approval from the four regional sales managers. Would you send each of them a facsimile copy for approval. Ask them to reply by electronic mail no later than 10 o'clock tomorrow morning."

"Also, Lynn, would you set up an emergency teleconference meeting with the plant managers in Reston, Becker, and Eugene. The topic will be the third-quarter production forecast."

"Consider it done. Each of them will have the message suggesting possible meeting times in their electronic mailboxes in a couple of minutes."

"Lynn, we'll also need to put a notice on Z-Buzz (Zimco's electronic bulletin board) about the availability of that new position in market research. That reminds me, don't let me forget to sit down this afternoon and run statistical summaries on the Stib research data. With our on-line statistics package, it shouldn't take more than a few minutes. It's hard to believe that I used to spend all day on these summaries." As Sally leaned back in her chair, she said, "You know Lynn, our automated office has sure made life a lot easier."

Secure in the fact that the day won't be all memos, calling, adding figures, and paper shuffling, Lynn responds, "I couldn't agree more."

As she sat down at her workstation to look over the Burpo report, Sally reminded Lynn, "I won't be in the office Friday. I'm going to telecommute and work on the annual market summary report."

### OFFICE AUTOMATION APPLICATIONS

As you could probably gather from the scenario between Sally Marcio and Lynn Lester in the Sales and Marketing Division, Zimco Enterprises is a showplace for application of **office automation**. This case study is devoted to describing applications of office automation at Zimco. The term "office automation" refers collectively to those computer-based applications associated with general office work. Office automation applications include *word processing*, *electronic mail*, *image processing*, *voice processing*, *office*

At Zimco, all office workers, including executives, are trained to use word processing and to send messages via electronic mail. Executives prefer editing their reports using word processing to making red-pencil revisions to a hard copy for a secretary to key in. They also like having the option of sending a memo electronically, thereby circumventing the time-consuming step of producing a hard copy.
(Quotron Systems, Inc.)

*information systems*, and *telecommuting*. All of these applications are available on both micro and mainframe computer systems at Zimco.

Peggy Peoples, VP of Personnel, did a study of the effects of office automation on the Personnel Division. The study revealed an increase in office productivity of almost 100 percent. The other divisions report improvements in office productivity of 50 to 75 percent. Preston Smith, the president, takes pride in the fact that "we are taking advantage of the potential of office automation." In the sections that follow, each of the applications of office automation is discussed in the context of how it is used at Zimco.

## WORD PROCESSING

Word processing, the cornerstone of office automation, revolves around written communication and is found virtually everywhere at Zimco. Managers, secretaries, engineers, and just about everyone else who has a need to write a memo, a letter, a report, or just jot down ideas has become a word processing addict. Word processing

means using the computer to enter, store, manipulate, and print text in letters, memos, reports, books, and so on.

Peggy Peoples explained: "The word is out on word processing. People love it! With word processing, managers and secretaries alike have only to key in the initial draft of whatever they are doing, be it a memo or a report; then they make revisions and corrections to the disk-based draft until it is ready to be printed in final form."

The fundamental concepts of word processing are discussed briefly below. These concepts are discussed in more detail in the special skills section of this text entitled, "Microcomputer Productivity Software."

**Formatting a Document.** When you *format* a document, you are describing the size of the print page and how you want the document to look when printed. As with the typewriter, you must set the left and right margins, the tab settings, line spacing, and character spacing. You can even justify on both the left and the right margins, such as in newspapers and books. Depending on the software, some or all of these specifications are made in a *layout line*.

**Entering Text.** To begin preparation of the document, all you have to do is start keying-in the text. Text is entered in **replace mode** or **insert mode.** When in replace mode, the character that you enter *overstrikes* the character in the cursor position. When in insert mode, you can enter *additional* text. Word processing permits *full-screen editing*. That is, you can move the **cursor** (the blinking character that indicates the location of the next input) to any position in the document to insert or replace text.

**Features.** Word processing features presented here are common to most word processing software packages. Two of the handiest features are the *copy* and *move* commands. With the copy feature, you can select a word, a phrase, or as much contiguous text as you desire, and copy it to another portion of the document. To do this, you simply issue the copy command, then tell the computer what to copy and where to put it. At the end of the copy procedure, two exact copies of the text are present in the document. The

```
To:      Field Sales Staff
From:    G. Brooks, Northern Sales Manager
Re:      Weekly Briefing Session

     The Sales Department's weekly briefing session will be
held at 9:00 a.m. this Thursday.  Last month's sales figures
and new sales strategies for the Tegler and Qwert will be
discussed.  See you Thursday!  We'll meet in the second floor
conference room.
```

```
To:      Field Sales Staff
From:    G. Brooks, Northern Sales Manager
Re:      Weekly Briefing Session

     The Sales Department's weekly briefing session will be
held at 9:00 a.m. this Thursday.  We'll meet in the second
floor conference room.  Last month's sales figures and new
sales strategies for the Tegler and Qwert will be discussed.
See you Thursday!
```

**FIGURE Z4–1**
**The Move Command in Word Processing**
In the first screen, the text to be moved is identified. The cursor is then positioned at the "move to" location—in our example, after the first sentence. In the second screen, the move command is issued and the designated text is "moved" to a location following the first sentence.

move command works in a similar manner, except that the text you select is moved to the location that you designate and the original text is deleted.

George Brooks, the Northern Regional Sales Manager, uses word processing to generate memos to his staff. Figure Z4–1 illustrates how George edited a memo to the field staff to make it more readable. He did this by "moving" the last sentence from the end of the memo to just after the first sentence.

The *search* or *find* feature permits George to search through the entire document and identify all occurrences of a particular character string. For example, George decided to switch the meeting announced in the memo of Figure Z4–1 from Thursday to Friday. If he wanted to

search the memo for all occurrences of "Thursday", he would simply initiate the search command and type in "Thursday". The cursor would be immediately positioned at the first occurrence of "Thursday". He can also *search and replace*. For example, he can selectively replace "Thursday" with "Friday". George, however, selected the option that allows him to *replace* all occurrences instantly with a *global search and replace* (see Figure Z4–2).

Several years ago, a letter to employees went out over President Preston Smith's signature. A couple of "typos" resulted in misspelled words and an embarrassment to Preston Smith. After that unfortunate mishap, Preston declared that "all letters must be checked electronically for misspelled words before they are sent." People use the *spell* feature to do this. The spell feature checks every word in the text against an electronic dictionary (usually from 75,000 to 150,000 words), then alerts the user if a word is not in the dictionary.

Other word processing features, such as *centering* of titles *indenting*, *boldface*, *underline*, *header* and *trailer labels*, and *pagination* (numbering of pages), are discussed in the special skills section, "Microcomputer Productivity Software."

Merging Text with a Data Base.   Besides providing a faster and easier way to type, the text generated by word processing can be merged with data from a data base. For example, a typical word processing application could involve the preparation of the same letter that is to be sent to a number of people.

When Zimco announced the enhanced version of the Qwert, each regional sales manager sent a "personal" letter to every Zimco customer in their respective regions. There are thousands of customers in each region. The secretary with a regular typewriter would have only two choices: either type thousands of separate letters or type one letter and photocopy it. In the business world in general and at Zimco in particular, the latter is not acceptable. Using word processing, a secretary can type the letter once, store it on the disk, then simply merge the customer name-and-address file (also stored on the disk) with the letter. The letters are then printed with the proper addresses and salutations. Figure Z4–3 illustrates how the Qwert announcement letter is merged with the customer name-and-address file to produce a "personalized" letter.

## ELECTRONIC MAIL

Because Zimco's computers, including PCs, are linked together in a *computer network*, employees are able to route messages to each other via **electronic mail**. A message can be a note, letter, report, chart, or even a procedures manual. Each person at Zimco is assigned an "electronic mailbox" on disk storage in which messages are received and stored. Preston Smith, or any other employee at Zimco, "opens" and "reads" his electronic mail by simply going to the nearest

**FIGURE Z4–2**
**The Global Search and Replace Command in Word Processing**
All occurrences of the word "Thursday" in the memo of Figure Z4–1 are replaced with "Friday" when a global search and replace command is issued.

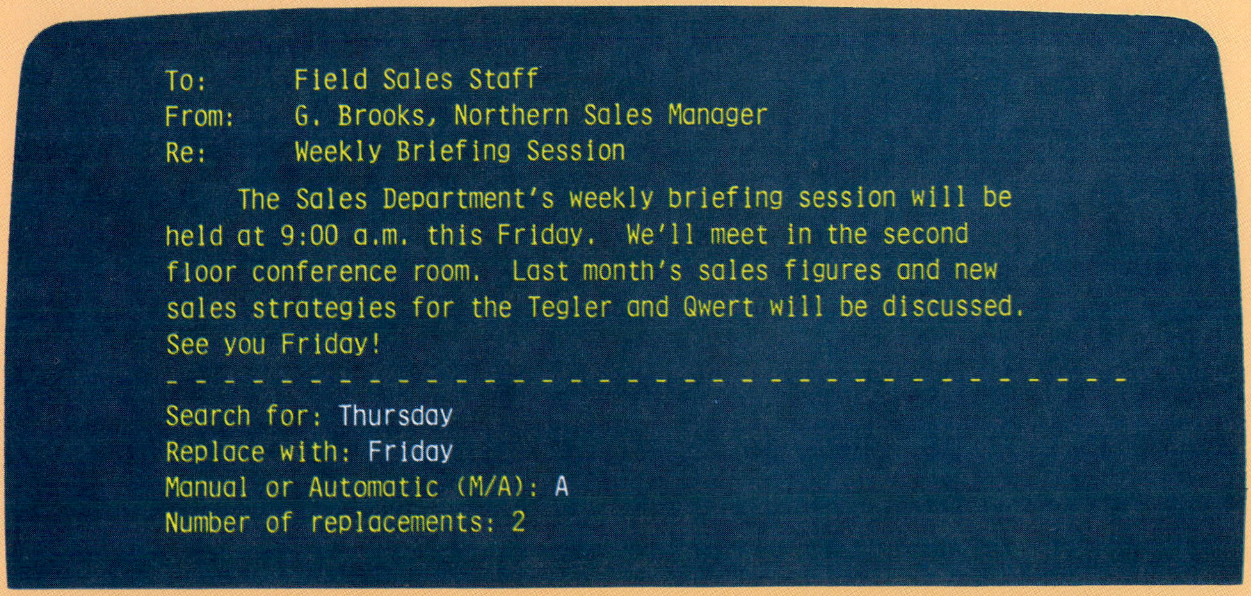

```
To:       Field Sales Staff
From:     G. Brooks, Northern Sales Manager
Re:       Weekly Briefing Session

    The Sales Department's weekly briefing session will be
held at 9:00 a.m. this Friday.  We'll meet in the second
floor conference room.  Last month's sales figures and new
sales strategies for the Tegler and Qwert will be discussed.
See you Friday!

- - - - - - - - - - - - - - - - - - - - - - - - - - - - - - - -

Search for: Thursday
Replace with: Friday
Manual or Automatic (M/A): A
Number of replacements: 2
```

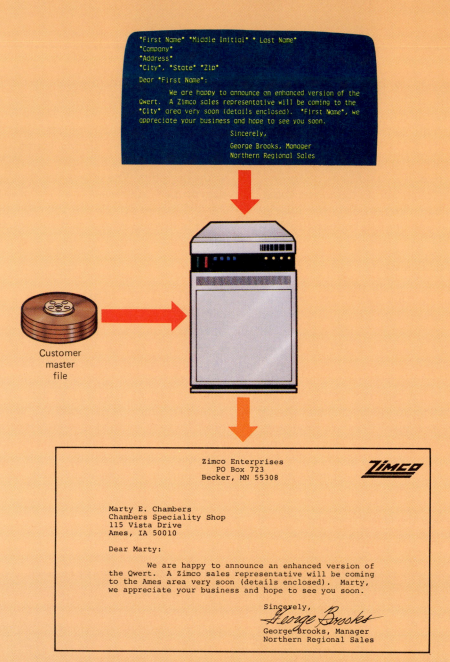

**FIGURE Z4-3**
**Merging Data with Word Processing**
The names and addresses from a customer master file are retrieved from secondary storage and merged with the text of a letter. In the actual letter, the appropriate data items are inserted for ∗First Name∗, ∗Company∗, ∗Address∗, ∗City∗, and so on. In this way, a "personalized" letter can be sent to each customer.

workstation and recalling the message(s) from storage.

Recently, Monroe Green, the VP of Finance and Accounting, asked his assistant to call a meeting for the purpose of discussing recent revisions to the federal tax code. She sent a message to each accounting manager via electronic mail, thereby avoiding the time-consuming ritual of "telephone tag." She entered a single message at her workstation and designated a preassigned routing code (all accounting managers). When sent, the message is routed to the electronic mailboxes of the all accounting managers. Each manager "opens the mail" by displaying the message at his or her workstation. At Zimco, an employee "logs on" by entering a password and authorization code at a workstation. A message, such as "Check mail", is displayed if there is any mail in his or her electronic mailbox.

Electronic mail is a common application at Zimco. It's a lot faster, more effective, and a good deal less expensive than interoffice mail.

## IMAGE PROCESSING

Image processing involves the creation, storage, and distribution of pictorial information. There are two levels of image processing sophistication at Zimco.

At the first level, *facsimile* equipment, which has been around since the 1960s, transfers hardcopy documents via telephone lines to another office. The process is similar to making a copy on a copying machine, except that the original is inserted in a facsimile machine at one office and a hard copy is produced on another facsimile machine in another office. In the office automation scenario at the first of this case study, Sally Marcio needed quick approval on a Qwert ad piece, so she sent facsimile copies of the ad piece to the regional sales managers.

Recent technological innovations have expanded the scope of image processing. Conrad Innis, the VP of CIS, has commissioned a feasibility study to assess the feasibility and applicability of offering more sophisticated image processing capabilities to users at Zimco, specifically an *image processor*. An image processor uses a camera to scan and digitize the image; then the digitized image is stored on a disk. The image can be handwritten notes, photographs, drawings, or anything that can be digitized. In digitized form, the image can be retrieved, displayed, altered, merged with text, stored, and sent via data communications to one or several remote locations.

Preliminary indications are that Zimco may remove all facsimile equipment and replace it with image processors. The image processors provide greater flexibility and can be integrated with existing MISs.

## VOICE PROCESSING

Voice processing applications at Zimco include *voice message switching* and *teleconferencing*. The workstation for voice message switching (a store-and-forward "voice mailbox" system) is a touch-tone telephone. Voice message switching accomplishes the same function as electronic mail, except that the hard copy is not available. When a manager sends a message, the voice is digitized and stored on a magnetic disk for later retrieval. The message is routed to the destination(s) the manager designates (using the telephone's keyboard); then it is heard upon request by the intended receiver(s). Zimco's voice store-and-forward system permits any employee to send one or many messages with just one phone call.

Twice a year, Zimco sales reps from the four regional offices meet to discuss sales strategies via teleconferencing. Teleconferencing enables people in different locations to see and talk to each other and to visually share charts and other meeting materials. Zimco doesn't have their own teleconferencing facility, so they use public facilities. Each facility has video cameras, monitors, and a meeting table. The voice and video of teleconferencing are supported by the telephone network. The idea behind teleconferencing is that people who are geographically scattered can meet without the need for time-consuming and expensive travel.

Zimco has elected not to use teleconferencing as a substitute for all travel. Otto Manning, the VP of Operations, observed that "the controlled teleconferencing environment does not transmit subtle nonverbal communication, which is so important to human understanding."

## OFFICE INFORMATION SYSTEMS

Zimco has several small information systems that address traditional office tasks. For example, one system allows employees to keep their personal *calendars* on-line. As workers schedule

The "calendar" is one of many timesaving office information systems at Zimco.
(Long and Associates)

activities, they block out times in their electronic calendars. There are definite advantages to having a central data base of personal calendars. Recently, Preston Smith's assistant scheduled a meeting of the VPs to review the impact of some unfavorable publicity. To do this, his assistant entered the names of the VPs and the expected duration of the meeting. The *conference scheduling* system searched the calendars of vice-presidents and suggested possible meeting times. Preston's assistant then selected a meeting time, and the VPs were notified by electronic mail. Of course, their calendars were automatically updated to reflect the meeting time.

One of the most popular office information systems at Zimco is the company *directory*. The directory contains basic personnel data: name, title, department, location, and phone number. To "look up" someone's telephone number, all an employee has to do is enter the person's name into the nearest workstation. Associated data are displayed within 2 seconds. The beauty of the directory data base is that it is always up to date, unlike the old hard-copy directories that Peggy Peoples said "never seemed to have the current titles or phone numbers."

Other office systems at Zimco allow employees to organize *personal notes*, keep *diaries*, document ideas in a *preformatted outline*, and

keep a *tickler* file. When employees log-on in the morning, the tickler file automatically reminds them of "things to do" for that day.

## TELECOMMUTING

Each department at Zimco has at least one, and usually a couple, of portable microcomputers. These micros fold up to about the size of an attaché case and can be easily carried between the office and home. Managers often take a micro home with them to take advantage of the peace and quiet. These portable micros can be used as stand-alone computer systems or they can serve as workstations linked to Zimco's mainframe computer system. The latter is known as **telecommuting.**

Zimco's commitment to the support of office automation and on-line access to information systems has made telecommuting very popular and a feasible alternative way to accomplish one's job. Each professional-level employee is permitted to telecommute up to one day per week, as long as the telecommuting is done on Monday or Friday. All group meetings are scheduled on the midweek days. Whenever someone needs a few hours, or perhaps a day, of uninterrupted time to accomplish a task that does not require direct personal interaction, they block out part or all of a Monday or Friday on their personal calendars, then telecommute.

Monroe Green, the VP of Accounting and Finance, says, "I telecommute to prepare the quarterly financial statements." All of the information he needs is at his fingertips and he finishes in one day at home what used to take him a week. Preston Smith stated emphatically: "I got sick and tired of spending nights up in my office. By telecommuting, I'm at least within earshot of my wife and kids. Also, I like to get into more comfortable clothes." Conrad Innis and numerous other Zimco employees have their own PC. Conrad explains one of his many uses of his PC: "Every Monday evening I write out the agenda for my Tuesday morning staff meeting. I then send a summary of the agenda via electronic mail to my managers so that they will see it first thing Tuesday morning when they log in."

At Zimco, telecommuting may never catch on as an alternative to working in the office, but it has proven to be a boon to productivity for many people. Zimco's management feels that telecommuting offers a lot of advantages to motivated workers who want to telecommute occasionally. They encourage telecommuting, but only in those instances where the opportunities for improved productivity are apparent.

## Discussion Questions

1. Identify all of the office automation applications mentioned, directly or indirectly, by Sally Marcio or Lynn Lester in the office scenario at the first of this case study.

2. When doing word processing, under what circumstances would you enter text in replace mode? In insert mode? Which mode would you use most often, and why?

3. Which office automation applications have the potential to reduce the amount of time that Zimco employees spend on the telephone? Explain.

4. After considerable debate, Zimco management decided to allow employees to telecommute one day each week. Some of the benefits of telecommuting were presented in the case study. What do you think were some of management's negative concerns about telecommuting?

5. What advantages does voice message switching have over electronic mail? What advantages does electronic mail have over voice message switching? Why do you suppose that Zimco opted to implement both?

6. How would the manager of the Customer Service Department at Zimco benefit from word processing?

7. Discuss the keystroke-by-keystroke procedures for sending and retrieving electronic mail at your college (your company).

8. What advantages does an image processor have over facsimile equipment?

# PART 3

# HARDWARE AND COMMUNICATIONS

*Today, in the decade of the 1980s, a company's success and survival is directly related to how well it is able to compete in the marketplace on technological grounds. It is imperative that we take full advantage of the opportunities that new and emerging information processing technology will offer us over the next few years. Systems and communications technologies are strategic weapons, not "cost centers."*

Robert F. McDermott
Chairman
USAA

# Computer Systems—Micros, Minis, and Mainframes

## CHAPTER
## 5

### STUDENT LEARNING OBJECTIVES

- To distinguish between microcomputers, minicomputers, and mainframes
- To illustrate typical hardware configurations for microcomputers, minicomputers, and mainframes.
- To distinguish between the different types of microcomputers.
- To demonstrate awareness of the relative size, scope, characteristics, and variety of available computer systems.

### FOCUS OF ZIMCO CASE STUDY

- Micros at Zimco.

## 5

## 5-1 COMPUTER SYSTEMS: A ROSE IS A ROSE IS A ROSE . . .

The most distinguishing characteristic of any computer system is its "size" or computing capacity. Computers have been classified as *microcomputers*, *minicomputers*, *superminicomputers*, *midicomputers*, *maxicomputers*, and *supercomputers*. From this list you might think that these terms were coined by fashion designers. Such is not the case. The minicomputer preceded the miniskirt!

Now, and even in the past, these computer classifications have defied definition. Even though it is doubtful that any two computer specialists would describe a minicomputer or a supercomputer in the same way, these terms are still used frequently. Rapid advances in computer technology have caused what used to be distinguishing characteristics (e.g., physical size, cost, memory capacity, and so on) to become blurred.

All computers, no matter how small or large, have the same fundamental capabilities: processing, storage, input, and output. Just as "a rose, is a rose, is a rose . . ." (Gertrude Stein), "a computer, is a computer, is a computer. . . ." Keep this in mind as we discuss the three basic categories of computers: *microcomputer systems*, *minicomputer systems*, and *mainframe computer systems*. It should be emphasized that these are relative categories, and what people call a minicomputer system today may be called a microcomputer system at some time in the future.

## 5-2 MICROCOMPUTERS: SMALL BUT POWERFUL

### The Evolution of the Microcomputer

Microprocessors.    Here is a tough one. What is smaller than a dime and found in wristwatches, sewing machines, and jukeboxes? The answer: a **microprocessor**. Microprocessors play a very important role in our lives. You probably have a dozen or more of them at home and may not know it. They are used in telephones, ovens, televisions, greeting cards, cars, and, of course, personal computers.

The microprocessor is a product of the microminiaturization of electronic circuitry; it is literally a "computer on a chip." The first fully operational microprocessor was demonstrated in March 1971. Since that time, these relatively inexpensive microprocessors have been integrated into thousands of mechanical and electronic devices, even elevators and ski boot bindings. In a few years, virtually everything that is mechanical or electronic will incorporate microprocessor technology into the design.

Many automobile engine functions are monitored and controlled by microprocessors. This one optimizes the shifting of gears in this 5-speed automatic transmission by controlling the throttle and clutch functions.
(Eaton Corporation)

This management consultant's micro is configured with a keyboard for input, a video monitor and a printer for output, and two disk drives for storage of data and programs.
(Dataproducts Corporation)

**Microcomputers.**   The microprocessor is sometimes confused with its famous offspring, the **microcomputer.** A keyboard, video monitor, and memory were attached to the microprocessor and—the microcomputer was born! Suddenly, owning a computer became an economic reality for individuals and small businesses.

In a microcomputer, the microprocessor, electronic circuitry for handling input/output signals from the peripheral devices, and "memory chips" are mounted on a single circuit board, called a **motherboard.** Before being attached to the circuit board, the microprocessor and other chips are mounted to a *carrier*. Carriers have standard-sized pin connectors that permit the chips to be attached to the motherboard.

The motherboard, the "guts" of a microcomputer, is what distinguishes one microcomputer from another. The motherboard is simply "plugged" into one of several slots designed for circuit boards. Most micros have several empty slots so that you can purchase optional capabilities in the form of *add-in* boards. For example, you can purchase more memory, a board that permits graphics output, or a modem (a device that permits data communications between computers). These capabilities are discussed in more detail in later chapters.

*Microcomputer Defined*.   But what is a micrcomputer? During the last decade, people have described microcomputers in terms of cost, physical dimensions, size of primary storage, and amount of data processed at a time, but all definitions proved confusing. A **micro** is just a small computer. Perhaps the best definition of a micro is *any computer that you can pick up and carry*. But don't be misled by the "micro" prefix. You can "pick up and carry" some very powerful computers!

A microcomputer is also called a **personal computer** or **PC.** The label "personal computer" was associated with microcomputers because they were designed for use by one person at a time. For the most part, this one-to-one relationship still holds true. However, some micros or PCs can handle several users simultaneously. Multiuser micros are discussed later.

An architect carries his blueprints and his lap PC to the construction site. The computer comes in handy when dealing with on-the-spot revisions to specifications. (GRiD Systems Corporation)

*Pocket, Lap, and Desktop PCs.* Personal computers come in three different physical sizes: *pocket PCs*, *lap PCs*, and *desktop PCs*. The pocket and lap PCs are light (a few ounces to 8 pounds), compact, and can operate without an external power source—so they earn the "portable" label as well. There are also a number of "transportable" desktop PCs on the market, but they are more cumbersome to move. They fold up to about the size of a small suitcase, weigh about 25 pounds, and usually require an external power source. Most desktop PCs are not designed for frequent movement and are therefore not considered portable.

The power of a PC is not necessarily in proportion to its size. A few lap PCs can run circles around some of the desktop PCs. Some user conveniences, however, must be sacrificed to achieve portability. For instance, the miniature keyboards on pocket PCs make data entry and interaction with the computer difficult and slow. On lap PCs, the display screen is small and does not hold as much text as a display on a desktop PC.

*Home and Business PCs.* Some people make a distinction between *home* and *business* microcomputers. Actually, the differences are primarily cosmetic. For example, home computers may use a television set for a monitor and the keyboard may be less durable, but internally these computers are very similar. For instance, they may have the same motherboard. The "home" and "business" labels are more for marketing than for technical differentiation.

Most "home" PCs cost less and have slightly less processing capacity than do "business" PCs, but the home computer is often found in the office, and vice versa. The bottom line is that any computer in a home is a home computer. For this reason, future discussions of micros and PCs will not distinguish between the home and business varieties. Ironically, the number one use of computers in the home is for business work done at home!

Parts inventory and customer records are maintained on this micro at an automobile service center. (Courtesy of Apple Computer, Inc.)

This project manager carries his transportable PC home on weekends to review the schedule of project activities for the coming week. To prepare the computer for movement, the keyboard is detached and fastened in position to cover the monitor. A handle is attached to the back of the micro. (Sperry Corporation)

128

The microcomputer is used in small businesses operated by druggists, veterinarians, attorneys, plumbers, and hundreds of other professions. To the engineer and scientist, the microcomputer has become almost as commonplace as the hand calculator of the 1970s and the slide rule before that.

## Why Are Micros and Personal Computers So Popular?

The minimal cost and almost unlimited applications for the microcomputer have made it the darling of the computer industry. A little more than a decade ago, very few people had heard of a microcomputer. Now, the dollar amount of microcomputer sales is about equal to that of mainframes that cost 10 to 2000 times as much. The number of microcomputers sold in one month today exceeds the total number of operational computers in existence in the United States 10 years ago.

When you use a micro or personal computer, the capabilities of a complete computer system are at the tip of your fingers. Some are more powerful than computers that once handled the data processing requirements of large banks. PCs and their support software are designed to be user friendly; therefore, they are easy to use and understand. The wide variety of software available for microcomputers offers something for almost everyone, from video games to word processing to education to home finances to inventory control.

These reasons for the micro's popularity pale when we talk of the *real* reason for its unparalleled success—it is just plain fun to use, whether for personal, business, or scientific computing.

## Configuring a Microcomputer System

Normally, computer professionals are called upon to select, configure, and install the hardware associated with minicomputers and mainframe computers. But individuals, often users, select, configure and install their own micros, so it is important to know what makes up a microcomputer system.

The microcomputer is the smallest computer system. Even so, it has the same components as mainframe computer systems: input, output, storage, and processing. As you might expect, the input/output components are much slower, and the storage component has a smaller capacity than the larger systems.

The computer and its peripheral devices are called the computer system **configuration.** The configuration of a microcomputer can vary. The most typical micro configuration consists of:

1. A computer
2. A keyboard for input
3. A televisionlike display called a **monitor** for **soft copy** (temporary) output
4. A printer for **hard copy** (printed) output
5. One or two disk drives for permanent storage of data and programs

A portable micro is configured here with all the trimmings: a printer, a power supply (in front of the carrying case), the keyboard and processor unit (which also contains one disk drive), a mouse (for input,) another disk drive, a modem (under telephone) for making connections to other computers, and a joy stick (far right). These add-ons are discussed in Chapters 7 and 8. The processor unit is the central focus of the system. Cables from each device are connected to the input/ output ports at the rear of the processor unit.
(Courtesy of Apple Computer, Inc.)

In some microcomputer systems these components are purchased as separate physical units, then linked together. In others, two, three, and even all of the components can be contained in a single unit. With a few rare exceptions, the printer is usually a separate unit.

The storage medium of most microcomputers is normally a **diskette** or a **microdisk.** The diskette can be compared to a phonograph record, but it is thinner, more flexible, and permanently enclosed within a 5¼-inch square jacket. Because the diskette is flexible, like a page in this book, it is also called a **flexible disk** or a **floppy disk.** Some microcomputers use rigid microdisks (3¼ or 3½ inches in diameter) for storage. The more powerful microcomputers use hard disks. These and other storage media are discussed in detail in Chapter 7, "Peripheral Devices: I/O and Data Storage."

Just about any input or output device that can be linked to a mainframe computer can also be linked to a microcomputer. The wide variety of input/output devices range from the *mouse* (a device that moves the blinking cursor on a display screen) to the *voice synthesizer* (both are discussed in Chapter 7).

In keeping with conversational computerese, we will drop the "system" from "microcomputer system." Therefore, all future references to a personal computer or a microcomputer imply a microcomputer *system*.

## Multiuser Micros

In the early 1960s, mainframe computer systems were able to service only one user at a time. By the mid-1960s, technological improvements made it possible for computers to service several users simultaneously. A quarter of a century later, some mainframes service thousands of users, all at the same time!

We can draw a parallel between what happened to the mainframe in the 1960s and what is happening to microcomputers today. Until recently, micros were "personal" computers—for individual use only. But technological improvements have been so rapid that it has become difficult for a single user to tap the full potential of state-of-the-art micros. To tap this unused potential, hardware and software vendors are marketing products that permit several users on the system at once.

Several other workstations can be connected to this microcomputer to make it a multiuser system.
(Courtesy of International Business Machines Corporation)

These multiuser micros are configured with up to 12 keyboard/ monitor pairs, called **workstations.** These workstations, often located in the same office, share the microcomputer's resources and its peripheral devices. With a multiuser micro, a secretary can be transcribing dictation at one workstation, a manager can be doing financial analysis at another workstation, and a clerk can be entering data to a data base at another workstation. All of this is taking place at the same time on the same multiuser micro.

## Micros as Workstations

A workstation is the hardware that allows you to interact with a computer system, be it a mainframe or a multiuser micro. A video display terminal (VDT) is a workstation. A microcomputer can also be a workstation. With the installation of an optional data communications adapter, a micro has the flexibility to serve as a *stand-alone* computer system or as an "intelligent" workstation to a multiuser micro, a minicomputer, or a mainframe computer.

The term "intelligent" is applied to workstations that can also operate as stand-alone computer systems, independent of any other computer system. For example, you can dial-up any one of a number of information services on travel, securities, and consumer goods, link your micro to the telephone line and remote computer, then use your micro as a workstation to obtain information. Both the micro and the VDT can transmit and receive data from a remote computer, but only the micro workstation can process and store the data independently. We will talk more about micros as workstations in Chapters 7 and 8.

## 5-3   MINICOMPUTERS

### Micros versus Minis and Mainframes

*Micros* are computer systems. *Minicomputers* and *mainframes* are computer systems. Each offers a variety of input and output alternatives, and each is supported by a wide variety of packaged software. There are, of course, obvious differences in size and capabilities. Everything associated with minicomputers and mainframes is larger in scope: execution of programs is faster; on-line disk storage has more capacity; printer speeds are much faster; minicomputers and mainframes service many workstations; and of course, they cost more.

Besides size and capability, the single most distinguishing characteristic of minicomputers and mainframe computers is the manner in which they are used. Mainframe computers, with their expanded processing capabilities, provide a computing resource that can be shared by an entire company, not just a single user. For example, it is common in a company for the finance, personnel, and accounting departments to share the resources of a minicomputer or mainframe, possibly all at the same time.

Until the late 1960s, all computers were mainframe computers, and they were expensive—too expensive for all but the largest companies.

Computing capacity

■ Micros

■ Minis

■ Mainframes

1975   1980   1985   1990

Minicomputers are being designed to operate in a normal office environment. Most minicomputers, such as the one in this management consulting firm, do not require special accommodations for temperature and humidity control.
(Harris Corporation, Computer Systems Division)

About that time vendors introduced smaller, but slightly "watered down," computers that were more affordable to smaller companies. The industry dubbed these small computers **minicomputers,** or simply **minis.** The name has stuck, even though some of today's so-called minis are many times as powerful as the largest mainframes of the early 1970s (see Figure 5–1).

## What Is a Mini and How Is It Used?

There is no clear-cut or generally accepted definition for a minicomputer. The passing of time and a rapidly changing technology have blurred the distinction between categories of computers. The more powerful multiuser micros look very much like small minis, but minis are now accomplishing processing tasks that have traditionally been associated with mainframes. Minis bridge the gap between micros and mainframes, but the manner in which they are used makes them more characteristic of mainframes than of micros. Creating a rigorous definition of a minicomputer is like trying to grab a speeding bullet. Since technology has created a moving target, we will describe the minicomputer simply as a small mainframe computer.

**FIGURE 5–1**
**Micro, Mini, and Mainframe Computing Capacities**
The computing capacity of a micro, mini, or mainframe increases with advancing technology.

Minicomputers usually serve as stand-alone computer systems for small businesses (10 to 400 employees) and as remote computer systems linked to a large centralized computer. The latter use of minis is described in Chapter 8, "Data Communications." Minis are also common in research groups, engineering firms, and colleges.

## Configuring a Minicomputer System

Minis have most of the operational capabilities of mainframe computers that may be 10 to 1000 times faster. They just perform their tasks more slowly. Minicomputer input, output, and storage devices are similar in appearance and function to those used on much larger systems. However, the printers are not quite as fast, the storage capacity is smaller, and fewer workstations can be serviced. Figure 5–2 illustrates a midsized minicomputer system configuration that provides information systems support for a mail-order sporting goods retailer with $40 million in sales. The components illustrated in Figure 5–2 are described in the following discussion.

■ *Processing*. It is premature to give you a technical description of processing capabilities. That will be done in Chapter 6, "Inside the Computer." We can, however, give you a feeling for the relative processing capabilities of a minicomputer by comparing it to one with which most of us have at least a casual familiarity—the microcomputer. The processor in the minicomputer system of Figure 5–2 has about 10 times the processing capability of a state-of-the-art single-user micro.

■ *Storage*. An organization's storage-capacity requirements increase even faster than its processing requirements. Typically, the first major upgrade from a microcomputer is away from diskette data storage. The "hard" disk alternative has a much greater capacity than the diskette or microdisk. The minicomputer system in Figure 5–2 has four disk drives (discussed in Chapter 7, "Peripheral Devices: I/O and Data Storage"), each capable of storing 800 megabytes (million characters) for a total capacity of 3,200 megabytes. The system also has two magnetic *tape drives*, each with a capacity of 200 megabytes of on-line sequential storage. Disk data files are periodically dumped, or loaded, to tape for backup. If, for some reason, the data on the disks are destroyed, the data on the backup tapes could be loaded to the disks so that processing could continue.

■ *Input*. The primary means of data input to the system are the 20 VDTs installed in the marketing and credit departments. The **operator console** in the machine room is also used to communicate instructions to the system. Seven workstations are used by programmers to enter, debug, and test their programs.

■ *Output*. A 1200-line-per-minute (lpm) printer provides hard copy output. The VDTs in the departments of marketing, credit, programming, and the console in the machine room provide soft copy output. Twelve VDTs are made available to middle and top management for on-line inquiry.

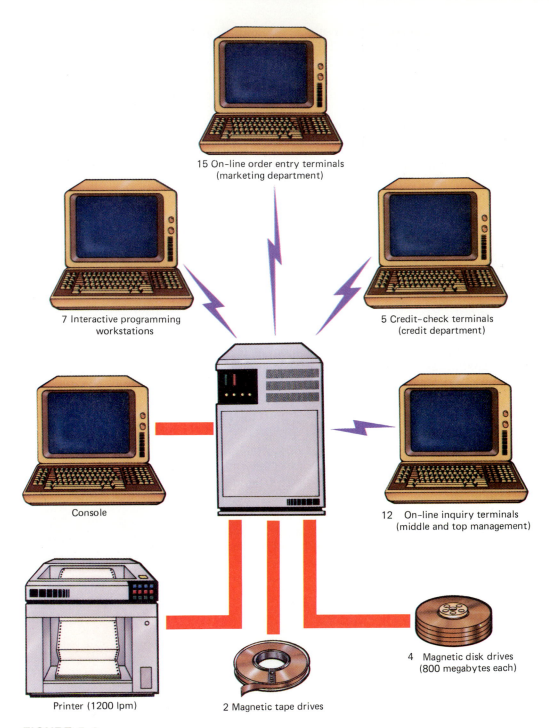

15 On-line order entry terminals
(marketing department)

7 Interactive programming
workstations

5 Credit-check terminals
(credit department)

Console

12   On-line inquiry terminals
(middle and top management)

Printer (1200 lpm)

2 Magnetic tape drives

4   Magnetic disk drives
(800 megabytes each)

**FIGURE 5–2**
**A Minicomputer System**
This system supports a mail-order sporting goods retailer with $40 million in
sales and is representative of a midsized minicomputer.

It is unlikely that you would find two minicomputers configured in exactly the same way. A company that prefers to use disk rather than tape backup would not need magnetic tape drives. Another may have a substantial volume of printed output and require two 2000-line-per-minute printers. Figure 5–2 is an example of one possible configuration.

As the definition of a minicomputer becomes more obscure, the term "minicomputer" will take its place beside "electronic brain." But for now, it remains a commonly used term, even though it lacks a commonly accepted definition.

## 5–4   MAINFRAME COMPUTER SYSTEMS

Besides the obvious difference in the speeds at which they process data, the major difference between minicomputers and other mainframe computers is in the number of remote workstations that they can service. As a rule of thumb, any computer that services more than 100 remote workstations can no longer be called a minicomputer. Some supercomputers, the fastest and most powerful of mainframes, provide service to over 10,000 remote workstations.

The speed at which medium and large mainframe computers can perform operations allows more input, output, and storage devices with greater capabilities to be configured in the computer system. The computer system in Figure 5–3 is used by the municipal government of a city of about 1 million people. This example should give you an appreciation for the relative size and potential of a medium-sized mainframe computer system. The hardware devices illustrated will be explained in detail in subsequent chapters. The components are described briefly on the following page.

The clean lines of this large mainframe computer system hide the thousands of integrated circuits, miles of wire, and even gold, that make up the inner workings of a computer system. This data center provides information processing support for hundreds of end users. (Courtesy Burroughs Corporation)

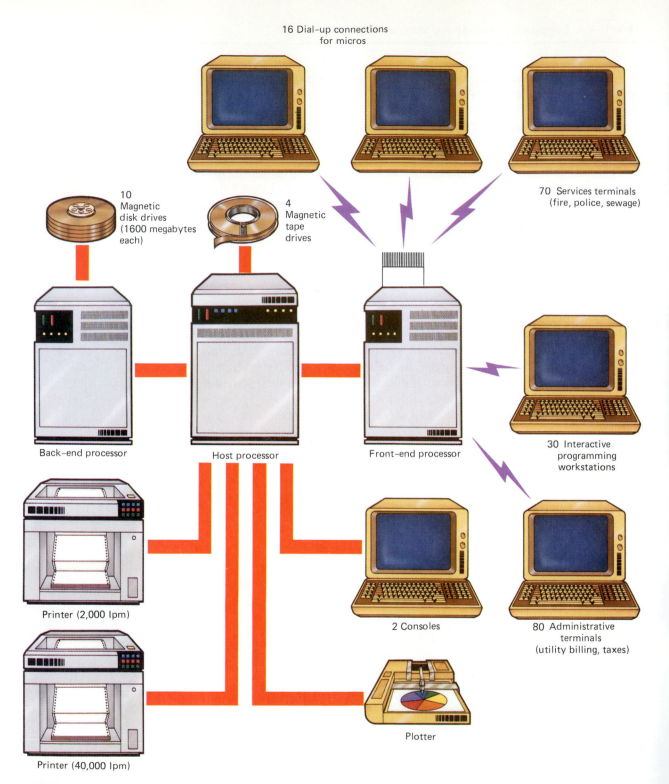

16 Dial-up connections
for micros

10 Magnetic disk drives (1600 megabytes each)

4 Magnetic tape drives

70 Services terminals (fire, police, sewage)

Back-end processor

Host processor

Front-end processor

30 Interactive programming workstations

Printer (2,000 lpm)

Printer (40,000 lpm)

2 Consoles

80 Administrative terminals (utility billing, taxes)

Plotter

**FIGURE 5-3**
**A Mainframe Computer System**
This midsized mainframe computer system supports the administrative processing needs for the municipal government of a city with a population of about 1 million.

■ *Processing*. Mainframe computer systems, including some minis, will normally be configured with the mainframe or **host processor** and several other processors. The host processor has direct control over all the other processors, storage devices, and input/output devices. The other processors relieve the host of certain routine processing requirements. For example, the **back-end processor** performs the task of locating a particular record on a data storage device. The **front-end processor** relieves the host processor of communications-related processing duties, that is, the transmission of data to and from remote workstations and other computers. In this way, the host can concentrate on overall system control and the execution of applications software.

A typical configuration would have a host processor, a *front-end processor*, and perhaps a *back-end processor*. The host is the main computer and is substantially larger and more powerful than the other *subordinate* processors. The front-end and back-end processors control the data flow in and out of the host processor. Although the host could handle the entire system without the assistance of the front-end and back-end processors, overall system efficiency would be drastically reduced without them.

■ *Storage*. All mainframe computer systems use similar direct and sequential storage media. The larger ones simply have more of them and they usually work faster. In Figure 5–3 there are four magnetic tape drives and 10 magnetic disk drives. The disk drives are *dual density* and can pack twice the data in the same amount of physical storage space as can the disks shown in Figure 5–2. The total data storage capacity in the example is 800 megabytes of sequential storage (tape) and 16,000 megabytes of direct-access storage (disk).

■ *Input*. The primary means of entering data to the system is the same, no matter what the size of the computer system. The only difference between a large and a small system is in the number and location of the workstations. In the example of Figure 5–3, 150 workstations are dedicated to service and administrative functions, 30 are used for programming, and 16 ports are available for those who might wish to use their PCs to dial-up and log-on to the mainframe computer. A port is an access point in a computer system that permits data to be transmitted between the computer and a peripheral device.

■ *Output*. As in the minicomputer system in Figure 5–2, the hard copy is produced on high-speed printers and the soft copy on workstations. In the example, there are two printers: a line printer with a speed of 2000 lines per minute and a page printer that uses laser printing technology to achieve printing speeds of over 40,000 lines per minute. The plotter, also pictured in the configuration, is used by city engineers to produce hard copies of graphs, charts, and drawings.

This mainframe computer, which is one of the world's fastest computers, is sometimes called a supercomputer. This one, which looks like a space-age sofa, helps an oil company to process mountains of data into pictures of the underground. (Phillips Petroleum Company)

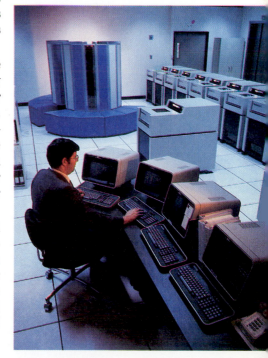

## 5–5   COMPUTER SYSTEMS SUMMARY

There has never been a common definition for terms such as microcomputer, minicomputer, and supercomputer. Consequently, their meanings become even more obscure with each leap in technological innovation. Nevertheless, people still use these terms to refer to general classes of computers. Just remember that one person's microcomputer may be another's minicomputer.

Perhaps the most important point to be made in this chapter is this: Whether we talk about a personal computer, a mainframe, a mini, or any other kind of computer system, they differ only in size and how they are applied.

## SUMMARY OUTLINE AND IMPORTANT TERMS

**5–1**   COMPUTER SYSTEMS: A ROSE IS A ROSE IS A ROSE. . . . The three basic computer categories are microcomputer, minicomputer, and mainframe. All computers, no matter how large or small, have the same fundamental capabilities: processing, storage, input, and output.

**5–2**   MICROCOMPUTERS: SMALL BUT POWERFUL.   **Microprocessors** not only set the stage for **microcomputers,** but they are found in dozens of devices about the home. The **motherboard** in a microcomputer contains the electronic circuitry for processing and I/O operations, and some memory. The **micro,** also called a **personal computer** or **PC,** comes in pocket, lap, and desktop sizes.

The most common **configuration** for a micro is a keyboard for input, a **monitor** for **soft copy** output, a printer for **hard copy** output, and disk drives for permanent storage of data on **diskettes** or **microdisks.** A diskette is also called a **flexible disk** or **floppy disk.** Multiuser micros are configured with several **workstations.** Micros can be used as stand-alone computer systems or they can serve as "intelligent" workstations to mainframe computers.

**5–3**   MINICOMPUTERS.   Micros are computer systems, but they differ greatly from **minicomputer** and mainframe computer systems in processing capabilities and in how they are used. The term "minicomputer," or **mini,** emerged about 20 years ago as a name for small computers. The name has stuck, even though some of today's minis are more powerful than the mainframes of the early 1970s. Minis now accomplish processing tasks that have been traditionally associated with mainframe computers. Minicomputers usually serve as stand-alone computer systems for small businesses and as remote computer systems linked to a large centralized computer. There is no generally accepted definition of a minicomputer.

**5–4**   MAINFRAME COMPUTER SYSTEMS.   Besides the obvious differences in processing speed, the major difference between minicomputers and medium-sized-to-large mainframes is in the number of remote workstations that can be serviced. A computer servicing more than 100 workstations is no longer a minicomputer.

A typical mainframe configuration might have a **host processor,** a **front-end processor,** and perhaps a **back-end processor.** The special-function processors help to improve overall system efficiency.

**5–5**   COMPUTER SYSTEMS SUMMARY.   A computer is a computer, whether it is called a PC, a mainframe, or a desktop computer. They differ only in size and how they are applied.

# REVIEW EXERCISES

## Concepts

1. What is a motherboard?
2. Describe the capabilities of a multiuser micro.
3. What is the relationship between a microprocessor and a microcomputer?
4. In terms of physical size, how are PCs categorized?
5. What is the name given to printed output? Output on a monitor?
6. Give two examples each of both input hardware and output hardware.
7. What is a dual-density disk drive?
8. What is the purpose of a mainframe computer's operator console?
9. Contrast the processing environment for mainframe computers to that of a microcomputer.
10. What is the difference between a diskette and a microdisk?
11. Describe an "intelligent" workstation.

## Discussion

12. The primary use of computers in the home is for business work done at home. Is there a contradiction when one speaks of "business" microcomputers and "home" microcomputers? Explain.
13. Is the use of terms such as microcomputer, minicomputer, midicomputer, supercomputer, and so on, a help or a hindrance to distinguishing between the processing capabilities of computer systems? Explain.
14. List at least 10 products that are smaller than a breadbox and use microprocessors. Select one and describe the function of its microprocessor.

**15.** What options would you like to have on your own personal micro that are not included in a minimum configuration? Why?

**16.** Discuss at least five domestic applications for personal computers.

**17.** How might a microcomputer help in the day-to-day administration of an appliance store (20 employees)?

**18.** Ask two people who know and have worked with computers for at least three years to describe a minicomputer. What can you conclude from their responses?

## SELF-TEST (by section)

**5–1.** The most distinguishing characteristic of any computer system is its computing capacity. (T/F)

**5–2.** **(a)** A microcomputer cannot be linked to a mainframe computer. (T/F)

**5–2.** **(b)** The processing component of a microcomputer is a _____ .

**5–2.** **(c)** The microdisk is also known as a floppy disk. (T/F)

**5–3.** **(a)** A minicomputer is referred to as a personal computer. (T/F)

**5–3.** **(b)** Minicomputers are now accomplishing processing tasks that have traditionally been associated with mainframe computers. (T/F)

**5–4.** **(a)** Each peripheral device is connected to a mainframe computer through a port. (T/F)

**5–4.** **(b)** The _____ relieves the host processor of communications-related processing duties.

**5–5.** There is no commonly accepted definition for a supercomputer. (T/F)

*Self-Test answers.*   5–1, T; 5–2 (a), F; (b), microprocessor; (c), F; 5–3 (a), F; (b), T; 5–4 (a), T; (b), front-end processor; 5–5, T.

# Zimco Enterprises

## MICROS AT ZIMCO

### MICROCOMPUTER APPLICATIONS AND OPPORTUNITIES

Shortly after Conrad Innis, VP of Computer and Information Services (CIS), began work at Zimco in 1981, he invited the other four VPs and the president, Preston Smith, to spend a Friday and Saturday with him in an informal round-table discussion. The topic was "Computer Applications at Zimco." The six executives met at Beaver Bend State Park in southeastern Oklahoma to get away from the everyday routine (and the telephone) at Zimco headquarters in Dallas.

Conrad's objective was to get Zimco's top management into "thinking computers and automation"—and it worked. Conrad made the point that every system does not have to be designed and developed by the Computer and Information Services Division. He brought the point home by announcing that Zimco was in the top 10 percent of all manufacturing companies in the number of micros per white-collar employee. He said, "Unlike most companies, Zimco has the hardware to support user-developed systems." When Sally Marcio, VP of Sales and Marketing, asked for an example, Conrad talked about using microcomputer-based word processing and database software to announce product promotional campaigns. "These software productivity tools enable us to send 'personalized' letters to our customers."

Conrad told Peggy Peoples of Personnel that "there is no need for us to produce a twice-weekly printout of all personnel records." He said, "The personnel system could be placed online such that records could be accessed and updated from any of the workstations in the Personnel Division."

Conrad came well prepared for the meeting. He had examples of how computers in general, and micros in specific, could be applied in the various divisions *to save time and money*, and *to allow managers to make better decisions*. He encouraged managers to "take advantage of the miracles of modern technology."

Conrad encouraged the VPs to buy micros for their divisions because of their *dual-purpose capabilities*. "You can use micros in stand-alone mode to handle small user-developed systems that are applicable to a particular department or individual. Or they can serve as workstations that can be linked to Zimco's mainframes." At present, Zimco has 345 workstations throughout the enterprise, about 200 of which are microcomputers.

The informal meeting at Beaver Bend State Park focused attention on the potential for computer applications at Zimco. Today, Zimco is a leader in all areas of computer-based automation, both in the office and in the plant. The following sections tell a little about how the four line divisions at Zimco are currently using micros to improve productivity and to provide better and more timely information. Case studies in other chapters address Zimco's management information system, which is supported by CIS.

### MICROS IN THE SALES AND MARKETING DIVISION

When the effervescent VP of Sales and Marketing, Sally Marcio, heard about all the things that micros could do for her division, she could hardly contain her excitement. Sally was definitely primed for ideas on further automation of sales

141

and marketing activities. She remarked bluntly that "if we fall behind our competition in the area of customer service, we'll lose market share. To provide the best customer service possible, we must take advantage of what computers have to offer." After that remark, Conrad couldn't resist quoting one of his MIS maxims: "Even if you're on the right track, you'll get run over if you just sit there!"

Today, Zimco is gaining, not losing, market share. Sally attributes their success in sales to "an energetic field staff and effective use of computers." Sally described just one of the many ways that micros are used in the Sales and Marketing Division.

"The Customer Service Department, which reports to me, responds to a variety of customer inquiries, from order status to price information. They do this from their microcomputer workstations, which are linked to the corporate data base. At the end of the day, each rep requests that the names and addresses of those customers with whom they have interacted be *downloaded* from the corporate data base to disk storage on their microcomputer workstations." She went on to explain that each customer service representative has a micro, with disk storage, and they share a desktop laser printer.

Sally said that during the last hour or so of the day, the customer service workstations become stand-alone computer systems so that representatives can use word processing and mail-merge software to write "personalized" letters to the customers that they talked with during the day. This activity is illustrated graphically in Figure Z5–1.

**FIGURE Z5–1**
**Downloading Data to Micro Workstations from the Mainframe**
Micros are used as workstations and for stand-alone operation in the Sales and Marketing Division. At the end of the day, customer service representatives request that data be downloaded to their micros. The representatives then use the data to write and send personalized follow-up letters to customers who called in during the day.

Integrated corporate data base

Download customer data

Local temporary customer data base for each customer service representative

"Personalized" follow up letters to customers

The basic form letter "confirms Zimco's continuing commitment to customer service." She said that about 50 percent of the time the reps add a sentence or so that relates to the customer's particular situation. The name and address and the body of the letter are on disk. The rep has only to merge the name and address with the appropriate form letter, perhaps add a personal note, then route the letter to the printer.

Sally says that this "immediate and personal follow-up to a customer's inquiry has provided immeasurable goodwill and set us apart from our competitors."

## MICROS IN THE FINANCE AND ACCOUNTING DIVISION

The Finance and Accounting Division has been the principal user of computers since the day the first computer arrived at Zimco in 1959. Ironically, prior to the high-level meeting at Beaver Bend, the VP of the Finance and Accounting Division, Monroe Green, was complacent with their level of automation (primarily accounts receivable, accounts payable, general ledger, and payroll) and had no desire to increase his division's "dependence on computers." He was convinced that "mainframe computers are for business and micros are toys."

Well, after Conrad demonstrated the potential of a microcomputer, Monroe changed his tune. Now he is gradually replacing the VDTs in his division with micros so that his people will have the best of both worlds—direct access to the integrated corporate data base on the mainframe and the potential for stand-alone operation as well.

One micro application that Monroe finds particularly helpful is an electronic spreadsheet *template* of Zimco's income statements for the past two years. The template, which is simply a spreadsheet model, contains a column that allows him to produce a pro rata income statement for next year (see Figure Z5–2). Monroe uses the spreadsheet software to create "what if" scenarios. For example, Otto Manning is implementing

a number of cost-cutting measures and he anticipates that the Operations Division can hold the "cost of goods sold" to a 1 percent increase, even though more products will be built and shipped. Sally Marcio predicts that next year will be a "great year" and net sales will increase by 20 percent. Preston Smith has asked all managers to "hold the line" on all selling and administrative expenses; therefore, these expenses are expected to remain about the same.

With spreadsheet software, Monroe was able to answer the question: "What if the cost-of-goods-sold increased by 1 percent, sales increased by 20 percent, and everything else remained the same for the coming year?" Monroe entered only the three forecast variables to get the pro rata income statement (the "Next Year" column) printout shown in Figure Z5–2. Other calculations (e.g., sales with a 20 percent increase, net profit, earnings per share, taxes) are performed automatically because the appropriate formulas are built into the spreadsheet template. Some entries are unchanged (e.g., depreciation, dividends, and interest); however, if Monroe wanted to reflect a change in depreciation, he would simply change the value of the "depreciation" entry.

Monroe says, "we at Zimco are very interested in monitoring the *price-earnings ratio*, or the relationship that exists between the *earnings per share* and the *market price* of our stock." Calculations for the price-earnings ratio are shown at the bottom of the spreadsheet in Figure Z5–2. The earnings per share is calculated by dividing the net profit by the number of shares outstanding (e.g., for "This Year," $6,645,000/6,000,000 = $1.11). The price-earnings ratio is calculated by dividing the current market price of Zimco stock by the earnings per share (e.g., for "This Year," $14.00/$1.11 = 12.64).

In the "Next Year" column of the price-earnings ratio section of the spreadsheet, Monroe asked: "What if we issued 300,000 new shares of stock and the market price of Zimco stock reached $21.25; what would the P-E ratio be?" Monroe can easily add other financial ratios (e.g., current ratio, net profit ratio) to the spreadsheet if he so desires because he has the balance sheet data on another part of the same spreadsheet template.

As you can imagine, the president, Preston Smith, was ecstatic with the projected profit and the price-earnings ratio. However, over the years Preston has learned to temper the always-optimistic estimates made by Otto and Sally with a touch of reality, so he created his own pessimistic pro rata income statement. This income statement reflects what he called the "worst case scenario." Again, Preston needed only to change the three forecast variables to get the results of Figure Z5–3. As Preston observed, "the estimated P-E ratio is very sensitive to the estimates for sales and expenses. There's a lot of difference

### FIGURE Z5–2
**An Optimistic Pro Rata Income Statement for Zimco**
Electronic spreadsheet software and a spreadsheet template were employed to prepare an optimistic pro rata income statement for Zimco for next year. The spreadsheet user enters only the values of the three forecast variables (sales, cost of goods sold, and administrative expenses); the rest of next year's income statement is filled in automatically.

A2:  'ZIMCO INCOME STATEMENT ($1000)

|    | A | B | C | D |
|----|---|---|---|---|
|    |   |   |   |   |
| 1  | ==================================================== | | | |
| 2  | ZIMCO INCOME STATEMENT ($1000) | Next Year | This Year | Last Year |
| 3  | ---------------------------------------------------- | | | |
| 4  | Net sales | $183,600 | $153,000 | $144,780 |
| 5  | Cost of sales & op. expenses | | | |
| 6  | Cost of goods sold | 116,413 | 115,260 | 117,345 |
| 7  | Depreciation | 4,125 | 4,125 | 1,500 |
| 8  | Selling & admin. expenses | 19,875 | 19,875 | 15,000 |
| 9  | | | | |
| 10 | Operating profit | $43,187 | $13,740 | $10,935 |
| 11 | Other income | | | |
| 12 | Dividends and interest | 405 | 405 | 300 |
| 13 | | | | |
| 14 | TOTAL INCOME | $43,592 | $14,145 | $11,235 |
| 15 | Less: interest on bonds | 2,025 | 2,025 | 2,025 |
| 16 | | | | |
| 17 | Income before tax | 41,567 | 12,120 | 9,210 |
| 18 | Provision for income tax | 18,777 | 5,475 | 4,160 |
| 19 | | | | |
| 20 | NET PROFIT FOR YEAR | $22,790 | $6,645 | $5,050 |

A34:  'FORECAST VARIABLES FOR NEXT YEAR'S PRO RATA INCOME STATEMENT

|    | A | B | C | D |
|----|---|---|---|---|
| 21 | ==================================================== | | | |
| 22 | | | | |
| 23 | | | | |
| 24 | | | | |
| 25 | Shares outstanding | 6,300,000 | 6,000,000 | 6,000,000 |
| 26 | Market price | $21.25 | $14.00 | $13.00 |
| 27 | Earnings per share | $3.62 | $1.11 | $0.84 |
| 28 | | | | |
| 29 | Price-earnings ratio | 5.87 | 12.64 | 15.45 |
| 30 | ==================================================== | | | |
| 31 | | | | |
| 32 | | | | |
| 33 | ==================================================== | | | |
| 34 | FORECAST VARIABLES FOR NEXT YEAR'S PRO RATA INCOME STATEMENT | | | |
| 35 | ---------------------------------------------------- | | | |
| 36 | Projected change in sales | | 20.00% | |
| 37 | Projected change in cost of goods sold | | 1.00% | |
| 38 | Projected change in administrative expenses | | 0.00% | |
| 39 | ==================================================== | | | |
| 40 | | | | |

between a P-E of 5.87 and a P-E of 17.94! "

Of course, the possibilities of what Monroe and Preston can do with electronic spreadsheet software and micros are endless. The special skills section in this book on "Microcomputer Productivity Software" includes details on the function, concepts, and uses of electronic spreadsheet software. This section also includes details

on how the income statement spreadsheet template of Figure Z5–2 is developed.

## MICROS IN THE PERSONNEL DIVISION

The Personnel Division receives announcements of position openings each day from several departments. They respond by preparing releases

**FIGURE Z5–3**
**A Pessimistic Pro Rata Income Statement for Zimco**
The same electronic spreadsheet template used to produce the printout of Figure Z5–2 was used to produce a pessimistic pro rata income statement. Again, the only entries needed to produce the pro rata income statement for the coming year are the three forecast variables.

A2: 'ZIMCO INCOME STATEMENT ($1000)

|   | A | B | C | D |
|---|---|---|---|---|
| 1 | ============================================= | | | |
| 2 | ZIMCO INCOME STATEMENT ($1000) | Next Year | This year | Last Year |
| 3 | --------------------------------------------- | | | |
| 4 | Net sales | $157,590 | $153,000 | $144,780 |
| 5 | Cost of sales & op. expenses | | | |
| 6 |    Cost of goods sold | 117,565 | 115,260 | 117,345 |
| 7 |    Depreciation | 4,125 | 4,125 | 1,500 |
| 8 |    Selling & admin. expenses | 20,670 | 19,875 | 15,000 |
| 9 | | --------- | --------- | --------- |
| 10 |    Operating profit | $15,230 | $13,740 | $10,935 |
| 11 | Other income | | | |
| 12 |    Dividends and interest | 405 | 405 | 300 |
| 13 | | --------- | --------- | --------- |
| 14 |    TOTAL INCOME | $15,635 | $14,145 | $11,235 |
| 15 | Less: interest on bonds | 2,025 | 2,025 | 2,025 |
| 16 | | --------- | --------- | --------- |
| 17 | Income before tax | 13,610 | 12,120 | 9,210 |
| 18 | Provisions for income tax | 6,148 | 5,475 | 4,160 |
| 19 | | --------- | --------- | --------- |
| 20 |    NET PROFIT FOR YEAR | $7,462 | $6,645 | $5,050 |

A34: 'FORECAST VARIABLES FOR NEXT YEAR'S PRO RATA INCOME STATEMENT

|   | A | B | C | D |
|---|---|---|---|---|
| 21 | ============================================= | | | |
| 22 | | | | |
| 23 | | | | |
| 24 | ============================================= | | | |
| 25 | Shares outstanding | 6,300,000 | 6,000,000 | 6,000,000 |
| 26 | Market price | $21.25 | $14.00 | $13.00 |
| 27 | Earnings per share | $1.18 | $1.11 | $0.84 |
| 28 | | --------- | --------- | --------- |
| 29 |    Price-earnings ratio | 17.94 | 12.64 | 15.45 |
| 30 | ============================================= | | | |
| 31 | | | | |
| 32 | | | | |
| 33 | ============================================= | | | |
| 34 | FORECAST VARIABLES FOR NEXT YEAR'S PRO RATA INCOME STATEMENT | | | |
| 35 | --------------------------------------------- | | | |
| 36 | Projected change in sales | | 3.00% | |
| 37 | Projected change in cost of goods sold | | 2.00% | |
| 38 | Projected change in administrative expenses | | 4.00% | |
| 39 | ============================================= | | | |
| 40 | | | | |

to local newspapers. These releases are usually, but not always, placed in the "classified ads" section.

Peggy Peoples, VP of Personnel, explained the problems associated with placing ads in the newspaper and a computer-based solution. "We are obligated by company policy," she said, "to make these positions available to existing employees before we solicit outside applicants." In the past, circulating position announcements internally took several days, and only one of eight position openings is filled from within. Managers complained that delaying a public release of the available positions meant that they had to operate shorthanded longer than necessary."

Conrad Innis suggested a solution: "Don't use hard copy to announce position openings. Use our **electronic bulletin board**." That's just what Peggy did. Now, minutes after a position opening is received from a department, it is posted on the Zimco Bulletin Board System (ZBBS). The ZBBS is affectionately known to Zimco employees as "Z-Buzz."

To post an item to Z-Buzz or scan its contents, employees simply log-on to the nearest workstation. Z-Buzz includes typical bulletin board items such as softball scores, "for sale" items, messages of all kinds, and of course, position announcements. Workstations, most of which are micros, are everywhere at Zimco, even in the halls, the cafeterias, and the executive washroom. Those employees that would like to transfer to another job or another office routinely scan the position announcements on Z-Buzz.

The position announcements appear immediately in the company's electronic bulletin board and they appear the same or the next day in local newspapers. The Personnel Division runs want ads in five to 12 newspapers every day of the year. For 30 years, they mailed or called in the ads to newspapers. Conrad Innis suggested that they will "save a lot of time and money by using their micros to transmit the ads electronically." Now people in the Personnel Division compose the text of the ads and insert standard electronic publishing symbols that designate size

A manager in the personnel division at Zimco uses his micro and electronic spreadsheet software to ask "what if" questions regarding a proposal for a new benefits package.
(Sperry Corporation)

```
/AT Zimco Enterprises

/CE !BREnd!NDuser Liason in Accounting!RM

/T        !BRZimco!RM is seeking a !IThighly motivated!RM individual
with at least a bachelor's degree in accounting and at least one year
of experience working directly with programmers and systems analysts.
The successful candidate will have the interpersonal skills needed to
encourage greater automation of accounting. Write Zimco or call Zimco
for an interview.
```

**END-USER LIASON IN ACCOUNTING**

ZIMCO is seeking a *highly motivated*
individual with at least a bachelor's
degree in accounting and at least one
year of experience working directly
with programmers and systems analysts.
The successful candidate will have the
interpersonal skills needed to encourage
greater automation of accounting.
Write Zimco or call Zimco for an
interview.

**FIGURE Z5–4**
**The Text of a Position Announcement**
The text of a position announcement is shown prior to its electronic distribution
to area newspapers and as it appears in the classified ads section.

of print, centering of text, and so on. They then use their data communications software to automatically "dial up" the computers at the newspapers and transmit the ads electronically. Compositors at the various newspapers simply insert the ads in the appropriate section. No other keystrokes are required. Figure Z5–4 illustrates what is sent and how it appears in the "Want Ads." Because Zimco enters and formats their own ads, they pay substantially less than do other advertisers.

## MICROS IN THE OPERATIONS DIVISION

Otto Manning, VP of Operations, said that "one of his division's biggest problems is planning and tracking projects." On numerous occasions in the past, he has requested help from CIS in implementing a mainframe-based project management system. The last system he proposed would cost $22,000 and require two person-months of programmer time to implement. His proposal, however, was a low-priority activity in the CIS backlog of user service requests.

Conrad Innis suggested to Otto that he consider a microcomputer-based project management system that cost $495. The system could be installed and used by the project managers in the Operations Division—without any assistance from CIS!

Otto took Conrad's advice. He even purchased a **site license** for $1600. The site license permits the duplication, distribution, and use of the software package within Zimco Enterprises. In contrast, the license agreement for the $495

QWERT–PLUS DEVELOPMENT PROJECT

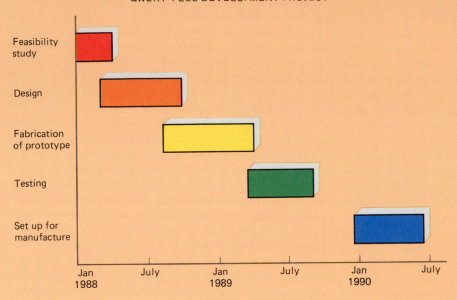

**FIGURE Z5–5**
**Bar Chart for the Qwert-Plus Development Project**
This bar chart is an output from a microcomputer-based project management
system that is used by the Research and Development Department to monitor
and track projects.

version prohibited duplication; therefore, it could be used only by one manager at a time. The hardware needed to run the project management system, that is, the micros and associated peripheral devices, was already available. Today, all projects within the Operations Division are scheduled and monitored using the micro-based project management system.

The Research and Development Department is currently developing a second-generation Qwert, tentatively named the Qwert-Plus. Figure Z5–5 illustrates a bar chart that was produced for the Qwert-Plus development project. The project management system produces bar charts and a variety of reports: "Ahead/Behind Report," "Project Personpower Utilization Report," and the "Project Costs Report," to mention a few.

Otto Manning later remarked: "And to think that we implemented a computer-based project management system with $1600, our existing micros, and without assistance from CIS." This is the trend, not only at Zimco, but elsewhere. Users are finding that they can attend to many of their

computing needs by simply taking full advantage of their existing micros and a plethora of user-friendly micro-based software packages.

## DISCUSSION QUESTIONS

1. Why do you think Conrad Innis, the VP of CIS, felt it necessary to invite Zimco's top management to an out-of-the-way retreat to talk about "Computer Applications at Zimco"?

2. Zimco is in the top 10 percent of all manufacturing companies in the number of micros per white-collar worker. Does this reflect frivolous spending or a conscious effort to make effective use of available technology. Explain.

3. Customer service representatives spend almost 70 percent of their day interacting directly with customers. Approximately one hour each day is spent preparing courtesy follow-up letters, primarily to enhance good-

will between Zimco and its customers. Do you think the "personalized" letters are a worthwhile effort? Why or why not?

4. The case study describes how the Sales and Marketing Division takes advantage of the dual-purpose capabilities of micros in the Customer Service Department. Discuss how other departments in the same division can do the same.

5. A company policy requires that a warning label be affixed to the front of every microcomputer at Zimco. The label reads: "This computer is not to be used for the unlawful duplication of copyright software." What do you suppose prompted Zimco's top management to implement such a policy?

6. Describe an electronic spreadsheet template that would be helpful to all four regional sales managers.

7. Compare Monroe Green's and Preston Smith's electronic spreadsheet analysis of Zimco's pro rata income statement for the coming year (Figures Z5–2 and Z5–3). If they were to compare notes, what do you think would be their next step in the analysis? Explain.

8. Besides announcing internal position openings, identify other management uses of Z-Buzz, Zimco's electronic bulletin board system, that involve the enterprise-wide distribution of information.

From the very start, our Company's commitment has been to the finest skin care teaching organization in the world. We have achieved this status by providing strong personal financial incentives and growth opportunities for our beauty consultants. We currently track the activities of more than 100,000 consultants selling 350 skin care and cosmetic products in 50 states and five foreign countries.

Our computers allow us to track the activities of each of these consultants and their eligibility for commissions, promotional awards and our famous Pink Cadillacs and Buicks. Behind the scenes, our computers process data relating to finances, inventories, production schedules, material requirements planning, production process control, product formuli, skin color analysis, robot controlled distribution centers, etc. We even have a voice response system called "BETTY" which synthesizes human speech, allowing our sales directors to converse directly with computers for up-to-date information about sales levels and opportunities.

Our future plans call for much more sophisticated computer support so that we can achieve even more personal, effective programs for our consultants and employees. As John Naisbitt says in Megatrends, we are becoming "HIGH TECH, HIGH TOUCH."

Mary Kay Ash
Chairman of the Board
Mary Kay Cosmetics, Inc.

# Inside the Computer

## CHAPTER 6

### STUDENT LEARNING OBJECTIVES

- ■ To describe how data are stored in a computer system.
- ■ To demonstrate the relationships between bits, bytes, characters, and encoding systems.
- ■ To translate alphanumeric data to a format for internal computer representation.
- ■ To explain and illustrate the principles of computer operations.
- ■ To identify and describe the relationships between the internal components of a computer.
- ■ To distinguish processors by their speed, memory capacity, and word length.

### STUDENT LEARNING OBJECTIVES
### (Appendix: Working with Numbering Systems)

- ■ To know why and when to use a particular numbering system.
- ■ To perform rudimentary arithmetic operations in the binary, octal, and hexadecimal numbering systems.

### FOCUS OF ZIMCO CASE STUDY

- ■ Microcomputer acquisition policy and procedures at Zimco.

## 6–1 DATA STORAGE

In Chapter 1 we learned that *data*, not *information*, are stored in a computer system. *Data are the raw material from which information is derived, and information is data that have been collected and manipulated into a meaningful form*. To manipulate data, we must have a way to store and retrieve them.

It is easy to understand data storage in a manual system. When, for example, a customer's address changes, we pull the folder, erase the old address, and write in the new one. We can see and easily interpret data that are manually kept. We cannot see or easily interpret data stored in a computer. This, of course, comes as no surprise. Data are represented and stored in a computer system to take advantage of the physical characteristics of electronics and computer hardware, not human beings.

Data are stored *temporarily* during processing in a section of the computer system called **primary storage** or **main memory**. Data are stored for *permanent* storage on **secondary storage** devices, such as magnetic tape and disk drives. We discuss primary storage in detail later in this chapter. Secondary storage is covered in Chapter 7, "Peripheral Devices—I/O and Data Storage." In this chapter we focus on the details of how data are represented internally in both primary and secondary storage, and on the internal workings of a computer.

## 6–2 A BIT ABOUT THE BIT

The computer's seemingly endless potential is, in fact, based on only two electrical states—*on* and *off*. The physical characteristics of the computer make it possible to combine these two electronic states to represent letters and numbers. An "on" or "off" electronic state is represented by a **bit**. "Bit" is short for *b*inary dig*it*. The presence or absence of a bit is referred to as *on-bit* and *off-bit*, respectively. In the **binary** numbering system (base 2) and in written text, the on-bit is a 1 and the off-bit is a 0.

Remember from Chapter 2 that the generations of computers were characterized by vacuum tubes, transistors, and integrated circuits. These electronic components enabled computers to distinguish between "on" and "off" and, therefore, to use binary logic.

Data are stored temporarily in primary storage during processing and permanently on secondary storage, such as magnetic disk.
(Protocol Computers, Inc.)

Physically, these states are achieved in a variety of ways. In primary storage the two electronic states are represented by the direction of current flow. Another approach is to turn the circuit on or off. In secondary storage the two states are made possible by the magnetic arrangement of the ferrous oxide coating on magnetic tapes and disks.

Bits may be fine for computers, but human beings are more comfortable with letters and decimal numbers (the base-10 numerals 0 through 9). Therefore, the letters and decimal numbers that we input to a computer system must be translated to 1s and 0s for processing and storage. The computer translates the bits back to letters and decimal numbers on output. This translation is performed so that we can recognize and understand the output, and it is made possible by encoding systems.

## 6–3   ENCODING SYSTEMS: COMBINING BITS TO FORM BYTES

**EBCDIC and ASCII.**   Computers do not talk to each other in English, Spanish, or French. They have their own languages, which are better suited to electronic communication. In these languages, bits are combined according to an **encoding system** to represent letters (**alpha** characters), numbers (**numeric** characters), and special characters (such as *, $, +, and &). For example, in the eight-bit **EBCDIC** encoding system (*E*xtended *B*inary-*C*oded *D*ecimal *I*nterchange *C*ode—pronounced *EBB-see-dik*), which is used primarily in mainframe computers, 11000010 represents the letter B, and 11110011 represents a decimal number 3. In the seven-bit **ASCII** encoding system (*A*merican *S*tandard *C*ode for *I*nformation *I*nterchange—pronounced *AS-key*), which is used primarily in micros and data communications, a B and a 3 are represented by 1000010 and 0110011, respectively. There is also an eight-bit version of ASCII, called **ASCII-8,** that is used on some mainframe computers.

Letters, numbers, and special characters are collectively referred to as **alphanumeric** characters. Alphanumeric characters are *encoded* to a bit configuration on input so that the computer can interpret them. The characters are *decoded* on output so that we can interpret them. This coding, which is based on a particular encoding system, equates a unique series of bits and no-bits with a specific character. Just as the words "mother" and "father" are arbitrary English-language character strings that refer to our parents, 11000010 is an arbitrary EBCDIC code that refers to the letter B. The combination of bits used to represent a character is called a **byte** (pronounced bite). Figure 6–1 shows the binary value (the actual bit configuration) and the decimal equivalent of commonly used characters in both EBCDIC and ASCII.

The seven-bit ASCII can represent up to 128 characters ($2^7$). EBCDIC and ASCII-8 can represent up to 256 characters ($2^8$). Even though the English language has considerably fewer than 128 alphanumeric characters, the extra bit configurations are needed to communicate a variety

An eight-bit encoding system, with its 256 unique bit configurations, is more than adequate to represent all of the alphanumeric characters used in the English language. The Japanese, however, need a 16-bit encoding system and a special keyboard to represent their 50,000 Kanji characters.
(Courtesy of International Business Machines Corporation)

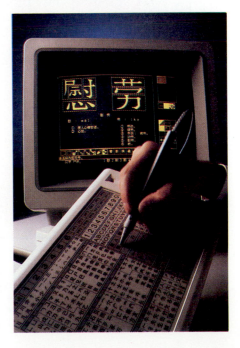

**FIGURE 6–1**
**EBCDIC and ASCII Codes**
This figure contains the binary and decimal values for the EBCDIC and ASCII codes for commonly used alphanumeric and special characters.

| Character | EBCDIC Code Binary Value | Decimal Value | ASCII Code Binary Value | Decimal Value |
|---|---|---|---|---|
| A | 1100 0001 | 193 | 100 0001 | 65 |
| B | 1100 0010 | 194 | 100 0010 | 66 |
| C | 1100 0011 | 195 | 100 0011 | 67 |
| D | 1100 0100 | 196 | 100 0100 | 68 |
| E | 1100 0101 | 197 | 100 0101 | 69 |
| F | 1100 0110 | 198 | 100 0110 | 70 |
| G | 1100 0111 | 199 | 100 0111 | 71 |
| H | 1100 1000 | 200 | 100 1000 | 72 |
| I | 1100 1001 | 201 | 100 1001 | 73 |
| J | 1101 0001 | 209 | 100 1010 | 74 |
| K | 1101 0010 | 210 | 100 1011 | 75 |
| L | 1101 0011 | 211 | 100 1100 | 76 |
| M | 1101 0100 | 212 | 100 1101 | 77 |
| N | 1101 0101 | 213 | 100 1110 | 78 |
| O | 1101 0110 | 214 | 100 1111 | 79 |
| P | 1101 0111 | 215 | 101 0000 | 80 |
| Q | 1101 1000 | 216 | 101 0001 | 81 |
| R | 1101 1001 | 217 | 101 0010 | 82 |
| S | 1110 0010 | 226 | 101 0011 | 83 |
| T | 1110 0011 | 227 | 101 0100 | 84 |
| U | 1110 0100 | 228 | 101 0101 | 85 |
| V | 1110 0101 | 229 | 101 0110 | 86 |
| W | 1110 0110 | 230 | 101 0111 | 87 |
| X | 1110 0111 | 231 | 101 1000 | 88 |
| Y | 1110 1000 | 232 | 101 1001 | 89 |
| Z | 1110 1001 | 233 | 101 1010 | 90 |
| a | 1000 0001 | 129 | 110 0001 | 97 |
| b | 1000 0010 | 130 | 110 0010 | 98 |
| c | 1000 0011 | 131 | 110 0011 | 99 |
| d | 1000 0100 | 132 | 110 0100 | 100 |
| e | 1000 0101 | 133 | 110 0101 | 101 |
| f | 1000 0110 | 134 | 110 0110 | 102 |
| g | 1000 0111 | 135 | 110 0111 | 103 |
| h | 1000 1000 | 136 | 110 1000 | 104 |
| i | 1000 1001 | 137 | 110 1001 | 105 |
| j | 1001 0001 | 145 | 110 1010 | 106 |
| k | 1001 0010 | 146 | 110 1011 | 107 |
| l | 1001 0011 | 147 | 110 1100 | 108 |
| m | 1001 0100 | 148 | 110 1101 | 109 |
| n | 1001 0101 | 149 | 110 1110 | 110 |
| o | 1001 0110 | 150 | 110 1111 | 111 |
| p | 1001 0111 | 151 | 111 0000 | 112 |
| q | 1001 1000 | 152 | 111 0001 | 113 |
| r | 1001 1001 | 153 | 111 0010 | 114 |
| s | 1010 0010 | 162 | 111 0011 | 115 |
| t | 1010 0011 | 163 | 111 0100 | 116 |
| u | 1010 0100 | 164 | 111 0101 | 117 |
| v | 1010 0101 | 165 | 111 0110 | 118 |
| w | 1010 0110 | 166 | 111 0111 | 119 |
| x | 1010 0111 | 167 | 111 1000 | 120 |
| y | 1010 1000 | 168 | 111 1001 | 121 |
| z | 1010 1001 | 169 | 111 1010 | 122 |

| Character | EBCDIC Code Binary value | Decimal value | ASCII Code Binary value | Decimal value |
|---|---|---|---|---|
| 0 | 1111 0000 | 240 | 011 0000 | 48 |
| 1 | 1111 0001 | 241 | 011 0001 | 49 |
| 2 | 1111 0010 | 242 | 011 0010 | 50 |
| 3 | 1111 0011 | 243 | 011 0011 | 51 |
| 4 | 1111 0100 | 244 | 011 0100 | 52 |
| 5 | 1111 0101 | 245 | 011 0101 | 53 |
| 6 | 1111 0110 | 246 | 011 0110 | 54 |
| 7 | 1111 0111 | 247 | 011 0111 | 55 |
| 8 | 1111 1000 | 248 | 011 1000 | 56 |
| 9 | 1111 1001 | 249 | 011 1001 | 57 |
| Space | 0100 0000 | 64 | 010 0000 | 32 |
| . | 0100 1011 | 75 | 010 1110 | 46 |
| < | 0100 1100 | 76 | 011 1100 | 60 |
| ( | 0100 1101 | 77 | 010 1000 | 40 |
| + | 0100 1110 | 78 | 010 1011 | 43 |
| & | 0101 0000 | 80 | 010 0110 | 38 |
| ! | 0101 1010 | 90 | 010 0001 | 33 |
| $ | 0101 1011 | 91 | 010 0100 | 36 |
| * | 0101 1100 | 92 | 010 1010 | 42 |
| ) | 0101 1101 | 93 | 010 1001 | 41 |
| ; | 0101 1110 | 94 | 011 1011 | 59 |
| , | 0110 1011 | 107 | 010 1100 | 44 |
| % | 0110 1100 | 108 | 010 0101 | 37 |
| — | 0110 1101 | 109 | 101 1111 | 95 |
| > | 0110 1110 | 110 | 011 1110 | 62 |
| ? | 0110 1111 | 111 | 011 1111 | 63 |
| : | 0111 1010 | 122 | 011 1010 | 58 |
| # | 0111 1011 | 123 | 010 0011 | 35 |
| @ | 0111 1100 | 124 | 100 0000 | 64 |
| ' | 0111 1101 | 125 | 010 0111 | 39 |
| = | 0111 1110 | 126 | 011 1101 | 61 |
| '' | 0111 1111 | 127 | 010 0010 | 34 |

of activities, from ringing a bell to signaling the computer to accept a piece of datum.

**The Nibble.** The eight-bit structure of EBCDIC and ASCII-8 gives these encoding systems an interesting and useful quality. Only four bit positions are needed to represent the 10 decimal digits. Therefore, a single

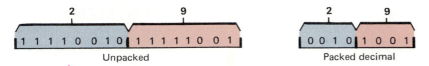

**FIGURE 6–2**
**Decimal 29 in EBCDIC**
Since all numeric codes in EBCDIC have 1111 in the first four positions, the 1s can be eliminated and two numeric digits can be "packed" into one byte. ASCII-8 numbers are packed in a similar manner.

numeric digit can be stored in a half-byte, or a *nibble*, as it is sometimes called. This enables us to store data more efficiently by "packing" *two* decimal digits into one eight-bit byte (see Figure 6–2).

Since two decimal digits can be packed into one byte, a byte is not always the same as a character. Even so, the terms "byte" and "character" are often used interchangeably, with an implied understanding that some bytes may contain two numeric characters.

Parity Checking.    Within a computer system, data in the form of coded characters are continuously transferred at high rates of speed between the computer, the input/output (I/O) and storage devices, and the remote workstations. Each device uses a built-in checking procedure to help ensure that the transmission is complete and accurate. This procedure is called **parity checking.**

Logically, an ASCII character may have seven bits, but physically there are actually *eight* bits transmitted between hardware devices. Confused? Don't be. The extra **parity bit,** which is not part of the character code, is used in the parity-checking procedure to detect whether a bit has been accidentally changed, or "dropped," during transmission. A dropped bit results in a **parity error.**

To maintain *odd parity* (see Figure 6–3), the extra parity bit is turned *on* when the seven-bit ASCII byte has an *even* number of on-bits. When the ASCII byte has an *odd* number of on-bits, the parity bit is turned *off*. The receiving device checks for this condition. A parity error occurs when an even number of on-bits is encountered. Some computer systems are designed to maintain *even parity*, but odd and even parity work in a similar manner.

**FIGURE 6–3**
**Parity Checking**
The letter B is entered and transmitted to the computer for processing. Since the ASCII "B" has an even number of bits, an on-bit must be added to maintain odd parity.

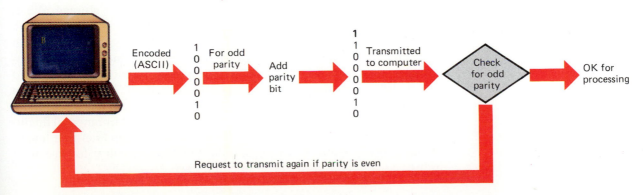

## 6–4   COMPONENTS OF A COMPUTER SYSTEM: A CLOSER LOOK AT THE PROCESSOR AND PRIMARY STORAGE

Let's review. We have learned that all computers have similar capabilities and perform essentially the same functions, although some might be faster than others. We have also learned that a computer system has input, output, storage, and processing components, that the *processor* is the "intelligence" of a computer system, and that a single computer system may have several processors. We have discussed how data are represented inside a computer system in electronic states called bits. We are now ready to expose the inner workings of the nucleus of the computer system—the processor.

The internal operation of a computer, or processor, is interesting, but there really is no mystery about it. The mystery is in the minds of those who listen to hearsay and believe science fiction writers. The computer is a nonthinking electronic device that has to be plugged into an electrical power source, just like a toaster or a lamp.

Literally hundreds of different types of computers are marketed by scores of manufacturers. The complexity of each type may vary considerably, but in the end, each processor, sometimes called the **central processing unit (CPU)**, has only two fundamental sections: the *control unit* and the *arithmetic and logic unit*. *Primary storage* also plays an integral part in the internal operation of a processor. These three—primary storage, the control unit, and the arithmetic and logic unit—work together. Let's look at their functions and the relationships between them.

### Primary Storage

The Technology.   Unlike magnetic secondary storage devices, such as tape and disk, primary storage has no moving parts. With no mechanical movement, data can be accessed from primary storage at electronic speeds, or close to the speed of light. Most of today's computers use CMOS (*C*omplementary *M*etal-*O*xide *S*emiconductor) technology for primary storage. A CMOS memory chip that is about one-eighth the size of a postage stamp can store about 1,000,000 bits, or over 100,000 characters of data!

But there is one major problem with semiconductor storage. When the electrical current is turned off or interrupted, the data are lost. Researchers are working to perfect a primary storage that will retain its contents after an electrical interruption. Several "nonvolatile" technologies, such as *bubble memory*, have emerged, but none has exhibited the qualities necessary for widespread application. However, bubble memory is superior to CMOS for use in certain computers. Bubble memory is highly reliable and is not susceptible to environmental fluctuations, and it can operate on battery power for a considerable length of time. These qualities make bubble memory a natural for use with industrial robots and in portable computers.

Modern technology has taken away some of the romance associated with the computer mystique. Today's computers don't have hundreds of multicolored blinking lights and swirling tapes. The processing component of this mainframe computer system is the box in the middle. It has only one switch—on/off.

(Courtesy of International Business Machines Corporation)

**Function.**   Primary storage, or main memory, provides the processor with *temporary* storage for programs and data. *All programs and data must be transferred to primary storage from an input device (such as a VDT) or from secondary storage (such as a disk) before programs can be executed or data can be processed.* Primary storage space is always at a premium; therefore, after a program has been executed, the storage space occupied by it is reallocated to another program that is awaiting execution.

Figure 6–4 illustrates how all input/output (I/O) is "read to" or "written from" primary storage. In the figure, an inquiry (input) is made on a VDT. The inquiry, in the form of a message, is routed to primary storage over a **channel** (such as a coaxial cable). The message is interpreted, and the processor initiates action to retrieve the appropriate program and data from secondary storage. The program and data are "loaded" or moved to primary storage from secondary storage. This is a *nondestructive* read process. That is, the program and data that

**FIGURE 6–4**
**Interaction between Primary Storage and Computer System Components**
All programs and data must be transferred from an input device or from secondary storage before programs can be executed and data can be processed. Output is transferred to the printer from primary storage.

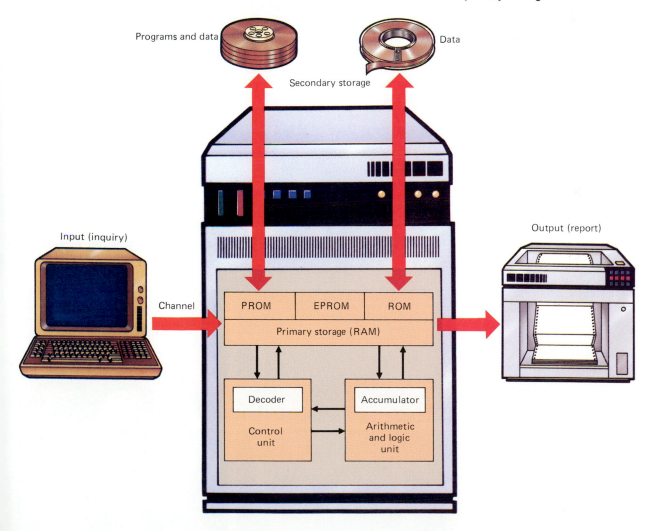

Programs and data

Data

Secondary storage

Input (inquiry)

Output (report)

Channel

PROM   EPROM   ROM

Primary storage (RAM)

Decoder

Accumulator

Control unit

Arithmetic and logic unit

are read reside in both primary storage (temporarily) and secondary storage (permanently). The data are manipulated according to program instructions, and a report is written from primary storage to a printer.

A program instruction or a piece of data is stored in a specific primary storage location called an **address.** Addresses permit program instructions and data to be found, accessed, and processed. The content of each address is constantly changing as different programs are executed and new data are processed.

RAM, ROM, PROM, and EPROM.   Another name for primary storage is **random-access memory (RAM).** A special type of primary storage, called **read-only memory (ROM),** cannot be altered by the programmer. The contents of ROM are "hard-wired" (designed into the logic of the memory chip) by the manufacturer and can be "read only." When you turn on a microcomputer system, a program in ROM automatically readies the computer system for use. Then the ROM program produces the initial display screen prompt.

A variation of ROM is **programmable read-only memory (PROM).** PROM is ROM into which you, the user, can load "read-only" programs and data. Some microcomputer software packages, such as electronic spreadsheets, are available as PROM units as well as on diskette. Once a program is loaded to PROM, it is seldom, if ever, changed. However, if you need to be able to revise the contents of PROM, there is EPROM, erasable PROM.

## The Control Unit

Just as the processor is the nucleus of a computer system, the **control unit** is the nucleus of the processor. The control unit has three primary functions:

1. To read and interpret program instructions
2. To direct the operation of internal processor components
3. To control the flow of programs and data in and out of primary storage

The four phases of chip manufacture are design, fabrication, testing, and packaging. Chips are designed (top left) to accomplish a particular function (e.g., a processor or primary storage). During fabrication (top right), the circuitry of several hundred chips is etched into these silicon wafers. The chips are tested (bottom left) while they are still part of the wafer. The chips are separated from the wafer and packaged (bottom right) in protective carriers that can be plugged into circuit boards. (Starting top left and running clockwise, photos courtesy of TRW, Inc.; Gould, Inc.; National Semiconductor Corporation; Intel Corporation.)

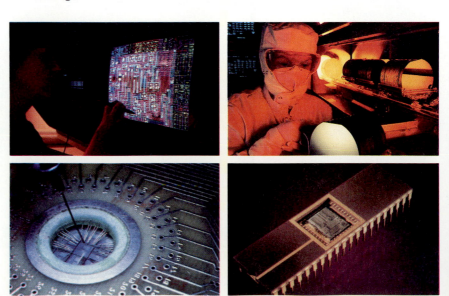

A program must first be loaded to primary storage before it can be executed. During execution, the first in a sequence of program instructions is moved from primary storage to the control unit, where it is **decoded** and interpreted. The control unit then directs other processor components to carry out the operations necessary to execute the instruction.

The control unit contains high-speed working storage areas called **registers** that can store no more than a few bytes. They are used for a variety of processing functions. For example, registers store status information, such as the *address* of the next instruction to be executed. Registers facilitate the movement of data and instructions between primary storage, the control unit, and the arithmetic-logic unit.

## Arithmetic and Logic Unit

The **arithmetic and logic unit** performs all computations (addition, subtraction, multiplication, and division) and all logic operations (comparisons).

Examples of *computations* include the payroll deduction for social security, the day-end inventory, the balance on a bank statement, and the like. A *logic* operation compares two pieces of data; then, based on the result of the comparison, the program "branches" to one of several alternative sets of program instructions. Let's use an inventory system to illustrate the logic operation. At the end of each day the inventory level of each item in stock is compared to a reorder point. For each comparison indicating an inventory level that falls below ($<$) the reorder point, a sequence of program instructions is executed that produces a purchase order. For each comparison indicating an inventory level at or above ($=$ or $>$) the reorder point, another sequence of instructions is executed.

The arithmetic and logic unit also does alphabetic comparisons. For example, when comparing Smyth and Smith, Smyth is evaluated as being alphabetically greater, so it is positioned after Smith.

## 6–5   COMPUTER OPERATION: FITTING THE PIECES TOGETHER

Some automobiles have the engine in the front, some have it in the rear, and a few have it in the middle. It's the same with computers. Computer architecture—the way in which they are designed—varies considerably. For example, one vendor's computers might have separate primary storage areas for data and programs. In some microcomputers the *motherboard*, a single circuit board, holds the electronic circuitry for the processor, memory, and the input/output interface with the peripheral devices. A knowledge of these idiosyncrasies is not required of the user; therefore, the following example focuses on the *essentials* of computer operation.

The BASIC program in Figure 6–5 computes and displays the sum of any two numbers. BASIC is a popular programming language. Figure

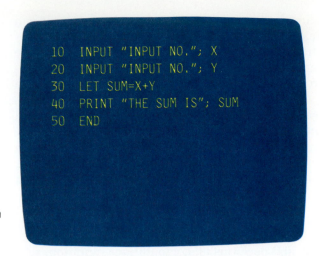

```
10   INPUT "INPUT NO."; X
20   INPUT "INPUT NO."; Y
30   LET SUM=X+Y
40   PRINT "THE SUM IS"; SUM
50   END
```

**FIGURE 6–5**
**A BASIC Program**
This program, written in the BASIC programming language, adds any two numbers and displays the sum. The execution of this program is illustrated in Figure 6–6.

6–6 illustrates how a processor works by showing the interaction among primary storage, the control unit, and the arithmetic and logic unit during the execution of the BASIC program in Figure 6–5. Primary storage in Figure 6–6 has only 10 primary storage locations, and these are used only for data. In practice, both program and data would be stored in primary storage, which usually has a minimum of 64,000 storage locations.

During execution of the BASIC program, one of the numbers (5, in the example) is loaded to a register called an **accumulator.** The other number in primary storage (2, in the example) is added to the 5 in the accumulator, and the value in the accumulator becomes 7. The following statement-by-statement discussion of the BASIC program of Figure 6–5 illustrates exactly what happens as each instruction is executed.

■ *Statement 10* (INPUT "INPUT NO."; X) permits the terminal operator to enter any numeric value. The control unit arbitrarily assigns the value to primary storage location *six*. In Figure 6–6, the value entered is 5. Future program references to X recall the content of the storage location whose address is *six*.

■ *Statement 20* (INPUT "INPUT NO."; Y) permits the terminal operator to enter any numeric value. The control unit arbitrarily assigns the value to primary storage location *seven*. In the figure, the value entered is 2.

■ *Statement 30* (LET SUM = X + Y) adds the content of location *six* to that of location *seven*. The sum is then stored in location *eight*. This addition is accomplished in three steps.
*Step 1.* The 5 in location *six* is copied to the *accumulator*. The 5 remains in location *six* and the value of the *accumulator* becomes 5.
*Step 2.* The content of location *seven* (value = 2) is added to the content of the *accumulator* (value = 5). The addition changes the content of the *accumulator* to 7.

**Statement 10**

INPUT "INPUT NO."; X

Accept a number and
store it in primary
storage location six.

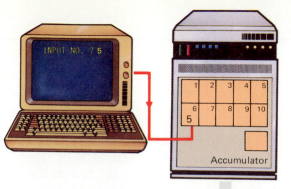

**FIGURE 6–6**
**Internal Computer**
**Operation**
This figure, which is explained
in the text, illustrates what
happens inside the computer
when the BASIC program of
Figure 6–5 is executed.
Primary storage is shown with
10 numbered storage
locations.

**Statement 20**

INPUT "INPUT NO."; Y

Accept a number and
store it in primary
storage location seven.

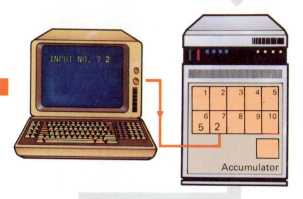

**Statement 30**

LET SUM = X + Y

STEP 1
Move a number to
the accumulator.

STEP 2
Add the other number
to the value in the accumulator.

STEP 3
Move the sum to primary
storage location eight.

**Statement 40**

PRINT "THE SUM IS"; SUM

Display sum.

**Statement 50**

END

Terminate execution.

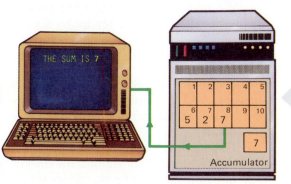

*Step 3.* The 7 cannot be outputted directly from the *accumulator*; therefore, the content of the *accumulator* (value = 7) is copied arbitrarily to location *eight*. The value of the *accumulator* is unchanged.

■ *Statement 40* (PRINT "THE SUM IS "; SUM) displays, on the workstation screen, "THE SUM IS " and the result of the addition (content of location *eight*), or 7 in the figure.

■ *Statement 50* (END) signals the end of the program.

More complex arithmetic and I/O tasks involve further repetitions of these fundamental operations. Logic operations are similar, with values being compared between primary storage locations, the accumulator, and registers.

## 6–6  DESCRIBING THE PROCESSOR: DISTINGUISHING CHARACTERISTICS

People are people, and computers are computers, but how do we distinguish one from the other? We describe people in terms of height, build, age, and so on. We describe computers or processors in terms of *speed*, the *capacity* of their associated primary storage, and the *word length*. For example, a computer might be described as a 1-MIP, 1M, 32-bit micro. Let's see what this means.

Processor Speed.  Processor speed is often measured in **MIPS,** millions of instructions per second. The processing speed of today's mainframe computers is in the range 20 to 1000 MIPS. We even have 1-MIP micros.

Processor speed is also measured in timed intervals called **machine cycles.** Normally, several machine cycles are required to *retrieve*, *interpret*, and *execute* a single program instruction. The shorter the machine cycle, the faster the processor. Machine cycles are measured in milliseconds, microseconds, and nanoseconds—or thousandths, millionths, and billionths of a second. As technology advances, machine cycles will eventually be measured in picoseconds—or trillionths of a second.

We seldom think in time units smaller than a second; consequently, it is almost impossible for us to think in terms of computer speeds. Imagine: Today's minicomputers can execute more instructions in a minute than you have had heartbeats since the day you were born!

Capacity of Primary Storage.  The capacity of primary storage is stated in terms of the number of bytes that can be stored. As we learned earlier in this chapter, a byte is roughly equivalent to a character (such as A, 1, &).

The memory capacity of microcomputers is usually stated in terms of **K,** a convenient designation for 1024 ($2^{10}$) bytes of storage. The memory capacity of mainframe computers is stated in terms of millions of bytes (**megabytes** or **M).** Memory capacities range from 64K bytes in small micros to 8 billion bytes in supercomputers.

This supercomputer being installed at a computer services company has a word size of 64 bits and offers up to 1,024 megabytes of primary storage. (Boeing Computer Services)

**Word Length.** A **word** is the number of bits that are handled as a unit for a particular computer system. The word size of modern microcomputers is normally 16 bits or 32 bits. Supercomputers have 64-bit words. Other common word lengths are 8 and 36 bits.

Now, if anyone ever asks you what a 1-MIP, 1M, 32-bit micro is, you've got the answer!

# APPENDIX: WORKING WITH NUMBERING SYSTEMS

This special appendix to Chapter 6 discusses the relationships between computers and the binary, octal, decimal, and hexadecimal numbering systems. It also presents the principles of numbering systems, discusses numbering-system arithmetic, and illustrates how to convert a value in one numbering system to its equivalent in another.

## Numbering Systems and Computers: Why Four Numbering Systems?

We human beings use a **decimal,** or base-10, numbering system, presumably because people have 10 fingers. If we had three fingers and a thumb on each hand, as does "the Extra Terrestrial," E.T., from the popular movie, then in all probability we would be using the **octal** numbering system, which has a base of 8.

Early computers were designed around the decimal numbering system. This approach made the design of the computer logic capabilities unnecessarily complex and did not make efficient use of resources. For example, 10 vacuum tubes were needed to represent one decimal digit. In 1945, as computer pioneers were struggling to improve this cumbersome approach, John von Neumann suggested that the numbering system used by computers should take advantage of the physical

```
38C070   29306294  4580623F  D20DD0AA  62A29640    8CECCC04  88F00010  80000004  88100010    41110003  5010D064  94FCD067  D703D06C
38C0A0   D06E0610  12114770  6202D203  D09F629D    4120D121  45B06236  5820D120  413062C4    477061A6  4810D06E  41110001  4010D06E
38C0D0   1A2C44E0  60701A1E  41818001  44F06076    9640D112  455062DA  94BFD112  4810D06C    02FF1302  FFC3C9D5  C5E240E2  C1D4C540
38C100   FF0098E0  D08012EE  47806310  D27CF000    48A0D06A  4BA0D06C  88A00002  45B0623E    D12094FC  D1235B00  D1201A10  5800D120
```

**FIGURE 6–7**
**A Hexadecimal Dump**
Each of the lines contains a hexadecimal representation of the contents of primary storage. The leftmost column of numbers is storage addresses. Each pair of hexadecimal digits represents the eight bits of an EBCDIC byte. The address of the first byte in the dump (29) is 0038C070 in hexadecimal or 0000000000111 00011000000001110000 in binary. You can see how much space is saved by displaying dumps in "hex" rather than binary.

In some programming languages, programmers display special characters that do not appear on the keyboard by entering the hexadecimal equivalent of their ASCII or EBCDIC code.
(Photo courtesy of Hewlett-Packard Company)

characteristics of electronic circuitry. To deal with the basic electronic states, "on" and "off," von Neumann suggested the use of the *binary* numbering system. His insight has vastly simplified the way that computers handle data.

Computers *operate* in binary and *communicate* to us in decimal. A special program translates decimal to binary on input, and binary to decimal on output. Under normal circumstances, a programmer would see only decimal input and output. On occasion, though, we must deal with long and confusing strings of 1s and 0s in the form of a **dump.** A dump is like a snapshot of the contents of primary storage (on-bits and off-bits) at a moment in time. To reduce at least part of the confusion of seeing only 1s and 0s on the output, the octal or the **hexadecimal** (base-16) numbering system is used as shorthand to display the binary contents of both primary and secondary storage (see Figure 6–7).

The decimal equivalents for binary, octal, and hexadecimal numbers are shown in Figure 6–8. We know that in decimal, any number greater than 9 is represented by a sequence of digits. When you count in decimal, you "carry" to the next position in groups of 10. As you examine Figure 6–8, notice that you carry in groups of 2 in binary, in groups of 8 in octal, and in groups of 16 in hexadecimal. Also, note that *three* binary bits can be represented by one octal digit and that *four* bits can be represented by one "hex" digit.

Octal and hexadecimal numbering systems are used only for the

| Binary (base 2) | Octal (base 8) | Decimal (base 10) | Hexadecimal (base 16) |
|---|---|---|---|
| 000 | 0 | 0 | 0 |
| 001 | 1 | 1 | 1 |
| 010 | 2 | 2 | 2 |
| 011 | 3 | 3 | 3 |
| 100 | 4 | 4 | 4 |
| 101 | 5 | 5 | 5 |
| 110 | 6 | 6 | 6 |
| 111 | 7 | 7 | 7 |
| 1000 | 10 | 8 | 8 |
| 1001 | 11 | 9 | 9 |
| 1010 | 12 | 10 | A |
| 1011 | 13 | 11 | B |
| 1100 | 14 | 12 | C |
| 1101 | 15 | 13 | D |
| 1110 | 16 | 14 | E |
| 1111 | 17 | 15 | F |
| 10000 | 20 | 16 | 10 |

**FIGURE 6–8**
**Numbering-System Equivalence Table**

convenience of the programmer when reading and reviewing the binary output of a dump (see Figure 6–7). Computers *do not operate or process* in these numbering systems. During the 1960s and early 1970s, programmers often had to examine the contents of primary storage to debug their programs (i.e., to eliminate program errors). Today's programming languages have sophisticated **diagnostics** (called error messages) and computer-assisted tools that aid programmers during program development. These diagnostics and development aids have minimized the need for applications programmers to convert binary, octal, and hexadecimal numbers to their decimal equivalents. However, if you become familiar with these numbering systems, you should achieve a better overall understanding of computers.

### MEMORY BITS

#### NUMBERING SYSTEMS

| Name | Base | Digits | Use |
|------|------|--------|-----|
| Binary | 2 | 0, 1 | Computer processing |
| Octal | 8 | 0–7 | Programmer convenience |
| Decimal | 10 | 0–9 | Human input/output |
| Hexadecimal (hex) | 16 | 0–9, A–F | Programmer convenience |

## Principles of Numbering Systems

Binary.   The binary numbering system is based on the same principles as the decimal numbering system, with which we are already familiar. The only difference between the two numbering systems is that binary uses only two digits, 0 and 1, and the decimal numbering system uses 10 digits, 0 through 9.

The value of a given digit is determined by its relative position in a sequence of digits. Consider the example in Figure 6–9. If we want to write the number 124 in decimal, the interpretation is almost

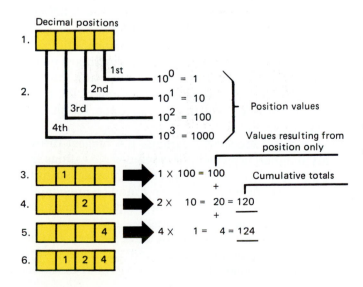

**FIGURE 6–9**
**Numbering-System Fundamentals**
Ralph, our eight-fingered Martian, who is used to counting in octal, might go through the thought process illustrated here when counting 124 marbles in decimal. Ralph's steps are discussed in the text.

automatic because of our familiarity with the decimal numbering system. To illustrate the underlying concepts, let's give Ralph, a little green eight-fingered Martian, a bag of 124 (decimal) marbles and ask him to express the number of marbles in decimal. Ralph, who is more familiar with octal, would go through the following thought process (see Figure 6–9).

- *Step 1*. Ralph knows that the relative position of a digit within a string of digits determines its value, whether the numbering system is binary, octal, or decimal. Therefore, the first thing to do is to determine the value represented by each digit position.

- *Step 2*. Ralph knows that as in any numbering system, the rightmost position has a value of the base to the zero power, or 1 ($10^0 = 1$). The second position is the base to the first power, or 10 ($10^1 = 10$). The third position is the base squared, or 100; and so on.

- *Step 3*. Since the largest of the decimal system's 10 digits is 9, the greatest number that can be represented in the *rightmost position* is 9 (9 × 1). The greatest number that can be represented in the *second position*, then, is 90 (9 × 10). In the *third position*, the greatest number is 900; and so on. Having placed the marbles in stacks of 10, Ralph knows immediately that there will be no need for a fourth-position digit (the thousands position). It is apparent, however, that a digit must be placed in the third position. Since placing a 2 in the third position would be too much (200 > 124), Ralph places a 1 in the third position to represent 100 marbles.

- *Step 4*. Ralph must continue to the second position to represent the remaining 24 marbles. In each successive position, Ralph wants to represent as many marbles as possible. In this case, a 2 placed in the second position would represent 20 of the remaining marbles ($2 \times 10^1 = 20$).

- *Step 5*. There are still four marbles left to be represented. This can be done by inserting a 4 in the rightmost, or "1s" position.

- *Step 6*. The combination of the three numbers in their relative position represents 124 (decimal).

Ralph would go through the same thought process if asked to represent the 124 (decimal) marbles using the binary numbering system (see Figure 6–10). To make the binary conversion process easier to follow, the computations in Figure 6–10 are done in the more familiar decimal numbering system. See if you can trace Ralph's steps as you work through Figure 6–10.

Octal and Hexadecimal. Perhaps the biggest drawback to using the binary numbering system for computer operations is that programmers may have to deal with long and confusing strings of 1s and 0s. To reduce the confusion, octal (base-8) and hexadecimal (base-16) numbering systems are used as a shorthand to display the binary contents of primary and secondary storage.

Notice that the bases of the binary, octal, and hex numbering systems are multiples of 2: 2, $2^3$, and $2^4$, respectively. Because of this, there is a convenient relationship between these numbering systems.

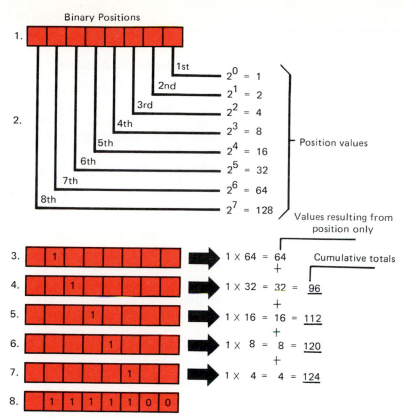

**Binary Positions**

1.

2.

$2^0 = 1$
$2^1 = 2$
$2^2 = 4$
$2^3 = 8$
$2^4 = 16$
$2^5 = 32$
$2^6 = 64$
$2^7 = 128$

Position values

Values resulting from position only

3. $1 \times 64 = 64$

4. $1 \times 32 = 32 = \underline{96}$

5. $1 \times 16 = 16 = \underline{112}$

6. $1 \times 8 = 8 = \underline{120}$

7. $1 \times 4 = 4 = \underline{124}$

8.

Cumulative totals

**FIGURE 6–10**
**Representing a Binary Number**
To represent 124 marbles in binary, we would follow the same thought process as we would in decimal (see Figure 6–9), but this time we have only two digits (0 and 1). For ease of understanding, the arithmetic is done in decimal.

The numbering-system equivalence table shown in Figure 6–8 illustrates that a single hexadecimal digit represents four binary digits (e.g., $0111_2$ = $7_{16}$, $1101_2$ = $D_{16}$, $1010_2$ = $A_{16}$, where subscripts are used to indicate the base of the numbering system). Notice that in hexadecimal, *letters* are used to represent the six higher-order digits.

An octal digit represents three binary digits (e.g., $111_2$ = $7_8$, $010_2$ = $2_8$, $101_2$ = $5_8$). Two hexadecimal digits can be used to represent the eight-bit byte of an EBCDIC equals sign (=) (e.g., $01111110_2$ is the same as $7E_{16}$). Figure 6–11 illustrates how a string of EBCDIC bits can be reduced to a more recognizable form using hexadecimal.

We will examine next how to convert a number of one numbering system to an equivalent number of another numbering system. For example, there are occasions when we might wish to convert a hexadecimal number to its binary equivalent. We shall also learn the fundamentals of numbering-system arithmetic.

**FIGURE 6–11**
**"System" Expressed in Different Ways**
The word "System" is shown as it would appear in input/output, internal binary notation, and hexadecimal notation.

| | S | y | s | t | e | m |
|---|---|---|---|---|---|---|
| Input/output (alphanumeric) | S | y | s | t | e | m |
| Internal representation (binary) | 1110 0010 | 1010 1000 | 1010 0010 | 1010 0011 | 1000 0101 | 1001 0100 |
| Hexadecimal equivalent | E 2 | A 8 | A 2 | A 3 | 8 5 | 9 4 |

## Converting Numbers from One Base to Another

**Decimal to Binary, Octal, or Hexadecimal.**   A decimal number can be easily converted to an equivalent number of any base by the use of the *division/remainder* technique. This two-step technique is illustrated in Figure 6–12. Follow these steps to convert *decimal to binary*.

- *Step 1*. Divide the number (19, in this example) repeatedly and record the remainder of each division. In the first division, 2 goes into 19 nine times, with a remainder of 1. The remainder will always be one of the binary digits, 0 or 1. In the last division, you will be dividing 1 by the base (2) and the remainder will be 1.
- *Step 2*. Rotate the remainders as shown in Figure 6–12; the result (10011) is the binary equivalent of a decimal 19.

Figure 6–13 illustrates how the same division/remainder technique is used to convert a decimal 453 to its hexadecimal equivalent (1C5). In a *decimal-to-hex* conversion, the remainders will always be one of the 16 hex digits. In *decimal-to-octal* conversion, the divisor is 8.

**Binary to Decimal, Octal, and Hexadecimal.**   To convert from *binary to decimal*, multiply the 1s in a binary number by their position values, then sum the products (see Figure 6–14). In Figure 6–14, for example, binary 11010 is converted to its decimal equivalent.

The easiest conversions are *binary to octal* and *binary to hex*. To convert binary to octal, simply begin with the 1s position on the right and segment the binary number into groups of three digits each, as shown in Figure 6–15. Then refer to the equivalence table in Figure 6–8 and assign each group of three binary digits an octal equivalent.

**FIGURE 6–12**
**Converting a Decimal Number to Its Binary Equivalent**
Use the two-step division/ remainder technique to convert a decimal number to an equivalent number of any base.

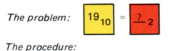

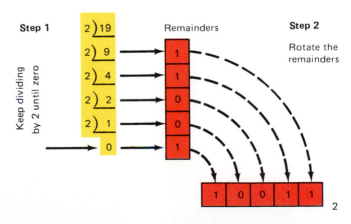

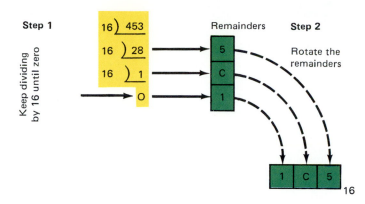

The problem:    $453_{10}$ = $?_{16}$

The procedure:

**FIGURE 6–13**
**Converting a Decimal Number to Its Hexadecimal Equivalent** The two-step division/remainder technique is used to convert a decimal number to its hex equivalent.

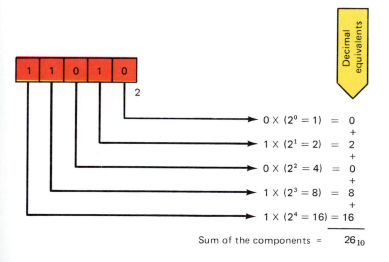

The problem: $11010_2$ = $?_{10}$

The procedure:

**FIGURE 6–14**
**Converting a Binary Number to Its Decimal Equivalent**
Multiply the 1s in a binary number by their position values.

$$0 \times (2^0 = 1) = 0$$
$$+$$
$$1 \times (2^1 = 2) = 2$$
$$+$$
$$0 \times (2^2 = 4) = 0$$
$$+$$
$$1 \times (2^3 = 8) = 8$$
$$+$$
$$1 \times (2^4 = 16) = 16$$

Sum of the components = $26_{10}$

**FIGURE 6–15**
**Converting a Binary Number to Its Octal or Hexadecimal**
Equivalent Place the binary digits in groups of three or four, then convert the binary number directly to octal or hexadecimal.

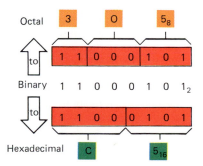

Combine your result, and the conversion is complete. Go through the same procedure for binary-to-hex conversions, except segment the binary number into groups of four digits each.

Octal and Hexadecimal to Binary.    To convert octal and hex numbers to binary, perform the grouping procedure for converting binary to octal and hex in reverse (see Figure 6–15).

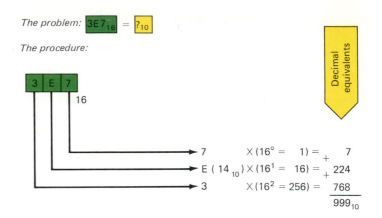

**FIGURE 6–16**
**Converting a Hexadecimal Number to Its Decimal Equivalent**
Multiply the digits in a hexadecimal number by their position values.

**Octal and Hexadecimal to Decimal.** Use the same procedure as that used for binary-to-decimal conversions (see Figure 6–14) to convert *octal to decimal* and *hex to decimal*. Figure 6–16 demonstrates the conversion of a hex 3E7 to its decimal equivalent of 999.

### Arithmetic in Binary, Octal, and Hexadecimal

The essentials of decimal arithmetic operations have been drilled into us so that we do addition and subtraction almost by instinct. We do binary arithmetic, as well as that of other numbering systems, in the same way that we do decimal arithmetic. The only difference is that we have fewer (binary) or more (hexadecimal) digits to use. Figure 6–17 illustrates and compares addition and subtraction in decimal with that in binary, octal, and hex. Notice in Figure 6–17 that you carry to, and borrow from, adjacent positions just as you do in decimal arithmetic.

**FIGURE 6–17**
**Binary, Octal, Decimal, and Hexadecimal Arithmetic Comparison**
As you can see, the only difference in doing arithmetic in the various numbering systems is the number of digits used.

|             | Binary                      | Octal             | Decimal           | Hexadecimal   |
|-------------|-----------------------------|-------------------|-------------------|---------------|
| Addition    | 1111100<br>+  10010<br>10001110 | 174<br>+  22<br>226 | 124<br>+  18<br>142 | 7C<br>+ 12<br>8E |
| Subtraction | 1111100<br>−  10010<br>1101010 | 174<br>−  22<br>152 | 124<br>−  18<br>106 | 7C<br>− 12<br>6A |

## SUMMARY OUTLINE AND IMPORTANT TERMS

**6–1**  DATA STORAGE.  Data, not information, are stored in a computer system. Data are stored temporarily during processing in **primary storage** or **main memory** and permanently on **secondary storage** devices, such as magnetic tape and disk drives.

**6–2**  A BIT ABOUT THE BIT.  The two electronic states of the computer are presented by a **bit,** short for "binary digit." Letters and decimal numbers are translated to bits for storage and processing on computer systems.

**6–3** ENCODING SYSTEMS: COMBINING BITS TO FORM BYTES. **Alphanumeric** characters are represented in computer storage by combining strings of bits to form unique bit configurations for each character. Characters are translated to these bit configurations, also called **bytes,** according to a particular coding scheme, called an **encoding system.** Popular encoding systems include **EBCDIC, ASCII,** and **ASCII-8.**

Parity-checking procedures ensure that data transmission between hardware devices is complete and accurate.

**6–4** COMPONENTS OF A COMPUTER SYSTEM: A CLOSER LOOK AT THE PROCESSOR AND PRIMARY STORAGE. The processor is the "intelligence" of a computer system. A processor has two fundamental sections, the **control unit** and the **arithmetic and logic unit,** which work together with primary storage to execute programs. The control unit interprets instructions and directs the arithmetic and logic unit to perform computation and logic operations.

Primary storage, or **RAM (random-access memory),** provides the processor with temporary storage for programs and data. All input/output, including programs, must enter and exit primary storage. Other variations of internal storage are **ROM (read-only memory), PROM (programmable read-only memory),** and **EPROM (erasable PROM).**

**6–5** COMPUTER OPERATION: FITTING THE PIECES TOGETHER. Data are passed between primary storage and the **accumulator** of the arithmetic and logic unit for both computation and logic operations.

**6–6** DESCRIBING THE PROCESSOR: DISTINGUISHING CHARACTERISTICS. A processor is described in terms of its speed, primary storage capacity, and word length. Speed is measured in **MIPS** and by timed intervals called **machine cycles.** Memory capacity is measured in **K** or **M** bytes. The **word** (the number of bits that are handled as a unit) length of computers ranges from 16 bits for the smaller micros to 64 bits for supercomputers.

APPENDIX: WORKING WITH NUMBERING SYSTEMS. The two primary numbering systems used in conjunction with computers are binary and **decimal.** Decimal is translated to binary on input and binary is translated to decimal on output. The **octal** and **hexadecimal** numbering systems are used primarily as a programmer convenience in reading and reviewing binary output, which may be in the form of a **dump.** The only difference between the decimal numbering system and the other numbering systems that are associated with computers is the number of digits that each numbering system has.

Use the division/remainder technique to convert decimal

to binary, octal, or hexadecimal. Convert binary, hex, and octal to decimal by summing the decimal equivalent of the respective position values. Convert octal and hex to binary and the reverse by working with binary digits in groups of three and four, respectively. The mechanics of arithmetic operations are the same for all numbering systems.

## REVIEW EXERCISES

### Concepts

1. Distinguish between RAM, ROM, PROM, and EPROM.
2. How many EBCDIC bytes can be stored in a 32-bit word?
3. Which two functions are performed by the arithmetic and logic unit?
4. List examples of alpha, numeric, and alphanumeric characters.
5. Write your first name as an ASCII bit configuration. Do it again, but this time include parity bits where appropriate to maintain an odd parity.
6. What are the functions of the control unit?
7. What advantage does the use of a nibble offer when using the ASCII-8 or EBCDIC encoding system?
8. We describe computers in terms of what three characteristics?
9. (Appendix exercise) What is the base of the following numbering systems: Binary? Octal? Hexadecimal? Decimal? What is the significance of each with respect to computers?
10. (Appendix exercise) Convert the following binary numbers to their decimal, octal, and hexadecimal equivalents.

    | (a) | 1001 | (d) | 1110 | (g) | 111 | (j) | 110110110 |
    |---|---|---|---|---|---|---|---|
    | (b) | 111000 | (e) | 110101 | (h) | 10 | (k) | 11111111 |
    | (c) | 101 | (f) | 11 | (i) | 110001 | (l) | 10000001 |

11. (Appendix exercise) Convert the following octal and hexadecimal numbers to their binary equivalents.

    | *Octal* | | *Hexadecimal* | |
    |---|---|---|---|
    | (a) | 2 | (e) | A |
    | (b) | 47 | (f) | 2E |
    | (c) | 651 | (g) | 389 |
    | (d) | 22 | (h) | CB |

12. (Appendix exercise) Express the number of people in your class in binary, octal, decimal, and hexadecimal.
13. (Appendix exercise) Write the numbers expressing $25_{10}$ to $35_{10}$ in binary, octal, and hexadecimal.
14. (Appendix exercise) Perform the following arithmetic operations.

    (a) $101_2 + 11_2$   (d) $60_{10} + F1_{16} - 1001001_2$
    (b) $734_8 - 6_8$   (e) $11_2 + 27_8 + 93_{10} - B_{16}$
    (c) $A1_{16} + BC_{16} + 10_{16}$

## Discussion

**15.** The letter K is used to represent 1024 bytes of storage. Would it not have been much easier to let K represent 1000 bytes? Explain.

**16.** Millions of bytes of data are transferred routinely between computing hardware devices without any errors in transmission. Very seldom is a parity error detected. In your opinion, is it worth all the trouble to add and check parity bits every time a byte is transmitted from one device to another? Why?

**17.** Create a five-bit encoding system that is used for storing upper-case alpha characters, punctuation symbols, and the apostrophe. Discuss the advantages and disadvantages of your encoding system relative to the ASCII encoding system.

## SELF-TEST (by section)

**6–1.** _____ are the raw material from which _____ is derived.

**6–2.** "Bit" is the singular for "byte." (T/F)

**6–3.** **(a)** The combination of bits used to represent a character is called a _____ .

   **(b)** The procedure that ensures complete and accurate transmission of data is called ASCII checking. (T/F)

**6–4.** **(a)** Data are loaded from secondary to primary storage in a nondestructive read process. (T/F)

   **(b)** The _____ is that part of the processor that reads and interprets program instructions.

   **(c)** The arithmetic and logic unit controls the flow of programs and data in and out of main memory. (T/F)

**6–5.** A single BASIC program instruction can cause several internal operations to take place. (T/F)

**6–6.** **(a)** The word length of most microcomputers is 64 bits. (T/F)

   **(b)** MIPS is an acronym for "millions of instructions per second." (T/F)

**App.** **(a)** A decimal 92 is the equivalent of an octal 5C. (T/F)

   **(b)** A dump is a snapshot of the contents of primary storage at a moment in time. (T/F)

   **(c)** The sum of an octal 77 and a binary 1001 is _____ in decimal.

*Self-Test answers.*   6–1, Data, information; 6–2, F; 6–3 (a), byte; (b), F; 6–4 (a), T; (b), control unit; (c), F; 6–5, T; 6–6 (a), F; (b), T; App. (a), F; (b), T; (c), 72.

# Zimco Enterprises

## MICROCOMPUTER ACQUISITION POLICY AND PROCEDURES AT ZIMCO

### THE PC PROLIFERATION PROBLEM

At present, Zimco has 345 workstations throughout the enterprise, about 200 of which are microcomputers. All micros can serve as stand-alone systems or as workstations. The overwhelming majority of these micros are HAL PCs or HAL-compatible PCs, but it wasn't always that way. This movement in the direction of HAL PCs or HAL compatibles is by design. When Conrad Innis, the VP of Computer and Information Services, arrived on the scene in 1981, his focus was mainframe activities. But by early 1983, the "PC proliferation problem" had become acute and needed attention.

In early 1983, Zimco had 42 micros: 10 Oranges, 12 HALs, 15 RTS-88s, and 5 others, all from different vendors. Conrad was concerned because micro users were depending on his CIS people to provide technical support. In an executive meeting, Conrad said: "Our CIS programmers and analysts are spending an inordinate amount of their time supporting micros from eight different vendors."

Initially, users viewed the purchase price of the micros as the majority of the expense associated with buying a micro. Some found out later that the successful implementation of a micro may result in costs of several times the purchase price. Conrad circulated a blunt memo to all Zimco employees who had enough discretionary buying power to purchase a micro. In effect, the

Over half of the workstations at Zimco are microcomputers. About half of those have a dedicated printer and the remainder share a printer with one or two other micros.
(Dataproducts Corporation)

memo said to cease and desist buying micros until you know what you are doing. Managers were buying micros without any forethought as to what they wanted to do with them.

Being responsible for the effective use of computer resources at Zimco, Conrad decided to confront the "PC proliferation problem" and establish a policy regarding the acquisition of micros. He wanted to avoid the plight of those companies that did not set a standard. These companies neded up with a wide variety of micros, and more often than not, the programs and data were not **compatible;** that is, programs and data prepared for one micro could not be used on another. The policy and associated guidelines established at Zimco for the acquisition of micros are discussed in this case study.

## ZIMCO'S MICROCOMPUTER REVIEW BOARD

The first action taken by Conrad to address PC proliferation at Zimco was to establish a *Microcomputer Review Board*. The board, which was to meet on the first working Wednesday of each month, was given five fundamental charges.

1. Establish guidelines for the acquisition of microcomputer hardware, specifying which micros and associated peripheral devices would be supported by CIS personnel.
2. Establish guidelines for the acquisition of microcomputer software, specifying which microcomputer productivity software tools (e.g., electronic spreadsheet, word processing, database, graphics, communications, and idea processor) would be supported by CIS personnel.
3. Review and approve/disapprove all user requests to purchase microcomputer hardware or software.
4. Set up and monitor a volume microcomputer purchase program that enables departments and employees to purchase a micro hardware and software at substantial discounts.
5. Educate users in the purchase and acquisition of microcomputer hardware and software.

The Microcomputer Review Board is composed of five department heads, one from each of the five divisions at Zimco. The chairperson is always the manager of the Programming Department in CIS, currently Gram Mertz.

### Selecting a "Standard" Micro for Zimco

As you can imagine, there was considerable debate as to which micro or micros should become the standard at Zimco. Before making their decision, the review board solicited input from throughout the enterprise. Preston Smith, the president, was a proponent of HAL PCs. Conrad Innis and Peggy Peoples, the VP of Personnel, were high on the Orange PCs. Virtually everyone in manufacturing wanted the new T&T multiuser PCs to be selected as the standard.

The board took the conservative route and selected a micro that had, in effect, become the de facto standard for business microcomputers— the HAL PC. They considered selecting another noncompatible micro as an "alternative standard," but the members unanimously agreed that having to provide technical support to two very different micros would place too much of a burden on CIS personnel. The board's decision to chose HAL PCs was based primarily on the availability of software. Chairperson Gram Mertz justified the board's decision: "We felt that even though several of the other top candidates were more user friendly, they simply don't offer the scope of software that is available for the HAL PC."

Because so much software was being written to run on the HAL PC, a number of companies manufacture HAL "clones," or micros that run the same software and accomplish the same functions as the HAL PC. The board designated one of these HAL PC-compatible micros, the Zap-100, as an acceptable alternative to the HAL PC. The Zap-100 was priced 30 percent lower than the HAL PC. This gave users a choice.

### Selecting "Standard" Software

The Microcomputer Review Board's charge was to evaluate and select only software that fit into one of six "productivity tool" categories: electronic spreadsheet, word processor, database, graphics, communications, and idea processor. There are literally hundreds of software packages in one or several of these categories. The board selected 12 software packages, several of which were integrated packages; that is, they performed the functions of several software packages (e.g., electronic spreadsheet, database, and graphics).

The evaluation and selection of software that relates to a particular application, such as accounting or marketing, is done by the people in the affected departments.

## The Microcomputer Purchase Request Form

Any micros purchased within Zimco must be approved by the Microcomputer Review Board. At first the idea of filling out a *Microcomputer Purchase Request Form* seemed a little silly, but when Conrad explained the logic behind the form, most agreed that it was necessary. In a general session for management personnel, Conrad explained the need for the form. "Look around you. Half of the micros at Zimco are either underutilized or they are just gathering dust. Too many people are buying micros without any plans as to how they will be used. It is our hope that the mandatory request form will encourage potential micro users to do a little up-front thinking. It's not our intention to discourage the purchase of micros; on the contrary, they're wonderful business tools, but Zimco can't afford the luxury of having a bunch of PCs around that are more cosmetic than functional."

## The Volume Purchase Program

Zimco employees were made aware that microcomputers and personal computers can be purchased at retail chains, such as Computerland, ENTRE Computer Center, 20/20, MicroAge, and other vendor product centers. However, Conrad wanted to offer Zimco employees a "computer perk." In cooperation with HAL and the HAL-compatible vendor, the Microcomputer Review Board makes volume purchases of PCs at discount rates, then resells "extras" to employees at substantial savings. This plan benefits everybody (except local retailers) because Zimco ob-

Some Zimco employees prefer to purchase their micros through a computer retail store rather than participate in the company program because they want a guarantee of immediate service if the system malfunctions. Salespersons at computer retail stores are usually happy to show customers what options are available for a particular microcomputer.
(Courtesy of International Business Machines Corporation)

tains PCs at volume prices for internal use; the manufacturers sell their computers; and the employees get an inexpensive PC. But the real reason Conrad encouraged this computer perk is to promote "computer literacy." He knew that employees would inevitably begin to use and understand their computers and, in the long run, their computer savvy would be translated into improved productivity in their jobs.

## Steps to Buying a Micro

The following is the actual text from Zimco's internal document entitled "Steps to Buying a Micro." The Microcomputer Review Board was aware that buying a computer can be a harrowing experience or it can be a thrilling and fulfilling one. As Gram Mertz said: "If you go about the acquisition of a micro methodically and with purpose, micros will add another dimension to your work. If not, you may curse the day that you decided to buy a micro." The following hints for the evaluation and selection of a microcomputer were compiled by the review board.

■ *Step 1. Achieve computer literacy*. You don't buy an automobile before you learn how to drive, and you shouldn't buy a microcomputer without a good understanding of its capabilities and limitations. Zimco's CIS education coordinator offers a self-paced course that will give you the knowledge to make informed decisions when buying a micro. Several local colleges offer such courses as well.

■ *Step 2. Determine your information and computer usage needs*. There is an old adage: "If you don't know where you are going, any road will get you there." The statement is certainly true of choosing a PC. "Knowing where you are going" can be translated to mean "How do you plan to use the PC?" You must answer this question in the Microcomputer Purchase Request Form.

■ *Step 3. Investigate software options*. Determine what software is available to meet your prescribed information needs. When evaluating available software, consider these items: Does it provide the functionality you need; would it be difficult to learn; does the software make effective use of the hardware (e.g., function keys on keyboard, color monitor); is the documentation clear, concise, and well organized; and is it easy to use? Be sure to look over the documentation and spend some time working with a software package before making a commitment to purchase.

■ *Step 4. Investigate hardware options*. If you select a specific software product in Step 3, your selection may dictate the general computer system configuration requirements. In all likelihood, you will have several, if not a dozen, hardware alternatives available to you. Become familiar with the features, and options, of each alternative system.

■ *Step 5. Determine features desired*. You can go with a "minimum" configuration, or you can add a few "bells and whistles." Expect to pay for each feature in convenience, quality, and speed that you add to the minimum configuration. For example, people are usually willing to pay a little extra for the added convenience of a two-disk system, even though one disk will suffice. On the other hand, a color monitor may be an unnecessary luxury for some applications. The peripherals that you select depend very much on your specific needs and volume of usage. For example, the type of printer that you choose would depend on the volume of hard-copy output that you anticipate, whether you need graphics output, whether you need letter-quality print, and so on.

■ *Step 6. "Test drive" several alternatives*. Once you have selected several software and hardware alternatives, spend enough time to gain some familiarity with them. Do you prefer one keyboard over another? Does a

Zimco employees are encouraged to familiarize themselves with the capabilities of a particular software package before making the decision to buy.
(Western Union Corporations)

word processing system fully use the features of the hardware? Is one system easier to understand and use than another? Use these sessions to answer any questions that you might have about the hardware or software. Salespeople at most retail stores are happy to give you a test drive; just ask.

■ *Step 7. Select and buy.* Apply your criteria, select, then buy your hardware and software.

---

### MEMORY BITS

**STEPS TO BUYING A MICROCOMPUTER**

1. Achieve computer literacy
2. Determine your information and computer usage needs
3. Investigate software options
4. Investigate hardware options
5. Determine features desired
6. "Test drive" several alternatives
7. Select and buy

---

## FACTORS TO CONSIDER WHEN BUYING A MICRO

During the fourth meeting of the Microcomputer Review Board, Gram Mertz discussed one of his many observations. He said: "Users still need more direction. They're still buying first and asking questions later. I think we should give them something to think about before buying." The result of Gram's comments is a pamphlet entitled, "Factors to Consider when Buying a Micro." The pamphlet, which is distributed along with each Micrcomputer Purchase Request Form, enumerates the following considerations.

1. *Future computing needs.* What will your computer and information processing needs be in the future? Most micros provide room for growth; that is, you can add more memory and other peripheral devices as you need them. Make sure that the system you select can grow with your needs.

2. *Who will use the system?* Plant not only for yourself but for others in your home or office who will also use the system. Get their input and consider their needs along with yours.

3. *Availability of software.* Software is developed for one or several microcomputers, but not for all microcomputers. As you might expect, a more extensive array of software is available for the more popular micros. Make sure that the micro you select has an array of available software that will support your short- and long-term information and processing needs.

4. *Service.* Computing hardware is very reliable. Even so, the possibility exists that one or several of the components will eventually malfunction and have to be repaired. Before purchasing a micro, identify a reliable source of hardware maintenance. Most retailers service what they sell. If a retailer says that the hardware must be returned to the manufacturer for repair, choose another retailer or another system.

5. *Obsolescence.* "I'm going to buy one as soon as the price goes down a little more." If you adopt this strategy, you may never purchase a computer. If you wait another six months, you will probably be able to get a more powerful micro for less money. But what about the lost opportunity?

6. *Other costs.* The cost of the actual microcomputer system is the major expense, but there are numerous incidental expenses that can mount up and may influence your selection of a micro. If you have a spending limit, consider these costs when purchasing the hardware (the cost ranges are for the business user at Zimco): software, $100 to $1500; instructional literature, $0 to $100; maintenance $0 to $500 per year; diskettes, $50 to $200; furniture, $0 to $350; insurance, $0 to $20; and printer cartridges, paper, and other supplies, $40 to $200.

## DISCUSSION QUESTIONS

1. Zimco standardized on the HAL PC and a HAL PC compatible, the Zap-100. Since the compatible costs 30 percent less than the actual HAL PC, why didn't Zimco just standardize on the compatible?

2. What was meant when people at Zimco referred to the "PC proliferation problem"?

3. Should a company specify what microcomputer hardware and software users can buy, or should users be permitted the flexibility to choose whatever they want? Justify your position.

4. Zimco encourages their micro users to be "computer literate" (Step 1 in the suggested steps to buying a micro) by providing an in-house education program for computer literacy. Should users study computers on company time or on their own time? Explain.

5. Zimco's Microcomputer Review Board now requires any employee desiring to purchase micro hardware or software to complete a Microcomputer Purchase Request Form. Why do you think the board implemented this requirement?

6. What would you look for when taking a word processing package for a "test drive"?

7. Identify the types of expenses that a product manager at Zimco can expect to incur during the first year if he or she purchases and uses a microcomputer system, primarily for word processing, spreadsheet applications, and as a workstation.

8. "I'm going to wait a few more months for the price to go down." How would you respond to a Zimco manager who, year after year, used this excuse for not buying a micro?

*The mission of an electric utility is to provide a reliable electric supply at the lowest possible cost. To that end, electric utilities were among the earliest users of computers to support customer information systems, both for automated customer billing and for real-time access to customer records. Today, computers are an integral part of every utility operation, from the complex engineering and economic modeling necessary for the selection of electric generation needed ten years in the future to the instantaneous control of existing generation as customer demands change.*

*Although there is always a need for improved technology, the critical resource is intelligent, resourceful people who can relate business needs to technology.*

James J. O'Connor
Chairman and President
Commonwealth Edison

# Peripheral Devices—
# I/O and Data Storage

## STUDENT LEARNING OBJECTIVES

- To describe the use and characteristics of the different types of workstations.
- To explain alternative approaches and devices for data entry.
- To describe the operation and application of common output devices.
- To distinguish between primary and secondary storage.
- To distinguish between secondary storage devices and secondary storage media.
- To describe the principles of operation, methods of data storage, and use of magnetic disk drives.
- To describe the principles of operation, methods of data storage, and use of magnetic tape drives.
- To discuss the applications and use of optical laser disk storage.

## FOCUS OF ZIMCO CASE STUDY

- Information systems at Zimco: finance and accounting.

## 7-1 I/O DEVICES: OUR INTERFACE WITH THE COMPUTER

Data are created in many places and many ways. Before data can be processed and stored, they must be translated to a form that the *computer* can interpret. For this, we need *input* devices. Once the data have been processed, they must be translated back to a form that we can understand. For this, we need *output* devices. These **peripheral** input/output (I/O) devices enable communication between us and the computer.

The diversity of computer applications has encouraged manufacturers to develop and market a variety of I/O methods and hardware. Innovative I/O devices are being continuously introduced to the marketplace. For example, voice recognition devices accept data (input) through simple verbal communication. Speech synthesizers permit verbal communication in the other direction (output).

This chapter is divided into four parts. In the first part, the focus is on the variety of workstations available, most of which are both input and output. The second part presents devices that are used primarily for entering data. The third part describes devices that are strictly output. The last part is devoted to the data storage category of peripheral devices.

## 7-2 WORKSTATIONS

A **workstation** is a device that allows us to interact with a computer from just about anywhere. A workstation's primary input mechanism is usually a *keyboard*, and the output is usually a televisionlike display screen called a *monitor*. Workstations, sometimes called **terminals**,

This department provides administrative support to three regional insurance claims offices. Because each of these "knowledge workers" routinely deals with computer-generated information, each person needs a workstation to interact with the computer.

come in all shapes and sizes and have a variety of input/output capabilities.

Although the common telephone is the most familiar workstation (keypad input and voice output), the *video display terminal* (*VDT*) and the *microcomputer* are the ones most commonly used for computer interaction. The VDT is affectionately known as the "tube," short for **cathode-ray tube**. From our past discussions (Chapter 4, "Computer Systems—Micros, Minis, and Mainframes"), we know that a microcomputer can serve as a stand-alone computer or as a workstation linked to a mainframe.

Workstations in the factory are becoming as common as steel-toed shoes. Shop floor workers set up and operate production facilities from their workstations.
(Reproduced with permission of AT&T)

**The Keyboard.**   Just about all workstations come equipped with a keyboard for input. The typical key-driven data entry device will have a standard *alphanumeric keyboard* with an optional numeric keyboard, called a *10-key pad*. Some keyboards will also have *special-function keys*, which can be used to instruct the computer to perform a specific operation that may otherwise require several keystrokes. Some keyboards are designed for a specific application, such as for use in fast-food restaurants.

**Other Input Devices.**   For some applications the keyboard is too cumbersome. For example, an engineer might need to "draw" a line to connect two points on the workstation's display screen. Such applications call for devices that go beyond the capabilities of keyboards. These devices permit random movement of the **cursor** to create the image. A cursor, or blinking character, always indicates the location on the screen of the next input. The light pen, joystick, track ball, digitizing tablet and pen, and mouse are among the most popular cursor movement and input mechanisms.

The *light pen* detects light from the cathode-ray tube when it is moved close to the screen. The cursor is automatically locked on to the position of the pen and tracks the movement of the pen over the screen. The *joystick* is a single vertical stick that moves the cursor in the direction in which the stick is pushed. The *track ball* is a ball that is inset in the worktable in front of the screen. The ball is "rolled" to move the cursor. The *digitizing tablet and pen* is a pen and a pressure-sensitive tablet with the same *X-Y* coordinates as the screen. The outline of an image drawn on a tablet is reproduced on the display screen.

There are two mice in this photo. Both move freely about the desktop. Both have tails. But only one eats cheese.
(Summagraphics Corporation)

The *mouse*, sometimes called the "pet peripheral," is now standard equipment for some workstations and micros. The mouse, attached to the computer by a cable, is a small device that when moved across a desktop, moves the cursor. The mouse is used for quick positioning of the cursor over a graphic image, called an *icon* (e.g., a file cabinet or a diskette) or a phrase that depicts some action (e.g., store file on disk). The action is initiated when a button on the mouse is pushed. Also, holding a button down and moving the mouse cause objects on the screen to be moved.

**The Monitor.**   Alphanumeric and graphic output are displayed on the workstation's monitor. The three primary attributes of monitors are

This CAD system illustrates the difference between a low-resolution monochrome monitor (left) and a high-resolution color monitor. A security specialist is using a digitizing board, a keyboard, and a joystick (above keyboard) to design the layout of an airport security checkpoint. (CalComp)

The computer operators in this data center interact with the computer through one of the operator consoles. (Courtesy Burroughs Corporation)

the *size* of the display screen, whether the display is *color or monochrome*, and the *resolution* or detail of the display. The size of the screen varies, the most common being that which displays up to 25 lines of 80 characters each. Other common screen sizes are 32 by 80 and 25 by 132. The diagonal dimension of the display screen varies from 5 to 25 inches. Output on a monitor is temporary and is available to the end user only until another display is requested.

Monitors are either monochrome or color. Monochrome monitors display images in a single color, usually white, green, or amber. Color monitors add the dimension of color, which highlights various aspects of the output.

Some monitors have a much higher **resolution**, or quality of output. Resolution refers to the number of addressable points on the screen—that is, the number of points to which light can be directed under program control. A strictly alphanumeric workstation has about 65,000 such points. A workstation used primarily for computer graphics and computer-aided design may have over 16 million points. The high-resolution monitors project extremely clear images that look almost like photographs.

## Workstation Summary

Workstations of every size and shape are used by secretaries for word processing, by programmers for interactive program development, by clerks for recording transactions, by commercial artists for creating ad pieces, by management for making decisions, by engineers for computer-aided design (CAD), by computer operators to communicate with the computer (via the operator console), by shop supervisors for line scheduling, and by thousands of other people for hundreds of applications.

The trend in workstations is to provide processing as well as I/O capability. This, in effect, means that by the second edition of this book, virtually all workstations will be microcomputers with stand-alone processing capability. Microcomputers are becoming so powerful that users are no longer completely dependent on mainframe capabilities for complex processing jobs. With these "intelligent" workstations, users can conduct interactive sessions with mainframe computers or download data for stand-alone processing. Data processed in stand-alone mode can also be uploaded to the mainframe such that they can be shared with users at other workstations.

> **MEMORY BITS**
>
> **WORKSTATION**
> - Input
>   Keyboard
>   Light pen
>   Joystick
>   Track ball
>   Digitizing tablet and pen
>   Mouse
> - Output
>   Monitor
>     Monochrome or color
>     Low or high resolution

## 7–3 DATA ENTRY: GETTING DATA INTO THE COMPUTER SYSTEM

The trend in data entry has been toward decreasing the number of transcription steps. This is accomplished by entering the data as close to the source as possible. For example, in sales departments, orders are input directly to the system by salespersons. In accounting departments, financial transactions are recorded and entered into the system by bookkeepers and accountants.

Until recently, data entry has been synonymous with *keystrokes*. The keystroke will be the basic mode of data entry for some time to come, but recent innovations have eliminated the need for key-driven data entry in certain applications. For example, you have probably noticed the preprinted bar codes on grocery products. At some supermarket checkout counters these bar codes have eliminated the need for most key entry. Checkers need only pass the product over the *laser scanner* and the price is entered.

Data entry is an area where enormous potential exists for increases in productivity. The technology of data entry devices is constantly changing. New and improved methods of transcribing raw data are being invented and put on the market each month. These data entry methods and associated devices are discussed next.

The trend in data entry is to minimize keystrokes and capture data as close to the source as possible in machine-readable form. For example, supermarket checkout systems use laser scanners to read the bar codes that identify each item. Price and product description are retrieved from a data base and recorded on the sales slip.
(Courtesy of International Business Machines Corporation)

### Optical Scanning

**Optical character recognition** (**OCR**) provides a way to encode (write) certain data in machine-readable format on the original source document. For example, the International Standard Book Number (ISBN) on the back cover of this book is written in machine-readable OCR. This eliminates the need for publishers and bookstore clerks to key these data manually. OCR equipment consists of a family of devices that encode and read OCR data.

OCR Scanners. OCR characters are identified through light-sensitive devices called **OCR scanners**. Both scanner technologies, *contact* and *laser*, bounce a beam of light off an image, then measure the reflected light to determine the value of the image. Hand-held *wand scanners* make contact as they are brushed over the printed matter to be read.

Stationary *laser scanners* are more versatile and can read data passed near the scanning area. Both can recognize printed characters and various types of codes.

OCR devices can "learn" to read almost any typeface, including this book! The "learning" takes place when the structure of the character set is described to the OCR device. OCR scanners can be classified into the following five categories:

- *Label scanners*. These devices read data on price tags, shipping labels, and the like. A hand-held wand scanner is a label scanner.
- *Page scanners*. These devices scan regular typewritten pages.
- *Document scanners*. Document scanners are capable of scanning documents of varying sizes (e.g., utility-bill invoice stubs and sales slips from credit card transactions).
- *Continuous-form scanners*. These devices read data printed on continuous forms, such as cash register tapes.
- *Optical mark scanners*. Optical mark scanners scan preprinted forms, such as multiple-choice test answer forms. The position of the "sense marks" indicates a particular response or character. Optical mark scanning is somewhat dated but still applicable where handwritten data entry is impractical.

## Applications of Optical Scanners

*Bar Codes.*   The stationary scanners, such as those in supermarkets, use lasers to interpret the bar codes printed on products. Bar codes represent alphanumeric data by varying the width and combination of adjacent vertical lines. Just as there are a variety of internal bit encoding systems, there are a variety of bar-coding systems (see Figure 7–1). One of the most visible of these systems is the Universal Product Code (UPC). The UPC, originally used for supermarket items, is gaining momentum and is now being printed on other consumer goods. The advantage of bar codes over characters is that the position or orientation of the item being read is not as critical to the scanner. In a supermarket, for example, the data can be recorded even if a bottle of ketchup is rolled over the laser scanner!

*Wand Scanners.*   The hand-held wand scanner is now common in point-of-sale (POS) systems in retail stores throughout the world. Clerks need only brush the wand over the price tag to record the sale. Since the POS terminal is on-line, the inventory is also updated as each item is sold.

*OCR Turnaround Documents.*   OCR devices are custom made for situations where data can be encoded by the computer system on a **turnaround document** and when visual recognition is important. A turnaround document is *computer-produced output* that is ultimately returned as *machine-readable input* to a computer system. The utility billing system of an electric company is a good example of this OCR application.

In the textile industry, pay is based on piecework. Employees affix labels with their employee number and part number to each item they complete. A hand-held wand scanner reads these data as input to the payroll system.
(CAERE Corporation)

**FIGURE 7–1**
**Various Codes That Can Be Interpreted by OCR Scanners**

The utility billing system procedures are shown in Figure 7–2.

1. The invoices from the electricity company (the turnaround documents) are generated from the customer master file and the electricity usage file. Data on the invoice are printed in a format that can be read by an OCR document scanner.

2. The customers return the OCR-readable invoice stubs with the payment. Clerks cross-check the payment amount against the amount due. Partial payments are separated out from full payments.

3. An OCR scanner reads the original turnaround document of full-payment customers to acknowledge receipt of payment.

4. The only data entry required is on partial payments. The amount of the payment is encoded on the partial-payment invoice stubs, and these are read by the OCR device.

5. The customer's account is credited by the amount of the payment.

*Original Source Data Collection.* Optical character recognition is also used for original source data collection. An example is data collection for credit card purchases (by VISA, MasterCard, and the like). When you make a credit card purchase, your card, a multicopy form, and a portable imprint device are used to record the sales data in machine-readable OCR format. On the form, the data recorded for most credit card purchases include the *account number of the buyer*, the *account number of the merchant*, and the *amount of the purchase*.

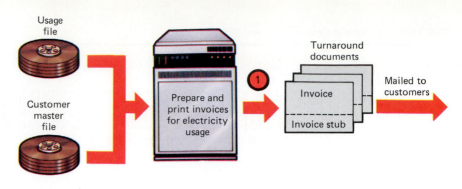

Usage file

Customer master file

Prepare and print invoices for electricity usage

① Turnaround documents

Invoice
Invoice stub

Mailed to customers

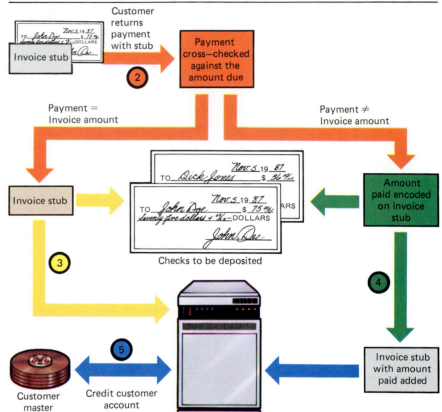

Customer returns payment with stub

Invoice stub

② Payment cross—checked against the amount due

Payment = Invoice amount

Payment ≠ Invoice amount

Invoice stub

③

Checks to be deposited

Amount paid encoded on invoice stub

④

Invoice stub with amount paid added

⑤ Credit customer account

Customer master file

**FIGURE 7–2**
**Electricity Utility Billing System**
This system invoices customers with OCR turnaround documents, thereby minimizing the amount of key entry required. The five steps are discussed in the text.

The telephone in this clothing store is actually a combination phone and terminal. Clerks get confirmation on credit purchases by sliding the credit card's magnetic stripe through the slot. The customer's account number and the amount of the purchase (entered by the clerk) are transmitted to a central computer for processing and a confirmation (or rejection) number is returned and displayed.
(Copyright 1984 GTE Telenet Communications Corporation)

188

Bank identification
number

Account number

Encoded on blank check

Amount
encoded when
received by bank

**FIGURE 7–3**
**A Magnetic Ink Character Recognition (MICR) Encoded Check**
Notice that the amount is entered on the check when it is received by the bank.

## Magnetic Ink Character Recognition

**Magnetic ink character recognition (MICR)** is similar to optical character recognition and is used exclusively by the banking industry. MICR readers are used to read and sort checks and deposits. You have probably noticed the *account number* and *bank number* encoded on all your checks and personalized deposit slips. The *date* of the transaction is automatically recorded for all checks processed that day; therefore, only the *amount* must be keyed in (see Figure 7–3).

## Magnetic Stripes and Smart Cards

The **magnetic stripes** on the backs of charge cards and badges offer another means of data entry. The magnetic stripes are encoded with data appropriate for the application. For example, the account number and privacy code are encoded on cards for automatic teller machines.

The **smart card**, which is similar in appearance to other cards, contains a microprocessor that retains certain security and personal data in its memory at all times. The smart card is really a portable computer that fits in a billfold. Since it will be almost impossible to duplicate, it may be the charge and/or identification card of the future.

## Voice Data Entry

Computers are great talkers, but they are not very good listeners. It is not uncommon for a **voice data entry** system to misinterpret the slamming of a door for a spoken word. Voice data entry, or **voice recognition**, devices can be used to enter limited kinds and quantities of data. Here's how it works. When you speak into a microphone, each sound is broken down and examined in several frequencies. The voice input, such as a spoken "one" or "stop," is then converted to digital signals that are matched against similarly formed *templates* in the computer's electronic dictionary.

Despite being limited to the ability to interpret relative few words,

voice data entry has a number of applications. Salespersons in the field can enter an order simply by calling the computer and stating the customer number, item number, and quantity. Quality control personnel, who must use their hands, call out defects as they are detected. Baggage handlers at airports call out the three-letter destination identifier, and luggage is routed to the appropriate conveyer system. Physicians in the operating room can request certain information on a patient while operating. A computer-based audio response unit or a speech synthesizer (both covered later in this chapter) make the conversation two-way.

## Vision systems

To give computers eyesight, a camera provides the input needed to create the data base. First a vision system, complete with camera, digitizes the images of all objects to be interpreted. The digitized form of each image is then stored in the data base. When in operation, the vision inputs are digitized; then the computer interprets them by matching the structure of the input with those in the data base.

As you can imagine, **vision input systems** are best suited to tasks where only a very few images will be encountered. These tasks are usually simple, monotonous ones, such as inspection and item selection. For example, a robot on an assembly line might perform several functions, depending on which one of three parts is coming down the line and whether it meets certain quality control specifications. A vision system can determine which part it is, perform rudimentary gauging inspections, then signal the robot's computer to take appropriate action.

## Portable Data Entry

**Portable data entry** devices are hand held and usually off-line. The typical portable data entry device would have a limited keyboard and a magnetic cassette tape on which to "capture" the data. After the data have been entered, they are batched to the host computer for processing.

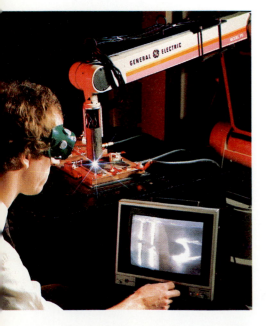

Stock clerks in supermarkets can use portable data entry devices to speed up the order process. To enter the product number, the clerk passes the scanner over the bar code; the number to be ordered is then entered on the keyboard. The data are collected off-line then transmitted to the mainframe for processing.
(MSI Data Corporation)

One portable data entry device combines a hand-held optical wand with a keyboard. Stock clerks in department stores routinely use such devices to collect and enter reorder data. As clerks check the inventory level visually, they identify the items to be restocked. First the price tag is scanned by the wand, then the number to be ordered is entered on the keyboard.

## 7–4 OUTPUT DEVICES

Output devices translate bits and bytes to a form that we can understand. Workstations are both input and output devices. The most common "output only" devices (printers, computer-output microfilm/microfiche, voice response units, and plotters) are discussed in this section.

### Printers

Printers produce hard-copy output, such as management reports, payroll checks, and program listings. Printers are generally classified as **serial printers, line printers,** or **page printers.** Printers are rated by their print speed. Print speeds for serial printers are measured in *characters per second* (*cps*), and for line and page printers they are measured in *lines per minute* (*lpm*). The print-speed ranges for the three types of printers are 40 to 450 cps, 500 to 3600 lpm, and 500 to 40,000 lpm, respectively.

Printers are further categorized as *impact* or *nonimpact*. An impact printer uses some type of hammer or hammers to "impact" the ribbon and the paper, much as a typewriter does. Nonimpact printers use chemicals, lasers, and heat to form the images on the paper.

Serial Printers. Serial printers are the primary hard-copy output unit for microcomputers, and they are often used in conjunction with one or several workstations to provide hard-copy capability. Impact serial printers rely on **dot-matrix** and **daisy-wheel** technology. Nonimpact serial printers employ **ink-jet** technology. Regardless of the technology,

**MEMORY BITS**

**DATA ENTRY**

- Keyboards
- Optical character recognition (OCR)
- Magnetic ink character recognition (MICR)
- Magnetic stripes and smart cards
- Voice recognition
- Vision input systems

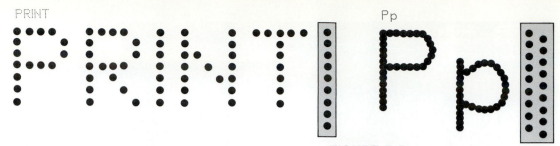

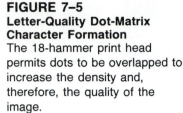

**FIGURE 7–5**
**Letter-Quality Dot-Matrix Character Formation**
The 18-hammer print head permits dots to be overlapped to increase the density and, therefore, the quality of the image.

**FIGURE 7–4**
**Dot-Matrix Printer Character Formation**
Each character is formed in a 7 × 5 matrix as the nine-hammer print head moves across the paper. The two bottom hammers are used for lowercase letters that extend below the line (e.g., g and p).

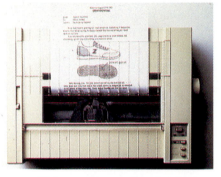

This graphics and text output shows the versatility of a dot-matrix printer. A dot-matrix printer can produce hard copies of graphic images (as they would appear on a screen) just as easily as it prints letters and reports.
(Courtesy of Apple Computer, Inc.)

The daisy-wheel printer is so named because its print mechanism resembles the shape of a daisy. Each of the "petals" of the daisy-wheel contains a fully-formed impression of a character. The interchangeable daisy-wheels are available in a wide variety of character sets.
(Dataproducts Corporation)

the images are formed *one character at a time* as the print head moves across the paper.

*The Dot-Matrix Printer.* The dot-matrix printer configures printed dots to form characters and all kinds of images in much the same way as lights display time and temperature on bank signs. One or several vertical columns of small print hammers are contained in a rectangular "print head." The hammers are activated independently to form a dot character image as the print head moves horizontally across the paper. The characters in Figure 7–4 are formed within a 7 × 5 dot matrix. The number of dots within the matrix varies from one printer to the next. The quality of the printed output is directly proportional to the density of the dots in the matrix (Figure 7–5).

Dot-matrix printers are more flexible than printers of fully formed characters. Depending on the model, dot-matrix printers can print a variety of sizes and types of characters (even old English and script characters), print graphics, and print bar codes.

*The Daisy-Wheel Printer.* The daisy-wheel printer produces *letter-quality* output for word processing applications. An interchangeable daisy wheel containing a set of fully formed characters is spun to the desired character. A print hammer strikes the embossed character on the print wheel to form the image. Daisy-wheel printers produce letter-quality text output, but they are the slowest of the serial printers and cannot produce graphic output.

*The Ink-Jet Printer.* Ink-jet printers squirt "dots" of ink on the paper to form images in a manner similar to that of the dot-matrix printer. The big advantage that ink-jet printers have over dot-matrix printers is that they can produce *multicolor* output.

**Line Printers.** Line printers are impact printers that print *a line at a time*. The two most popular types of line printers are the band printer and the matrix line printer.

*Band and Chain Printers.* Band and chain printers have a print hammer for each print position in the line of print (usually 132). On a band printer, several similar character sets of fully formed characters are embossed on a horizontal band that is continuously moving in front of the print hammers. On a chain printer, the characters are embossed on each link of the print chain. On both types, the paper is momentarily stopped and as the desired character passes over a given column, the hammer is activated and the image is formed on the paper.

*The Matrix Line Printer.* Matrix line printers print a line of *dots* at a time. Needlelike hammers are lined up across the width of the paper. Like serial matrix printers, the characters are formed in rectangular dot configurations and they are capable of producing graphic output.

Page Printers. Page printers are of the nonimpact type and use electro-photographic and laser printing technology to achieve high-speed hard-copy output by printing *a page at a time*. Operating at peak capacity during an eight-hour shift, a high-speed page printer can produce almost a quarter of a million pages—that's 50 miles of output. This enormous output capability is normally directed to persons outside an organization. For example, large banks use page printers to produce statements for checking and savings accounts; insurance companies print policies on page printers; and electric utility companies use them to bill their customers.

Desktop laser page printers produce letter-quality output at 8 to 10 pages per minute. Page printers have the capability to print graphs and charts, and they offer considerable flexibility in the choice of size and style of print.

Printer Summary. Hundreds of printers are produced by dozens of manufacturers. There is a printer manufactured to meet the hard-copy output requirements of any company or individual. Almost any combination of features can be obtained. You can specify the speed, quality of output, color requirements, flexibility requirements, and even noise level. Printers sell for as little as a good pair of shoes or for as much as a small office building.

The nozzles on the print head of a color ink-jet printer expel thousands of droplets per second to produce color images.
(BASF)

This line printer uses an operator-changeable steel band and prints 1,500 lines per minute. To load the continuous-feed paper, the acoustical enclosure is raised and the "gate" containing the band and ribbon is swung open.
(Storage Technology Corporation)

Inside this desktop laser page printer, laser beams scan across the print drum to create text and graphics at speeds of over eight pages per minute.
(Sperry Corporation)

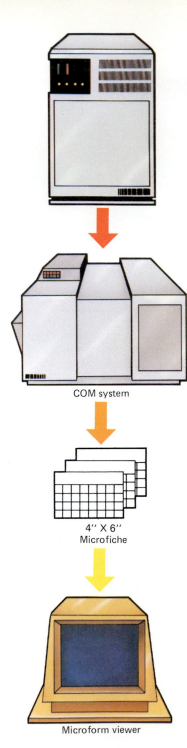

COM system

4″ X 6″
Microfiche

Microform viewer

**FIGURE 7–6**
**The Computer Ouput**
**Microfilm/Microfiche (COM)**
**Process**
In the on-line COM process, data
are routed directly from the
computer to the COM system.

## Computer Output Microfilm/Microfiche

**Computer output microfilm/microfiche (COM)** devices prepare microfilm and microfiche that can be read on microfilm viewers. Each COM device contains an image-to-film recorder and a duplicator for making multiple copies of a microfiche.

In the COM process (see Figure 7–6), the images (output) to be miniaturized are prepared, as if to be printed, on a computer system. This output is then sent to the COM device. Here the images are miniaturized for microform viewers.

In the miniaturization process, images are displayed on a small high-resolution video display. A camera exposes a small segment of the microfilm for each display, thereby creating a grid pattern of images, or frames. The microfilm is then developed and cut into 4- by 6-inch sheets of microfiche, each containing up to 270 frames. The duplicator section makes multiple copies of the microfiche. Each sheet of microfiche is titled and indexed so that the appropriate frame or "page" can be retrieved quickly on a viewer.

COM is an alternative to an on-line computer-based system when up-to-the-minute information is not critical. COM is also used extensively instead of hard copy for archival storage (e.g., old income tax records).

## Voice Response Units

There are two types of **voice response units:** one uses a *recording* of a human voice and other sounds, and the other uses a *speech synthesizer*. The first type of voice response unit selects output from user-recorded words, phrases, music, alarms, or anything that you might record on tape, just as a printer would select characters. Most of us have probably heard, "The number you have dialed has been changed to eight-six-one-four-zero-three-eight." The initial phrase and the numbers are "outputted" using a voice response unit.

Speech synthesizers convert raw data to electronically produced speech. Some micros have built-in speech synthesizers. Press a button and the speech synthesizer reads aloud in English whatever words appear on the screen. These devices combine sounds resembling the phonemes (basic sound units) that make up speech. A speech synthesizer is capable of producing at least 64 unique sounds. The existing technology produces synthesized speech with only limited vocal inflections and phrasing. Still, the number of applications is growing. In one application, an optical-character reader scans books to retrieve the raw data. The speech synthesizer then translates the printed matter into spoken words for blind persons.

Today, we must see and touch our workstations to interact with a computer, but in a few years, we'll be talking with computers as we move about our homes and offices.

An interior view of this reading machine shows an optical scanner reading a typewritten letter. The scanner's output is automatically converted to computer signals which in turn are converted to full-word English speech using a speech synthesizer.
(Kurzweil Computer Products)

## Plotters

A **pen plotter** is a device that converts computer-generated graphs, charts, and line drawings to high-precision hard-copy output. There are two basic types of pen plotters: the *drum plotter* and the *flatbed plotter*. Both types have one or more pens that move over the paper to produce the image. Several pens are required to vary the width and color of the lines. Pens are selected and manipulated under computer control. On the drum plotter, the pens and the drum move concurrently in different axes to produce the image. On the flatbed plotter, the pen moves in both axes while the paper remains stationary.

**Electrostatic plotter/printers** produce a "quick and dirty" hard copy of graphic images for plot previewing. The final plot is completed on the high-precision drum or flatbed plotter.

## 7-5   DATA STORAGE DEVICES AND MEDIA

### Secondary Storage: Permanent Data Storage

Within a computer system, programs and data are stored in *primary storage* and in *secondary storage* (see Figure 7–7). Programs and data are stored *permanently* for periodic retrieval in **secondary storage,** also called **auxiliary storage.** Programs and data are retrieved from secondary storage and stored *temporarily* in high-speed primary storage for processing. If an employee's address is updated during process-

A research economist uses this eight-pen flatbed plotter to draw a map of the United States that is divided into economic regions.
(Houston Instrument)

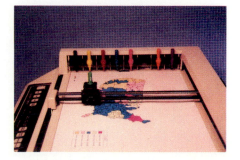

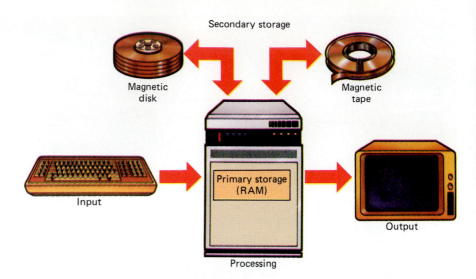

Secondary storage

Magnetic disk

Magnetic tape

Input

Primary storage (RAM)

Output

Processing

**FIGURE 7–7**
**Primary and Secondary Storage**
Programs and data are stored permanently in secondary storage and temporarily in primary storage.

ing, the personnel master file on secondary storage is updated to reflect the change.

The various types of **magnetic disk drives** and their respective storage media are the state of the art for on-line storage of programs and data. **Magnetic tape drives** complement magnetic disk storage by providing inexpensive backup capability and off-line storage. In this section we focus on the terminology, principles, operation, and trade-offs of these secondary storage devices. We also discuss the potential and applications of the emerging **optical laser disk** technology.

An important consideration in both the design of an information system and the purchase of a computer system is the way that data are accessed. Magnetic tape is for **sequential access** only. Magnetic disks have **random-** or **direct-access** capabilities as well as sequential access capabilities. You are quite familiar with these concepts, but you may not realize it. Magnetic tape is operationally the same as the one in home and car tape decks. The magnetic disk can be compared to the phonograph record. When playing music on a cassette tape you have to wind the tape forward to search for the song you want. With a phonograph record, all you would have to do is move the needle "directly" to the track containing the desired song. This simple analogy demonstrates the two fundamental methods of storing and accessing data—*sequential* and *random*. Both methods are discussed in detail in the pages that follow.

## Magnetic Disks

Hardware and Storage Media.    Magnetic disk drives are secondary storage devices that provide a computer system with **random** *and* **sequential processing** capabilities. In random processing, the desired programs and data are accessed *directly* from the storage medium. In sequential processing, the computer systems must search through the storage medium to find the desired programs or data.

The rigid 3½ inch microdisks can fit in a shirt pocket.
(Courtesy of Apple Computer, Inc.)

Several companies distribute their annual report with a supplemental software diskette. The software on the diskette provides stockholders the opportunity to interactively view financial data that are displayed in a variety of graphic formats. (Intelligent Systems Corporation)

Because of its random and sequential processing capabilities, magnetic disk storage is the overwhelming choice of both micro and mainframe users. A variety of magnetic disk drives (the hardware device) and magnetic disks (the media) are manufactured for different business requirements. The different types of *interchangeable* magnetic disks, in order of increasing storage capacity, are the $3\frac{1}{2}$-inch **microdisk,** the $5\frac{1}{4}$-inch **diskette,** the 8-inch diskette, the **disk cartridge,** and the **disk pack.** In contrast to the flexible diskettes, or "floppies," the microdisk, disk cartridge, and disk pack are hard or rigid disks.

Not all disk storage media are interchangeable. In fact, the trend is to permanently installed or *fixed* disks. All fixed disks are rigid. Today, because integrated software and data bases require all data and programs to be on-line at all times, the trend is to fixed disks, away from interchangeable disks.

**Random Processing.**   Magnetic disks are used for information systems where the data must be accessed directly or where the data are on-line. An airline reservation system provides a good example of this need. Direct-access capability is required to retrieve the record for any flight at any time from any reservations office. The data must be current, or flights may be overbooked or underbooked.

File and data base organization for random processing, also called **direct processing,** and sequential processing are discussed in detail in Chapter 11, "Data Organization and File Processing."

**Principles of Operation.**   The manner in which data are stored is similar for interchangeable and fixed hard disks. First we focus on hard disks, then discuss how floppy disks differ from hard disks.

*Cylinder Disk Organization*.   The hard-disk storage medium for a single drive may consist of one or a stack of several metal platters, each with a thin film coating of cobalt or iron oxide. The thin film coating on the disk can be electronically magnetized by the *read/write* head

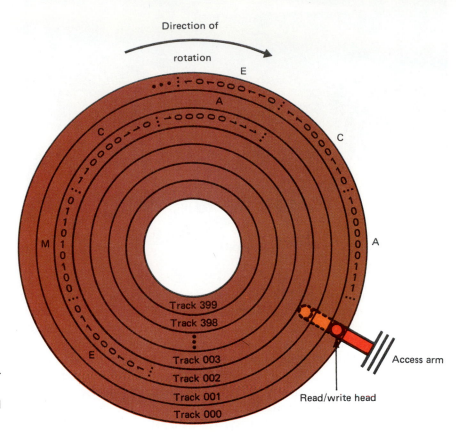

Direction of rotation

**FIGURE 7–8**
**Top View of a Magnetic Disk with Cylinder Organization**
Data are read or written serially in tracks. In the figure, the read/write head is first positioned over cylinder 000, then moved to cylinder 002 to access the record for the ACME company.

Track 399
Track 398
Track 003
Track 002
Track 001
Track 000

Access arm

Read/write head

The trend in disk storage is toward permanently-installed storage media. The access arms for this fixed disk move the read/write heads to the appropriate track to retrieve the data.
(International Memories, Inc.)

to represent the absence or presence of a bit (0 or 1). Data are recorded **serially** in concentric circles called *tracks* by magnetizing the surface to represent bit configurations (see Figure 7–8).

A rigid disk spins continuously at a high speed, typically 3600 revolutions per minute. Unlike rigid disks, which are constantly spinning, the floppy is set in motion only when a command is issued to read or write to disk. The rotational movement of the disk passes all data under/over a read/write head, thereby making all data available for access on each revolution of the disk.

Disk drives contain a rigid disk with 1 to 20 metal platters. To illustrate, we will use 11 platters, a common number. Data are stored on all *recording surfaces* except for those surfaces on the top and bottom of the stack. A disk with 11 platters has 20 recording surfaces on which data can be stored. A disk drive will have at least one read/write head for each recording surface. The heads are mounted on **access arms** that move in tandem and literally float on a cushion of air over the spinning recording surfaces.

To read or write a record, the access arms are moved under program control to the appropriate *cylinder*. Collectively, the cylinder references all *tracks* of the same number. For example, each recording surface has a track numbered 002 and the disk has a cylinder numbered 002. If the record to be accessed is on recording surface 03, track 002, the access arm and the read/write heads for all 20 recording surfaces are moved to cylinder 002.

In Figure 7–8, the access arm is positioned over track 000 (cylinder 000). In this position, the ACE Company record or any other record on cylinder 000 can be accessed without further movement of the access arm. If the ACME Company record is to be read, the access arm must be positioned over track 002 (cylinder 002) until the ACME record passes under the read/write head.

Fortunately, the software automatically monitors the location or **address** of our files and programs on disk storage. We need only enter employee's name to retrieve his or her record. The computer system locates the record and loads it to primary storage for processing. Although the addressing schemes vary considerably between disks, the address will normally reference the *cylinder*, the *recording surface*, and the *relative position* of a record on a track (e.g., the fourth record).

*Access Time*. The **access time** is the interval of time between the instant when a computer makes a request for a transfer of data from a secondary storage device and the instant when this operation is completed. The access of data from secondary storage depends on mechanical apparatus.

The *seek time*, which comprises the greatest amount of the total access time, is the time it takes the mechanical access arm to move to the desired cylinder. The *rotational delay time* is the time it takes for the appropriate record to be positioned under the read/write head. On the average, this would be half the time it takes for one revolution of the disk, or about 8 milliseconds at 3600 rpm. The *transmission time*, or the time that it takes to transmit the data to primary storage, is negligible. The average access time for most hard-disk drives is less than 20 milliseconds—still very slow compared with the microsecond-to-nanosecond processing speeds of computers.

*Sector Disk Organization*. Floppy disks and some rigid disks use **sector organization** to store and retrieve data. Sector organization is similar to the cylinder-type organization, except that each recording surface is divided into sectors, from 8 to 16 (see Figure 7–9). Each sector is assigned a unique number; therefore, the *sector number* and *track number* are all that is needed to comprise an address.

Disk summary. Disks come in a wide variety of shapes and storage capacities. The type used would depend on the volume of data that you have and the frequency with which those data are accessed. All types of disks are available for both micros and mainframes; however, most micros use microdisks, floppies, or small fixed disks called *Winchester disks*.

Magnetic disks range in storage capacity from low-capacity floppy disks that can store about 320,000 characters to very high-density rigid disks that can store over 30 million characters on 1 square inch of recording surface. That's the equivalent of the text of this and 20 other books on a space the size of a postage stamp!

| MEMORY BITS |
| --- |
| **DISK ACCESS TIME =** |
| ■ Seek time + |
| ■ Rotational delay time + |
| ■ Transmission time |

Interchangeable magnetic disk packs sit atop rows of disk drives in one of NASA's computer centers. Each disk pack has 11 disks with 20 recording surfaces. (NASA)

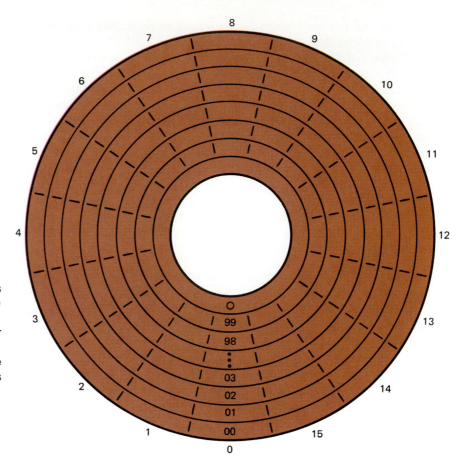

**FIGURE 7–9**
**Top View of a Magnetic Disk with Sector Organization**
Photoelectric cells sense light as it passes through the index hole in sector 0. This feedback enables the computer to monitor which sector is over the read/ write head at any given time. The number of sectors that a disk has varies from 1 to 32, depending on the computer system. As in cylinder organization, data are read or written serially in tracks, within a given sector.

The traditional $10\frac{1}{2}$ inch tape reel is contrasted with the high-density tape cartridge. The much smaller cartridge can store 200 million characters, about 20% more than the reel.
(Courtesy of International Business Machines Corporation)

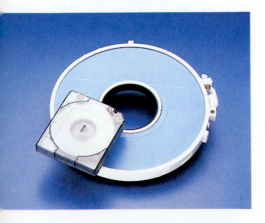

## Magnetic Tape

Magnetic tape storage is used primarily as a backup medium for magnetic disk. On occasion, a magnetic tape may be used for an application that involves only *sequential processing*. A **reel** or **cassette** tape can be conveniently mounted to a tape drive for processing, then removed for off-line storage. A cassette is also called a **cartridge.** For backup, a tape is taken from off-line storage, mounted to a tape drive, and the contents of a disk file are "dumped" from the disk to the tape. The tape is removed and placed in off-line storage as a backup to the operational disk master file. Details of backup procedures are discussed and illustrated in Chapter 10, "Data Organization and File Processing."

Hardware and Storage Media.    The device on which a reel ($\frac{1}{2}$-inch width) or cassette ($\frac{1}{4}$-inch width) of magnetic tape (the storage medium) is mounted and processed is known as a tape drive. The mechanical operation of a magnetic tape drive is similar to that of a reel-to-reel or cassette audio tape deck. A thin Mylar tape passes under a **read/ write head** and the data are either (1) read and transmitted to primary storage, or (2) transmitted from primary storage and written to the tape.

A tape drive is rated by the **density** at which the data can be stored on a magnetic tape as well as by the speed of the tape as it passes under the read/write head. Combined, these determine the **transmission rate,** or the number of characters per second that can be transmitted to primary storage. Tape density is measured in **bytes per inch (bpi)** or the number of bytes (characters) that can be stored per linear inch of tape. Tape density varies from 800 to 20,000 bpi. A 6250-bpi tape, a common density, traveling under the read/write head at 300 inches per second is capable of a transmission rate of 1,875,000 characters per second.

Magnetic tape reels and cassettes come in a variety of lengths, the most common being 2400 feet. The capacity of a tape is equal to the tape density (bpi) times the length of the tape (in inches). A 6250-bpi, 2400-foot (28,800-inch) tape has a capacity of approximately 180 megabytes (million bytes).

**Principles of Operation.**   Because of the physical nature of magnetic tapes, files must be processed sequentially from beginning to end for each computer run. On any given computer run, a *single* tape is either input or output, not both. One tape, however, can be just an input tape and another just an output tape. Sequential processing with magnetic tape is discussed in detail in Chapter 10, "Data Organization and File Processing."

The principles of tape data storage are illustrated in Figure 7–10. The thin film coating of the tape is electronically magnetized by the

Time-lapse photography catches this reel-to-reel tape drive in the middle of a "read" operation.
(Storage Technology Corporation)

**FIGURE 7–10**
**Cross Section of a Magnetic Tape**
This cross section of magnetic tape contains two records from a customer master file. Those tracks in which an "on-bit" appears most often (0, 1, 2, P, 3) are clustered in the center of the tape. Those tracks that are least likely to be magnetized to an on bit (4, 6, 7, 5) are placed toward the outside so that the data on a tape with damaged edges are less likely to be affected. The tape travels past the write head, then the read head. This enables the computer to read and check the data immediately after they are written to the tape.

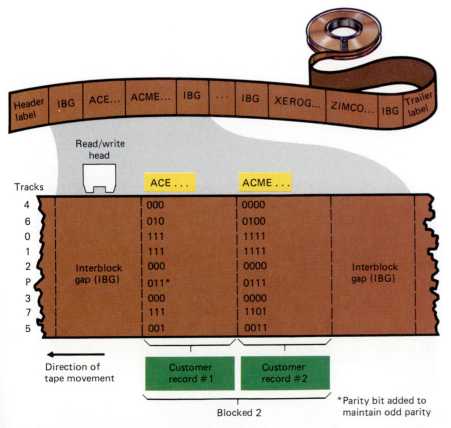

Photomicrography techniques are used to show how bits are recorded in parallel on a nine-track magnetic tape.
(AT&T Technologies)

read/write head to form bit configurations. In EBCDIC, eight bits (the EBCDIC code) plus the parity bit are needed to represent a character. Each of the nine bits is stored in one of nine *tracks* that run the length of the tape. In the nine-track tape of Figure 7–10, characters are represented by parallel EBCDIC bit configurations. This method of storing data in adjacent bit configurations is known as **parallel representation.** Compare this parallel representation with the serial representation of magnetic disks in Figure 7–8.

Figure 7–10 portrays a cross section of a magnetic tape that contains a *customer master file*. The data relating to each customer are grouped and stored in a *customer record*. The records are stored *alphabetically by customer name* (from ACE, ACME, . . . , to ZEROG, ZIMCO).

Records are usually grouped in blocks of two or more, separated by an **interblock gap (IBG).** The IBGs not only signal a stop to the reading process but also provide some margin for error in the rapid *start/stop* operation of the tape drive.

**Blocking** permits additional records to be transmitted with each "read" or "write." Each time the computer is instructed to read from a magnetic tape, all data between adjacent interblock gaps are transmitted to primary storage for processing. The next read transmits the next **block** of records to primary storage. When the computer is instructed to write to a tape, the data are transmitted from primary storage to the tape drive. Then a block of data and an IBG are written to the tape.

In Figure 7–10, the records have a blocking factor of 2 and are said to be "blocked two." Figure 7–11 shows how the same file would appear blocked three and unblocked. Notice how the tape blocked three contains more records per linear length of the tape.

To signal the beginning and end of a particular tape file, the computer adds a **header label** and a **trailer label,** respectively. The header label contains the name of the file and the date it was created. The

**FIGURE 7–11**
**Customer Records Blocked Three (top) and Unblocked (bottom)**

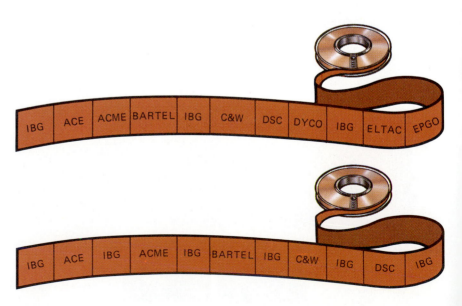

An alternative to disk and tape storage is the mass storage device. Mass storage devices are used when on-line access is required for very large data bases. A half trillion characters of data can be stored in this mass storage device. Inside, data cartridges are retrieved from honeycomb-like storage bins and loaded to the read/write station for processing.
(Courtesy of International Business Machines Corporation)

trailer label is written at the end of the data file and contains the number of records in the file (see Figure 7–10).

| MEMORY BITS | | |
|---|---|---|
| **CHARACTERISTICS OF MAGNETIC TAPE AND DISK** | | |
| | **Tape** | **Disk** |
| *Type access* | Sequential | Direct (random) or sequential |
| *Data representation* | Parallel | Serial |
| *Storage scheme* | IBG separation | Cylinder, sector |

## Optical Laser Disks: From Megabytes to Gigabytes

Some industry analysts have predicted that **optical laser disk** technology, now in its infant stage of development, may eventually make magnetic disk and tape storage obsolete. With this technology, the read/write head of magnetic storage is replaced with two lasers. One laser beams light to the light-sensitive recording surface of the disk to write the data, and another laser reads the data. A light beam is easily deflected to the desired area of the optical disk, so an access arm is not needed.

The density of data stored on optical disks is 20 times that on magnetic disks. To put this into perspective, a single 12-inch optical disk can store up to 4 **gigabytes** (billion bytes) of data. That is the equivalent of the text for the entire *Encyclopaedia Britannica*! Moreover, optical disks are less sensitive to environmental fluctuations, store *images* as well as *digital* data, and cost less per megabyte of storage than magnetic disks.

By now you are probably off to purchase some optical laser disks—but perhaps you should reconsider. Most optical laser disks are *write once*. That is, once the data have been written to the medium, they

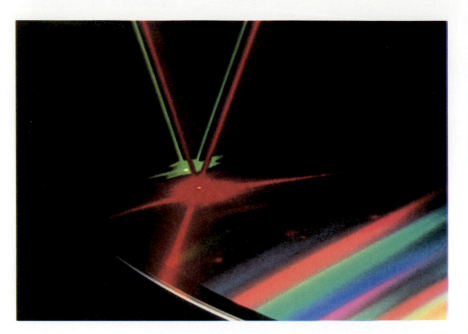

We may be approaching the technological limits of magnetic data storage. When this happens, sophisticated optics and lasers (light amplification by stimulated emission of radiation) may help to take up the slack. When this 14-inch platter is loaded to an optical laser disk drive, four billion characters (four gigabytes) of data are available for on-line access.
(Storage Technology Corporation)

Furniture retailers recall the images of interior design items from optical laser disk storage. The images are then displayed on high-resolution color monitors.
(Information Handling Services—An ITG Company)

can only be read, not updated or changed. A laser is used to score microscopic pits into a disk and to read them. However, erasable optical laser disks with read/write capabilities are beginning to be available commercially.

Optical disk storage is a feasible alternative to magnetic tape for archival storage. For example, a company might wish to keep a permanent record of all financial transactions during the last year. Another popular application of optical disks is in information systems that require the merging of text and images that do not change for a period of time. A good example is a "catalog." A customer can "thumb through the pages" of a retailer's electronic catalog on a VDT, or perhaps a PC, and view the item while reading about it. With a few keystrokes the customer can order the item as well.

As optical laser disk technology matures to reliable, cost-effective read/write operation, it may eventually dominate secondary storage in the future as magnetic disk and tape do today.

## SUMMARY OUTLINE AND IMPORTANT TERMS

**7-1**  I/O DEVICES: OUR INTERFACE WITH THE COMPUTER.  A variety of **peripheral** input and output devices complement the computer system to provide the interface between us and the computer system.

**7-2**  WORKSTATIONS.  We interact with a computer system through a **workstation** or **terminal.** VDTs and micros are the most common workstations. The input mechanism is usually a keyboard, and the output is normally a display screen, called a monitor. Other input devices associated with workstations include the light pen, the joystick, the track ball, the digitizing tablet and pen, and the mouse.

The three attributes of monitors are size (diagonal dimension 5 to 25 inches), color (monochrome or color), and **resolution** (quality of output).

Workstations are quickly becoming companions to workers in most fields of endeavor.

**7–3**   DATA ENTRY: GETTING DATA INTO THE COMPUTER SYSTEM.   The trend in data entry is to minimize the number of transcription steps by entering data on-line, at the source. **Optical character recognition** eliminates the need for some manual data entry by encoding certain data in machine-readable format. **OCR scanners** recognize printed characters and certain coded symbols, such as **bar codes.** OCR scanners are used for original source data collection and with **turnaround documents. Magnetic ink character recognition** devices, which are used almost exclusively in banking, are similar to OCR in function but have increased speed and accuracy.

**Magnetic stripes** and **smart cards** provide input to card and badge readers. **Voice data entry** or **voice recognition devices** can be used to enter limited kinds and quantities of data. **Vision input systems** are best suited for tasks that involve only a few images. **Portable data entry** devices are hand held and are normally used to collect data off-line.

**7–4**   OUTPUT DEVICES.   Output devices translate data stored in binary to a form that can be interpreted by the end user. Workstations are both input and output devices. Printers prepare hard-copy output at speeds of 40 characters per second to 40,000 lines per minute. **Serial printers** are both impact and nonimpact, where **line printers** are impact only and **page printers** are nonimpact only. The technologies used to produce the image vary widely from one printer to the next.

**Computer output microfilm/microfiche (COM)** devices prepare microfilm and microfiche as a space- and timesaving alternative to printed output. **Voice response units** provide recorded or synthesized voice output. **Pen plotters** and **electrostatic plotter/printers** convert stored data to hard-copy graphs, charts, and line drawings.

**7–5**   DATA STORAGE DEVICES AND MEDIA.   Data and programs are stored on **secondary** or **auxiliary** storage for permanent storage. The **magnetic disk drives** and **magnetic tape drives** are the state of the art for both on-line and off-line storage. **Optical laser disk** technology is emerging as an alternative to storage medium.

Data are stored sequentially on magnetic tape; they are stored randomly on magnetic disks. **Sequential access** requires the file to be searched record by record until the desired record is found. **Random access** enables the desired record to be retrieved directly from its storage location.

The different types of interchangeable magnetic disks are the **microdisk,** the **diskette,** the **disk cartridge,** and the **disk pack.** The trend is away from interchangeable disks to fixed disks.

Magnetic disk drives provide the computer system with direct-access and **random processing** capabilities. Data are stored serially on each recording surface by tracks. Each record that is stored on a disk is assigned an **address** that designates the physical location of the record. An **access arm,** with read/write heads for each recording surface, is moved to the appropriate track or cylinder to retrieve a record.

In **sector organization,** each disk recording surface is divided into sectors.

A thin Mylar tape is spun on a **reel** or encased in a **cassette** or **cartridge** to create a magnetic tape. This magnetic tape is loaded to a tape drive, where data are read or written as the tape is passed under a **read/write head.** The physical nature of the magnetic tape results in data being stored and accessed sequentially. Data are stored using **parallel representation,** and they are **blocked** to minimize the start/stop movement of the tape. The standard nine-track 2400-foot tape stores data at a density of 6250 **bpi.**

**Optical laser disk** storage, now in its infant stage of development, has the capability to store data at 20 times the density of magnetic disks.

## REVIEW EXERCISES

### Concepts

1. List devices, other than key-driven, that are used to input source data to a computer system.
2. Which types of printers print fully formed characters?
3. What is a turnaround document? Give two examples.
4. Identify all input and output methods employed by an automatic teller machine.
5. What is the relationship between a light pen and a cursor?
6. Give three example applications for bar codes.
7. What are alternative names for flexible disks? Auxiliary storage? Direct processing?
8. What is the purpose of the interblock gap?
9. How many megabytes does it take to make a gigabyte?
10. A program issues a "read" command for data to be retrieved from a magnetic tape. Describe the resulting movement of the data.
11. Using the initials of your name and EBCDIC, graphically contrast parallel and serial data representation.

12. A company's employee master file contains 120,000 employee records. Each record is 1800 bytes in length. How many 2400-foot, 6250-bpi magnetic tapes (interblock gap = 0.6 inch) will be required to store the file? Assume that records are blocked five. Next, assume that records are unblocked, and perform the same calculations.

13. A disk pack has 20 recording surfaces and 400 cylinders. If a track can store 10,000 bytes of data, how much data can be stored on eight such disk packs?

## Discussion

14. Department stores use hand-held wand scanners to interpret the bar codes imprinted on the price tags of the merchandise. Why don't they use slot scanners as supermarkets do?

15. What input/output capabilities are available at your college? At your place of employment?

16. Compare today's vision input systems with those portrayed in such films as *2001* and *2010*. Do you believe that we will have a comparable vision technology by the year 2001?

17. If increasing the blocking factor for a magnetic tape file improves tape utilization, why not eliminate all IBGs and put all the records in one big block? Explain.

18. A floppy disk does not move until a read or write command is issued. Once the command is issued, the floppy begins to spin, and it stops spinning after the command is executed. Why is a disk pack not set in motion in the same manner? Why is a floppy not made to spin continuously?

19. Every Friday night, a company makes backup copies of all master files and programs. Why is this necessary? The company has both tape and disk drives. What storage medium would you suggest for the backup? Why?

## SELF-TEST (by section)

7-1. (a) Input devices translate data to a form that can be interpreted by a computer. (T/F)

   (b) The primary function of I/O peripherals is to facilitate computer-to-computer data transmission. (T/F)

7-2. (a) The input device that is rolled over a desktop to move the cursor is called a joystick. (T/F)

   (b) The quality of output on a workstation's monitor is determined by its _____ .

7-3. (a) Optical character recognition is a means of original source data collection. (T/F)

   (b) The _____ card contains a tiny microprocessor.

**(c)** Bar codes represent alphanumeric data by varying the width and combination of adjacent vertical lines. (T/F)

**7–4.** **(a)** Ink-jet printers are classified as impact printers. (T/F)

**(b)** Dot-matrix printer technology is available in serial and line printers. (T/F)

**7–5.** **(a)** Data are retrieved from temporary auxiliary storage and stored permanently in main memory. (T/F)

**(b)** Magnetic disks have both _____ and _____ access capabilities.

**(c)** In a disk drive, the read/write heads are mounted on an access arm. (T/F)

**(d)** The method of storing data on tape in adjacent bit configurations is known as _____ .

**(e)** Rotating data storage devices will be obsolete by 1990. (T/F)

*Self-Test answers.*  7–1 (a), T; (b), F; 7–2 (a), F; (b), resolution; 7–3 (a), T; (b), smart; (c), T; 7–4 (a), F; (b), T; 7–5 (a), F; (b), direct (or random), sequential; (c), T; (d) parallel representation; (e), F.

# Zimco Enterprises

## INFORMATION SYSTEMS AT ZIMCO: FINANCE AND ACCOUNTING

### FACS: FINANCE AND ACCOUNTING CONTROL SYSTEM

Zeke Zimmers, Jr., then the president of Zimco Enterprises, walked into the accounting office just after a visibly tired group of accountants had completed the year-end closing for 1933. He announced very bluntly: "I've hired an automation expert and I want all of you to cooperate with him. Let's bring our accounting procedures into the twentieth century. We should not have to work night and day for months just to close our books each year. Technology has provided us with machines to help us and we should be using them!"

It was apparent to Zeke that accounting was the obvious place to begin automating Zimco's administrative activities. Automation expenses were easy to justify with accounting applications. The tasks were repetitive, they involved numerous calculations, and they required the periodic storage and retrieval of data.

Zimco's administrative activities have continued to evolve with the technology. Fifty-plus years later, the Finance and Accounting Division has a sophisticated system they proudly call the Finance and Accounting Control System, or FACS. FACS, which was developed in-house by CIS in close cooperation with the Finance and Accounting Division, is the envy of a good many businesses in the Dallas–Ft. Worth area. Monroe Green, the VP of Finance and Accounting, is always willing to demonstrate "his" system to non-competitive companies.

The beauty of FACS is that it is one of four functional components of Zimco's integrated Management Information System (MIS). It is no coincidence that the four systems correspond to the four functional divisions at Zimco (see Figure Z3-3). Zimco's MIS is an on-line, interactive, menu-driven system that puts data processing and information gathering at the fingertips of end users. The functional components of Zimco's MIS are:

- *FACS*: Finance and Accounting Control System (Process 1 of MIS: Finance and Accounting)
- *PERES*: Personnel Resources System (Process 2 of MIS: Personnel)
- *PICS*: Production and Inventory Control System (Process 3 of MIS: Operations)
- *SAMIS*: Sales and Marketing Information System (Process 4 of MIS: Sales and Marketing)

All the MIS component systems share a common data base, thereby eliminating much of the data redundancy that plagues other nonintegrated companies. FACS, which is Process 1 (Finance and Accounting) of Zimco's MIS overview data flow diagram (see Figure Z3–3), is discussed in this case study. PERES, PICS, and SAMIS (processes 2, 3, and 4 of the Zimco MIS) are discussed in the Zimco case studies following Chapters 9, 10, and 11, respectively.

Zimco, like just about every other company, created acronyms for their system to make everyday conversation among workers a little more efficient. Conrad Innis, the VP of CIS, explained the need for acronyms very succinctly: "It's a whole lot easier to say 'picks' (for PICS) than it is to say 'Production and Inventory Control System'."

## THE FIVE SUBSYSTEMS OF FACS

During the early stages of the FACS development project, the project team spent a week mapping out the information and control flows that involve the Finance and Accounting Division. An overview result of that work is shown in Figure Z7-1. The systems analysts, accountants, and financial people on the team decided to divide the system into five logical subsystems (see Figure Z7-1). The subsystems are not necessarily aligned with particular departments because FACS is an integrated system that is designed to support the needs of the organization as a whole.

Notice that each of the four components of the Zimco MIS are numbered 1, 2, 3, and 4. The numbering scheme is used in data flow diagrams to identify subordinate processes. Since the Finance and Accounting process (FACS) is numbered "1," the first-level subordinate systems are identified as 1.1, 1.2, 1.3, and so on. The five subsystems are:

**1.1** Asset Management
**1.2** Receipt Control
**1.3** Disbursement Control
**1.4** Financial Planning
**1.5** Financial Reporting

Perhaps the best way to explain the operation of FACS is to focus on the interaction between these five subsystems and their interaction with the external (e.g., financial institutions) and internal (e.g., managers) entities (see Figure Z7-1). All subsystems interact frequently with the integrated data base, but some of these interactions are omitted in Figure Z7-1 so that the information flow between the subsystems is more visually apparent.

### Asset Management (1.1)

Just as data are input to and output from a computer system, money is input to and output from the Asset Management Subsystem (see Figure Z7-1). Monroe Green explains: "Money is the common denominator at Zimco and in the business world in general. The Asset Management Subsystem releases funds and takes in funds as needed. The funds, of course, are kept in various financial institutions. Zimco's accounting and financial people are responsible for ensuring that enough liquid funds are on hand to meet the ongoing operational needs of the company."

Funds received from the Receipt Control Subsystem (1.2), primarily payments from customers, are deposited with financial institutions. Funds are withdrawn and distributed to the Disbursement Control Subsystem (1.3) so that these funds can be used to meet the ongoing financial obligations of Zimco. Since the Asset Management Subsystem does most of the interaction with financial institutions, the periodic payments for bonds and loans are made through the Asset Management Subsystem rather than through the Disbursement Control Subsystem.

The Asset Management Subsystem periodically generates asset utilization reports as input to the Financial Planning Subsystem (1.4). In turn, the Financial Planning Subsystem feeds the Asset Management Subsystem with asset demand forecasts. Based on the demand forecasts, the Asset Management Subsystem does the processing required to ensure that liquid funds are made available to meet short- and long-term obligations.

Data generated by the Asset Management Subsystem become part of the integrated data base and are used by the Financial Reporting Subsystem (1.5) to produce Zimco's financial statements.

### Receipt Control (1.2)

The primary function of the Receipt Control Subsystem (see Figure Z7-1) is the *accounts receivable* application. In a nutshell the Sales and Marketing Division is responsible for getting the order; the Operations Division is responsible for the manufacture and delivery of the order; and the Finance and Accounting Division is responsible for collecting for the order. The accounts receivable application keeps track of money owed the company on charges for products sold (Stibs, Teglers, Qwerts, and Farkles) or services rendered (primarily the maintenance of products). When a Zimco customer purchases goods or services, the customer record in the integrated data base is updated to reflect the charge.

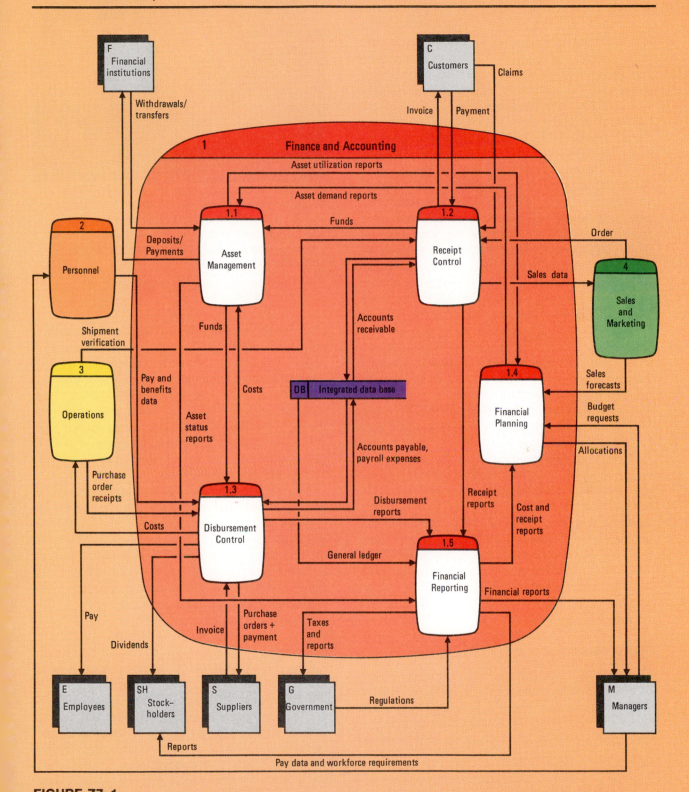

**FIGURE Z7–1**
**Zimco's Finance and Accounting Control System (FACS)**
This data flow diagram is the explosion of the Finance and Accounting (1) process
of the MIS overview data flow diagram of Figure Z3–3.

As soon as an order is verified within the Sales and Marketing Information Systems (SAMIS), order information is automatically recorded on the customer record and an invoice, which reflects the balance due, is sent to the customer. Upon receipt of payment, the amount due is decreased by the amount of the payment in the data base.

Management relies on the Receipt Control Subsystem (accounts receivable) to identify overdue accounts. Reports are generated that "age" accounts to identify those customers whose accounts are overdue by more than 30 days, 60 days, or 90 days. As Monroe Green puts it: "Those accounts that are 30 days overdue, we call and remind; those that are 60 days overdue, we notify that shipment of orders has been suspended; those that are 90 days overdue go on our deadbeat list and we take legal action."

Monroe Green states proudly: "Our accounts receivable system is strictly top drawer. We still do traditional data processing activities, such as aging of accounts and producing invoices, but we have tremendous flexibility in what we can do. For example, we can provide customers with a variety of discounts to encourage their timely payment. We also have access to the information we need to do our jobs right. Customer credit histories are on-line and the data are up-to-the-minute. We can provide sales analysis by multiple criteria for our sales and marketing managers. That is, they can request analysis by salesperson, territory, product, and so on. Because FACS is integrated, each accounts receivable transaction becomes an automatic entry in the *general ledger* portion of the integrated data base. We couldn't ask for a better system."

## Disbursement Control (1.3)

The Disbursement Control Subsystem (see Figure Z7-1) ensures that all external creditor entities (except financial institutions) and employees are paid promptly. The primary applications in this subsystem are *accounts payable* and *payroll*.

Accounts Payable. "Zimco purchases everything from paper clips to 18-wheelers on credit," says Monroe Green. "Our accounts payable ap-

People in the accounts payable department tap directly into Zimco's integrated data base to obtain the information they need to be able to respond to supplier inquiries regarding payment and receipt of orders. (Honeywell, Inc.)

plication is the other side of our accounts receivable application. That is, an invoice from a supplier company's accounts receivable system becomes input to our accounts payable application. When we receive an invoice, the accounts payable application generates a check and adjusts the balance owed." Monroe added: "Of course, our accounts payable application is carefully designed to take advantage of available discounts for prompt payment."

Purchase orders are generated in every department, but the Operations Division generates most of them. The purchase order is a flag to the Disbursement Control Subsystem to expect an invoice from a supplier. When the invoice is received from the supplier and receipt of the item is verified by the ordering department on the integrated data base, payment is then authorized and the supplier is sent a check.

Like accounts receivable transactions, accounts payable transactions are automatically fed to the general ledger application. The features of Zimco's accounts payable application are numerous. It has an audit program to check entries. Invoices can be selected interactively by date or vendor. For any given invoice the system computes the optimal discount strategy. The invoice aging report, purchase journal, and a variety of other timely reports help managers to control purchased inventory and overhead expenses.

**Payroll.** The payroll application at Zimco is a combined effort between the Personnel Division and the Finance and Accounting Division. The Personnel Division is responsible for the benefits program and for wage and salary administration. Prior to each pay period, the people in the Personnel Division verify pay and benefits data on the integrated data base. The mechanics of producing and distributing the payroll checks are handled by the Disbursement Control Subsystem in the Finance and Accounting Division. The two primary outputs of the payroll application are the payroll check and stub, which are distributed to the employees, and the payroll register, which is a summary report of payroll transactions. These transactions, of course, are logged automatically on the general ledger portion of the integrated data base.

The payroll application handles all calculations associated with gross pay, taxes, and user-defined deductions. The payroll application is capable of generating a variety of management reports, such as the federal tax summary report and the retirement contribution summary report.

Any disbursement, be it pay, dividends, or payment for goods or services, is noted in the appropriate record(s) in the integrated data base. Summary and detailed disbursement reports are input to the Financial Reporting Subsystem (1.5).

## Financial Planning (1.4)

The Financial Planning Subsystem (see Figure Z7-1) operates in support of the budgeting process. Monroe Green, himself an active participant in the budgeting process, says that "each year our financial planners, in cooperation with management, must decide how the company's revenues can be allocated to over 400 accounts."

Zimco's accounting is done on a calendar-year basis, so the budgeting process begins during the late summer and, if all goes well, takes effect at the beginning of the new year. During a prescribed period, managers enter their budget requests, with line-item detail, into the Financial Planning Subsystem from their workstations. Concurrent with the preparation of budget requests, the Sales and Marketing Division prepares a forecast of sales for the coming year.

The Financial Planning Subsystem helps translate these sales into projected revenues.

Managers often spend months preparing their departmental budgets for the coming year. To aid in this task, the *budget* application provides each manager with historical information on past line-item expenditures (e.g., salaries, office equipment, office supplies, and so on). Based on this information and projected budget requirements, each manager can make budget requests for the next fiscal year.

Financial planners and top management match requests for funds against projected revenues. "At Zimco," says Monroe Green, "managers invariably ask for more than they need, knowing full well that they will never get what they request." Eventually, a workable budget is established.

Managers at Zimco frequently use the Financial Planning Subsystem to monitor expenditures in their departments. For example, Figure Z7-2 illustrates the display that was generated when the manager of the Purchasing Department inquired about the status of her department's travel budget. She entered only the coded travel account number (30300) to obtain the budget status of her travel account. Other managers routinely make similar inquires. Inordinate budget variances, such as the one shown in Figure Z7-2, prompt managers to take immediate action to get certain budget items under control.

## Financial Reporting (1.5)

The Financial Reporting Subsystem (see Figure Z7-1) includes the *general ledger* application—the glue that integrates all the other accounting applications. In the not-too-distant past, accountants manually posted debits and credits for each account in a ledger book, thus the name "general ledger" for today's electronic system. Other "account" applications (accounts receivable, accounts payable, payroll, and so on) are sources of financial transactions and feed data to the general ledger application.

The general ledger application records every monetary transaction that occurs within Zimco. Payment of a bill, an interdepartmental transfer of funds, receipt of payment for an order, a contri-

```
                    BUDGET STATUS INQUIRY

        Enter account number:  30300
                 Purchasing Department: travel
                 Date: April 1

        Total budget amount              $12,000.00
        Prorated budget amount to date     3,000.00
        Actual expenses to date            5,972.41

        Amount over prorated budget       $2,972.41
```

**FIGURE Z7–2**
**Management Budget Inquiry**
The Financial Planning Subsystem of FACS enables Zimco managers to make
on-line budget inquiries regarding budgets.

bution to an employee's retirement fund—all are examples of monetary transactions. The general ledger system keeps track of these transactions and provides the input necessary to produce Zimco's financial statement.

For the purposes of accounting, Zimco is divided up into 14 general accounting categories, such as current assets, current liabilities, cost of goods sold, and so on. These, in turn, are subdivided into as many accounts as are needed to accurately reflect monetary flow within Zimco. Monetary transactions are recorded as a debit or a credit to a particular account. The *balance sheet*, one of two major components of Zimco's financial statement, reflects a summary of these accounts at the end of a particular day. The balance sheet is so named because the company's assets are equated with its liabilities. Since all monetary transactions are recorded on-line as they occur via FACS, managers can request a display of the balance sheet on any day of the year, not just at the end of each quarter.

The other major component of the financial statement is the *profit and loss statement*. Often called the "income statement," the profit and loss statement reflects how much Zimco makes or loses during a given period, usually a quarter or a year (see Figure Z5-2 for an example of an income statement).

The financial planners at Zimco routinely tap into the Financial Reporting Subsystem to ask "what if" questions. For example, they use decision support software to ask: "What if gross sales are increased by 10 percent and the cost of goods sold is decreased by 5 percent, how would net earnings be affected?" Managers also find prior-year comparisons helpful.

The Securities and Exchange Commission (SEC) requires publicly held companies such as Zimco to file quarterly financial statements. Every three months Zimco and thousands of other companies transmit these reports to the SEC electronically via data communications.

## MAINTAINING FACS

All FACS subsystems are on-line 24 hours a day. Any authorized Zimco employee can tap into the interactive, menu-driven FACS system to make inquiries or to add, delete, or revise data. The Finance and Accounting Division is responsible for maintaining that portion of the integrated data base that deals with monetary accounting, even though much of the input comes from the other divisions. On occasion, this causes some problems. Monroe Green admits that "sometimes the Personnel Division has to be prodded to get the pay and benefits data in on time. However, you can always depend on the sales reps in the field to get their expense reports in on time."

## DISCUSSION QUESTIONS

1. Explain why the expense of automating accounting applications is easy to justify. Give examples.

2. Why did the FACS project team decide to design the system around five logical subsystems rather than along organizational lines?

3. Do acronyms, such as FACS and PERES, foster cyberphobia, or do they serve to simplify interaction between users and computer professionals? Explain.

4. Draw a data flow diagram explosion of the Receipt Control Subsystem (1.2) showing the primary information flows between appropri-ate processes, the customer entity, and the integrated data base. Label subordinate processes 1.2.1, 1.2.2, and so on.

5. Explain the relationship between Zimco's accounts payable application and a supplier's accounts receivables application.

6. Draw a data flow diagram explosion of the Financial Reporting Subsystem (1.5) showing the primary information flows between appropriate processes, the managers and government entities, and the integrated data base. Label subordinate processes 1.5.1, 1.5.2, and so on.

7. Getting out the payroll at Zimco is a joint effort between the Personnel Division and the Finance and Accounting Division. Could the payroll application be made more efficient by consolidating it in one division or the other? Explain.

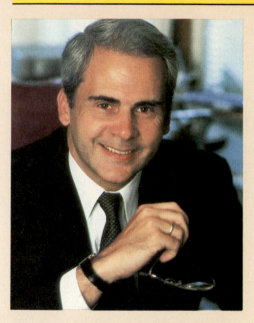

*The management and dissemination of operational, financial, and customer information has become the strategic imperative in almost every large organization. Federal Express' early recognition of this fact, and our extensive application of computer and telecommunications technologies to lower costs and improve performance, have been key elements in our substantial growth.*

Frederick W. Smith
Chairman, President
and Chief Executive Officer
Federal Express Corporation

# Data Communications

## CHAPTER 8

### STUDENT LEARNING OBJECTIVES

■ To demonstrate an understanding of data communications terminology.

■ To detail the function and operation of data communications hardware.

■ To describe the alternatives and sources for data transmission services.

■ To illustrate the various types of computer networks.

### FOCUS OF ZIMCO CASE STUDY

■ Zimco's computer network.

This stock broker uses the data communications capabilities of a telephone in conjunction with his portable workstation to keep in touch with office activities and retrieve critical information wherever he travels.
(Copyright 1984 GTE Telenet Communications Corporation)

In this on-line, transaction-oriented dispatch system, service coordinators take calls from customers with malfunctioning computers and assign service engineers to handle the problems. Sevice engineers carry hand-held terminals that enable them to transmit service status and parts orders directly to the system.
(Courtesy of International Business Machines Corporation)

## 8–1 DATA COMMUNICATIONS: FROM ONE ROOM TO THE WORLD

For many years we have depended on telephone conversations and the postal service to communicate data and information from one location to another. Now, thousands of memos and charts can be sent to locations around the world in a matter of seconds. This is possible because of **data communications** capabilities. Data communications is, very simply, the collection and distribution of "electronic" data from and to remote facilities. Data are transmitted from computers to workstations and other computers over land, in the air, and under the sea. Telephone lines, satellites, and coaxial cable on the ocean floor are a few of the many ways that data are transmitted.

Our society is becoming more dependent on data communications capabilities. Government, business, and individuals have an increased need to communicate with one another. We might even say that our society is shrinking (figuratively, of course), for between data communications and computer technology, it is just as easy to communicate with someone in another state as it is to communicate with someone in the next building.

Through the 1960s, a company's computing hardware was located in a single room, called the machine room. Since that time, microcomputers, workstations, and data communications have made it possible to move hardware and information systems "closer to the source" and to the people who use them. Before long, workstations will be as much a part of our work environment as desks and telephones are now.

Several other terms describe the general area of data communications. **Telecommunications** encompasses not only data communications, but any type of remote communication, such as the transmission of a television signal. **Teleprocessing (TP)** is the combination of *tele*communications and data *processing* and is often used interchangeably with the term "data communications." The integration of computer systems, workstations, and communications links is referred to as a **computer network**.

## 8–2 WHY "GO ON-LINE"?

Easily accessible data communication facilities and the widespread availability of workstations just about signal the end of the batch processing era. In batch processing, transactions are periodically batched for processing, and reports are generated and distributed daily or weekly. Today, people want information *now*, and they want it to be *current*. These demands cannot be met with batch-oriented information systems.

Organizations use communications-based information systems—that is, they "go on-line"—to get an *immediate response* to an inquiry from an *up-to-the-minute data base*. For example, in a department store, a sale is recorded immediately on a POS terminal. With an up-to-the-minute data base, an illegal charge card or a customer's exceeding the charge limit can be detected before the sale is completed. In a batch system, an illegal charge card could be used all day before being detected.

*Increased capability* and *flexibility* are important features of on-line systems. Business executives have the corporate data base at their fingertips. Before leaving home in the morning, a company president can use a PC to review a list of slow-selling products, then inform all vice-presidents, via electronic mail, of a meeting to address these problem areas.

## 8–3  DATA COMMUNICATIONS HARDWARE

Data communications hardware is used to transmit data in a computer network between workstations and computers and between computers. This hardware includes modems, down-line processors, front-end processors, and data PBXs. The integration of these devices (except the data PBX) with workstations and computer systems is illustrated in Figure 8–1 and discussed below.

**FIGURE 8–1**
**Hardware Components in Data Communications**
Devices that handle the movement of data in a computer network are the modem, down-line processor, front-end processor, and host processor.

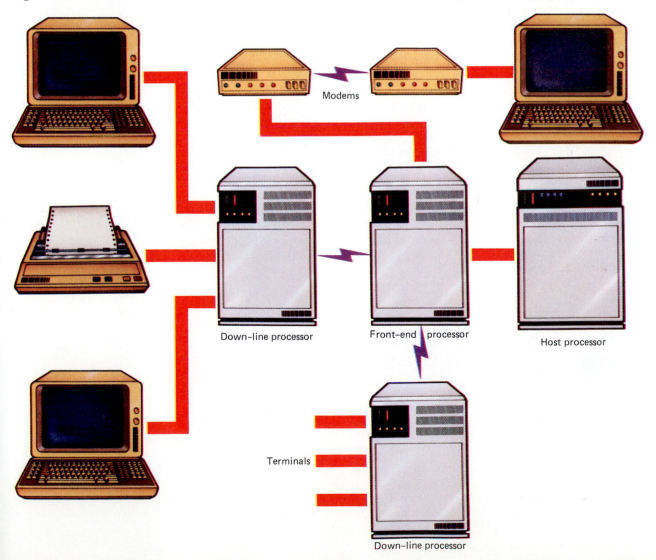

Modems

Down-line processor      Front–end processor      Host processor

Terminals

Down-line processor

If every desk is expected to have a telephone, a personal computer, and a modem, why not combine them into a single unit? Some manufacturers have: This voice/data workstation permits communication with other people and other computers.
(AT&T Information Systems)

## FIGURE 8–2
**The Modulation/Demodulation Process**
Electrical digital signals are modulated to analog signals for transmission over telephone lines, then demodulated for processing at the destination.

## The Modem

Telephone lines were designed for voice communication, not data communication. The **modem** (*mo*dulator/*dem*odulator) converts computer-to-workstation electrical *digital* signals to *analog* signals so that the data can be transmitted over telephone lines (see Figure 8–2). The digital electrical signals are "modulated" to make sounds similar to those you hear on a touch-tone telephone. Upon reaching their destination, the analog signals are "demodulated" by another modem to computer-compatible electrical signals for processing. The process is done in reverse for workstation-to-computer communication.

On most workstations, the modem is an optional device that is contained on a circuit board and simply plugged into an empty slot in the workstation. To make the connection with a telephone line, you simply plug the telephone line into the modem, just as you would if connecting a telephone. Modems have varying degrees of "intelligence." For instance, some modems can automatically dial-up the computer (*auto-dial*), then establish a link (*log on*), and even answer incoming calls from other computers (*auto-answer*).

For transmission media other than telephone lines, the modulation/demodulation process is not required. A modem is always required when you "dial-up" the computer on a telephone line. If you need a telephone hookup (for a voice conversation) on the same line and do not want to hassle with disconnecting the phone with each use, you can purchase a modem with an **acoustical coupler.** To make the connection, you mount the telephone handset directly on the acoustical coupler. Some workstations have not only a built-in modem but a built-in telephone as well.

## The Down-Line Processor

The **down-line processor** is remote from the *host processor*. It collects data from a number of low-speed devices, such as workstations and serial printers. The down-line processor then transmits "concentrated" data over a *single* communications channel (see Figure 8–3).

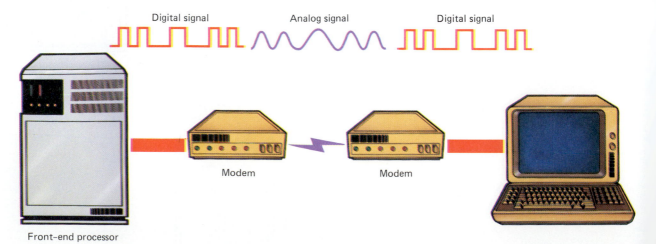

Digital signal          Analog signal          Digital signal

Front-end processor          Modem          Modem

This office is one of 27 regional customer support centers. Each workstation is connected to a concentrator (foreground) that is connected via a high-speed communications line to the company's headquarters office in Columbus, Ohio.
( (c) MICOM Systems, Inc., 1983)

## FIGURE 8–3
### "Concentrating" Data for Remote Transmission
The down-line processor "concentrates" the data from several low-speed devices for transmission over a single high-speed line. Data received from a front-end processor are interpreted by the down-line processor and routed to the appropriate device.

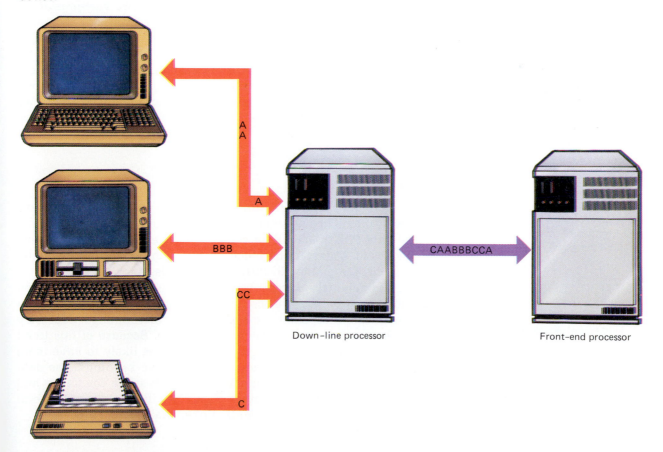

Down-line processor                                    Front-end processor

The down-line processor, also called a **concentrator** or **multiplexor,** is an economic necessity when several low-speed workstations are located at one remote site. One high-speed line connecting the down-line processor to the host is considerably less expensive than several low-speed lines connecting each workstation to the host. An airport airline reservations counter might have four workstations. Each workstation is connected to a down-line processor, which in turn is connected to a central host computer. An airport might have one or several down-line processors, depending on volume of passenger traffic.

## The Front-End Processor

The workstation or computer sending a **message** is the *source*. The workstation or computer receiving the message is the *destination*. The **front-end processor** (described briefly in Chapter 5) establishes the link between source and destination in a process called **handshaking.**

If you think of messages as mail to be delivered to various points in a computer network, the front-end processor is the post office. Each computer system and workstation is assigned an **address.** The front-end processor uses these addresses to route messages to their destination(s). The content of a message could be anything from a program instruction to an "electronic" memo. Figure 8–4 illustrates how a memo would be sent from the president of a company to two vice-presidents and the plant manager. It is not uncommon for a front-end processor to control communications between a dozen down-line processors and 100 or more workstations.

The front-end processor relieves the host processor of communications-related tasks, such as message routing, parity checking, code translation, editing, and cryptography (the encryption/decryption of data). This processor "specialization" permits the host to operate more efficiently and to devote more of its resources to processing applications programs.

## The Data PBX

The old-time telephone PBX (private branch exchange) switchboard has given its name to a new generation of devices for **data PBX** switching. The data PBX is actually a computer that electronically connects computers and workstations much as telephone operators manually connected people on the old PBX switchboards.

There is definitely a trend to **distributed processing.** "Distributed processing" is a term that was coined to describe an information system that is made more responsive to end users by "distributing" processing capabilities closer to the people who use them. Because of this trend to distributed processing, a single organization is likely to have more than one mainframe computer and a bunch of workstations. The data PBX, serving as the hub of data activity, permits these computers and workstations to talk to one another. Figure 8–5 illustrates how several mainframe computer systems can be linked via a data PBX.

A data PBX connects computing devices for data communication in a manner similar to the way operators used to connect telephones for voice communication. With the data PBX, however, it's all automatic. (AT&T Technologies)

MEMORY BITS

**HARDWARE FOR DATA COMMUNICATIONS**
- Modem
- Down-line processor (concentrator or multiplexor)
- Front-end processor
- Data PBX

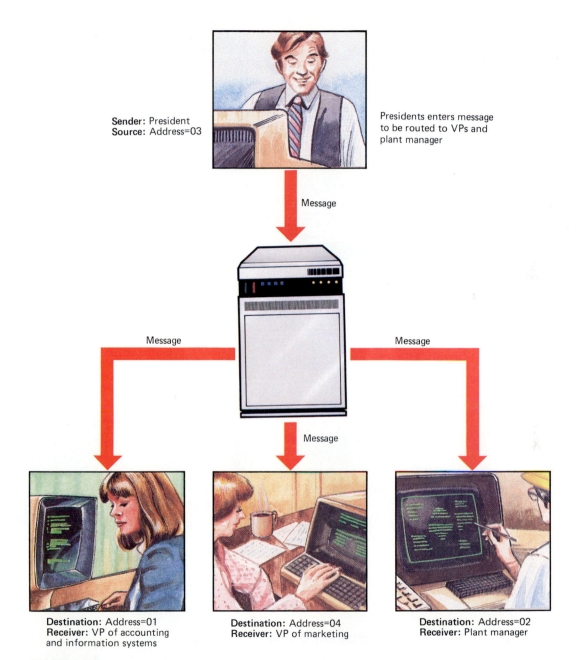

**Sender:** President
**Source:** Address=03

Presidents enters message
to be routed to VPs and
plant manager

Message

Message                                                          Message

Message

**Destination:** Address=01
**Receiver:** VP of accounting
and information systems

**Destination:** Address=04
**Receiver:** VP of marketing

**Destination:** Address=02
**Receiver:** Plant manager

**FIGURE 8–4**
**Message Routing**
In the illustration, the president sends a message to two VPs and the plant
manager.

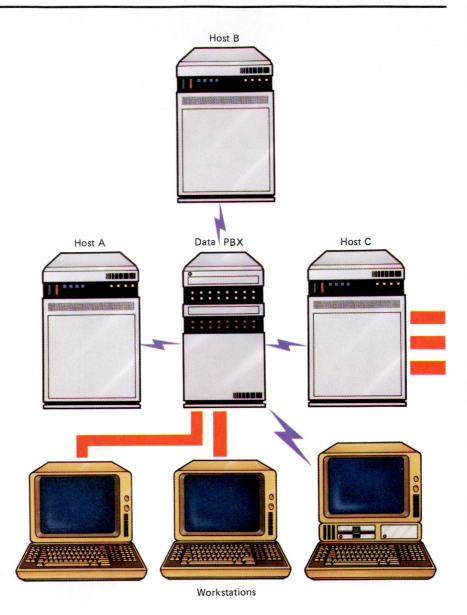

**FIGURE 8–5**
**Computers and Workstations Linked to a Data PBX**
Any two of the host computers or workstations can be linked together for data transmission by the data PBX.

Host B

Host A          Data PBX          Host C

Workstations

## 8–4   THE DATA COMMUNICATIONS CHANNEL: DATA HIGHWAYS

### Transmission Media

A **communications channel** is the facility by which data are transmitted between locations in a computer network. Data are transmitted as combinations of bits (0s and 1s). A channel's *capacity* is rated by the number of bits that can be transmitted per second. A regular telephone line can transmit up to 9600 bits per second (bps), or 9.6K bps (thousands of bits per second). Under normal circumstances, a 9.6K bps line would fill a video monitor in 1 or 2 seconds. Data rates of 1500K bps are available through common carriers, such as American

Telephone and Telegraph (AT&T). The channel, also called a **line** or a **data link,** may be comprised of one or a combination of the transmission media discussed below.

**Telephone Lines.**   The same transmission facilities that we use for telephone conversations can also be used to transmit data. This capability is provided by communications companies throughout the country and the world.

**Optical Fiber.**   Very thin transparent fibers have been developed that will eventually replace the copper wire traditionally used in the telephone system. These hairlike fibers carry data faster and are lighter and less expensive than their copper-wire counterpart.

Copper wire in the telephone network is being replaced by the more versatile optical fiber. Laser-generated light pulses are transmitted through these ultrathin glass fibers. A pair of optical fibers can simultaneously carry 1,344 voice conversations and interactive data communications sessions.
(TRW Inc.)

The differences in the data transmission rates of copper wire and optical fiber are tremendous. In the time it takes to transmit a single page of Webster's *Unabridged Dictionary* over copper wire (about 6 seconds), the entire dictionary could be transmitted over a single optical fiber.

Another of the many advantages of optical fiber is its contribution to data security. It is much more difficult for a computer criminal to intercept a signal sent over optical fiber (via a beam of light) than it is over copper wire (an electrical signal).

**Coaxial Cable.**   Coaxial cable contains electrical wire and is constructed to permit high-speed data transmission with a minimum of signal distortion. Coaxial cable is laid along the ocean floor for intercontinental voice and data transmission. It is also used to connect workstations and computers in a "local" area (from a few feet to a few miles).

Microwave repeater stations, such as this one atop a skyscraper, relay signals to transceivers or other repeater stations.
(Ericsson)

**Microwave.**   Communications channels do not have to be wires or fibers. Data can also be transmitted via microwave radio signals. Transmission of these signals is line-of-sight; that is, the radio signal travels in a direct line from one repeater station to the next until it reaches its destination (see Figure 8–6). Because of the curvature of the earth, microwave repeater stations are placed on the tops of mountains and towers, usually about 30 miles apart.

**FIGURE 8–6**
**Microwave Data Transmission**
The curvature of the earth requires that line-of-sight microwave signals be carried via microwave repeater stations.

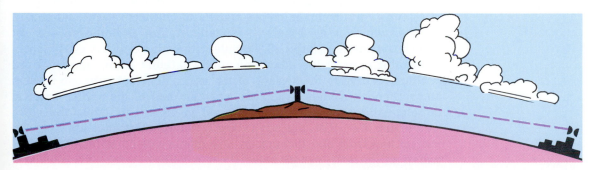

**FIGURE 8–7**
**Satellite Data Transmission**
Three satellites in geosynchronous orbit provide worldwide
data transmission service.

Satellites have made it possible to overcome the line-of-sight problem. Satellites are routinely launched into orbit for the sole purpose
of relaying data communication signals to and from earth stations. A
satellite, which is essentially a repeater station, is launched and set
in a geosynchronous orbit 22,300 miles above the earth. A geosynchronous orbit permits the communications satellite to maintain a fixed
position relative to the surface of the earth. Each satellite can receive
and retransmit signals to slightly less than half of the earth's surface;
therefore, three satellites are required to effectively cover the earth
(see Figure 8–7). The big advantage of satellites is that data can be
transmitted from one location to any number of other locations anywhere on (or near) our planet.

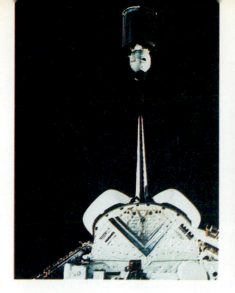

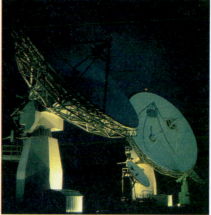

This communications satellite is being released from the space shuttle enroute to a geosynchronous orbit 22,300 miles above the earth. (NASA)

In satellite communications, data are first transmitted to an earth station, where giant antennas route signals to another earth station via a communications satellite. The signals are then transmitted to their destination over another type of communications channel. (Western Union Corporation)

## Data Transmission in Practice

A communications channel from computer A in Seattle, Washington, to computer B in Orlando, Florida (see Figure 8–8), would usually consist of several different transmission media. The connection between computer A and a workstation in the same building is probably coaxial cable. The Seattle company might use a communications company,

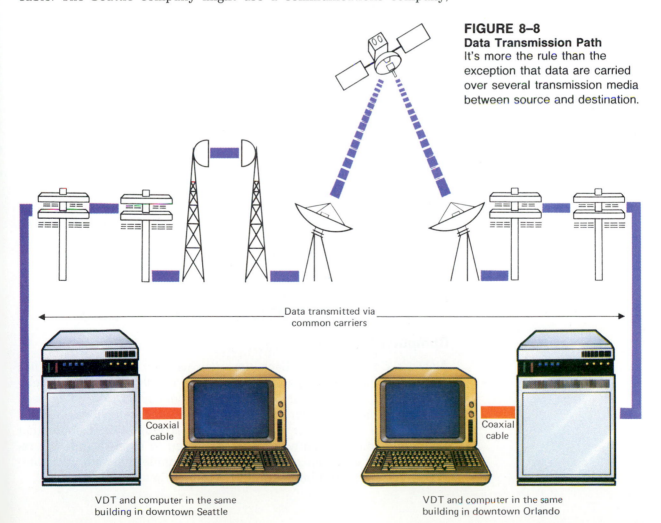

**FIGURE 8–8**
**Data Transmission Path**
It's more the rule than the exception that data are carried over several transmission media between source and destination.

Data transmitted via common carriers

Coaxial cable

Coaxial cable

VDT and computer in the same building in downtown Seattle

VDT and computer in the same building in downtown Orlando

such as AT&T, to transmit the data. The company would then transmit the data through a combination of transmission facilities that might include copper wire, optical fiber, and microwave.

## 8-5   DATA TRANSMISSION SERVICES

### Common Carriers

It is impractical, not to mention illegal, for companies to string their own coaxial cables between Philadelphia and New York City. It is also impractical for them to set their own satellites in orbit. Therefore, companies turn to **common carriers,** such as AT&T and Western Union, to provide channels for data communications. Data communications common carriers, which are regulated by the Federal Communications Commission (FCC), offer two basic types of service: private lines and switched lines.

A **private line** (or **leased line**) provides a dedicated data communications channel between any two points in a computer network. The charge for a private line is based on channel capacity (bps) and distance (air miles).

A **switched line** (or **dial-up line**) is available strictly on a time-and-distance charge, similar to a long-distance telephone call. You make a connection by "dialing-up" the computer; then a modem sends and receives data.

As a rule of thumb, a private line is the least expensive alternative if you expect to use the channel more than three hours per day and you do not need the flexibility to connect with several different computers.

### Specialized Common Carriers

A **specialized common carrier,** such as a **value-added network (VAN),** may or may not use the transmission facilities of a common carrier; but in each case, it "adds value" to the transmission service. The value added over and above the standard services of the common carriers may include electronic mail, data encryption/decryption, and code conversion for communication between noncompatible computers.

## 8-6   NETWORKS: LINKING COMPUTERS AND WORKSTATIONS

### Computer Networks

Network Configurations. Each time you use the telephone, you use the world's largest computer network—the telephone system. A telephone is an end point, or a **node,** that is connected to a network of computers that route your voice signals to another telephone, or node. The node in a computer network can be a workstation or another computer. Computer networks are configured to meet the specific requirements of an organization. The basic computer network configurations—star, ring, and bus—are illustrated in Figure 8–9.

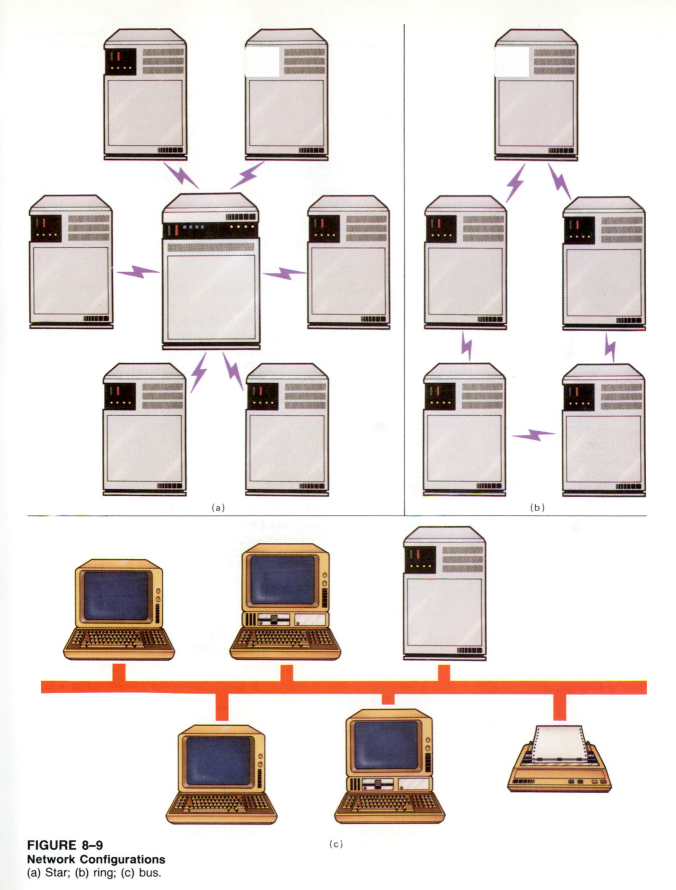

(a)

(b)

(c)

**FIGURE 8–9**
**Network Configurations**
(a) Star; (b) ring; (c) bus.

The **star configuration** involves a centralized host computer that is connected to a number of smaller computer systems. The smaller computer systems communicate with one another through the host and usually share the host computer's data base. Both the central computer and the distributed computer systems are connected to workstations (micros or VDTs). Any workstation can communicate with any other workstation in the network. Banks usually have a large home-office computer system with a star network of minicomputer systems in the branch banks.

The **ring configuration** involves computer systems that are approximately the same size, and no one computer system is the focal point of the network. Each intermediate computer system must read a message and pass it along to the destination computer system.

The **bus configuration** permits the connection of workstations, peripheral devices, and microcomputers along a central cable. Devices can be easily added to or deleted from the network. Bus configurations are most appropriate when the devices linked are close to one another (see the discussion of local area networks that follows).

A pure form of any of these three configurations is seldom found in practice. Most computer networks are *hybrids*—that is, combinations of these configurations.

**The Micro/Mainframe Link.**   Micros, initially designed for use by a single individual, have even greater potential when they can be linked with mainframe computers. To give micros this dual-function capability, vendors developed the necessary hardware and software to have **micro/mainframe links.** There are three categories of micro/mainframe links:

1. The microcomputer serves as a dumb terminal (i.e., I/O only with no processing) that is linked to the mainframe.
2. Microcomputer users request that data be downloaded from the mainframe to their micros for processing.
3. Both microcomputer and mainframe work together to process data and produce information.

Micro/mainframe links of the first two types are well within the state of the art, but achieving the third is no easy task. The tremendous differences in the way computers and software are designed make complete micro/mainframe integration of activities difficult and, for some combinations of micros and mainframes, impossible.

## Local Area Networks

A **local area network (LAN),** or **local net,** is a system of hardware, software, and communications channels that connects devices on the same premises, such as a suite of offices. A local net permits the movement of data (including text, voice, and graphic images) between mainframe computers, personal computers, workstations, I/O devices, and even data PBXs. For example, your micro can be connected to another micro, to mainframes, and to shared resources, such as printers and

At the end of each month, this plant manager downloads cost data from the company's mainframe computer to his microcomputer (see modem under the telephone). He then uses micro-based graphics software to compare expenditures for the Boston plant with those of the Phoenix and Indianapolis plants.
(Management Science America, Inc. (MSA))

A local area network links microcomputers so that students and instructors can share hardware and software resources.
(Courtesy of International Business Machines Corporation)

disk storage. The distance separating devices in the local net may be a few feet to a few miles.

The unique feature of a local net is that a common carrier is not necessary to transmit data between computers, workstations, and shared resources. Because of the proximity of devices in local nets, a company can install its own communications channels (such as coaxial cable or optical fiber).

Like computers, cars, and just about everything else, local nets can be built at various levels of sophistication. At the most basic level they permit the interconnection of PCs in a department so that users can send messages to one another and share files and printers. The more sophisticated local nets permit the interconnection of mainframes, micros, and the gamut of peripheral devices throughout a large, but geographically constrained, area, such as a cluster of buildings.

In the near future, you will be able to plug a workstation into a communications channel just as you would plug a telephone line into a telephone jack. This type of data communications capability is being installed in the new "smart" office buildings and even in some hotel rooms.

Local nets are often integrated with "long-haul" networks. For example, a bank will have home-office teller workstations linked to the central computer via a local net. But for long-haul data communication, the bank's branch offices must rely on common carriers.

## 8–7 LINE CONTROL: RULES FOR TRANSMITTING DATA

### Polling and Contention

When a workstation or a microcomputer is connected to a computer over a single communications channel, this is a **point-to-point** connection. When more than one workstation or micro is connected to a single communications channel, the channel is called a **multidrop** line. Workstations on a multidrop line must share the data communications channel. Since all workstations cannot use the same channel at once,

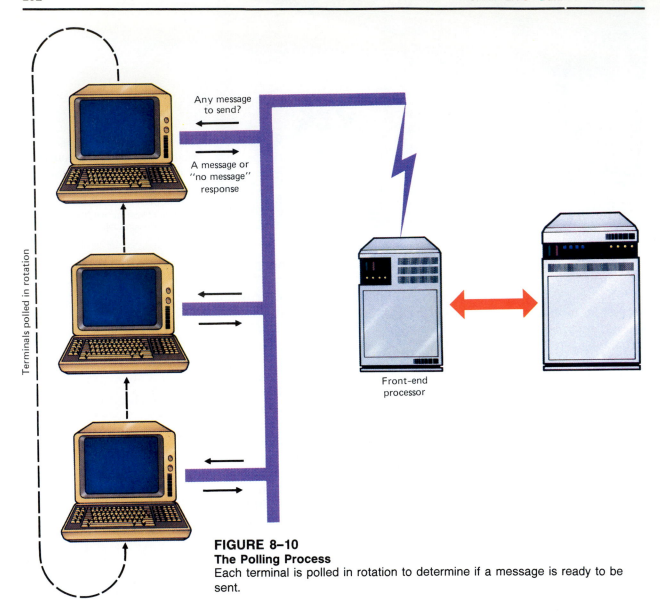

**FIGURE 8-10**
**The Polling Process**
Each terminal is polled in rotation to determine if a message is ready to be
sent.

line-control procedures are needed. The most common line-control procedures are **polling** and **contention.**

In polling, the front-end processor "polls" each workstation in rotation to determine whether a message is ready to be sent (see Figure
8–10). If a particular workstation has a message to be sent and the
line is available, the front-end processor accepts the message and polls
the next workstation.

Programmers can adjust the polling procedure so that some workstations are polled more often than others. For example, tellers in a
bank are continuously interacting with the system. A loan officer, however, may average only two inquiries in an hour. In this case, the teller
workstations might be polled four times for each poll of a loan-officer
workstation.

In contention, a workstation with a message to be sent automatically requests service from the host processor. A request might result in a "line busy" signal, in which case the workstation waits a fraction of a second and tries again, and again, until the line is free. Upon assuming control of the line, the workstation sends the message and then relinquishes control of the line to another workstation.

## Communications Protocols

Communications **protocols** are rules established to govern the way that data are transmitted in a computer network. The two general classifications of protocols, **asynchronous** and **synchronous,** are illustrated in Figure 8–11.

In asynchronous data transmission, data are transferred at irregular intervals on an as-needed basis. *Start/stop bits* are appended to the beginning and end of each message. The start/stop bits signal the receiving workstation/computer at the beginning and end of the message. A message could be a single character or a string of characters, depending on the communications protocol. Asynchronous transmission, sometimes called start/stop transmission, is best suited for data communication involving low-speed I/O devices, such as VDTs and serial printers.

In synchronous transmission, the source and destination operate in timed synchronization to enable high-speed data transmission. Start/stop bits are not required in synchronous transmission. Data transmission between computers and between down-line processors and front-end processors normally is synchronous.

**FIGURE 8–11**
**Asynchronous and Synchronous Transmission of Data**
Asynchronous data transmission takes place at irregular intervals, where synchronous data transmission requires timed synchronization.

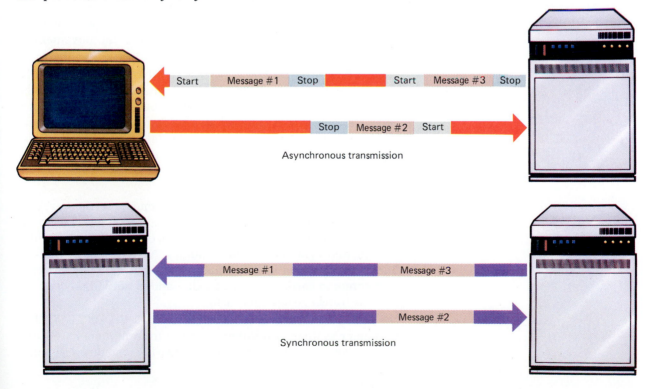

Asynchronous transmission

Synchronous transmission

## SUMMARY OUTLINE AND IMPORTANT TERMS

**8–1** DATA COMMUNICATIONS: FROM ONE ROOM TO THE WORLD. Modern businesses use **data communications** to transmit data and information at high speeds from one location to the next. Data communications, or **teleprocessing (TP),** makes an information system more accessible to the people who use it. The integration of computer systems via data communications is referred to as a **computer network.**

**8–2** WHY "GO ON-LINE"? Companies are converting existing batch systems to on-line systems for a variety of reasons: to get a faster response to inquiries, to keep the data base current at all times, and to get more capability and flexibility in the system design.

**8–3** DATA COMMUNICATIONS HARDWARE. The data communications hardware used to facilitate the transmission of data from one remote location to another includes **modems, down-line processors, front-end processors,** and **data PBXs.** Modems modulate and demodulate signals so that data can be transmitted over telephone lines. The latter three are special-function processors; they not only convert the signal to a format compatible with the transmission facility but also relieve the host processor of a number of processing tasks associated with data communications. One of the duties of the front-end processor is to establish the link between the source and the destination in a process called **handshaking.**

The availability of data communications hardware is helping to fuel a trend to **distributed processing,** the movement of processing capabilities closer to the people who use them.

**8–4** THE DATA COMMUNICATIONS CHANNEL: DATA HIGHWAYS. A **communications channel (line,** or **data link)** is the facility by which data are transmitted between locations in a computer network. A channel may be composed of one or more of the following transmission media: telephone lines, optical fiber, coaxial cable, and microwave radio signal. A channel's capacity is rated by the number of bits that can be transmitted per second.

**8–5** DATA TRANSMISSION SERVICES. **Common carriers** provide communications channels to the public, and lines can be arranged to suit the application. A **private,** or **leased, line** provides a dedicated communications channel. A **switched,** or **dial-up, line** is available on a time-and-distance charge basis. **Specialized common carriers,** such as **value-added networks,** offer expanded transmission services.

**8–6** NETWORKS: LINKING COMPUTERS AND WORKSTATIONS. Computer systems are linked together to form a computer network. The basic patterns for configuring computer systems within a computer network are **star, ring,** and **bus.** In practice, most networks are actually hybrids of these configurations.

The connection of microcomputers to a mainframe computer is called a **micro/mainframe link.**

**8–7**   LINE CONTROL: RULES FOR TRANSMITTING DATA.   A communications channel servicing a single workstation is a **point-to-point** connection. A communications channel servicing more than one workstation is called a **multidrop** line. The most common line-control procedures are **polling** and **contention.**

Data communications **protocols** are rules for transmitting data. The **asynchronous** protocol begins and ends each message with start/stop bits and is used primarily for low-speed data transmission. The **synchronous** protocol permits the source and destination to communicate in timed synchronization for high-speed data transmission.

# REVIEW EXERCISES

## Concepts

1. What is meant by "geosynchronous orbit," and how does it relate to data transmission via satellite?

2. What is the purpose of a multiplexor?

3. What is the relationship between teleprocessing and a computer network?

4. What device converts digital signals to analog signals for transmission over telephone lines? Why is it necessary?

5. Why is it not advisable to spread microwave relay stations 200 miles apart?

6. Briefly describe the function of a data PBX.

7. Describe circumstances for which a leased line would be preferred over a dial-up line.

8. Consider this situation: A remote line printer is capable of printing 800 lines per minute (70 characters per line average). Line capacity options are 2.4K, 4.8K, or 9.6K bps. Data are transmitted according to the ASCII encoding system. What capacity would you recommend for a communications channel to permit the printer to operate at capacity?

## Discussion

9. Suppose that you are a systems analyst for a municipal government. You have been asked to justify the conversion from a batch to an on-line incident-reporting system to the city council. What points would you make?

10. How is a specialized common carrier, such as a value-added

network, able to improve on the services offered by a common carrier and offer these services at a reduced cost?

11. The five PCs in the purchasing department of a large consumer goods manufacturer are used primarily for word processing and data base applications. What would be the benefits and burdens associated with connecting the PCs in a local area network?

## SELF-TEST (by section)

8-1. The general area of data communications encompasses telecommunications. (T/F)

8-2. Getting an immediate response to an inquiry is one of several reasons to "go on-line." (T/F)

8-3. (a) The _____ converts digital signals to analog signals for the purpose of transmitting data over telephone lines.

(b) Another name for a front-end processor is "multiplexor." (T/F)

(c) _____ is a term that describes moving processing capabilities closer to the people who use them.

8-4. (a) It is more difficult for a computer criminal to tap into an optical fiber than a copper telephone line. (T/F)

(b) A _____ orbit enables a communications satellite to maintain a fixed position relative to the surface of the earth.

8-5. The two basic types of service offered by common carriers are private line and leased line. (T/F)

8-6. (a) The _____ network configuration involves a centralized host computer.

(b) A LAN is designed for "long-haul" data communications. (T/F)

8-7. In asynchronous data transmission, start/stop bits are appended to the beginning and end of each message. (T/F)

*Self-Test answers.*   8–1, F; 8–2, T; 8–3 (a), modem; (b), F; (c), distributed processing; 8–4 (a), T; (b), geosynchronous; 8–5, F; 8–6 (a), star; (b), F; 8–7, T.

# Zimco Enterprises

## ZIMCO'S COMPUTER NETWORK

### THE DECENTRALIZATION OF INFORMATION PROCESSING

Centralization versus Decentralization. Through the mid-1970s, the prevailing thought at Zimco was to take advantage of the economies of scale and *centralize* all computer-based information processing in the Computer and Information Services Division. At the time, Zimco could get more computing capacity for its dollar by continuing to upgrade their centralized mainframe computer system. This is no longer true at Zimco or anywhere else.

Conrad Innis, VP of CIS, first talked about a new era in computer support during the annual executive retreat in 1984. He said: "The computer center at Dallas has grown so big and complex that we have begun to lose our ability to be responsive to user information needs. It is this lack of responsiveness that has caused us to reevaluate our current centralized mode of operation. Otto Mann, our VP of Operations, has suggested that we *decentralize* by moving more in the direction of *distributed processing,* and we in CIS agree. We can get an outstanding price-performance ratio by networking micros and minis to our mainframe in Dallas."

The Push to Distributed Processing. Distributed processing is both a technological and an organizational concept. Conrad Innis had convinced Zimco's management group that information processing can be more effective if computer *hardware* (usually micros and minis), *data, software,* and in some cases, *personnel* are moved physically closer to the people who use these resources. That is, if the people in the Operations Division need access to a computer and its information, these resources are made available to

them in their work area. They don't need to go to the Computer and Information Services Division for every request. As Otto Mann says, "With distributed processing, users control their 'information' destiny."

At Zimco, computer systems are arranged in a computer network, with each system connected to one or more other systems. Distributed processing is usually designed around a combination of geographical and functional considerations. Figure Z8–1 illustrates the implementation of distributed processing at Zimco. At the headquarters location in Dallas, Zimco has *functionally* distributed processing systems in the Finance and Accounting Division, the Sales and Marketing Division, and the home office plant. These are supported by people in CIS. *Geographically* distributed processing systems are located at each of the three plant/distribution center sites in Eugene, Becker, and Reston. Each of the remote plant sites is supported by a small staff of computer professionals.

All six distributed systems are minicomputers with similar configurations. The basic configuration is shown in Figure Z8–2. Each has its own magnetic disk storage for a "local data base" and its own low-speed, letter-quality laser printer. Each distributed mini services the workstations in the local area.

### THE COMPUTER NETWORK

The host computer system at Dallas serves as the hub of Zimco's computer network, maintains the integrated data base, and services all areas of Zimco operation. The distributed processing systems can function as part of the Zimco computer network, or, since they are entirely self-

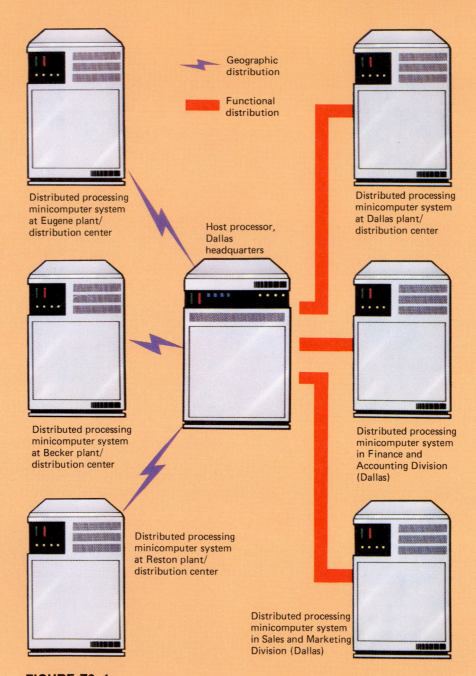

**FIGURE Z8–1**
**A Distributed Processing Network**
The distributed processing network of Zimco Enterprises demonstrates both geographic and functional distribution of processing.

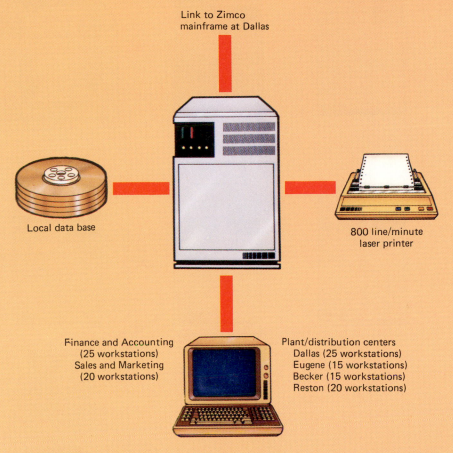

Link to Zimco
mainframe at Dallas

Local data base

800 line/minute
laser printer

Finance and Accounting
(25 workstations)
Sales and Marketing
(20 workstations)

Plant/distribution centers
Dallas (25 workstations)
Eugene (15 workstations)
Becker (15 workstations)
Reston (20 workstations)

**FIGURE Z8–2**
**Configuration of Minicomputer Systems in Zimco's Distributed Processing
Network.**
The distributed minis at the plants and at the home office (see Figure Z8–1)
have similar configurations. Each has a disk for a local data base, a laser printer,
and from 15 to 25 workstations.

contained, they also can operate as stand-alone
systems.

The Mainframe Configuration at Dallas.   Conrad
Innis likes to say: "What we have at Zimco is
a host of computers." The mainframe computer
system at the Dallas computer center has three
processors: a host, a front-end processor, and a
back-end processor (see Figure Z8–3). The central mainframe is the focal point of the star network that services the six distributed minicomputers.

    Each of the special-function processors at
Zimco is strategically located in the computer

network to increase efficiency and **throughput,**
or the rate at which work can be performed by
a computer system.

The Need for Special-Function Processors.   Recently, Gram Mertz, the manager of the Programming Department, explained the need for
special-function processors to a group of new
programmers. He said: "A processor executes
only one instruction at a time, even though it
appears to be handling many tasks simultaneously. A **task** is the basic unit of work for a processor. At any given time, several tasks will compete for processor time. For example, one task

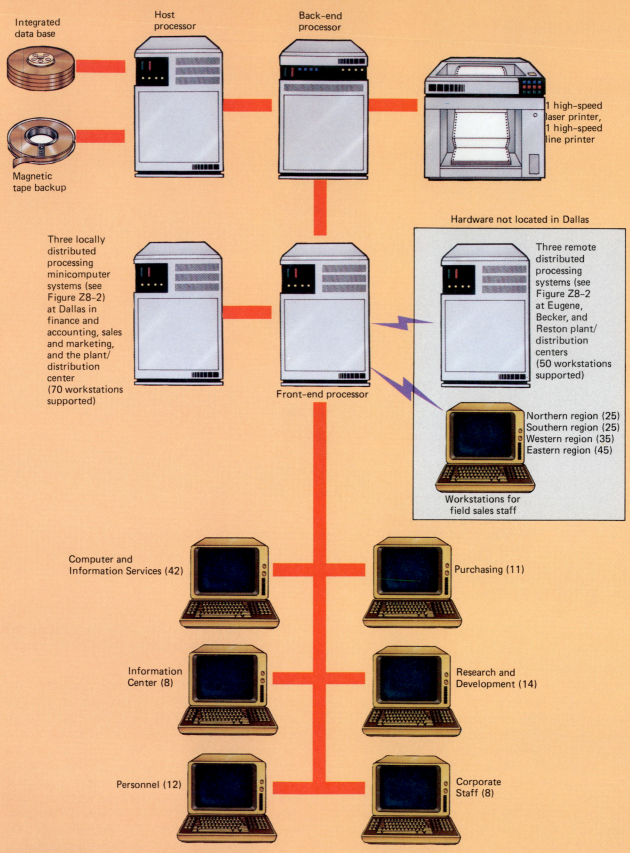

**FIGURE Z8-3**
**The Computer Network at Zimco Enterprises**
The host processor is the hub of a computer network that includes two special-function processors, six distributed minicomputers, and over 300 workstations. The configuration of the six distributed minis is shown in Figure Z8-2.

might involve printing sales reports and another calculating finance charges.''

Gram continued by discussing the limitations of a single-processor environment. "Since a single processor is capable of executing only one instruction at a time, one task will be given priority and the others will have to wait. The processor rotates between competing tasks so quickly, however, that it appears as if all are being executed at once. Even so, this rotation eventually takes its toll on processor efficiency. To improve the overall efficiency of a computer system, the *processing load* is *distributed* among several other special-function processors."

The manager of the Programming Department explained to the new hires that the host processor in the computer center at Zimco's Dallas headquarters is responsible for overall control of the computer system and for the execution of certain applications programs. Other processors in the computer system are under the control of and subordinate to the host.

At Zimco, the front-end processor relieves the host processor of communications-related processing duties. All data being transmitted *to* the host processor *from* remote computers or workstations or *from* the host processor *to* remote computers or workstations are handled by the front-end processor.

The back-end processor, which is also called a *database machine* by some CIS personnel, handles tasks associated with the retrieval and manipulation of data stored on secondary storage devices (see Figure Z8–3). Gram Mertz explained the concept. "Suppose that a program executing in the host needs Conrad Innis's record from the data base. The host issues a request to the back-end processor to retrieve Conrad's record. The back-end processor then issues the commands necessary to retrieve Conrad's record and transmits the record to the host for processing. This helps to reduce the processing load of the host, thereby increasing its efficiency."

## THE DISTRIBUTED MINIS

Otto Mann is a real proponent of distributed processing. He said: "In the past, when the mainframe went down, our plants went down. Our

manufacturing, inventory, and shipping activities are so dependent on PICS (Production and Inventory Control System) that the computer system must be up at all times for us to remain fully operational. Now, with distributed processing we can go to stand-alone operation in the plants if the Dallas mainframe goes down. If one of the plant minis goes down, the computer center at Dallas provides backup so we can continue operation."

Each of the distributed processors is essentially a "host" processor system that is "distributed" or physically located in a functional area or at a plant/distribution center site. These minicomputer systems have their own input/output (I/O), workstations, and storage capabilities, and can operate as a stand-alone (i.e., independent of the host) or as a distributed system (i.e., part of the Zimco computer network).

According to Otto Mann: "Most of the routine processing and data base activities are handled locally by the distributed systems in the four plants. For example, when I want information that deals strictly with the production of stibs, I tap into the local data base on the mini at the Dallas plant. However, when I need a summary of missed workdays due to illness, I tap into the integrated data base on the host at headquarters. When I make an inquiry about the Tegler inventory levels at the Reston Distribution Center, my request is routed to the local data base at Reston via the host in Dallas."

## SERVICING REMOTE AND LOCAL PROCESSING

Figure Z8–3 graphically illustrates the scope of Zimco's computer network. Over 300 workstations, about 200 of which are micros, permit users to access the integrated data base supported on the host or to access one or more of the local data bases supported on the distributed minis. Zimco has a policy that limits data base access to employees with a "need to know." Conrad Innis explained: "Each employee at Zimco is assigned a password and an authorization code. The password gets them on to the system and the authorization code determines what data they can access."

Approximately half of the workstations are located outside Dallas and are therefore *remote* to the host computer system. Fifty workstations are serviced by the minis at the three remote plant sites (Eugene, Becker, and Reston). Each field sales representative has a portable personal computer that doubles as a workstation. While in a customer's office, the field reps establish a link with the Zimco computer network to enter orders, to make inquires about the status of orders, and to determine the delivery schedule for a particular product.

Almost 100 *local* workstations in Dallas are connected directly to the host. The bulk of these are in CIS and are used primarily for system development and maintenance work. Eight are located in the Information Center. The remainder are used by people in purchasing, research and development, personnel, and the corporate staff.

Conrad Innis explained: "Since our integrated MIS is part and parcel of just about everything we do, it is important that we make the system available to all who need it. Our goal is to provide every white-collar worker with a workstation by the end of this decade—and we're well on our way toward meeting that goal."

## ON-LINE APPLICATIONS AT ZIMCO

Zimco's computer network puts its users on-line so that they can take advantage of a variety of data communications applications. Dale Connors, Manager of Data Communications, said: "Our computer network has made it possible for CIS to be even more responsive to end-user needs."

Dale continued discussing the "pluses" of Zimco's on-line, transaction-oriented environment. "Being on-line, our users can make a variety of inquiries from their workstations. For example, Peggy Peoples in Personnel can easily call up an employee's training record; or a field rep can inquire about a customer's credit limit. At Zimco, time is money, so we try to keep our response time to under 1 second." **Response time** is the elapsed time between when a message is sent and when a response is received.

Only 10 years ago, data entry was the responsibility of CIS, but now virtually all data are entered on-line, directly from the source location. For example, the sales staff enters the data for call-in orders directly into SAMIS (Sales and Marketing Information Systems) while they are talking with customers.

Scores of specialized programs are supported on the host computer system. Dale Connors says: "If a user requests a particular software package and the cost of the software is within reason, we get it and put it on-line." These programs, which are available to all Zimco employees, are used for a variety of remote processing tasks on an as-needed basis. For example, the product managers in marketing are frequent users of the statistical packages. All programmers and many users, especially in research and development, write their programs interactively at workstations while in direct communication with the computer.

Conrad Innis points with pride to the fact that valuable information is as close as the nearest workstation. "Our full-scale support of an on-line, integrated MIS has made it possible for managers, administrative personnel, and programmers to work at home on their own workstations." Zimco encourages this "electronic cottage" concept by permitting employees the flexibility of "telecommuting" up to one day a week. Conrad said, "with the elimination of travel time, coffee breaks, idle conversations, and numerous office distractions, we have found that conscientious, self-motivated employees can be more productive at home when working on certain projects." Of course, there are differing opinions on the merits of the electronic cottage. Sally Marcio, VP of Sales and Marketing says: "I'm more productive working at the office, where household and family distractions fade into the distance."

## DISCUSSION QUESTIONS

1. Discuss centralization and decentralization as they are applied to computers and information processing.

2. Elaborate on Zimco management's rationale for moving in the direction of distributed processing.

3. Discuss how special-function processors can

enhance the throughput of Zimco's host computer system.

4. Would you classify Zimco's computer network as a star network or a hybrid network? Explain.

5. The trend at Zimco is to distributed processing. Besides processing, what else is distributed?

6. The only functional division at Zimco that does not have at least one distributed minicomputer system is the Personnel Division. Discuss possible reasons for not implementing a distributed system in the Personnel Division.

7. Conrad Innis would like to see a workstation on the desktop of every white-collar worker at Zimco. Some workers simply don't want a workstation. Should they be excluded from Conrad's plan? Explain.

8. Only 20 percent of the professional people at Zimco routinely take advantage of the opportunity to telecommute one day each week. If you worked at Zimco, would you telecommute? Why or why not?

# PART 4

# SOFTWARE AND DATA MANAGEMENT

*The impact of computers in business has increased dramatically since 1968 when Cullinet Software, Inc., was founded. At that time, most larger institutions such as banks and insurance companies had mainframe computers. Many hardware vendors believed that software, although necessary in the short term, would eventually go away.*

*However, when I worked for a computer programming firm in the mid 1960s that wrote customized applications software, it seemed obvious that there was great potential for packaged software products. It just didn't make good sense to re-invent the software wheel. Others, as well, recognized the opportunity and as a result the software industry has grown to such an extent that software, once dominated by hardware, now often drives hardware sales.*

*An array of business application software is necessary to run many companies today, regardless of size. Research and development continues to push back the boundaries of computer technology while exploring such areas as artificial intelligence, expert systems, and robotics. This work will change still further the way people around the world do business. However, the future of database, applications, and the aforementioned decision support systems distribution over mainframe, departmental, and end user work stations will require developments in software technology integration. The components exist but they must be integrated, which is not a simple task.*

John J. Cullinane
Chairman of the Board
Cullinet Software, Inc.

# Programming Languages and Software Concepts

## CHAPTER 9

## STUDENT LEARNING OBJECTIVES

- To discuss the terminology and concepts associated with programming languages and software.
- To distinguish between and give examples of applications software and systems software.
- To characterize each generation of programming languages.
- To categorize programming languages by generation.
- To describe the function of compilers and interpreters.
- To detail the purpose and objectives of an operating system.

## FOCUS OF ZIMCO CASE STUDY

- Information systems at Zimco: personnel.

Programs written to address a specific business processing task, such as providing on-line directory information to telephone operators, are called applications software.
(Reproduced with permission of AT&T)

At the end of each day, this operator calls a program that copies critical magnetic disk files to magnetic tape for backup. Such general software is referred to as systems software.
(Quotron Systems, Inc.)

## 9-1  PROGRAMMING AND SOFTWARE

In Chapters 5 through 8 we discussed the operation and application of computer hardware. Most people in the business community will agree that computers have become an integral part of virtually all business activities. We can touch them and see the results of their seemingly endless capabilites. But the computer-literate person recognizes that hardware is useless without **software,** and software is useless without hardware.

A computer system does nothing until directed to do so. A **program,** which consists of instructions to the computer, is the means by which we tell a computer to perform certain operations. These instructions are logically sequenced and assembled through the act of **programming. Programmers** use a variety of **programming languages,** such as COBOL and BASIC, to communicate instructions to the computer.

We use the term "software" to refer to the programs that direct the activities of the computer system. Software falls into two general categories: applications and systems. **Applications software** is designed and written to perform specific personal, business, or scientific processing tasks, such as payroll processing, order entry, or financial analysis.

**Systems software** is more general than applications software and is usually independent of any specific application area. Systems software programs support *all* applications software by directing the basic functions of the computer. For example, when the computer is turned on, an initialization program prepares and readies all devices for processing. Software that permits us to write programs in COBOL and BASIC is also systems software. The operating system, discussed later in this chapter, is classified as systems software.

| MEMORY BITS | |
|---|---|
| **SOFTWARE** | |
| **Applications** | **Systems** |
| Claims processing (insurance) | Programming language compilers/ interpreters |
| Tax collection (local government) | Operating systems |
| Order entry processing (manufacturing) | Utility programs |
| Registration (university) | Communications software |
| Satellite trajectory tables (NASA) | Database management systems |

## 9-2  GENERATIONS OF PROGRAMMING LANGUAGES

We "talk" to computers within the framework of a particular programming language. There are many different programming languages, most of which have highly structured sets of rules. The selection of a programming language depends on who is involved and the nature of "conversation." The president of a company may prefer a different type of language than that preferred by a professional programmer; languages used for payroll processing may not be appropriate for ad hoc (one-time) inquiries. The use and application of the more common business programming languages is discussed in Sections 9–3 and 9–8.

Like computers, programming languages have evolved in generations. With each new generation, fewer instructions are needed to instruct the computer to perform a particular task. That is, a program written in a first-generation language that computes the total sales for each sales representative, then lists those over quota, may require 100 or more instructions; the same program in a fourth-generation language may have fewer than 10 instructions.

The hierarchy of programming languages, shown in Figure 9–1, illustrates the relationships between the six generations of programming languages. The later generations do not necessarily provide us with greater programming capabilites, but they do provide a *more sophisticated programmer/computer interaction*. In short, each new generation is easier to understand and use. For example, in the fourth, fifth, and sixth generations, we need only instruct the computer system *what to do*, not necessarily *how to do it*. When programming in one of the first three generations of languages, you have to tell the computer what to do *and* how to do it.

The ease with which the later generations can be used is certainly appealing, but the earlier languages also have their advantages. All six generations of languages are in use today.

**FIGURE 9–1**
**The Hierarchy of Programming Languages**
As you progress from one generation of programming languages to the next, fewer instructions are required to perform a particular programming task.

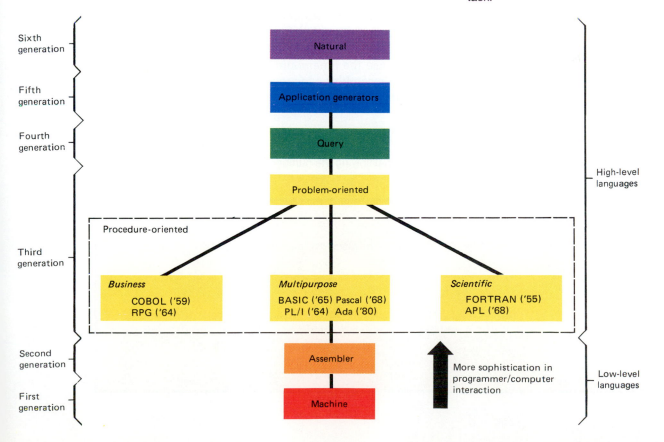

## 9–3   THE FIRST AND SECOND GENERATIONS: "LOW-LEVEL"

### Machine Language

Each computer has only *one* programming language that can be executed—the **machine language.** We talk of programming in COBOL, Pascal, and BASIC, but all of these languages must be translated to the machine language of the computer on which the program is to be executed. These and other high-level languages are simply a convenience for the programmer.

Machine-language programs, the *first generation*, are written at the most basic level of computer operation. Because their instructions are directed at this basic level of operation, machine language and assembler language (see below) are collectively called **low-level languages.** In machine language, instructions are coded as a series of 1s and 0s. As you might expect, machine-language programs are cumbersome and difficult to write. Early programmers had no alternative. Fortunately, we do.

### Assembler Language

A set of instructions for an **assembler language** is essentially one to one with those of a machine language. Like machine languages, assembler languages are unique to a particular computer. The big difference between the two types is the way the instructions are represented by the programmer. Rather than a cumbersome series of 1s and 0s, assembler languages use easily recognized symbols, called **mnemonics,** to represent instructions (see Figure 9–2). For example, most assembler languages use the mnemonic "MUL" to represent a "Multiply" instruction. The assembler languages ushered in the *second generation* of programming languages.

**FIGURE 9–2**
**An Assembler Program Procedure**
These assembler instructions compute PAY by multiplying the number of HOURS times the RATE.

```
COMP$PAY           PROC PUBLIC
;
;       COMP$PAY - procedure to compute gross pay (PAY = HOURS * RATE)
;
        MOV        AX,HOURS                   ;multiplicand
        MUL        RATE+2                     ;   times second word of multiplier
        MOV        PAY+2,AX                   ;store the product in PAY
;
        MOV        AX,HOURS                   ;multiplicand
        MUL        RATE                       ;   times first word of multiplier
        ADD        PAY+2,AX                   ;add the product to PAY
        ADC        PAY,DX                     ;add the carry, if any
        RET                                   ;end procedure
COMP$PAY           ENDP
```

## 9–4  COMPILERS AND INTERPRETERS: PROGRAMS FOR PROGRAMS

No matter which **high-level** language (third through sixth generations) a program is written in, it must be translated to machine language before it can be executed. This conversion of high-level instructions to machine-level instructions is done by systems software programs called compilers and interpreters.

### Compilers

The **compiler** program translates the instructions of a high-level language, such as COBOL, to machine-language instructions that the computer can interpret and execute. A separate compiler (or an interpreter, discussed in the next section) is required for each programming language intended for use on a particular computer system. That is, to execute both COBOL and Pascal programs, you must have a COBOL compiler and a Pascal compiler. High-level programming languages are simply a programmer convenience; they cannot be executed in their source, or original, form.

The actual high-level programming-language instructions, called the **source program,** are translated or **compiled** to machine-language instructions by a compiler. The circled numbers in Figure 9–3 cross-reference the following numbered discussion of the compilation process.

1. Suppose that you want to write a COBOL program. You first enter the instructions into the computer system through an on-line workstation. Having done so, you identify the language (COBOL) in which you wrote the program and request that the program be compiled.

2. The COBOL compiler program is called from secondary storage and loaded to primary storage along with the COBOL source program. [*Note*: Step 3 will be attempted but not completed if the source program has errors or **bugs** (see step 4).]

3. The COBOL compiler translates the source program to a machine-language program called an **object program.** The object program is the output of the compilation process. At this point, the object program resides in primary storage and can be executed upon your command.

   The compilation process can be time consuming, especially for large programs. Therefore, if you intend to execute the program at a later time, perhaps during another session, you should store the object program on secondary storage for later recall. On most mainframe computer systems this is done automatically.

4. If the source program contains a **syntax error** (e.g., an invalid instruction format), the compiler will display an error message, or diagnostic, on the workstation screen, then terminate the compilation process. A diagnostic identifies the program statement or statements in error and the cause of the error. Syntax errors usually

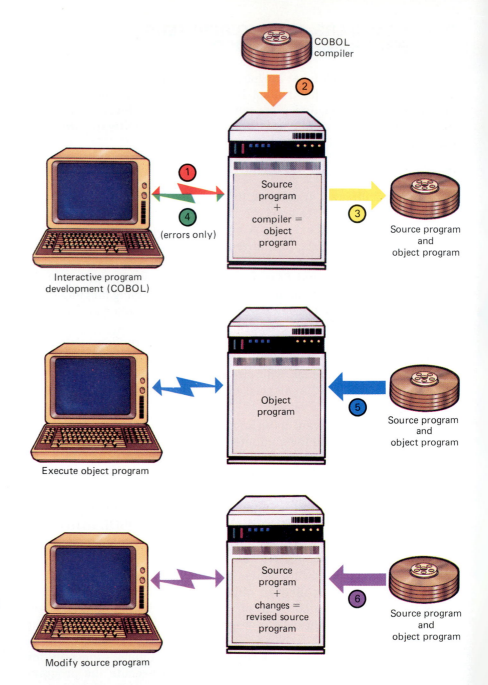

COBOL
compiler

Source
program
+
compiler =
object
program

(errors only)

Interactive program
development (COBOL)

Source program
and
object program

Object
program

Execute object program

Source program
and
object program

**FIGURE 9–3**
**The Compilation Process**
A source program is translated
to an object program for
execution. Steps of the
compilation process are
discussed in the text.

Source
program
+
changes =
revised source
program

Modify source program

Source program
and
object program

involve invalid instructions. Consider the following COBOL statement: DISPLY "WHOOPS." The statement is invalid because DIS-
PLAY is misspelled.

As a programmer, you will make the necessary corrections and
attempt the compilation over, and over, and over again, until the
program compiles and executes. Don't be discouraged. Very few
programs compile on the first, second, or even third attempts. When

your program finally compiles and executes, don't be surprised if the output is not what you expected. A "clean," or error-free, compilation is likely to surface undetected **logic errors.** For example, your program logic might result in an attempted division by zero; this is mathematically and logically impossible and will result in a program error. In most cases, you will need to remove a few such bugs in the program logic and in the I/O formats before the program is finished.

5. Suppose that you come back the next day and wish to execute your COBOL program again. Instead of repeating the compilation process of step 2, you simply call the object program from secondary storage and load it to primary storage for execution. Since the object program is already in machine language, no compilation is necessary.

6. If you want to make any changes to the original source programs, you will: recall the original source code from secondary storage, make the changes, recompile the program, and create an updated object program (repeat steps 1 through 4).

Programs that are run frequently are stored and executed as object programs. Recompilation is necessary only when the program is modified.

## Interpreters

An **interpreter** is a system software program that ultimately performs the same function as a compiler—but in a different manner. Instead of translating the entire source program in a single pass, an interpreter translates *and* executes each source program instruction before translating and executing the next.

The obvious advantage of interpreters over compilers is that an error in instruction syntax is brought to the attention of the programmer immediately, thereby prompting the programmer to make corrections during program development. This is a tremendous help.

This telecommuter programmer/ analyst takes advantage of the convenience of an interpreter to write and debug programs. She compiles completed programs that are to be used for routine processing because they make more efficient use of the hardware.
(Photo courtesy of Hewlett-Packard Company)

As we know, advantages are usually accompanied by disadvantages. The disadvantage of interpreters is that they do not use computing resources as efficiently as a program that has been compiled. Since the interpreter does not produce an object program, it must perform the translation process each time a program is executed.

For programs that are to be run often, programmers take advantage of the strengths of both interpreters and compilers. First, they develop and debug their programs using an interpreter. Then they compile the finished program to create a more efficient object program that can be used for routine processing.

## 9–5  THE THIRD GENERATION: FOR PROGRAMMER CONVENIENCE

A quantum leap in programmer convenience accompanied the introduction of the *third generation* of programming languages. A third-generation language is placed in one of two categories: **procedure-oriented languages** or **problem-oriented languages** (review Figure 9–1).

### Procedure-Oriented Languages

The flexibility of procedure-oriented languages permits programmers to model almost any scientific or business procedure. Instructions are **coded,** or written, sequentially and processed according to program specifications.

Unless triggered by program logic to do otherwise, the processor selects and executes instructions in the sequence in which they are written. In a production payroll system, for example, a particular sequence of program instructions is executed for each salaried employee; another sequence is executed for each hourly employee.

Procedure-oriented languages are classified as *business*, *scientific*, or *multipurpose*. These are illustrated in Figure 9–1 and discussed below.

**Business Languages.**    Business programming languages are designed to be effective tools for developing business information systems. The strength of business-oriented languages lies in their ability to store, retrieve, and manipulate alphanumeric data.

The arithmetic requirements of most business systems are minimal. Although sophisticated mathematical manipulation is possible, it is cumbersome to achieve, so it is best left to scientific languages.

*COBOL.*    **COBOL,** the first business programming language, was introduced in 1959. It remains the most popular. The original intent of the developers of COBOL (*CO*mmon *B*usiness *O*riented *L*anguage) was to make its instructions approximate the English language. Here is a typical COBOL *sentence*: "IF SALARY-CODE IS EQUAL TO 'H' MULTIPLY SALARY BY HOURLY-RATE GIVING GROSS-PAY ELSE PERFORM SALARIED-EMPLOYEE-ROUTINE." Note that the sentence contains several instructions and even a period.

The minicomputer computer system at this west coast textile warehouse helps administrative personnel keep track of orders and shipping information. The applications software for this system was written in COBOL. (Courtesy of NEC Information Systems, Inc.)

```
0100 IDENTIFICATON DIVISION.
0200 PROGRAM-ID.              PAYPROG.
0300 REMARKS.                 PROGRAM TO COMPUTE GROSS PAY.
0400 ENVIRONMENT DIVISION.
0500 DATA DIVISION.
0600 WORKING-STORAGE SECTION.
0700 01 PAY-DATA.
0800         05 HOURS       PIC 99V99.
0900         05 RATE        PIC 99V99.
1000         05 PAY         PIC 9999V99.
1100 01 LINE-1.
1200         03 FILLER      PIC X(5)        VALUE SPACES.
1300         03 FILLER      PIC X(12)       VALUE "GROSS PAY IS  ".
1400         03 GROSS-PAY   PIC $$$$9.99.
1500 01 PRINT-LINE          PIC X(27).
1600 PROCEDURE DIVISION.
1700 MAINLINE-PROCEDURE.
1800         PERFORM ENTER-PAY.
1900         PERFORM COMPUTE-PAY.
2000         PERFORM PRINT-PAY.
2100         STOP RUN.
2200 ENTER-PAY.
2300         DISPLAY "ENTER HOURS AND RATE OF PAY".
2400         ACCEPT HOURS, RATE.
2500 COMPUTE-PAY.
2600         MULTIPLY HOURS BY RATE GIVING PAY ROUNDED.
2700 PRINT-PAY.
2800         MOVE PAY TO GROSS-PAY.
2900         MOVE LINE-1 TO PRINT-LINE.
3000         DISPLAY PRINT-LINE.
```

```
Enter hours and rate of pay
43, 8.25
   Gross pay is $354.75
```

**FIGURE 9–4**
**A COBOL Program**
This COBOL program accepts the number of *hours* worked and the pay *rate* for an hourly wage earner, then computes and displays the gross *pay* amount. The resultant input/output is shown in an interactive session.

The American National Standards (ANS) Institute has established standards for COBOL and other languages. The purpose of these standards is to make COBOL programs *portable*. A program is said to be portable if it can be run on a variety of computers. Unfortunately, the ANS standards are followed only casually; consequently, it is unlikely that a COBOL program written for a Burroughs computer, for example, can be executed on a Data General computer without some modification.

Figure 9–4 illustrates a COBOL program that computes gross pay for hourly wage earners. Notice that the program is divided into four divisions: identification, environment, data, and procedure. The procedure division contains the logic of the program; that is, the sequence of instructions that instructs the computer to accept, process, and display data.

For the purpose of comparison, the COBOL program in Figure

The computer systems on-board the space shuttle collect flight data that are relayed to earth and analyzed by programs written in FORTRAN.
(NASA)

9–4 and all other examples of third-generation programs (Figures 9–5 through 9–8) are written to perform the same input, processing, and output activities: compute gross pay for hourly wage earners. The interactive session (see Figure 9–4) is the same for all these programs.

*RPG*. **RPG** (*R*eport *P*rogram *G*enerator) was originally developed in 1964 for IBM's entry-level punched-card business computers and for the express purpose of generating reports. As punched cards went the way of vacuum tubes, RPG remained—evolving from a special-purpose problem-oriented language to a general-purpose procedure-oriented language. Its name has made RPG the most misunderstood of the programming languages. People who do not know RPG still associate it with report generation when, in fact, it has become a powerful programming language that matured with the demands of RPG users.

RPG has always differed somewhat from other procedure-oriented languages in that the programmer specifies certain processing requirements by selecting the desired programming options. That is, during a programming session, the programmer is presented with *prompting formats* at the bottom of the workstation screen. The programmer requests the prompts for a particular type of instruction, then responds with the desired programming specifications.

**Scientific Lanugages.** Scientific languages are algebraic/formula-type languages. These are specifically designed to meet typical scientific processing requirements, such as matrix manipulation, precision calculations, iterative processing, the expression and resolution of mathematical equations, and so on. For example, engineers and actuaries turn to scientific languages when writing programs for statistical analysis.

*FORTAN*. **FORTRAN** (*Fo*rmula *Tran*slator), the first procedure-oriented language, was developed in 1955. It was, and it remains, the most popular scientific language. The FORTRAN program in Figure 9–5 performs the same processing functions as the COBOL program in Figure 9–4.

*APL*. **APL** (*A P*rogramming *L*anguage), introduced in 1968, is a symbolic interactive programming language that is popular with engineers,

## FIGURE 9–5
### A FORTRAN Program
This FORTRAN program accepts the number of *hours* worked and the pay *rate* for an hourly wage earner, then computes and displays the gross *pay* amount. The resultant interactive session is the same as that of Figure 9–4.

```
      program payprog
c
c     payprog        - Program to compute the pay for an employee,
c                      given hours worked and the employee's pay rate.
c
      real hours, rate, pay                     !define the variables
c
      write(6,1)                                !input prompt
1     format(1H,'Enter hours and rate of pay')
      read(5,*) hours, rate                     !accept hours & pay rate
      pay = hours * rate                        !compute pay
      write(6,2) pay                            !display gross pay
2     format(1H,5X,'Gross pay is $',F7.2)
      end
```

```
100 REM payprog          Program to compute the pay for an employee,
110 REM                  given hours worked and the employee's pay rate.
120 REM
130 PRINT "Enter hours and rate of pay"      'input prompt
140 INPUT HOURS, RATE                        'accept hours & pay rate
150 LET PAY = HOURS * RATE                   'compute pay
160 PRINT TAB(5);"Gross pay is $";PAY        'display gross pay
170 END
```

mathematicians, and scientists. A special keyboard with "shorthand" symbols helps speed the coding process.

**Multipurpose Languages.** Multipurpose languages are equally effective for both business and scientific applications. These languages are an outgrowth of the need to simplify the programming environment by providing programmers with one language that is capable of addressing all of a company's programming needs.

*BASIC.* **BASIC,** developed in 1964, is the primary language supported by millions of personal computers. BASIC is also used extensively on mainframe computer systems, primarily for one-time "quick and dirty" programs.

BASIC is perhaps the easiest language to learn and use (see Figure 9–6). It is commonly used for both scientific and business applications—and even for developing video games. The widespread use of BASIC attests to the versatility of its features. In fact, BASIC is the only programming language that is supported on virtually every computer.

The special skills section, "BASIC Programming," at the back of the book contains more background information and a comprehensive tutorial on the BASIC programming language.

*Pascal.* During the last decade, **Pascal,** named after the seventeenth-century French mathematician Blaise Pascal, has experienced tremendous growth. Introduced in 1968, Pascal is considered the state of the art among widely used procedure-oriented languages (see Figure 9–7).

Pascal's power, flexibility, and self-documenting structure have made it the language of choice in many computer science curriculums

**FIGURE 9–6**
**A BASIC Program**
This BASIC program accepts the number of *hours* worked and the pay *rate* for an hourly wage earner, then computes and displays the gross *pay* amount. The resultant interactive session is the same as that of Figure 9–4.

**FIGURE 9–7**
**A Pascal Program**
This Pascal program accepts the number of *hours* worked and the pay *rate* for an hourly wage earner, then computes and displays the gross *pay* amount. The resultant interactive session is the same as that of Figure 9–4.

```
program payprog(input,output);
{       Program to compute the pay for an employee,
        given hours worked and the employee's pay rate. }

var     hours, rate, pay : real;                     {define the variables}

begin
  writeln(output,'Enter hours and rate of pay');     {input prompt}
  readln(input,hours,rate);                          {accept hours & pay rate}
  pay := hours * rate;                               {compute pay}
  writeln(output,'     Gross pay is $',pay:0:2)      {display gross pay}
end.
```

```
/*       payprog.c       - Program to compute the pay for an employee,
                           given hours worked and the employee's pay rate. */

main()
{
        float hours, rate, pay;                    /* define the
                                                      variables used */
        printf("Enter hours and rate of pay\n");   /* input prompt */
        scanf("%f %f", &hours, &rate);             /* accept hours
                                                      and pay rate */

        pay = hours * rate;                        /* compute pay */
        printf("\tGross pay is $%.2f\n",pay);      /* print gross pay */
}
```

**FIGURE 9–8**
**A C-Language Program**
This C program accepts the number of *hours* worked and the pay *rate* for an hourly wage earner, then computes and displays the gross *pay* amount. The resultant interactive session is the same as that of Figure 9–4.

Computer-aided design (CAD) enables engineers to see, test, and modify a design from any viewpoint. The components of this automobile universal yoke are highlighted in different colors. Pascal, a multipurpose programming language, is often used to develop software for CAD.
(Reprinted with permission from Computervision Corporation, Bedford, MA)

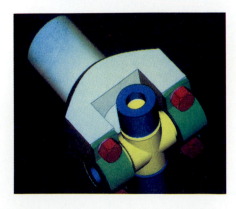

and for many developers of systems software. Currently, only 1 to 2 percent of the business-system programs are written in Pascal, but it is enjoying a growing acceptance in the business community.

*C.*   The results of a recent employment survey showed **C** programmers to be in the greatest demand. Developers of proprietary packaged software are very interested in C because it is considered more transportable than other languages. That is, it is relatively machine independent: a C program written for one type of computer (see Figure 9–8) can be run on another type with little or no modification.

*PL/I.*   **PL/I (***Programming Language/I***),** introduced in 1964, was hailed as the answer to many of the shortcomings of existing programming languages, such as COBOL and FORTRAN. It has not, however, won the widespread acceptance that was originally anticipated, but it is widely used.

*Ada.*   **Ada** is the most recent and perhaps the most sophisticated procedure-oriented language. Ada is a multipurpose language developed for the United States Department of Defense. The language was named to honor the nineteenth-century pioneer, Lady Augusta Ada Lovelace, considered by some to be the first programmer. Ada developers are optimistic that as more people begin to study it, Ada will gain widespread acceptance not only in the military but in the private sector as well.

## Problem-Oriented Languages

A problem-oriented language is designed to address a particular application area or to solve a particular set of problems. Problem-oriented languages do not require the programming detail of procedure-oriented ones. The emphasis of problem-oriented languages is more on *input and the desired output* than on the *procedures or mathematics involved.*

Problem-oriented languages have been designed for scores of applications: simulation (e.g., GPSS, SLAM); programming machine tools (e.g., APT); and analysis of stress points in buildings and bridges (e.g., COGO).

Programs for computerized machine tools, such as this lathe, are written in problem-oriented languages.
(General Electric Company)

## 9–6 THE FOURTH GENERATION: QUERY LANGUAGES _____

**Query Languages.** Over the years, most companies have accumulated large amounts of computer-based data. Prior to *fourth-generation* languages (mid-1970s), these data were not directly accessible to users. Users had to describe their information needs to a professional programmer, who would then write a program in a procedure-oriented language to produce the desired information. Fulfilling a typical user request would take at least a couple of days and as much as two weeks. By then, the information might no longer be timely. With fourth-generation **query languages,** these same ad hoc requests, or *queries*, can be completed in minutes by the user, without involving computer professionals!

**Principles and Use.** Query languages use high-level English-like instructions to retrieve and format data for user inquiries and reporting. Most of the procedure portion of a query-language program is generated automatically by the computer and the language software. As a programmer in query languages, you need only specify "what to do," *not* "how to do it"; a programmer using a procedure-oriented language would have to write instructions depicting "what to do" *and* "how to do it." Thus the use of query languages for certain information needs yields substantial improvements in programming productivity.

The features of a query language include English-like instructions, limited mathematical manipulation of data, automatic report formatting, sequencing (sorting), and record selection by criteria. An example query language output and program are presented in the Zimco case study following this chapter (Figures Z9–2 and Z9–3).

These managers are being taught the use and application of fourth-generation query languages. After completing a one-day seminar they will be able make certain inquiries to the corporate data base without the assistance of a computer specialist.
(Courtesy of International Business Machines Corporation)

With four to eight hours of training and practice, you can learn to write query-language programs, make inquiries, and get reports—without the assistance of a professional programmer. With query languages, it may be easier and quicker to sit down at the nearest workstation and write a program than it is to relate inquiry or report specifications to a programmer. Now managers can attend to their own seemingly endless numbers of ad hoc requests. Query languages benefit everyone concerned. Users get the information that they need quickly, and programmers can devote their time to an ever-increasing backlog of information systems projects. Professional programmers use query languages to increase their productivity as well.

**Entrepreneurial Innovation.** Procedure-oriented languages, such as FORTRAN and COBOL, were designed by volunteer committees and individuals, primarily for the public domain. Companies such as CDC and IBM then developed compilers and interpreters to support these languages. The fourth-, fifth-, and sixth-generation languages are products of entrepreneurial innovation. That is, these languages (e.g., NOMAD2, EASYTRIEVE Plus) are developed to be marketed and sold. The demand for very high-level languages is so great that many entrepreneurs have produced products for this highly competitive market. Each of the last three generations may have a dozen or more equally popular languages. Customers will, of course, purchase a language that will best meet their information processing needs.

## 9–7   THE FIFTH GENERATION: APPLICATION GENERATORS

**Principles and Use.** **Application generators** are designed primarily for use by computer professionals. The concept of an application generator is not well defined, nor will it ever be, as entrepreneurs are continually working to provide better ways to create information systems. In contrast to the ad hoc orientation (one-time information requests) of fourth-generation query languages, application generators are designed to assist in the *development* of full-scale information systems.

During the development of an information system with an application generator, also called a code generator, programmers specify, through an interactive dialogue with the system, what information processing tasks are to be performed. This is essentially a fill-in-the-blank process. After programmers enter their specifications, the actual procedure-level instructions are generated automatically. In the creation of an information system, you would describe the data base, then specify screen layouts for file creation and maintenance, data entry, management reports, and menus. The application generator software consists of modules of **reusable code** that are pulled together and integrated automatically to complete the system.

**Improved Productivity.** Application generators are currently in the infant stage of development. Existing application generators do not have the flexibility of procedure-oriented languages; therefore, the generic reusable code of application generators must occasionally be supplemented with *custom code* to handle unique situations. Normally, about 10 to 15 percent of the code would be custom code. Application generators provide the framework by which to integrate custom code with generated code.

When used for the purposes intended, application generators can increase programmer and systems analyst productivity by as much as 500 percent. As they mature, application generators will play an ever-increasing role in information systems development.

## 9–8   THE SIXTH GENERATION: NATURAL LANGUAGES

The next step in the sophistication of programming languages is the **natural language**: the sixth generation. The premise behind a natural language is that the programmer or user needs little or no training. He or she simply writes, or perhaps verbalizes, specifications without regard for instruction format or syntax. To date, there is no such language. Researchers are currently working to develop pure natural languages that will permit an unrestricted dialogue between us and a computer. Although the creation of such a language is difficult to comprehend, it is probably inevitable.

In the meantime, natural languages with certain syntax restrictions are available. And for limited information processing tasks, such as ad hoc inquiries and report generation for a specific application area, existing natural languages work quite well. With certain limitations, existing natural languages permit users to express queries in normal, everyday English. You can phrase a query any way you want. For example, you could say, "Let me see the average salaries by job category in the marketing department." Or you would get the same results if you said; "What is the average salary in the marketing department for each job classification?" If your query is unclear, the natural-language software might ask you questions that will clarify any ambiguities. Other typical natural-language queries might be:

- Are there any managers between the ages of 30 and 40 in the northwest region with MBA degrees?
- Show me a pie chart that compares voter registrations for Alabama, Georgia, North Carolina, South Carolina, and Florida.
- What are the top 10 best-selling fiction books in California?

## 9–9   THE OPERATING SYSTEM: THE BOSS

Just as the processor is the nucleus of the computer system, the **operating system** is the nucleus for all software activity. The operating system is a family of *systems software* programs that are usually, though not always, supplied by the computer system vendor.

When using a natural language, all you have to do is ask. To produce this bar chart, a sales manager entered the following request: "Show total actual to plan by region for international." The tabular and graphic summaries are generated automatically in response to the request.
(© Artificial Intelligence Corporation)

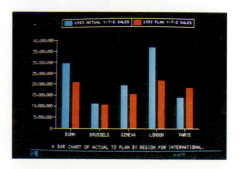

## Mainframe Operating Systems

Design Objectives.   All hardware and software, both systems and applications, are under the control of the operating system. You might even call the operating system the "boss." The logic, structure, and nomenclature of the different operating systems vary considerably. However, each is designed with the same three objectives in mind:

1. Minimize turnaround time [elapsed time between submittal of a job (e.g., print payroll checks) and receipt of output]
2. Maximize throughput (amount of processing per unit time)
3. Optimize the use of the computer system resources (processor, primary storage, and peripheral devices)

The Supervisor.   One of the operating system programs is always *resident* in primary storage (see Figure 9–9). This program, called the **supervisor,** loads other operating system and applications programs to primary storage as they are needed. For example, when you request a COBOL program compilation, the supervisor loads the COBOL compiler

**FIGURE 9–9**
**Software, Storage, and Execution**
The supervisor program is always resident in primary storage and calls other programs, as needed, from secondary storage. All programs must be in object format to be executed. Applications programs rely on data base management system software to assist in the retrieval of data from secondary storage. Software in the front-end processor handles data communications-related tasks.

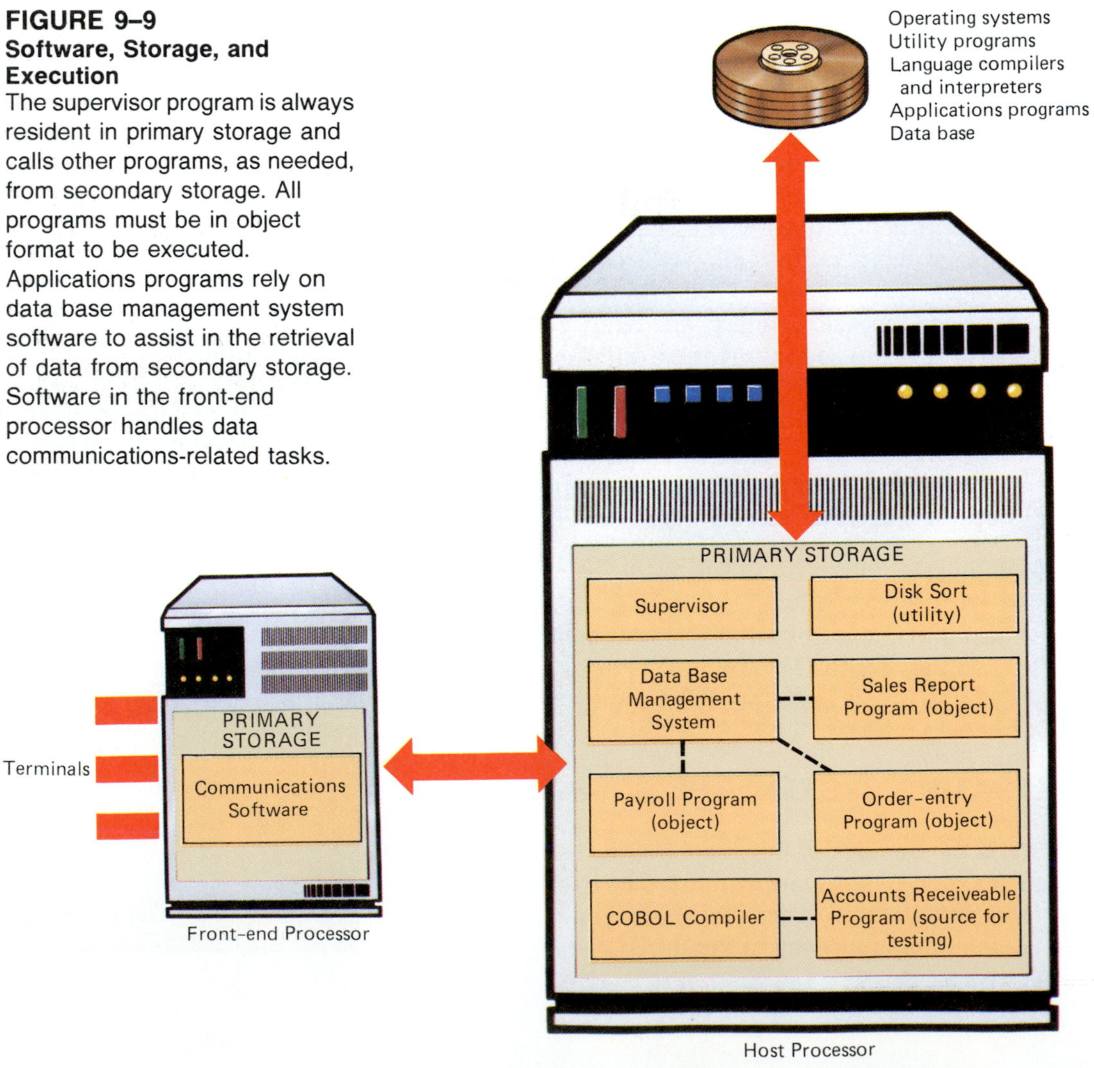

to primary storage and links your source program to the compiler to create an object program. In preparation for execution, another program, the **linkage editor,** assigns a primary storage address to each byte of the object program.

Allocating Computer Resources.   In a typical computer system, several jobs will be executing at the same time. The operating system determines which computer system resources are allocated to which programs. As an example, suppose that a computer system with only one printer has three jobs whose output is ready to be printed. Obviously, two must wait. The operating system continuously resolves this type of resource conflict to optimize the allocation of computer resources.

Operator Interaction.   The operating system is in continuous interaction with computer operators. The incredible speed of a computer system dictates that resource-allocation decisions be made at computer speeds. Most of these decisions are made automatically by the operating system. For decisions requiring human input, the operating system interrogates the operators through the operator console. The operating system also sends messages to the operator. A common message is "Printer no. 1 is out of paper."

Compatibility Considerations.   There are usually several operating system alternatives available for medium-sized and large computers. The choice of an operating system depends on the processing orientation of the company. Some operating systems are better for *timesharing* (i.e., servicing multiple end users), others for *batch processing*, and others for *distributed processing*.

Applications programs are not as portable between operating systems as we would like. An information system is designed and coded for a specific *compiler*, *computer*, and *operating system*. This is true for both micros and mainframes. Therefore, programs that work well under one operating system may not be compatible with a different operating system.

## Microcomputer Operating Systems

The objectives and functions of microcomputer operating systems are similar to mainframe operating systems. Although some vendors of microcomputers supply their own operating systems, many use **MS DOS, CP/M,** or **UNIX.** MS DOS, developed by Microsoft Corporation, CP/M, developed by Digital Research Corporation, and UNIX, developed by AT&T, have become the unwritten standards for the microcomputer industry. MS DOS and CP/M have a long tradition of acceptance in the single-user microcomputer environment. UNIX has a similar tradition of acceptance in the multiuser mainframe environment.

Some of today's micros are more powerful than the UNIX-based mainframe computers of the early 1980s. This increased capacity enabled micro vendors and AT&T to adapt the very popular UNIX operating system for *multiuser*, *multitasking* (able to handle different processing tasks at the same time) microcomputers. MS DOS and CP/M have

Although some personal computers can service several workstations, the operating systems for most personal computers are oriented to servicing a single user.
(AT&T Information Systems)

been upgraded to handle the multiuser, multitasking environment also. You may encounter spin-offs of these operating systems. For example, PC DOS for the IBM PC is based on Microsoft's MS DOS, and XENIX is a spin-off of UNIX. Because these operating systems are so widely used, hundreds of software vendors have developed systems and applications software that are compatible with them.

Before you can use a microcomputer, you must "**boot** the system." The procedure for booting the system on most micros is simply to load the operating system from disk storage into primary storage. For some micros, this is as easy as flipping the "on" switch. A few seconds later, with the operating system in memory, you are ready to begin processing.

### Other System Software Categories

In this chapter we have discussed two system software categories: *programming-language compiler/interpreters* and *operating systems*. Other system software categories are *utility programs*, *communications software*, and *database management system software*.

**Utility programs** are service routines that eliminate the need for us to write a program every time we need to perform certain common computer operations, such as copying or sorting files. **Communications software** controls the flow of traffic (data) to and from remote locations. **Database management system (DBMS)** software provides the interface between application programs and the data base. DBMS concepts are discussed in greater detail in Chapter 10, "Data Organization and File Processing."

## 9–10   SOFTWARE CONCEPTS _____

### Multiprogramming

All computers, except small micros, have **multiprogramming** capability. Multiprogramming is the *seemingly simultaneous execution* of more than one program at a time. In Section 9–3 we learned that a computer can execute only one program at a time. But the internal processing speed of a computer is so fast that several programs can be allocated a "slice" of computer time in rotation; this makes it appear to us that several programs are being executed at once.

The great difference in processor speed and the speeds of the peripheral devices makes multiprogramming possible. A 40,000-line-per-minute printer cannot even challenge the speed of an average mainframe processor. The processor is continually waiting for the peripheral devices to complete such tasks as retrieving a record from disk storage, printing a report, or copying a backup file onto magnetic tape. During these "wait" periods, the processor just continues processing other programs. In this way, computer system resources are used efficiently.

In a multiprogramming environment, it is not unusual for several programs to require the same I/O device. For example, two or more

The operating system of this large host computer system is the nerve center of a network of distributed computer systems. The system services hundreds of on-line users in a multiprogramming environment.
(Cullinet Software, Inc.)

programs may be competing for the printer. Rather than hold up the processing of a program by waiting for the printer to become available, both programs are executed and the printer output for one is temporarily loaded to magnetic disk. As the printer becomes available, the output is called from magnetic disk and printed. This process is called **spooling.**

## Virtual Memory

We learned in Chapter 6, "Inside the Computer," that all data and programs must be resident in primary storage to be processed. Therefore, primary storage is a critical factor in determining the *throughput*, or how much work can be done by a computer system per unit of time. Once primary storage becomes full, no more programs can be executed until a portion of primary storage is made available.

**Virtual memory** is a systems software addition to the operating system that effectively expands the capacity of primary storage through the use of software and secondary storage. This allows more data and programs to be resident in primary storage at any given time.

The principle behind virtual memory is quite simple. Remember, a program is executed sequentially—one instruction after another. Programs are segmented into **pages,** so only that portion of the program being executed (one or more pages) is resident in primary storage. The rest of the program is on disk storage. Appropriate pages are *rolled* (moved) into primary storage from disk storage as they are needed to continue execution of the program. The paging process and use of virtual memory is illustrated graphically in Figure 9–10.

The advantage of virtual memory is that primary storage is effectively enlarged, giving programmers greater flexibility in what they can do. For example, some applications require several large programs to be resident in primary storage at the same time (e.g., the order-processing and credit-checking programs illustrated in Figure 9–10).

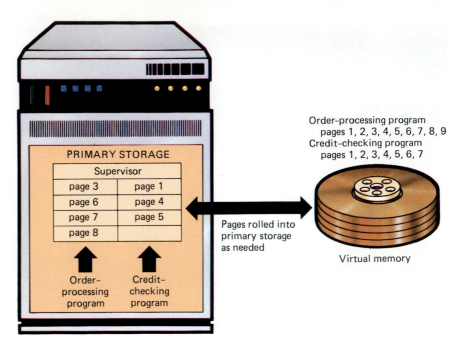

Order–processing program
pages 1, 2, 3, 4, 5, 6, 7, 8, 9
Credit-checking program
pages 1, 2, 3, 4, 5, 6, 7

Pages rolled into
primary storage
as needed

Virtual memory

**FIGURE 9–10**
**Virtual Memory**
Pages of the order-processing
and credit-checking programs
are rolled from virtual memory on
disk into "real" memory (primary
storage) as they are needed.

If the size of these programs exceeds the capacity of "real" primary storage, then virtual memory can be used as a supplement to complete the processing.

The disadvantage of virtual memory is the cost in efficiency during program execution. A program that has many branches to many pages will execute slowly because of the time required to roll pages from secondary to primary storage. Excessive page movement results in too much of the computer's time being devoted to page handling and not enough to processing. This excessive data movement is appropriately named *thrashing* and can actually be counterproductive.

## SUMMARY OUTLINE AND IMPORTANT TERMS

**9–1**   PROGRAMMING AND SOFTWARE.   A **program** directs a computer to perform certain operations. The program is produced by a **programmer,** who uses any of a variety of **programming languages** to communicate with the computer. Programs are referred to as **software.**

Software is classified as either **applications software** or **systems software.** Applications software is designed to perform certain personal, business, or scientific processing tasks. Systems software is more general and supports the basic functions of the computer.

**9–2**   GENERATIONS OF PROGRAMMING LANGUAGES.   Like computers, programming languages have evolved in generations. With each new generation comes a more sophisticated programmer/computer interaction.

**9–3** THE FIRST AND SECOND GENERATIONS: "LOW-LEVEL." The first two generations of programming languages are **low-level languages;** that is, the programmer must identify each fundamental operation that the computer is to perform. The **machine language** is the only language that can be executed on a particular computer. **High-level languages** have surpassed machine language and **assembler language** in terms of human efficiency.

**9–4** COMPILERS AND INTERPRETERS: PROGRAMS FOR PROGRAMS.   High-level languages must be translated to machine language to be executed. High-level languages are a programmer convenience and facilitate the programmer/computer interaction. A **compiler** is needed to translate a **source program** in a high-level language to an **object program** in machine language for execution. An **interpreter** performs a function similar to a compiler, but it translates one instruction at a time.

**9–5** THE THIRD GENERATION: FOR PROGRAMMER CONVENIENCE.   Third-generation languages are either **procedure-oriented languages** or **problem-oriented languages.** Procedure-oriented languages are classified as business (**COBOL** and **RPG**), scientific (**FORTRAN** and **APL**), or multipurpose (**BASIC, Pascal, C, PL/I,** and **Ada**). Problem-oriented languages are designed for a particular application.

**9–6** THE FOURTH GENERATION: QUERY LANGUAGES. In fourth-generation **query languages,** the programmer need only specify "what to do," not "how to do it." The features of query languages include English-like instructions, limited mathematical manipulation of data, automatic report formatting, sequencing (sorting), and record selection by criteria.

**9–7** THE FIFTH GENERATION: APPLICATION GENERATORS. **Application generators,** the fifth generation, are designed to assist in the development of full-scale information systems. Application generators consist of modules of **reusable code** that are pulled together and integrated automatically to complete the system.

**9–8** THE SIXTH GENERATION: NATURAL LANGUAGES.  The sixth-generation **natural language** will someday enable programmers to write or verbalize program specifications without regard to instruction format or syntax. In the meantime, natural languages with certain syntax restrictions are available for limited information processing tasks.

**9–9** THE OPERATING SYSTEM: THE BOSS.   The design objectives of an **operating system,** the nucleus of all software activity, are to minimize turnaround time, maximize throughput, and optimize the use of computer resources. Operating systems are oriented to a particular type of processing environment, such as timesharing, batch, or distributed processing.

  **MS DOS, CP/M,** and **UNIX** are popular operating systems for microcomputers. Until recently, micro operating systems were oriented to servicing a single user. Today, the more sophisticated micro operating systems support the multiuser, multitasking environment.

Systems software categories include programming-language compilers/interpreters, operating systems, **utility programs,** communications software, and **database management systems.**

**9-10**   SOFTWARE CONCEPTS.   **Multiprogramming** is the seemingly simultaneous execution of more than one program at a time on a single computer. **Virtual memory** effectively expands the capacity of primary storage through the use of software and secondary storage.

## REVIEW EXERCISES

### Concepts

1.  Associate each of the following with a particular generation of languages: reusable code, mnemonics, and Ada.

2.  What are the four divisions in a COBOL program? Which contains the program logic?

3.  Name two types of program errors.

4.  Name two procedure-oriented programming languages in each of the three classification areas—business, scientific, and multipurpose.

5.  What are the programs called that translate source programs to machine language? Which one does the translation on a single pass? Which one does it one statement at a time?

6.  Contrast fourth-generation to fifth-generation languages.

7.  Why is it necessary to spool output in a multiprogramming environment?

8.  Give two examples each of applications and systems software.

9.  Name the systems software category associated with: (a) a company's data base, (b) file backup, and (c) overall software and hardware control.

### Discussion

10.  Discuss the difference between a program and a programming language.

11.  If each new generation of languages enhances interaction between programmers and the computer, why not write programs using the most recent generation of languages?

12.  Which generations of languages would a public relations manager be most likely to use? Why?

13.  Suppose you are a programming manager and find that 12 of the 16 programmers would prefer to switch to COBOL from

RPG. Would you support the switch, given that all 600 existing programs are written in RPG and only three programmers are proficient in COBOL? Why or why not?

14. Describe the circumstances that result in the use of virtual memory becoming counterproductive.

## SELF-TEST (by section)

**9-1.** _____ software is more general than _____ software.

**9-2.** When programming in one of the first three generations of languages, you tell the computer "what to do," not "how to do it." (T/F)

**9-3.** Assembler-level languages use mnemonics to represent instructions. (T/F)

**9-4.** An object program is always free of logic errors. (T/F)

**9-5.** A COBOL program has _____ (how many) divisions.

**9-6.** A fourth-generation program will normally have fewer instructions than the same program written in a third-generation language. (T/F)

**9-7.** Application generators are used almost exclusively for ad hoc requests for information. (T/F)

**9-8.** An individual must undergo extensive training before he or she can write programs in a natural language. (T/F)

**9-9.** The operating system program that is always resident in main memory is called the supervisor. (T/F)

**9-10.** Programs are segmented into pages before they are spooled. (T/F)

*Self-Test answers.*   9-1, Systems, applications; 9-2, F; 9-3, T; 9-4, F; 9-5, four; 9-6, T; 9-7, F; 9-8, F; 9-9, T; 9-10, F.

# Zimco Enterprises

## INFORMATION SYSTEMS AT ZIMCO: PERSONNEL

### PERES: PERSONNEL RESOURCES SYSTEM

PERES, which is pronounced like the French city, is an acronym for Zimco's Personnel Resource System. "PERES is one of the four major components of Zimco's corporate-wide MIS [see Figure Z3–3 in the case study following Chapter 3]," says Peggy Peoples, VP of Personnel. "PERES is essentially a personnel accounting system that maintains pertinent data on employees. Besides routine historical data, such as educational background, salary history, and so on, PERES includes data on performance reviews, skills, and professional development."

PERES is divided into three subsystems:

**2.1** Recruiting
**2.2** Pay and Benefits Administration
**2.3** Training and Education

These subsystems are graphically illustrated in the data flow diagram of Figure Z9–1. Figure Z9–1 shows the explosion of the "personnel" component of the Zimco MIS. Each of these subsystems is described in the following sections.

### THE THREE SUBSYSTEMS OF PERES

#### Recruiting Subsystem (2.1)

Peggy Peoples explained Zimco's recruiting policy. "It has long been a tradition at Zimco to hire quality people and promote from within. At the beginning of each quarter, the division VPs enter their work force requirements into PERES; it is our job to find candidates to fill these positions. Our Recruiting Subsystem (see Figure Z9–

1) has proven to be a real help in landing the best people available."

The Recruiting Subsystem (2.1) automatically distributes predefined job descriptions to selected colleges and to several personnel search agencies. About 20 percent of these are distributed via electronic mail; the rest are generated in hard copy and sent via the postal service. The colleges and agencies suggest possible candidates; then the Recruiting Department conducts a preliminary interview. The results of the interview, which are entered into PERES, are on-line and readily accessible to management.

Managers can make on-line inquiries directly from their workstations. The following are examples of some of the on-line reports made available by the menu-driven Recruiting Subsystem.

- Work Force Summary: Current and Authorized
- Current Openings: By Division By Department
- Current Candidate Summary

Peggy says that "the first day a new hire comes to work, he or she reports to us. We give them a couple of minutes' instruction on the use of our workstations, then ask them to enter their personal data into PERES. This serves two purposes. We get the data into the system, but most important, the new hire realizes that computers are very much a part of how we conduct business at Zimco. This is the first activity of a two-day orientation that we give every new hire."

Classified ads, announcing Zimco job openings, are sent to local newspapers electronically in a format that needs no further editing by typesetters. This approach saves time and Zimco gets

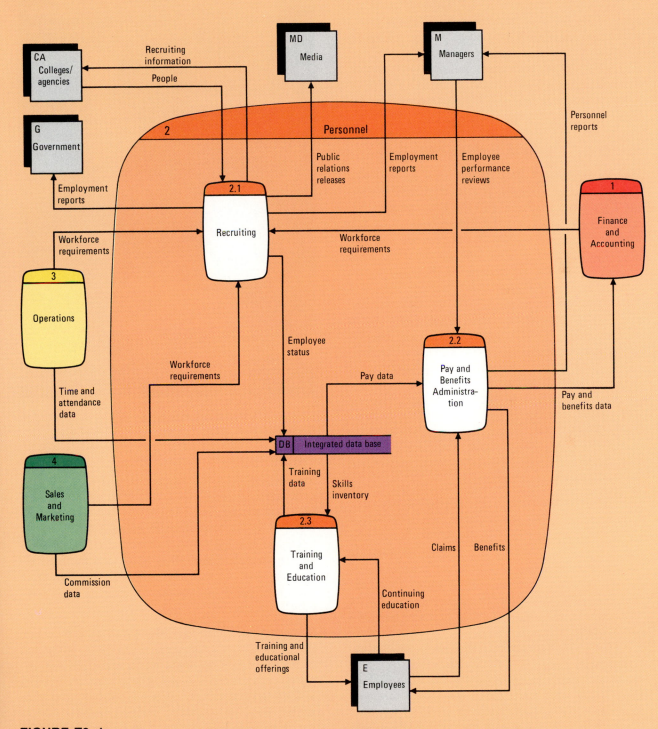

**FIGURE Z9–1**
**Zimco's Personnel Resource System (PERES)**
This data flow diagram is the explosion of the personnel (2) process of the
MIS overview data flow diagram of Figure Z3–3.

a discount for delivering machine-readable ad copy. This facet of the Recruiting Subsystem is explained in the Zimco case study following Chapter 5.

A variety of mandatory government reports, dealing primarily with equal opportunity employment, are generated from the Recruiting Subsystem.

## Pay and Benefits Administration (2.2)

Maintenance and Preparation of Payroll Data. The *payroll application* is a joint effort between the Personnel Division and the Finance and Accounting Division (see the Zimco case study following Chapter 7 on FACS, the Finance and Accounting Control System). Peggy Peoples once described the Pay and Benefits Administration Subsystems (see Figure Z9–1) as the "heart of the *wage and salary administration application*." She explained that "supervisors enter hours-worked data for hourly personnel directly into their workstations. We make any adjustments to pay, such as an optional purchase of Zimco stock, directly to an employee's record on the integrated data base. Then, prior to each pay period, we verify pay and benefits data on the integrated data base. Once the data are prepared, the actual preparation and distribution of the checks is handled by the Disbursement Control Subsystem (1.3) of FACS."

Performance Reviews. At Zimco, every employee has a semiannual performance review—even Preston Smith, the president. Each employee is evaluated by his or her immediate manager in six areas: ability to work with others, innovativeness, contribution through achievement of goals, potential for advancement, ability to communicate, and expertise in his or her area of specialty.

Many managers record their numeric evaluations, from 1 to 10, and add a verbal support statement while interacting directly with PERES. Opie Rader, the manager of the Operations Department in the CIS Division says: "I conduct performance reviews with my people while both of us are seated in front of the tube. When a subordinate comes in my office for the interview, I have already done the rating, usually on the

Many Zimco managers interact simultaneously with the Personnel Resources System (PERES) and their subordinates during a performance review.
(Photo courtesy of Hewlett-Packard Company)

low side. If, by virtue of other information, a subordinate can convince me that he or she should be rated higher, I change the rating on the spot. I feel that there should be some give and take between manager and subordinate. The PERES system gives me and other managers the flexibility to render a mutually agreeable performance review without unnecessarily causing hard feelings."

Management Reports.  Managers at Zimco use the company's fourth-generation query language to make ad hoc requests for information and reports. A manager obtains information by writing a short program that, in turn, "queries" the integrated data base. Such queries can be made to the data base for information in any functional area, not just personnel.

The *query language* used at Zimco is called INGEN (for Information Generator). INGEN, pronounced "engine," was developed by a Dallas entrepreneur. Ed Cool, the education coordinator in CIS, presents a four-hour training session on INGEN during the first week of each month. Ed says: "Seventy percent of the managers at Zimco, including top management, know, use, and love INGEN. INGEN is user friendly and managers can get the information they need without having to wait in line for a programmer."

A recent INGEN request by Monroe Green in the Finance and Accounting Division illustrates the use and applicability of fourth-generation languages. Monroe Green described what information he wanted: "There had been some rumblings about pay discrimination in two of my departments, so I used INGEN to find out for myself. I wrote a short INGEN program to print a list of the employees in each department along with other data, including last month's gross and net pay."

The six-instruction program that Monroe Green wrote (Figure Z9–2) is a good example of how a query language can be used to generate a management report. Monroe's 4GL (fourth-generation language) program is described below.

■ *Instruction 1* specifies that the payroll data are stored on a FILE called PAYROLL in the integrated data base. Although the data of only one file are needed in this example, requests requiring data from several files are no more difficult.

■ *Instruction 2* specifies that the information in the report is to be *sorted* (department 911 before 914) and LISTed BY DEPARTMENT. All "900"-level departments are in the Fi-

nance and Accounting Division. The codes "911" and "914" refer to the Financial Planning and Credit Departments. Instruction 2 also specifies which data elements within the file are to be included in the report of Figure Z9–3. If Monroe had written the instruction as LIST BY DEPARTMENT BY NAME, the employee names would be listed in alphabetical order for each department.

■ *Instruction 3* specifies the criterion by which records are SELECTed. Monroe Green is interested only in those employees from DEPARTMENTs 911 and 914. Other criteria could be included for further record selections. For example, the criterion "GROSS > 400" could be added to select only those people (from departments 911 and 914) whose gross pay is greater than $400.00.

■ *Instruction 4* causes SUBTOTALS to be computed and displayed BY DEPARTMENT.

■ *Instructions 5 and 6* allow Monroe to enhance the appearance and readability of the report by including a title and labeling the columns. Instruction 5 produces the report title, and instruction 6 specifies descriptive column headings.

The COBOL equivalent of this request would require the efforts of a professional programmer from CIS and over 150 lines of code!

Monroe Green's authorization code permits him access to payroll data for those employees within his realm of responsibility—no one else. If he had requested the same report for a "600" department (Personnel Division), he would have received a message on his display screen denying him access to these data.

**FIGURE Z9–2**
**Query-Language Program to Produce Report of Figure Z9–3**
Each instruction is discussed in detail in the case study.

```
1.   FILE IS PAYROLL
2.   LIST BY DEPARTMENT NAME ID SEX NET GROSS
3.   SELECT DEPARTMENT = 911, 914
4.   SUBTOTALS BY DEPARTMENT
5.   TITLE: "PAYROLL FOR DEPARTMENTS 911, 914"
6.   COLUMN HEADINGS:  "DEPARTMENT", "EMPLOYEE, NAME";
     "EMPLOYEE, NUMBER"; "SEX"; "NET, PAY"; "GROSS, PAY"
```

PAYROLL FOR DEPARTMENTS 911, 914

| DEPARTMENT | EMPLOYEE NAME | EMPLOYEE NUMBER | SEX | NET PAY | GROSS PAY |
|---|---|---|---|---|---|
| 911 | ARNOLD | 01963 | 1 | 356.87 | 445.50 |
| 911 | LARSON | 11357 | 2 | 215.47 | 283.92 |
| 911 | POWELL | 11710 | 1 | 167.96 | 243.20 |
| 911 | POST | 00445 | 1 | 206.60 | 292.00 |
| 911 | KRUSE | 03571 | 2 | 182.09 | 242.40 |
| 911 | SMOTH | 01730 | 1 | 202.43 | 315.20 |
| 911 | GREEN | 12829 | 1 | 238.04 | 365.60 |
| 911 | ISAAC | 12641 | 1 | 219.91 | 313.60 |
| 911 | STRIDE | 03890 | 1 | 272.53 | 386.40 |
| 911 | REYNOLDS | 05805 | 2 | 134.03 | 174.15 |
| 911 | YOUNG | 04589 | 1 | 229.69 | 313.60 |
| 911 | HAFER | 09764 | 2 | 96.64 | 121.95 |
| DEPARTMENT TOTAL | | | | 2,522.26 | 3,497.52 |
| 914 | MANHART | 11602 | 1 | 250.89 | 344.80 |
| 914 | VETTER | 01895 | 1 | 189.06 | 279.36 |
| 914 | GRECO | 07231 | 1 | 685.23 | 1,004.00 |
| 914 | CROCI | 08262 | 1 | 215.95 | 376.00 |
| 914 | RYAN | 10961 | 1 | 291.70 | 399.20 |
| DEPARTMENT TOTAL | | | | 1,632.83 | 2,403.36 |
| FINAL TOTAL 17 RECORDS TOTALED | | | | 4,155.09 | 5,900.88 |

**FIGURE Z9–3**
**A Payroll Report**
This payroll report is the result of the execution of the query-language program of Figure Z9–2.

Query languages are effective tools for generating responses to a variety of requests for information. Short query-language programs, similar to the one in Figure Z9–2, are all that is needed to respond to the following typical Zimco management requests:

- Which employees have accumulated over 20 sick days since January 1?
- List departments that have exceeded their total budget allocation for the month of June in alphabetical order by department name.

Terri Suttor, manager of the Technical Support Department in CIS, is investigating the feasibility of implementing a natural language. She said: "It would be easier for managers to use (than INGEN), but they will be more limited in the kinds of requests they can make. State-of-the-art natural-language software can interpret no more than a one-sentence query at a time. A natural-language equivalent of the query-language program of Figure Z9–2 would be: "Show me a report of employee payroll data for departments 911 and 914." Department and overall summary data are automatically generated.

## Training and Education (2.3)

The Training and Education Subsystem (2.3) monitors and tracks the ongoing career development of Zimco employees. Any external or internal training or education received by an employee is entered into his or her "skills inventory." Included in an employee's skills inventory are any special skills or knowledge. As a matter of policy, managers first conduct an internal search to fill openings. They do this by listing desired skills, knowledge, and so on, then initiating an automatic search of the skills inventory section of the integrated data base. Frequently, there is a match and an opportunity for promotion is extended to an existing employee.

The Personnel Division administers ongoing in-house training programs and evaluates employee requests for external educational support. The Training and Education Subsystem automatically informs employees of in-house offerings by posting a notice on Z-Buzz, the name employees have given to Zimco's electronic bulletin board.

## DISCUSSION QUESTIONS

1. A proposal being seriously considered by Zimco's top management is to change all hourly employees to salaried employees. If adopted, what impact would this proposal have on the Pay and Benefits Administration Subsystem?

2. Monroe Green would like to produce a report that lists the employees in department 911 alphabetically by sex. He wants the name, employee number, department, net pay, and gross pay listed for each new employee. How would you modify the query-language program in Figure Z9–2 to generate this report?

3. Opie Rader and other Zimco managers conduct performance reviews with their subordinates while interacting with PERES. Discuss the pros and cons of this approach.

4. Zimco is one of the few companies that asks new hires to enter their own personal data into the corporate data base. Discuss the advantages of this approach.

5. Describe three management reports that you might expect to be generated by the Training and Education Subsystem.

6. Describe the information flow between PERES and FACS. Be specific.

7. What are the advantages of having an on-line skills inventory for all employees?

© *Thomas Victor*

*Publishing and information services is an industry unlike any other, one in which instinct and intuition play as key a role in decision making as do statistics and data. Publishers serve as the catalytic agent that brings together the creative thinking of the authors with the hunger for knowledge and entertainment of millions of readers. Computers help us do this faster, more efficiently, and to a greater degree than ever before in history. Soon there will be a paperless path from the author's imagination to the printed page—already in some cases even the printed page has been eliminated, as in database services. The computer is the vehicle, the tool, that allows us to access and process a vast amount of information quickly. But the quality of the product remains dependent on the human aspect, our ability to make judgments. The life blood of the publishing process will always be the creative energy, talent, and passion of those who write, edit, and market our products.*

Richard E. Snyder
Chairman and CEO
Simon & Schuster, Inc.

# Data Organization and File Processing

## CHAPTER 10

## STUDENT LEARNING OBJECTIVES

- To identify sources of data.
- To describe and illustrate the relationships between the levels of the hierarchy of data organization.
- To describe how data are stored, retrieved, and manipulated in computer systems.
- To demonstrate an understanding of the principles and use of sequential and random processing.
- To demonstrate an understanding of the principles and use of database management systems.
- To discuss the differences between file-oriented and data base organization.

## FOCUS OF ZIMCO CASE STUDY

- Information systems at Zimco: Operations

## 10–1   DATA: THE KEY TO INFORMATION _____

### Data Management

Data management encompasses the storage, retrieval, and manipulation of data. In this chapter we discuss the concepts and methods involved in computer-based data management. We first discuss the traditional methods of data organization, then database management systems.

Your present or future employer will probably use both the traditional and the data base approaches to data management. Many existing information systems were designed using traditional approaches to data management, but the trend now is to use the data base approach to develop new information systems.

### Sources of Data

So far, we have discussed data with respect to information and computer hardware. But where do data come from? And how are data compiled?

Obtaining the data necessary to extract information and generate output is always one of the more challenging tasks in information processing. Data have many sources. They can be compiled as a result of a *telephone call*; received in the form of *letters* and *turnaround documents*; and collected on *remote workstations*, perhaps as part of a point-of-sale or airline reservation system. Some data are *generated outside the company* (e.g., when a customer submits an order specifying type and quality of products). Most data, however, are *generated internally* (e.g., expenses, inventory activity, hours worked, and so on).

Data can come from strange places. For example, metal sensors in the streets relay data to a central computer that controls traffic.

The stock exchange is the source of thousands of pieces of trading data. An information system continually updates a securities data base so that stock brokers in offices all over the country have access to up-to-the-minute quotations on stocks, bonds, and commodities.
(General Instrument Corporation)

Long-distance telephone calls generate destination and duration data for billing purposes. The digitizing of an image, perhaps an x-ray, creates data. Even hardware errors provide a source of data.

The data that we need are not always readily available. Existing data are usually not in the proper format, or they are not complete or up to date. Once consistent and reliable sources of data have been identified for a particular application, procedures must be established to obtain these data. To do this, users and computer specialists work together to establish a scheme of data organization and a method by which to manage the data. The material in this chapter will provide some insight into how this is done.

## 10–2   THE HIERARCHY OF DATA ORGANIZATION: WHICH COMES FIRST— THE BIT OR THE BASE?

In this section we expand on the *hierarchy of data organization*, a concept that was introduced in Chapter 1. Recall that each information system has a hierarchy of data organization, and that each succeeding level in the hierarchy is the result of combining the elements of the preceding level (see Figure 10–1). Data are logically combined in this fashion until a data base is achieved. The six levels of the hierarchy are *bit*, *character*, *data element*, *record*, *file*, and *data base*. The first level, bits, is handled automatically, without action on the part of either the programmer or the end user. The other five levels are important design considerations for any information processing activity. In the following sections we discuss each level of the hierarchy and how each relates to the succeeding level.

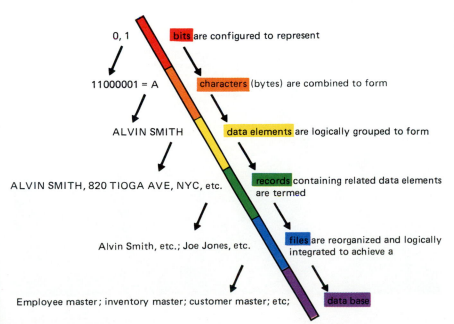

**FIGURE 10–1
The Hierarchy of Data Organization**

0, 1     bits are configured to represent

11000001 = A     characters (bytes) are combined to form

ALVIN SMITH     data elements are logically grouped to form

ALVIN SMITH, 820 TIOGA AVE, NYC, etc.     records containing related data elements are termed

Alvin Smith, etc.; Joe Jones, etc.     files are reorganized and logically integrated to achieve a

Employee master; inventory master; customer master; etc;     data base

## Bits and Characters

A **character** is represented by a group of **bits** that are configured according to an encoding system, such as ASCII or EBCDIC. Whereas the bit is the basic unit of primary and secondary storage, the character is the basic unit for human perception. When we enter a program instruction on a workstation, each character is automatically encoded to a bit configuration. The bit configurations are decoded on output so that we can read and understand the output. In terms of data storage, a character is usually the same as a **byte** (see Chapter 6, "Inside the Computer").

## Data Elements

The **data element** is the lowest-level *logical* unit in the data hierarchy. For example, a single character (e.g., "A") has little meaning out of context. But when characters are combined, they form a logical unit, such as a name (e.g., "Alicia" or "Alvin"). A data element is best described by example: social security number, first name, street address, marital status—all are data elements. A data element is also called a **field.**

An "address" is not necessarily *one* element, but *four* data elements—street address, city, state, and zip code. If we treated the entire address as one data element, it would be cumbersome to print, since the street address is normally placed on a line separate from city, state, and zip code. Also, since name-and-address files are often sorted by zip code, it is a good idea to store the zip code as a separate data element.

When it is stored on secondary storage, a data element is allocated a certain number of character positions. The number of positions allocated is the *field length*. The field length of a telephone area code is 3. The field length of a telephone number is 7.

Whereas data elements are the general, or generic, reference, the

When you travel by air and check your luggage through to your destination, a three-character destination tag (e.g., LAX is Los Angeles, OKC is Oklahoma City) is attached to each piece of luggage. At some airports, this coded data element (destination) is read by an optical scanner and your luggage is automatically routed, via conveyor, to the appropriate pick-up station.
(AT&T Technologies)

| DATA ELEMENTS | DATA ITEMS |
|---|---|
| Employee/social security number | 445447279 |
| Last name | SMITH |
| First name | ALVIN |
| Middle initial | E |
| Department (coded) | ACT |
| Sex (coded) | M |
| Marital status (coded) | S |
| Salary (per week) | 800.00 |

**FIGURE 10–2**
**A Portion of an Employee Record**
The data elements listed are commonly found in employee records. Example data items appear next to each data element.

specific "value" of a data element is called the **data item.** For example, a social security number is a data element, but "445487279" and "440214158" are data items. Street address is a data element, but "1701 El Camino" and "134 East Himes Street" are data items.

## Records

A **record** is a description of an event (e.g., a sale, a hotel reservation) or a thing (e.g., a person or a part). Related data elements describing an event or a thing are logically grouped to form a record. For example, Figure 10–2 contains a partial list of data elements for a typical employee record—it also shows the data items for an *occurrence* of a particular employee record: "Department," "Sex," and "Marital status" are *coded* for ease of data entry and to save storage space.

The record is the lowest-level logical unit that can be accessed from a file. For example, if the personnel manager needs to know just the marital status of Alvin E. Smith, his entire record will be retrieved from secondary storage and transmitted to primary storage for processing.

## Files

A **file** is a collection of related records. The employee master file contains a record for each employee. An inventory file contains a record for each inventory item. The accounts receivable file contains a record for each customer. The term "file" is also used to refer to a named area on a secondary storage device that contains a *program* or *textual material* (such as a letter).

## Data Base

The **data base** is the data resource for all computer-based information systems. In a data base, the data are integrated and related so that data redundancy is minimized. In a situation where an employee moves and records are kept in a traditional file environment, the address must be changed in all files that maintain address data. In a data base, employee address data are stored only *once* and made available to all departments. Therefore, only one update is needed.

The data base supporting the air traffic control system contains the location, altitude, and flight path of all aircraft. The system gives controllers a visual and audible warning when adequate aircraft separation is violated. (Courtesy of International Business Machines Corporation)

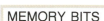

**MEMORY BITS**

**HIERARCHY OF DATA ORGANIZATION**

- Bit
- Character (byte)
- Data element, or field
- Record
- File
- Data base

Database management system (DBMS) software (discussed in Sections 10–6 through 10–9) has enabled many organizations to move from traditional file organization to data base organization, thereby enjoying the benefits of a higher level of data management sophistication.

## 10–3 TRADITIONAL APPROACHES TO DATA MANIPULATION AND RETRIEVAL

In traditional file processing, files are sorted, merged, and processed by a **key data element.** For example, in a payroll file the key might be "employee name," and in an inventory file the key might be "part number."

When you write programs based on the traditional approaches, data are manipulated and retrieved either *sequentially* or *randomly*. You might recall that sequential and random (or direct) access were discussed briefly in Chapter 7, "Peripheral Devices: I/O and Data Storage." Remember, an analogy was made between sequential processing and cassette tapes, and between random processing and phonograph records. Sequential and random processing are presented in detail in the sections that follow.

## 10–4 SEQUENTIAL PROCESSING: ONE AFTER ANOTHER

**Sequential files,** used for **sequential processing,** contain records that are ordered according to a key data element. The key, also called a **control field,** in an employee record might be social security number or employee name. If the key is social security number, the employee records are ordered and processed *numerically* by social security number. If the key is employee name, the records are ordered and processed *alphabetically* by last name. *A sequential file is processed from start to finish. The entire file must be processed, even if only one record is to be updated.*

The principal storage medium for sequential files is magnetic tape. Direct-access storage devices (DASD), such as magnetic disks, can be used also for sequential processing (see Section 10–5).

## Principles of Sequential Processing

Sequential processing procedures for updating an inventory file are illustrated in Figures 10–3, 10–4, and 10–5. Figure 10–3 lists the contents of an inventory *master file*, which is the permanent source of inventory data, and a *transaction file*, which reflects the daily inventory activity.

*Prior to processing, the records on both files are sorted and arranged in ascending sequence by part number (the key).* A utility sort program takes a file of unsequenced records and creates a new file with the records sorted according to the values of the key. The sort process is illustrated in Figure 10–4.

Figure 10–5 shows both the inventory master and transaction files as input and the *new inventory master file* as output. Since the technology does not permit records to be "rewritten" on the master file, a new master file tape is created to reflect the updates to the master file. *A new master file is always created in sequential processing for master file updates.* The processing steps are illustrated in Figure 10–5 and explained as follows:

■ *Prior to processing.* If the two input tapes are *not sorted* by part number, they must be sorted as shown in Figure 10–4. The sorted tapes are then mounted on the tape drives. A blank tape, mounted on a third tape drive, will ultimately contain the updated master file. The arrows under the part numbers in Figure 10–5 indicate which records are positioned before the read/write heads on the respective tape drives. These records are the *next* to be read. Each file has an **end-of-file marker (EOF)** that signals the end of the file.

■ *Step 1.* The first record (4) on the transaction file (T) is read and loaded to primary storage. Then the first record (2) on the master file (M) is loaded to primary storage. A comparison is made of

Magnetic tape is currently the preferred medium for backup and archival storage. This tape librarian is filing recently produced backup tape cassettes for off-line storage.
(Courtesy of International Business Machines Corporation)

**FIGURE 10–3**
**Inventory Master and Transaction Files**
Both files are sorted by part number. The numbers in brackets, [ ], reflect the inventory master file after the update. Figures 10–5 and 10–6 graphically illustrate the update process.

Inventory master file (sorted by part number)

| Part no. | Price | No. used to date | No. in stock |
|---|---|---|---|
| 2 | .25 | 40 | 200 |
| 4 | 1.40 | 100 [106] * | 100 [94] |
| 8 | .80 | 500 | 450 |
| • | • | • | • |
| • | • | • | • |
| • | • | • | • |
| 20 | 4.60 | 60 [72] | 14[2] |
| 21 | 2.20 | 50 | 18 |

One record ➤ (points to record: 2    .25    40    200)

Transaction file (sorted by part number)

| Part no. | No. used today |
|---|---|
| 4 | 6 |
| 20 | 12 |

* [   ] reflects updated values

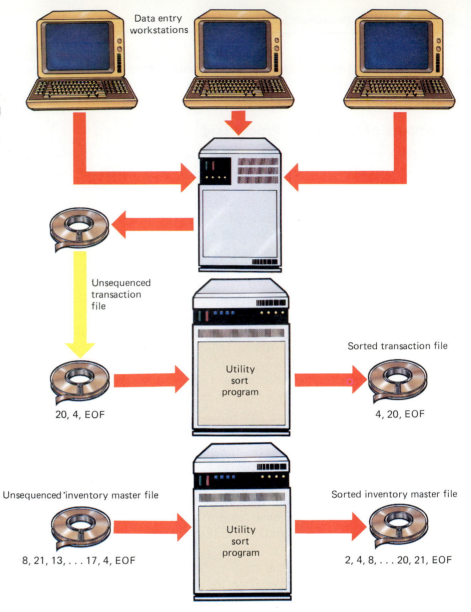

**FIGURE 10–4**
**Sorting**
Unsequenced inventory master and transaction files are sorted prior to sequential processing. Normally, the master file would be sorted as a result of prior processing.

Data entry workstations

Unsequenced transaction file

20, 4, EOF

Utility sort program

Sorted transaction file

4, 20, EOF

Unsequenced inventory master file

8, 21, 13, . . . 17, 4, EOF

Utility sort program

Sorted inventory master file

2, 4, 8, . . . 20, 21, EOF

the two keys. Because there is not a match [4 ≠ (is not equal to) 2], the first record on the master file is written to the new master file tape without being changed.

■ *Step 2*. The next record (4) on the master file is read and loaded to primary storage. After a positive comparison (4 = 4), the record of part number 4 is updated (see Figure 10–3) to reflect the use of 6 items and then written to the new master file. In Figure 10–3 note that the "number in stock" data item is reduced from 100 to 94 and the "number used to date" is increased from 100 to 106. Updated records in Figure 10–5 are enclosed in boxes.

■ *Step 3*. The next record from the transaction file (20) and the next record from the master file (8) are read and loaded to primary storage. A comparison is made. Since the comparison is negative

$(20 \neq 8)$, the record for part number 8 is written to the new master file without being changed.

■ *Step 4*. Records from the master file are individually read and loaded, and the part number is compared to that of the transaction record (20). With each negative comparison (e.g., $20 \neq 17$), the record from the old master file is written, without change, to the new master file. The read-and-compare process continues until a match is made $(20 = 20)$. Record 20 is then updated and written to the new master file.

■ *Step 5*. A read is issued to the transaction file and an end-of-file marker is found. All records on the master file following the record for part number 20 are written to the new master file, and the end-of-file marker is recorded on the new master file. All tapes

**FIGURE 10–5**
**Sequential Processing**
An inventory master file is updated using sequential processing and magnetic tapes. Processing steps are discussed in the text. Notice in Step 5 that the backup is a by-product of sequential processing.

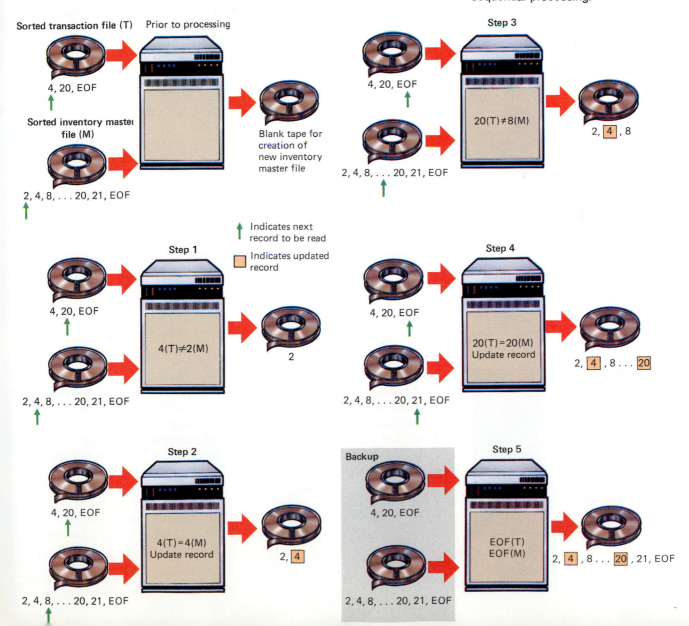

are then automatically rewound and removed from the tape drives for off-line storage and processing at a later time.

## Backup

The transaction file and old master file are retained as *backup* to the new master file. Fortunately, *backup is a by-product of sequential processing*. After the new master file is created, the old master file and the transaction file become the backup. If the new master is destroyed, the transaction file can simply be run against the old master file to recreate the new master file.

Backup files are handled and maintained by *generation*, with the up-to-date master file being the current generation. This tape cycling procedure is called the **grandfather-father-son method** of file backup. The "son" file is the up-to-date master file. The "father" generation is noted in Step 5 of Figure 10–5. Most computer centers maintain a grandfather file (from the last update run) as a backup to the backup.

## 10–5   RANDOM OR DIRECT-ACCESS PROCESSING: PICK AND CHOOSE _____

A **direct-access file,** or a **random file,** is a collection of records that can be processed randomly (in any order). This is called **random processing.** Only the value of the record's key field is needed in order for a record to be retrieved or updated. More often than not, magnetic disks are the primary storage medium for random processing.

You can access records on a direct-access file by more than one key. For example, a salesperson inquiring about the availability of a particular product could inquire by *product number* and, if the product number is not known, by *product name*. The file, however, must be created with the intent of having multiple keys.

### Random-Access Methods

The procedures and mechanics of the way a particular record is accessed directly are, for the most part, transparent to users, and even to programmers. However, some familiarity will help you understand the capabilities and limitations of direct-access methods. The **indexed sequential-access method,** or **ISAM** (pronounced *Eye-sam*) is a popular method that permits both sequential and random processing.

An ISAM file is actually two files: The *data file* contains the records (e.g., for each student, for each inventory item); the smaller *index file* contains the key and disk address of each record on the data file. A request for a particular record is first directed to the index file, which, in turn, "points" to the physical location of the desired record on magnetic disk (see Chapter 7, "Peripheral Devices: I/O and Data Storage").

A micro user can take advantage of many information services, such as electronic shopping, by establishing a communications link with a large computer system. Once on-line, the user has access to a random access file that contains descriptions of thousands of items. The user shops by selecting an item from a "video catalog." Forecasters estimate that by 1990 up to 20% of all retail sales will be transacted from personal computers.
(Mindset Corporation)

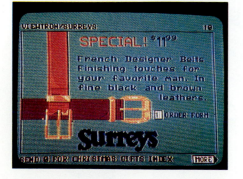

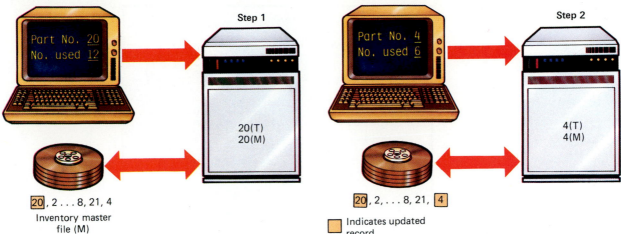

Step 1

Part No. 20
No. used 12

20(T)
20(M)

20, 2 . . . 8, 21, 4
Inventory master
file (M)

Step 2

Part No. 4
No. used 6

4(T)
4(M)

20, 2, . . . 8, 21, 4
Indicates updated
record

**FIGURE 10–6**
**Random Processing**
An inventory master file is
updated using random
processing and magnetic disks.
Processing steps are discussed
in the text.

## Principles of Random Processing

In Figure 10–6, the inventory master file of Figure 10–3 is updated from
an *on-line* workstation to illustrate the principles of random processing.
The following activities take place during the update:

- *Step 1*. The first transaction (for part number 20) is entered into
  primary storage from an on-line workstation. The computer issues
  a read for the record of part number 20 on the inventory master
  file. The record is retrieved and transmitted to primary storage
  for processing. The record is updated and written back to the *same*
  location on the master file. The updated record is simply written
  over the old record.

- *Step 2*. A second transaction (for part number 4) is entered into
  primary storage. The computer issues a read for the record of part
  number 4 on the inventory master file. The record is retrieved and
  transmitted to primary storage for processing. The record is then
  updated.

Since only two updates are to be made to the inventory master
file, processing is complete. However, unlike sequential processing,
where the backup is built in, random processing requires a special
run to provide backup to the inventory master file. In the backup activity
illustrated in Figure 10–7, the master file is "dumped" from disk to
tape at frequent intervals, usually daily. If the inventory master file

**FIGURE 10–7**
**Backup Procedure for Random
Processing**
Unlike sequential processing, a
separate run is required to create
the backup for random
processing.

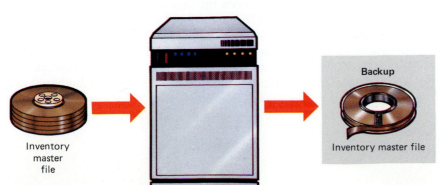

Backup

Inventory
master
file

Inventory master file

| | Sequential Processing | Random Processing |
|---|---|---|
| Primary Storage Medium | | |
| Preprocessing | Files must be sorted | None required |
| File Updating | Requires complete processing of file and creation of new master file | Only active records are processed, then rewritten to the same storage area |
| Data Currency | Batch (at best, data are a day old) | On-line (up-to-the-minute) |
| Backup | Built-in (old master file and transaction file) | Requires special provisions |

**FIGURE 10–8**
**Differences Between Sequential and Random Processing**

is destroyed, it can be recreated by dumping the backup file (on tape) to disk (the reverse of Figure 10–7).

As you can see, random processing is more straightforward than sequential processing, and it has those advantages associated with on-line, interactive processing. Figure 10–8 summarizes the differences between sequential and random processing.

## 10–6  DATA INTEGRATION: SOLVING THE DATA PUZZLE

Our discussion thus far has focused on traditional file processing. These files are usually designed to meet the specific requirements of a particular functional-area department, such as accounting, sales, or production. Consequently, different, but in many ways similar, files are created to support these functions. Many of the data elements on each of these files are common. For example, each of these functional areas has a need to maintain such data as customer name, customer address, and the contact person at the customer location. When the name of the contact person changes in a traditional file environment, each file must be updated separately.

*Data redundancy* is costly, but it can be minimized by designing an *integrated data base* to serve the organization as a whole, not just one specific department. The integrated data base is made possible by **database management system (DBMS)** software. Some of the DBMS software packages on the market include IMS, dBASE III, TOTAL, IDMS, IDMS/R, DL1, System 2000, RAMIS, ADABAS, Ingress, SQL/DS, and Encompass. Notice that "database" is one word when it refers to the software that manages the data base. "Data base" is two words when it refers to the highest level of the hierarchy of data organization (see Figure 10–1).

## 10–7   WHAT'S TO BE GAINED FROM A DATA BASE ENVIRONMENT?

**Greater Access to Information.**   Most organizations have accumulated a wealth of data, but translating these data to meaningful information has, at times, proven difficult, especially in a traditional file environment. The structure of an integrated data base provides enormous *flexibility* in the types of reports that can be generated and the types of on-line inquiries that can be made.

**Minimizing of Data Redundancy.**   A database management system minimizes data redundancy through advanced *data structures*, or the manner in which the data elements and records are related to each other.

**Software Development Made Easier.**   The programming task is simplified with a database management system because data are more readily available. In a data base, data are *independent* of the applications programs. That is, data elements can be added, changed, and deleted from the data base, and this does not affect existing programs. Adding a data element to a record of a traditional file may require the modification and testing of dozens, and sometimes hundreds, of programs.

The processing constraints of traditional files are overcome by database management systems software. To do this, database management systems rely on sophisticated data structures. The examples presented in Sections 10–8 and 10–9 should help you to better understand the principles and advantages of database management systems. The examples present two types of database management systems that are commonly found in practice. The first example illustrates the principles of *CODASYL* (*Co*nference for *Da*ta *Sy*stems *L*anguages) DBMSs, sometimes called *network* DBMSs, and the second example illustrates the principles of *relational* DBMSs.

High density storage media and data base management systems have made it possible to maintain readily accessible "electronic libraries." A trust officer of a savings and loan company is browsing through the earnings reports of various companies before investing her company's funds.
(Mead Data Central)

## 10–8   CODASYL DATABASE MANAGEMENT SYSTEMS

**A CODASYL DBMS Example.**   Consider the following situation. A library currently maintains a file that contains the following data elements on each record:

- Title
- Author(s)
- Publisher
- Publisher's address
- Classification
- Publication year

The head librarian wants more flexibility in obtaining decision-making information. Many of the librarian's requests would be impractical with the existing traditional file (see Figure 10–9). A data base administrator recommended restructuring the file for a CODASYL database manage-

| Title | ISBN number | Publication year | Publisher | Publisher's address | Author 1 | Author 2 | Author 3 | Author 4 |
|---|---|---|---|---|---|---|---|---|

**FIGURE 10–9**
**Record Layout**
This record layout is for a traditional book inventory file in a library.

Libraries are converting their cumbersome card catalogs to computer data base systems. These systems almost eliminate data redundancy and provide library patrons with immediate on-line access to subject, title, and author information. Publishers are already supplying libraries with "index card" data in machine-readable format. (University of Oklahoma)

ment system. The data base administrator is a computer specialist who designs and maintains the data base.

Not surprisingly, the analysts found certain data redundancies in the existing file. Since each book or title has a separate record, the *name* of an author who has written several books is repeated for each book written. A given publisher may have hundreds, even thousands, of books in the library—but in the present file, the *publisher* and *publisher's address* are repeated for each title.

To eliminate these data redundancies, the data base administrator suggested the records shown in Figure 10–10. The **data base record** is similar to the record of a traditional file in that it is a collection of related data elements and is read from, or written to, the data base as a unit.

Next, the data base administrator establishes the relationships between the records. There is a *one-to-many* relationship between the publisher and title records. That is, one publisher may publish any number of titles. The publisher-title relationship is represented in Figure 10–10 by a connecting line between the two records. A double arrow toward the title record represents the possibility of more than one title per publisher. The publisher-title combination is called a **set.** Other sets defined by the data base administrator are title-author and author-

**FIGURE 10–10**
**A Data Base Schema**
The record layout of the traditional book inventory file in Figure 10–9 is reorganized into data base records and integrated into a data base schema to minimize data redundancy. Relationships are established among the data base records so that authors, titles, and publishers can be linked as appropriate.

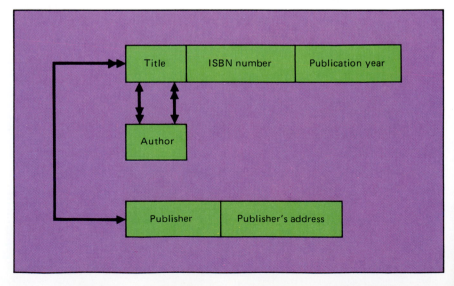

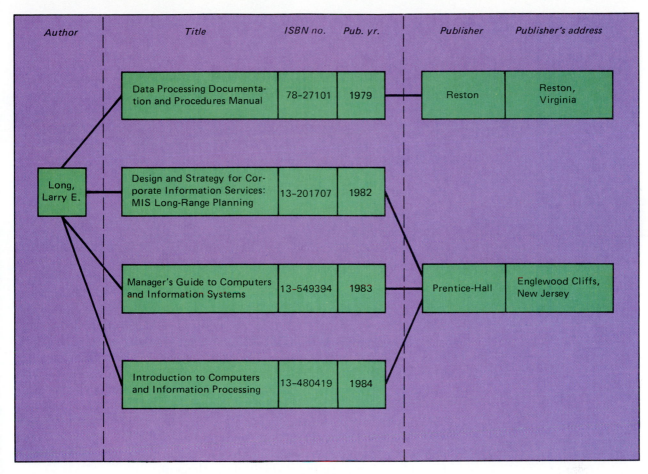

| Author | Title | ISBN no. | Pub. yr. | Publisher | Publisher's address |
|--------|-------|----------|----------|-----------|---------------------|
| | Data Processing Documentation and Procedures Manual | 78-27101 | 1979 | Reston | Reston, Virginia |
| Long, Larry E. | Design and Strategy for Corporate Information Services: MIS Long-Range Planning | 13-201707 | 1982 | | |
| | Manager's Guide to Computers and Information Systems | 13-549394 | 1983 | Prentice-Hall | Englewood Cliffs, New Jersey |
| | Introduction to Computers and Information Processing | 13-480419 | 1984 | | |

**FIGURE 10–11**
**An Occurrence of the Data Base Structure of Figure 10–10**
Notice that publishers can be linked to authors via the title record, and vice versa.

title. Figure 10–10 is a graphic representation of the logical structure of the data base, called a **schema** (pronounced *SKEE-muh*).

In the data base schema of Figure 10–10, a particular author's name appears only once. The author's name is then linked to the title records of those books that he or she has authored. The publisher record is linked to all the titles that it publishes. When accessing a record in a program, you simply request the record of a particular title, author, or publisher. Once you have the author's record, you can use the links between records to retrieve the titles of the books written by that author. Similarly, if you request the record of a particular publisher, you can obtain a list of all titles published by that publisher.

**Occurrences.**   Figure 10–10 is a representation of the schema, and Figure 10–11 is an *occurrence* of the data base structure. The schema and the occurrence are analogous to the data element and the data item (e.g., publisher: Prentice-Hall). One is the definition—the category or abstract—and the other is the actual value or contents.

**Queries to the Data Base.**   This data base design eliminates, or at least minimizes, data redundancy and permits the head librarian to make a wide range of inquiries. For example:

■ What titles were written by Mark Twain?

■ List those titles published in 1986 by Prentice-Hall (alphabetically by title).

Responses to these and other similar inquiries are relatively easy to obtain with a database management system. Similar inquiries to the library's existing file would require not only the complete processing of the file, but perhaps several data preparation computer runs for sorting and merging.

If the head librarian decides after a year to add, for example, the Library of Congress number to the title record, the data base administrator can make the revision without affecting existing programs.

## 10–9   RELATIONAL DATABASE MANAGEMENT SYSTEMS

**Relational versus CODASYL DBMSs.**   The relational approach to database management systems has been gaining momentum through the 1980s. In contrast to the CODASYL DBMS, data are accessed by *content* rather than by *address*. That is, the relational approach uses the computer to search the data base for the desired data rather than accessing data through a series of indices and physical addresses, as with CODASYL DBMSs. In relational DBMSs, the data structures, or relationships between data, are defined in *logical,* rather than *physical*, terms. That is, the relational data base has no predetermined relationship between the data, such as the one-to-many sets in the CODASYL schemas (see Figure 10–10). In this way, data can be accessed at the *data element* level. In CODASYL structures, the entire record must be retrieved to examine a single data element.

**A Relational DBMS Example.**   Let's stay with library applications for our relational DBMS example, but let's shift emphasis from book inventory to book circulation. The objective of a circulation system is to keep track of who borrows which books, then monitor the timely return of the books. In the traditional file environment, the record layout might appear as shown in Figure 10–12. In the record shown, a library patron can borrow from one to four books. Precious storage space is wasted for patrons who borrow infrequently, and the four-book limit may force prolific readers to make more frequent trips to the library.

The data base administrator recommended the relational DBMS organization shown in Figure 10–13. The data base contains two *tables*, each containing rows and columns of data. A row is roughly equivalent to the occurrence of a CODASYL record. The column headings, called *attributes*, are analogous to data elements.

The first table contains patron data and the second table contains data relating to books out on loan. Each new patron is assigned a number and issued a library card with a number that can be read with an optical wand scanner. The patron's card number, name, and address are added to the data base. When the patron borrows a book,

---

### MEMORY BITS

#### APPROACHES TO DATA MANAGEMENT

■ Sequential processing

■ Random (or direct) processing
  Indexed sequential-access method (ISAM)
  Direct access

■ Database management systems (DBMS)
  CODASYL
  Relational

| Card No. | First Name | Last Name | Address | | | | Book #1 (ISBN) | Due Date | Book #2 (ISBN) | Due Date | Book #3 (ISBN) | Due Date | Book #4 (ISBN) | Due Date |
|---|---|---|---|---|---|---|---|---|---|---|---|---|---|---|
| | | | Street | City | ST | ZIP | | | | | | | | |

**FIGURE 10–12**
**Record Layout**
This record layout is for a traditional book circulation file in a library.

Patron Data

| Card No. | First Name | Last Name | Address | | | | 
|---|---|---|---|---|---|---|
| | | | Street | City | ST | ZIP |
| 1243 | Jason | Jones | 18 W. Oak | Ponca City | OK | 74601 |
| 1618 | Kay | Smith | 108 10th St. | Newkirk | OK | 74647 |
| 2380 | Heather | Hall | 2215 Pine Dr. | Ponca City | OK | 74604 |
| 2644 | Brett | Brown | 1700 Sunset | Ponca City | OK | 74604 |
| 3012 | Melody | Beck | 145 N. Brook | Ark. City | KS | 67005 |
| 3376 | Butch | Danner | RD#7 | Tonkawa | OK | 74653 |
| 3859 | Abe | Michaels | 333 Paul Ave. | Kaw City | OK | 74641 |

Books-on-Loan Data

| Card No. | Book No. (ISBN) | Due Date |
|---|---|---|
| 1618 | 89303-530 | 4/7 |
| 1243 | 13-201702 | 4/20 |
| 3859 | 13-48049 | 4/9 |
| 2644 | 18-23614 | 4/14 |
| 2644 | 71606-214 | 4/14 |
| 2644 | 22-68111 | 4/3 |
| 1618 | 27-21675 | 4/12 |

**FIGURE 10–13**
**A Relational Data Base Organization**
The record layout of the traditional book circulation file record of Figure 10–12 is reorganized and integrated into a relational data base with a "Patron Data" table and a "Books-on-Loan Data" table.

the librarian at the circulation desk uses a wand scanner to enter the card number and the book's ISBN number. These data and the due date, which are entered on a keyboard, become a row in the "on loan" table. Notice that by using a relational DBMS there is no limit to the number of borrowed books that the system can handle for a particular patron.

Queries to the Data Base. Suppose that the circulation librarian wanted a report of overdue books as of April 8 (4/8). The query would be: "List all books overdue" (query date is 4/8). The search criterion "due date < (before) 4/8" is applied to the "due date" column in the "on loan" table (see Figure 10–14). The search surfaces two overdue books; then the system uses the card numbers to cross-reference delinquent patrons in the "patron" table to obtain their names and addresses. The report at the bottom of Figure 10–14 is produced in response to the librarian's query. Data on each book, including publisher, author,

| Card No. | Book No. (ISBN) | Due Date | Overdue? (Due Date < 4/8) |
|---|---|---|---|
| 1618 | 89303-530-0 | 4/7 | Yes |
| 1243 | 13-201702-5 | 4/20 | No |
| 3859 | 13-48049-8 | 4/9 | No |
| 2644 | 18-23614-1 | 4/14 | No |
| 2644 | 71606-214-0 | 4/14 | No |
| 2644 | 22-68111-7 | 4/3 | Yes |
| 1618 | 27-21675-2 | 4/12 | No |

**FIGURE 10–14**
**Queries to a Relational Data Base**
The figure graphically illustrates the resolution and output of an April 8 query to the data base: "List all books overdue."

| Overdue Books (4/8) | | | |
|---|---|---|---|
| Card No. | Name | Due Date | ISBN Number |
| 1618 | Kay Smith | 4/7 | 89303-530-0 |
| 2644 | Brett Brown | 4/3 | 22-68111-7 |

and ISBN number, might be maintained in another table in the relational data base.

We all keep data, both at our place of business and at home. DBMS software and the availability of computing hardware make it easier for us to extract meaningful information from these data. In time, working with data bases will be as familiar to us as reaching in a desk drawer for a file folder.

## SUMMARY OUTLINE AND IMPORTANT TERMS

**10–1**   DATA: THE KEY TO INFORMATION.   Most organizations use both the traditional and data base approaches to data management. The trend is to the data base approach.

Data come from many sources. The source and method of data entry are important considerations in information processing. Some data are generated outside the organization, but most are generated as a result of internal operations.

**10–2**   THE HIERARCHY OF DATA ORGANIZATION: WHICH COMES FIRST—THE BIT OR THE BASE?   The six levels of the hierarchy of data organization are **bit, character** (or **byte**), **data element, record, file,** and **data base.** The first level is transparent to the programmer and end user, but the other five are integral to the design of any information processing activity. A string of bits is combined to form a character. Characters are combined to represent the values of data elements. Related data elements are combined to form records. Records with the same data elements combine to form a file. The data base is the company's data resource for all information systems.

**10–3**   TRADITIONAL APPROACHES TO DATA MANIPULATION AND RETRIEVAL.   In traditional file processing, files are sorted, merged, and processed by a **key data element.** Data are retrieved and manipulated either sequentially or randomly.

**10–4**   SEQUENTIAL PROCESSING: ONE AFTER ANOTHER.   **Sequential files,** used for **sequential processing,** contain records that are ordered according to a key, also called a **control field.**

A sequential file is processed from start to finish, and a particular record cannot be updated without processing the entire file.

In sequential processing, the records on both the transaction and the master file must be sorted prior to processing. A new master file is created for each computer run in which records are added or changed.

**10–5**   RANDOM OR DIRECT-ACCESS PROCESSING: PICK AND CHOOSE.   The **direct-access** or **random file** permits **random processing** of records. The primary storage medium for direct-access files is magnetic disk.

The **indexed sequential-access method (ISAM)** is one of several access methods that permit a programmer random access to any record on the file. In ISAM, the access of any given record is, in effect, a series of sequential searches through several levels of an index file. This search results in the disk address of the record in question.

In random processing, the unsorted transaction file is run against a random master file. Only the records needed to complete the transaction are retrieved from secondary storage.

**10–6**   DATA INTEGRATION: SOLVING THE DATA PUZZLE.   A traditional file is usually designed to meet the specific requirements of a particular functional-area department. This approach to file design results in the same data being stored and maintained in several separate files. Data redundancy is costly and can be minimized by designing an integrated data base to serve the organization as a whole and not any specific department. The integrated data base is made possible by **database management system (DBMS)** software.

**10–7**   WHAT'S TO BE GAINED FROM A DATA BASE ENVIRONMENT?   The benefits of a data base environment have encouraged many organizations to convert information systems that use traditional file organization to an integrated data base. Database management systems permit greater access to information, minimize data redundancy, and provide programmers more flexibility in the design and maintenance of information systems.

Database management systems rely on sophisticated data structures to overcome the processing constraints of traditional files. Two common types of DBMSs are CODASYL and relational.

**10–8**   CODASYL DATABASE MANAGEMENT SYSTEMS.   In CODASYL data bases, data links are established between **data base records.** One-to-one and one-to-many relationships between data base records are combined to form **sets.** The data base **schema** is a graphic representation of the logical structure of these sets.

**10–9**   RELATIONAL DATABASE MANAGEMENT SYSTEMS.   In relational DBMSs, data are accessed by content rather than by address. There is no predetermined relationship between the data; therefore, the data can be accessed at the data element level. The data are organized in tables in which each row is roughly equivalent to an occurrence of a CODASYL record.

# REVIEW EXERCISES

## Concepts

1. What are the six levels of the hierarchy of data organization?
2. What is the lowest-level logical unit in the hierarchy of data organization?

3.  What is the logical structure of a CODASYL data base called?

4.  Name two possible key data elements for a personnel file. Name two for an inventory file.

5.  In the grandfather-father-son method of file backup, which of the three files is the most current?

6.  What is the purpose of an end-of-file marker?

7.  Under what circumstances is a new master file created in sequential processing?

8.  What is meant when someone says that data are program independent?

9.  Use the technique of Figure 10–5 to illustrate graphically the sequential processing steps required to update the inventory master file of Figure 10–3. The transaction file contains activity for part numbers 8 and 21. Assume that the transaction file is unsequenced.

10. Use the technique of Figure 10–6 to illustrate graphically the random processing steps required to update the inventory master file of Figure 10–3. The transaction file contains activity for part numbers 8 and 21. Provide for backup.

11. The attribute of a relational DBMS is analogous to which level of the hierarchy of data organization?

## Discussion

12. Contrast the advantages and disadvantages of sequential and random processing. Do you feel there will be a place for sequential processing in 1990? If so, where?

13. Assume that the registrar, housing office, and placement service at your college all have computer-based information systems that rely on traditional file organization. Identify possible redundant data elements.

14. Identify the sources of data that eventually become input to an accounting information system.

15. The author contends that a fundamental knowledge of the capabilities and limitations of ISAM is important, even though ISAM storage and search procedures are transparent to the programmer. Do you agree or disagree? Why?

16. What do you feel is the most significant advantage to using a database management system? Why?

## SELF-TEST (by section)

10–1. Since a turnaround document is machine readable, it is not considered a source of data. (T/F)

10–2. _____ is another name for field.

**10–3.** A key data element is not needed for sequential processing. (T/F)

**10–4.** The entire sequential file must be processed if only one record is to be updated. (T/F)

**10–5.** In ISAM organization, the data file contains the key and disk address. (T/F)

**10–6.** Integrated data bases are made possible by DBMS software. (T/F)

**10–7.** One of the disadvantages of DBMS software is that applications programs must be modified when the data base design is changed. (T/F)

**10–8.** The CODASYL schema and the occurrence are analogous to the data element and the _____ .

**10–9.** In relational DBMSs, the data structures are defined in logical, rather than physical, terms. (T/F)

*Self-Test answers.*   10–1, F; 10–2, Data element; 10–3, F; 10–4, T; 10–5, F; 10–6, T; 10–7, F; 10–8, data item; 10–9, T.

# Zimco Enterprises

## INFORMATION SYSTEMS AT ZIMCO: OPERATIONS

### PICS: PRODUCTION AND INVENTORY CONTROL SYSTEM

PICS, Zimco's Production and Inventory Control System, supports the Operations Division and is one of the four functional components of Zimco's integrated Management Information System (see Figure Z3–3 in the case study following Chapter 3). PICS is the central focus of this case study. FACS, the Finance and Accounting Control System, and PERES, the Personnel Resources System, are presented in the case studies following Chapters 7 and 9, respectively. SAMIS, the Sales and Marketing Information System, is featured in the case study following Chapter 11.

Figure Z10–1 graphically illustrates the scope of PICS by showing the explosion of Process 3, "Operations," of the Zimco MIS overview data flow diagram (Figure Z3–3). PICS is logically divided into five subsystems. These are:

**3.1** Production
**3.2** Research and Development
**3.3** Schedule and Monitor Production
**3.4** Acquire and Manage Materials
**3.5** Shipping

The Operations Division's user liaison, Ursula Lain, is the interface between CIS people (programmers, systems analysts, and the data base administrator) and users. She made a valuable contribution to PICS during its design and implementation by facilitating and fostering verbal communication between CIS and user personnel. Ursula explained how the project team came up with the five subsystems. "The project team analyzed the Operations Division from an information processing perspective, not from a departmental perspective. Because the information and processing requirements of the various departments overlapped substantially, it seemed only logical that we design PICS as an integrated system. Although there is some correlation between the subsystems and departmental lines, this was not a criterion during the design phase. Our primary concern was to design a system that would best meet the needs of the Operations Division, while complementing Zimco's overall MIS."

### TRANSITIONING TO A DATA BASE ENVIRONMENT

Otto Manning, the VP of Operations, was the real force behind the development and implementation of PICS and he was very much a proponent of designing it around an integrated data base. He said: "The Operations Division is very dynamic and hopelessly intertwined with everything we do here at Zimco. We get input from marketing, R&D, and accounting. Marketing tells us what products to make, how many to make, and when to have them in stock. R&D tells us how to make them and accounting tells us how much we can spend. All too often marketing wants the product before R&D is finished with the design, and accounting doesn't allocate enough money to cover the cost of production. These and other conflicts between divisions highlight the need for people throughout the company to be better informed. To help alleviate some of our misinformation problems, we decided that the nerve center of PICS should be an integrated data base."

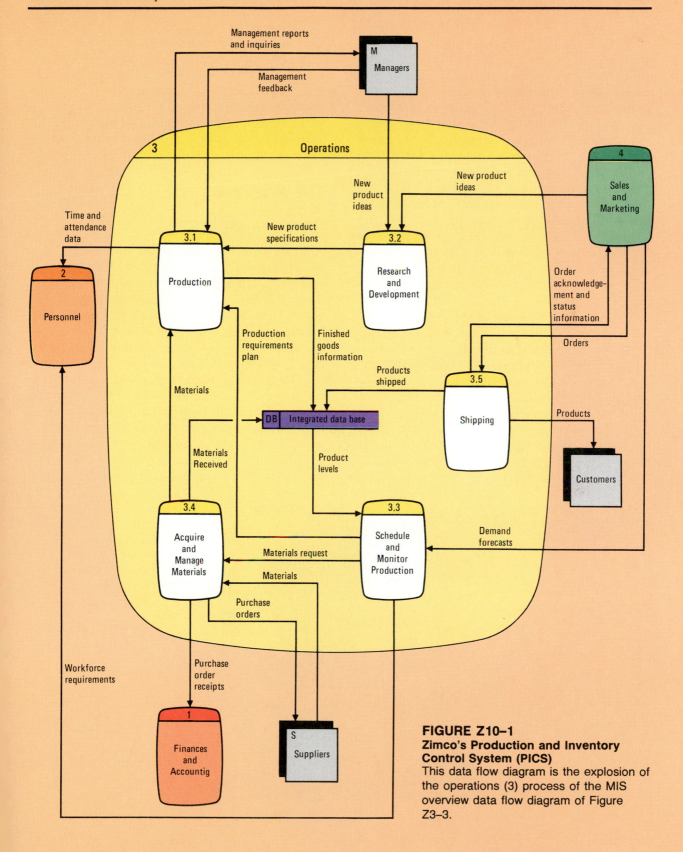

**FIGURE Z10–1**
**Zimco's Production and Inventory
Control System (PICS)**
This data flow diagram is the explosion of
the operations (3) process of the MIS
overview data flow diagram of Figure
Z3–3.

Both users and CIS people knew that transitioning to an integrated data base from a traditional file environment would be a major undertaking. During the decision period in the early 1980s, Terri Suttor, the manager of the Technical Support Department in CIS, would often get on her soapbox to cite the tremendous advantages of having an integrated data base. According to Terri: "The traditional approach to data organization revolves around the file and our many sequential and direct access files are fraught with data redundancy." Terri liked to say: "We may be data rich but we are information poor. A DBMS can turn our wealth of data into a wealth of information."

Terri, who manages the data base administrators, would discuss the benefits of an integrated data base with anyone who would listen. "An integrated data base supported by a good database management system (DBMS) will inevitably expand the scope of available information and enable Zimco managers to make more informed and, therefore, better decisions." Terri said that "by minimizing data redundancy, data collection and update procedures are simplified. We can have greater confidence in the integrity of our data because we make the update in only one place—the data base."

Terri was also quick to point out that having an integrated data base would have a very positive impact on CIS. "The data base environment opens new doors for programmers and systems analysts. It gives them greater flexibility in the initial design of the system. And with a DBMS, system maintenance is much easier and less expensive."

## THE FIVE SUBSYSTEMS OF PICS

### Production (3.1)

All activities in the Operations Division function to support the production process, and so it is with PICS. All other subsystems support the Production Subsystem (3.1). Plant managers get the specifications for new products and product enhancements from the Research and Development Subsystem (3.2). For example, the design of the new Qwert Plus is in an electronic format. When the prototypes of the new Qwert Plus pass acceptance testing, production will use the electronic form of the design to program the machine tools that will make the parts for the Qwert Plus.

Each day, plant managers at the four plant/distribution center sites tap into the Schedule and Monitor Production Subsystem (3.3) to moni-

Workstations strategically located throughout Zimco plants and warehouses make production and shipping information readily available to authorized persons.
(Honeywell, Inc.)

tor production levels. The Acquire and Manage Materials Subsystem (3.4) ensures that raw materials needed during production are at the right place at the right time. And, of course, the Shipping Subsystem (3.5) gets the products out the door to the customer.

Plant managers rely heavily on the linear programming and other mathematical models that are embodied in the Production Subsystem to help them make the most effective use of available resources. These models help schedule the arrival of raw materials and components, the use of machine tools and assembly stations, the use of the work force, and maintenance shutdowns.

An important aspect of the production process is quality control. Zimco uses sampling techniques to maintain a high level of quality control. Each plant has inspectors on the floor who examine both work-in-process and finished goods for defects. Inspectors enter defect data directly into the Production Subsystem. The subsystem then does the necessary statistical analysis and provides inspectors with immediate feedback as to whether a lot should be sampled further or deemed defective.

## Research and Development (3.2)

Many data elements in the PICS data base are coded. Otto Manning says: "We try to code every data element we can, both to save data entry keystrokes and to save storage space." For example, the R&D "project code" data element (see Figure Z10–2) is coded. Engineers and supervisors need only enter a five-character code when making inquiries about a particular project. The code identifies whether the project is a development or applications project, whether it deals with a new product or an enhancement to an existing product, and if it is an enhancement, the code associates the project with one of the current Zimco products (e.g., Stib). The project code has a unique numerical identifier to distinguish between similar projects (e.g., multiple "DES" projects).

Otto says that "since many of our data elements are coded, they have special meaning and provide information to the user." For example, the project code DES03 describes a development project (#03) to enhance the Stib (see Figure Z10–2).

**FIGURE Z10–2**
**Coded Data Elements**
The figure illustrates the coding scheme for a five-position R&D project code. Example coded data elements are shown at the bottom.

| Position | A/N | Code | Description |
| --- | --- | --- | --- |
| 1 | Alpha | D | Development |
|  |  | A | Application |
| 2 | Alpha | N | New product |
|  |  | E | Enhancement |
| 3 | Alpha | S | Stib |
|  |  | T | Tegler |
|  |  | Q | Qwert |
|  |  | F | Farkle |
|  |  | X | Not application |
| 4–5 | Numeric | not applicable | Unique numerical project identifier |

Examples:

DES03 — Development project #03 to enhance the Stib
AET01 — Application project #01 to improve production of the Tegler
DNX08 — New product development project #08

## Schedule and Monitor Production (3.3)

The Schedule and Monitor Production Subsystem receives the demand forecast for the various Zimco products from the sales and marketing component (4) of the overall Zimco MIS. These forecasts are what drive the production process.

Mathematical models built into the Schedule and Monitor Production Subsystem retrieve data from the integrated data base to generate a production requirements plan. This plan specifies week-by-week in-stock requirements for Stibs, Teglers, Farkles, and Qwerts. The plan tells the plant manager what the rate of production for a particular product should be over a period of time, usually six months. Plant managers take immediate action if the information they get from this subsystem suggests that production levels may fall below production requirements.

The materials request, which is a by-product of the production requirements plan, is automatically generated and routed to the Acquire and Manage Materials Subsystems (3.4).

## Acquire and Manage Materials (3.4)

*Materials Requirements Planning.* Built into the overall Zimco MIS, and specifically the Acquire and Manage Materials Subsystem, is the philosophy of *material requirements planning*, often called *MRP*. MRP is essentially a set of mathematical models that accepts data for production requirements and translates these requirements into an optimal schedule for the ordering and the delivery of the components and raw materials needed to manufacture Zimco's products.

*Inventory Management and Control.* The Acquire and Manage Materials Subsystem gets the materials request from the Schedule and Monitor Production Subsystem (3.3). The subsystem then generates purchase orders for the raw materials and components needed to meet production schedules. These purchase orders are sent to the suppliers, some via intercompany networking. An "electronic flag" is added to the integrated data base to notify the Finance and Accounting Division of the order.

Manufacturing companies such as Zimco must manage stock (components and raw materials) and finished-goods inventories. This subsystem (3.4) monitors the quantity on hand and the location of each inventory item. Figure Z10–3 illustrates the interactive, user-friendly nature of PICS with a few of the menus and input/output displays that are generated by the Acquire and Manage Materials Subsystem. The inventory inquiries in Figure Z10–3 are made by a user to Zimco's integrated data base, a CODASYL-based data base.

The data base subschema in Figure Z10–4 illustrates that portion of the integrated data base that relates specifically to the *inventory management and control application*. *The arrows indicate the one-to-many relationships between the five data base records*; *that is*, *one* record for a Zimco product will have cross-references to the *many* records of the stock items that make up that product.

The data base subschema in Figure Z10–4 is designed to minimize data redundancy. The *product* data base record contains a list of those items (e.g., components and raw materials) that are combined to produce a Zimco product. The two inventory records, *finished-goods* and *item*, maintain stock and order data. The *purchase order* record indicates what was ordered. The *supplier* record includes pertinent data about each supplier. The entire schema for Zimco's CODASYL-based integrated data base, which is not shown, includes relationships between these and other data base records.

## Shipping (3.5)

In any manufacturing company, a product is conceived, designed, manufactured, sold, and ultimately shipped to the customer. The Shipping Subsystem (3.5) supports the last major activity in the manufacturing cycle. The orders are entered into SAMIS (Sales and Marketing Information System) by the field sales staff. Once an order is verified, a shipping notice is automatically sent to the Distribution Department via the Shipping Subsystem. Once the product is sent to the customer, acknowledgment is sent simultaneously to the Sales and Marketing Division and to the Finance and Accounting Division via the

**FIGURE Z10–3**
**Interactive Session with an On-Line Inventory System**
(a) The main menu presents the user with six processing options. The user enters option "5" to obtain an inventory exception report. (b) This exception report is produced when main menu option "5" is selected. Only those inventory items whose quantity on hand is too high or too low are listed. (c) From the main menu, the user selected option "1" to get the transaction menu. (d) This screen is produced when main menu option "1" is selected. Desiring to update quantity on hand, the user selects transaction option "1." (e) From this transaction display screen, the user enters *item number* (1015), *number received* (2000), and *number used* (300) to update quantity on hand for Farkle valves.

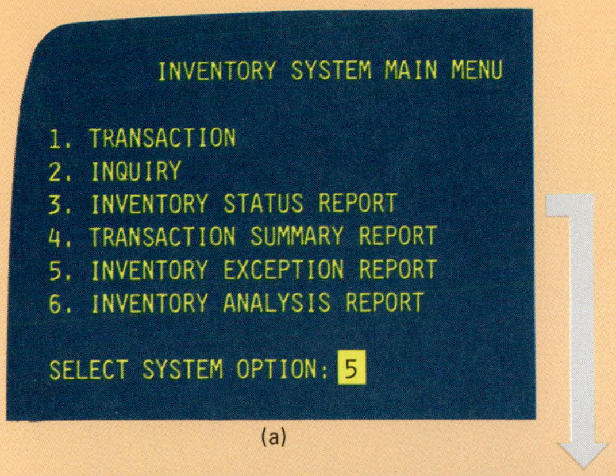

INVENTORY SYSTEM MAIN MENU

1. TRANSACTION
2. INQUIRY
3. INVENTORY STATUS REPORT
4. TRANSACTION SUMMARY REPORT
5. INVENTORY EXCEPTION REPORT
6. INVENTORY ANALYSIS REPORT

SELECT SYSTEM OPTION: 5

(a)

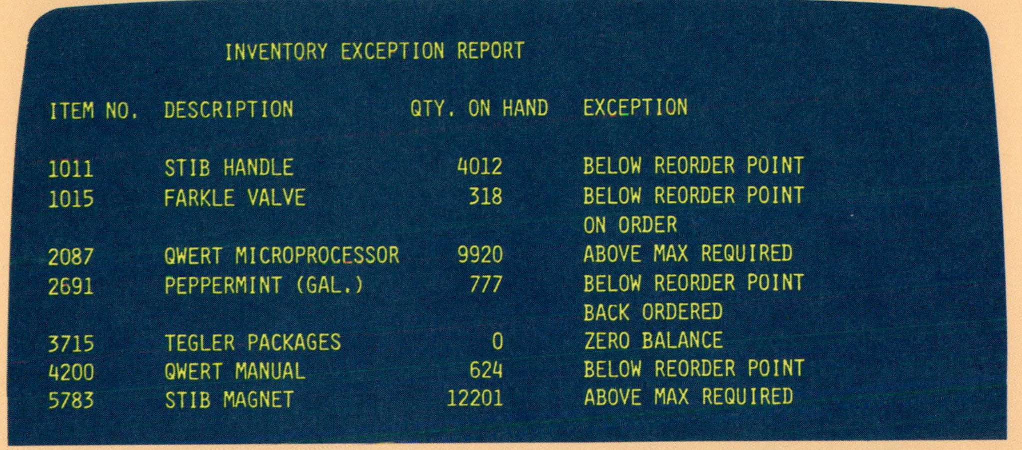

INVENTORY EXCEPTION REPORT

| ITEM NO. | DESCRIPTION | QTY. ON HAND | EXCEPTION |
|---|---|---|---|
| 1011 | STIB HANDLE | 4012 | BELOW REORDER POINT |
| 1015 | FARKLE VALVE | 318 | BELOW REORDER POINT ON ORDER |
| 2087 | QWERT MICROPROCESSOR | 9920 | ABOVE MAX REQUIRED |
| 2691 | PEPPERMINT (GAL.) | 777 | BELOW REORDER POINT BACK ORDERED |
| 3715 | TEGLER PACKAGES | 0 | ZERO BALANCE |
| 4200 | QWERT MANUAL | 624 | BELOW REORDER POINT |
| 5783 | STIB MAGNET | 12201 | ABOVE MAX REQUIRED |

(b)

INVENTORY SYSTEM MAIN MENU

1. TRANSACTION
2. INQUIRY
3. INVENTORY STATUS REPORT
4. TRANSACTION SUMMARY REPORT
5. INVENTORY EXCEPTION REPORT
6. INVENTORY ANALYSIS REPORT

SELECT SYSTEM OPTION: 1

(c)

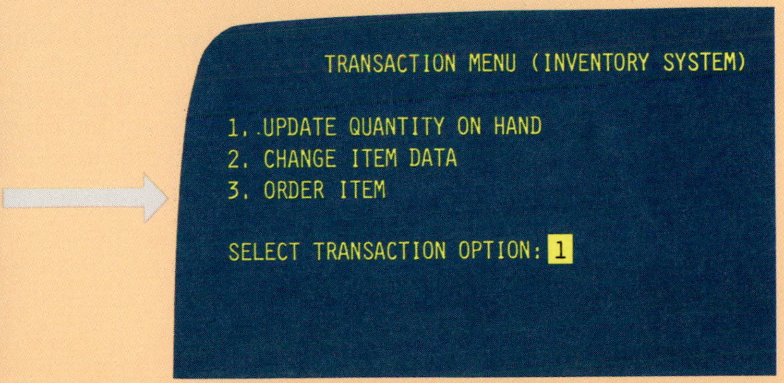

TRANSACTION MENU (INVENTORY SYSTEM)

1. UPDATE QUANTITY ON HAND
2. CHANGE ITEM DATA
3. ORDER ITEM

SELECT TRANSACTION OPTION: 1

(d)

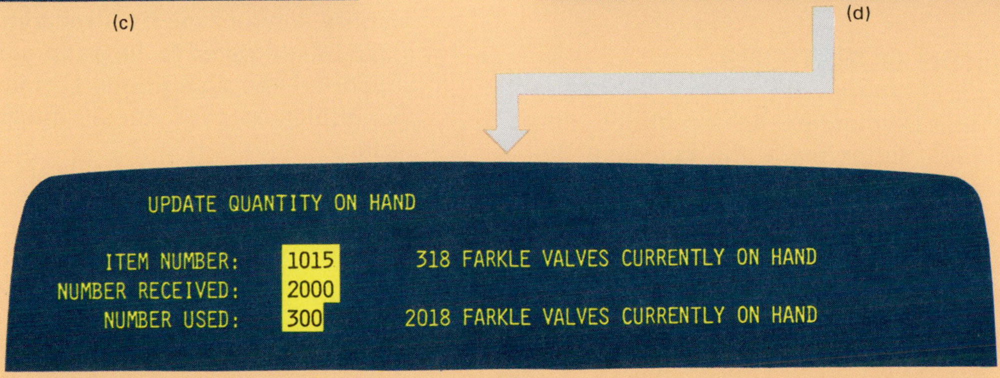

UPDATE QUANTITY ON HAND

ITEM NUMBER:     1015     318 FARKLE VALVES CURRENTLY ON HAND
NUMBER RECEIVED: 2000
NUMBER USED:     300      2018 FARKLE VALVES CURRENTLY ON HAND

(e)

301

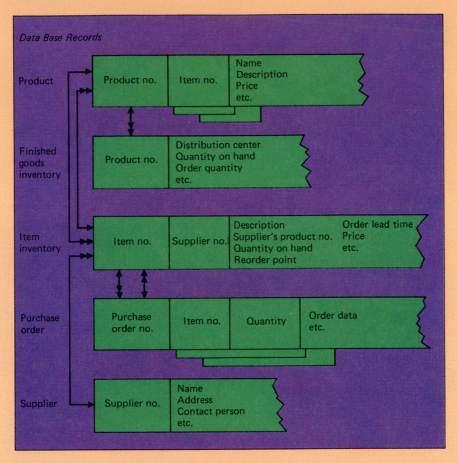

**FIGURE Z10–4**
**Data Base Subschema for the Inventory Management and Control Application**
This data base subschema is that portion of Zimco's integrated data base that deals directly with inventory management and control. Links with these data base records and other data base records in accounting and finance are not shown.

integrated data base. The sales force monitors the progress of the order and accounting sends the customer an invoice.

## DISCUSSION QUESTIONS

1. Prior to implementing an integrated data base, Terri Suttor made the comment that Zimco may be data rich but it is information poor. Explain how Zimco can be data rich but information poor.

2. Ursula Lain, the Operations Division user li-

aison, was instrumental in the development and implementation of PICS. What can she do now to make PICS an even more effective tool for people in the Operations Division?

3. Identify some of the data redundancies that might have existed in the traditional files that supported the Operations Division prior to the implementation of an integrated data base.

4. Terri Suttor said: "With a DBMS, system maintenance is much easier and less expensive." Why?

5. Draw a data flow diagram explosion of the

Schedule and Monitor Production Subsystem (3.3) showing the primary information flows between appropriate processes, the supplier entity, and the integrated data base. Label subordinate processes 3.3.1, 3.3.2, and so on.

6. A Zimco supplier manufactures screws and Zimco uses every type of screw that they make. They make all screws of both brass and steel. Currently, the screw lengths range from $\frac{1}{4}$ to 2 inches in $\frac{1}{4}$-inch increments, but the supplier plans to expand the product line to $3\frac{1}{2}$ inches. Each length of screw is manufactured with three types of heads—round, hex, and flat. Currently, production workers have to verbally describe the screw they want. Otto Mann would like an easier way to identify a particular screw.

In that regard, he has asked that you set up a coding scheme to do this. The screw number should be coded within a minimum of positions to save disk storage. What coding scheme would you suggest?

# PART 5
# INFORMATION SYSTEMS DEVELOPMENT

The medical care field presents some very special challenges to computer technology and its relationship to the concept that information is a resource. Medical services are dependent on information and there is a continuing need to manage this resource.

The primary challenge from the medical care field to the information systems industry is to relay important information to the physician in an efficient and economic way, and yet guard against usurping the physician's prerogatives or making the patient feel as though technology has taken first place to compassion and caring. This

challenge notwithstanding, the medical care field faces some very real needs for increased efficiency and productivity. Computer technology offers a means to deal with those needs. Data transfer, improved clerical efficiency, and improved utilization of physicians' time are all areas in which computer technology may provide substantial benefits.

R. W. Fleming
Chairman
Department of Administration
Mayo Clinic

# The Systems Development Process

## STUDENT LEARNING OBJECTIVES

- To describe the four stages of the system life cycle.
- To discuss the characteristics and benefits of a systems development methodology.
- To describe and order the systems development activities for:
  Phase I—Prototyping
  Phase II—Systems Analysis and Design
  Phase III—Programming
  Phase IV—Conversion and Implementation
  Phase V—Post-Implementation Evaluation
- To explain the concept of prototyping.
- To demonstrate a knowledge of system design techniques.
- To place the programming task in perspective with respect to the systems development process.
- To distinguish between the different approaches to system conversion.
- To know what to look for during the post-implementation evaluation.

## FOCUS OF ZIMCO CASE STUDY

- Information systems at Zimco: sales and marketing.

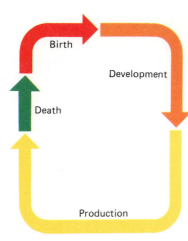

**FIGURE 11-1**
**The System Life Cycle**
A system is not immortal. It is born, grows, matures, and eventually dies.

An idea often signals the birth of an information system. These construction supervisors are discussing the possibility of designing a system that will help them to better schedule the arrival of construction materials from suppliers.
(Honeywell, Inc.)

## 11-1  THE SYSTEM LIFE CYCLE

An information system is analogous to the human life form. It is born, grows, matures, and eventually dies. The **system life cycle** has four stages, as shown in Figure 11-1.

**Birth Stage.**  In the *birth stage* of the system life cycle, someone has an idea as to how the computer can assist in providing better and more timely information.

**Development Stage.**  The idea becomes a reality during the *development stage* of the system life cycle. During the development stage, systems analysts, programmers, and users work together to analyze a company's information processing needs and design an information system. The design specifications are then translated into programs, and the system is implemented.

**Production Stage.**  Upon implementation, the information system enters the *production stage* and becomes operational, serving the information needs of the company. The production stage is the longest of the four stages and will normally last from four to seven years. During the production stage, information systems are continuously modified, or "maintained," to keep up with the changing needs of the company.

**Death Stage.**  The accumulation of system modifications to a dynamic information system eventually takes its toll on system efficiency. The *death stage* arrives when an information system becomes so cumbersome to maintain that it is no longer economically or operationally effective. At this time, the system is discarded and the system life cycle is repeated.

## 11-2  TURNING AN IDEA INTO AN INFORMATION SYSTEM

In this chapter we present the state of the art in systems development, which is currently a combination of the traditional approach and the latest technological tools and design aids. Since systems development is a *team* effort, most companies have adopted a standardized **systems development methodology** that provides the framework for cooperation. This step-by-step approach to systems development is essentially the same whether it be for an airline reservation system or a personnel system.

A company's methodology is usually presented in a manual and depicts the following:

1. Activities to be performed
2. The relationship and sequence of these activities
3. The key evaluation and decision **milestones** [significant points in the development process (e.g., programming is completed)]

In recent years, methodologies have encouraged greater user involvement, emphasized the design aspects, and relied more on fourth- and fifth-generation languages to generate the software. These trends are included in the methodology presented in this chapter.

Information is critical to economists, plant supervisors, engineers, nurses, and people in scores of other professions. In the search for better and more timely information, these people often find themselves working closely with programmers and systems analysts in the development of an information system. Because users are taking on a more active role in systems development, it is important that the user community have a solid understanding of their role in the system development process.

## The Service Request: Lights, Camera, Action!

The **service request**, which is normally compiled by the user, gets the ball rolling. When user departments do not have the technological expertise or resources to meet certain information needs, they submit a service request to the information services department to request that a *new information system be developed* or that *an existing system be enhanced*. Because the extent of the requests usually exceeds the available personnel and computer resources, each request must be evaluated relative to its contribution to corporate need. A completed service request would include explanations of the following:

- The objectives for the proposed system
- The fundamental operation of the proposed system
- The scope of the proposed system
- The problems associated with the present system
- The justification for the proposed system
- The long-range objectives for the proposed system

The more extensive service requests prompt a **feasibility study**. The objective of a feasibility study is to determine whether the proposed project is economically and procedurally feasible. Typically, a benefit/cost analysis (see Chapter 3, "Management Information Systems") is used to determine the economic feasibility of a proposed project. Based on the results of the feasibility study, a decision is made either to *table* the project or to *approve* it. Approval triggers one of two activities: the purchase and implementation of a proprietary software package or the beginning of the systems development methodology. A five-phase methodology is the focus of the remainder of this chapter.

## A Five-Phase Systems Development Methodology

The five-phase systems development methodology discussed in this chapter should give you an overview of what is involved in developing and implementing an information system. The phases are:

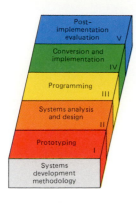

- *Phase I—Prototyping.* During Phase I, information requirements are identified and a *prototype system* is developed that serves as a model for the development of the full-scale system.

- *Phase II—Systems Analysis and Design.* During Phase II, systems analysts and users work together to compile detailed system specifications. These specifications are submitted to programmers for coding in Phase III.

- *Phase III—Programming.* During Phase III, the software needed to support the system is developed.

- *Phase IV—Conversion and Implementation.* During Phase IV, data files are created, and the new system is implemented and put into operation.

- *Phase V—Post-Implementation Evaluation.* Phase V begins the *production stage* of the life cycle (see Figure 11–1). During this stage the system is evaluated periodically to ensure that it continues to meet the information processing needs of the company.

These five phases are equally applicable to systems development in small, one-person businesses and in large companies with several layers of management. In practice, the systems development process may be divided into three, five, or even ten phases, but the chronology of the activities remains essentially the same.

## A Responsibility Matrix: Defining Who Does What, and When

We are about to discuss the information systems development process in the context of the five-phase systems development methodology discussed above. In this way, you can more easily identify *who* does *what*, and *when*. To help you, the methodology is illustrated graphically in Figure 11–2 in the form of a *responsibility matrix*.

The major activities for each of the five phases are listed along the left-hand side of the responsibility matrix. Although some of the activities are accomplished at the same time, they are generally pre-

At the start of the project, it is always a good idea for the project team leader to assemble the team, go over the system development methodology, and make sure responsibility areas are clearly understood.
(Living Videotext, Inc.)

| Key:<br>**A** = Approval<br>**C** = Consultation<br>**R** = Primary responsibility<br>**P** = Participating responsibility | Individuals and groups involved | | |
|---|---|---|---|
| | Project team | IS management | User management |
| **Phase I — Prototyping** | | | |
| I-1. Appoint project team and establish project schedule | | R | P |
| I-2. Document present system | R | | C |
| I-3. Interview users | R | | C |
| I-4. Complete general system design of the proposed system | R | | C |
| I-5. Develop prototype system | R | | P/A |
| **Phase II — Systems Analysis and Design** | | | |
| II-1. Specify data base requirements | R | | |
| II-2. Establish controls | R | | |
| II-3. Complete detailed system design | R | | C |
| II-4. Conduct structured walkthrough | P | R | A |
| II-5. Prepare layouts | R | | C |
| **Phase III — Programming** | | | |
| III-1 Review systems specifications | R | | |
| III-2. Identify and describe programs to be written | R | | |
| III-3. Write, Test, and document programs | R | | |
| **Phase IV — Conversion and Implementation** | | | |
| IV-1. Conduct system test | R | | P |
| IV-2. Convert to new system | R | | P |
| **Phase V — Post-Implementation Evaluation** | | | |
| V-1. Conduct post-implementation evaluation | R | | C |
| V-2. System maintenance | | P | R |

sented in the order in which they are begun. The phases and numbered activities in the responsibility matrix are the basis for our discussion of the systems development process.

The individuals and groups directly involved in the development of an information system are listed across the top of the matrix. Each is described as follows:

- *Project team*. The project team will normally consist of systems analysts, programmers, perhaps the data base administrator, and one or two people who will eventually use the system (users). Systems analysts design the system and develop the system specifications. The programmers use these "specs" as guidelines to write the programs. The data base administrator assists the team in designing and creating the data base.

- *Information services management*. This group includes the director and other managers in the information services department.

- *User management*. This group encompasses all user managers (e.g., director of personnel, VP of marketing) who affect or are affected by the proposed development project.

**FIGURE 11–2**
**Systems Development Responsibility Matrix**
The project team has direct responsibility for most systems development activities, but information services and user managers have participating responsibilities and are called upon for consultation and approval.

Not all information systems are developed in cooperation with the information services department. Some systems, especially micro-based systems, are developed entirely by users. (Photograph provided by Tandem Computers Incorporated)

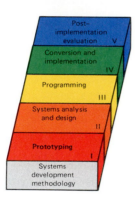

The entries in the matrix reflect the extent and type of involvement for each of the foregoing individuals and groups.

- **A** Denotes *approval* authority.
- **C** Denotes that the individual/group may be called in for *consultation*.
- **R** Denotes who has primary *responsibility* for a particular activity.
- **P** Denotes that although the individual or group does not have primary responsibility, they have *participating responsibility*.

## 11–3 PHASE 1—PROTOTYPING

The objective of Phase I—Prototyping is to analyze the current situation, identify information needs, and develop a prototype system. A prototype system is a scaled-down model of the proposed system. The prototype system would normally handle the main transaction-oriented procedures, produce the critical reports, and permit rudimentary inquiries. In effect, the prototype system permits users a "sneak" preview of the completed system. Having gained some hands-on experience, users can better relate their exact information processing needs to the project team.

Until about 1982, it was not economically feasible to develop a prototype system. In fact, it would probably have cost almost as much to do a prototype as it would to develop the entire system. But today the project team can use fourth- and fifth-generation languages to create a subset of the proposed system that, to the user at a workstation, appears and acts very much like the finished product.

The following numbered activities for Phase I correspond to the responsibility matrix of Figure 11–2.

### I–1. Appoint Project Team and Establish Project Schedule

A project team is appointed by managers of the information services department and the affected user departments. One member of the team is appointed the **project leader**.

Every information system project has a deadline. The project team leader is assigned so many programmers, systems analysts, and users. Based on the deadline and the resources available, the project leader establishes an implementation schedule.

A typical project schedule is illustrated in the **bar chart** of Figure 11–3. A *start date* and a *completion date* are estimated for each phase. Figure 11–4 is presented to give you a feeling for how much of the project team's effort is spent on each of the five phases. A range of "percent effort" is presented to reflect the variations in emphasis between companies.

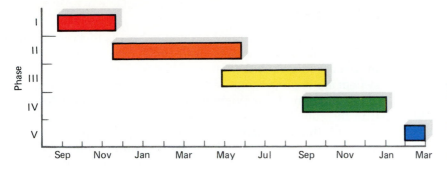

**FIGURE 11–3**
**Bar Chart of a Project Schedule**
Systems development project teams often use bar charts to schedule activities and track progress toward implementation.

## I–2. Document Present System

Before you can design a new system, you must have a good grasp of the existing flow of information, be it manual or computer-based. If the existing system is computer-based, it is usually accompanied by some type of documentation. If the existing system is manual, the project team may need to compile a basic documentation package that includes a list and examples of all reports and documents, system data elements and files, and a graphic illustration of the information and work flow of the present system.

The information and work flow of the present system is documented by reducing the system to its basic component parts: *input*, *processing*, and *output*. A variety of design techniques can be used to depict graphically the logical relationship between these parts. Perhaps the most popular, although not necessarily the best for all situations, is **flowcharting**. Other more "structured" techniques include **data flow diagrams** and **hierarchical plus input-processing-output** (**HIPO**). Flowcharting is discussed in Chapter 12; programming and data flow diagrams are introduced in the Zimco case study following Chapter 3. The use of HIPO is explained later in this chapter in Phase II, Activity II–3, Complete Detailed System Design.

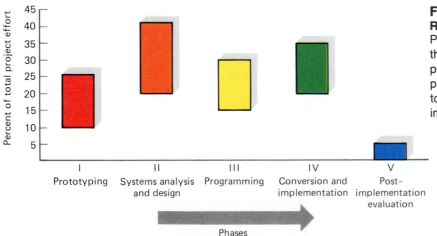

**FIGURE 11–4**
**Relative Project Effort**
Programming is usually no more than 15 to 30 percent of the total project effort. The bulk of a project team's effort is devoted to analysis, design, and implementation.

### I–3. Interview Users

One of the first activities for project team members is to exercise their communicative skills and talk with the people who are going to use the system. User feedback is the basis for the project team's specifications for system input, processing, and output requirements (information needs). The evaluation of the existing system (I–2) also provides valuable input to the specifications or **specs**.

At this point, the emphasis turns toward *output requirements*. In the system design process, you begin with the desired output and work back to determine input and processing requirements. Outputs are printed reports, workstation displays (e.g., graphic art for an ad piece), or some kind of transaction (e.g., purchase order, payroll check).

### I–4. Complete General System Design of the Proposed System

From the information gathered thus far, the project team analyzes the existing system and assesses information needs, then develops a *general system design* of the proposed system. The general system design, and later the detailed design (in Phase II), involves continuous communication between members of the project team and all levels of users. After evaluating several alternative approaches, the project team translates the system specs into a general system design.

The general design of the proposed system is documented both by a graphic illustration (e.g., data flow diagrams), showing the fundamental operation of the proposed system, and by a supporting written description.

### I–5. Develop Prototype System

Throughout the twentieth century, manufacturers have built prototypes of everything from toasters to airplanes. Automobile manufacturers build a prototype car according to original design specifications. Every aspect of the prototype is tested and—if engineers see possibilities for improvement—it is modified. Prototyping is now becoming SOP (standard operating procedure) for software development.

Defining System Specifications.   Traditionally, a rough spot in the systems development process has been that of defining the systems specifications. In the past this activity was usually done in cooperation with users and was done as early in the project as possible. The reason for defining specifications so quickly was this: Once the design and programming were begun, the technology (primarily third-generation languages and traditional file processing) did not permit much flexibility to make design changes.

Design changes were costly and, if possible, were avoided. When users failed to accurately express all of their information requirements to the project team, the system specifications often were ill defined and incomplete. Eventually, these information oversights caused the project team to backtrack and make costly modifications. To avoid

With application generators and other very high-level languages, a prototype system can actually be developed in interactive consultation with the user.
(Photo courtesy of Hewlett-Packard Company)

this, the project team at a certain point would "freeze" the specs, after which no more changes could be made before the system was implemented. Well, frozen specs are like ice cubes—when enough heat is applied, they melt!

With the current fourth- and fifth-generation languages and database management systems, the specs are only cooled, not frozen. These tools make it possible to develop a working prototype system, which is usually a subset of the proposed system. Even though it is a subset, the prototype system will have menus, reports, various input/output screens, and a data base. To the user, the prototype version will look very much like the real thing. Depending on the complexity of the system, the prototype can be completed with a minimum of programming effort.

Creating the Prototype System.    To create a prototype system, project team members first rough out the logic of the system and how the elements fit together, then suggest to the user the I/O interfaces (system interaction with user). The project team members sit down with users to create and modify whatever interactive display screens are required to meet their information processing needs. Remember, with fifth-generation languages, called application generators (see Chapter 9), all you have to do is describe the screen image (menus, reports, inquiries, etc.) and the programming code is automatically generated for you. If a data base, other than the existing one, is needed, perhaps a new data base will have to be created.

Users can actually sit down at a workstation and test out the prototype system. As they do so, new information needs usually surface and they find better ways to do certain activities. In effect, the prototype is the beginning. From here, the system is expanded and refined to meet the users' total information needs. Fifth-generation languages are limited in what they can do, so the typical system may require a considerable amount of **custom coding**, probably in third- and fourth-generation languages.

# 11-4  PHASE II—SYSTEMS ANALYSIS AND DESIGN

Once the prototype system is in operation, Phase II—Systems Analysis and Design is begun. The prototype forms the foundation. In Phase II, the format and content of *all* input and output are described, the prototype system is refined, the data base specifications are prepared, and the detailed system design is completed.

To this point, little or no custom code for detailed programs has been written. However, much remains to be done before the system is fully conceptualized and detailed programming can begin. Doing detailed programming at this stage of the process is like beginning the construction of a skyscraper without a blueprint. Programming is the brick, mortar, and steel of an information system and should not be started until the detailed system design (the blueprint) is completed.

The following numbered activities for Phase II correspond to the responsibility matrix of Figure 11–2.

## II–1. Specify Data Base Requirements

The date base is the common denominator in any system. It contains the raw material (data) necessary to produce the output (information). In manufacturing, for example, you decide what you are going to make, then you order the raw material. In the process of developing an information system, you decide what your output requirements are, then you determine which data are needed to produce the output. In a sense, the output requirements can be thought of as an input to data base design.

With the trend to integrated on-line systems and DBMS technology, at least part, and perhaps all, of the data base may already exist. Creation of the data base may not be necessary; however, it is likely that data elements will need to be added to the data base.

The first step in data base design is to compile a **data dictionary**. A data dictionary, illustrated in Figure 11–5, is simply a listing of all data elements in the data base. An existing data base will already have a data dictionary. The data elements, together with certain descriptive information, are listed along the left-hand side of the data dictionary "matrix."

The matrix portion of Figure 11–5 is completed *after* the data base organization has been determined and *after* the reports and input screens are designed. The data elements are then cross-referenced to reflect their occurrence in data base records, reports, and input screens.

## II–2. Establish Controls

An information system should run smoothly under normal circumstances. But as Murphy has taught us, "If anything can go wrong, it will." We, as users, programmers, and operators, make oversights and

**FIGURE 11–5**
**Data Dictionary**
Companies maintain an up-to-date data dictionary with descriptive information for all data elements. The use or occurrence of these data elements is cross-referenced to appropriate files, reports, and source documents. The entry in the "Format" column describes the data element's length and whether it is numeric (9) or alphanumeric (X).

| No. | Name | Description | Format | Coded | Responsibility | Best sellers list (R) | Over due report (R) | On-loan report (R) | Patron data base (D) | Book data base (D) | Checkout display (S) | Acq. data entry (S) | Data base update (S) |
|---|---|---|---|---|---|---|---|---|---|---|---|---|---|
| 1 | TITLE | Complete title of book | X(150) | No | Acquisitions | X | X | X | | X | X | X | X |
| 2 | ISBN | ISBN number | 9(13) | No | Acquisitions | | | | X | X | X | X | X |
| 3 | PUBYR | Year of publication | 9(2) | No | Acquisitions | X | | | | X | | X | X |
| 4 | AUTHOR | Name of an author | X(25) | No | Acquisitions | X | | | | X | | X | X |
| 5 | PUBL | Name of publisher | X(25) | No | Acquisitions | | | | | X | | X | X |
| 6 | DUE | Due date of book | 9(6) | No | Circulation | | X | | X | | X | | |
| 7 | CARDNO | Patron card number | 9(4) | Yes | Circulation | | | | X | | X | | |
| 8 | FNAME | First name of patron | X(10) | No | Circulation | | X | | X | | X | | |

errors in judgment. But to err is human. Computers may not be human, but they are machines and machines sometimes fail.

Because of the ever-present potential for human and hardware errors, coupled with the threat of computer crime, it is important that we build in controls to ensure the accuracy, reliability, and integrity of the system. Without controls, an enterprising computer criminal might be able to supplement his or her checking account without making a deposit. An erroneous data entry error could result in the delivery of a red car instead of a blue one. Someone expecting a monthly pay check of $2500 might receive $250,000. A computer operator could cause chaos by forgetting to do the daily audit run. This activity (II–2) is conducted to prevent these, and any of a thousand other, undesirable events from happening.

Information system controls minimize or eliminate errors before, during, and after processing so that the data entered and the information produced are complete and accurate. Controls also minimize the possibility of computer fraud. There are four types of controls: *input controls*, *processing controls*, *output controls*, and *procedural controls*.

**Input Controls.**   Data are checked for accuracy when entered into the system. In on-line data entry, the data entry operator verifies the data by sight checks. Also, a variety of checking procedures are designed into the software. Two of these software control procedures are discussed below.

- *Reasonableness check*. Suppose that a Zimco customer's maximum order to date is 250 Farkles, and an order is entered for 2000 Farkles. Since an order of 2000 is much greater than the maximum order to date of 250, the entry is historically unreasonable, and the probable error is brought to the attention of the data entry operator.
- *Limits check*. A limits check assesses whether the value of an entry is out of line with that expected. For example, Zimco Enterprise's policy guarantees 40 hours of work per week for each employee and limits overtime to 15 hours per week. A limits check on the "hours-worked" entry guarantees that a value between 40 and 55, inclusive, is entered.

**Processing Controls.**   Systems analysts and programmers use a variety of techniques to validate that processing is complete and accurate. Control totals and consistency checks are a few of the many techniques that can be built into the software.

- *Control total*. A control total, or hash total, is a value that is known to be the accumulated sum of a particular data element. Control totals are used primarily to verify that processing is complete. For example, when the Zimco payroll checks are printed, the employee numbers are added together and compared to a known value. If the accumulated control total is not equal to the known value, the computer operator knows immediately that some checks were not processed or that some checks were processed that should not have been.

The opportunity for any wrong-doing is diminished when operators are not involved in programming and programmers are not involved in operations. (Management Science America, Inc. (MSA))

**QUERY:  Let me see the daily delivery report.**

| ROUTE NO. | COLA | FIZZ | BURP | ROUTE TOTAL |
|-----------|------|------|------|-------------|
| 1 | 41 | 68 | 32 | 141 |
| 2 | 29 | 18 | 64 | 111 |
| 3 | 71 | 65 | 48 | 184 |
| 4 | 67 | 58 | 56 | 181 |
| TOTAL | 208 | 209 | 200 | 617 |

**FIGURE 11–6**
**Crossfoot Checking**
The sum of the row totals equals
the sum of the column totals.

- *Consistency check*. The consistency check compares like data items for consistency of value. For example, if Zimco's electricity bill for March is 300 percent higher than the bill for March of last year, the invoice would not be processed. Zimco management would then ask the electric utility company to check the accuracy of the meter reading.

**Output Controls.**  Some people take for granted that any computer-produced output is accurate. Such is not always the case. There are too many things that can go wrong. One of many methods of output control is *crossfoot checking*. This technique is used in reports, such as the one in Figure 11–6, that have column and row totals with some arithmetic relationship to one another. In Figure 11–6, the column totals for each beverage type should equal the total for all delivery routes.

**Procedural Controls.**  In an information system, the work is done either by the computer system or by people. Programs tell the computer what to do. People are guided by procedures. Some procedures are built into the system for control purposes. For example, many companies subscribe to the *separation-of-duties* procedure. The theory behind this procedure is that if responsibilities for input, processing, and output are assigned to different people, most attempts to defraud the system will be foiled. It is unlikely that would-be computer criminals could solicit that much cooperation.

## II–3. Complete Detailed System Design

The *detailed system design* is the result of analysis of feedback from users of the prototype system, and of detailed input/output, processing, and control requirements. The *general system design* of Phase I depicts the relationship between major processing activities and has enough detail for development of a prototype system. The detailed design includes *all* processing activities and the input/output associated with them.

The detailed design is the cornerstone activity of the system development process. It is here that the relationships between the various

---

**MEMORY BITS**

**SYSTEM CONTROLS**
- Input controls
  Reasonableness check
  Limits check
- Processing controls
  Control totals
  Consistency check
- Output controls
  Crossfoot checking
- Procedural controls
  Separation of duties

components of the system are defined. The system specifications and the prototype system are integrated with the project team's imagination and skill to create an information system. The detailed system design is the culmination of all previous work. Moreover, it is the *blueprint* for all project team activities that follow.

A number of techniques aid programmers and analysts in the design process. Each of these techniques permits the design of the system to be illustrated graphically. One of these techniques, HIPO, is discussed briefly below.

**Hierarchy Plus Input-Processing-Output.**   **Hierarchy plus input-processing-output**, or **HIPO** (pronounced *HI-poe*), is a top-down design technique that permits the project team to divide the system into independent modules for ease of understanding and design. HIPO follows the "divide and conquer" line of reasoning.

HIPO has several standard forms. A *structure chart* breaks a system down into a hierarchy of modules. For example, a structure chart for a payroll system is shown in Figure 11–7. Each module is then broken into finer levels of input-processing-output detail in an *overview diagram*. In Figure 11–8, an overview diagram is shown for Module 1.3.1 of Figure 11–7, weekly payroll processing.

The primary advantage of HIPO is that it encourages analysts and programmers to examine the system from the top down (i.e., from the general to the specific). The result is a more structured design. This advantage is, to some extent, offset by the cumbersome volume of paperwork required to document the system.

**FIGURE 11–7**
**HIPO Structure Chart**
This structure chart breaks a payroll system down into a hierarchy of modules.

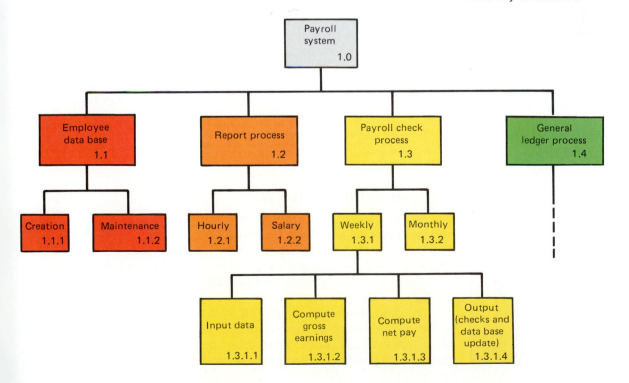

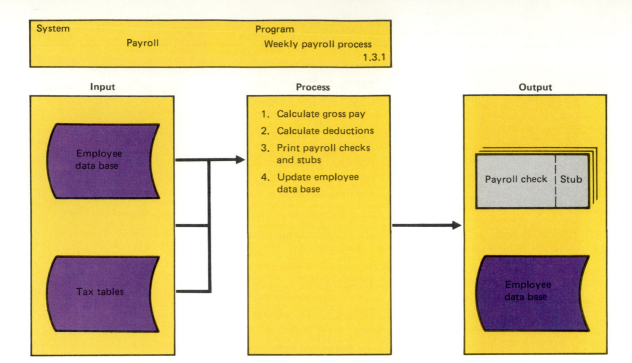

| System | Program |
|---|---|
| Payroll | Weekly payroll process |
| | 1.3.1 |

**Input**

Employee data base

Tax tables

**Process**

1. Calculate gross pay
2. Calculate deductions
3. Print payroll checks and stubs
4. Update employee data base

**Output**

Payroll check | Stub

Employee data base

**FIGURE 11–8**
**HIPO Overview Diagram**
The example overview diagram illustrates the input, processing, and output components of Module 1.3.1 of Figure 11–7.

During a structured walkthrough, the logic of a proposed system design is carefully examined by a peer group. In the photo, two project team members are "walking through" the specs for a proposed system that will provide credit department personnel and management with more timely customer credit information.
(Intergraph Corporation)

**Design Technique Summary.** There is no one best analytical or design technique. If you elect to take more advanced courses, you will gain a deeper understanding of HIPO and other techniques. Like HIPO, data flow diagrams (**DFDs**) document the system at several levels of generality and encourage top-down design. The use of DFDs is explained in the Zimco case study following Chapter 3, and DFDs are used to illustrate the information flow within Zimco in the case studies following Chapters 3, 7, 9, 10, and 11. Flowcharting and several other techniques are discussed in Chapter 12, "Programming Concepts." The best approach to system design is to use a combination of techniques that fits the circumstances for a particular company, system, or program.

The principles of HIPO, data flow diagrams, flowcharting, or any of a dozen other design techniques are not difficult to learn. But applying these techniques to the design of information systems requires practice, practice, and more practice. You can learn how to type, but that does not mean that you are going to write the great American novel. These techniques are just tools. It's your skill and imagination that make an information system a reality.

## II–4. Conduct Structured Walkthrough

We are human beings, and we make mistakes. We overlook things and don't always select the best way to design a program or a system. To do the best job possible, project team members often ask other interested and knowledgeable persons to review and evaluate what they have done. This peer-review procedure is called a **structured walkthrough**.

The procedures of a structured walkthrough are simple. The material to be reviewed (a system design in our example) is distributed several days in advance to appropriate persons. During the actual walkthrough, the person(s) who did the work explains the design and the accompanying documentation. This is done by "walking through" the system, step by step, perhaps with the aid of one of the design tools (e.g., HIPO charts). After the walkthrough, the project team evaluates all recommendations and incorporates the good ideas into the system design.

Several structured walkthroughs are scheduled for most system development projects, and they have proven to be a very effective tool. When project team members know their work is going to be scrutinized by their colleagues, they try hard to do a good job. Wouldn't you?

## II–5. Prepare Layouts

So far, except for the screen displays designed in the prototype system, most of the output requirements have only been identified and described briefly. The programmer, however, needs specifics. So detailed output specifications, called **layouts**, are prepared. These show programmers exactly where the output information should be placed on printed reports and workstation screen displays. The layout shows the specific location of such items as *report title*, *column headings*, and in the case of workstation screens, *input formats* for data entry.

Figure 11–9 illustrates a screen layout for a departmental payroll

**FIGURE 11–9**
**Screen Layout**
Detailed layouts are prepared for each hard- and soft-copy output.

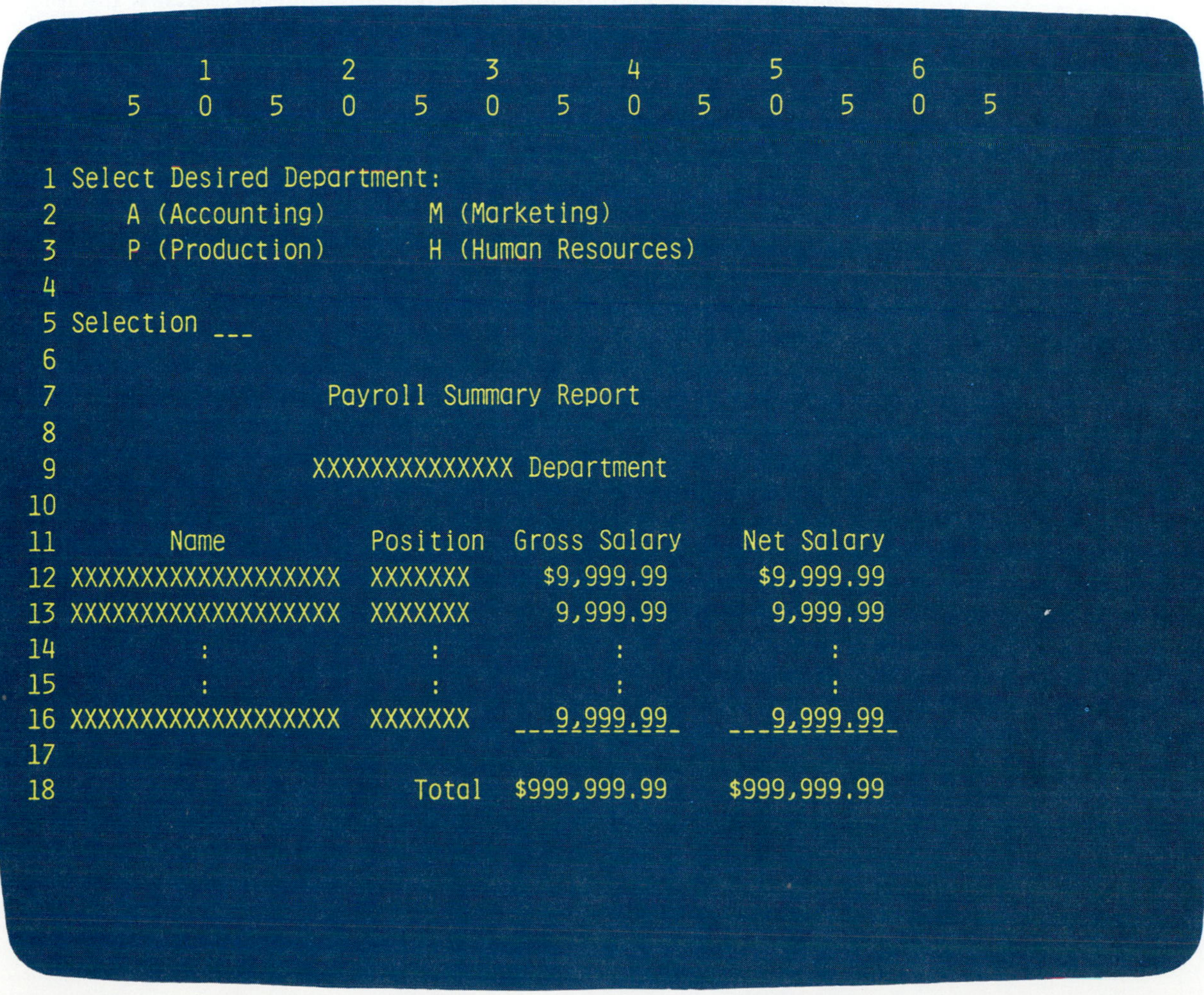

summary report. All the example reports and interactive screen displays pictured in photographs throughout this book were produced from a layout similar to that of Figure 11–9.

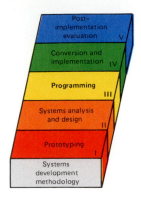

## 11–5   PHASE III—PROGRAMMING

With detailed specifications in hand, we are now ready to write the programs needed to make the proposed system operational. Some of the program code was generated when we used fifth-generation languages (i.e., applications generators) to develop and refine the prototype system. During Phase III the remainder of the programs are written. The four major activities of this phase (see Figure 11–2) are discussed below.

### III–1. Review System Specifications

During Phase III, programming becomes the dominant activity, and the programmers really go to work. The system specifications completed in Phase II—Systems Analysis and Design are all that is needed for programmers to write, or "code," the programs to implement the information system. Before getting started, programmers review the following system specifications:

- Printer output layouts of reports and transactions
- Workstation input/output screen layouts
- Data dictionary
- Files and data base design
- Controls and validation procedures
- Data entry specifications
- General and detailed systems design

Once programmers have reviewed and understood these specs, the programming task is begun. A superior programming effort will go for naught if the system specifications are incomplete and poorly written. As the saying goes, "Garbage in, garbage out."

### III–2. Identify and Describe Programs to Be Written

An information system needs an array of programs to create and update the data base, print reports, permit on-line inquiry, and so on. Depending on the scope of the system and how many programs can be generated with fifth-generation languages, as few as three or four or as many as several hundred programs may need to be written before the system can be implemented. At this point all programs needed to make the system operational are identified an described. Each program description includes the following:

- Type of programming language (e.g., COBOL, BASIC, fourth generation)

In programming, two heads are sometimes better than one. A programmer can become so close to a program that he or she may overlook obvious errors in logic. These errors often shine as bright as a neon light when the program design is discussed with a colleague.
(Reproduced with permission of AT&T)

- A narrative of the program, describing the tasks to be performed
- Frequency of processing (e.g., daily, weekly, on-line, etc.)
- Input to the program
- Output produced by the program
- Limitations and restrictions (e.g., sequence of input data, response-time maximums, etc.)
- Detailed specifications (e.g., specific computations and logical manipulations, any tables, etc.)

## III–3. Write, Test, and Document Programs

Armed with system specifications and program descriptions, we are now ready to write the programs. The development of a program is actually a *project within a project*. Just as there are certain steps that the project team takes to develop an information system, there are certain steps a programmer takes to write a program. Each of the following program development steps is described in greater detail in Chapter 12, "Programming Concepts."

1. Describe the problem to be addressed by the programmer.
2. Analyze the problem.
3. Design the general logic of the program.
4. Design the detailed logic of the program.
5. Code the program.
6. Test and debug the program.
7. Document the program.

Once all programs are written, Phase III is complete and we are ready to go on to Phase IV—Conversion and Implementation. In Phase IV all the work comes together, and the information system becomes a reality.

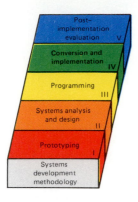

## 11-6   PHASE IV—CONVERSION AND IMPLEMENTATION

During Phases I, II, and III the information system is designed and the programs are written and individually tested. But we're not home free yet—much remains to be done before the system becomes operational. The primary objective of Phase IV—Conversion and Implementation is to install the information system and make it operational.

Even though the programs of the system have been individually or *unit tested* (Phase III), there is no guarantee that the programs will work as a system. Therefore, integrated *systems testing* is accomplished in Phase IV. In addition, the project team provides user training on the operation of the information system and creates (or revises) the data base. At the completion of Phase IV, the system is turned over to the users as an operational information system.

In Phases I, II, and III the project team integrates input, output, processing, and storage requirements to design and code an information system. In Phase IV the project team is confronted with a different challenge. They must now integrate *people*, *software*, *hardware*, *procedures*, and *data*. The four major activities of Phase IV are described briefly below and illustrated in the responsibility matrix, Figure 11–2.

### IV–1. Conduct System Test

The individual programs were tested and debugged in Phase III, but they have not been integrated and tested as a system. An information system for inventory management and control may have a hundred programs and a comprehensive data base; these must be tested together to ensure harmony of operation. The purpose of the system test is to validate all software, input/output, procedures, and the data base. It is a safe bet that a few design errors, procedural errors, or oversights will surface during system testing. Minor modifications in design and programming may be required to complete the system test to the satisfaction of the users.

### IV–2. Convert to New System

Now we are ready to implement the system; this normally involves a "conversion" from the existing system to the new one. An organization's approach to system conversion depends on their *willingness to accept risk* and the *amount of time available* for the conversion. Four common approaches are parallel conversion, direct conversion, phased conversion, and pilot conversion. These approaches are graphically illustrated in Figure 11–10 and discussed below.

During system testing, systems analysts are constantly gathering feedback from users. Analysts are especially interested in hearing about errors and parts of the system where interaction is cumbersome or slow.
(Honeywell, Inc.)

Parallel Conversion.   In **parallel conversion**, the existing system and the new system operate simultaneously, or in parallel, until the project team is confident that the new system is working properly. The two principal advantages of parallel conversion are that (1) the existing system serves as a backup, in case the new system fails to operate as expected, and (2) the results of the new system can be compared to the results of the existing system.

There is less risk with this strategy because the present system provides backup, but it also imposes a double work load on personnel and hardware resources during the conversion. The duration of parallel

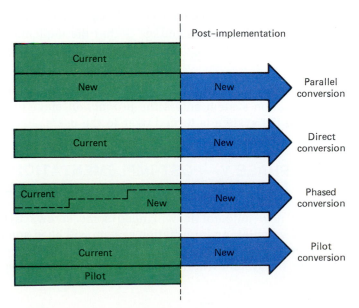

**FIGURE 11–10**
**Common Approaches to System Conversion**

conversion is usually one month or a major system cycle. For a public utility company, this might be one billing cycle, which is usually a month.

Direct Conversion.    As companies improve their system testing procedures, they begin to gain confidence in their ability to implement a working system. Some companies forgo parallel conversion for a **direct conversion**. A greater risk is associated with direct conversion because there is no backup in case the system fails.

Companies select this "cold turkey" approach when there is no existing system or when the existing system is substantially different. For example, all on-line hotel reservations systems are implemented cold turkey.

Phased Conversion.    In **phased conversion**, an information system is implemented one module at a time by either parallel or direct conversion. For example, in a point-of-sale system, the first phase might be to convert the sales accounting module. The second phase could be the inventory management module. The third might be the credit check module.

Phased conversion has the advantage of spreading out the demand for resources so that the demand is not as heavy as it might be at any one time. The disadvantages are that the conversion takes longer, and there must be a system interface between the existing and new system after each new module is implemented.

Pilot Conversion.    In **pilot conversion**, the new system is implemented by parallel, direct, or phased conversion as a "pilot" system in only one of the several areas for which it is targeted. For example, suppose that a company wanted to implement a manufacturing resources planning system in its eight plants. One plant would be selected as a *pilot* and the new information system would be implemented there first.

The advantage of pilot conversion is that the inevitable bugs in a system can be removed before the system is implemented at the other locations. The disadvantage is that the implementation time for the total system takes longer than if the entire system were implemented at one time.

The User Takes Control.    Once the conversion has been completed, the information system enters the *production* stage of the system life cycle, and the system is turned over to the users.

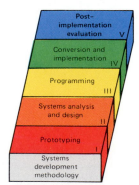

## 11–7    PHASE V—POST-IMPLEMENTATION EVALUATION

Just as a new automobile will need some screws tightened after a few hundred miles, an information system will need some "fine tuning" just after implementation. Over the production stage of the system life cycle, the system will be modified many times to meet the changing needs of the company. The two activities of Phase V—Post-Implementation Evaluation (see Figure 11–2), which are discussed below, deal with what takes place after implementation.

## V–1. Conduct Post-Implementation Evaluation

The **post-implementation evaluation** is a critical examination of the system after it has been put into production. The evaluation is conducted three to six months after implementation. This waiting period allows several factors to stabilize: the resistance to change, the anxieties associated with change, and the learning curve. It also allows time for unanticipated problems to surface.

The post-implementation evaluation focuses on the *actual* versus the *anticipated* performance objectives. Each facet of the system is assessed with respect to present criteria. If any part of the system is judged deficient, plans are made to correct the problems.

Also, it is a good idea to document what went wrong. No information system has ever been developed without mistakes being made. The best way to avoid making the same mistakes again is to identify the mistakes, then write them down.

Three to six months after the hardware, software, people, procedures, and data have been integrated into an operational information system, key members of the project team are conducting a post-implementation evaluation to assess the overall effectiveness of an aircraft maintenance system.
(Courtesy of International Business Machines Corporation)

## V–2. System Maintenance

Once an information system is implemented and "goes on-line," the emphasis is switched from *development* to *operations*. In a payroll system, supervisors begin to enter hours-worked on their workstations, and the computer center produces and issues payroll checks. Once operational, an information system becomes a cooperative effort between the users and the information services department.

An information system is dynamic and must be responsive to the changing needs of the company and those who use it. The process of modifying an information system to meet changing needs is known as *system maintenance*.

There are two approaches to system maintenance. The first, and least desirable, is the "reactive" approach. That is, *do nothing unless requested to do so* by the people who use it. The more effective, "proactive" approach requires the project team to *review the system* once or twice a year to see where it can be improved. During this review, they look into such things as the following:

- Effectiveness of the system
- Turnaround time
- Response time
- Relevance of information
- Input/output formats and content
- File and data base organization
- Update, control, and backup procedures
- Currency of system documentation

The results of periodic system reviews, service requests, and occasionally, a bug in the system are what prompt system maintenance activities.

An information system cannot live forever. The accumulation of modifications and enhancements will eventually make any information system cumbersome and inefficient. Minor modifications are known as **patches**. Depending on the number of patches and enhancements, an information system will remain operational, or in the production stage, from four to seven years.

Toward the end of the useful life of an information system, it is more trouble to continue patching the system than it is to redesign the system from scratch. The end of the production stage signals the "death" stage of the information system life cycle (see Figure 11–1). A new system is then "born" of need, and the system development process is repeated.

## SUMMARY OUTLINE AND IMPORTANT TERMS

**11–1**  THE SYSTEM LIFE CYCLE.  The four stages of a computer-based information system comprise the **system life cycle**. They are birth, development, production, and death.

**11-2**   TURNING AN IDEA INTO AN INFORMATION SYSTEM.   The process of developing a computer-based information system is essentially the same, regardless of the information system being developed. Some companies follow a **systems development methodology** that provides the framework for cooperation between the various people involved in a development project.

A **service request**, which is usually prepared by the user, signals the beginning of a systems development project. The service request is for an enhancement to an existing system or for the development of a new system. A decision, based on a feasibility study, is made to either approve or table the project.

Systems development methodologies vary in scope, complexity, sophistication, and approach. A five-phase methodology is presented in a responsibility matrix to help you understand the activities and responsibilities for the development of an information system. The matrix shows when and to what extent individuals and groups are involved in each activity of the systems development process.

**11-3**   PHASE I—PROTOTYPING.   The objective of Phase I is to analyze the current situation, identify information needs, and develop a **prototype system**, or a subset of the proposed system. A **project leader's** first activity is to establish a project schedule and graphically illustrate it in a **bar chart**.

After familiarizing themselves with the existing system, the project team completes a general system design so that they can better understand the scope of the system. To do this, they use design techniques, such as **flowcharting**, **data flow diagrams**, and **HIPO**.

A prototype system is created, primarily with fifth-generation languages, that will enable users to test out the fundamental operation of the proposed system prior to full implementation.

**11-4**   PHASE II—SYSTEMS ANALYSIS AND DESIGN.   During Phase II the format and content of all input and output are described, the prototype system is refined, the data base specifications are prepared, and the detailed system design is completed.

After the **data dictionary** has been compiled, controls are built into the system to ensure the accuracy, reliability, and integrity of the information system. Input, processing, output, and procedural controls are designed to detect system errors so that corrective action can be taken as quickly as possible.

A detailed system design is completed that integrates feedback from the prototype system with a synthesis of the input/ output, processing, and control requirements. At this point in the system development process the project team integrates the system specifications with their own technical and procedural innovations to create an information system. To do this they use any of a number of helpful design techniques.

To ensure that something was not overlooked or designed incorrectly, a **structured walkthrough** is conducted. The project team then completes Phase II with the input/output **layouts** and the data entry specifications.

**11–5**  PHASE III—PROGRAMMING.  During Phase III of the systems development methodology, programs are written, creating the software necessary to make the information system operational.

Programmers review the system specifications (from Phase II) with systems analysts and users on the project team. Each program to be written is identified and described. For each program, the programmer does the following: describes the problem; analyzes the problem; designs the general, then the detailed logic; then codes, tests, and documents the program.

**11–6**  PHASE IV—CONVERSION AND IMPLEMENTATION.  In Phase IV the work of Phases I, II, and III is integrated with people, software, hardware, procedures, and data, and the information system becomes operational.

A system test is conducted to ensure that the various components of the system work correctly and in harmony. After a satisfactory system test, the system is converted. Approaches to the conversion of a system are **parallel**, **direct**, **phased**, and **pilot conversion**.

**11–7**  PHASE V—POST-IMPLEMENTATION EVALUATION.  In Phase V the system is fine tuned shortly after implementation; then it is modified as needed to meet the changing needs of the company.

About three to six months after implementation, a **post-implementation evaluation** is conducted. This evaluation is a critical examination of the information system after it becomes operational.

An information system is dynamic and must be responsive to the changing needs of the company. The process of adjusting information systems to meet these needs is known as systems maintenance. An information system can be revised only so many times before it becomes too cumbersome to use and maintain. This signals the "death" of the information system and the "birth" of its successor. The system life cycle is then repeated.

## REVIEW EXERCISES

### Concepts

1.  What is the objective of prototyping?
2.  What are patches?
3.  What advantage does direct conversion have over parallel conversion? Parallel over direct conversion?

4.  In which stage of the information system life cycle are systems "conceived"? "Maintained"?

5.  What are the consequences of omitting a structured walk-through of a detailed system design?

6.  Name three system design techniques.

7.  What is a structure chart, and how is it used?

8.  What is the purpose of a bar chart in project scheduling?

9.  Give two examples of uses of a control total.

10. Design a screen layout for an on-line hospital admittance system. Design only that screen with which the hospital clerk would interact to enter basic patient data. Distinguish between input and output by underlining the input.

## Discussion

11. Why is it important to spend time documenting and understanding the existing system if it is to be discarded after a new system is developed?

12. What dangers are involved in developing an information system without following a methodology?

13. Would it be easier for one person or five people to do a relatively simple program? Draw a parallel to the size of a project team.

14. Some managers consider it a waste of time for two programmers to be familiar with each program. Argue for *or* against this attitude.

15. A bank programmer developed an algorithm to determine the check digit for the bank's credit card numbers. The programmer sold the algorithm, one of the bank's control procedures, to an underground group that specialized in counterfeit credit cards. A year later the programmer was caught and pleaded guilty. What do you feel is a just sentence for this crime?

16. Do you feel that operator sight checks are a valid approach to data entry verification? Why or why not?

17. Discuss specific input, processing, output, and procedural controls that could be built into a payroll system.

## SELF-TEST (by section)

11-1. The system becomes operational in the _____ stage of the system life cycle.

11-2. The service request is normally compiled by users. (T/F)

11-3. (a) A prototype system is developed in Phase _____ of the system development process.

     (b) A prototype system is essentially a complete information system, but without the data base. (T/F)

**11–4.** **(a)** The limits check is a procedural control. (T/F)

**(b)** A _____ is a listing of all data elements in a data base.

**11–5.** Phase III—Programming is the only phase that can be completed out of sequence. (T/F)

**11–6.** Greater risk is associated with direct conversion than with phased conversion. (T/F)

**11–7.** The post-implementation evaluation is normally conducted one year after system implementation. (T/F)

*Self-Test answers.*    11–1, production; 11–2, T; 11–3 (a), I (one); (b), F; 11–4 (a), F; (b), data dictionary; 11–5, F; 11–6, T; 11–7, F.

# Zimco Enterprises

## INFORMATION SYSTEMS AT ZIMCO: SALES AND MARKETING

### MAKE VERSUS BUY

Zimco's original MIS Strategic Plan called for the in-house development of all four components of Zimco's MIS: FACS (finance and accounting), PERES (personnel), PICS (operations), and SAMIS (sales and marketing). Figure Z3–3 (in the case study following Chapter 3) contains an overview data flow diagram of Zimco's MIS. Limited resources dictated that the integrated MIS be developed and implemented in stages. The plan called for FACS to be implemented first, followed by PERES and PICS. SAMIS, the Sales and Marketing Information System, had the lowest priority, for two reasons. First, and perhaps most significant, Sally Marcio, VP of Sales and Marketing, was less vocal about the need for SAMIS than the other VPs were about their systems. Second, Sally was relatively satisfied with the information that she and her managers were receiving from an outside timesharing service.

The "Make" Alternative.   Several years ago during the early summer, Sally stormed into Conrad Innis's (VP of CIS) office and said: "The competition is getting the jump on us with better information. Also, that darned timesharing service has doubled rates! We can't wait any longer; we've got to have SAMIS by the end of the year to stay competitive!"

At that time, work was not scheduled to begin on SAMIS for another 18 months. Conrad told Sally: "We simply don't have the resources to commit to a major new in-house development project. As an alternative, would you consider buying a commercial software package?"

The "Buy" Alternative.   Zimco's Computer and Information Services (CIS) Division, like most centralized computer centers, suffers from a shortage of human resources. To help alleviate this problem, Zimco managers have occasionally opted to purchase and install commercially available software packages. The "package," sold by software vendors, consists of the programs (software) and their associated documentation. For larger, more complex packaged systems, vendors also provide training and consultation as part of the package.

Sally Marcio did not believe that the Sales and Marketing Division could wait a couple of years for CIS to develop an in-house (the "make" alternative) information system. She decided to take Conrad's advice and began looking for a packaged sales and marketing system (the "buy" alternative). After evaluating seven such systems, a search team recommended a package developed by a firm in Cleveland. Sally said: "With a few minor modifications, this system will fit our needs to a tee." Since the packaged system was compatible with Zimco's database management system, the modifications were relatively minor.

Because of the immediacy of the need and the availability of a product, Zimco management decided to "buy" rather than "make" the fourth component of the Zimco MIS. SAMIS went online in November, five months after Sally first related her sense of desperation to Conrad.

### SAMIS: SALES AND MARKETING INFORMATION SYSTEM

SAMIS is that component of the integrated MIS that services the Sales and Marketing Division.

The system interacts frequently with the other three MIS components: FACS, PERES, and PICS. Sally Marcio calls SAMIS the "wizard of Zimco" because of the way it helps to coordinate all activities within the Sales and Marketing Division. The five subsystems of SAMIS match up perfectly with the functions of the five departments in the Sales and Marketing Division. If you will remember, this is in contrast to the subsystems of FACS, PERES, and PICS which are not aligned with the organizational structures of their respective divisions. The five subsystems of SAMIS are:

**4.1** Market Research Subsystem

**4.2** Advertising and Promotion Subsystem

**4.3** Customer Services Subsystem

**4.4** Sales and Order Processing Subsystem

**4.5** Sales Forecasting and Analysis Subsystem

The second-level data flow diagram of Figure Z11–1 is the explosion of the "sales and marketing" component of the Zimco MIS (see Figure Z3–3). Each of the five subsystems is described in the following sections.

## THE FIVE SUBSYSTEMS OF SAMIS

### Market Research Subsystem (4.1)

The Market Research Department systematically gathers all kinds of data that may in some way provide information that will help managers to make better decisions regarding the marketing and sale of Zimco products. Unlike accounting or personnel systems, the data gathered for input to the Market Research Subsystem are very volatile (see Figure Z11–1); that is, data that are seemingly accurate today may be erroneous tomorrow. Because of the everchanging nature of market research data, the data must be constantly updated so that the information derived from the data is representative of the current market. Inputs to the Market Research Subsystem are:

- Data on the marketing activities of competitors
- Demographic data
- Economic indicators
- Data on consumer behavior
- Customer responses to surveys

Zimco subscribes to several commercially available data bases that provide much of these data. The company obtains the rest of the data by periodically distributing surveys, from Zimco's integrated data base, and from feedback from the field sales representatives.

People in the Market Research Department use SAMIS to keep an eye on demographics and customer buying trends so that they can identify untapped niches in the market. Sally Marcio says: "Without SAMIS, certain segments of the marketplace would forever remain hidden. For example, for years we aimed the Farkles (inflatable cushions) sales pitch at commuters. A survey conducted by market research surfaced numerous domestic uses for Farkles. By broadening the scope of our advertising we were able to increase Farkle sales by 18 percent during the next year."

The Market Research Subsystem automatically gathers ideas for new products and enhancements to existing products from Zimco managers and from the Customer Service Subsystem. Last year one of Zimco's distributors reported that several women complained about the "unattractive" color of the Farkle. In response, the Market Research Department worked closely with the Operations Division to produce Farkles in pastel colors. Before releasing the pastel Farkles, Zimco test marketed them in Cincinnati and used SAMIS to monitor sales on a daily basis. The new brightly colored Farkles test marketed very well and are now a part of the product line.

The Market Research Subsystem includes a number of models that help researchers analyze and interpret the data. For example, each week the system determines if there is any satistically significant correlation between sales trends for the various Zimco products and other trends. For example, statistical techniques are used to correlate product sales to the consumer price index, unemployment level, furniture sales, and numerous other factors that might in some way influence the sale of a Zimco product. If a correlation exists, market researchers can identify trends early and give management some time to react, perhaps with an unscheduled price adjustment.

**FIGURE Z11–1**
**Zimco's Sales and Marketing Information System (SAMIS)**
This data flow diagram is the explosion of the sales and marketing (4) process of the MIS overview data flow diagram of Figure Z3–3.

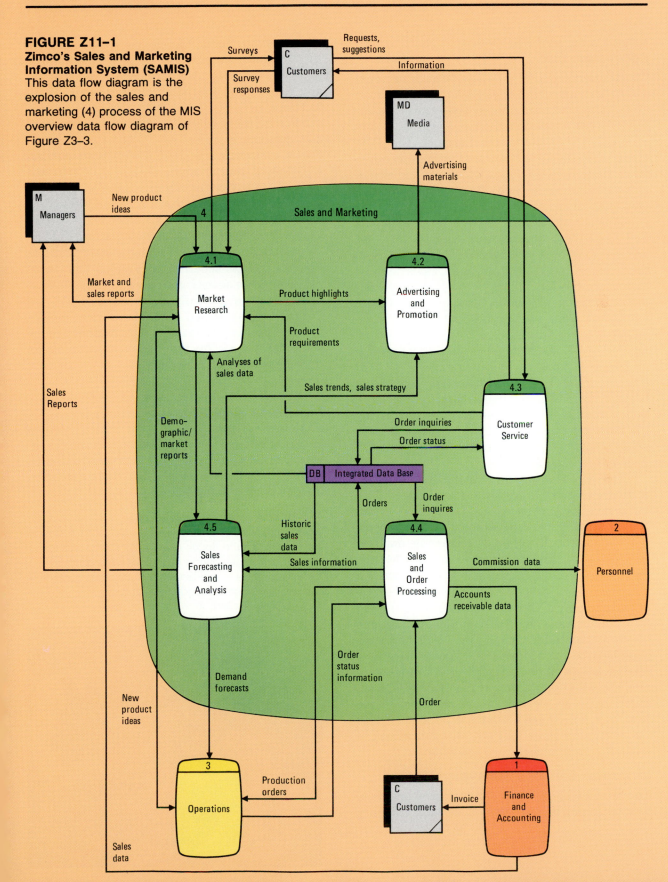

## Advertising and Promotion Subsystem (4.2)

Zimco promotes their products through personal selling (exclusively to retailers and wholesalers), advertising, and promotional campaigns. The latter two are supported by the Advertising and Promotion Subsystem (see Figure Z11–1). The catalyst for the advertising and promotion activity is the information on sales trends and strategies provided by the Sales Forecasting and Analysis Subsystem.

Zimco routinely advertises in newspapers and magazines. The copy and graphics for these ads are generated on-line and routed directly to the print media via electronic mail. Occasionally, they advertise on television and radio. About three times a year, Zimco has promotional campaigns for each of their products. These campaigns usually involve price reductions or rebates. SAMIS has made it possible for the people at Zimco to analyze the effectiveness of their ads and promotional campaigns on a day-to-day basis. Sally Marcio is proud of SAMIS's contribution to her division's bottom line: "By identifying the most effective advertising medium, SAMIS helps Zimco managers to maximize the value of their advertising dollars."

The purchase price of SAMIS included the software and hardware for a computerized dialing system for *telemarketing*. The system, which is part of the Advertising and Promotion Subsystem, automatically dials a telephone number, then plays a prerecorded message. Sally Marcio decided to use this component of the subsystem to kick off a new promotional campaign. The telephone numbers of Zimco customers were entered into the system, then dialed automatically, one after another. Sally Marcio said: "Telemarketing sounded like a good idea, but it wasn't. Customer feedback was all negative. They let us know immediately that they didn't appreciate these 'computer' calls, so we turned the machine off the next day and haven't turned it on since." This incident reminds us that not all applications of computer technology are worthwhile.

## Customer Services Subsystem (4.3)

The function of customer service representatives is to respond to any type of customer inquiry or complaint. Sally Marcio says: "Because of SAMIS, our customer service reps have on-line access to the integrated data base and just about any information that the customer would want to know."

For the more routine inquiries, many of Zimco's customers prefer the "Zimco Connection." Zimco customers are given a telephone number, a password, and an authorization code that will allow them to tap directly into SAMIS from their own workstations. Customers routinely establish an on-line link with the Customer Service Subsystem (see Figure Z11–1) to track orders and shipments and to get the latest pricing information. Of course, security precautions limit what customers can access and they can't change anything. According to Sally: "The Customer Service Subsystem has helped to build customer loyalty and has made relations with our customers much smoother. They know that if they have a question they can ask us or they can query our data base directly."

One of the activities of the Customer Service Department is discussed in the Zimco case study following Chapter 5. That case study explains how customer service representatives use the integrated data base to send courtesy follow-up letters to customers with whom they have interactions during the day.

The Sales and Marketing Information System (SAMIS) provides Zimco customers with two methods for making inquiries about the status of an order. They can make their inquiry by telephone or they can use data communications to tap directly into customer-accessible portions of Zimco's integrated data base.
(Computer Consoles, Inc.)

## Sales and Order Processing Subsystem (4.4)

The Sales and Order Processing Subsystem (see Figure Z11–1) provides the facility for Zimco's field sales reps and Zimco's customers to enter orders directly into SAMIS and the integrated data base. Every field sales rep has a portable workstation. The rep can enter an order, make an inquiry, or send a message while in a customers office. To do this, the rep simply dials the number of the Dallas mainframe on a telephone. Upon hearing the computer's high whistle "greeting," the rep inserts the telephone handset into the workstation's built-in modem. This makes the connection between the workstation and Zimco's mainframe computer.

Sally says that "the use of portables in the field has resulted in faster delivery to the customer, far less paperwork, and a better cash flow to Zimco. More often than not a sales rep can guarantee the customer that his order will be shipped within twenty-four hours. The customer appreciates that."

Just having the portable workstations gives the field reps a psychological boost. They know that they have a direct link to literally everyone in the company, even though they work out of their homes. All of them routinely get and receive electronic mail. Since the portable workstations double as microcomputers, the sales reps use them in stand-alone mode to do spreadsheet analysis and word processing.

The Sales and Order Processing Subsystem also provides support for *intercompany networking*. Some customers prefer to enter their orders directly from their mainframe computers into Zimco's mainframe at Dallas. Customers send the order data in a standard format and the order is confirmed with a return message from Zimco's mainframe computer. Sally reports: "Intercompany networking benefits our customer and us. Zimco customers are able to cut their inventories since they get quicker delivery. It cuts our paperwork substantially, thereby reducing the overall cost of sales."

## Sales Forecasting and Analysis Subsystem (4.5)

The Sales Forecasting and Analysis Subsystem (see Figure Z11–1) uses mathematical models to combine the historical sales data, sales forecasts, and other predictive data to extrapolate sales trends for Zimco products. The production levels at each of the plants are based on the sales forecasts. Each month, the Sales Forecasting and Analysis Subsystem generates a 6-Month Demand Schedule for each of Zimco's products. Figure Z11–2 illustrates the March–August 6-Month Demand Schedule for Stibs.

The Operations Division uses these demand reports to schedule production levels at the plants and to set minimum finished-goods inventory levels at each of the warehouses. Each month the "6-Month Demand Schedule" is updated to reflect current information. Notice the "% Chg." columns in Figure Z11–2. These figures indicate the percent change in the product demand estimate from the previous month's (Febru-

**FIGURE Z11–2**
**6-Month Demand Schedule**
This report is generated each month to help plant managers set production and finished-goods inventory levels. The "% Chg." columns indicate the percent change in the product demand estimate from the previous month's (February) "6-Month Demand Report."

```
                    6-Month Demand Schedule (Stibs)
                Anticipated Unit Demand by Warehouse (1000s of units)

            Dallas % Chg.  Eugene  % Chg.  Benton  % Chg.  Reston  % Chg.  Total  % Chg
March        101    1.0%    210     1.5%    192     3.0%    222     0.5%    725    1.5%
April         97   -1.2%    215     4.0%    182    -2.0%    219    -1.0%    713    0.2%
May          105    5.0%    213     3.0%    183    -1.5%    225     2.0%    726    1.8%
June         109    8.0%    221     7.0%    197     6.0%    239     8.0%    766    7.2%
July          99    1.0%    206    -0.5%    184    -1.0%    230     4.0%    719    1.0%
August       110   -0.5%    205    -1.0%    187     0.5%    223     1.0%    725    0.1%
```

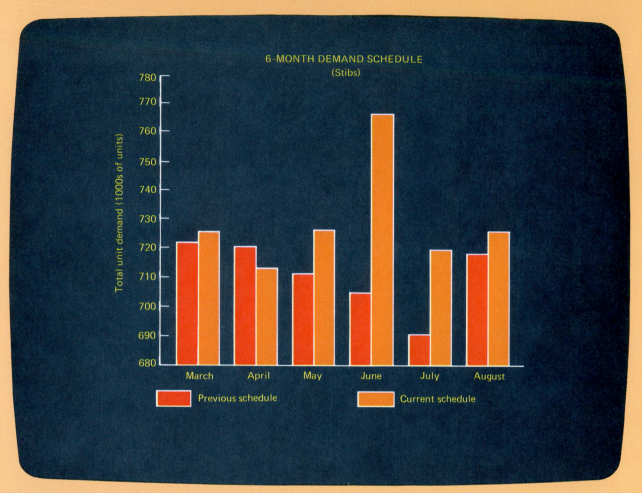

**FIGURE Z11–3**
**Bar Chart for 6-Month Demand Schedule**
This bar chart graphically highlights any major changes in the total product demand forecast (e.g., June) by comparing the demand estimates for the current "6-Month Demand Schedule" with the estimates on the previous month's schedule.

ary) "6-Month Demand Schedule." For example, the March Stibs demand for the Dallas warehouse is forecast to be 1 percent greater than it was a month ago. The bar chart in Figure Z11–3 graphically highlights any major changes in the monthly total demand estimates. From the figure, it is obvious that there will be a far greater demand for Stibs in June than was earlier expected.

## SAMIS Summary

The examples presented in this case study represent only a small fraction of the capabilities of SAMIS. Sales managers can request a sales summary of the top 10 accounts in their regions. Orders can be received, processed, and billed with-

out human intervention. When sales fall below the historical norm in a particular sales territory, the appropriate regional sales manager is automatically notified via electronic mail. Sally Marcio summed up her impressions of SAMIS very succinctly. "Before SAMIS, we had too much data and not enough information. Now we use information as a competitive weapon."

## DISCUSSION QUESTIONS

1. Zimco management is routinely confronted with a "make versus buy" decision regarding software. Discuss the advantages and disadvantages of each alternative.

2. The Sales and Order Processing Subsystem permits field sales reps to make inquiries to the integrated data base from their portable workstations while in a customer's office. Discuss the types of inquiries that a sales rep might make.

3. Describe the benefits of intercompany networking for both Zimco and for Zimco's customers.

4. Zimco follows the five-phase system development methodology presented in Figure 11–2. Only part of the methodology was applied to SAMIS, since it is a software package. Identify these activities.

5. A search team, made up of people from both the CIS and Sales and Marketing Divisions, was formed to evaluate commercially available sales and marketing software packages. Discuss the criteria they might have used to select SAMIS.

6. What observations can you make about the information presented in the "6-Month Demand Schedule for Stibs" in Figures Z11–2 and Z11–3?

7. Currently, Zimco's computerized dialing system is unused. Suggest applications for this system that would benefit Zimco.

*In a world of constant change, it is very important for business judgements to be made based on reliable information. Computers provide up-to-date, fast and accurate information and assist management in making intelligent decisions.*

John H. Johnson
Editor and Publisher
Johnson Publishing Company, Inc.

# Programming Concepts

## STUDENT LEARNING OBJECTIVES

- To identify approaches to solving a programming problem.
- To describe the concept of structured programming.
- To demonstrate an understanding of the principles and use of flowcharting and other program design techniques.
- To classify the various types of program instructions.
- To describe the steps and approaches to program development.

## FOCUS OF ZIMCO CASE STUDY

- Productivity Improvement at Zimco.

## 12–1 PROGRAMMING IN PERSPECTIVE

A computer is not capable of performing calculations or manipulating data without exact step-by-step instruction. These instructions take the form of a computer program. Five, fifty, or even several hundred programs may be required for an information system. Electronic spreadsheet software is made up of dozens of programs that work together so that you can perform spreadsheet tasks. The same is true of word processing software.

Most of the programs that you develop while you are a student will be independent of those developed by your classmates and, more often than not, independent of one another. In a business environment, programs are often complementary to one another. For example, you might write a program to collect the data and another program to analyze the data and print a report.

There is no such thing as an "easy" program. A programming task, whether it be in the classroom, in business, or at home, should challenge your intellect and logic capabilities. As soon as you develop competence at one level, your instructor will surely assign you a program that is more difficult than anything you have done in the past. Even when doing recreational programming on your personal computer, you won't be satisfied with an "easy" program. You will probably challenge yourself with increasingly complex programs.

Programming can be enormously frustrating, especially at first. *Don't despair*! Just when you think that the task confronting you is impossible, a little light will turn on and open the door to the joy of learning to program. That light has turned millions of people on to programming, and it will turn you on, too (if it hasn't already).

## 12–2 PROBLEM SOLVING AND PROGRAMMING LOGIC

A single program addresses a particular problem: to compute and assign grades, to permit an update of a data base, to monitor a patient's heart rate, to analyze marketing data, and so on. In effect, when you write a program, you are solving a *problem*. To solve the problem you must derive a *solution*. And to do that, you must use your powers of *logic*.

A program is like the materials used to construct a building. Much of the brainwork involved in the construction of a building goes into the blueprint. The location, appearance, and function of a building are determined long before the first brick is laid. And so it is with programming. The design of a program, or its programming logic (the blueprint), is completed before the program is written (or the building is constructed). This section and the next discuss approaches to designing the logic for a programming task. Later in this chapter we discuss the program and the different types of program instructions.

(Dahlgren Museum, Naval Surface Weapons Center)

(National Computer Systems)

Programming has come a long way since the late 1940s when programmers set electrical switches to create programs. Today, programming is done interactively at sophisticated programmer workstations and often in consultation with people who will use the system.

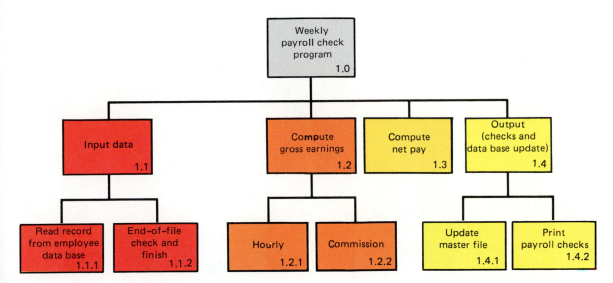

**FIGURE 12–1**
**Program Structure Chart**
The logic of a payroll program to
print weekly payroll checks can
be broken into modules for ease
of understanding, coding, and
maintenance.

## Structured Program Design: Divide and Conquer

Figure 12–1 illustrates a *structure chart* for a program to print weekly payroll checks. Hourly and commission employees are processed weekly. A structure chart for a program to print monthly payroll checks for salaried employees would look similar, except that task 1.2, compute gross earnings, would not be required. The salary amount can be retrieved directly from the employee data base.

The structure chart permits a programming problem to be broken down into a hierarchy of tasks. A task can be broken down into subtasks, as long as a finer level of detail is desired. The most effective programs are designed so they can be written in **modules,** or independent tasks. It is much easier to address a complex programming problem in small, more manageable modules than as one big task. This is done using the principles of **structured programming.**

In structured programming, the logic of the program is addressed hierarchically in logical modules (see Figure 12–1). In the end, the logic of each module is translated into a sequence of program instructions that can be executed independently. By dividing the program into modules, the structured approach to programming reduces the complexity of the programming task. Some programs are so complex that if taken as a single task, they would be almost impossible to conceptualize, design, and code. Again, we must "divide and conquer."

## 12–3   PROGRAM DESIGN TECHNIQUES

A number of techniques are available to help programmers analyze a problem and design the program. Data flow diagrams, presented in the Zimco case study following Chapter 3, and HIPO, presented briefly in Chapter 11, can be used as *program* design aids as well as *system*

Every other workstation in this computer center is a microcomputer. The other workstations are linked to the mainframe in the background. The techniques used in designing computer programs are the same for both micros and mainframes. (Control Data Corporation)

design aids. Both can capture graphically the logic of systems (the general level) or programs (the detailed level). The process symbol in a *system* data flow diagram might represent one or several programs (e.g., print payroll checks), whereas a process symbol in a *program* data flow diagram might represent a computation (e.g., compute federal tax deduction). In this section, three more design techniques—*flow-charting*, *pseudocode*, and *decision tables*—are presented as they would be used in the design of a program's logic. These techniques can also be used as system design tools.

## Flowcharting

One of the most popular design techniques is **flowcharting.** Flowcharts illustrate data, information, and work flow through the interconnection of *specialized symbols* with *flow lines*. The combination of symbols and flow lines portrays the logic of the program or system. The more commonly used flowchart symbols are shown in Figure 12–2.

Flowcharting Symbols.   Each symbol indicates the *type of operation to be performed*, and the flowchart graphically illustrates the *sequence in which the operations are to be performed*. *Flow lines* ⟶ depict the sequential flow of the program logic. A rectangle ☐ signifies some type of *computer process*. The process could be as specific as "compute an individual's grade average" (in a program flowchart) or as general as "prepare class schedules for the fall semester" (in a system flowchart). The *predefined process* ◫, a special case of the process symbol, is represented by a rectangle with extra vertical lines. The predefined process refers to a group of operations that may be detailed in a separate flowchart. The parallelogram ▱ is a generalized *input/output* symbol that denotes any type of input to, or output from, the program or system. The diamond-shaped symbol ◇ marks the point at which a *decision* is to be made. In a program flowchart, a particular set of instructions is executed based on the outcome of a

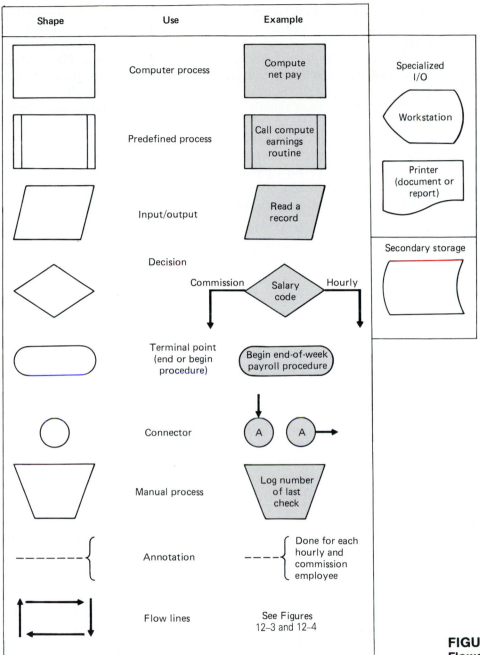

**FIGURE 12–2**
**Flowchart Symbols**

decision. For example, in a payroll program, gross pay is computed differently for hourly and commission employees; therefore, for each employee processed, a decision is made as to which set of instructions are to be executed.

Each flowchart must begin and end with the oval *terminal point* symbol ⬭. A small circle ○ is a *connector* and is used to break and then link flow lines. The connector symbol is often used to avoid having to cross lines. The trapezoid ▽ indicates that a *manual pro-*

*cess* is to be performed. Contrast this to a computer process represented by a rectangle. The bracket ---{ permits descriptive notations to be added to flowcharts.

The *on-line data storage symbol* ⬭ represents a file or data base. The most common *specialized input/output* symbols are the *workstation* ⬭ and the *printer* (hard copy) ⬭ symbols.

These symbols are equally applicable to system and program flowcharting and can be used to develop and represent the logic for each. A *system* flowchart for a payroll system is illustrated in Figure 12–3. Contrast this system flowchart to the *program* flowchart of Figure 12–4. The program flowchart portrays the logic for the structure chart of Figure 12–1. The company in the example of Figure 12–1 processes hourly and commission employee checks each week (salary employee

**FIGURE 12–3**
**General Systems Flowchart**
This flowchart graphically illustrates the relationship between I/O and major processing activities in a payroll system.

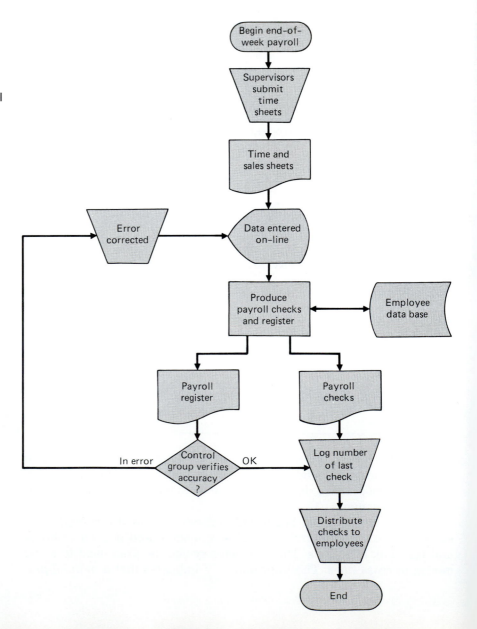

checks are processed monthly). Gross earnings for hourly employees are computed by multiplying hours-worked times the rate of pay. For salespeople on commission, gross earnings are computed as a percentage of sales.

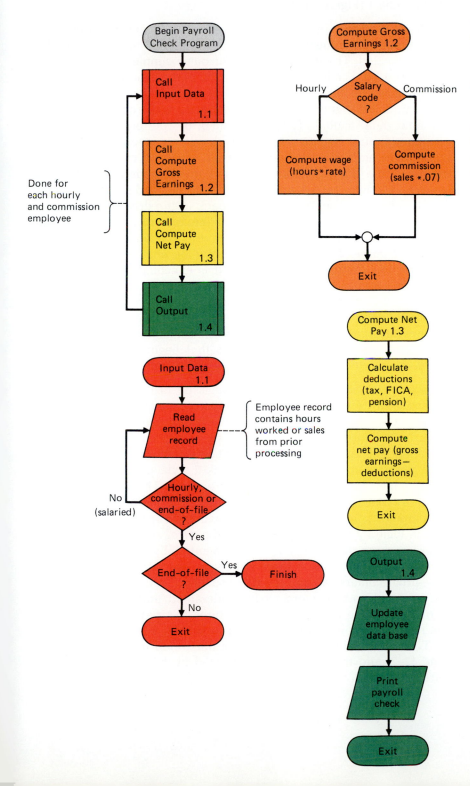

**FIGURE 12–4**
**Program Flowchart**
This flowchart portrays the logic of a program to compute and print payroll checks for commission, hourly, and salaried employees (see the structure chart of Figure 12–1). The logic is designed so that a driver module calls subroutines as they are needed to process each employee.

If you'll remember from Chapter 11, "The Systems Development Process," we discussed a HIPO example for a payroll system. The structure chart of Figure 12–1 and the flowchart of Figure 12–4 represent the *program* logic to accompany Module 1.3.1 of the Chapter 11 *system* structure chart (Figure 11–7).

The Driver Module.   In structured programming, each program has a **driver module** that causes other program modules to be executed as they are needed. The driver module for our example payroll program (see Figure 12–4) is a **loop** that "calls" each of the subordinate modules, or **subroutines,** as they are needed for the processing of each employee. The program is designed such that when the payroll program is initiated, the "input data" module (1.1) is executed, or "performed" first. After execution, control is then returned to the driver module, unless there are no more employees to be processed, in which case execution is terminated (the "Finish" terminal point). For each hourly or commission employee, Modules 1.2, 1.3, and 1.4 are performed, and at the completion of each subroutine, control is passed back to the driver module.

When dividing the logic of a program into modules, a good guideline to follow is that each module should have a *single entry point* and a *single exit point*. That is, a program module should begin and end with the same instructions each time it is executed. Thus transfer of control into and out of a particular program module occurs only at the entry and exit points. The single-entry/single-exit-point guideline encourages good program logic, because it does not permit multiple branches to other modules. An excess of branches tends to confuse the logic of the program. The modules that begin or end a program may have an extra entry/exit point to begin or end program execution.

Programming Control Structures.   Through the 1970s, programmers unknowingly wrote what is now referred to as "spaghetti code." It was so named because their program flowcharts appeared more like a plate of spaghetti than like a logical analysis of a programming problem. The redundant and unnecessary branching (jumps from one portion of the program to another) of a spaghetti-style program resulted in confusing logic, even to the person who wrote it. These programs were difficult to write and debug, and even harder to maintain.

Computer scientists thwarted this dead-end approach to developing program logic by identifying three basic *control structures* into which any program, or subroutine, can be segmented. By conceptualizing the logic of a program in these three structures—*sequence*, *selection*, and *loop*—programmers can avoid writing spaghetti code and thus produce programs that can be more easily understood and maintained. The use of these three basic control structures has paved the way for a more rigorous and scientific approach to solving a programming problem. These three control structures are illustrated in Figures 12–5, 12–6, and 12–7, and their use is demonstrated in the payroll example of Figure 12–4.

**FIGURE 12–5**
**Sequence Control Structures**

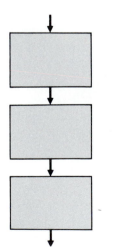

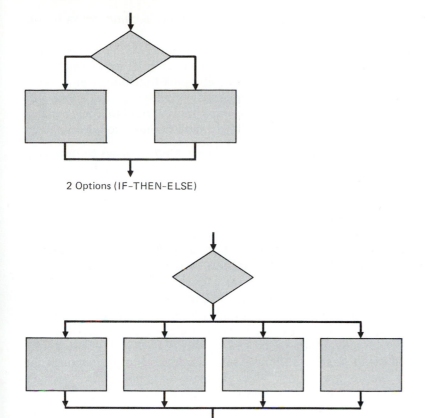

**FIGURE 12-6**
**Selection Control Structures**
Any number of options can result from a decision in a selection control
structure.

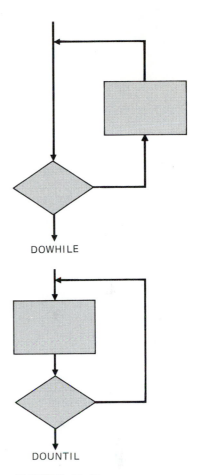

**FIGURE 12-7**
**Loop Control Structures**
The two types of loop structures
are DOWHILE and DOUNTIL.

*Sequence Structure.* In the sequence structure (Figure 12–5), the processing steps are performed in sequence, one after another. Modules
1.3 and 1.4 in Figure 12–4 are good examples of sequence structures.

*Selection Structure.* The selection structure (Figure 12–6) depicts the
logic for selecting the appropriate sequence of statements. In Figure
12–4, our example payroll program, the selection structure is used to
illustrate the logic for the computation of gross pay for hourly and
commission employees (Module 1.2). In the selection structure, a decision is made as to which sequence of instructions is to be executed
next. In Module 1.2, is the salary code for an employee record "hourly"
or "commission"? In the actual payroll program, a different sequence
of instructions is executed for hourly and commission employees. The
two-option selection structure is sometimes referred to as *IF-THEN-
ELSE*. For example, *IF* the salary code is hourly, *THEN* compute wages,

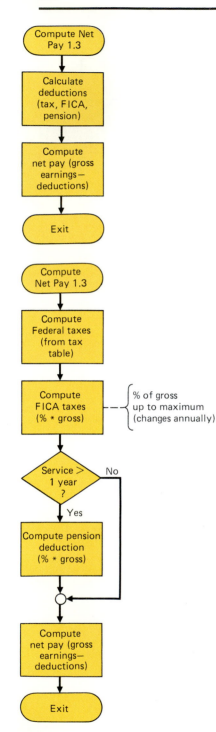

**FIGURE 12–8**
**Level of Detail in Flowcharts**
The logic of Module 1.3, Compute Net Pay, of Figures 12–1 and 12–4 is depicted in a general and a more detailed flowchart.

*ELSE* compute commission (employee pay type is commission by default).

The selection structure of Module 1.2 presents two decision options: hourly or commission. Other circumstances might call for three or more decision options. For example, suppose that part-time hourly employees are treated differently than full-time hourly employees, and salary employees are also paid weekly. In this case, there would be four decision options: hourly (full-time), hourly (part-time), commission, and salary.

*Loop Structure.*   The loop structure (Figure 12–7) is used to represent the program logic when a portion of the program is to be executed repeatedly until a particular condition is met. There are two variations of the loop structure (see Figure 12–7): When the decision, or *test-on-condition*, is placed at the beginning of the statement sequence, it becomes a *DOWHILE loop*; when placed at the end, it becomes a *DOUNTIL loop* (pronounced *doo while* and *doo until*). Notice that the leading statements in a DOUNTIL structure will always be executed at least once. In the example payroll flowchart of Figure 12–4, that portion of the input data module (1.1) that reads an employee record is illustrated in a DOUNTIL loop. Employee records, containing hours-worked and sales data, are read sequentially. Since only hourly or commission employees are processed weekly, the loop is repeated until the record of an hourly or commission employee is read, or until the end-of-file marker is reached. When an hourly or commission employee record is read, control is returned to the driver module, which in turn passes control to Module 1.2.

**Level of Flowchart Detail.**   The example program flowchart of Figure 12–4 is made somewhat general so that the concepts can be demonstrated more easily. A flowchart showing greater detail could be compiled, if desired. For example, Figure 12–8 illustrates how Module 1.3, Compute Net Pay, can be expanded to show more detail.

In program flowcharting, the level of detail is a matter of personal preference. Some programmers complete a general flowchart that outlines the overall program logic, then flesh it out with a more detailed flowchart. Many other examples of program flowcharting can be found in the special section "BASIC Programming" at the end of the book.

## Pseudocode

Another design technique that is used almost exclusively for program design is called **pseudocode.** While the other techniques represent the logic of the program graphically, pseudocode represents the logic in programlike statements written in plain English. Since pseudocode does not have any syntax guidelines (i.e., rules for formulating instructions), you can concentrate on developing the logic of your program. Once you feel that the logic is sound, the pseudocode is easily translated to a procedure-oriented language that can be executed. In Figure 12–9, the logic of a simple program is represented in pseudocode and with a flowchart.

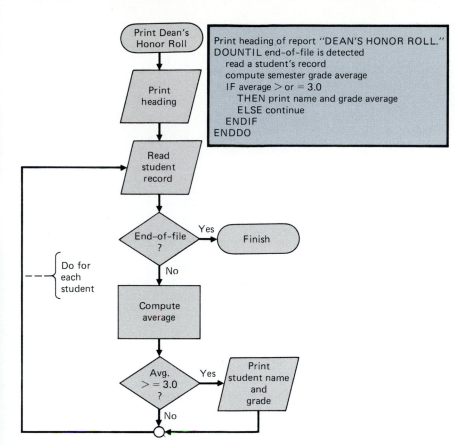

**FIGURE 12–9**
**Pseudocode Example with Flowchart**
This pseudocode program depicts the logic of a program to compile a list of students who have qualified for the dean's honor roll. The same logic is shown in a flowchart.

## Decision Tables

The **decision table** is a handy tool that analysts and programmers use to graphically depict what happens in a system or program for occurrences of various circumstances. The decision table is based on "IF . . . THEN" logic. *IF* this set of conditions is met, *THEN* take this action. Decision tables are divided into quadrants (see Figure 12–10). Conditions that may occur are listed in the *condition stub* (the upper left quadrant). The possible occurrences for each condition type are noted in the *condition entries* (the upper right quadrant). Each possible set of conditions, called a *rule*, is numbered at the top of each column. Actions that can result from various combinations of conditions, or rules, are listed in the *action stub* (the lower left quadrant). For each rule, an action-to-be-taken entry is made in the *action entries* (the lower right quadrant).

The decision table in Figure 12–11 illustrates what action is taken for each of several sets of conditions. For example, *IF* the employees to be processed are salaried and it is the end of the month (rule 1), *THEN* both paychecks and a payroll register are printed. *IF* the employees to be processed are on a commission and it is the end of the week (rule 4), *THEN* paychecks only are printed.

**FIGURE 12–10**
**Decision-Table Format**
Decision tables are divided into four quadrants: condition stub, condition entries, action stub, and action entries.

|  | Heading | Rules |
|---|---|---|
| "IF" | Condition stub | Condition entries |
| "THEN" | Action stub | Action entries |

| Payroll type/output chart | Rules | | | | |
|---|---|---|---|---|---|
| | 1 | 2 | 3 | 4 | 5 |
| Salaried employee | Y | N | N | N | N |
| Hourly employee | N | Y | Y | N | N |
| Commission employee | N | N | N | Y | Y |
| End of week | N | Y | N | Y | N |
| End of month | Y | N | Y | N | Y |
| Print paychecks | X | X | | X | X |
| Print payroll register | X | X | X | | X |

**FIGURE 12–11**
**Decision Table**
This decision table depicts what payroll outputs would be generated for various payroll types and conditions.

The decision table is not a good technique for illustrating work flow. It is, however, very helpful when used in conjunction with flowcharts, data flow diagrams, and HIPO charts. The major advantage of decision tables is that a programmer or analyst must consider *all* alternatives, options, conditions, variables, and so on. With decision tables, the level of detail is dictated by the circumstances. With flowcharts and other design techniques, the level of detail (contrast Figures 12–4 and 12–8) is more a matter of personal preference.

There is no substitute for good sound logic in programming. If you follow the guidelines of structured programming and make judicious use of these program design techniques, your program will be easier to write, use, and maintain.

## MEMORY BITS

### SYSTEM AND PROGRAM DESIGN TECHNIQUES
- Flowcharting
- Data flow diagrams (DFD)
- Hierarchical plus input-processing-output (HIPO)
- Pseudocode
- Decision tables

## 12–4  SO WHAT'S A PROGRAM?: CONCEPTS AND PRINCIPLES OF PROGRAMMING

A computer program is made up of a sequence of instructions that are executed one after another. These instructions, also called **statements,** are executed in sequence unless the order of execution is altered by a "test-on-condition" instruction or a "branch" instruction.

The flowchart of our example payroll program (Figure 12–4) is recreated in Figure 12–12, together with a sequence of language-independent instructions. Except for the computation of gross earnings, the processing steps are similar for both types of employees. Two sequences of instructions are needed to compute gross earnings for *hourly* and *commission* employees. We can also see from the flowchart that the sequence in which the instructions are executed may be altered at three places (decision symbols), depending on the results of the test-on-condition. In Module 1.2, for example, the sequence of instructions to be executed depends on whether the test-on-condition detects an hourly or a commission employee.

To the right of the flowchart in Figure 12–12 is a representation of a sequence of language-independent instructions and the order in which they are executed. *Statement numbers* are included, as they are in most program listings. This program could be written in any procedure-oriented language. The purpose of the discussion below is to make you familiar with general types of programming instructions, not those of any particular programming language. Each language has an instruction set with at least one instruction in each of the following *instruction classifications*: input/output, computation, control, data transfer and assignment, and format.

**Input/Output.**   Input/output instructions direct the computer to "read from" or "write to" a peripheral device (e.g., printer, disk drive). *Statement 50* of Figure 12–12 requests that an employee record, including pay data, be read from the data base. *Statement 320* causes a payroll check to be printed.

**Computation.**   Computation instructions perform arithmetic operations (add, subtract, multiply, divide, and raise a number to a power). *Statement 160* (PAY = HOURS * RATE) computes gross earnings for hourly employees. *Statement 190* (PAY = SALES * .07) computes gross earnings for commission employees, where the commission is 7 percent of sales.

**Control (Decision and/or Branch).**   Control instructions can alter the sequence of the program's execution. *Unconditional* and *conditional* instructions prompt a decision and, perhaps, a branch to another part of the program or to a subroutine. In Figure 12–12, *statements 10–40*, *80*, *110*, *130*, *140*, *210*, *270*, and *340* are control instructions.

*Unconditional Instructions.*   Statements 10 through 40 are unconditional branch instructions. An unconditional branch instruction disrupts the normal sequence of execution by causing an unconditional branch to another part of the program or to a subroutine. In *statements 10–40*, the branch is from the driver module to a subroutine. The CALL statement works in conjunction with the RETURN statement to branch to another location, then RETURN control back to the statement following the CALL. For example, the CALL at *statement 10* passes control to the "Input Data" module (1.1) at *statement 50*; then the RETURN at *statement 120* passes control back to the driver module at *statement 20*.

Another unconditional branch instruction, very popular before structured programming, is the GOTO (pronounced *go too*) instruction. The GOTO statement causes control of execution to "go to" another portion of the program. A GOTO instruction is placed at *statement 170* so that once the hourly pay is calculated, control is passed directly to the RETURN statement in order to bypass that portion of module 1.2 that deals with commission employees.

The GOTO at *statement 170* was included for demonstration purposes, but in an actual program it should have been avoided when possible. Programming gurus advocate that the GOTO statement be used sparingly. Excessive use of GOTOs destroys the logical flow of the program and makes it difficult to divide the program into modules.

These programmers write programs in COBOL, BASIC, and C. Although these programming languages are substantially different in their capabilities and uses, the concepts embodied in these languages are similar enough that these programmers have no trouble writing in one language in the morning and another in the afternoon.
(Cromemco, Inc.)

**FIGURE 12–12**
**Program Flowchart with Language-Independent**
**Instructions**
The flowchart (same as Figure 12–4) presents the logic of a payroll program to compute and print payroll checks for commission, hourly, and salaried employees. The accompanying "program" has a few language-independent instructions to help illustrate the concepts and principles of programming. A detailed discussion of this figure is presented in the text.

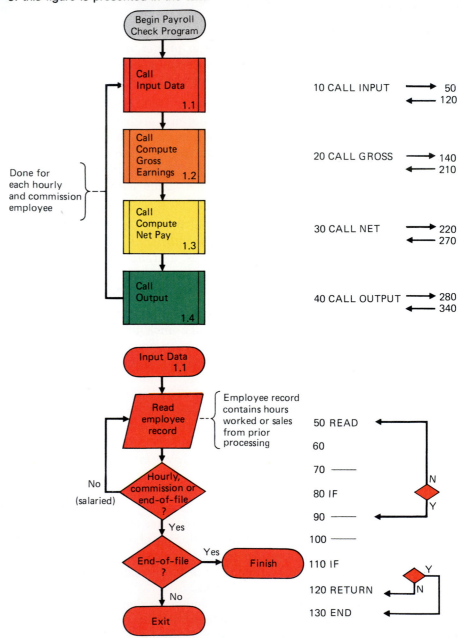

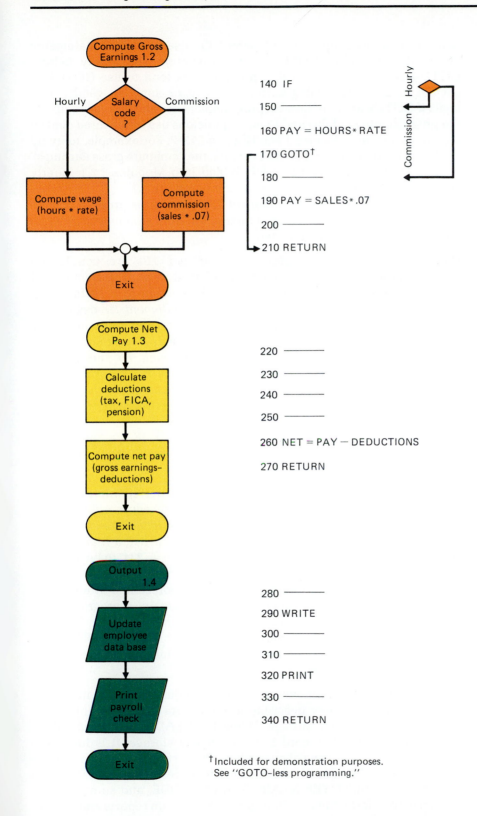

140 IF

150 ————

160 PAY = HOURS * RATE

170 GOTO†

180 ————

190 PAY = SALES * .07

200 ————

210 RETURN

220 ————

230 ————

240 ————

250 ————

260 NET = PAY — DEDUCTIONS

270 RETURN

280 ————

290 WRITE

300 ————

310 ————

320 PRINT

330 ————

340 RETURN

† Included for demonstration purposes.
  See "GOTO-less programming."

Some companies simply do not permit the use of GOTO statements at all, thus the term **GOTO-less programming.** The theory behind GOTO-less programming is that programmers tend to use GOTOs to get out of a "programming corner" instead of applying good sound logic. If GOTOs are not allowed, programmers are encouraged to divide the program into modules and to make judicious use of the three control structures shown in Figures 12–5, 12–6, and 12–7. For example, to avoid the GOTO statement (160) in the example, the "compute gross earnings" module (1.2) could have been subdivided into Modules 1.2.1 (hourly computation) and 1.2.2 (commission computation).

The END instruction at *statement 130* terminates program execution. Control is passed to the END instruction from *statement 110* when the end-of-file marker is detected.

*Conditional Instructions.   Statements 80 and 110* are conditional branch instructions and are generally referred to as IF statements: If certain conditions are met, then a branch is made to a certain part of the program. The conditional branch at *statement 80* causes the program to "loop" until the employee record read is for either an hourly or a commission employee, or the end-of-file marker is reached. The sequence of instructions, *statements 50 through 80*, comprise a DOUNTIL loop. The IF at *statement 110* causes the program to terminate if there are no more employees to be processed. Each programming language offers one or more specialized instructions for the express purpose of creating loops.

In *statement 140*, the salary code is checked. IF the salary code is "commission," THEN a branch is made to *statement 180* and processing is continued.

Data Transfer and Assignment.   Data can be transferred internally from one primary storage location to another. In procedure-oriented languages, data are transferred or "moved" by *assignment instructions*. These instructions permit a *string constant*, also called a *literal value*, such as "The net pay is", or a *numeric value*, such as 234, to be assigned to a named primary storage location.

In a program, a primary storage location is represented by a **variable name** (e.g., PAY, HOURS, NET). A variable name in a program statement refers to the *contents* of a particular primary storage location. For example, a programmer may use the variable name HOURS in a computation statement to refer to the numeric value of the *hours worked* by a particular employee.

Format.   Format instructions are used in conjunction with input and output instructions; they describe how the data are to be entered or outputted from primary storage. When the READ at *statement 50* retrieves an employee's record from secondary storage, it is loaded to primary storage as a string of characters. The format instruction enables the program to distinguish which characters are to be associated with the variables EMPLOYEE-NAME, SALARY-CODE, and so on.

On output, format instructions print headings on reports and present data in a readable format. For example, PAY may be computed to be 324750; however, on output, you would want to "edit" 324750 and insert a dollar sign, a decimal point, and perhaps a comma, for readability ($3,247.50). This is called *editing* the output.

With these few types of instructions, you can model almost any business or scientific procedure, whether it be sales forecasting or guiding rockets to the moon. This discussion is paralleled in the special section "BASIC Programming" at the end of the book, with actual BASIC examples being given for each instruction type.

## 12–5  WRITING PROGRAMS

If you are writing programs to implement an information system, any programming assignment would be accompanied by the systems specifications and program descriptions from Phase II—Systems Analysis and Design. The contents of the specifications and descriptions are summarized in Chapter 11, "The Systems Development Process," Activities III-2 and III-3. If you are writing a single program, you may need to do some analytical work that might otherwise have been done in Phase II.

Remember, writing a program is a project within itself. The following steps, first listed in Chapter 11, are followed for each programming project.

- *Step 1.* Describe the problem.
- *Step 2.* Analyze the problem.
- *Step 3.* Design the general logic of the program.
- *Step 4.* Design the detailed logic of the program.
- *Step 5.* Code the program.
- *Step 6.* Test and debug the program.
- *Step 7.* Document the program.

Programming is no longer limited to technical specialists. End users in marketing, entertainment, and a hundred other fields are acquiring their own micros and learning to program. For short programs, it may take less time for end users to write their own programs than to describe the problem to a professional programmer.
(SCM Corporation)

A team of programmers is usually assigned to work on big projects. The programming team meets as a group at least once per week to coordinate efforts, discuss problems, and report on individual and team progress.
(Management Science America, Inc. (MSA))

355

**Step 1. Describe the Problem.**   The "problem" is described in the program descriptions completed in Activity III-3 (see Chapter 11). For example, a problem might be to write a program that accepts numeric quiz scores and assigns a letter grade. Another problem might be to write a program that identifies and prints the names of customers whose accounts are delinquent. Your instructor will probably define the problem for programs that you might do as class assignments.

**Step 2. Analyze the Problem.**   In this step you break the problem into its basic components for analysis. Remember: "Divide and conquer." Although different programs have different components, a good place to start with most programs is to analyze the *output*, *input*, *processing*, and *file-interaction* components. You would then identify important considerations in the design of the program logic. At the end of the problem analysis stage, you should have a complete understanding of what needs to be done and a good idea of how to do it.

**Steps 3 and 4. Design the General and Detailed Logic of the Program.** Next, you have to put the pieces together in the form of a logical program design. Like the information system, the program is also designed in a hierarchical manner, or from the general to the specific.

*The General Design* (*Step 3*).   The *general* design of the program is oriented primarily to the major processing activities and the relationships between these activities. The structure chart of Figure 12–1 and the flowchart of Figure 12–4, both discussed earlier in this chapter, illustrate the general design of a weekly payroll program to compute and print paychecks. By first completing a general program design, you make it easier to investigate alternative design approaches. Once you are confident of which approach is best, a more detailed design may be completed.

*The Detailed Design* (*Step 4*).   The *detailed* design results in a graphic representation of the program logic that includes *all* processing activities and their relationships, calculations, data manipulations, logic operations, and all input/output. Figure 12–8, discussed earlier, contrasts general and detailed program design.

It is best to test the logic of a program in graphic format (e.g., flowchart or data flow diagram) before you code the instructions. If you rush into Step 5 (Code the Program), you will spend a lot of unnecessary time backtracking to fix the things you overlooked. Resist the urge to start coding before you have the logic of the program firmly fixed in your mind—and on paper. After all, if you don't have time to do it right the first time, how could you possibly have time to do it over?

**Step 5. Code the Program.**   Whether you "write" or "code" the program is a matter of personal preference. In this context, the terms are the same. In Step 5, the graphic and narrative design of program development Steps 1 to 4 is translated into machine-readable instructions, or programs. If the logic is sound and the design documentation (e.g., flowcharts, pseudocode, and so on) is thorough, the coding process is relatively straightforward.

The best way to write a program is to work directly from the design documentation and compose the program interactively at a workstation or PC. Remember, programs are much easier to write when broken down into several small and more manageable modules. Programmers have shown time and time again that it takes less time to code ten 50-line modules than it does to code a single 500-line program.

When you write a program, you should have appropriate documentation on hand. This documentation may consist of some or all of the following:

- The data dictionary (with standardized names for variables, e.g., NET, HOURS)
- The coding scheme for coded data elements
- The file layouts and data base schemas
- Printer and video display layouts
- Data entry specifications
- The program design documentation (e.g., HIPO charts, flowcharts, program descriptions, etc.)

Much of a programmer's time is spent on program maintenance, that is, the modification of existing programs to meet the changing needs of the organization. The program maintenance task is much easier if the program logic is well documented with a flowchart, pseudocode, or some other design technique.
(Cromemco, Inc.)

You may not need to write original code for every programming task. Many organizations maintain libraries of frequently used program modules, called **reusable code.** For example, several programmers might use the same reusable code for an input subroutine.

Step 6. Test and Debug the Program.   Once the program has been entered into the system, it is likely that you will encounter at least one of those cantankerous **bugs.** A bug is an error in program syntax and logic. Ridding a program of bugs is the process of **debugging.**

*Syntax Errors.*   Debugging a program is a repetitive process, whereby each successive attempt gets you one step closer to a working program. The first step is to eliminate *syntax errors* or **diagnostics;** you get a syntax error when you violate one of the rules for writing instructions (e.g., placement of parentheses, spelling of commands, and so on). The diagnostics on the first run are mostly typos (e.g., REED instead of READ). Most compilers and interpreters identify the number of the statement causing the diagnostic and give you an **error message.** As you will quickly find out, if you haven't already, error messages are not always totally explanatory. The error message points you in the right direction, but some extra effort may be required to isolate the exact cause of the error.

*Logic and I/O Errors.*   Once the diagnostics have been removed, the program can be executed. A diagnostic-free program is not necessarily a working program. You now have to debug the *logic of the program* and the *input/output formats*. To do this, you need to create *test data* and, perhaps, a *test data base* so that you know what to expect as output. For example, suppose that you write a program to average

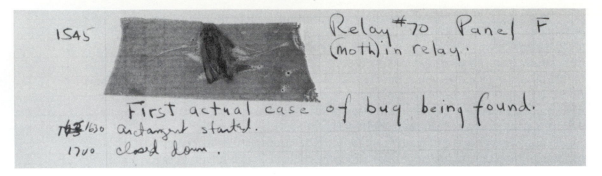

This is the first computer "bug." In 1945, computer pioneer Grace Hopper was asked to isolate why the Mark I computer had stopped. She found this moth which "had been beaten to death" in an electronic relay. Thereafter, the process of correcting a hardware or software error became known as "debugging." (Dahlgren Museum, Naval Surface Weapons Center)

three grades and assign a letter grade. If your test data are 85, 95, and 75, you would expect the average to be an 85 and the letter grade to be "B". If the output is not 85 and "B", there is a bug in the program logic.

A program whose logic is sound might have input or output formats that need to be "cleaned up" to meet layout specifications. Suppose that your output looked like this:

    THE LETTER GRADE ISB

and the layout specs called for this:

    THE LETTER GRADE IS B

Then you would need to modify the output format to include a blank space between IS and the letter grade.

*Test Data.*    Test data are an integral part of the test procedure. Test data are made up so that all possible circumstances or branches within the program are tested. Good test data contain both valid and erroneous data. It's always a good idea to introduce erroneous data deliberately to see if error routines are working properly. For example, in a program that averages grades, you might wish to include an error routine that questions grades greater than 100. To test this routine, you simply enter a grade of, say, 108. If the program works properly, the error routine will detect the erroneous data and display an error message. A good programmer lives by Murphy's Law, which assumes that if it can happen, it will! Don't assume that whoever uses your program will not make certain errors in data entry.

A program may be bug-free after *unit testing*, but eventually it will have to pass *systems testing*, where all programs are tested together. Thorough testing is essential to high-quality information systems; otherwise, a "bug" might fly up and "byte" you at the worst possible time. It has happened before.

**Step 7. Document the Program.**   When you write a program in a college course, you turn it in, it's graded, and then it's returned. Your effort contributes to your knowledge and expertise, but in all probability the program you wrote will not be used again. In a business environment, however, a program that you write may be used every day— for years!

Over the life of the system, procedures and information requirements change. For example, because the social security tax rate is revised each year, certain payroll programs must be modified. To keep up with these changes, programs must be updated periodically, or maintained. Program maintenance can be difficult if the program documentation is not complete and up to date.

The programs you write in college are not put into production and are therefore not maintained. You may ask, "Why document them?" The reason is simple. Good documentation now helps to develop good programming habits that will undoubtedly be carried on in your future programming efforts. *Documentation* is part of the *programming process*. It's not something you do after the program is written. A good program documentation package includes the following items:

- ■ *Program title.* A brief descriptive title (e.g., PRINT_PAYROLL-_CHECKS)
- ■ *Language.* The language in which the program is written (e.g., CO-BOL, BASIC)
- ■ *Narrative description.* A word description of the functions performed
- ■ *Variables list.* A list containing the name and description of each variable used in the program
- ■ *Source listing.* A hard-copy listing of the source code
- ■ *Detailed program design.* The flowcharts, decision tables, and so on
- ■ *Input/output layouts.* The printer and workstation display layouts; examples of hard-copy output (e.g., payroll check)
- ■ *Frequency of processing.* How often the program is run (e.g., daily, weekly, on-line)
- ■ *Detailed specifications.* The arithmetic computations, sorting and editing criteria, tables, control totals, and so on
- ■ *Test data.* A test package that includes test data and expected results (The test data are used to test and debug the program after each program change.)

Some of these documentation items can be included in the actual program as *internal* documentation. Descriptive programmer remarks throughout the program make a program easier to follow and to understand. Typically, the program title, a narrative description, and the variables list would also be included as internal documentation. All of the example BASIC programs in the special section "BASIC Programming" at the back of the book illustrate internal documentation.

# SUMMARY OUTLINE AND IMPORTANT TERMS _____

**12-1** PROGRAMMING IN PERSPECTIVE.  We direct computers to perform calculations and manipulate data by describing step-by-step instructions in the form of a program. Learning to program can be somewhat frustrating at first, but with a little practice, programming is just plain fun.

**12-2** PROBLEM SOLVING AND PROGRAMMING LOGIC.  Programs can provide solutions to particular problems. The creativity in programming is in the application of logic to problem solving.

The most effective programs are designed so that they can be written in **modules.** Addressing a programming problem in logical modules is known as **structured programming.**

**12-3** PROGRAM DESIGN TECHNIQUES.  Data flow diagrams and HIPO can also be applied to programming logic. Design techniques such as **flowcharting, pseudocode,** and **decision tables** are commonly used to represent systems and programming logic.

**Flowcharts** illustrate data, information, and work flow through the interconnection of specialized symbols with flow lines. In structured programming, each program is designed with a **driver module** that calls **subroutines** as they are needed.

Program logic can be conceptualized in three basic control structures: sequence, selection, and **loop.** There are two variations on the loop structure: DOWHILE and DOUNTIL.

Pseudocode represents program logic in programlike statements that are written in plain English. There are no syntax guidelines for formulating pseudocode statements.

Decision tables are used by both programmers and analysts to depict what happens for occurrences of various circumstances.

**12-4** SO WHAT'S A PROGRAM?: CONCEPTS AND PRINCIPLES OF PROGRAMMING.  A computer program is made up of a sequence of instructions or **statements.** There are five classifications of instructions.

- Input/output instructions direct the computer to read or write to a peripheral device.
- Computation instructions perform arithmetic operations.
- Control instructions can alter the sequence of a program's execution.
- Data transfer and assignment instructions permit data to be transferred internally.
- Format instructions describe how data are to be entered or outputted from primary storage.

**12-5** WRITING PROGRAMS.  The writing of a program is a project within itself and follows the following seven steps:

- *Step 1.* Describe the problem.

- *Step 2.* Analyze the problem. Examine the output, input, processing, and file-interaction components.
- *Step 3.* Design the general logic of the program.
- *Step 4.* Design the detailed logic of the program.
- *Step 5.* Code the program. Use appropriate documentation and **reusable code.**
- *Step 6.* Test and debug the program. Programs are **debugged** to eliminate **diagnostics** and logic errors and to clean up the input/output.
- *Step 7.* Document the program.

## REVIEW EXERCISES

### Concepts

1. Draw the flowcharting symbols for manual process, terminal point, workstation, and decision.
2. Where is the test-on-condition placed in a DOWHILE loop? In a DOUNTIL loop?
3. Assign meaningful variable names to at least six data elements that you might expect to find in a personnel record.
4. Write a pseudocode program that represents the logic of Module 1.1 (Input Data) in Figure 12–4.
5. Give an original example of a computation instruction.
6. Name and illustrate the three basic program control structures.
7. What common program instructions are associated with conditional and unconditional statements?
8. What is the purpose of a test-on-condition instruction?
9. Describe the characteristics of good test data.
10. What are the benefits of structured programming?
11. What is meant by the remark "garbage in, garbage out" as applied to systems specifications and programming?
12. In a decision table, in which quadrant is the condition stub? The action entries?

### Discussion

13. Discuss the rationale for the "divide and conquer" approach to programming.
14. What is the rationale for completing a general design of a program's logic before completing a detailed design?
15. Break up into groups of four so that each group can conduct several structured walkthroughs (walkthrough procedures are discussed in Chapter 11). Rotate the role of presenter so that each member has a chance to walkthrough the logic and I/O of a recent programming assignment.

**16.** Discuss the justification for the extra effort required to document a program fully.

## SELF-TEST (by section)

**12–1.** **(a)** The software for an electronic spreadsheet package is contained in a single program. (T/F)

**(b)** Computer programs direct the computer to perform calculations and manipulate data. (T/F)

**12–2.** **(a)** Programs are written in _____ , or independent tasks.

**(b)** The effectiveness of structured programming is still a matter of debate. (T/F)

**12–3.** **(a)** Flowcharting is used primarily for program design and rarely for systems design. (T/F)

**(b)** IF-THEN-ELSE logic is associated with the selection structure. (T/F)

**12–4.** **(a)** There is a direct relationship between the number of GOTO instructions in a program and how well the program's design is structured. (T/F)

**(b)** "Subtotal Amount" is a _____ constant.

**12–5.** **(a)** Program modules that are used frequently in different programs and maintained in libraries are called reusable code. (T/F)

**(b)** Once a program has been unit tested, no further testing is required. (T/F)

*Self-Test answers.*   12–1 (a), F; (b), T; 12–2 (a), modules; (b), F; 12–3 (a), F; (b), T; 12–4 (a), F; (b), string; 12–5 (a), T; (b), F.

CASE
STUDY

# Zimco Enterprises

## PRODUCTIVITY IMPROVEMENT AT ZIMCO

### THE PRODUCTIVITY IMPROVEMENT PROGRAM

Three years ago, Preston Smith, Zimco's president, initiated a "Productivity Improvement Program" and challenged his management team to "do more work with less by increasing productivity." When he kicked off the program, he said: "The opportunities to increase productivity are staring us in the face. It's up to us to make a concerted effort to take advantage of them."

Preston was well aware of the fact that the "Productivity Improvement Program" (PIP to Zimco insiders) would be met with some resistance. People tend to resist change. In a half-encouraging and a half-threatening way, he told managers "to stop thinking status quo management and to get ready to make some bold decisions. If we plan to compete in a world economy, we can't rest on our laurels. We must agressively pursue every opportunity to make a better product at a lower cost."

This case study discusses some of the steps that Conrad Innis and his managers took to meet Preston Smith's challenge to improve productivity in the Computer and Information Services Division.

### INCREASING PRODUCTIVITY IN CIS

During the first three months of the PIP program, Conrad Innis held weekly roundtable meetings with his managers for the express purpose of exchanging ideas on how the CIS Division could improve productivity. Literally hundreds of ideas were discussed, but the management group decided to focus on implementing only those that showed the most promise. Several of the more effective approaches are discussed in the following sections.

Adopting a Standardized Systems Development Methodology. Besides providing a framework for coordinating the many activities during system development, a systems development methodology encourages project teams to do it right the first time. An oversight (perhaps an error in system logic) left undetected becomes more and more difficult to correct as the project progresses. A logic error that would take one hour to correct in Phase II would take nine days to correct in Phase V (see Figure Z12–1)!

With the systems development methodology now in place (see Chapter 11, "The Systems Development Process"), rigorous attention to detail causes errors to surface in the early stages of development.

Starting a Comprehensive In-House Education Program. Conrad knew that there is a direct correlation between productivity and education, so he hired an education coordinator and provided funding for up to one month of education, for all technical professionals in CIS. In his argument to get funding for the education program, Conrad told Preston Smith: "Before we can realize the full potential of the division's productivity efforts, the people in CIS must learn to exploit the latest technology." Today, the education program is credited with making programmers, analysts, and other specialists much more productive

363

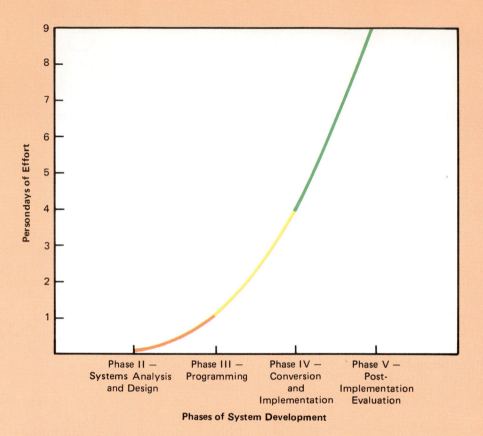

**FIGURE Z12–1**
**The Cost of an Error**
This chart depicts the relative personnel time required to correct a logic error
when first detected in the different phases of development.

Through Zimco's in-house
education program, users and
computer specialists learn new
and better ways to use computer
technology to improve their
productivity.
(Cromemco, Inc.)

because they are constantly learning new and betters ways to apply the tools of their trade.

### Establishing an Information Center.

Three years ago, three out of every four user service requests were for one-time, ad hoc reports. And as Conrad is often fond of saying: "The users always want these reports yesterday." Today, Zimco users, from clerks to top management, routinely go to an information center to get the information they need, usually in less time than it would take to explain their need to a CIS programmer. The information centers (see Chapter 1, "The World of Computers") are located at the headquarters office and at each of the plants. The availability of information centers has reduced time-consuming one-time requests by 80 percent. Programmers and analysts now have more time to devote to ongoing development projects.

### Capturing Data Closer to the Source.

Three years ago, CIS still had 18 data entry operators; today, only two remain. Methodically, data entry is being moved as close to the source as possible.

Throughout Zimco, data are captured as close to the source as possible. Instead of filling out a hard-copy source document that must be transcribed into machine-readable format, workers enter data directly to the integrated data base from their workstations.
(Mohawk Data Sciences Corporation)

For example, field sales reps use their portable computers to enter orders directly into the mainframe computer at Dallas. In the past, data entry operators had to transcribe the data from the order form, usually from one to five days after the field sales rep filled out the form. Also in the order processing area, customers sometimes send in their orders via intercompany networking (data are sent computer to computer).

### Implementing a Project Management System.

When Conrad arrived at Zimco in 1981, he observed that when a project got behind schedule, the tendency was to "throw people at the project in an attempt to meet an unrealistic deadline." Inevitably, the extra people caused more problems than they did good. This prompted Conrad to order a computer-based project management system that would permit managers to monitor and control project progress. Gram Mertz, the manager of the Programming Department, said: "With the project management system, we are better able to isolate problems and make adjustments before things get out of hand."

### Initiating Mandatory Periodic System Reviews.

Opie Rader, the manager of the Operations Department, was convinced that much of the computer capability and information that CIS was providing was not used. Opie said: "Over time, some of the services we provide became useless to our users, but nobody bothered to tell us. Now, each year we conduct a system review on all major systems. Each review usually results in our discontinuing certain marginal services."

### Implementing a Chargeback System.

Before implementation of a chargeback system, the CIS Division was an information "candy store" and the candy was free. Users didn't appreciate the scope of their requests. Today, users are charged for all services provided by CIS. Conrad explained: "We implemented a chargeback system to encourage the judicious use of Zimco's computer and information resources. People, by nature, are more deliberate about what they ask for when they are spending their own money."

### Encouraging Technology Transfer.

"Why reinvent the wheel?" asked Conrad Innis. "We should be applying existing technology whenever possible." Zimco has adopted a policy that requires systems analysts and programmers to evaluate the possibility of using commercially available proprietary software as an alternative to developing original software in house. Gram Mertz, manager of Programming, said: "It's a lot less expensive to buy a software package that the user likes than it is to make one ourselves from scratch."

### Using Fourth- and Fifth-Generation Languages.
"Since we decided to use fourth- and fifth-generation languages, our programming productivity has increased at least 75 percent," says Gram Mertz. "We still do about half of our program development work in COBOL and Pascal (third-generation languages), but all of our quick-and-dirty reports are done with INGEN, our query language, and much of our production code is generated with our application generator."

### Inviting Advice from Consultants.
Only recently did CIS begin using outside consultants. Old-timer Sybil Allen, manager of the Systems Analysis Department, said: "For years, if we got in a technical bind, we would drop everything and spend endless amounts of time fighting through the learning curve. Now if we have an occasional problem, we call in an expert consultant rather than disrupt operations." Zimco found out that by using consultants wisely, they could save money and time. Conrad retained a consultant to help CIS personnel create and implement their current systems development methodology.

### Promoting Better Keyboarding Skills.
Every professional in the CIS division spends an average of four hours per day at a workstation. Ironically, only one out of three had any formal keyboard skills training—most used the "hunt-and-peck" method. Conrad said: "If we can improve the keyboarding skills of the people in CIS, we could improve productivity substantially." Those with marginal keyboarding skills were asked to spend 30 minutes a day for a month working with a self-paced microcomputer-based keyboarding tutorial. By learning better keyboarding skills, programmers and analysts have improved their interactive effectiveness to the point that they save from 30 minutes to one hour a day!

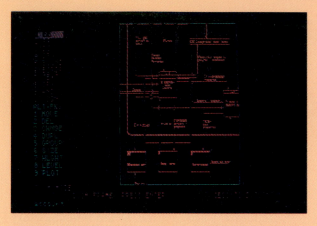

Software packages are available that enable programmers to design programs interactively at their workstations. Zimco programmers and systems analysts have made significant strides in productivity improvement since they began using an automated package, called DFDraw, to create data flow diagrams. (Long and Associates)

### Using Automated Design Tools.
Just two years ago, programmers and analysts at Zimco were spending untold hours meticulously drafting and revising flowcharts and data flow diagrams. Now, they design programs and information systems using automated design tools. Instead of using pencils, paper, templates, and erasures, they use computers and graphics software. For example, analysts create data flow diagrams interactively on a display screen by designating the type of symbol, where it is to go, and its caption. Once all the symbols and flow lines are on the screen, they can be moved, added, deleted, and revised to test out various solutions to a problem. Sybil Allen claims that "by using these on-line interactive design tools my analysts effectively work an extra hour a day."

### More Ways to Improve CIS Productivity.
CIS took steps, other than those discussed in previous sections, to improve productivity. Other efforts included: reorganizing CIS to be more responsive to user needs; implementing a database management system to minimize data redundancy; rearranging the work areas for more efficient person/person and person/machine interactions; and soliciting ongoing worker feedback through quality circles.

## "THERE IS A BETTER WAY"

Conrad Innis often made the point, "there is a better way." He encouraged everyone in CIS to search for this better way, apply it, then tell others about it. Just three years after the initiation of Zimco's Productivity Improvement Program, CIS is claiming an overall increase in productivity of almost 100 percent. By religiously seeking a "better way," CIS has been able to keep pace with Zimco's ever-increasing demand for information and data processing services.

## DISCUSSION QUESTIONS

1. Certainly, one of the advantages of a chargeback system is that user managers tend to be more judicious about the kinds of service that they request from CIS. What are the disadvantages of a chargeback system?

2. Figure Z12–1 illustrates how it is increasingly time consuming to correct a logic error in a system design as the project progresses. Explain why this is the case.

3. Conrad Innis said: "Before we can realize the full potential of the division's productivity efforts, the people in CIS must learn to exploit the latest technology." Give a couple of example in support of Conrad's comment.

4. Why is the use of fourth- and fifth-generation languages considered a means to improve productivity?

5. How does having a systems development methodology help a project team to "do it right the first time"?

6. Sally Marcio, VP of Sales and Marketing, encouraged her division's participation in the PIP program. Do you think the Sales and Marketing Division would be dependent on the CIS Division to help implement some of their productivity improvement measures? Explain.

7. Rather than take advantage of an information center to make their own ad hoc inquiries, a few Zimco users still rely on CIS personnel. What arguments would would you make to convince these people that Zimco's information centers can benefit them, the company, and CIS?

# PART

# 6

# OPPORTUNITY AND CHALLENGE

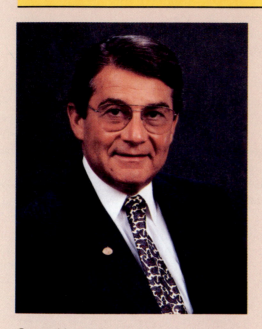

*Our rapid growth could never have been accomplished without a network of more than 2000 electronic point-of-sale terminals on-line with state-of-the-art computer hardware and software. Hess's sophisticated systems enable us to forecast the future of our business. By taking the mass of data and organizing it, refining it, and presenting it to our management team in a usable form, we have been able to keep well-balanced retail stocks in our stores and to maximize sales and service to our customers.*

Irwin Greenberg
President and CEO
Hess's Department Stores, Inc.

# Computers Tomorrow— Career Opportunities and Applications

## STUDENT LEARNING OBJECTIVES

- To identify computer specialist positions in information services departments and in user departments.
- To identify job opportunities in organizations that provide computer-related products or services.
- To become aware of the relationship between career mobility and computer knowledge.
- To identify possible computer applications of the future.

## FOCUS OF ZIMCO CASE STUDY

- Zimco's MIS strategic plan.

## 13-1 THE JOB OUTLOOK

### Opportunities for Users with Computer Knowledge

Whether you are seeking employment (or perhaps a promotion) as an economist, an accountant, a salesperson, a financial broker, or in any of a hundred other jobs, one question is frequently asked: "What do you know about computers?" Already, well over half of all white-collar workers routinely work with computers. By 1990, virtually all white-collar workers and a good portion of the blue-collar workers will spend a significant portion of their day interacting with a computer.

Upon completion of this course, you will be part of the computer-literate minority and able to respond affirmatively to this inquiry. But what about that 95 percent of our society that must answer "nothing" or "very little"? These people will find themselves at a disadvantage.

### Opportunities for Computer Specialists

If you are planning a career as a computer specialist, opportunity abounds. Almost every company, no matter how small or large, employs computer specialists. And most of those companies are always looking for qualified people.

For the last decade, people with computer/information systems education have been at or near the top of the "most wanted" list. With millions (yes, millions!) of new computers being purchased and installed each year, it is a good bet that this trend will continue. Of course, the number of people being attracted to the booming computer fields is also increasing. Even so, the most pessimistic forecasters predict a doubling of the demand for computer specialists during the next decade.

Career Opportunities in an Information Services Department.    Today, the majority of computer specialist positions, such as systems analysts and programmers, are in a company's information services department. The Zimco case study following Chapter 2 describes the computer specialist positions in Zimco's Computer and Information Services Division. These include *systems analysts*, *applications programmers*, *programmer/analysts*, *systems programmers*, *data communications specialists*, *data base administrators*, *computer operators*, *control clerks*, *data entry operators*, *librarians*, *education coordinators*, and of course, the *managers* of the various groups. Figure 13–1 shows how these positions are aligned with the groups in a typical information services department.

"Distributed" Career Opportunities.    The trend to distributed processing has prompted a movement of computer specialists to the user departments. Some people are predicting that as many as 75 percent of the computer specialist positions will be in the user groups by 1990 (see Figure 13–2). Even now, virtually every type of user group, from R&D to distribution, is vigorously recruiting people with computer expertise.

| The Information Services Department | |
|---|---|
| Management<br>  Director<br>  Group managers | Managers in each of the groups that follow perform the traditional management functions: planning, organizing, staffing, directing, and controlling. |
| Systems analysis<br>  Systems analyst | The systems analysis group analyzes, designs, and implements computer-based information systems. |
| Programming<br>  Applications programmer<br>  Programmer/analyst | The programming group translates system design specifications produced by systems analysts into programs. |
| Data communications<br>  Data communications<br>   specialist | The data communications group designs computer networks and implements hardware and software that permits data transmission among computers and workstations. |
| Technical support<br>  Data base<br>   administrator<br>  Systems programmer | The technical support group designs, develops, maintains, and implements systems software (i.e., generalized software, such as the operating system and database management system). |
| Operations<br>  Computer operator<br>  Control clerk<br>  Data entry operator<br>  Librarian | The operations group performs those machine room activities associated with the running of operational information systems (e.g., loading tapes, scheduling, and running jobs). Operations also includes control functions and data entry. The trend to on-line data entry is causing the data entry function to be "distributed" to the user areas. |
| Education<br>  Education coordinator | The education group is responsible for the continuing education of computer specialists and for training users in the operation of hardware and information systems. |

**FIGURE 13–1**
**Computer Specialist Positions by Group in an Information Services Department**

A product manager for a soft drink company monitors the success of marketing campaigns by gathering and analyzing data from regional distribution offices. Computer specialists at a regional office develop and maintain a variety of administrative information systems. Both need a solid foundation of computer knowledge to accomplish their jobs effectively.

(Copyright 1984 GTE Telenet Communications Corporation)

(Control Data Corporation)

The jobs of office automation specialists are not limited to implementation of hardware and software. One of their challenges is to design computer work areas that will be aesthetically pleasing while providing comfort and efficiency.
(TRW Inc.)

Information center specialists assist users in the use and application of hardware and software until they can become self sufficient.
(Courtesy of International Business Machines Corporation)

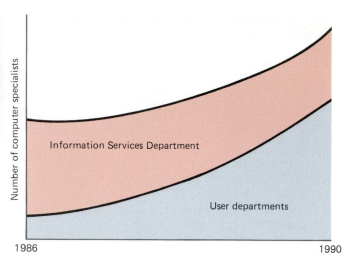

**FIGURE 13–2**
**Computer Specialist Positions in Transition**
The trend to distributed processing has increased the number of computer specialists in the user areas.

Today it's not just the information services department that has computers. Computers are found in every area. Besides the computer specialists in the traditional areas (e.g., programming, systems analysis), a new breed of computer specialists is emerging in the user areas. These include *office automation specialists*, *microcomputer specialists*, *information center specialists*, and *user liaisons*.

*Office Automation Specialists.* Office automation encompasses those computer-based applications generally associated with office work, such as word processing, image processing, and electronic mail (for details, see the Zimco case study following Chapter 4). **Office automation specialists** are being hired to help with the growing demand for automating office activities. They help users to implement, then make effective use of office systems.

*Microcomputer Specialists.* From the popularity of microcomputers has emerged a new career path, sometimes referred to as **microcomputer specialist.** Users do not always have the time to learn the details of using microcomputers and their software. Rather than have each person in an office learn micros and micro software packages (e.g., electronic spreadsheet) inside out, a firm can have a micro specialist help users over the rough spots, as well as develop new systems.

*Information Center Specialists.* An **information center** is a facility in which computing resources are made available to various user groups. The information center is described in Chapter 1, "The World of Computers." **Information center specialists** conduct training sessions, answer questions, and help users to help themselves.

*User Liaisons.* **User liaisons,** introduced in the Zimco case study following Chapter 2, serve as the technical interface between the information services department and the user group. The user liaison coordinates system conversions and is the catalyst for new systems development.

Other Career Opportunities: Services, Hardware, Software, and Education.   There are a host of computer specialist career opportunities in organizations that provide computer-related products or services. We can divide these organizations into four groups: services, hardware vendors, software vendors, and education.

*Service Vendors*.   The computer revolution is creating a tremendous demand for computer-related services. In response to this demand, a number of service organizations have emerged. These include *service bureaus*, *consulting firms*, and *computer repair stores*, to mention a few. Service bureaus provide almost any kind of information processing services. These services include, but are not limited to, developing and implementing information systems, providing computer time (time-sharing), and transcribing source data. A service bureau is essentially a public computer center. Therefore, it needs people in most of the traditional computer career specialities. Consulting firms provide advice relating to the use of computers and the information resource. One of the fastest-growing service groups is computer repair stores.

*Hardware Vendors*.   The most visible hardware vendors are the computer system manufacturers, such as Digital Equipment Corporation (DEC), Apple, IBM, and Hewlett-Packard (HP). These companies manufacture the processor and usually some or all of the peripheral equipment (disk drives, printers, workstations, and so on). Plug-compatible manufacturers, or *PCMs*, make peripheral devices that can be attached directly to another manufacturer's computer. Original-equipment manufacturers, or *OEMs*, integrate the hardware and software of several vendors with their own software, then sell the entire package.

At the "Mac Fac" (Macintosh Factory), microcomputers are "burned in" for several days before shipment to lower the probability that a system will fail on delivery.
(Courtesy of Apple Computer, Inc.)

Hardware vendors market and service hardware. To do so, they need *marketing representatives* to sell the products and *systems engineers* to support them once they have been installed. Marketing representatives hold a technical sales position that requires a broad knowledge of the company's products and their capabilities. The systems engineer is the technical "expert" and is often called on by customers for advice on technical matters.

*Software Vendors.*   Companies that produce and market software are called *software vendors* or "software houses." What you buy from a software house is a proprietary **software package** for a particular computer-based system or application. When a company purchases or leases a software package, the company receives a *license agreement* to use the copyright software.

A variety of computer specialists work together to create a software package for the commercial market. Many stories are told about successful software enterpreneurs who turned an idea into millions of dollars. These opportunities still exist today, and thousands of aspiring entrepreneurs are creating companies and placing their software on the market each year. Some struggle to marginal success and some fail, but a few make it big—real big!

*Education.*   The computer explosion in the last few years has created an insatiable demand for computer-related education. This demand for computer education is taxing the resources of our educational institutions and has given rise to a tremendous demand for *professors* and *instructors*. Instructors are needed in industry as well. Programmers, analysts, and users are forever facing the announcement of a new technological innovation or the installation of a new system. In-house education is focused on the specific educational needs of the organization.

## Career Mobility and Computer Knowledge

Computer literacy is already a prerequisite to employment in some professions, such as business and engineering. Within a few years, computer literacy may well be a prerequisite for success in most professions. Career mobility is becoming forever intertwined with an individual's current and future knowledge of computers.

The jobs of managers who continue to ignore the computer revolution are vulnerable to those who aspire to their positions. Aggressive people in the business community recognize that an understanding of computers is becoming prerequisite knowledge for anyone pursuing a management position.

Just as advancing technology is creating new jobs, it is changing old ones. Some traditional jobs will change, or even disappear. For example, office automation is radically changing the function and role of secretaries and office managers. With computer-aided design (CAD), draftspersons are learning new ways to do their jobs.

Career advancement, of course, ultimately depends on your abilities, imagination, and performance. Your understanding of computers can only enhance your opportunities. If you cultivate your talents and you aspire to leave your mark on your chosen profession, the sky is the limit.

## 13–2   COMPUTER APPLICATIONS OF THE FUTURE

It seems as if the computer is everywhere—yet, in reality, we are only scratching the surface of possible computer applications. The outlook for innovative, exciting, and beneficial computer applications is bright—very bright indeed.

### Expectations and Reality

The short-term expectations that the general public has for computer technology are probably excessive. Intense media coverage has given the computer novice the impression that bedmaking, dishwashing domestic robots are just around the corner; that computer-controlled organ transplants are almost perfected; and that computers have all the answers! To be sure, we are making progress in leaps and bounds, but we have a long way to go before such applications are feasible. Nevertheless, these rising expectations are a challenge to computer professionals to deliver.

Of course, no one can see into the future, but we can extrapolate from trends and our knowledge of current research. This section paints a futuristic picture of some computer applications that are sociologically, economically, and technologically feasible within the next decade.

The state of the art of the technology enables this tiny megabit chip to hold a million pieces of data—but it's not enough. Our largest and fastest computers are still not capable of simulating an entire airplane in flight. Of course, aerospace engineers want it all. Their expectations are representative of people in other professions who already have plans for computers that are not even developed. (Reproduced with permission of AT&T)

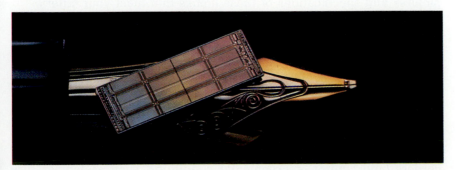

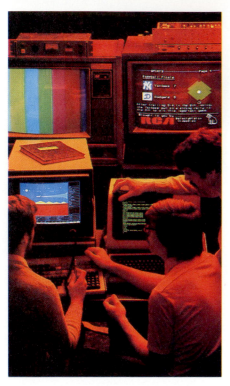

A new "page" of information is being created and added to the data base of a commercial information network. The screens, such as the one showing a baseball score, can be accessed by those who subscribe to the information service.
(RCA)

## Information Networks

As the percentage of homes with micros increases, so does the potential for *information networks*. Information networks, a number of which exist today, provide certain services to an end user through a communications link to a workstation. Several currently available services provided by information networks are described in Chapter 1, "The World of Computers." The two-way system provides the end user with information (e.g., airline flight schedules) and permits the end user to enter data (e.g., reservations for airline flights).

The four components of an information network are the central computer, the data base, the network, and the workstations. The central computer system is accessed by end users who desire a particular service. The data base contains data and screens of information (e.g., perhaps a graphic display of a refrigerator with price and delivery information) that are presented to users. The transmission media in the network can be the telephone system, two-way cable TV, or any of a variety of digital data transmission media (see Chapter 8, "Data Communications"). As workstations and microcomputers proliferate, a greater variety of information networks will be made available to more and more people. Even now, workstations that can access these networks are available in many airplanes and hotel rooms.

Hotel guests can communicate with their homes, companies, or virtually anyone else through the use of computers in their rooms. They can obtain theater or airline tickets, shop or order gifts, scan restaurant menus, and even play video games. In a few years, all major hotels will provide their guests with access to workstations and information networks.

Commercially available information networks have an endless number of applications. For example, let's take real estate. Suppose that you live in Tuscon, Arizona, and have been transferred to Salt Lake City, Utah. It is only a matter of time before you will be able to gain access to a nationwide information network that maintains an up-to-date listing of every home in the country that is for sale. Here is how it will work. You will enter your purchase criteria: Salt Lake City, Utah: $80,000 to $100,000; no more than 1 mile from an elementary school; double garage; and so on. The system will then present pictures and specifications of those homes that meet your criteria.

## Communications

The telephone as we know it will probably disappear. In the relatively near future, the function of the telephone will be incorporated into our home computers and workstations so that we can not only hear, but see, the person on the other end of the line. Moreover, we will be able to pass data and information back and forth as if we were sitting at the same table. From our remote workstations we'll be able to operate home appliances, such as answer machines and video recorders, and control environmental conditions, such as temperature and lighting.

Computers and data communications have turned our world into a "global village." This satellite, which has served as a data communications link between North America with Europe, is being loaded in the bay of a space shuttle craft and brought back to earth for repair. (NASA)

Currently, voice and data are transmitted as both analog and digital signals (see Chapter 8, "Data Communications"). In the future, all communication will be digital, including television. A digital television signal will provide TV sets with greater versatility. Our sets will function much like computer workstations. The display screen will be larger, and each set will have a keyboard for two-way communication. If you so desire, you can split the screen and watch two, or even three, programs at once. You can continue to watch a program and request that the stock reports be subtitled across the screen. During a news program, newscasters can sample the thinking of tens of thousands of people in a matter of minutes. As they ask the questions, we at home respond on our keyboard. Our responses are immediately sent to a central computer for analysis. The results can be reported almost immediately. In this way, television news programs will keep us abreast of public opinion on critical issues and the feeling toward political candidates on a day-to-day basis.

For this manufacturer's sales representative, her home is her office. She uses data management software to maintain a data base that contains pertinent client information, such as name, address, and product preferences. (Courtesy of Apple Computer, Inc.)

## In the Office

The traditional letter may never become obsolete, but electronic mail will become an increasingly popular alternative, especially since most of us will have our own workstations, both at home and at work. To prepare and send a letter, an executive will dictate, not to a secretary, but to a computer! The executive's words will be transcribed directly into text, without key entry. The letter will then be routed to appropriate destinations via electronic mail. The recipient of the letter can request that it be displayed at a workstation or read, using synthesized speech.

With professionals spending a greater percentage of their working day interacting with the computer, look for the "electronic cottage" concept to gain momentum. At least a part of the work of most professionals will be done at home. For many professionals, their work is at their fingertips, whether at home or the office.

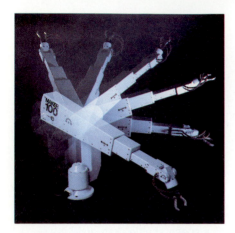

The robot shown here (in multiple exposures) can be programmed to "pick and place" an item from anywhere to anywhere within the reach of the telescopic manipulator arm. Before robots, workers in assembly plants were primarily involved with manual tasks; now they are concerned with tasks that tap their cognitive resources. These tasks include production scheduling, quality control, and the design and programming of robots.
(United States Robots, Square D Company)

## A Peek at the Crystal Ball: Business and Government

**Manufacturing.**  In the face of growing competition from international markets, manufacturing companies, especially those that are labor intensive, are being confronted with three choices: "automate, migrate, or evaporate." They can *automate*, thereby lowering cost and increasing productivity. They can *migrate* (move) to countries that offer less expensive labor. Or they can *evaporate*. Most have elected to automate, even with the blessing of organized labor. As one labor leader put it; "If we don't do it, I'm convinced we'll lose the jobs anyway."

With the trend to greater use of automation, we can anticipate an increase in the number of industrial robots (see Chapter 4). As the smokestack industries become more "high tech," the complexion of their work force will change. There will be a shift of emphasis from brawn to brains. A few unmanned plants already exist: this number will grow. These radical changes are a by-product of our transition from an industrial society to an information society. Traditional jobs will change or be lost forever, but new, and hopefully more challenging, jobs will emerge to replace them.

**Retail.**  Information networks will enable us to do our shopping electronically. Instead of walking through the aisle of a grocery store or thumbing through stacks of shirts, we will be able to use our personal computer in conjunction with an information network to select and purchase almost any retail item. The items selected will be automatically picked, packaged, and, possibly, delivered to our doorstep. This information service will help speed the completion of routine activities, such as grocery shopping, leaving us more time for leisure, travel, and the things we enjoy.

Time consuming check authorizations at grocery stores may be a thing of the past with the introduction of cash dispensing systems. This customer uses his bank card (with magnetic stripe) and a keyboard to withdraw cash from his bank account.
(Diebold, Incorporated)

**Financial Services.**   The overwhelming acceptance of automatic teller machines has fueled the trend to more electronic funds transfer (EFT). Over the next decade, transaction documents, such as checks and credit card purchase slips, will begin to disappear. Monies will be electronically transferred at the time of the purchase from the seller's account to the buyer's account. Total EFT will require an enormously complex communications network that links the computers of all financial institutions with virtually all businesses. Such a network is technologically and economically feasible today, but sociologically we are a few years away.

**Publishing.**   Certainly, books, magazines, newspapers, and the "printed word," in general, will prevail for casual reading and study. However, it is not unreasonable to expect that publishers will offer *soft-copy* publishing as an alternative to *hard-copy* publishing. We'll be able to receive books, magazines, and newspapers in electronic format, perhaps via data communications on our home computers or on a disk. A few specialized computer trade magazines are available now on disks, but in a few years a wide variety of magazines will be distributed via data communications or disks.

Can you imagine a bookstore without books? It's possible! With customized printing on demand, you will be able to browse through virtually any current book from a workstation; then, if you wish to purchase the book, it will be printed and bound while you wait!

**Transportation.**   Someday soon, computer-based automobile navigation systems will be standard equipment on cars. There are already enough satellites in the sky for an on-board automobile navigation system to obtain a fix. A fix establishes the location of the car. The car's location will be noted on a video display of a road map. You will be able to call up appropriate regional or city maps from an on-board optical laser disk storage, and you will even be able to plot your course and track progress.

By now you are probably saying that this Buck Rogers-type application is a bit far fetched. Well, prototypes of automobile navigation systems are now being tested—and they work!

An information service makes the full text of newspapers, wire services, magazines, newsletters, and government publications available for immediate on-line access. Subscribers to this service use key words to enter the data base and zero in on a particular topic (e.g., computer crime, soy bean futures). Eventually, information services will make the full text of books available for perusal.
(Mead Data Central)

Crowded skies have resulted in a rash of "near misses" in recent years. Airlines and the Federal Aviation Adminstration are counting on sophisticated computer systems to eliminate or minimize the risk of mid-air collisions.
(Reproduced with permission of AT&T)

It's hard to find a more people-oriented entertainment facility than Walt Disney World's Epcot Center—yet much of the action is computer controlled. Epcot's "Communicore" computer center controls your movement through the various exhibits, the movement of hundreds of life-like animals and people, the sounds you hear, and even the temperature of the buildings.
(Long and Associates)

**Entertainment.**  How about interactive soap operas? Yes, because of the two-way communication capabilities of your television/workstation, you can be an active participant in how a story unfolds. The soaps will be shot so that they can be pieced together in a variety of ways. Imagine, you can decide whether Michelle marries Clifton or Patrick!

It won't be long before the rough drafts for television series scripts are written by computers. Many of the weekly television shows have a formula plot. For instance, heroes are presented with a problem situation, they confront the problem, they get in trouble, they get out of trouble, stick the bad guys, and live to do it again next week. Formula plots lend themselves nicely to computer-produced rough-draft scripts. The computer system will already have the names of the key characters on file. The systems will also have dialogues for a variety of situations. The names of nonregulars (e.g., the bad guys) are randomly generated by the computer. The script writers enter a story-line sketch, then the computer pieces together dialogues and scenes within the restrictions of the show's formula plot and the story line. The script writers then refine the draft script.

In the arts, sculptors may someday become more productive with the aid of computers. For example, a sculptor can create three-dimensional "sketches" on a computer, similar to the way an engineer designs a part using computer-aided design (CAD). The computer activates a robotlike sculpting tool that roughs-out the general shape of the figure. The sculptor then adds the creative touches that make a piece of clay a work of art.

**Health Care.**  Expert systems have already benefited physicians by helping them diagnose physical illnesses (see Chapter 4, "Computers and Information Systems in Business and Government"). In the near future we can anticipate expert systems that help diagnose and treat mental illnesses and emotional problems as well. Psychologists and psychiatrists will continue to work with patients in the classical manner, but with the added advantage of a "partner." This "partner" can tap a vast storehouse of knowledge and recommend everything from lines of questioning to diagnosis and treatment.

The handicapped can look forward to improved mobility and independence. Sophisticated prostheses can be activated by voice, motion, muscle activity, breathing, and even blinking of the eyes. Research is under way that may enable paraplegics to walk by substituting a computer for a nervous system that has ceased to function.

Medical and technical researchers have dared to contemplate the integration of computers with the brain. That is, we may eventually electronically connect tiny computer implants to the brain for the purpose of enhancing the brain's computational and factual-recall capabilities.

**Government.**   Computer-enhanced photography will enable us to break out the finer details in photographs. Its immediate application is in the area of military intelligence; with computer-enhanced photography, the headlines in a newspaper can be read from a photograph taken 150 miles above the earth.

Local, state, and federal elections might not require an army of volunteers. Politicians might not have to worry about rain on Election Day. We will eventually record our votes from home or business workstations. Such a system will encourage greater voter participation. Of course, security and voter authenticity will be a concern. One possible solution would be to ask voters to identify themselves with their social security number and a voter registration security code that is known only to the voter. A few years later we won't need to carry cards or remember numbers; each voter's identity will be validated when the system reads our fingerprints and our voiceprint. All we will have to do to identify ourselves will be to enter our voiceprint by speaking a few words and our fingerprint by placing our finger near an optical laser scanner.

The IRS will tighten up on tax cheaters by feeding taxpayer lifestyle data into sophisticated models. Descriptive data, such as neighborhood and automobile type, will be used to predict whether people are underpaying taxes.

## Artificial Intelligence

We have artificial sweeteners, artificial grass, artificial flowers—why not artificial intelligence? In Chapter 1, "The World of Computers," artificial intelligence (AI) is defined as an expansion of the capabilities of computers to include the ability to reason, to learn, to strive for self-improvement, and to simulate human sensory capabilities. Chapter 1 focuses on state-of-the-art applications of artificial intelligence, but what does the future hold for AI?

Today's computers can produce reams of paper, perform billions

Computers have enabled medical doctors to make a quantum leap in the quality of health care. This system allows doctors to electronically examine enhanced images, such as X-rays, from the next room or from across the country.
(Reproduced with permission of AT&T)

Only recently have legislators at both the state and Federal levels begun to take advantage of the capabilities of computers. This legislator and his staff just received a preliminary draft for new legislation via electronic mail.
(General Instrument Corporation)

Until only recently most oil field applications of computer technology were administrative in nature. Expert systems and other computer-based innovations are rapidly changing the manner and effectiveness of oil exploration.
(Phillips Petroleum Company)

of calculations, and control the flow of thousands of messages, but at the day's end, they know no more than they did at its start. Much of the research in the area of artificial intelligence is aimed at giving computers the ability to emulate human reasoning and, therefore, learn. Now computer "knowledge" is derived from human knowledge. Perhaps, in the future, computers will learn and contribute to their own knowledge base.

Researchers in artificial intelligence hold out great promise for tomorrow's *expert systems*, one of several areas of AI research. Crude but effective expert systems (see Chapter 4) are now being commercialized for medical diagnosis, oil exploration, and several other areas. An expert system is a knowledge-based system to which preset rules are applied to solve a particular problem, such as determining a patient's illness. Present expert systems are based primarily on factual knowledge—a definite strength of computers. We human beings, though, solve problems by combining factual knowledge with our strength—*heuristic knowledge*—that is, intuition, judgment, and inferences.

The really tough decisions involve both factual *and* heuristic knowledge. For this reason, researchers are working to improve the computer's ability to gather and use heuristic knowledge. This formidable technological hurdle stands in the way of humanlike expert systems. However, this hurdle will eventually be cleared, and expert systems will abound for virtually every profession. Attorneys will have mock trials with expert systems to "pre-try" their cases. Doctors will routinely ask a "second opinion." Architects will "discuss" the structural design of a building with an expert system. Military officers can "talk" with the "expert" to plan battlefield strategy. City planners will "ask" an expert system to suggest optimal locations for recreational facilities.

AI research is continually enhancing the abilities of computers to simulate human sensory capabilities. In the not-too-distant future, we will be able to have meaningful verbal conversations with computers. These computers will be able to talk, listen, and even smell the roses!

## 13-3   YOUR CHALLENGE

Having mastered the contents of this book and this course, you are now poised to exploit the benefits of the computer in your personal and business lives. This course, however, is only the beginning. The computer learning process is ongoing. The dynamics of a rapidly advancing computer technology demands a constant updating of skills and expertise. Perhaps the excitement of technological innovation and ever-changing opportunities for application is part of the lure of computers.

By their very nature, computers bring about change. With the total amount of computing capacity in the world doubling every two years, we can expect even more dramatic change in the future. The cumulative effects of these changes are altering the basic constructs of society and the way we conduct business.

Never before has such opportunity presented itself so vividly. This generation, *your generation*, has the technological foundation and capability to change dreams to reality.

## SUMMARY OUTLINE AND IMPORTANT TERMS

**13–1** THE JOB OUTLOOK. People who can claim computer knowledge on their résumés will have an advantage over those who cannot. This is true in a great many professional disciplines.

Virtually every company employs or is considering employing computer specialists. Some of the most visible career paths are found in a company's information systems department. These include systems analysts, applications programmers, programmer/analysts, systems programmers, data communications specialists, data base administrators, computer operators, control clerks, data entry operators, librarians, education coordinators, and of course, the managers of the various groups.

A new breed of computer specialists is emerging in the user areas. **Office automation specialists** help users make effective use of office systems. The **microcomputer specialist** stays on top of the latest micro hardware and software technology and helps implement this technology in a user area. **Information center specialists** work in an **information center** and help users to help themselves. The **user liaison** serves as the technical interface between the information services department and the user groups.

There are a host of career opportunities that are not in an information services department or a user group. These opportunities are found with vendors of computer services, hardware, and software and in the area of computer education.

Computer literacy is a prerequisite to employment in some professions, and in a few more years it may well be a prerequisite in most professions.

**13–2** COMPUTER APPLICATIONS OF THE FUTURE. The number and variety of computer applications is expected to grow rapidly in the coming years. In the near future, we can anticipate an even greater variety of services available through information networks, telephones integrated into workstations, the widespread acceptance and use of electronic mail, unmanned manufacturing facilities, electronic shopping, less use of cash, soft-copy publishing, automobile navigation systems, create-your-own-story soaps on television, robot sculptors, computer-controlled artificial limbs, and expert systems that help us with business and domestic decisions.

**13–3** YOUR CHALLENGE. The computer offers us the opportunity to improve the quality of our lives. It is our challenge to harness the power of the computer and direct it to the benefit of society.

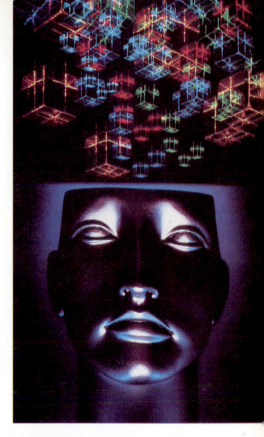

Albert Einstein said, "Imagination is more important than knowledge, for knowledge is limited while imagination embraces the entire world." You now have a base of computer knowledge. Combine this knowledge with your innate creative abilities and you are poised to make a significant impact on the business world. The photo contains computer-generated art.
(TRW Inc.)

## REVIEW EXERCISES

### Concepts

1. What is the function of a user liaison?
2. Name six computer specialist positions commonly represented in a company's information services department.
3. Describe the business of OEMs.
4. What is the product of a software house?
5. Contrast the jobs of systems engineer and marketing representative. How do they complement each other?
6. Briefly describe two uses for expert systems.
7. Based on your knowledge of the capabilities of computers, now and in the future, speculate on at least three futuristic applications that we can expect within the next five years.
8. Briefly describe a application in the retail industry that would use an information network.

### Discussion

9. Of the job functions described in this chapter, which would you prefer? Why?
10. Discuss the advantages of distributed processing from the standpoint of career mobility.
11. Some companies will have only one level of programmer or systems analyst, where other companies will have two, three, and even four levels. Discuss the advantages of having several levels for a particular position (e.g., Programmer I, Programmer II, and so on).
12. A company recruits people to become programmer/analysts. All project team members do both programming and systems analysis. In what ways would this affect the systems development methodology discussed in Chapter 12? Discuss the effects this arrangement would have on career development.
13. Discuss the merit of systems analysts having programming experience.
14. Select five position announcements from the classified ads section of *Computerworld*. Describe what you feel would be appropriate experience and education requirements for each of the positions.
15. Why do some senior managers have an unfavorable view of young people who have computer knowledge?
16. "Automate, migrate, or evaporate." Discuss this statement from the points of view of manufacturing management and of labor.
17. During the implementation of computer applications, managers have traditionally focused on hardware and software. Now they realize that they must pay more attention to the human needs as well. What are these needs?

**18.** Discuss possible futuristic applications of computers in health care.

**19.** Compare your perspective on computers today with what it was four months ago. How have your feelings and attitudes changed?

## SELF-TEST (by section)

**13-1. (a)** The trend to distributed processing is causing more and more computer specialists to move to the user departments. (T/F)

**(b)** "Office automation specialist" is a fancy name for a word processor. (T/F)

**(c)** PCM stands for _____ .

**(d)** Computer literacy is not yet a prerequisite for employment in any profession. (T/F)

**13-2. (a)** The use of electronic mail is on the rise. (T/F)

**(b)** The magazine-on-a-disk has been discussed but is beyond the state of the art. (T/F)

**(c)** _____ are knowledge-based systems to which preset rules are applied to solve a particular problem.

**(d)** In the future, users of a computer system may identify themselves by entering a _____ and a fingerprint.

**13-3.** The total computing capcacity in the world is increasing at slightly less than 25 percent per year. (T/F)

*Self-Test answers.*   13-1 (a), T; (b), F; (c), plug-compatible manufacturer; (d), F; 13-2 (a), T; (b), F; (c), expert systems; (d) voiceprint; 13-3, F;

# Zimco Enterprises

## ZIMCO'S MIS STRATEGIC PLAN

### MIS PLANNING AT ZIMCO ENTERPRISES

Three years ago Preston Smith, Zimco's president, made a rather profound statement during the annual meeting. He said: "At Zimco, our Computer and Information Services Division is no longer simply a data processing support function. With the capability to provide managers with valuable information on a timely basis, CIS is emerging as one of Zimco's most valuable strategic tools." This statement by Preston Smith set the stage for the development of Zimco's first *MIS Strategic Plan*. The first comprehensive plan was created in 1985 and it has been updated annually to reflect new directions in the area of computers and information processing.

The MIS Strategic Plan is compiled at two levels: the *strategic level* and the *operational level*. The more general strategic level contains the strategic objectives for the Computer and Information Services Division and is aimed primarily at top management. The operational portion of the plan identifies the specific activities that must be accomplished in order to achieve the strategic objectives, and it serves as a working document for CIS managers.

### MIS Strategic Planning

**The Need for Planning.** The MIS strategic planning effort evolved at Zimco because of a desperate need for corporate coordination of the development of the data base and in information dissemination. The MIS Strategic Plan is subordinate to, and supportive of, Zimco's corporate *Five-Year Long-Range Plan*. The Five-Year Long-Range Plan focuses on the company's products

and the MIS Strategic Plan focuses on the company's information and data processing needs. Conrad Innis, the VP of CIS, knew that it is easier to coordinate plans with the same planning horizon, so he chose a five-year planning horizon for the MIS Strategic Plan.

Even after Preston Smith made his statement at the annual meeting, the concept of MIS strategic planning had to be sold to management. Conrad Innis knew that if the plan was to be successful, he had to have the full cooperation of all managers at Zimco. To develop a viable plan, CIS planners need direction from top management and from user managers throughout the enterprise. Conrad used another one of his maxims to solicit their cooperation. He told them: "The time and money that you spend on helping us plan your information future is easily justified when you consider the potential cost of not planning."

**Focus and Scope of the MIS Strategic Plan.** Conrad Innis says: "At Zimco, the compilation of the MIS Strategic Plan is viewed as an opportunity to recognize the shortcomings of the past and to lay the groundwork for a more responsive information services function in the future." The *focus* of the MIS Strategic Plan is on the *strategic objectives* and the *one-time and ongoing activities* that will enable CIS to provide the computer/information services support necessary to accommodate the growth and flexibility requirements of Zimco. The *scope* of the plan includes the *events and activities that are affected by or under the control of CIS*. Applications of computer technology are so pervasive at Zimco that the scope of the plan includes just about every area of corporate activity.

# THE INFORMATION SYSTEMS POLICY COMMITTEE

CIS resources are not adequate to handle all user requests for service. Therefore, these requests must be prioritized for the overall good of the company. Conrad says: "I am not in a position to choose an accounting project over a manufacturing project. Wisely, Preston Smith decided that the best approach is to let those who are affected make these critical decisions. To do this, he created the Information Systems Policy Committee. We call it the ISPC for short." The members of the ISPC, Zimco's five vice-presidents, are charged with the following duties:

- Approve or reject requests for major MIS services.
- Set priorities among approved major information systems projects.
- Monitor the progress of major information systems development projects.
- Monitor the performance of ongoing information systems (e.g., PICS and PERES).
- Arbitrate differences between departments and/or divisions arising from CIS operations.
- Set policy that relates to computers and information processing.

The ISPC meets on the second Wednesday of each month. Inevitably, there are serious problems and priorities to be resolved. Conrad says: "If I made all the decisions regarding computer applications at Zimco, I wouldn't have very many friends. We have many heated debates during ISPC meetings, but ultimately, the cumulative thinking of top management determines what is best for Zimco."

# THE CIS SITUATION ASSESSMENT

Zimco's MIS Strategic Plan is updated annually to reflect more current information and changing circumstances. The first planning activity, which is always conducted during the month of January, is the *situation assessment*. The situation assessment is an in-depth investigation of CIS by CIS managers. The end product of the situation as-

sessment is a status report on the CIS Division. The investigation has three primary objectives:

1. To provide a candid assessment of where Zimco Enterprises stands with respect to the computer/information services technology as compared to other similar companies and the state of the art of the technology

2. To highlight areas for improvement within CIS and within the enterprise

3. To provide a foundation for the initiation of the annual CIS strategic and operational planning efforts

"The situation assessment is our report card," says Conrad Innis. "It tells what we've done right and it points out areas in which we need improvement." Some of the areas investigated during the situation assessment include: staffing, morale, operations and controls, standards, priorities, quality and effectiveness of information systems, hardware capacity, security, and relations with users.

# STRATEGIC OBJECTIVES FOR CIS

Zimco's strategic objectives, which are listed in the following sections for each of 13 planning areas (see Figure Z13–1), are complementary to one another and to the focus of the overall plan. The strategic objectives (the bulleted items) are followed by a brief discussion of several of the activities that would need to be accomplished to achieve these strategic objectives. These activities would be prioritized and scheduled in the operational portion of the MIS Strategic Plan.

**FIGURE Z13–1**
**Strategic Planning Areas**

Service
Policy
Information systems
Hardware
Systems software
Communications
Organization
Personnel
Management
Operations
Standards and procedures
Facilities
Office automation

One of the objectives outlined in Zimco's MIS Strategic Plan is to support the information requirements of all levels of business activity in a timely, responsive, and cost-effective manner.
(Photo courtesy of Hewlett-Packard Company)

### Service

■ To support the information requirements of all levels of business activity in a timely, responsive, and cost-effective manner

### Policy

■ To establish policy for computer and information resources that provides guidelines for common situations and a framework by which CIS, corporate, and user management can cope with exceptional situations

### Information Systems

■ To integrate existing and proposed information systems in a data base environment
■ To provide on-line inquiry capability in appropriate proposed and existing systems
■ To emphasize user friendliness and distributed processing in systems design
■ To make judicious use of proprietary software packages
■ To conduct periodic system reviews

### Hardware

■ To continue to upgrade and expand existing hardware to accommodate the growing data processing and information needs of the corporation

One of the objectives outlined in Zimco's MIS Strategic Plan is to provide greater user accessibility to the computer and information services through distributed processing. The Sales and Marketing Division has a distributed minicomputer for local processing. Division personnel can access the mini or Zimco's mainframe computer.
(Courtesy of Wang Laboratories, Inc.)

- To provide greater user accessibility to the computer and information services through distributed processing
- To integrate state-of-the-art hardware technology into the design of existing and proposed systems

## Systems Software

- To provide systems software support for distributed processing
- To support user-oriented query languages

## Communications

- To emphasize data communications in the design of future information systems
- To implement more effective approaches to verbal and written communication

## Organization

- To structure the organization within CIS to meet operational commitments and be responsive to Zimco's information services needs

## Personnel

- To recruit and retain outstanding individuals with management potential
- To improve the quality of existing CIS personnel through career development
- To provide career alternatives for personnel who are not inclined to management
- To maintain a high level of CIS morale

## Management

- To recognize the importance of good management
- To improve management's ability to manage through the effective use of proven management approaches and techniques

## Operations

- To provide sufficient operational capability to achieve acceptable response times and turnaround times during peak periods

One of the objectives outlined in Zimco's MIS Strategic Plan is to implement more effective approaches to verbal and written communication. The plant manager at Eugene, Oregon feels that the presentation of summary data in graphic format is more effective than a tabular presentation of the same data.
(Photo courtesy of Hewlett-Packard Company)

## Standards and Procedures

- To develop and implement the standards and standardized procedures necessary to create the proper framework for information systems development and maintenance, and for effective interaction with users

## Facilities

- To provide ergonomically sound working space for CIS personnel
- To work with corporate facility planners to ensure consideration of future communications, hardware, and security requirements
- To establish and maintain information centers at headquarters and at all plant sites

## Office Automation

- To coordinate the integration of office automation equipment and applications into the Zimco computer network and into future information systems designs
- To encourage office automation in support of increased productivity for office personnel

## THE OPERATIONAL PORTION OF THE PLAN

The details for achieving the strategic objectives are explained and illustrated in the operational portion of the MIS Strategic Plan. In this part of the plan, the anticipated start and completion dates and the commitment of resources (e.g., person-months) for all activities within CIS are identified. A few of the many activities listed on the current plan include: the hiring of three new programmers and seven new analysts, a mainframe upgrade in the Dallas computer center, an enhancement to PICS, updating the programming standards manual, the presentation of four bimonthly user seminars on presentation graphics, and 55 other major activities to be accomplished over the next five years.

Identifying Specific Activities. Since CIS resources are scheduled and allocated by activity, specific activities necessary to carry out the strategic objectives set forth in the strategic objectives are identified. At Zimco, management identifies two types of activities: *project-oriented* (one-time) and *ongoing* activities.

Examples of project-oriented activities that were scheduled as a result of a previous Zimco MIS Strategic Plan include:

- The development of a prototype system for FACS
- An MIS security audit
- An enhancement to the Customer Service Subsystem of SAMIS
- The presentation of three in-house seminars on "The Effective Use of Business Graphics"
- A mainframe upgrade

Examples of ongoing activities that were scheduled as a result of a previous Zimco MIS Strategic Plan include:

- Operational support, control, and maintenance of PERES
- MIS strategic planning
- Compilation and distribution of "Compu-Talk," the monthly CIS newsletter

Setting Priorities and Scheduling.   Once the specific activities needed to carry out the strategic objectives have been identified, the ISPC (Information Systems Policy Committee) determines the priorities for major activities and CIS management prioritizes minor activities. The activities are now ready to be scheduled by CIS planners. The scheduling process requires that preliminary estimates of cost and personnel be made for each activity proposed.

The scheduling of CIS activities is essentially a trade-off between maintaining the priorities set by the ISPC and CIS management and minimizing the fluctuation in personnel requirements (i.e., *work-load leveling*). At any given time, CIS has 50 to 70 approved activities that are ready to be scheduled. A portion of the CIS Project Schedule Chart is shown in Figure Z13–2. The complete chart graphically illustrates the scheduled start and end dates for all approved projects.

*Summary*.   Conrad Innis is very outspoken in his praise for the benefits of MIS strategic planning. "MIS planning will never be easy. It requires a commitment of support and cooperation from CIS managers, users managers, and top management. But in the long run, all of us would be hard pressed to find a more cost-effective investment opportunity than MIS strategic planning."

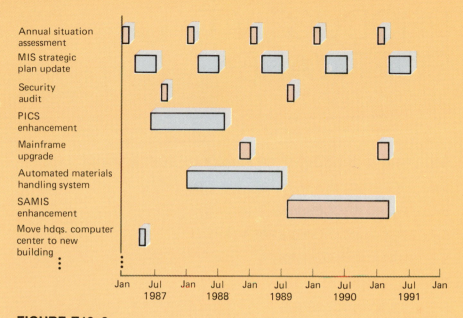

**FIGURE Z13–2**
**CIS Project Schedule Chart (Partial)**
The CIS Project Schedule Chart is a by-product of the operational portion of
the MIS Strategic Plan. It graphically illustrates the scheduled start and end dates
for all approved projects.

## DISCUSSION QUESTIONS

1. Both the MIS Strategic Plan and the corporate Five-Year Long-Range Plan deal with all facets of Zimco operation. Why not combine them into a single plan?

2. What did Conrad Innis mean when he told Zimco managers to "consider the potential cost of not planning"?

3. The scope of the MIS Strategic Plan includes the events and activities that are affected by or under the control of CIS. Describe areas within the Operations Division and within the Sales and Marketing Division that would be within the scope of the MIS Strategic Plan. What areas in these two divisions would not be considered within the scope of the MIS Strategic Plan?

4. Discuss the relationship between the strategic portion and the operational portion of the MIS Strategic Plan?

5. One of the charges of the Information Systems Policy Committee (ISPC) is to set priorities among major information systems projects that have been approved for development. Prior to the formation of the ISPC, Conrad Innis set all MIS priorities. Discuss the advantages of having the ISPC set the priorities.

6. Discuss the criteria that the Information Systems Policy Committee might use to set priorities for major information systems development projects.

7. Several of the CIS managers were very outspoken against conducting an annual situation assessment. Why?

8. Besides the MIS Strategic Plan, CIS also maintains a contingency plan that details what to do if some extraordinary event (e.g., fire in the machine room) drastically disrupts the operation of the headquarters computer center in Dallas. What kinds of information do you think would be included in the contingency plan?

# MICROCOMPUTER PRODUCTIVITY SOFTWARE

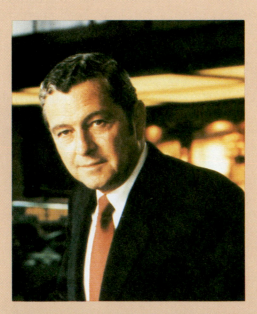

*At our company, the microcomputer is revolutionizing the engineering process in about the same way the gasoline engine changed the transportation industry!*

B.C. Bartlett
President
Deere & Company
Moline, Illinois

## S-1  THE MICROCOMPUTER FAMILY OF PRODUCTIVITY SOFTWARE _____

Thousands of commercially available software packages run on micro-computers, but the most popular business software is the family of "productivity" software packages. These programs are the foundation of personal computing in the business world. The microcomputer productivity tools include:

- ■ *Word processing*. Word processing software permits users to enter, store, manipulate, and print text.

- ■ *Electronic spreadsheet*. Electronic spreadsheet software permits users to work with the rows and columns of a matrix (or spreadsheet) of data. Several spreadsheets can be contained in a single worksheet.

- ■ *Data management*. Data management or **database** software permits users to create and maintain a data base and to extract information from the data base.

- ■ *Graphics*. Graphics software permits users to create charts and line drawings that graphically portray the data in an electronic spreadsheet or data base.

- ■ *Idea processors*. Idea processor software helps users to organize and document their thoughts and ideas.

- ■ *Communications*. Communications software permits users to send and receive transmissions of data to/from remote computers, and to process and store the data as well.

The *function*, *concepts*, and *use* of each of these micro software tools are the focus of this special skills section.

"This used to take me over a week, and now I do it in 30 minutes!" Similar statements have been made by thousands of business micro users. These six categories of software packages are now proven productivity tools in any field that requires people to work with text, numbers, graphics, or ideas (and that list doesn't leave out many people!). These packages are often characterized as productivity tools because they help to relieve the tedium of many time-consuming manual tasks.

No more retyping—thanks to word processing software. Electronic spreadsheets permit us to perform certain arithmetic and logic operations without writing programs. With data management software we can format and create a data base in minutes. Say goodbye to grid paper, plastic templates, and the manual plotting of data: graphics software prepares bar, pie, and line charts without our drawing a single line. When brainstorming with idea processors, the result is a logical outline of conclusions, not indecipherable notes on a yellow pad. And communications software helps to minimize redundant data entry by permitting the transfer of files between computers.

In each productivity tool category, there are dozens of commercially available software packages from which to choose. The software packages in each category accomplish essentially the same functions. They differ primarily in the scope and variety of the special features they have to offer and in their "user friendliness."

## S-2   INTERACTING WITH THE SYSTEM

**User Friendly.**   Software is said to be **user friendly** when someone with relatively little computer experience has little difficulty using the system. User-friendly systems communicate easily understood words and phrases to the end user, thus simplifying the user's interaction with the computer system. A central focus of the design of micro productivity software is user friendliness.

There are, of course, degrees of user friendliness. At the first level, it is assumed that the user has little or no experience and that the user's interaction with the software will be tentative and deliberate. At this level, the system offers some welcome "hand holding." For example, some software packages use **icons** or pictographs, rather than words or phrases, to communicate with the end user. When you wish to issue a file handling command, for example, you position the cursor near the icon representing files (perhaps a file cabinet or a diskette). When you select a particular icon, you are then presented with a menu of file handling choices. Your choices might be to save, retrieve, or delete a file.

The first level of user friendliness may be too friendly, and even cumbersome, for the seasoned user. Too much hand holding forces experienced users to work more slowly than they would like; therefore, micro software provides alternatives. As you become familiar with the software, you can learn and use techniques that offer more efficient interaction with the system.

A handy feature available on most software packages is the **help command.** When you find yourself in a corner, you can press the "help" key, and more explanation or instruction is displayed on the screen. When you are finished reading the help information, the system returns you to your work at the same point that you left it.

A director of personnel in a consumer goods company uses electronic spreadsheet and data management software to ask "what if" questions regarding a proposal for a new benefits package for the company's 1,200 union workers.
(Quotron Systems, Inc.)

The reaction of this nurse and doctor confirms what millions have already learned: micros and productivity software can be very user friendly.
(Photo supplied courtesy of Epson America)

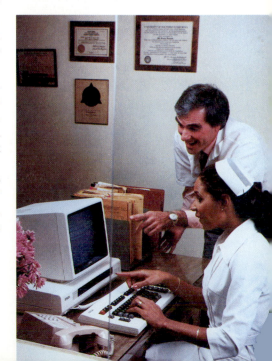

The primary input and control device on a microcomputer is the keyboard. The two primary output devices are the video monitor and the printer.
(Dataproducts Corporation)

**Input and Control.**   A microcomputer's *keyboard* is normally the primary input and control device. You enter data and issue commands via the keyboard. It has, besides the standard typewriter keyboard, *function keys*, also called *soft keys*. When pressed, these function keys trigger the execution of software, thus the name "soft" key. For example, pressing a particular function key might call up a menu of possible activities that can be performed. Another function key might rearrange the words in a paragraph for right and left justification. Some keyboards are equipped with a *10-key pad* (numbers for rapid numeric data entry).

A keyboard also has *cursor control keys*. These "arrow" keys allow you to move the cursor up, down, left, and right. Pressing the *HOME* key results in different actions for different packages, but often, the cursor is moved to the beginning of a work area (e.g., the start of the document in word processing).

Other important keys common to most keyboards are the *backspace* (*BKSP*), *escape* (*ESC*), *control* (*CTRL*), and *alternate* (*ALT*) keys. Press the BKSP key to move the cursor one position to the left and delete the character in that position. The ESC key may have many functions, depending on the software package, but in most situations you can press the ESC key to negate the current command. The CTRL and ALT keys are used in conjunction with another key. You hold down a CTRL or ALT key to give another key new meaning. For example, on some word processing systems you press HOME to move the cursor to the top left corner of the screen. When you press CTRL and HOME together, the cursor is positioned at the beginning of the document.

Another device used for input and control is the *mouse*. The hand-held mouse is connected to the computer by an electrical cable (the mouse's tail) and rolled over a desktop to move the cursor. Buttons on the mouse are activated to select a menu item or to perform certain tasks, such as moving blocks of data from one part of the screen to another.

**Menus.**  When using these productivity tools, you issue commands and initiate operations by selecting activities to be performed from a *hierarchy of menus*. These hierarchies are sometimes called "menu trees." When you select an item in the *main menu*, you are normally presented with another menu of activities, and so on—thus the "tree." Depending on the items you select, you may progress through as many as eight levels of menus before processing is initiated. The menus appear in a *control panel* or a *pull-down menu*. The control panel is usually, but not always, located at the bottom or top of the screen. The pull-down menus are superimposed in a **window** over whatever is currently on the screen. You select a particular menu item by positioning the cursor over or next to the desired menu item with the cursor control keys or a mouse.

The main menu of a graphics software package might give you the choice of what type of chart you want produced: *bar chart*, *pie chart*, or *line chart*. If you select *bar chart*, then another menu gives you more choices: Do you wish to *create* a new one or *revise* an existing one? If you select *create*, then more menus are presented that permit you to describe the appearance of the chart (e.g., labels) and to identify what data are to be charted.

At some point in the menu hierarchy, the user is asked to enter the specifications for data to be charted (graphics software) or the size of the output paper (word processing software), and so on. As a convenience to the user, many of the specification options (size of output paper) are already filled in to reflect common situations (e.g., document size is set at $8\frac{1}{2}$ by 11 inches). If the user is satisfied with these **default options,** no further specifications are required. The user can easily revise the default options to accommodate the less common situations. For example, to print a document on legal-size paper, the default paper length of 11 inches would need to be revised to 14 inches.

**The Operating System.**  The nucleus of a microcomputer system is its **operating system.** All hardware and software, including micro productivity software, are under the control of the operating system. It is to the advantage of the users of micro software to learn something about the operating system for their particular micro. Beside being the "boss" program, the operating system enables users to run application programs such as word processing and it provides users with a variety of file handling capabilities. Unfortunately, the logic, structure, and nomenclature of the different operating systems vary considerably, so we'll not present operating system specifics in this section. Your instructor will tell you what you need to know to run a particular software package.

*Micro Operating Systems*.  The operating system is usually, though not always, supplied by the micro vendor. Some of the more popular micro operating systems are MS DOS, developed by Microsoft Corporation, CP/M, developed by Digital Research Corporation, and UNIX, developed by AT&T. You may encounter spin-offs of these operating systems. For example, PC DOS for the IBM PC is based on Microsoft's MS DOS, and XENIX is a spin-off of UNIX.

Some systems are designed with a windowing feature that lets users view several outputs on the screen at the same time. With this kind of design, the user is not limited to viewing only text or only graphics output. The windowing feature also permits a window of menu options to be superimposed over an existing display.
(Courtesy of International Business Machines Corporation)

*Booting the System.*   Before you can use a microcomputer, you must "**boot** the system." The procedure for booting the system on most micros is simply to load the operating system from disk storage into main memory. For most micros, this is no more difficult than inserting an operating system diskette (floppy disk) in a disk drive and flipping the "on" switch. On some systems all you have to do is turn the system on. A few seconds later, with the operating system in memory, you are ready to begin processing. Some operating systems give you the option to enter date and time data before displaying the **system prompt.**

*Running a Software Package.*   The system prompt is the operating system's message to you, the user, so that you can now enter a *system command* (e.g., to copy files from one diskette to another) or the name of the program (e.g., if you wish to run an applications program such as an electronic spreadsheet). The form of the system prompt varies among operating systems. A common prompt is the "greater than" symbol prefaced by a disk drive specification (e.g., A> is the prompt when the disk drive "A" is the active or default drive). Other common system prompts are the "$" (dollar sign) and the "]" (close bracket).

Once you have loaded the operating system to memory and the system prompt is displayed on the screen, you are ready to run a graphics package, a word processing package, or any other software package. To run a software package, you simply insert the diskette containing the software in the appropriate disk drive (if needed), then enter the name of the file that contains the applications software. For example, to run a particular word processing package on an MS DOS-based micro, you would load the software diskette to drive A, then key in "wp" (the name of the program file) after the system prompt. The command would look like this:

    A> wp

The next thing you would see would be the opening screen and eventually the main menu for the word processing package. All micro productivity tools are run in the same manner, unless they are made to be *self-booting* (i.e., the operating system and the applications software are on the same diskette). By making a software package self-booting, you can bypass the step that requires you to enter the name of the program file after the prompt.

*Utility Programs.*   The operating system contains certain utility programs that allow you to perform such activities as:

- Formatting (preparing) a diskette for processing
- Copying the contents of one diskette to another diskette
- Renaming, copying, or deleting a file
- Listing the files on a particular **directory**

A directory is a named area on disk in which files are stored. Hard disks can be divided into several logical directories. All files on a particular diskette take on the directory designation for the disk drive into which the diskette is loaded (e.g., the directory for drive A).

**Learning to Use Micro Productivity Tools.** The fundamental operation of the various word processing software packages is essentially the same. The same is true of the other productivity tools. Their differences are primarily in the way the software interacts with the user (e.g., menus options, presentation of output). The software tutorials in this special skills section are designed to give you a strong conceptual understanding of the features and use of these micro productivity tools.

*SuperSoftware*, one of the software supplements to this text, contains generic hands-on tutorials that demonstrate the features and operation of these tools. Between the textual material, hands-on experience with SuperSoftware, and in-class lectures, you should develop skills that can easily be translated to using any of the software packages that you might encounter at your college or place of business.

When you purchase a software package, you will receive at least one manual, the software on diskettes, and a *tutorial disk*. It is a good idea to go over the tutorial disk to get a feeling for the menu options and how the software interacts with the user. When you load the tutorial disk on the micro, an instructional program interactively walks you through a simulation (demonstration) of the features and use of the software. Once you have an overview understanding of the features and how the components fit together, it is easy to go to the manual for specific operational questions.

A microcomputer software package, such as Lotus Development Corporation's 1–2–3 (an integrated electronic spreadsheet and graphics package), will normally include a set of reference manuals, a function-key template (a keyboard overlay), and several diskettes containing the software and on-line tutorials.
(Lotus Development Corporation)

## REVIEW EXERCISES (S-1 and S-2)

1. Name and briefly describe the six microcomputer productivity tools.
2. What is the function of soft keys? Of cursor control keys?
3. Name microcomputer input devices other than the keyboard.
4. Describe the attributes of user-friendly software.
5. Contrast a control panel and a pull-down menu.
6. Most word processing packages have a default document size. What other defaults would a word processing package have?
7. What is meant by "booting the system"?

## S-3  WORD PROCESSING

### Function

Word processing, the "glamor" software of the 1970s, has become the mainstay application of computers in virtually every office. Word processing is using the computer to enter, store, manipulate, and print text in letters, reports, books, and so on. Once you have used word processing, you will probably wonder (like a million others before you) how in the world you ever survived without it!

Word processing has virtually eliminated the need for opaque correction fluid and the need to re-key revised letters and reports. Revising

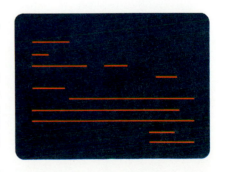

Many executives have become so accustomed to writing memos, preparing meeting agendas, and documenting ideas with word processing software that they take a portable computer along when they travel.
(Courtesy of Apple Computer, Inc.)

a hard copy is time consuming and cumbersome, but revising the same text in electronic format is quick and easy. You simply make corrections and revisions to the text on the computer before the document is displayed or printed in final form.

## Concepts

**Formatting a Document.**   When you *format* a document, you are describing the size of the print page and how you want the document to look when it is printed. As with the typewriter, you must set the left and right margins, the tab settings, line spacing (e.g., lines/inch), and character spacing (e.g., characters/inch). Depending on the software package, some or all of these specifications are made in a *layout line*. You can have as many layout lines as you want in a single document. Text is printed according to specifications in the most recent layout line until another layout line is defined. You must also specify the size of the output document, then set margins for the top and bottom of the text. The default document size is almost always 8½ by 11 inches.

As an option, you can even *justify* (line up) both the left and the right margins, like the print in newspapers and this book. Word processing software is able to produce "clean" margins on both sides by adding small spaces between characters and words in a line.

**Entering Text.**   To begin preparation of a document, all you have to do is begin typing. Text is entered in **replace mode** or **insert mode.** When in replace mode, the character that you enter *overstrikes* the character at the cursor position. For instance, suppose that you typed the word "the", but you wanted to type "and". To make the correction in replace mode, you would position the cursor at the "t" and type a-n-d, thereby replacing the "the" with "and".

On most word processing systems, you "toggle" or switch between replace and insert mode by pressing a key. When in insert mode, you can enter *additional* text. Let's use a memo written by George Brooks, the Northern Regional Sales Manager for Zimco Enterprises to illustrate the effects of insert mode data entry. George often uses word processing to generate memos to his staff. The first draft of one of George's memos is shown in Figure S-1. George wanted to emphasize that an upcoming meeting was to be on Thursday, so he decided to insert "See you Thursday! " just before the last sentence. To do this, he selected the insert mode, placed the cursor on the "W" in "We'll", and entered "See you Thursday! " (see Figure S-2).

Word processing permits *full-screen editing*. That is, you can move the cursor to any position in the document to insert or replace text. You can browse through a multiscreen document by *scrolling* a line at a time or a "page" (a screen) at a time. You can edit any part of any screen.

When you enter text, you press the carriage return key only when you wish to begin a new line of text. As you enter text in replace mode, the computer automatically moves the cursor to the next line.

```
To:     Field Sales Staff
From:   G. Brooks, Northern Sales Manager
Re:     Weekly Briefing Session

     The Sales Department's weekly briefing session will be
held at 9:00 a.m. this Thursday.  Last month's sales figures
and new sales strategies for the Tegler and Qwert will be
discussed.  We'll meet in the second floor conference room.
```

**FIGURE S-1**
**Word Processing: Memorandum**
This first-draft memo is revised for illustrative purposes in Figures S-2 through
S-6.

```
To:     Field Sales Staff
From:   G. Brooks, Northern Sales Manager
Re:     Weekly Briefing Session

     The Sales Department's weekly briefing session will be
held at 9:00 a.m. this Thursday.  Last month's sales figures
and new sales strategies for the Tegler and Qwert will be
discussed.  See you Thursday!  We'll meet in the second floor
conference room.
```

**FIGURE S-2**
**Word Processing: Insert Mode**
This memo is the result of the sentence "See you Thursday!     " being inserted
before the last sentence of the memo of Figure S-1. Notice how the text wraps
around to make room for the addition of a sentence.

In insert mode, the computer manipulates the text such that it *wraps
around*, sending words that are pushed past the right margin into the
next line, and so on, to the end of the paragraph. In Figures S-1 and
S-2, notice how the words "conference room". (in the last sentence)
are wrapped around to the next line when "See you Thursday! " is
inserted.

**Block Operation.** Features common to most word processing software packages are mentioned and discussed briefly in this section. The *block* operations are among the handiest of word processing features. They are the block *move*, the block *copy*, and the block *delete* commands. Let's discuss the move command first. These commands are the electronic equivalent of a "cut and paste" job. With the move feature, you can select a block of text (e.g., a word, a sentence, a paragraph, a section of a report, or as much contiguous text as you desire) and move it to another portion of the document. To do this, follow these steps:

1. Issue the move command (a main menu option or a function key).
2. Indicate the start and ending positions of the block of text to be moved (*mark* the text).
3. Move the cursor to the beginning of the designation location (where you wish the text to be moved).
4. Press the carriage return (or the appropriate function key) to complete the move operation.

At the end of the move procedure, the entire block of text that you select is moved to the location that you designate and the original is deleted. The sequence of the text is adjusted accordingly.

The following example demonstrates the procedure for marking and moving a block of text. After reading over the memo (of Figure S-2), George decided to edit his memo to the field staff to make it more readable. He did this by "moving" the last sentence from the end of the memo to just after the first sentence. To perform this operation, he first selected the move option (a function key on his word processing system) and designated the beginning ("W" in "We'll") and end ("." at end of paragraph) of the block. On most word processing systems, the portions of text that are marked for a block operation are usually displayed in *reverse video* (see Figure S-3). After marking the block, George then positioned the cursor at the designation location (just after the first sentence) and pressed the appropriate key (a function key) to complete the operation (see Figure S-4).

The copy command works in a similar manner, except that the text block you select is copied to the location that you designate. At the completion of the operation, two exact copies of the text are present

**FIGURE S-3**
**Word Processing: Marking Text for a Block Operation**
The last sentence of the memo of Figure S-2 is marked to be moved.

```
To:     Field Sales Staff
From:   G. Brooks, Northern Sales Manager
Re:     Weekly Briefing Session

    The Sales Department's weekly briefing session will be
held at 9:00 a.m. this Thursday.  Last month's sales figures
and new sales strategies for the Tegler and Qwert will be
discussed.  See you Thursday! We'll meet in the second floor
conference room.
```

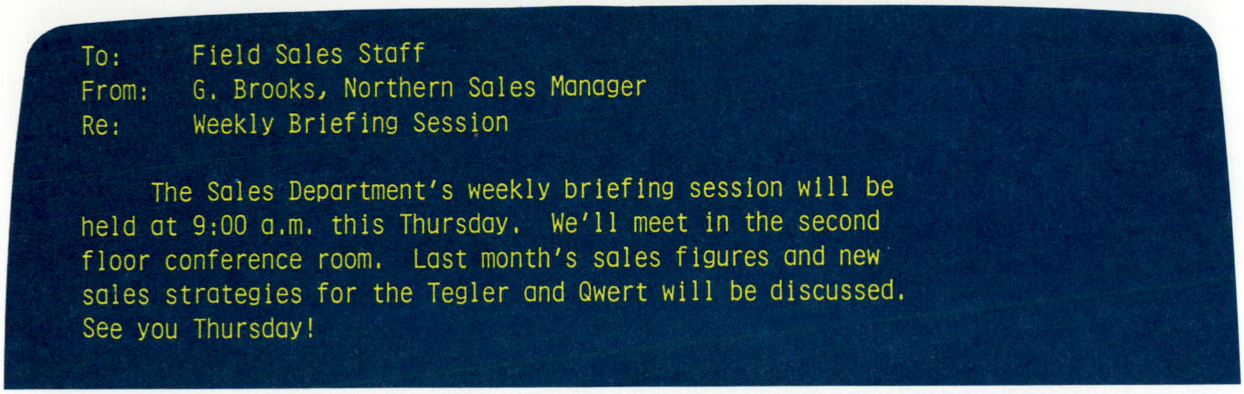

```
To:      Field Sales Staff
From:    G. Brooks, Northern Sales Manager
Re:      Weekly Briefing Session

     The Sales Department's weekly briefing session will be
held at 9:00 a.m. this Thursday.  We'll meet in the second
floor conference room.  Last month's sales figures and new
sales strategies for the Tegler and Qwert will be discussed.
See you Thursday!
```

in the document. To delete a block of text, mark the block in the same manner, then select the delete block option.

The "Search" Features.   Just as George Brooks was about to print his memo (Figure S-4), he learned that an important client was coming to town on Thursday, so he decided to switch the meeting from Thursday to Friday. He can make the necessary revisions to the memo by using any of several word processing features. One option is to use the *search* or *find* feature. This feature permits George to search through the entire document and identify all occurrences of a particular character string. For example, if George wanted to search for all occurrences of "Thursday" in his memo of Figure S-4, he would simply initiate the search command and type in the desired *search string*, "Thursday" in this example. The cursor is immediately positioned at the first occurrence of the character string "Thursday" so he can easily edit the text to reflect the new meeting day. From there, he can "find" other occurrences of "Thursday" by pressing the appropriate key.

As an alternative approach to making the Thursday-to-Friday change, George could use the *search and replace* feature. This feature enables George to selectively replace occurrences of "Thursday" in his memo with "Friday". Since he knew that he wanted *all* occurrences of "Thursday" to be replaced by "Friday", he performed a *global search and replace* (see Figure S-5).

**FIGURE S-4**
**Word Processing: Move Text**
This memo is the result of the marked block in Figure S-3 being moved to a position following the first sentence.

**FIGURE S-5**
**Word Processing: Search and Replace**
With the search and replace command, the two occurrences of "Thursday" in Figure S-4 are located and replaced automatically (option "A") with "Friday."

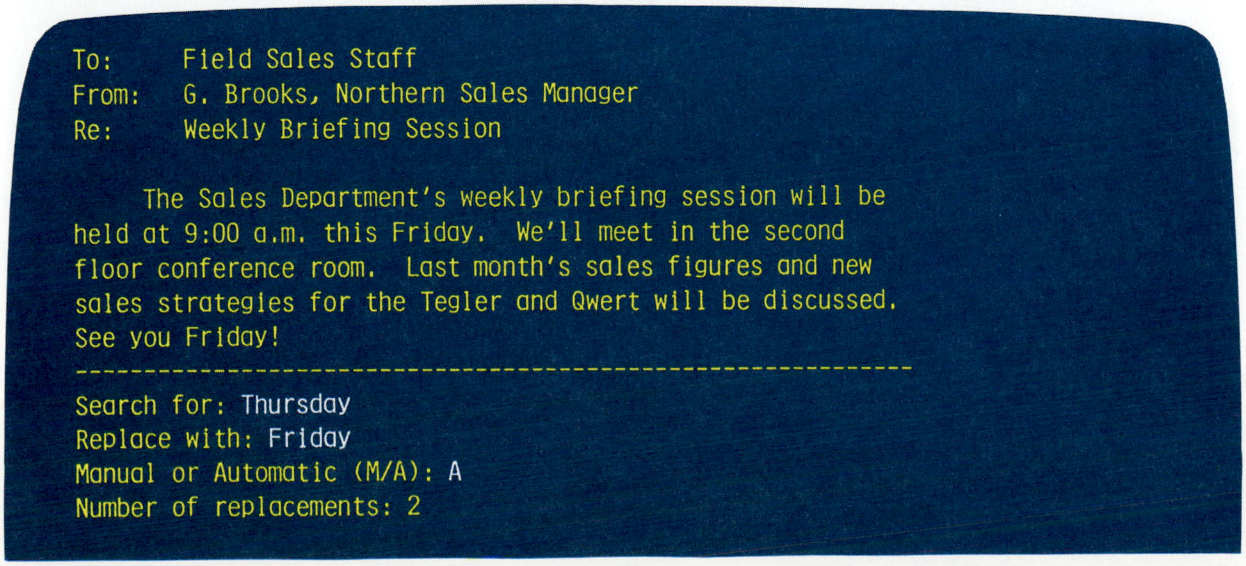

```
To:      Field Sales Staff
From:    G. Brooks, Northern Sales Manager
Re:      Weekly Briefing Session

     The Sales Department's weekly briefing session will be
held at 9:00 a.m. this Friday.  We'll meet in the second
floor conference room.  Last month's sales figures and new
sales strategies for the Tegler and Qwert will be discussed.
See you Friday!
--------------------------------------------------------------
Search for: Thursday
Replace with: Friday
Manual or Automatic (M/A): A
Number of replacements: 2
```

**bMEMORANDUMb**

```
To:      Field Sales Staff
From:    G. Brooks, Northern Sales Manager
Re:      Weekly Briefing Session


     The Sales Department's weekly briefing session will be
held at 9:00 a.m. this Thursday.  We'll meet in the second
floor conference room.  Last month's sales figures and new
sales strategies for the Tegler and Qwert will be discussed.
uSee you Thursdayu!
```

(a)

MEMORANDUM

```
To:      Field Sales Staff
From:    G. Brooks, Northern Sales Manager
Re:      Weekly Briefing Session


     The Sales Department's weekly briefing session will be
held at 9:00 a.m. this Thursday.  We'll meet in the second
floor conference room.  Last month's sales figures and new
sales strategies for the Tegler and Qwert will be discussed.
See you Thursday!
```

(b)

**MEMORANDUM**

```
To:      Field Sales Staff
From:    G. Brooks, Northern Sales Manager
Re:      Weekly Briefing Session


     The Sales Department's weekly briefing session will be
held at 9:00 a.m. this Thursday.  We'll meet in the second
floor conference room.  Last month's sales figures and new
sales strategies for the Tegler and Qwert will be discussed.
See you Thursday!
```

(c)

**FIGURE S-6**
**Word Processing: Boldface and Underline**
Text to be in boldface type or underlined is displayed differently, depending on
the word processing system and the color or resolution of the monitor.

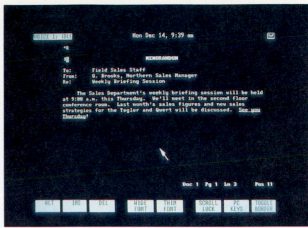

The memo of Figure S-6 was prepared and printed with three popular word processing packages. The first photo illustrates how the memo would be displayed using WordStar (WordStar is a trademark of MicroPro International Corporation). The second photo illustrates how the memo would be displayed using WordPerfect (WordPerfect is a trademark of Satellite Software International). The third photo illustrates how the memo would be displayed using Writing Assistant (Writing Assistant is a trademark of IBM Corporation).
(Long and Associates)

**Features That Enhance Appearance and Readability.**   George used several other valuable word processing features to enhance the appearance and readability of his memo before distributing it to his staff. First, he decided to enter the word "MEMORANDUM" at the top of his memo and use the automatic *centering* feature to position it in the middle of the page. On his word processing system, all he has to do to center whatever is on a particular line is to move the cursor to that line and press the "center" function key. The rest is automatic (see Figure S-6).

Word processing provides the facility to *boldface* and/or *underline* parts of the text for emphasis. In the memo of Figure S-6a, the reverse video "b" before and after the word "MEMORANDUM" causes it to appear in boldface print on output (see Figure S-7). The reverse video "u" before and after the sentence "See you Thursday!" (see Figure S-6a) causes it to be underlined on output (see Figure S-7). Some word processing systems display text that is to be in boldface type or underlined on output in reverse video. On a color monitor, the distinction can be made by displaying the text in different colors (see Figure S-6b). Systems with high-resolution monitors permit text to be displayed in boldface and underlined directly on the display screen (see Figure S-6c).

MEMORANDUM

```
To:       Field Sales Staff
From:     G. Brooks, Northern Sales Manager
Re:       Weekly Briefing Session

     The Sales Department's weekly briefing session will be
held at 9:00 a.m. this Thursday.  We'll meet in the second
floor conference room.  Last month's sales figures and new
sales strategies for the Tegler and Qwert will be discussed.
See you Thursday!
```

**FIGURE S-7**
**Word Processing: Printing Text**
The memo of Figure S-6 is printed on letterhead paper.

In creating the memo of Figure S-7, George Brooks used many, but not all of the features commonly used to enhance appearance and readability. He did not need the feature that allows him to *indent* a block of text. Also, his word processing software automatically prints *header* and *trailer labels*. The *pagination* feature automatically numbers the pages. On long reports, George usually repeats the report title at the top of each page (header label) and numbers each page at the bottom (pagination). These and other word processing features are illustrated in Figure S-8.

**Printing a Document.** To print a document, all you have to do is ready the printer (turn it on and align the paper) and select the print option on the main menu. Some word processing systems present you with a few final options. For example, you can choose to print the document as single or double spaced, or you are given the option to print specific pages or the whole document. Depending on the type of software and printer you have, you may even be able to mix the size and style of type fonts in a single document. For example, George could print the word "MEMORANDUM" in 48-point (about $\frac{1}{2}$ inch high) old English print if he wanted to.

For some word processing packages, what you see is what you get. That is, what is displayed on the screen is what the document will look like when it is printed. Other word processing packages use embedded commands (e.g., a reverse video "b" to indicate the start and end of boldface text). These packages usually have a *preview* feature that permits you to "format" and display the document as it would appear when printed.

**File Features.** Certainly, one of the most important features of a word processing package is the ability to store a document on disk storage for later recall. The stored version of a document is referred to as a *text file*. The *file* feature permits you to save, retrieve, and *delete* a text file. To perform a file operation, select the "file" option on the main menu, then select "save", "retrieve", or "delete". No matter which option you choose, you are asked by the system to identify the file (document). You would then enter an arbitrary name that in some way identifies the document (e.g., "MEMO"). Enter the file name of an existing file to retrieve or delete a file.

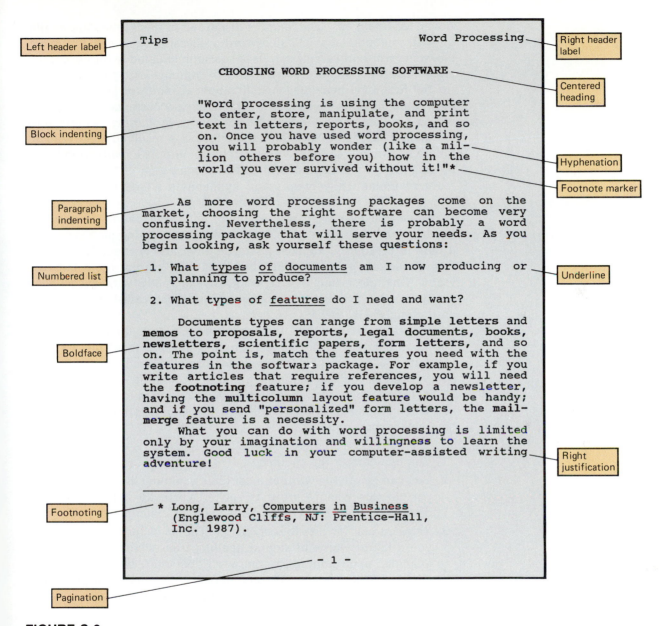

**FIGURE S-8**
**Word Processing: Features Overview**
Many of the more common capabilities of word processing software are illustrated
in this example printout of a text file.

George Brooks "saved" his memo (stored it on disk) under the
file name "MEMO". He stored it on disk because he knew that he
was planning a similar meeting next week at the same time and place
to discuss sales and strategies for Farkles and Stibs. Since he had
already prepared the memo of Figure S-6, all that he would have to
do to prepare a memo to announce next week's meeting would be to
retrieve the "MEMO" file and change the phrase "Tegler and Qwert"
to "Farkle and Stib".

**Advanced Features.** The features discussed in this section are available with the more sophisticated word processing packages. For example, some word processing software has sophisticated features for writers. A simple command creates a *table of contents* with page references for the first-level headings. An alphabetical *index of key words* can be created that lists the page numbers for each occurrence of designated words. One of the most tedious typing chores, *footnoting*, is done automatically (see Figure S-8). Footnote spacing is resolved electronically before anything is printed. Another feature permits a *multicolumn* output (e.g., one or more columns of text on a single page). The *hyphenation* feature automatically breaks and hyphenates words that fall at the end of the line on output (see Figure S-8).

Have you ever been writing along and been unable to put your finger on the right word? Well, some word processing packages have a built-in *thesaurus*! Suppose that you have just written: "The Grand Canyon certainly is beautiful." But "beautiful" is not quite the right word. Your electronic thesaurus is always ready with suggestions: pretty, elegant, exquisite, angelic, pulchritudinous, ravishing, . . . . Pulchritudinous? Oh, well.

If spelling is a problem, then word processing is the answer. Once you have entered the text and formatted the document the way you want it, you can call on the *spell* feature. The spell feature checks every word in the text against an electronic dictionary (usually from 75,000 to 150,000 words), then alerts you if a word is not in the dictionary. Upon finding an unidentified word, the spell function will normally give you several options.

1. You can correct the spelling.
2. You can ignore the word and continue scanning the text. Normally, you do this when a word is spelled correctly but is not in the dictionary (e.g., a company name such as Zimco).
3. You can ask for possible spellings. The spell function then gives you a list of words of similar spelling from which to choose. For example, upon finding the nonword "persors", the spell function might suggest: person, persona, persons, personal, and personnel.
4. Or you can add the word to the dictionary and continue scanning.

Another advanced feature—*numbered lists*—is illustrated in the list above and in Figure S-8. When using the numbered list feature, all you have to do is enter the items in the list. The spacing and the addition of the numbers are automatic.

The *grammar* feature highlights grammatical concerns and deviations from conventions. For example, it highlights split infinitives, phrases with redundant words (e.g., "very highest"), misuse of caps (e.g., JOhn or MarY), sexist phrases, double words (e.g., and and), and sentences that are written in the passive voice (versus the active voice).

## Use

You can create just about any kind of text-based document with word processing (see Figure S-8): letters, reports, books, articles, forms, memos, tables, and so on. The features of some word processing packages go beyond the generation of text documents. For example, some word processing systems provide the capability to merge parts of the data base with the text of the document. For example, a common application of word processing is to merge the names and addresses in a data base with the text of a letter to create "personalized" letters. An example of this merge application is illustrated in Figure S-9 and discussed in detail in the Zimco case study, "Office Automation at Zimco."

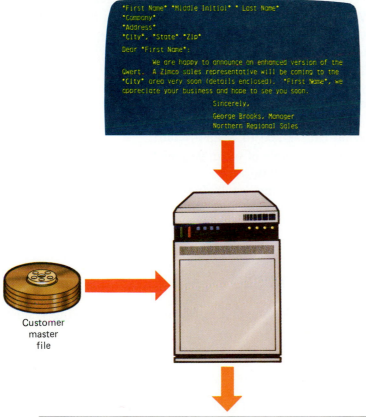

**FIGURE S-9**
**Merging Data with Word Processing**
The names and addresses from a customer master file are retrieved from secondary storage and merged with the text of a letter. In the actual letter, the appropriate data items are inserted for *First Name*, *Company*, *Address*, *City*, and so on. In this way, a "personalized" letter can be sent to each customer.

When working with word processing software, you are likely to enter long, continuous strings of text, as opposed to commands and data for the other types of micro software. Therefore, if you expect to use word processing capabilities frequently, you might consider acquiring a solid foundation in keyboarding skills, if you have not already done so. SuperSoftware, one of the software supplements that accompanies this text, includes a comprehensive keyboarding tutorial.

## REVIEW EXERCISES (S-3)

1. What is the function of word processing software?
2. What must be specified when formatting a document?
3. What is meant when a document is formatted to be right and left justified?
4. Text is entered in either of what two modes? What mode would you select to change "the table" to "the long table"? What mode would you select to change "pick the choose" to "pick and choose"?
5. What causes text to wrap around?
6. Give an example of when you might issue a global search and replace command.
7. When running the "spell" function, what options does the system present to you upon encountering an unidentified word?

## HANDS-ON EXERCISES

1. Enter the following text into your word processing system:

   Too Much Paper!

Last year, the Public Relations Department's paper budget was overrun by $350. Therefore, Public Relations personnel are requested to learn word processing. It is apparent that Public Relations has not taken full advantage of the word processing capabilities of its microcomputers.

Use the default layout line options (normally $8\frac{1}{2}$- by 11-inch document size, 1-inch right and left margins, 6 lines per inch, and so on). Justify on the right margin. Print the document.

In the exercises that follow, make the changes cumulative; that is, revise whatever text is left after the previous revision. Each exercise builds on the results of the previous exercise.

2.  In insert mode, insert the word "all" before "Public" in the second sentence. In replace mode, replace the lowercase letters in the title with capital letters. Print the document.

3.  Center the title. Print the document.

4.  At the end of the second sentence, add "by the end of the month". Observe how words at the end of the line wrap around to the next line. Print the document.

5.  Use the move command to move the second sentence to the end of the document. Print the document.

6.  Designate the word "all" to be underlined and the title to be in boldface when printed. Print the document.

7.  Place the "page" (new page) marker at the end of the document and use the copy command to produce another copy of the entire document just below the original. Print the documents.

8.  Use the search and replace command to replace all occurrences of "Public Relations" in the second document with "Research and Development". Revise $350 in the second document to be $525. Print the documents.

9.  Run the spell function. Print the document. If you performed all the hands-on exercises, your printed output should be similar to the examples that follow. Since the default margins vary among word processing systems, the lines in your printouts may break differently than those of the following example outputs.

### TOO MUCH PAPER!

Last year, the Public Relations Department's paper budget was overrun by $350. It is apparent that Public Relations has not taken full advantage of the word processing capabilities of its microcomputers. Therefore, *all* Public Relations personnel are requested to learn word processing by the end of the month.

### TOO MUCH PAPER!

Last year, the Research and Development Department's paper budget was overrun by $525. It is apparent that Research and Development has not taken full advantage of the word processing capabilities of its microcomputers. Therefore, *all* Research and Development personnel are requested to learn word processing by the end of the month.

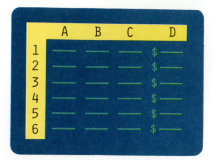

## S-4   THE ELECTRONIC SPREADSHEET

### Function

In 1978, a Harvard student convinced a couple of recent MIT graduates to rewrite their new business software to run on a personal computer. The software, called VisiCalc, became the first electronic spreadsheet. The 1979 introduction of VisiCalc revolutionized the way people perceived microcomputers. Suddenly, microcomputers were no longer just for games or education; they could also be a valuable asset for business.

The name "electronic spreadsheet" describes the software's fundamental application. The spreadsheet has been a common business tool for centuries. Before computers, the ledger (a spreadsheet) was the accountant's primary tool for keeping the books. Professors' grade books are set up in spreadsheet format.

Electronic spreadsheets are simply an electronic alternative to thousands of traditionally manual tasks. No longer are we confined to using pencils, erasers, and hand calculators for applications that deal with rows and columns of data. Think of anything that has rows and columns of data and you have identified an application for spreadsheet software. For example, how about income (profit and loss) statements (see Figure S-10), personnel profiles, demographic data, and budget summaries—to mention a few? Because electronic spreadsheets so closely resemble many of our manual tasks, they are enjoying widespread acceptance.

All commercially available electronic spreadsheet packages provide the facility to manipulate rows and columns of data. However, the *user interface*, or the manner in which the user enters data and commands, differs from one package to the next. The conceptual coverage that follows is generic and is applicable to all electronic spreadsheets. The examples, however, are oriented to Lotus 1–2–3 and Symphony, products of Lotus Development Corporation.

The use of voice recognition systems is gaining in popularity, especially in situations where "no hands" computer control is useful or required. This voice recognition system interprets and enters spoken spreadsheet commands and numbers.
(Texas Instruments, Inc.)

### Concepts

The example that we will use to illustrate and demonstrate electronic spreadsheet concepts is the Zimco income statement that was first presented in the Zimco case study, "Micros at Zimco" (Figures Z5-2 and Z5-3). Monroe Green, the VP of Finance and Accounting at Zimco, often uses an electronic spreadsheet **template** of Zimco's income statements for the past two years to do financial planning. The template, which is simply a spreadsheet model, contains a column that allows him to produce a pro rata income statement for next year (see Figure S-10). In Figure S-10, the actual income statement is shown on the first screen. The second screen contains the calculations for the price-earnings ratio and the display of the variables used to produce the pro rata income statement for next year. Since only 20 lines of the spreadsheet can be displayed at once, Monroe Green must "page up" or "page down" to see all of this spreadsheet.

C4: 153000

| | A | B | C | D |
|---|---|---|---|---|
| 1 | ================================================ | | | |
| 2 | ZIMCO INCOME STATEMENT ($1000) | Next Year | This Year | Last Year |
| 3 | ------------------------------------------------ | | | |
| 4 | Net sales | $183,600 | $153,000 | $144,780 |
| 5 | Cost of sales & op. expenses | | | |
| 6 |   Cost of goods sold | 116,413 | 115,260 | 117,345 |
| 7 |   Depreciation | 4,125 | 4,125 | 1,500 |
| 8 |   Selling & admin. expenses | 19,875 | 19,875 | 15,000 |
| 9 | | ------------ | ------------ | ------------ |
| 10 |     Operating profit | $43,187 | $13,740 | $10,935 |
| 11 | Other income | | | |
| 12 |   Dividends and interest | 405 | 405 | 300 |
| 13 | | ------------ | ------------ | ------------ |
| 14 |     TOTAL INCOME | $43,492 | $14,145 | $11,235 |
| 15 | Less: interest on bonds | 2,025 | 2,025 | 2,025 |
| 16 | | ------------ | ------------ | ------------ |
| 17 | Income before tax | 41,567 | 12,120 | 9,210 |
| 18 | Provision for income tax | 18,777 | 5,475 | 4,160 |
| 19 | | ------------ | ------------ | ------------ |
| 20 |     NET PROFIT FOR YEAR | $22,790 | $6,645 | $5,050 |

A34: 'FORECAST VARIABLES FOR NEXT YEAR'S PRO RATA INCOME STATEMENT

| | A | B | C | D |
|---|---|---|---|---|
| 21 | ================================================ | | | |
| 22 | | | | |
| 23 | | | | |
| 24 | ================================================ | | | |
| 25 | Shares outstanding | 6,300,000 | 6,000,000 | 6,000,000 |
| 26 | Market price | $21.25 | $14.00 | $13.00 |
| 27 | Earnings per share | $3.62 | $1.11 | $0.84 |
| 28 | | ------------ | ------------ | ------------ |
| 29 |   Price-earnings ratio | 5.87 | 12.64 | 15.45 |
| 30 | ================================================ | | | |
| 31 | | | | |
| 32 | | | | |
| 33 | ================================================ | | | |
| 34 | FORECAST VARIABLES FOR NEXT YEAR'S PRO RATA INCOME STATEMENT | | | |
| 35 | ------------------------------------------------ | | | |
| 36 | Projected change in sales | | 20.00% | |
| 37 | Projected change in cost of goods sold | | 1.00% | |
| 38 | Projected change in administrative expenses | | 0.00% | |
| 39 | ================================================ | | | |
| 40 | | | | |

**FIGURE S-10**
**Electronic Spreadsheet: An Income Statement Template**
This electronic spreadsheet template (both screens) is the basis for the explanation and demonstration of spreadsheet concepts. The "Next Year" pro rata income statement is extrapolated from the data in the "This Year" income statement and the values of forecast variables. The price-earnings ratio is calculated for each year.

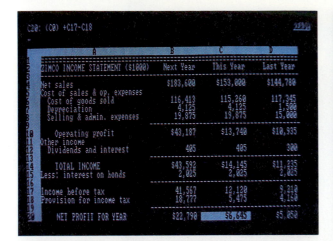
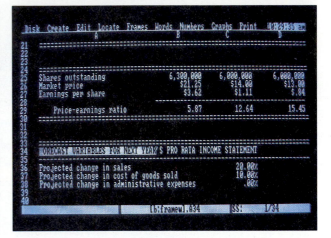
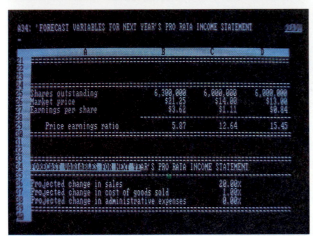

The income statement template of Figure S-10 was prepared using two popular electronic spreadsheet packages: The first two photos (shown vertically) illustrate how the template would be displayed using Lotus 1–2–3 (1–2–3 is a trademark of Lotus Development Corporation). The second two photos illustrate how the template would be displayed using Framework, an integrated package (Framework is a trademark of Ashton-Tate).
(Long and Associates)

**Organization.** Electronic spreadsheets are organized in a *tabular structure* with **rows** and **columns.** The intersection of a particular row and column designates a **cell.** As you can see in Figure S-10, the rows are *numbered* and the columns are *lettered*. Single letters identify the first 26 columns and double letters are used thereafter (A, B, . . . , Z, AA, AB, . . . , AZ, BA, BB, . . . , BZ). The number of rows or columns available to you depends on the size of your micro's RAM (random-access memory). Most spreadsheets permit hundreds of columns and thousands of rows.

Data are entered and stored in a cell, at the intersection of a column and a row. During operations, data are referenced by their **cell address.**

A cell address identifies the location of a cell in the spreadsheet by its column and row, with the column designator first. For example, in the income statement example of Figure S-10, C2 is the address of the column heading "This Year," and C4 is the address of net sales amount for this year ($153,000).

A movable highlighted area "points" to the *current cell*. This highlighted area, which is appropriately called the **pointer,** can be moved around the spreadsheet with the cursor control keys to any cell address. To add, delete, or edit an entry at a particular cell, the pointer must be located at the desired cell. The address and content of the current cell (location of the pointer) are displayed in the *control panel* (C4 and A4 in Figure S-10) and the content or resultant value (from a formula) of the current cell is displayed in reverse video (e.g., black on white with monochrome monitors) in the spreadsheet display.

Cell Entries. To make an entry in the spreadsheet, simply move the pointer with the cursor control keys to the appropriate cell and key in the data. To *edit* or replace an existing entry, you also move the pointer to the appropriate cell. The new or revised entry appears first in the control panel beside the cell address (see Figure S-10). Once you have completed work on a particular entry, press the carriage return or a cursor control key to make the entry in the actual spreadsheet. For example, let's say that "Net sales" in A4 was incorrectly entered initially as "New sales". To make the correction, the user would move the pointer to A4, indicate that the cell value is to be edited (usually an edit key), then delete the "w", insert a "t", and press the carriage return.

*Numeric*, *Label*, *and Formula Entries*. An entry to a cell is classified as a *numeric*, a *label*, or a *formula* entry. In Figure S-10, the entries in C4 and D4 are numeric. A label is a word, phrase, or any string of alphanumeric text (spaces included) that occupies a particular cell. In the example of Figure S-10, "This Year" in cell C2 is a label entry, as is "Net Sales" in A4 and "FORECAST VARIABLES FOR NEXT YEAR'S PRO RATA INCOME STATEMENT" in A34. Notice that the label in A34 extends across columns B and C. If an entry were made in B34, only the first 30 positions, or the width of column A, would be visible on the spreadsheet (e.g., "FORECAST VARIABLES FOR NEXT YE"). Spreadsheet packages permit the user to vary the column width to improve readability. The column width for columns B, C, and D is set at 15 positions.

Unless otherwise specified, numeric entries are right justified (lined up on the right) and label entries are left justified. However, you can specify that entries be left or right justified, or centered in the column. Note that the column heading in A2 is left justified and that the column headings in B2, C2, and D2 are right justified to improve the appearance of the spreadsheet.

Cells C10 and C14 contain formulas, but it is the numeric results (e.g., $13,740 and $14,145) that are displayed in the spreadsheet. The formula value of C10 (see Figure S-11) computes the operating profit

```
C10: +C4-C6-C7-C8
```

|    | A | B | C | D |
|----|---|---|---|---|
| 1  | ================================================================ | | | |
| 2  | ZIMCO INCOME STATEMENT ($1000) | Next Year | This Year | Last Year |
| 3  | ---------------------------------------------------------------- | | | |
| 4  | Net sales | $183,600 | $153,000 | $144,780 |
| 5  | Cost of sales & op. expenses | | | |
| 6  |   Cost of goods sold | 116,413 | 115,260 | 117,345 |
| 7  |   Depreciation | 4,125 | 4,125 | 1,500 |
| 8  |   Selling & admin. expenses | 19,875 | 19,875 | 15,000 |
| 9  | | ------------------------------------------- | | |
| 10 |   Operating profit | $43,187 | $13,740 | $10,935 |

**FIGURE S-11**
**Electronic Spreadsheet: Formulas**
The actual content of C10 is the formula in the control panel in the upper left-hand part of the screen. The result of the formula appears in the spreadsheet at C10.

(e.g., net sales less the cost of sales and operating expenses or +C4−C6−C7−C8). With the pointer at C10, the formula appears in the control panel and the actual numeric value appears in the spreadsheet. When the pointer is moved six rows up to C4, the actual numeric value (153000) is displayed in the control panel and an optional *edited* version (with $ and comma) is displayed in cell C4 (see Figure S-11).

Spreadsheet formulas use standard notation for **arithmetic operators:** + (add), − (subtract), * (multiply), / (divide), ˆ (raising to a power, or exponentiation). The formula contained in C10 (top of Figure S-11) computes the operating profit for "This Year". Compare this formula:

    +C4−C6−C7−C8

to the formula in cell D10 (below):

    +D4−D6−D7−D8

The formulas are similar, but the first formula references those amounts in column C and the second formula references those amounts in column D.

*Relative and Absolute Cell Addressing.* Monroe Green, Zimco's VP of Finance and Accounting, uses the income statement spreadsheet template of Figure S-10 to create "what if" scenarios. For example, the VP of the Operations Division has told him that he is implementing a number of cost-cutting measures. He anticipates that the Operations Division can hold the "cost of goods sold" to a 1 percent increase, even though more products will be built and shipped. The VP of Sales and Marketing has predicted that next year will be a "great year" and net sales will increase by 20 percent. The president of Zimco has asked all managers to "hold the line" on all selling and administrative expenses; therefore, these expenses are expected to remain about the same.

With spreadsheet software, Monroe was able to answer the question: "What if the cost-of-goods-sold increased by 1 percent, sales increased by 20 percent, and everything else remained the same for the coming year?" Monroe entered only the three forecast variables in C36, C37, and C38 (see Figure S-10) to get the pro rata income statement (the "Next Year" column of Figure S-10). All calculations (e.g., sales with a 20 percent increase, net profit, earnings per share, taxes) are performed automatically because the appropriate formulas are built into the spreadsheet template. The formulas that compute the "Next Year" values for net sales (B4), cost of goods sold (B6), and selling and administrative expenses (B8) are:

B4:   +C4*(1+$C$36)
B6:   +C6*(1+$C$37)
B8:   +C8*(1+$C$38)

Some entries are unchanged (e.g., depreciation, dividends, and interest); however, if Monroe wanted to reflect a change in depreciation, he would simply change the value of the "depreciation" entry in the "Next Year" column. The "provision for income tax" entry is extrapolated from the "This Year" column data by a formula that assumes the taxes will be paid at the same rate as the previous year [e.g., B18: (C18/ C17)*B17]. The distinction between the way the dollar amounts and the forecast variables are represented in the formulas highlights a very important concept of electronic spreadsheets, that of **relative cell addressing** and **absolute cell addressing.**

In creating the spreadsheet template for the income statement of Figure S-10, Monroe Green entered the operating profit formula only once: in C10 (see Figure S-11). Then spreadsheet commands were selected that *copied* or *replicated* the formula into cell D10. You can see from the results in Figure S-10 that the exact formula was not copied. Instead, the formula in D10 (+D4−D6−D7−D8) manipulates the data in the cells for "Last Year", not "This Year" (as in the formula in C10: +C4−C6−C7−C8). The same is true of other formulas that were copied from the "This Year" column to the "Last Year" column.

The formula in C10 references cells that have a "relative" position to C10, the location of the formula. When the formula in C10 is copied to D10, the electronic spreadsheet software revises these *relative cell addresses* so they apply to a formula that is located in D10. As you can see, the formula in D10 references cells that contain the data for "Last Year".

Each of the three forecast variables (C36 . . C38) is assigned an *absolute cell address*. The absolute cell address does not change when a formula in which it appears is copied from row to row or from column to column. The formula in B4 will always reference the forecast variable in cell C36, even if copied to any other location in the spreadsheet. In a formula, an absolute cell address is denoted by a dollar sign ($) prefix before the column and before the row (e.g., $C$36).

*The relative cell address is based on its position relative to the cell containing the formula.* When you copy or replicate a formula to another cell, the relative cell addresses are revised to reflect their

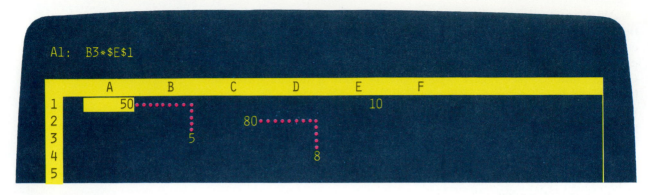

**FIGURE S-12**
**Electronic Spreadsheet:**
**Relative and Absolute Cell**
**Addressing**
When the formula in A1 is copied to C2, the formula in C2 becomes D4*$E$1.

new position relative to the new location of the formula. The absolute cell addresses remain unchanged. The two types of cell addressing are illustrated in the spreadsheet in Figure S-12. Suppose that the formula B3*$E$1 is in cell A1. B3 is a relative cell address that is one column to the right of and two rows down from A1. If this formula is copied to C2, the formula in C2 is D4*$E$1. Notice that D4 has the same relative position to the formula in cell C2: one column to the right and two rows down. The absolute cell address remains the same in both formulas.

You might ask: "Why beat around the bush? Why not just enter the value of the forecast variables directly in the formula?" Well, you could, but then Monroe would have to revise the formulas to do "what if" analysis.

Ranges.    Many electronic spreadsheet operations ask you to designate a **range.** The four types of ranges are highlighted in Figure S-13:

1. A single cell (example range is B12)

2. All or part of a column of adjacent cells (example range is A17 . . A20)

3. All or part of a row of adjacent cells (example range is B2 . . D2)

4. A rectangular block of cells (example range is B6 . . D8)

A particular range is depicted by the addresses of the endpoint cells and separated by two periods (some packages use only one period, e.g., C6.D8). Any cell can comprise a single cell range. The range for the total income amounts in Figure S-13 is B14 . . D14 and the range for the row labels is A4 . . A20. The range of the dollar amounts in the three income statements for "Next Year", "This Year", and "Last Year" data is depicted by any two opposite corner cell addresses (e.g., B4 . . D20 or D4 . . B20).

Many spreadsheet operations require users to designate one or several ranges. Do this by moving the pointer to an endpoint cell. Then you *anchor* the pointer by pressing a particular key, often a tab or a period. Once you have set the anchor (e.g., C6), move the pointer to the other endpoint (e.g., D8), press return, and you have defined the range (C6 . . D8). Ranges can also be defined by simply keying in the addresses of the endpoint cells.

|      | A | B | C | D |
|------|---|---|---|---|
| 1  | ============================================= | | | |
| 2  | ZIMCO INCOME STATEMENT ($1000) | Next Year | This Year | Last Year |
| 3  | ---------------------------------------- | | | |
| 4  | Net sales | $183,600 | $153,000 | $144,780 |
| 5  | Cost of sales & op. expenses | | | |
| 6  |   Cost of goods sold | 116,413 | 115,260 | 117,345 |
| 7  |   Depreciation | 4,125 | 4,125 | 1,500 |
| 8  |   Selling & admin. expenses | 19,875 | 19,875 | 15,000 |
| 9  | | | | |
| 10 |    Operating profit | $43,187 | $13,740 | $10,935 |
| 11 | Other income | | | |
| 12 |   Dividends and interest | 405 | 405 | 300 |
| 13 | | | | |
| 14 |    TOTAL INCOME | $43,492 | $14,145 | $11,235 |
| 15 | Less: interest on bonds | 2,025 | 2,025 | 2,025 |
| 16 | | | | |
| 17 | Income before tax | 41,567 | 12,120 | 9,210 |
| 18 | Provision for income tax | 18,777 | 5,475 | 4,160 |
| 19 | | | | |
| 20 |    NET PROFIT FOR YEAR | $22,790 | $6,645 | $5,050 |

The copy operation requires users to define a "copy from" range and a "copy to" range. When the operating profit formula in C10 was copied to the adjacent cell in the "Last Year" column, C10 was defined as the "copy from" range, and D10 was the "copy to" range. When you want to erase a portion of the spreadsheet, you first define the range that you wish to erase. For example, if you wish to erase the line of =s on row 1, you define the range to be A1 . . D1, then issue the erase command.

**Formatting Data for Readability.** The appearance of data in a spreadsheet can be modified to enhance readability. For example, the value .2 was entered as the projected change in sales in C36 (Figure S-10), but it appears in the spreadsheet display as a percent (20 percent). This is because the range C36 . . C38 was *formatted* so that the values are automatically displayed as percents rather than fractions (i.e., 0.2 becomes 20 percent). The methods of formatting data vary considerably between spreadsheet software packages.

Currency amounts can be formatted so that commas and a dollar sign are inserted. For example, in Figure S-10 the value for net sales

**FIGURE S-13**
**Electronic Spreadsheet: Ranges**
The four types of ranges are highlighted: cell (B12), column (A17..A20), row (B2..D2), and block (B6..D8).

for "This Year" is entered as 153000 in C4, which is formatted for currency. Notice that it is displayed as $153,000.

Numeric data can be defined so that they are displayed with a fixed number of places to the right of the decimal point. In Figure S-10, the format of the net sales data in the range B4 . . D4 is currency with the number of decimal places fixed at zero. The format of the market price data in the range B26 . . D26 is currency with the numbers of decimal positions fixed at two. Numbers with more decimal digits than specified in the format are rounded when displayed.

Creating Spreadsheet Formulas.   The three types of cell entries are numbers, labels, and formulas. This section expands on the use and application of formulas—the essence of spreadsheet operations.

A formula causes the spreadsheet software to perform numeric and/or string calculations and/or logic operations that result in a numeric value (e.g., 13740) or an alphanumeric character string (e.g., "ABOVE 25% LIMIT"). A formula may include one or all of the following: *arithmetic operations*, *functions*, and *logic operations*. Each is discussed below in more detail. The *string operations* (e.g., joining or concatenating character strings) capabilities are beyond the scope of this presentation.

When you design the spreadsheet, keep in mind where you want to place the formulas and what you want them to accomplish. Since formulas are based on relative position, you will need a knowledge of the layout and organization of the data in the spreadsheet. When you define a formula, you must first determine what you wish to achieve (e.g., calculate net profit). Then select a cell location for the formula (e.g., C20) and create the formula by connecting relative and absolute cell addresses with operators, as appropriate. In many instances, you will copy the formula to other locations (e.g., C20 was copied to D20) in Figure S-10.

Spreadsheet applications begin with a blank screen and an idea. The spreadsheet that you create is a product of skill and imagination. What you get out of a spreadsheet is very dependent on how effectively you use formulas.

*Arithmetic Operations*.   Formulas containing arithmetic operators are resolved according to a hierarchy of operations. That is, when more than one operator is included in a single formula, the spreadsheet software uses a set of rules to determine which operation to do first, second, and so on. In the hierarchy of operations, illustrated in Figure S-14, exponentiation has the highest priority, followed by multiplication-division and addition-subtraction. In the case of a tie (e.g., * and /, or + and −), the formula is evaluated from *left to right*. *Parentheses*, however, override the priority rules. Expressions placed in parentheses have priority and are evaluated innermost first, and left to right.

The formula that results in the value in B4 (183600) of Figure S-10 is shown below:

+C4*(1+$C$36)

| The Hierarchy of Operations | |
| --- | --- |
| **OPERATION** | **OPERATOR** |
| Exponentiation | ∧ |
| Multiplication-Division | *        / |
| Addition-Subtraction | +        − |

**FIGURE S-14**
**Hierarchy of Operations**

The parentheses in the cell B4 formula cause the expression inside the parentheses to be evaluated first; then the value of the expression is multiplied times the value in cell C4. All of the formulas in the spreadsheet of Figure S-10 are listed in Figure S-15.

Remember, once entered, these formulas can be copied such that they apply to a different set of data. For example, the earnings-per-share formula was entered in B27 and copied to the range C27 . . D27. Compare these three formulas in Figure S-15.

*Functions.* Electronic spreadsheets offer users a wide variety of pre-defined operations called **functions.** These functions can be used to create formulas that perform mathematical, logical, statistical, financial, and character-string operations on spreadsheet data. To use a function, simply preface the desired function name (e.g., AVG for average) with a prefix symbol (e.g., "@"; the symbol may vary between software packages), and enter the **argument.** The argument, which is placed in parentheses, identifies the data to be operated on. The argument can be one or several numbers, character strings, or ranges that represent data.

In the spreadsheet example of Figure S-10, the operating profit (C10) can be calculated (see the formula in Figure S-15) by subtracting the individual cell values under the "cost of sales and operating expenses" heading (C6, C7, and C8) from the net sales (C4).

C10: +C4−C6−C7−C8

Or the total of the "cost of sales and operating expenses" items can be computed with a function and its argument:

C10: +C4−@SUM(C6 . . C8)

The use of predefined functions can save a lot of time. What if the range to be summed was C6 . . C600?

In the same spreadsheet template, Monroe Green created a "THREE-YEAR SUMMARY DATA" section in the range A121 . . D127. He did this by copying the range A1 . . D20 (see Figure S-10) to the range A121 . . D140. He then edited the heading information to be as shown in row 122 of Figure S-16. Monroe then deleted unneeded rows of data to end up with the spreadsheet section in Figure S-16. In this section of the spreadsheet, Monroe used functions to calculate the overall average and to determine the minimum and maximum values for selected entries in the three-year income statement. To do this,

```
              A                        B            C            D
 1  ================================================================================
 2  ZIMCO INCOME STATEMENT ($1000)    Next Year    This Year    Last Year
 3  --------------------------------------------------------------------------------
 4  Net sales                         +C4*(1+$C$36)   153000      144780
 5  Cost of sales & op. expenses
 6    Cost of goods sold              +C6*(1+$C$37)   115260      117345
 7    Depreciation                    +C7             4125        1500
 8    Selling and admin. expenses     +C8*(1+$C$38)   19875       15000
 9                                    ------------------------------------
10       Operating profit            +B4-B6-B7-B8  +C4-C6-C7-C8  +D4-D6-D7-D8
11  Other income
12     Dividends and interest         +C12            405         300
13                                    ------------------------------------
14       TOTAL INCOME                 +B10+B12      +C10+C12    +D10+D12
15  Less: interest on bonds           +C15            2025        2025
16                                    ------------------------------------
17  Income before tax                 +B14-B15      +C14-C15    +D14-D15
18  Provision for income tax          (C18/C17)*B17   5475        4160
19                                    ------------------------------------
20       NET PROFIT FOR YEAR          +B17-B18      +C17-C18    +D17-D18
21  ================================================================================
22
23
24  ================================================================================
25  Shares outstanding                6300000       6000000     6000000
26  Market price                      21.25         14          13
27  Earnings per share                (B20*1000)/B25 (C20*1000)/C25 (D20*1000)/D25
28                                    ------------------------------------
29       Price-earnings ratio         +B26/B27      +C26/C27    +D26/D27
30  ================================================================================
31
32
33  ================================================================================
34  FORECAST VARIABLES FOR NEXT YEAR'S PRO RATA INCOME STATEMENT
35  --------------------------------------------------------------------------------
36  Projected change in sales                         0.2
37  Projected change in cost of goods sold            0.01
38  Projected change in administrative expenses       0
39  ================================================================================
```

**FIGURE S-15**
**Electronic Spreadsheet: Actual Content of Spreadsheet Cells**
This figure illustrates the actual content of all cells in Figure S-10. In an actual spreadsheet display, the formulas would be resolved when displayed (e.g., C10 would appear as $13,740) and the values would be displayed according to a preset format (e.g., C36 would appear as 20%).

**FIGURE S-16**
**Electronic Spreadsheet: Functions**
The average, maximum, and minimum spreadsheet functions are used to compute summary data in the range B124..D127.

```
B124: @AVG(B4..D4)

            A                B            C            D
121  ====================================================================
122  THREE-YEAR SUMMARY DATA    Average     Minimum      Maximum
123  --------------------------------------------------------------------
124  Net sales                  $160,460    $144,780     $183,600
125    Operating profit         $22,621     $10,935      $43,187
126    TOTAL INCOME             $22,991     $11,235      $43,592
127    NET PROFIT FOR YEAR      $11,495     $5,050       $22,790
```

he entered the following functions in B124, C124, and D124, respectively:

```
B124: @AVG(B4 . . D4)
C124: @MIN(B4 . . D4)
D124: @MAX(B4 . . D4)
```

The argument for each of these functions is the range of cells that represents the net sales for each of the three income statements. To complete the segment of the spreadsheet shown in Figure S-16, Monroe copied the contents of B4 [@AVG(B4 . . D4)] to the range B125 . . B127 (the "average" column), thereby making every entry in this column an average of the three years. He performed the same type of operation for the other two columns. These copy operations are possible because the formulas are automatically revised "relative" to their new position.

Other spreadsheet functions include: trigonometric functions, square root, comparisons of values, manipulations of strings of data, computation of Julian dates, computation of net present value and internal rate of return, and a variety of techniques for statistical analysis. Vendors of spreadsheet software create slightly different names for their functions.

*Logic Operations*.   Logical operations involve the use of **relational operators** and **logical operators** (see Figure S-17) to compare numeric and string values. The result of a logical operation is that an expression is either *true* or *false*.

Logical operations are used primarily in defining conditions for record selection (discussed in data management section) and in formulas containing an IF function. The format of the IF function is

@IF(*condition*, *result* [*condition true*], *result* [*condition false*])

The result in an IF function can be a number, a character string, or even another formula. The logical operators AND and OR (see Figure S-17) permit us to combine relational expressions in an IF function.

Suppose that Monroe wanted to include some data entry validation procedures in his spreadsheet template. He could ensure that realistic values are entered for the forecast variables by displaying a warning message in C40 in Figure S-10 if any of the values is above 25 percent.

| Relational Operators | |
|---|---|
| **COMPARISON** | **OPERATOR** |
| Equal to | = |
| Less than | < |
| Greater than | > |
| Less than or equal to | < = |
| Greater than or equal to | > = |
| Not equal to | <> |

| Logical Operators AND and OR | |
|---|---|
| **OPERATION** | **OPERATOR** |
| For the condition to be true: | |
| Both sub-conditions must be true | AND |
| At least one subcondition must be true | OR |

**FIGURE S-17**
**Relational and Logical Operators**

```
C40: @IF(C36>0.25#OR#C37>0.25#OR#C38>0.25, "ABOVE 25% LIMIT","")
```

|  | A | B | C | D |
|---|---|---|---|---|
| 33 | ================================================ | | | |
| 34 | FORECAST VARIABLES FOR NEXT YEAR'S PRO RATA INCOME STATEMENT | | | |
| 35 | ------------------------------------------------ | | | |
| 36 | Projected change in sales | | 50.00% | |
| 37 | Projected change in cost of goods sold | | 1.00% | |
| 38 | Projected change in administrative expenses | | 0.00% | |
| 39 | ================================================ | | | |
| 40 | | | ABOVE 25% LIMIT | |

**FIGURE S-18**
**Electronic Spreadsheet: Logical Operations**
An IF function in C40 (see discussion in text) serves as a data entry validation procedure. If any of the three forecast variables exceeds 25 percent, as is the case in this figure, the message, "ABOVE 25% LIMIT," is displayed in C40.

The following formula would perform the check on the data entered for the forecast variables.

@IF(C36>.25 # OR # C37>.25 # OR # C38>.25,"ABOVE 25% LIMIT","")

In the case of Figure S-10, where all forecast variables are less than 25 percent, no message ("" represents a null entry) is displayed because the condition is false. If any of the three forecast variables exceeds 25 percent, as in the case in Figure S-18, the message "ABOVE 25% LIMIT" is displayed in C40.

**Adding and Deleting Rows and Columns.** You can insert or delete entire rows and columns. For example, Monroe Green deleted rows in a duplicate copy of the income statement of Figure S-10 to produce the basis for compiling the spreadsheet of Figure S-16. If Monroe so desired, he could insert another "Year After Next" column in Figure S-10 such that what is now in columns B, C, and D would be moved over one column to columns C, D, and E. The "Year After Next" data would be in column B. The spreadsheet software automatically adjusts the relative cell addresses in the original spreadsheet data.

**Viewing Data in a Spreadsheet.** What if the spreadsheet template of Figure S-10 reflected data for the past five years? Since the screen on the monitor can display only a certain amount of information, Monroe would need to *scroll* horizontally through the spreadsheet to the first three years. To view spreadsheet areas that extend past the bottom of the screen, he would need to scroll vertically (e.g., the two parts of Figure S-10). Scrolling through a spreadsheet is much like looking through a magnifying glass as you move it around a page of a newspaper. You scroll left-right and/or up-down to view various portions of a large spreadsheet (see Figure S-19).

If Monroe were to scroll horizontally to view data from past years, row headings (e.g., Net sales, TOTAL INCOME, etc.) disappear from the screen to make room for other years of data. As you can imagine, data without labels can be very confusing. However, spreadsheet software has a solution to this dilemma: You can *freeze* selected columns or rows. In the example of Figure S-20, Monroe has frozen the leftmost

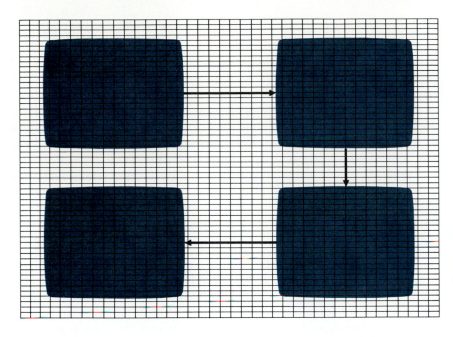

**FIGURE S-19**
**Electronic Spreadsheet:**
**Scrolling**
Scroll vertically and horizontally
to view those portions of a
spreadsheet that do not fit on a
single screen.

column (A), the row headings, at the left side of the screen so that
they are always visible when scrolling horizontally through the income
statements. When you freeze a portion of the screen, you are creating
a new border with labels, and everything moves on the screen but
the labels. Notice in Figure S-20 that the the "Next Year" and "This
Year" columns are off the screen, but the row labels remain. These
columns are returned to the screen when Monroe scrolls in the other
direction. The pointer cannot be positioned in a frozen area.

You can also freeze the rows at the top of the screen, the ones
that usually label a column. The freeze feature is particularly helpful
when the spreadsheet contains many rows or columns of data and
you want to work with only a few columns at a time.

**FIGURE S-20**
**Electronic Spreadsheet:**
**Freeze Column**
When column A is frozen at the
left of the screen, it is always
visible when scrolling
horizontally. In the figure, column
D is now adjacent to column A.

```
D10:   +D4-D6-D7-D8
                            A                    D
 1   ==================================================
 2   ZIMCO INCOME STATEMENT ($1000)      Last Year
 3   --------------------------------------------------
 4   Net sales                            $144,780
 5   Cost of sales & op. expenses
 6      Cost of goods sold                 117,345
 7      Depreciation                         1,500
 8      Selling and admin. expenses        15,000
 9                                        ----------------
10      Operating profit                  $10,935
```

## Use

Spreadsheet Templates.   The electronic spreadsheet of Figure S-10 is a *template*, or a model, of past years' income statements and a pro rata income statement. It can be used over and over for different purposes by different financial analysts. A template is analogous to a production program and a data base. It can be used again and again by different people with different sets of data. Next year the data now in the "This Year" column will be moved to the "Last Year" column and a new set of data will be entered for "This Year".

With electronic spreadsheets, a template is easily modified to fit a variety of situations. Another analyst may wish to modify the template slightly to handle quarterly income statements (only the column headings would be changed).

"What If" Analysis.   The real beauty of an electronic spreadsheet is that if you change the value of a cell in a spreadsheet, all other affected cells are revised accordingly. This capability makes spreadsheet software the perfect tool for "what if" analysis. For example, by using the spreadsheet template of Figure S-10, Monroe Green, Zimco's VP of Finance and Accounting, was able to answer the question: "What if sales increased by 20 percent, the cost of goods sold increased by 1 percent, and everything else remained the same for the coming year?" To produce the pro rata income statement (the "Next Year" column of Figure S-10), he entered appropriate values for the three forecast variables in C36, C37, and C38 (i.e., 0.2, 0.01, and 0 in Figure S-10).

Besides the pro rata income statement for "Next Year", Monroe wanted to monitor the *price-earnings ratio*, or the relationship that exists between the *earnings per share* and the *market price* of Zimco's stock. Data and the calculations for the price-earnings ratios are in the range B25 . . D29 in Figure S-10. The formulas and entries in the range B25 . . D29 are shown in Figure S-15. The earnings per share is calculated by dividing the net profit by the number of shares outstanding [e.g., for "This Year", $6,645,000/6,000,000 = $1.11, which is calculated by the formula in C27: (C20*1000)/C25 ]. The price-earnings ratio is calculated by dividing the current market price of Zimco stock by the earnings per share [e.g., for "This Year", $14.00/$1.11 = 12.64, which is calculated by the formula in C29: +C26/C27 ].

In the "Next Year" column of the price-earnings (P-E) ratio section of the spreadsheet, Monroe asked: "What if Zimco issued 300,000 new shares of stock and the market price of Zimco stock reached $21.25, what would the P-E ratio be?"

Over the years Zimco's president, Preston Smith, has learned to temper the optimistic estimates of his VPs with a touch of reality, so he used the spreadsheet template of Figure S-10 to create his own pessimistic pro rata income statement. This income statement reflects what he called the "worst-case scenario." Preston Smith needed only to change the three forecast variables (C36 . . C38) to get the results of Figure S-21. The results confirmed Preston's belief that the estimated P-E ratio is very sensitive to the estimates for sales and expenses. Compare the price-earnings ratio of the optimistic pro rata income statement in Figure S-10 (5.87) with the pessimistic pro rata income statement in Figure S-21 (17.94).

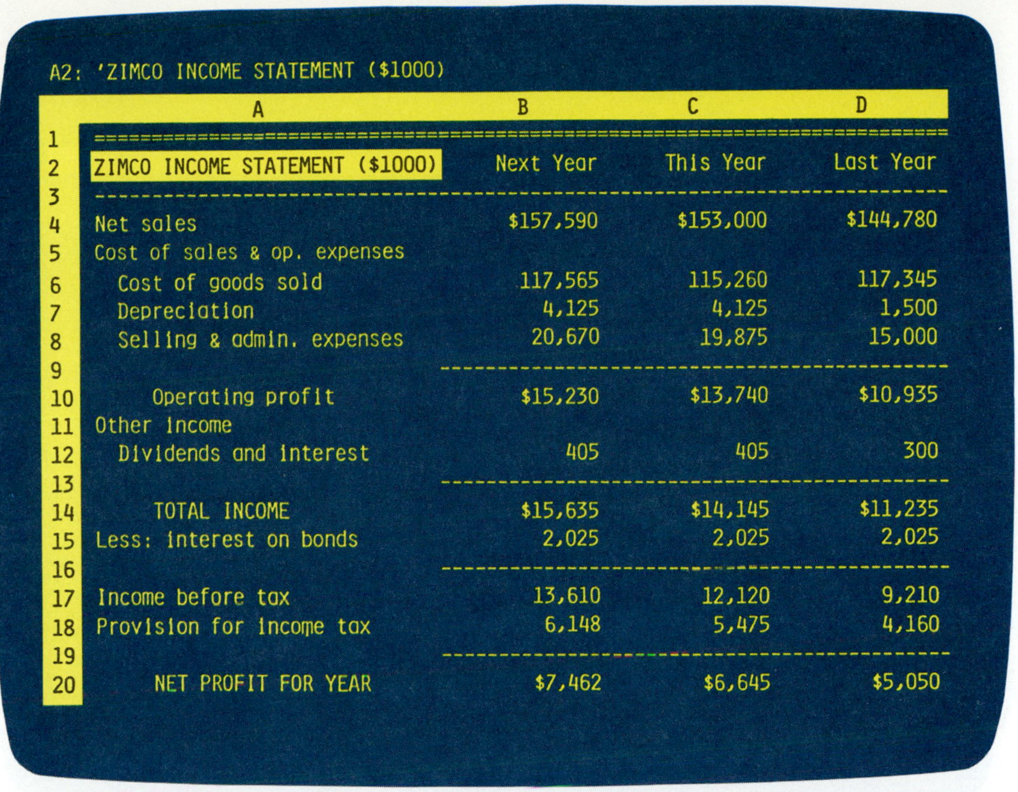

```
A2: 'ZIMCO INCOME STATEMENT ($1000)
```

|     | A | B | C | D |
|-----|---|---|---|---|
| 1   | ======================================= |
| 2   | ZIMCO INCOME STATEMENT ($1000) | Next Year | This Year | Last Year |
| 3   | ---------- |
| 4   | Net sales | $157,590 | $153,000 | $144,780 |
| 5   | Cost of sales & op. expenses | | | |
| 6   | Cost of goods sold | 117,565 | 115,260 | 117,345 |
| 7   | Depreciation | 4,125 | 4,125 | 1,500 |
| 8   | Selling & admin. expenses | 20,670 | 19,875 | 15,000 |
| 9   | | --------- | --------- | --------- |
| 10  | Operating profit | $15,230 | $13,740 | $10,935 |
| 11  | Other income | | | |
| 12  | Dividends and interest | 405 | 405 | 300 |
| 13  | | --------- | --------- | --------- |
| 14  | TOTAL INCOME | $15,635 | $14,145 | $11,235 |
| 15  | Less: interest on bonds | 2,025 | 2,025 | 2,025 |
| 16  | | --------- | --------- | --------- |
| 17  | Income before tax | 13,610 | 12,120 | 9,210 |
| 18  | Provision for income tax | 6,148 | 5,475 | 4,160 |
| 19  | | --------- | --------- | --------- |
| 20  | NET PROFIT FOR YEAR | $7,462 | $6,645 | $5,050 |

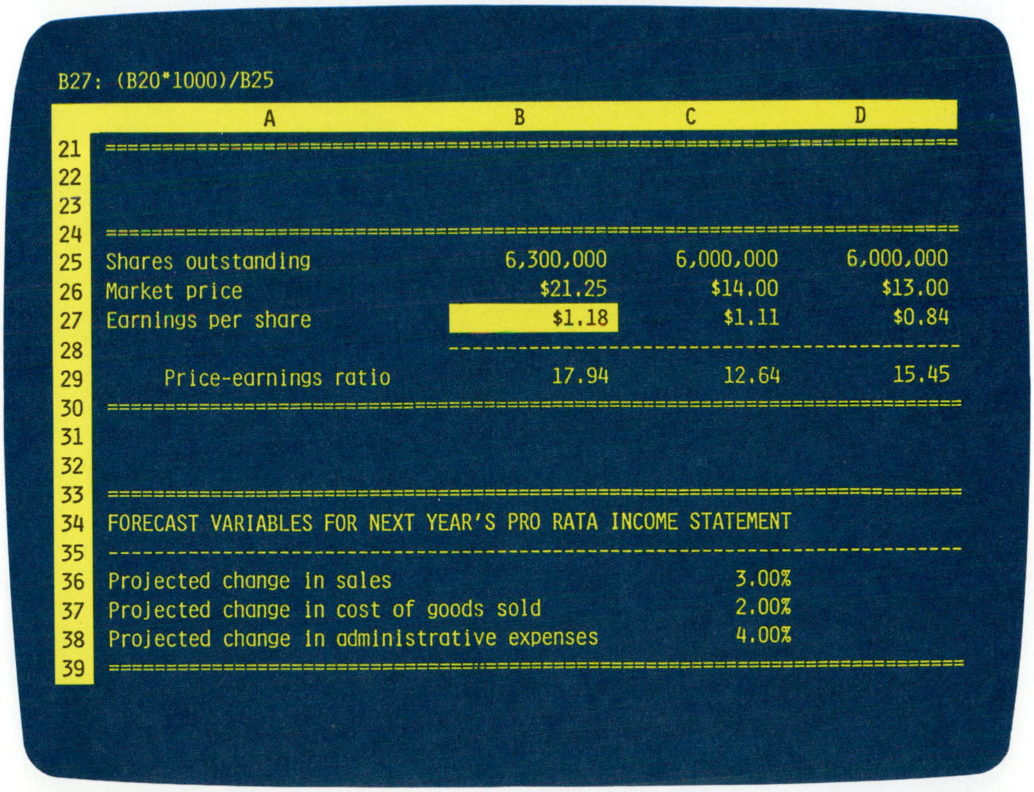

```
B27: (B20*1000)/B25
```

|     | A | B | C | D |
|-----|---|---|---|---|
| 21  | ======================================= |
| 22  | |
| 23  | |
| 24  | ======================================= |
| 25  | Shares outstanding | 6,300,000 | 6,000,000 | 6,000,000 |
| 26  | Market price | $21.25 | $14.00 | $13.00 |
| 27  | Earnings per share | $1.18 | $1.11 | $0.84 |
| 28  | | --------- | --------- | --------- |
| 29  | Price-earnings ratio | 17.94 | 12.64 | 15.45 |
| 30  | ======================================= |
| 31  | |
| 32  | |
| 33  | |
| 34  | FORECAST VARIABLES FOR NEXT YEAR'S PRO RATA INCOME STATEMENT |
| 35  | ---------- |
| 36  | Projected change in sales | | 3.00% | |
| 37  | Projected change in cost of goods sold | | 2.00% | |
| 38  | Projected change in administrative expenses | | 4.00% | |
| 39  | ======================================= |

**FIGURE S-21**
**Electronic Spreadsheet: An Income Statement Template**
This electronic spreadsheet display is the same as the one in Figure S-10 except that the forecast variables
in C36..C38 have been changed from 20%, 1%, and 0% to 3%, 2%, and 4%, respectively.

C53:   @SUM (C47..C51)

| | A | B | C | D |
|---|---|---|---|---|
| 41 | ============================================ | | | |
| 42 | ZIMCO BALANCE SHEET ($1000) | | This Year | Last Year |
| 43 | -------------------------------------------- | | | |
| 44 | ASSETS | | | |
| 45 | -------------------------------------------- | | | |
| 46 | Current assets | | | |
| 47 |   Cash | | $6,750 | $4,500 |
| 48 |   Marketable securities @ cost | | $12,750 | $6,900 |
| 49 |   Accounts receivable | | | |
| 50 |     Less: bad debt allowance | | $30,000 | $28,500 |
| 51 |   Inventories | | $40,500 | $45,000 |
| 52 | | | ------------ | ------------ |
| 53 |     Total current assets | | $90,000 | $84,900 |
| 54 | | | | |
| 55 | Fixed assets | | | |
| 56 |   Land | | 6,750 | $6,750 |
| 57 |   Building | | $55,500 | $52,500 |
| 58 |   Machinery | | $14,250 | $12,750 |
| 59 |   Office equipment | | $1,500 | $1,425 |
| 60 | | | ------------ | ------------ |

C71:   +C53+C64+C67+C69

| | A | B | C | D |
|---|---|---|---|---|
| 61 | | | $78,000 | $73,425 |
| 62 |     Less: accum. depreciation | | $27,000 | $22,500 |
| 63 | | | ------------ | ------------ |
| 64 |     Net fixed assets | | $51,000 | $50,925 |
| 65 | | | | |
| 66 | | | | |
| 67 | Prepayments & deferred charges | | $1,500 | $1,350 |
| 68 | | | | |
| 69 | Intangibles (goodwill, patents) | | $1,500 | $1,500 |
| 70 | | | ------------ | ------------ |
| 71 | TOTAL ASSETS | | $144,000 | $138,675 |
| 72 | | | ============================================ | |
| 73 | | | | |
| 74 | -------------------------------------------- | | | |
| 75 | LIABILITIES | | | |
| 76 | -------------------------------------------- | | | |
| 77 | Current liabilities | | | |
| 78 |   Accounts payable | | $15,000 | $14,100 |
| 79 |   Notes payable | | $12,750 | $15,000 |
| 80 |   Accrued expenses payable | | $4,950 | $4,500 |

```
C100: +C89+C98
```

| | A | B | C | D |
|---|---|---|---|---|
| 81 | Federal income taxes payable | | $4,800 | $4,350 |
| 82 | | | ------------- | ------------- |
| 83 | Total current liabilities | | $37,500 | $37,950 |
| 84 | | | | |
| 85 | Long-term liabilities | | | |
| 86 | First mortgage bonds; | | | |
| 87 | 9% interest, due 2000 | | $40,500 | $40,500 |
| 88 | | | ------------- | ------------- |
| 89 | Total liabilities | | $78,000 | $78,450 |
| 90 | ------------- | | ------------- | ------------- |
| 91 | STOCKHOLDERS' EQUITY | | | |
| 92 | | | ------------- | ------------- |
| 93 | Common stock, $5 par; | | | |
| 94 | 6,000,000 shares outstanding | | $30,000 | $30,000 |
| 95 | Capital surplus | | $10,500 | $10,500 |
| 96 | Retained earnings | | $25,500 | $19,725 |
| 97 | | | ------------- | ------------- |
| 98 | Total stockholders' equity | | $66,000 | $60,225 |
| 99 | ------------- | | ------------- | ------------- |
| 100 | TOTAL LIABILITIES & STOCKHOLDERS' EQUITY | | $144,000 | $138,675 |

**FIGURE S-22**
**Electronic Spreadsheet: A Balance Sheet Template**
Shown on page 428 and above, the electronic spreadsheet representation of the Zimco balance sheets for the last two years is included in rows 41 through 100 of a spreadsheet template. The income statement template of Figures S-10 and S-21 is on rows 1 through 40 of the same spreadsheet.

## Spreadsheet Summary

The possibilities of what Monroe Green, Preston Smith, you, and others can do with electronic spreadsheet software and micros are endless. For example, Monroe can add the Zimco balance sheets for the last two years (see Figure S-22) to the spreadsheet of Figure S-10 to create even more "what if" scenarios. With the income statement and the balance sheet in the same spreadsheet, he can change values in Zimco's financial statements to see how various financial indices, such as the net working capital (current assets minus current liabilities), the current ratio (current assets divided by current liabilities), and the inventory turnover (net sales divided by inventories), are affected. The formulas for the "This Year" balance sheet in Figure S-22 are listed in Figure S-23 to give you one more example of how formulas are used in an electronic spreadsheet template.

| Cell | Formula |
|---|---|
| C53 | @ SUM (C47 . . C51) |
| C61 | @ SUM (C56 . . C59) |
| C64 | +C61−C62 |
| C71 | +C53+C64+C67+C69 |
| C83 | @ SUM (C78 . . C81) |
| C89 | +C83+C87 |
| C98 | @ SUM (C94 . . C96) |
| C100 | +C89+C98 |

**FIGURE S-23**
**Electronic Spreadsheet: Formulas in Balance Sheet Template of Figure S-22**
These are the formulas for the "This Year" column of the balance sheet spreadsheet in Figure S-22.

## REVIEW EXERCISES (S-4)

1.  Describe the layout of an electronic spreadsheet.
2.  Give an example cell address. Which portion of the address depicts the row and which portion depicts the column?
3.  On what is a relative cell address based?
4.  Give an example of each of the four types of ranges.
5.  Give examples of the three types of entries that can be made in an electronic spreadsheet.
6.  What types of operators are used to compare numeric and string values?
7.  Write the equivalent formula for @AVG(A1 . . D1) without the use of functions.
8.  If the formula B2*$B$1 is copied from C1 to E3, what is the formula in E3? If the formula in E3 is copied to D45, what is the formula in D45?
9.  What is the difference between the pointer and the cursor?
10. List three alternatives descriptors for the range A4 . . P12.
11. When do you "anchor the pointer"?
12. What would you use in a formula to override the priority rules for arithmetic operators?
13. What formula would be entered in A5 to sum all numbers in the range A1 . . A4?
14. When would you need to scroll horizontally? Vertically?
15. What is a spreadsheet template?

## HANDS-ON EXERCISES

1.  The following data represent the unit sales data for the past year for Diolab, Inc., a manufacturer of a diagnostic laboratory instrument that is sold primarily to hospitals and clinics.

| | DIOLAB INC. SALES (UNITS) | | | |
|---|---|---|---|---|
| REGION | QTR1 | QTR2 | QTR3 | QTR4 |
| NE REGION | 214 | 300 | 320 | 170 |
| SE REGION | 120 | 150 | 165 | 201 |
| SW REGION | 64 | 80 | 60 | 52 |
| NW REGION | 116 | 141 | 147 | 180 |

Enter the title, headings, and data in an electronic spreadsheet. Place the title in the range B1, the column headings in the range

A2 . . E2, the row headings in the range A3 . . A6, and the
sales data in the range B3 . . E6.

If the following assignments are to be handed in, print out
the initial spreadsheets, then print them out again for each
revision.

2. Add another column heading called SALES/YR in F2 of the
Diolab spreadsheet. Enter a formula in F3 that sums the sales
for each quarter for the northeast region. Copy the formula
to the range F4 . . F6. SALES/YR should be 1004 for the NE
Region and 636 for the SE Region.

3. Add average sales per quarter, AVG/QTR, in column G. AVG/
QTR should be 251 for the NE Region and 159 for the SE Region.

4. Add two more columns that reflect sales per salesperson. In
column H, add number of salespersons per region, PERSONS:
5, 3, 2, and 4, respectively. In column I, add formulas that compute sales per person, SALES/PER (from the data in SALES/
YR and PERSONS columns). SALES/PER should be 200.8 for
the NE Region and 212 for the SE Region.

5. In the range B8 . . F8, use functions to total sales for each
quarter and for the year. The total sales for all regions should
be 2480.

6. Copy the range A2 . . A6 to A12 . . A16 and B2 . . E2 to
B12 . . E12. Diolab, Inc., sales are estimated to be 120 percent
of last year's sales. Complete the newly created spreadsheet
by multiplying last year's quarterly sales data by 1.2 and placing
the result in the spreadsheet. Title this set of data ESTIMATED
DIOLAB INC. SALES - NEXT YEAR. The NE Region first-quarter sales should be 257 (rounded) and the SE Region second-
quarter sales should be 180.

7. Each of the lab analysis units sells for $2000. Add formulas
in column F to compute estimated GROSS sales ($2000 times
the total of the estimated quarterly sales) for each region. Also
format the GROSS sales values as currency with no decimal
places such that the NE Region amount appears as $2,409,600
(SE Region is $1,526,400). You may need to expand the width
of column F to 11 positions.

## S-5  DATA MANAGEMENT

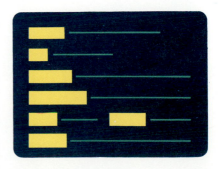

### Function

With data management software, you can create and maintain a data
base and extract information from the data base. To use data management or "database" software, you first identify the format of the data,
then design a display format that will permit interactive entry and
revision of the data base. Once the data base is created, its *records*
(related data about a particular event or thing) can be deleted or revised
and other records can added to the data base. "Database," as one

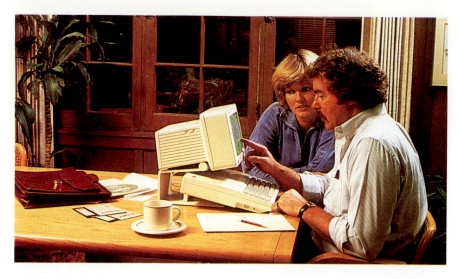

When learning to use a data base package or any other micro productivity tool, it is always handy to have a knowledgeable friend (or instructor) who can help you over the rough spots.
(Courtesy of Apple Computer, Inc.)

word, is an alternative terminology for data management software. "Data base," as two words, refers to the highest level of the hierarchy of data organization.

All database software packages have the following fundamental capabilities:

1. Create and maintain (e.g., add, delete, and revise records) a data base.
2. Extract and list all records or only those records that meet certain conditions.
3. Make an inquiry (e.g., the average value of a particular field in a series of records).
4. Sort records in ascending or descending sequence by primary, secondary, and tertiary fields.
5. Generate formatted reports with subtotals and totals.

The more sophisticated packages include a variety of other features, such as spreadsheet-type computations, graphics, and programming.

## Concepts

Many similarities exist between commercially available word processing packages and between commercially available electronic spreadsheet packages. With word processing, the user sees and manipulates lines of text. With electronic spreadsheets, the user sees and manipulates data in numbered rows and lettered columns. This is not the case with data management packages. All commercial software packages permit the creation and manipulation of data bases, but what the user sees on the screen may be vastly different for the various packages. However, the concepts embodied in these database packages are very similar. The conceptual coverage that follows is generic and can be applied to all database packages; however, the examples are oriented to dBASE II and dBASE III products of Ashton-Tate.

The organization of the data in a microcomputer data base is similar to the traditional hierarchy of data organization. Related **fields,** such as course identification number, course title, and course type are grouped to form **records** (e.g., the course record in the COURSE data base in Figure S-24). A collection of related records make up a data **file** or a **data base.** In data management software terminology, "file" and "data base" are often used interchangeably.

### FIGURE S-24
**Data Management: COURSE Data Base and TRAINING Data Base**
The COURSE data base contains a record for each course that Zimco offers to its employees. The TRAINING data base contains a record for each Zimco employee who is enrolled in or has taken a course.

| Record# | ID | TITLE | TYPE | SOURCE | DURATION |
|---|---|---|---|---|---|
| 1 | 100 | MIS Orientation | in-house | Staff | 24 |
| 2 | 201 | Micro Overview | in-house | Staff | 8 |
| 3 | 2535 | Intro to Info. Proc. | media | Takdel Inc | 40 |
| 4 | 310 | Programming Stds. | in-house | Staff | 6 |
| 5 | 3223 | BASIC Programming | media | Takdel Inc | 40 |
| 6 | 7771 | Data Base Systems | media | Takdel Inc | 30 |
| 7 | CIS11 | Business COBOL | college | St. Univ. | 45 |
| 8 | EX15 | Local Area Networks | vendor | HAL Inc | 30 |
| 9 | MGT10 | Mgt. Info. Systems | college | St. Univ. | 45 |
| 10 | VC10 | Elec. Spreadsheet | media | VidCourse | 20 |
| 11 | VC44 | 4th Generation Lang. | media | VidCourse | 30 |
| 12 | VC88 | Word Processing | media | VidCourse | 18 |

COURSE data base

| Record# | ID | EMPLOYEE | DEPARTMENT | START | STATUS |
|---|---|---|---|---|---|
| 1 | VC10 | Bell, Jim | Marketing | 01/12/87 | I |
| 2 | VC10 | Austin, Jill | Finance | 01/12/87 | I |
| 3 | VC10 | Targa, Phil | Finance | 01/12/87 | C |
| 4 | VC88 | Day, Elizabeth | Accounting | 03/18/87 | C |
| 5 | VC88 | Fitz, Paula | Finance | 04/04/87 | I |
| 6 | MGT10 | Mendez, Carlos | Accounting | 01/15/87 | I |
| 7 | EX15 | Adler, Phyllis | Marketing | 02/10/87 | W |
| 8 | 100 | Targa, Phil | Finance | 01/04/87 | C |
| 9 | 100 | Johnson, Charles | Marketing | 01/10/87 | C |
| 10 | 100 | Klein, Ellen | Accounting | 01/10/87 | C |

TRAINING data base

The best way to illustrate and demonstrate the concepts of data management software is by example. Ed Cool, Zimco's education coordinator, uses a micro-based data management software package to help him with his record-keeping tasks. To do this, Ed created two data bases. The COURSE data base (see Figure S-24) contains a record for each course that Zimco offers to their employees and for several courses at State University, for which Zimco provides tuition reimbursement. Each record in the COURSE data base contains the following fields:

- Identification number (supplied by Zimco for in-house courses, by vendors, and by State University)
- Title of course
- Type of course (in-house seminar, multimedia, college or vendor seminar)
- Source of course (Zimco staff or supplier of course)
- Duration (number of hours required to complete course)

The TRAINING data base (see Figure S-24) contains a record for each Zimco employee who is enrolled in or has taken a course. Each record contains the following fields:

- Identification number (cross-reference to COURSE data base)
- Employee (name of Zimco employee)
- Department (department affiliation of employee)
- Start (date course was begun)
- Status (employee's status code: I = incomplete, W = withdrawn from course, C = completed course)

Creating a Data Base.     To create a data base, the first thing you do is to set up a *screen format* that will enable you to enter the data for a record. The data entry screen format is analogous to a hard-copy form that contains labels and blank lines (e.g., medical questionnaire, employment application). Data are entered and edited (deleted or revised) with data management software one record at a time, like they are on hard-copy forms.

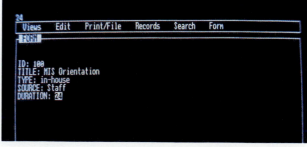

| Field no. | Field name | Field type | Field length | Decimal positions |
|-----------|-----------|-----------|-------------|-------------------|
| 1 | ID | Character | 5 | |
| 2 | TITLE | Character | 20 | |
| 3 | TYPE | Character | 8 | |
| 4 | SOURCE | Character | 10 | |
| 5 | DURATION | Numeric | 4 | 0 |

**FIGURE S-25**
**Data Management: Structure of the COURSE Data Base**

*The Structure of the Data Base.* To set up a data entry screen format you must first specify the *structure* of the data base by identifying the characteristics of each field in the data base. This is done interactively, with the system prompting you to enter the field name, field type, and so on (see Figure S-25). For example, the ID field in Figure S-25 is a five-character field. The *field name* is ID; the *field length* is five characters; and the *field type* is character. A character field type can be a single word or any alphanumeric (i.e., numbers, letters, and special characters) phrase up to several hundred characters in length. For numeric field types, you must specify the maximum number of digits (field length) and the number of decimal positions that you wish to have displayed. Since the course durations are all defined in whole hours, the number of decimal positions for the DURATION field is set at zero (see Figure S-25).

*Entering and Editing a Data Base.* The screen format for entering, editing, and adding records to the COURSE data base is shown in Figure S-26. This screen is generated automatically from the specifications outlined in the structure of the COURSE data base (see Figure S-25). To create the COURSE data base, Ed Cool issued a command

The data entry screen for the training data base of Figure S-24 is shown as it would appear for three popular data management packages. The first photo illustrates how the data entry screen would be displayed using dBASE III (dBASE III is a trademark of Ashton-Tate). The second photo illustrates how the data entry screen would be displayed using Reflex, an integrated package (Reflex-The Analyst is a trademark of BORELAND Analytica, Inc.). The third photo illustrates how the data entry screen would be displayed using Symphony, also an integrated package (Symphony is a trademark of the Lotus Development Corporation).
(Long and Associates)

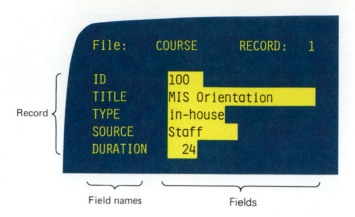

**FIGURE S-26**
**Data Management: Data Entry Screen Format**
Illustrated is the screen format for entering, editing, and adding records to the COURSE data base. This screen is automatically generated from the specifications outlined in structure of the COURSE data base (see Figure S-25).

that called up the data entry screen of Figure S-26, then he entered the data for first record, then the second record, and so on. On most data management systems, the records are automatically assigned a number as they are entered. The reverse video portion of the screen in Figure S-26 comprises the data for the five fields in record "1".

To add a record to an existing COURSE data base, Ed would issue a command such as *append* or *add*. This command displays the format screen of Figure S-26 (without data) so that he can enter the data for the new record(s). Each additional record is assigned the record number that is one greater than the current total. To edit a record, Ed would issue a command such as *edit* in conjunction with the desired record number (e.g., record 1) or a qualifier (e.g., ID='100'). The desired record would then appear superimposed over the format screen, as in Figure S-26. Changes are made to fields in the format screen in much the same way that you would change text in a word processing document.

Setting Conditions for Record Selection.  Data management software also permits you to retrieve, view, and print records based on preset conditions. You set conditions for the selection of records by composing a *relational expression* that reflects the desired conditions. The relational expression normally compares one or more field names to numbers or character strings using the *relational operators* discussed in the skills section on electronic spreadsheet software (see Figure S-17). Several expressions can be combined in a single condition with *logical operators* (see Figure S-17).

Ed Cool wanted a listing of all in-house seminars, so he issued commands to *locate* (*search* for) then *list* the records of all courses that are of TYPE "in-house" in the COURSE data base (see Figure S-24). To retrieve these records, he set the condition to

TYPE='in-house'

Depending on the data management package, the *search string* is enclosed in single or double quotes (e.g., "in-house"). We'll use single quotes. To produce the output of Figure S-27, Ed keyed in the command

LIST FOR TYPE='in-house'

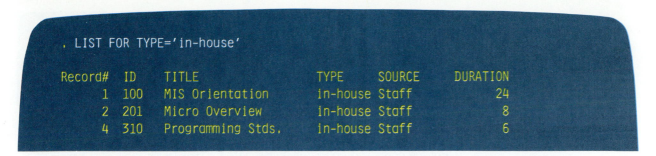

**FIGURE S-27**
**Data Management: Conditional Search and List**
For the command, LIST FOR TYPE='in-house,' only the records from the
COURSE data base (Figure S-24) for which TYPE='in-house' are displayed.

Of course, one of the options is to route the output to a display screen
or to a printer. If Ed wanted only the ID and TITLE for those records
that meet the condition TYPE='in-house', he would enter a command
like this:

    LIST ID, TITLE FOR TYPE='in-house'

Figure S-28 shows the output.

**Data Base Inquiries.**   You can "page" through the data base by moving
from record to record. You can view a particular record by entering
the record number that is supplied by the software or by entering certain
selection condition(s) (e.g., ID='EX15'). Database software also permits
inquiries that involve parts or all of one or more records. To extract,
then list (display, print, or edit) selected records from a data base,
you must first establish the condition or conditions. The following relational expressions establish conditions that will select or extract records (noted to the right of the expression) from the COURSE data
base of Figure S-24.

| | |
|---|---|
| TYPE='in-house' .AND. DURATION<=10 | records 2 and 4 (see Figure S-29) |
| SOURCE='VidCourse' .OR. SOURCE='Takdel Inc' | records 3, 5, 6, 10, 11, 12 |
| DURATION>15 .AND. DURATION<25 | records 1, 10, 12 |
| ID='CIS11' | record 7 |

```
. LIST ID,  TITLE FOR TYPE='in-house'

    Record#  ID    TITLE
          1  100   MIS Orientation
          2  201   Micro Overview
          4  310   Programming Stds.
```

**FIGURE S-28**
**Data Management: Conditional
Search and List, Specified**
Fields Only For the command,
LIST ID, TITLE FOR TYPE='in-
house,' only the ID and TITLE
fields for the records from the
COURSE data base (Figure S-
24) for which TYPE='in-house'
are displayed.

```
, LIST FOR TYPE='in-house' .AND. DURATION<=10
  Record# ID      TITLE                TYPE      SOURCE      DURATION
        2 201     Micro Overview       in-house  Staff              8
        4 310     Programming Stds.    in-house  Staff              6
```

**FIGURE S-29**
**Data Management: Conditional Expression with AND Operator**
For the command, TYPE='in-house' .AND. DURATION<=10, only the records
from the COURSE data base (Figure S-24) for which TYPE='in-house' *and*
DURATION <=(less than or equal to) 10 are displayed.

The process of selecting records by setting conditions is sometimes
called *filtering*; that is, those records or fields that you don't want
are "filtered out" of the display.

Besides filtering, you can also make inquiries to the data base
that result in a display of calculated information. For example, Ed
Cool wanted to know the total number of in-house seminar hours that
are made available to Zimco employees. To do this, he issued the
following command for the COURSE data base:

SUM DURATION FOR SOURCE='Staff'

The result, 38 (24+8+6), is displayed on the screen. To obtain the average duration of all courses, Ed issued this command:

AVERAGE DURATION

This command causes the average of all course durations (28) to be
displayed on the screen. Similarly, Ed issued this command to COUNT
the number of 'VidCourse' courses in the COURSE data base:

COUNT FOR SOURCE='VidCourse'

The result of 3 is displayed on the monitor.

**Sorting Records.**   Data can also be sorted for display in a variety of
formats. For example, the COURSE data base in Figure S-24 has been
sorted and is displayed in ascending order by course identification
number (ID). To obtain this sequencing of the data base records, Ed
Cool selected ID as the *key field* and requested an ascending sort of
the COURSE data base. Numbers are considered "less than" alphabetic
characters; therefore, the numeric IDs are listed before those that begin
with a letter.

Ed also wanted a presentation of the COURSE data base that was
sorted by ID within SOURCE. This involves the selection of a *primary*
and a *secondary key field*. Ed selected SOURCE as the primary key
field, but he wanted the courses offered by each source to be listed
in ascending order by ID. To achieve this record sequence, he selected
ID as the secondary key field. In most database packages, the issuing
of a sort command results in the compilation of a temporary data base.
After the sort operation, the temporary data base contains the records
in the order described in the sort command (see Figure S-30). Notice

```
    Record#  ID    TITLE                 TYPE     SOURCE       DURATION
          1  EX15  Local Area Networks   vendor   HAL Inc          30
          2  CIS11 Business COBOL        college  St. Univ.        45
          3  MGT11 Mgt. Info. Systems    college  St. Univ.        45
          4  100   MIS Orientation       in-house Staff            24
          5  201   Micro Overview        in-house Staff             8
          6  310   Programming Stds.     in-house Staff             6
          7  2535  Intro to Info. Proc.  media    Takdel Inc       40
          8  3223  BASIC Programming     media    Takdel Inc       40
          9  7771  Data Base Systems     media    Takdel Inc       30
         10  VC10  Elec. Spreadsheet     media    VidCourse        20
         11  VC44  4th Generation Lang.  media    VidCourse        30
         12  VC88  Word Processing       media    VidCourse        18
```

**FIGURE S-30**
**Data Management: COURSE Data Base Sorted by ID within SOURCE**
This display is the result of a sort operation on the COURSE data base with
the SOURCE field as the primary key field and the ID field as the secondary
key field.

in Figure S-30 that the SOURCE field entries are in alphabetical order
and the three "Staff" records (i.e., records 4, 5, and 6) are in sequence
by ID (e.g., 100, 201, 310).

Ed used the temporary data base of Figure S-30 to produce the
listing of Figure S-31. To do this he issued the following command:

    LIST SOURCE, ID FOR TYPE='vendor' .OR. TYPE='media'

Because the entries in the SOURCE field are alphabetized in Figure
S-30, the selected SOURCE entries in Figure S-31 are also alphabetized.

**FIGURE S-31**
**Data Management: Conditional Expression with OR Operator**
For the command, LIST SOURCE, ID FOR TYPE='vendor' .OR. TYPE='media,'
only the records from the COURSE data base (as sorted in Figure S-30) for
which TYPE='vendor' or TYPE='media' are displayed.

```
. LIST SOURCE, ID FOR TYPE='vendor' .OR. TYPE='media'
Record#  SOURCE       ID
      1  HAL Inc      EX15
      7  Takdel Inc   2535
      8  Takdel Inc   3223
      9  Takdel Inc   7771
     10  VidCourse    VC10
     11  VidCourse    VC44
     12  VidCourse    VC88
```

## Report Generation

*"Quick and Dirty" Reports.*   A data base is a source of information and data management software provides the facility to get at this information. A *report* is the presentation of information that is derived from one or more data bases. The simple listings of selected records and fields in Figures S-27 through S-30 are "quick and dirty" reports. Such reports are the bread and butter of data base capabilities. These listings may not be fancy, but in most instances the user is more interested in the information than the format in which it is displayed. The generation of formatted reports is discussed in a later section.

*Combining Two Data Bases.*   Ed Cool wanted to produce a "quick and dirty" status report that contained an alphabetical listing of those

**FIGURE S-32**
**Data Management: Combining Two Data Bases**
A common ID field enables the "joining" of the TRAINING data base with the COURSE data base to produce the TEMP1 data base.

TRAINING data base

| Record# | ID | EMPLOYEE | DEPARTMENT | START | STATUS |
|---|---|---|---|---|---|
| 1 | VC10 | Bell, Jim | Marketing | 01/12/87 | I |
| 2 | VC10 | Austin, Jill | Finance | 01/12/87 | I |
| 3 | VC10 | Targa, Phil | Finance | 01/12/87 | C |
| 4 | VC88 | Day, Elizabeth | Accounting | 03/18/87 | C |
| 5 | VC88 | Fitz, Paula | Finance | 04/04/87 | I |
| 6 | MGT10 | Mendez, Carlos | Accounting | 01/15/87 | I |
| 7 | EX15 | Adler, Phyllis | Marketing | 02/10/87 | W |
| 8 | 100 | Targa, Phil | Finance | 01/04/87 | C |
| 9 | 100 | Johnson, Charles | Marketing | 01/10/87 | C |
| 10 | 100 | Klein, Ellen | Accounting | 01/10/87 | C |

+

COURSE data base

| Record# | ID | TITLE | TYPE | SOURCE | DURATION |
|---|---|---|---|---|---|
| 1 | 100 | MIS Orientation | in-house | Staff | 24 |
| 2 | 201 | Micro Overview | in-house | Staff | 8 |
| 3 | 2535 | Intro to Info. Proc. | media | Takdel Inc | 40 |
| 4 | 310 | Programming Stds. | in-house | Staff | 6 |
| 5 | 3223 | BASIC Programming | media | Takdel Inc | 40 |
| 6 | 7771 | Data Base Systems | media | Takdel Inc | 30 |
| 7 | CIS11 | Business COBOL | college | St. Univ. | 45 |
| 8 | EX15 | Local Area Networks | vendor | HAL Inc | 30 |
| 9 | MGT10 | Mgt. Info. Systems | college | St. Univ. | 45 |
| 10 | VC10 | Elec. Spreadsheet | media | VidCourse | 20 |
| 11 | VC44 | 4th Generation Lang. | media | VidCourse | 30 |
| 12 | VC88 | Word Processing | media | VidCourse | 18 |

TEMP1 data base

| Record# | EMPLOYEE | ID | TITLE | STATUS |
|---|---|---|---|---|
| 1 | Bell, Jim | VC10 | Elec. Spreadsheet | I |
| 2 | Austin, Jill | VC10 | Elec. Spreadsheet | I |
| 3 | Targa, Phil | VC10 | Elec. Spreadsheet | C |
| 4 | Day, Elizabeth | VC88 | Word Processing | C |
| 5 | Fitz, Paula | VC88 | Word Processing | I |
| 6 | Mendez, Carlos | MGT10 | Mgt. Info. Systems | I |
| 7 | Adler, Phyllis | EX15 | Local Area Networks | W |
| 8 | Targa, Phil | 100 | MIS Orientation | C |
| 9 | Johnson, Charles | 100 | MIS Orientation | C |
| 10 | Klein, Ellen | 100 | MIS Orientation | C |

employees who had completed courses (i.e., STATUS='C' on TRAIN-ING data base of Figure S-24) along with the IDs and TITLEs of the courses they had taken. He also wanted a similar status report for those employees whose STATUS was incomplete (i.e., STATUS='I'). Producing these reports is a little more challenging because the data required are on two different data bases. The EMPLOYEE name and STATUS fields are on the TRAINING data base and the course ID and TITLE fields are on the COURSE data base. Since the two data bases have a common field (ID), Ed can *join* the two data bases to get the reports he wants.

The following command "joins" the TRAINING data base with the COURSE data base and generates the temporary data base (TEMP1) of Figure S-32.

```
JOIN [TRAINING] WITH COURSE TO TEMP1 FOR COURSE–>ID=ID
FIELDS EMPLOYEE, ID, TITLE, STATUS
```

Since Ed wants the employee names to be listed alphabetically, he had to sort the resultant data base (TEMP1) on the EMPLOYEE field and create another temporary data base called TEMP2. He then issued the following commands to get the reports he wanted (Figure S-33):

```
LIST FOR STATUS='C'
LIST FOR STATUS='I'
```

The resultant reports are shown in Figure S-33.

**FIGURE S-33**
**Data Management: Reports Made Possible by Combining Two Data Bases**
For the command, LIST FOR STATUS='C,' only the records from the TEMP1 data base (Figure S-30) for which STATUS='C' (completed course) are displayed in the first list. For the command, LIST FOR STATUS='I,' only those records for which STATUS='I' (incomplete) are displayed in the second list.

```
. LIST FOR STATUS='C'
Record#  EMPLOYEE          ID      TITLE              STATUS
      4  Day, Elizabeth    VC88    Word Processing    C
      6  Johnson, Charles  100     MIS Orientation    C
      7  Klein, Ellen      100     MIS Orientation    C
      9  Targa, Phil       VC10    Elec. Spreadsheet  C
     10  Targa, Phil       100     MIS Orientation    C

. LIST FOR STATUS='I'
Record#  EMPLOYEE          ID      TITLE              STATUS
      2  Austin, Jill      VC10    Elec. Spreadsheet  I
      3  Bell, Jim         VC10    Elec. Spreadsheet  I
      5  Fitz, Paula       VC88    Word Processing    I
      8  Mendez, Carlos    MGT10   Mgt. Info. Systems I
```

*Customized Reports.* Data management software provides the capability to create customized or formatted reports. This capability allows you to design the *layout* of the report. This means that you have some flexibility in spacing and can include titles, subtitles, column headings, separation lines, and other elements that make a report more readable. The user describes the layout of the *customized* report interactively, then stores it for later recall. The result of the description, called a *report form*, is recalled from disk storage and merged with a data base to create the customized report. Managers often use this capability to generate periodic reports (e.g., weekly training status report).

Once a month Ed Cool generates four reports that summarize the courses being offered for each type of course; that is, one report summarizes Zimco's course offerings for TYPE='in-house', another for TYPE='media' (multimedia), and so on. One of these formatted reports is shown in Figure S-34. This summary report of "MULTIMEDIA COURSES" was compiled by merging a predefined report format with the COURSE data base (as sorted in Figure S-30). The layout of the report form called for a title, column headings, subheadings (for each SOURCE of TYPE='media'), plus subtotals and a total for DURATION. The formatted report of Figure S-34 is one of dozens that Ed Cool generates on a weekly and monthly basis by using data management software.

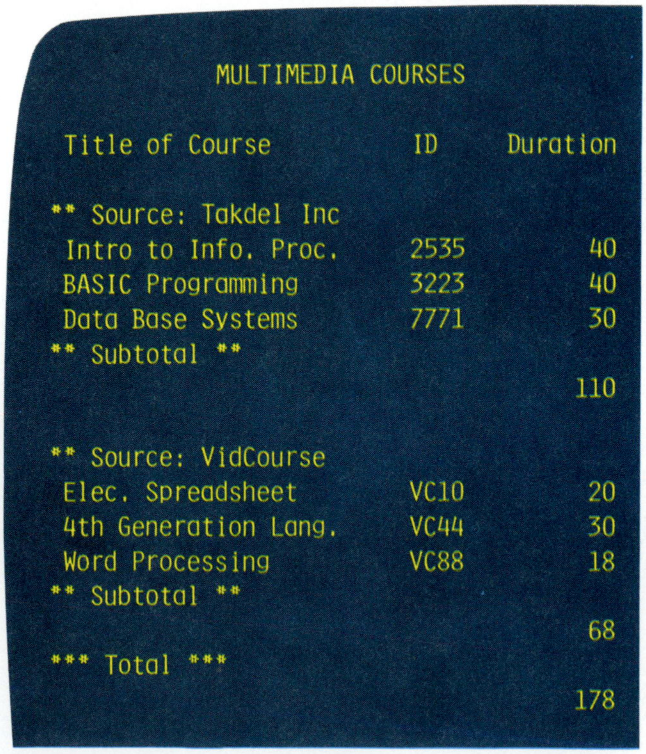

**FIGURE S-34**
**Data Management: Formatted Reports**
This formatted report was compiled by merging a predefined report format with the COURSE data base (as sorted in Figure S-30).

```
              MULTIMEDIA COURSES


   Title of Course         ID      Duration


   ** Source: Takdel Inc
    Intro to Info. Proc.    2535         40
    BASIC Programming       3223         40
    Data Base Systems       7771         30
   ** Subtotal **
                                        110


   ** Source: VidCourse
    Elec. Spreadsheet       VC10         20
    4th Generation Lang.    VC44         30
    Word Processing         VC88         18
   ** Subtotal **
                                         68

   *** Total ***
                                        178
```

## Use

Data management software earns the "productivity tool" label by providing users with the capability to organize data into an electronic data base that can be easily maintained and queried (permit user inquiries). The examples illustrated and discussed in the "concepts" section merely scratch the surface of the potential of database software. With relative ease, you can generate some rather sophisticated reports that involve subtotals, calculations, and even programming. You can change the structure of a data base. For example, if Ed Cool wanted to add an END field (data course was completed) to the structure of the TRAINING data base in Figure S-24, he could do so without having to recreate the data base.

Many of the capabilities of electronic spreadsheet software are embodied in data management software. For example, you can also make "what if" inquiries with database software. Ed Cool might ask: "What if we discontinued the VidCourse contract, how many courses would we have left to offer." You might observe that this and some other queries illustrated in this section might best be answered by simply examining a hard copy of the 10- and 12-record data bases. But what if Ed Cool had 120 different courses in his COURSE data base and 1500 employees in his TRAINING data base? These numbers are much more realistic for a company the size of Zimco, but procedures for making the inquiries to a data base with 1500 records are no more difficult than making inquiries to a data base with 10 records.

## REVIEW EXERCISES (S-5)

1. Describe the capabilities of data management software.
2. What characteristics describe a field in a data base record?
3. What is the purpose of setting conditions for a data base?
4. In data base terminology, what is meant by the term "filtering"?
5. Describe two types of inquiries to a data base that involve calculations.
6. What is the relationship between a field, a record, and the structure of a data base?
7. Give examples and descriptions of at least three other fields that might be added to the record for the COURSE data base.
8. Give examples and descriptions of at least three other fields that might be added to the record for the TRAINING data base.
9. What would be the employee name for the third record if the TRAINING data base were sorted such that the primary and secondary key fields were DEPARTMENT and EMPLOYEE, respectively?

## HANDS-ON EXERCISES

1. **(a)** Design a data entry screen to accept the following sales data for Diolab, Inc., a manufacturer of a diagnostic laboratory instrument that is sold primarily to hospitals and clinics.

| | DIOLAB INC. SALES (UNITS) | | | |
|---|---|---|---|---|
| REGION | QTR1 | QTR2 | QTR3 | QTR4 |
| NE REGION | 241 | 300 | 320 | 170 |
| SE REGION | 120 | 150 | 165 | 201 |
| SW REGION | 64 | 80 | 60 | 52 |

   **(b)** What is the data base record?

   **(c)** What are the field names, types, and lengths?

2. **(a)** Enter the Diolab data above into a data base.

   **(b)** Revise the NE Region first-quarter sales to be 214.

   **(c)** Add the following NW Region record to the data base.

| REGION | QTR1 | QTR2 | QTR3 | QTR4 |
|---|---|---|---|---|
| NW REGION | 116 | 141 | 147 | 180 |

   **(d)** Obtain a printout of the data base and store the data on a disk file named DIOLAB.

3. **(a)** What conditions would be needed to select all Diolab regions (records) that sold more than 150 units in the fourth quarter (all but SW Region)?

   **(b)** What conditions would be needed to select all Diolab regions (records) that sold more than 150 units in the fourth quarter *and* for which fourth-quarter sales are greater than third-quarter sales (SE and NW Regions)?

   **(c)** What command and conditions would be needed to select and display only the REGION and QTR4 fields of those Diolab regions for which the average sales for the first three quarters is less than the sales for the fourth quarter (SE and NW Regions)?

4. **(a)** Make an inquiry to the Diolab data base that results in a display of the average unit sales for each quarter (QTR1=128).

**(b)** Make an inquiry to the Diolab data base that results in a display of the total unit sales for each quarter (QTR1=514).

5. **(a)** Sort the Diolab data base in ascending order by QTR1 sales. What regions are first and last?

   **(b)** Sort the Diolab data base in descending order by QTR4 sales. What regions are first and last?

6. Generate a formatted report from the sorted data base of Exercise 5(a) that is entitled "DIOLAB INC. SALES (UNITS) and has the following column headings: Sales Region, 1st Qtr, 2nd Qtr, 3rd Qtr, and 4th Qtr. The report should include the total sales for each quarter.

# S-6   GRAPHICS

## Function

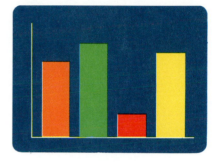

With the graphics software, you can create a variety of presentation graphics from data in an electronic spreadsheet of a data base. Among the most popular presentation graphics are **bar charts, pie charts,** and **line charts** (as seen in Figures S-36, S-39, and S-40, respectively). Other types of charts are possible. Each of these charts can be annotated with chart *titles*, *labels* for axes, and *legends*.

Some graphics software lets you create and store original drawings. To do this, however, your personal computer must be equipped with a mouse, joystick, digitizing board, or some type of device that permits the input of curved and angular lines. To make drawing easier to do, such software even offers a data base filled with a variety of frequently used symbols, such as rectangles, circles, cats (yes, even cats), and so on. Some companies draw and store the image of their company logo so it can be inserted on memos, reports, and charts.

Graphic representations of data have proven to be a very effective means of communication. It is easier to recognize problem areas and trends in a chart than it is in a tabular summary of the same data. For many years, the presentation of tabular data was the preferred approach to communicating tabular information. This was because it was simply too expensive and time consuming to produce presentation graphics manually. Today, you can use graphics software to produce perfectly proportioned, accurate, and visually appealing charts in a matter of seconds. Prior to the introduction of graphics software, the turnaround time was at least a day, and often a week.

## Concepts

The data needed to produce a chart already exist in a spreadsheet or data base. The graphics software leads you through a series of prompts, the first of which asks you what type of graph is to be pro-

With graphics software, you can prepare professional-looking visuals for presentations. The plotter draws the image directly on a blank acetate. When the acetate is placed on an overhead projector, the graphic image is projected on a large screen. (Tektronix, Inc.)

duced: bar chart, pie chart, line chart, and so on. You then select the spreadsheet ranges (or data base fields) that are to be plotted. You can also select spreadsheet ranges or data base field names for the labels. Once you have identified the source of the data and labels, and perhaps added a title, you can display, print, or plot the graph. Any changes made to data in a spreadsheet or data base are reflected in the charts as well.

## Use

Sally Marcio, the VP of Sales and Marketing at Zimco, is an avid user of spreadsheet and graphics software. The spreadsheet of Figure S-35 is an annual summary of the sales for each of Zimco's four products by sales region. This spreadsheet is used in the following sections to demonstrate the compilation of bar, pie, and line charts.

Bar Charts.   To prepare the bar chart of Figure S-36, Sally first had to specify appropriate ranges; that is, the values in the "Total" column (range F5 . . F8 of Figure S-35) are to be plotted and the values in the "Sales Region" column (range A5 . . A8 of Figure S-35) are to be inserted as labels along the horizontal or $x$ axis. Sally also added a title for the chart (Sales Summary by Region), titles for the $x$ axis (Region) and the vertical or $y$ axis [[Sales ($1000)].

The sales figures for each region in Figure S-35 (range B5 . . E8) can be plotted in a *clustered-bar chart*. The resultant chart, shown in Figure S-37, permits Sally to better understand the regional distribution of sales. The *stacked-bar chart* in Figure S-38 is an alternative presentation to the clustered-bar chart in Figure S-37. The clustered-bar chart visually highlights the relative contribution that each product made to the total sales for each region.

**FIGURE S-35**
**Graphics: Sales Data**
These data are used to produce the bar, pie, and line charts of Figures S-36 through S-40.

F10: aSUM(F5..F8)

| | A | B | C | D | E | F |
|---|---|---|---|---|---|---|
| 1 | | ANNUAL SALES FOR ZIMCO ENTERPRISES BY REGION ($1000) | | | | |
| 2 | | | | | | |
| 3 | Sales Region | Stibs | Farkles | Teglers | Qwerts | Total |
| 4 | ------------- | -------- | -------- | -------- | -------- | -------- |
| 5 | Southern | $7,140 | $5,460 | $3,150 | $5,250 | $21,000 |
| 6 | Western | $14,790 | $11,310 | $6,525 | $11,875 | $44,500 |
| 7 | Northern | $13,260 | $10,140 | $5,850 | $10,750 | $40,000 |
| 8 | Eastern | $15,810 | $12,090 | $6,975 | $12,625 | $47,500 |
| 9 | ------------- | -------- | -------- | -------- | -------- | -------- |
| 10 | Totals | $51,000 | $39,000 | $22,500 | $40,500 | $153,000 |

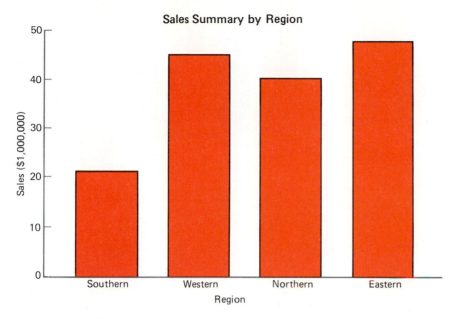

**Sales Summary by Region**

**FIGURE S-36**
**Graphics: Bar Chart**
The "Total" sales for each region in Figure S-35 are graphically represented in
this bar chart.

The bar chart of Figure S-37 was prepared using two popular graphics packages.
The first photo illustrates how the chart would be displayed using Symphony,
an integrated package (Symphony is a trademark of the Lotus Development
Corporation). The second plot illustrates how the chart would be displayed using
Reflex, also an integrated package (Reflex-The Analyst is a trademark of
BORELAND Analytica, Inc.).
(Long and Associates)

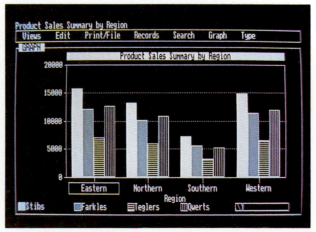

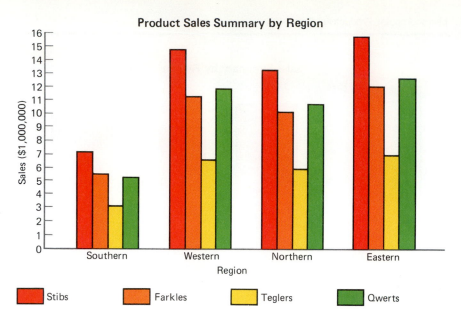

**FIGURE S-37**
**Graphics: Clustered-Bar Chart**
Regional sales for each of the
four products in Figure S-35 are
graphically represented in this
clustered-bar chart.

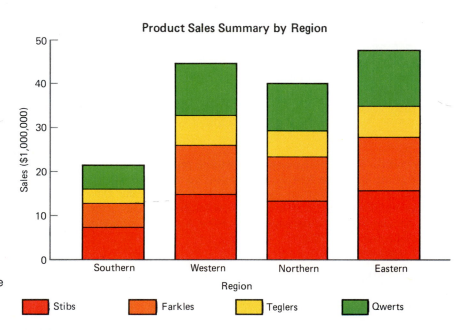

**FIGURE S-38**
**Graphics: Stacked-Bar Chart**
Regional sales for each of the
four products in Figure S-35 are
graphically represented in this
stacked-bar chart.

Pie Charts. Pie charts are the most basic of presentation graphics.
A pie chart graphically illustrates each "piece" of data in its proper
relationship to the whole "pie." To illustrate how a pie chart is constructed and used, refer again to the "Annual Sales" spreadsheet in
Figure S-35.

Sally Marcio produced the sales-by-product pie chart in Figure S-
39 by specifying that the values in the "Totals" row (range B10 . . E10
of Figure S-35) to be "pieces" of the pie. She specified further that
selected values in the column headings row (range B3 . . E3) be inserted as labels and she added a title. The numbers in parentheses
represent what percent each piece (i.e., total sales for a particular prod-

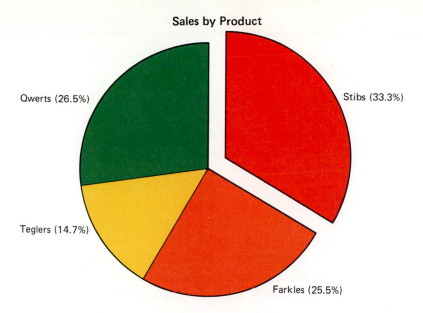

**Sales by Product**

Qwerts (26.5%)

Stibs (33.3%)

Teglers (14.7%)

Farkles (25.5%)

**FIGURE S-39**
**Graphics: Pie Chart**
Total sales by product (i.e., the "Totals" row, B10..E10) in Figure S-35 are graphically represented in this pie chart. The "Stibs" piece of the pie is exploded for emphasis.

uct) is of the whole (i.e., total sales or the value of F10). To emphasize the product with the greatest contribution to total sales, Sally decided to *explode* (or separate) the Stibs piece of the pie.

Line Charts. A line chart connects similar points on a graph with one or several lines. Sally Marcio used the clustered-bar chart of Figure S-37 to visually highlight relative product sales by region. She used the same data in the spreadsheet of Figure S-35 to generate the line chart of Figure S-40. The line chart makes it easy for Sally to compare sales between regions for a particular product.

In the line chart of Figure S-40, four ranges of data from the spreadsheet of Figure S-35 (B5 . . E5, B6 . . E6, and so on) are plotted and connected with a line, one for each product. The chart clearly indicates that the proportion of product sales is similar for each region.

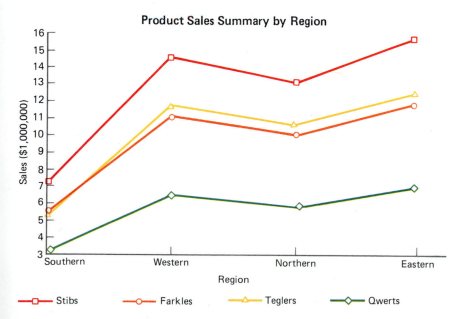

**Product Sales Summary by Region**

Sales ($1,000,000)

Region

Southern — Western — Northern — Eastern

Stibs — Farkles — Teglers — Qwerts

**FIGURE S-40**
**Graphics: Line Chart**
This line chart shows a plot of the data of Figure S-37. A line connects the sales for each product by region.

449

## REVIEW EXERCISES (S-6)

1.  Name three types of charts commonly used for presentation graphics.
2.  What is the source of the data needed to produce the charts?
3.  Name and graphically illustrate (by hand) two variations on the bar chart.
4.  What types of input devices enable you to produce original line drawings?
5.  Under what circumstances is a graphic representation of data more effective than a tabular presentation of the same data?
6.  What is meant when a portion of a pie chart is exploded?
7.  Is it possible to present the same information in a stacked bar and a line chart? How about stacked bar and pie charts?

## HANDS-ON EXERCISES

1.  The following Diolab, Inc., sales data are reproduced from the Hands-on Exercises in Sections S-5 and S-6. Produce the accompanying bar chart showing the total unit sales by region for Diolab, Inc. Label the y and x axes as shown.

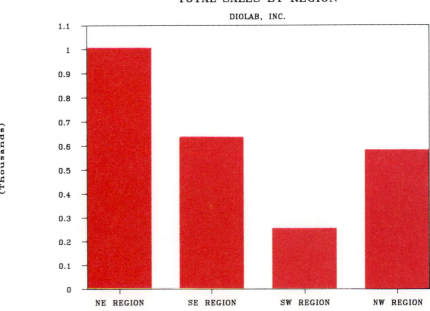

TOTAL SALES BY REGION

| DIOLAB INC. SALES (UNITS) | | | | |
| REGION | QTR1 | QTR2 | QTR3 | QTR4 |
| --- | --- | --- | --- | --- |
| NE REGION | 214 | 300 | 320 | 170 |
| SE REGION | 120 | 150 | 165 | 201 |
| SW REGION | 64 | 80 | 60 | 52 |
| NW REGION | 116 | 141 | 147 | 180 |

**2.** Produce the accompanying pie chart showing the total unit sales by region for Diolab, Inc. Title the chart and label each piece as shown.

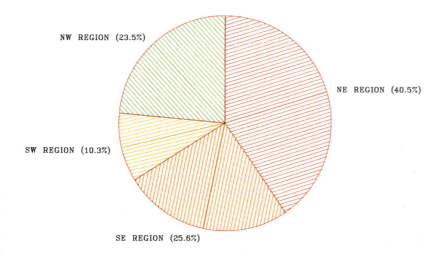

TOTAL SALES BY REGION
DIOLAB, INC.

**3.** Compare the information portrayed in the bar and pie charts above.

**4.** Produce the accompanying clustered-bar chart showing quarterly unit sales by region for Diolab, Inc. Title the chart, label the axes, and include a legend as shown.

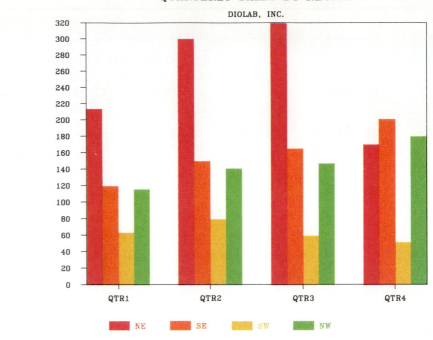

QUARTERLY SALES BY REGION

DIOLAB, INC.

5. Produce the accompanying line chart showing quarterly unit sales by region for Diolab, Inc. Title the chart, label the axes, and include a legend as shown.

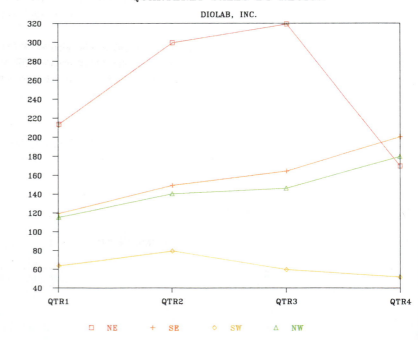

QUARTERLY SALES BY REGION

DIOLAB, INC.

6. Compare the information portrayed in the clustered-bar and line charts above.

## S-7  IDEA PROCESSORS

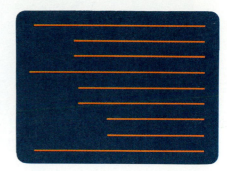

### Function

An idea processor is a productivity tool that allows you to organize and document your thoughts and ideas. Such software can be used for brainstorming, outlining project activities, developing speeches and presentations, compiling notes for meetings and seminars, and a myriad of other uses. Idea processors let you work with one idea at a time within a hierarchy of other ideas such that you can easily organize and reorganize your ideas.

Some people have referred to idea processor software as an electronic version of the yellow note pad. When you use an idea processor, you can focus your attention on the thought process by letting the computer help with the task of documenting your ideas.

### Concepts

Like word processing software, idea processor packages permit the manipulation of text, but with a different twist. They deal with one-line explanations of *items*: "ideas," points, notes, things, and so on. Idea processors, which are also called *outliners*, can be used to organize these single-line items into an outline format. You create an outline by entering items, then using the capabilities of the software to arrange them into a well organized outline.

Preston Smith, Zimco's president, dictates his letters, memos, and reports from outlines that he prepares using idea processor software. He also prepares notes for his meetings with an idea processor. For example, he prepared the agenda outlined in Figure S-41 for an "executive planning session". This example is the basis for demonstrating outliner concepts.

The Item Orientation of Outliners.  Just as a block of text in a word processing document can be moved, copied, and deleted, one or more items in an outline can be moved, copied, or deleted. First-level items are flush with the left margin. Second-level items are indented to show subordination to a first-level item. Third-level items are indented under second-level items, and so on (see Figure S-41 and the level indicators at the top left corner of the display). One of the handy features of an outliner is that you can easily change the level of an item by shifting it to the left or to the right. For example, the "5 year" and "10 year" items in Figure S-41 were originally fourth-level items under a third-level heading called "Alternatives", but Preston decided to delete the "Alternatives" heading and shift the "Planning horizon" options to the third level.

The first draft of Preston's agenda outline did not include any third-level headings under "Approach to long-range planning at Zimco". However, Preston wanted to emphasize two types of "Objectives", so he *inserted* the two third-level headings, "Qualitative results" and "Quantitative results" (see Figure S-41).

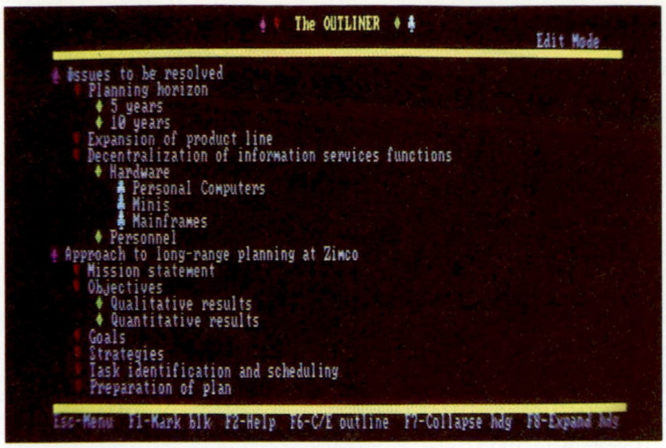
The OUTLINER
Edit Mode
Issues to be resolved
Planning horizon
5 years
10 years
Expansion of product line
Decentralization of information services functions
Hardware
Personal Computers
Minis
Mainframes
Personnel
Approach to long-range planning at Zimco
Mission statement
Objectives
Qualitative results
Quantitative results
Goals
Strategies
Task identification and scheduling
Preparation of plan
Esc-Menu F1-Mark blk F2-Help F6-C/E outline F7-Collapse hdg F8-Expand hdg

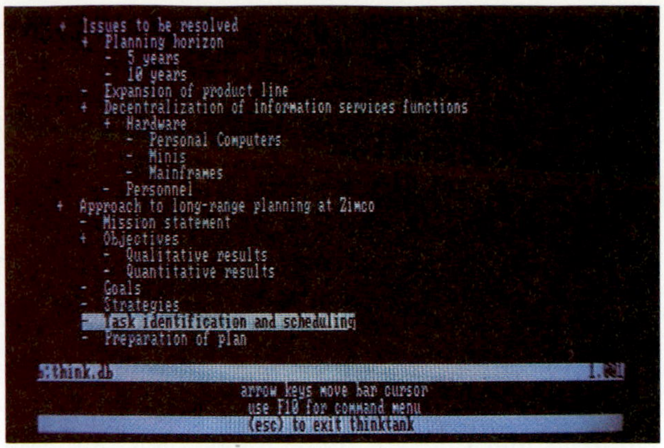
Issues to be resolved
Planning horizon
5 years
10 years
Expansion of product line
Decentralization of information services functions
Hardware
Personal Computers
Minis
Mainframes
Personnel
Approach to long-range planning at Zimco
Mission statement
Objectives
Qualitative results
Quantitative results
Goals
Strategies
Task identification and scheduling
Preparation of plan
think.db
arrow keys move bar cursor
use F10 for command menu
(esc) to exit thinktank

The outline of Figure S-41 was prepared using two popular idea processor packages. The first photo illustrates how the outline would be displayed using The OUTLINER (Long and Associates). The second photo illustrates how the outline would be displayed using ThinkTank. (ThinkTank is a trademark of Living Videotext, Inc.)
(Long and Associates)

**FIGURE S-41**
**Idea Processor: Display of an Outline**
The outline shown is an example of an agenda for an "executive planning session." The levels of the items can be equated to the level indicators in the top left corner of the display.

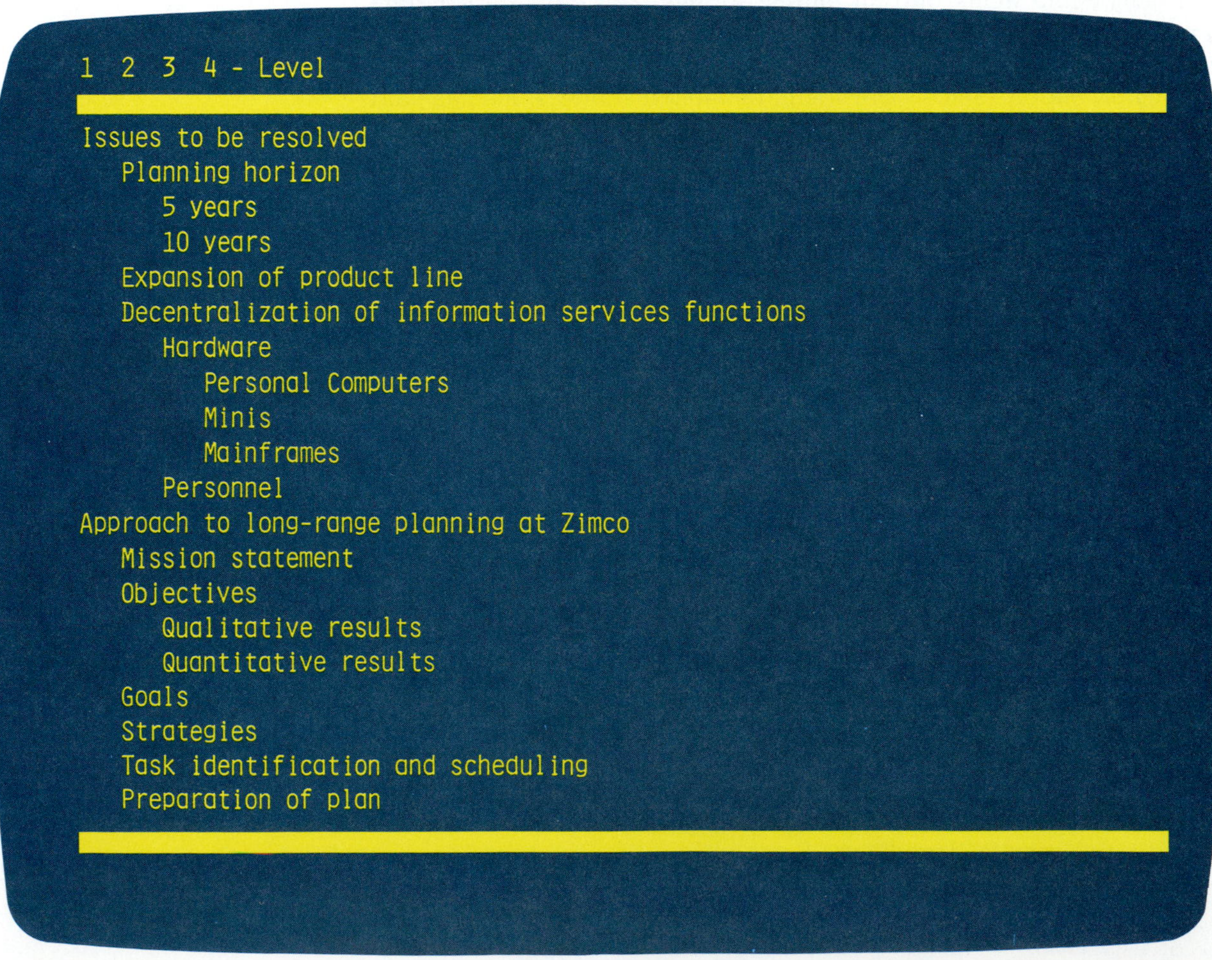
1 2 3 4 - Level
Issues to be resolved
Planning horizon
5 years
10 years
Expansion of product line
Decentralization of information services functions
Hardware
Personal Computers
Minis
Mainframes
Personnel
Approach to long-range planning at Zimco
Mission statement
Objectives
Qualitative results
Quantitative results
Goals
Strategies
Task identification and scheduling
Preparation of plan

Until moments before the planning session, Preston had the "Approach to long-range planning at Zimco" as the first item on the session's agenda. Once he decided to make "Issues to be resolved" the first item, he made the revision to the outline by *marking* the lines to be moved, then issuing a block move command. The resultant outline is shown in Figure S-41.

Collapsing/Expanding an Outline. In outliner terminology, the relationship between an item and its subordinate items is that of a *parent* and children. An item, no matter what level, is a parent if it has subordinate items, or children. For example, in Figure S-41, the second-level heading "Planning horizon" is the parent to its children "5 years" and "10 years". Notice that the "Planning horizon" item is also a child to "Issues to be resolved". Thus it is both a child and a parent.

The user can selectively *collapse* an outline to "hide" the children of a particular parent. That is, the children are deleted from the visual display of the outline, but they remain in main memory as part of the complete outline. This feature enables a user to "hide" children from the view of the user for those circumstances where all that is needed is a display of the parent item. For example, Preston Smith collapsed his entire session outline (see Figure S-41) to the second level (see Figure S-42). In most outliner packages, the parents with hidden children are marked with a "+" (see Figure S-42). His plans were to print out the more detailed outline of Figure S-41 for himself and the overview outline of Figure S-42 for the VPs attending the planning session.

An entire outline can be collapsed to a given level or the children of a single item can be hidden. To redisplay the hidden children, you issue an *expand* command. Again, the expand can be applied to any item marked with a plus or it can be applied collectively to an entire outline.

**FIGURE S-42**
**Idea Processor: Display of an Outline with Hidden Children**
The outline of Figure S-41 is displayed after being collapsed to the second level.

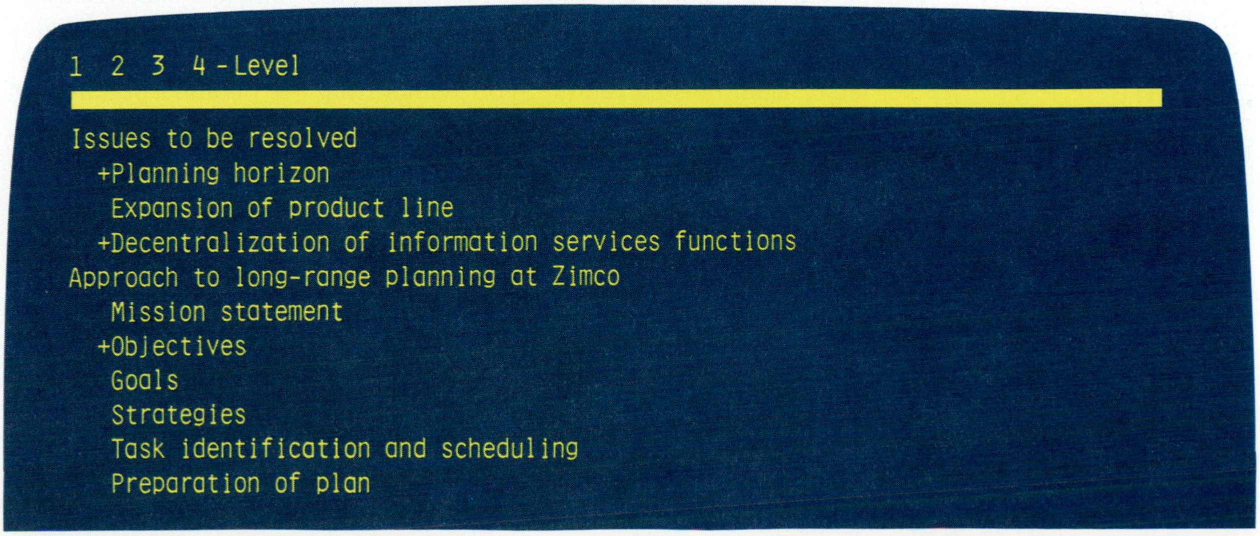

```
1  2  3  4 - Level

Issues to be resolved
   +Planning horizon
    Expansion of product line
   +Decentralization of information services functions
Approach to long-range planning at Zimco
    Mission statement
   +Objectives
    Goals
    Strategies
    Task identification and scheduling
    Preparation of plan
```

**FIGURE S-43**
**Idea Processor: Printout of an Outline**
On output, the hierarchy of items displayed in Figure S-41 is transformed to a traditional outline format.

```
            EXECUTIVE PLANNING SESSION

I.          Issues to be resolved
            A.  Planning horizon
                1.  5 years
                2.  10 years
            B.  Expansion of product line
            C.  Decentralization of information services functions
                1.  Hardware
                    a.  Personal Computers
                    b.  Minis
                    c.  Mainframes
                2.  Personnel
II.         Approach to long-range planning at Zimco
            A.  Mission statement
            B.  Objectives
                1.  Qualitative results
                2.  Quantitative results
            C.  Goals
            D.  Strategies
            E.  Task identification and scheduling
            F.  Preparation of plan
```

**Printing an Outline.** While organizing your thoughts, a meeting, the day's activities, and so on, by using an idea processor, the relationship between the ideas is purely positional (sequence and level of heading). However, on output (to a printer or a text file), the hierarchical display of items on the monitor is transformed into a traditional outline format. The hard-copy output of the Figure S-41 is shown in Figure S-43. The outline in Figure S-43 is presented in the traditional outline format. Some outliner packages use the alternative format (i.e., 1, 1.1, 1.1.1, 1.1.2, 1.2, 1.3, and so on, versus I, A, 1, 2, B, C, and so on).

## Use

People use idea processors or outliners to organize their thinking, their meetings, their presentations, their dictation, and anything else that can be documented in the hierarchical style of an outline. The number and variety of applications for an idea processor are limitless. Sybil Allen, Zimco's manager of the Systems Analysis Department, has created an outline template for her weekly team meeting. The outline contains a generic list of topics (items) that are common to all meetings, such as progress reports, problem areas, work schedules for coming week. Prior to the meeting, she fills in the details (e.g., itemizing problems). Like Preston Smith, Sybil works from the detailed outline and hands out an overview outline to members of the team.

## REVIEW EXERCISES (S-7)

1. Describe what advantages an idea processor has over a yellow note pad during brainstorming sessions.
2. Relate the parent/children concept to collapsing and expanding an outline.
3. Describe a business, a domestic, and a student application for idea processors.

## HANDS-ON EXERCISES

1. Using idea processor software, create an outline that you might use to deliver a 10-minute verbal presentation on word processing, electronic spreadsheet, and data management software. Make these three productivity tools the first-level headings and give each of them the following children: function, concepts, and use. Fill in third- and fourth-level headings to complete the outline. Print the outline.

2. Use block moves to rearrange the outline that you prepared in Exercise 1 such that data management is first, followed by electronic spreadsheet and word processing. Edit the outline if necessary. Print the outline.

3. Collapse the outline that you prepared in Exercise 2 to the second level, then expand the "function" items. Print the outline.

## S-8  COMMUNICATIONS

### Function

Communications software makes the microcomputer more than a small stand-alone computer. With communications software, a micro can transmit and receive data to/from a remote computer. Communications software automatically "dials up" a remote computer (another micro or a mainframe), then "logs-on" (establishes a link with a remote computer). Once on-line, you can communicate and share data with a remote computer.

After logging on, communications software allows you to **download** files; that is, you can request and receive data or program files that are transmitted from a remote computer. Once the files have been downloaded to your micro, you can select any of the microcomputer productivity tools to work with the files. Once processing is complete, you can use the communications software to **upload** the file to a remote computer. Uploading is the opposite of downloading.

### Concepts

You use the communications software to link your microcomputer via telephone lines to another computer system anywhere in the world. However, to do this, your micro must be equipped with a *modem*. The modem links your micro with the telephone line that connects the two computers. On most microcomputers the modem is an optional plug-in circuit board. You can purchase it with your micro or you can add it later as the need arises. A modem can also be purchased as a separate unit and connected to the micro with an electrical cable.

The communications software can be set up to dial and log-on automatically to frequently accessed computer systems. It will even redial if a busy signal is detected.

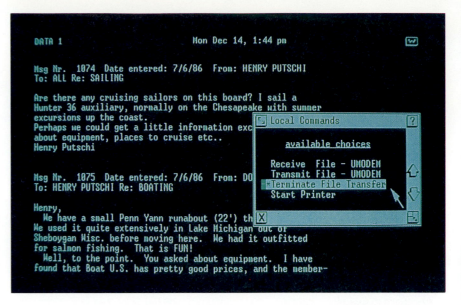

A "pull-down" menu and an options window for a communications software package are superimposed over a display of messages from a local electronic bulletin board. The user selects one of the bulletin boards shown in the menu and the software dials up the bulletin board and makes the connection. The specifications for this bulletin board, which have already been defined, are shown in the options window.
(Long and Associates)

A micro with a modem and communications software can be on the receiving end as well. That is, it can automatically answer "calls" from other computers.

## Use

Many *information services*, such as flight and hotel information, stock quotes, and even restaurant menus, are available to microcomputer owners with communications capabilities. A few information services are gratis, but most require a fee. The fee normally consists of a set monthly charge plus an amount based on usage.

Just about every city with a population of 25,000 or more has at least one *computer bulletin board*, often sponsored by a local computer club. Members "post" messages, announcements, for-sale notices, and so on, to the computer bulletin board by transmitting them to a central computer, usually another micro. To scan the bulletin board, members again use communications software to link up to the central computer. This software component also opens the door to sending and receiving *electronic mail*.

In the coming years, we'll probably see a shift to smaller briefcases. Why? With communications software and an ever-growing number of home computers, people won't need to lug their paperwork between home and office every day. For a great many white-collar workers, at all levels, much of their work is on computers. Continuing their work at home is simply a matter of establishing a link between their home and office computers.

The combination of microcomputers and communications software has fueled the growth of *cottage industries*. The world has been made a little more compact with the computer revolution. Stock brokers, financial planners, writers, programmers, and people from a wide variety of professions may not need to "go to the office." They can live wherever they choose. Micros make it possible for these people to access needed information, communicate with their clients, and even deliver products of their work (e.g., programs, stories, or recommendations).

## REVIEW EXERCISES (S-8)

1. What is the function of communications software?
2. Why would you download data? Upload data?
3. Why is a modem needed to upload data via telephone lines?
4. Some communications software has automatic dial and redial capabilities. Describe these capabilities.
5. One popular information service is home banking. Describe an interactive session with at least one transaction to both a checking and savings account. Begin from the time you turn on your microcomputer.

## HANDS-ON EXERCISES

1. Upload the text file of the memo you created in the Hands-on Exercises in Section S-3 to another computer. Download the same file to your microcomputer.
2. Send a message via electronic mail to a friend.
3. Tap into and scan a local computer bulletin board. Respond to one of the messages.

## S-9  INTEGRATED MICRO SOFTWARE: A "WINDOW" TO INFORMATION

### Function

Seldom do we produce a chart (graphics) without adding some explanatory text (word processing). Producing a hard copy of a memo (word processing) may be unnecessary if we can send it via electronic mail (communications). If you think about it, all of the micro productivity tools can be integrated to increase the capabilities of the individual software packages.

In contrast to software that is designed for a *specific* application, **integrated microcomputer software** is *general-purpose* software and provides the framework for a great number of business and "personal" applications. Integrated micro software, or simple **integrated software,** is the integration of two or more of the six major productivity tools (i.e., word processing, electronic spreadsheet, data management, graphics, idea processors, and communications software). These integrated packages permit us to work as we always have—on several projects at a time—but with the assistance of a computer.

With integrated software
packages, you can create and
print a letter in one window while
referencing an electronic
spreadsheet in another window.
(Digital Research Inc.)

## Concepts

Integrated software lets you work the way you think, and think the way you work. Several projects are at the tips of your fingers, and you can switch easily between them with relative ease. When you do this, you are switching from one *window* (e.g., spreadsheet) to another window (e.g., word processing). You can even "look through" several windows on a single display screen; however, you can only manipulate text or data in one window at a time. This is called the "current" window. Windows can overlap one another on the display screen.

You can perform work in one of several windows on a display screen or you can **zoom** in on a particular window. That is, the window you select is expanded to fill the entire screen. Press a key and you can return to a multiwindow display. A multiwindow display permits you to view how a change in one window affects another window. For example, as you change the data in a spreadsheet, you can view how an accompanying pie chart is revised to reflect the new data.

You can even create **window panes!** As you might expect, a window is divided into panes so that you can view several parts of the same window subarea at a time. For example, suppose that you were writing a long report in a word processing window; then you might wish to write the conclusions to the report in one window pane while viewing portions of the report in another window pane.

A handy feature available with most micro software packages is the **macro.** A macro is a sequence of frequently used operations or keystrokes that can be recalled as you need them. You create a macro by entering the sequence of operations or keystrokes, then storing them on disk for later recall. To *invoke* or execute the macro, you either refer to it by name (perhaps in the text of a word processing file) or enter the series of keystrokes that identify the desired macro (e.g., ALT-8, CTRL-F4). Three common user-supplied macros in word processing could be the commands necessary to format the first-, second- and third-level headings in a report. For example, the first-level heading is centered, boldface, and followed by two spaces; the second level is flush left, boldface, and followed by an indented paragraph; and the third level is flush left, underlined, and followed on the same line by the beginning of the first paragraph. In electronic spreadsheets, macros are commonly used to produce charts "automatically" from spreadsheet data.

## Use

A manager might use all micro productivity tools to handle a variety of administrative duties. In one window, a manager might use electronic spreadsheet software to track product sales by region. At the end of each week the manager might summarize and plot sales data in a bar chart in another window. In still another window the manager might write a memo recommending the top field sales representatives for special recognition. Another window might contain personal "things-to-do" notes in an outline format. The manager can distribute the memo via electronic mail by uploading it to the company's mainframe (via communications software). This example illustrates how the capabilities of the individual software packages complement the capabilities of the others.

## S-10  SUMMARY

Several hundred micro "productivity" software packages are available commercially. Over 30 integrated micro software packages are available. Commercially available software packages vary greatly in capabilities and price. Before buying, have an idea of how you plan to use the software, then check it out thoroughly to make sure it has the features you want. Ask the salesperson to demonstrate the package.

Software with essentially the same capabilities may be priced as much as several hundred dollars apart. Some graphics software creates displays of charts in seconds, while others take minutes. Some software packages are easy to learn and are accompanied by good documentation; others are not. Considering the amount of time that you might spend using micro software, any extra time you spend in evaluating the software will be time well spent.

Not all micro software packages are as "user friendly" as vendors would have us believe. Vendors are sometimes overzealous in their use of the phrase "easy to learn." However, hundreds of thousands of computer novices and experts have mastered the use of these valuable productivity tools, and with a little study and practice, you will too.

During the learning stages, keep a list of error messages handy; you will probably need them. A word of warning: Manuals and disk tutorials tell you everything you *can* do but say very little about what you *cannot* do. That may take a bit of "trial and error" to learn.

Perhaps the best way to learn micro software is to use it. Anticipate some frustrations, but before you know it, you too will be a software wizard. What you do with the software, though, is 10 percent skills and 90 percent imagination.

## REVIEW EXERCISES (S-9 and S-10)

1. Briefly describe the concept of integrated microcomputer software.
2. Why would a user of an integrated software package use the zoom feature?
3. What is a macro and how can the use of macros save time?
4. What do you look for when buying a microcomputer software package?
5. If you are in the market for micro software, test out at least two packages at a computer store and write up a brief comparison, noting the strengths and weaknesses of each.

This "BASIC Programming" section contains BASIC's fundamentals and many of its more advanced features. Depending on how much material you cover, you can achieve a beginning (Learning Modules I, II, and III), intermediate (Learning Modules IV, V, and VI), or advanced (Learning Modules VII, VIII, and IX) level of competency.

**ANS BASIC.** An American National Standard (ANS) for Minimal BASIC was established in 1978 and another more comprehensive standard, ANS BASIC, was introduced in 1985. However, even with a standard, hardware and software vendors tend to alter ANS BASIC to better accommodate the features of their products. As a result, a number of slightly different versions, or "dialects," exist for BASIC. The BASIC presented in Learning Modules I through VIII is a "BASIC-in-practice." That is, the instructions presented are applicable to most versions of BASIC. Any "nonstandard" features presented are widely accepted and are more the rule than the exception.

The BASIC presented in Learning Module IX—"The 'New' ANS BASIC"—adheres strictly to the standards set forth in the 1985 ANS BASIC. Kurtz, the co-developer of the original BASIC, served as chairman of the ANS committee charged with developing the new standard for BASIC. Currently, relatively few existing versions of BASIC adhere to the 1985 ANS BASIC. Widespread implementation of a new programming standard will typically take three to five years.

## B-3 METHOD OF PRESENTATION

**A Single Application.** The focus of this "BASIC Programming" section is to present material so that you can understand BASIC programming. Application is the secondary focus: therefore, all example programs are based on straightforward business applications involving sales data.

The "sales" example is presented in a series of programs, each of increasing challenge and complexity. The first example program illustrates a BASIC program to compute the total of three sales amounts. Eventually, example programs illustrate on-line reporting and inquiry, disk file processing, and graphics. Each of the example programs introduces and demonstrates the use of additional BASIC programming instructions and techniques.

**Structured Programming.** A *program description*, a *structure chart*, a *flowchart*, and an example *interactive session* accompany a *listing* of each of the 12 example programs. Figure B-1 highlights these items for Example Program #1. Example Program #1 is repeated and discussed in Learning Module II, "Getting Started in BASIC."

A structure chart breaks a programming problem into a hierarchy of tasks. A task can be broken down into subtasks, as long as a finer level of detail is desired. The most effective programs are designed so they can be designed and written in **modules,** or independent tasks.

# EXAMPLE PROGRAM #1

This program accepts three sales figures, then computes and displays the total.

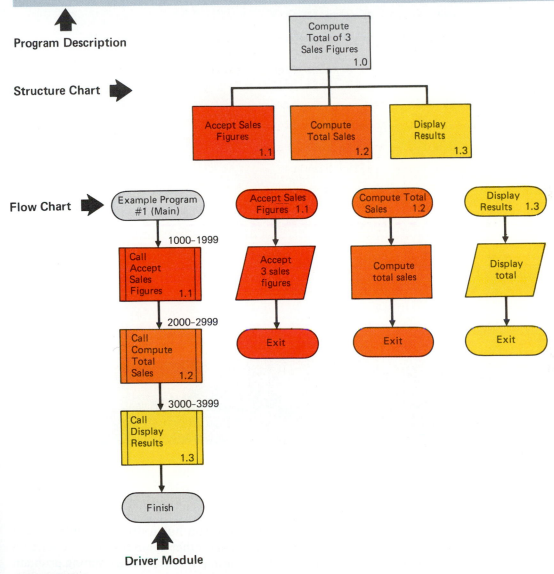

Program Description

Structure Chart ▶

Flow Chart ▶

Driver Module

**FIGURE B-1**
**Presentation Format of Example Programs**
Each example program listing is accompanied by a program description, a
structure chart, a flowchart, and an interactive session. The logic of each program
is structured so that a driver program calls subordinate modules as they are
needed.

continued

**Figure B-1** continued

Program Listing

```
2    REM           **** Example Program #1 ****
4    REM   Description:
6    REM     This program accepts three sales figures, then computes and
8    REM     displays the total.
10   REM   Variables list:
12   REM     S1, S2, S3              - Sales figures (Stibs, Farkles, Teglers)
14   REM     TOTAL                   - Total sales
99   REM
100  REM   <<<< Start Main >>>>
110  REM
120  REM   Call Module 1.1 - Accept Sales Figures
130  GOSUB 1000
140  REM   Call Module 1.2 - Compute Total Sales
150  GOSUB 2000
160  REM   Call Module 1.3 - Display Results
170  GOSUB 3000
180  END
190  REM   <<<< End Main >>>>
999  REM
1000 REM   ==== Module 1.1 - Accept Sales Figures
1010 INPUT S1, S2, S3
1999 RETURN
2000 REM   ==== Module 1.2 - Compute Total Sales
2010 LET TOTAL = S1 + S2 + S3
2999 RETURN
3000 REM   ==== Module 1.3 - Display Results
3010 PRINT TOTAL
3999 RETURN
```

Interactive Session

```
run
? 32000,28000,25000
 85000
ok
```

In structured programming, each program has a **driver module** (called "Main" in our examples) that causes other modules to be executed as they are needed. It is much easier to address a programming problem in small, more manageable modules than as one big task. This is done using the principles of **structured programming.**

In structured programming, the logic of the program is addressed hierarchically in logical modules (see Figure B-1). In the end, the logic of each module is translated into a sequence of program instructions that are called and executed as a unit. By dividing the program into modules, you can use the structured approach to program development and thereby reduce the complexity of the programming task. Some programs are so complex that if taken as a single task, they would be almost impossible to conceptualize, design, and code. The idea behind structured programming is to "divide and conquer." See Chapter 12, "Programming Concepts," for a detailed explanation of structured programming.

Flowcharting, one of the most popular design techniques, permits you to illustrate data, information, and work flow through the interconnection of *specialized symbols* with *flow lines*. The combination of symbols and flow lines portrays the logic of the program. Each symbol indicates the *type of operation to be performed*, and the flowchart graphically illustrates the *sequence in which the operations are to be performed*. Flow lines depict the sequential flow of the program logic. The more commonly used flowchart symbols are: computer process ☐, predefined process ▢▢, generalized input/output ▱, decision ◇, connector ○, and termination ⬭. Flowcharting and other flowchart symbols are discussed in Chapter 12, "Programming Concepts."

The numbers just outside the upper right-hand corner of all predefined functions provide cross references to appropriate program *statement numbers* in the program listing (see Figure B-1).

**Input/Output.**  The *interactive* nature of BASIC makes it necessary to distinguish between end-user input and computer output. To do this, example interactive sessions present *output* in yellow type and *input* in white type. In the textual material, output is shown in light type and input in **bold type.** For example,

Enter employee name and hours worked? **L. James, 38**

**Presentation of Example Programs.**  The 12 example programs are the basis for demonstrating the principles of programming in BASIC. Each example is presented with a *program description*, a *structure chart*, a *flowchart*, a *program listing*, and an example *interactive session*. These five items, which always appear together, are collectively referenced as Example Program #1, Example Program #2, and so on. To avoid confusion, only support graphics and special program segments will have figure numbers. Unless otherwise stated, any textual reference to an example program (e.g., Example Program #1) refers to all elements that comprise the documentation of the program.

# B-4  VARIABLES AND CONSTANTS

Numeric and alphanumeric values, such as 14 and "DP101", are stored in primary storage locations within the computer and recalled by **identifiers.** Identifiers are used to name these storage locations, which are called **variables.** Identifiers are also used to name arrays (discussed in Learning Module IV), functions (Learning Module VI), and programs.

Numeric values are refereced by *numeric identifiers*. Alphanumeric values are referenced by *string identifiers*. These identifiers, or **variable names,** represent the actual values of the storage locations. In the input/output example above, the values of "L. James" and 38 are stored in locations referenced by the variable names EMPLOYEE$ and HOURS. "L. James" is a **string constant** (also called a **literal value**) and 38 is a **numeric constant.** When found in programming instructions, string constants like "DP101" and "L. James" are placed within quotation marks. This convention is followed in the discussion material as well.

The range of allowable numeric and string values depends on the version of BASIC used. The minimum and maximum values for numeric constants normally range from $1 * 10^{-99}$ to $1 * 10^{+99}$. The maximum length of string constants varies from 256 to 32,000 characters.

Most versions of BASIC in use today use the following naming conventions. The identifier:

1. Is normally no more than 40 characters in length
2. Must begin with a letter
3. Contains only letters and digits (no spaces)
4. Becomes a string variable name when a dollar sign ($) is appended to the end of the name
5. Does not distinguish between upper- and lowercase letters (i.e., Part = PART)

Example identifiers for numeric and string values are listed below.

| Numeric Variables Names | String Variable Names |
|---|---|
| B | Z$ |
| PartNumber | PARTNAME$ |
| BIOLOGY318 | U11a |

In some versions of BASIC, *only the first two characters are interpreted by the computer*. For these versions, "Part Number" would be interpreted as "PA" and "U11a$" would be interpreted as "U1$". The remaining characters are purely for programmer convenience and documentation. For example, the numeric variable name TOTAL in the program listing of Figure B-1 (Example Program #1) is more descriptive than simply TO.

In the program of Figure B-1 (Example Program #1), the variable names for sales figures are S1, S2, and S3. You might say: "Why not use SALES1, SALES2, and SALES3?" If your version of BASIC only recognizes the first two characters as being significant, then SALES1, SALES2, and SALES3 would all be interpreted as a single variable name—SA.

The most common configuration for a microcomputer is a video monitor, a processor, at least one disk drive, and a printer.
(Dataproducts Corporation)

Another consideration in naming variables is that you must avoid using **reserved words,** such as READ, PRINT, and END. These words are reserved for the exclusive use of the BASIC interpreter and will be assumed to be a command, not a variable name.

## B-5 STYLE AND SPACING

In BASIC, each program statement can be automatically assigned a **line number.** You, as the programmer, can select the beginning number and the increment. Programmers often begin each second-level module (i.e., those that are called from the driver module) with some multiple of a thousand, then increment by 10 (see Figure B-1). This makes it easier to distinguish between modules and permits you to insert statements at a later date. The numbering scheme in the examples is designed to make it easier for you to cross-reference the program listing, the textual material, the structure chart, and the flowchart. For each example program (see Figure B-1), statements are numbered as follows:

| | | |
|---|---|---|
| Program description: | 10–99 | (increment 2) |
| Driver module (Main): | 100–999 | (increment 10) |
| | | |
| Module 1.1: | 1000–1999 | (increment 10) |
| Module 1.2: | 2000–2999 | (increment 10) |
| Module 1.3: | 3000–3999 | (increment 10) |
| Module 1.4: | 4000–4999 | (increment 10) |
| Module 1.5: | 5000–5999 | (increment 10) |
| Module 1.6: | 6000–6999 | (increment 10) |
| Module 1.7: | 7000–7999 | (increment 10) |

The increment is set to 5 when the number of statements in a module exceeds 99. Modules called by a second-level module (e.g., Module 1.1.2 or Module 1.3.1) are contained within the statement number range of the calling module. That is, Module 1.1.2 might begin with statement number 1350, which is within the Module 1.1 range of 1000–1999.

BASIC is a **free-form** language. This means that you have a lot of flexibility in the way the statements are entered. There is only one requirement. There must be at least one space between each of the following: variable names, constants, and reserved words. You may place operators [+ − * / ^ = < >], symbols [* ( ) "], and delimiters [, ; :] next to each of these items, or you can insert spaces for better readability. The following statements are the same:

```
2010 LET TOTAL=S1+S2+S3

2010 LET TOTAL = S1 + S2 + S3
```

To include more than one BASIC *instruction* on a single numbered *statement*, separate the instructions with a colon (:) [some systems use a backslash (\) ]. For example:

```
2010 LET TOTAL = Q1 + Q2 + Q3: LET AVERAGE = TOTAL / 3
```

It's a good idea to adopt a personal style, then be consistent throughout your program. A well-formatted program is easier to debug and revise. Indenting certain parts of the program will improve readability of the source code and help you to spot program modules, remarks, loops, and so on, more quickly.

In the example programs, all variable names (e.g., TOTAL) and BASIC commands (e.g., INPUT, PRINT, END) are in uppercase letters. All remarks are in upper/lowercase letters. The start and end of the "Main" driver program are indicated as follows:

```
REM <<<< Start Main >>>>
    ⋮
REM <<<< End Main >>>>
```

The boundaries of each subordinate module are indicated as follows:

```
1000 REM ---- Module 1.1—Accept Sales Figures
    ⋮
1999 RETURN
```

Program sequences are often indented to improve readability.

## REVIEW EXERCISES (LEARNING MODULE I)

1. Classify each of the following as a string or a numeric constant.
   (a) 12.456      (c) "Rocky Mountains"      (e) 789
   (b) "12.456"    (d) "ROCKY"                (f) 987654.0

   Which of the above are literal values?

**2.** Identify legal and illegal variable names from the following list. Explain what rule or rules are violated for the illegal variable names. Which are numeric and which are string variable names?

(a)  A1111                        (g)  *SCORE
(b)  B$                           (h)  ECONOMICORDERQUANTITY
(c)  ALPHA1A                      (i)  DESCRIP$
(d)  NET PAY                      (j)  SUM
(e)  5SALARY                      (k)  SUM1
(f)  END

**3.** In an inventory control program, variable A contains "parts on hand," variable B contains "parts used," and variable C contains "parts added." Rename the variables in the following statement so that they can be more easily understood.

```
100 LET A=A-B+C
```

**4.** The following special characters are used to formulate BASIC instructions. Classify each as being an operator, a symbol, or a delimiter.

(a)  *          (d)  :          (g)  ^
(b)  ,          (e)  )          (h)  +
(c)  /          (f)  =          (i)  "

**5.** What is the purpose of: (a) a driver module? (b) a line number?

**6.** For your computing environment, determine the following:
(a)  minimum and maximum values for numeric constants
(b)  maximum length of string constants
(c)  maximum length of variable names
(d)  number of significant characters in variable names

# LEARNING MODULE II

# Getting Started in Basic

## B-6  BASIC INSTRUCTION SET: LEARNING MODULE II GROUP

BASIC instructions are executed sequentially unless the sequence of execution is altered by a *control* instruction. Like other languages, BASIC's instruction set has at least one instruction in each of the major instruction categories. The instructions that we will discuss fall into the following categories:

- Input/output instructions
- Data transfer and assignment instructions
- Computation instructions
- Control instructions
- Format instructions
- Other instructions

Chapter 12, "Programming Concepts," contains a detailed explanation of all instruction categories. For ease of reference, a summary of BASIC instructions can be found at the end of the book.

A chart on the page preceding the start of Learning Module I summarizes the BASIC instructions in each instruction category and by the Learning Module in which they are introduced. The Learning Module II instruction set, presented below in this section, contains several of the most commonly used BASIC instructions. The use of these instructions is illustrated in Example Programs #1 and #2. The same pattern of introduction and illustration is followed in subsequent learning modules. Some of the advanced features of the instructions are introduced in context with the discussions of the example programs.

The line numbers have been omitted in most of the examples that are given in the textual material to help you focus on the **syntax,** or the rules of formulating instructions. The general format and at least one example are presented for each new instruction.

### Input/Output Instructions

Input.   An INPUT instruction causes program execution to pause and an optional *prompt* to be displayed on the terminal. When a semicolon (;) follows the prompt, a *question mark* (?) is displayed to signal the user that the program is waiting for data to be entered. When a comma (,) follows the prompt, the *question mark* (?) does not appear.

*Format*:   INPUT "prompt"; list of variables

*Examples*:

*Without prompt*

INPUT EMPLOYEE$, HOURS

*With prompt*
INPUT "Enter employee name and hours worked"; EMPLOYEE$, HOURS

If you executed a program with the INPUT instruction above, a prompt and question mark would appear as shown below.

Enter employee name and hours worked? **L. James, 38**

The variables take on the corresponding input data. In the example, EMPLOYEE$ takes on the value of "L. James", and HOURS takes on the value of 38. Good interactive programs have plenty of input prompts. If you did not have a prompt and saw only a question mark (or nothing), how would you know what to enter?

PRINT. When BASIC was developed, most terminals were teleprinters with key input and printer output (no monitor). Therefore, it was only logical that the primary output instruction be called PRINT. The PRINT instruction has stuck, even though most output is soft copy on video display terminals (VDTs) or microcomputer monitors. The PRINT instruction causes output to be displayed on a monitor or printed on a teleprinter terminal, depending on which one you are using.

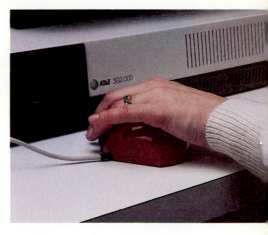

The keyboard is our primary means of entering data into a computer system. Another input device, called the mouse, is rolled across the desktop to move the cursor quickly about the screen.
(AT&T)

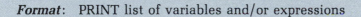

*Format*:   PRINT list of variables and/or expressions

The PRINT instruction displays (or prints) the values of variables, constants, and the results of any arithmetic expressions.

*Example*:   PRINT "The pay of", EMPLOYEE$, "is", HOURS $* 8.50$

Using the values from the INPUT example above (L. James, 38), the output would be as follows:

The pay of            L. James            is                         323

The *value* of EMPLOYEE$ and the two other string constants are displayed as is. The arithmetic expression (38*8.50 = 323) is resolved and displayed. In BASIC, the asterisk (*) is the symbol for the multiplication operation.

A numeric constant is, itself, an arithmetic expression. See what happens when a single number is included in the PRINT list.

*Example*:   PRINT "Hours worked is", 38

The output becomes

Hours worked is                      38

The *delimiters* (, ;) that separate the items in the print list determine *where* the values and constants are displayed on the line. The display line is divided into *zones* (see Figure B-2). The first item in the print list is displayed (or printed) in the first zone, the second item in the second zone, and so on. Some versions of BASIC have a preset zone

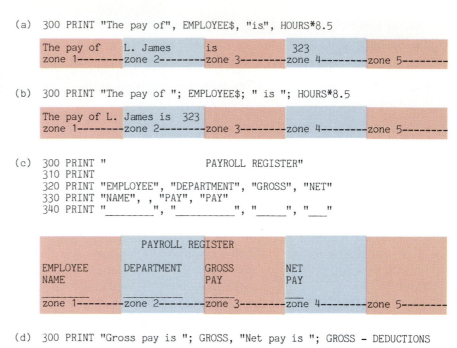

(a)  300 PRINT "The pay of", EMPLOYEE$, "is", HOURS*8.5

```
The pay of      L. James       is             323
zone 1--------  zone 2-------- zone 3-------- zone 4-------- zone 5--------
```

(b)  300 PRINT "The pay of "; EMPLOYEE$; " is "; HOURS*8.5

```
The pay of L. James is  323
zone 1--------  zone 2-------- zone 3-------- zone 4-------- zone 5--------
```

(c)  300 PRINT "                    PAYROLL REGISTER"
     310 PRINT
     320 PRINT "EMPLOYEE", "DEPARTMENT", "GROSS", "NET"
     330 PRINT "NAME", , "PAY", "PAY"
     340 PRINT "_____", "_____", "_____", "___"

```
                    PAYROLL REGISTER

EMPLOYEE        DEPARTMENT     GROSS          NET
NAME                           PAY            PAY
_____        _____     _____          ___
zone 1--------  zone 2-------- zone 3-------- zone 4-------- zone 5--------
```

**FIGURE B-2**
**Uses of the PRINT Instruction**
These outputs are discussed in
the text material.

(d)  300 PRINT "Gross pay is "; GROSS, "Net pay is "; GROSS - DEDUCTIONS

```
Gross pay is  323            Net pay is  280
zone 1--------  zone 2-------- zone 3-------- zone 4-------- zone 5--------
```

width, usually from 14 to 18 character positions wide. On others, you can set the zone width to be whatever you want. For the purposes of illustration, we will assume a zone width of 14 characters in all examples.

The two print list delimiters, the *comma* (,) and the *semicolon* (;), serve a dual purpose. The delimiters separate the items in the print list and position the cursor of VDTs and micros, or the print head for teleprinter terminals.

- The *comma* positions the cursor/print head at the *beginning of the next complete zone*.

- The *semicolon* positions the cursor/print head at the *next display/ print position*. When separated by a semicolon, items in the print list would be displayed next to one another.

Figure B-2 illustrates how the PRINT instruction can be used for a variety of display requirements. Figure B-2(a) is a repeat of the example above. Notice that the 323 in Figure B-2(a) begins in the second position of zone 4. All numbers are displayed with a leading space to permit a minus sign for negative numbers.

Figure B-2(b) shows what happens when semicolons are used as delimiters. Figure B-2(c) illustrates how a report title and column headings can be generated with a series of PRINT instructions. Notice that a PRINT instruction with no item list (statement 310) causes a blank line to be displayed. Figure B-2(d) illustrates how readability can be improved by using commas and semicolons in combination. Notice that the character strings "Gross pay is " and "Net pay is " both have a blank space at the end of the string. This provides a space between the string and the following number.

**LPRINT.** Use the LPRINT instruction when you are working on a VDT or micro, have a printer available, and want a hard-copy output. LPRINT causes the output line to be routed to a printer.

## Data Transfer and Assignment Instructions

**LET.** The LET expression can be used to assign values to variables and to perform computations. The LET computation capabilities are discussed later in the computation instruction category.

*Format*: LET variable = variable or constant value

*Examples*:  LET SCORE = 95
LET GRADE$ = "A"
LET X = Y
LET EMPLOYEE$ = E$

Use the LPRINT instruction to route an output line to a printer. Mailing labels are being printed on this printer. Printers vary in output speeds from 40 characters per second to 40,000 lines per minute.

In the assignment examples above, the constant values of 95 and "A" are assigned to storage locations referenced by the variable names SCORE and GRADE$, respectively. In the latter two examples, the values of the data referenced by the variables Y and E$ are transferred to the storage locations referenced by X and EMPLOYEE$, respectively. The values of Y and E$ are unchanged. The values previously in SCORE, GRADE$, X, and EMPLOYEE$ are replaced with the values of the constants and variables on the right-hand side.

In those versions of BASIC released prior to the new ANS BASIC standard, the addition of the reserved word LET is optional. However, in ANS BASIC, the LET is part of the command structure and is, therefore, required.

Any variable that is used in an instruction and has not been previously assigned a value is set equal to *zero* (0) for numeric variables and to the *null* ("") character for string variables. The null character is a string value that has no length.

## Computation Instructions

**LET.** The LET instruction is also used for computation.

*Format*:   LET variable = expression

*Example*:   LET X = (A+B−C)⌃3

An *expression* consists of numeric variables and constants, and **arithmetic operators** (+ − * / ⌃). Arithmetic expressions are more cumbersome in all programming languages because they must be entered on the same level (or one continuous line). In our handwritten calculations, we put the numerator physically over the denominator (e.g., ½) and

| OPERATION | OPERATOR |
|---|---|
| Exponentiation | $\wedge$ or $\uparrow$ or $**$ |
| Multiplication – Division | $*$  $/$ |
| Addition – Subtraction | $+$  $-$ |

denote exponentiation with superscripts (e.g., $A^2$). In programming, however, we have to put the numerator, denominator, and superscripts on the same level.

When more than one operator is included in a single expression, the computer must determine which to perform first. Because of this, a standard **hierarchy of operations** was established to provide rules by which the computer evaluates arithmetic expressions. The hierarchy is illustrated in Figure B-3. Exponentiation ($\wedge$, $\uparrow$, or $**$) has the highest priority, followed by multiplication-division ($*$,$/$) and addition-subtraction ($+$,$-$). Notice that multiplication and division have the same priority, and addition and subtraction have the same priority. In the case of a tie, the expression is evaluated from *left to right*.

Parentheses override the priority rules for the hierarchy of operations. What would happen if we removed the parentheses from the arithmetic expression $X = (A+B-C)\wedge3$? Without the parentheses, the first operation would be the exponentiation, $C^3$. The parentheses override the hierarchy priority and cause the expression within the parentheses to be resolved first. The result of $A+B-C$ is then raised to the third power. *When in doubt, use parentheses*. When you have a set of parentheses within a set of parentheses, the innermost expression is evaluated first. Always make sure that you have the same number of open and close parentheses in arithmetic expressions. Figure B-4 illustrates the order in which the expression for the future value of an annuity would be resolved by a computer.

**FIGURE B-4**
**Evaluation of an Arithmetic Expression**
The formula for the future worth of an annuity is shown algebraically and as a BASIC computation instruction. The expression is resolved by the computer in stages, according to the hierarchy of operations.

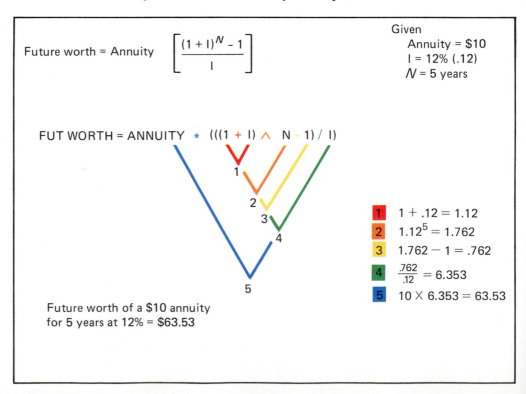

$$\text{Future worth} = \text{Annuity} \left[ \frac{(1 + I)^N - 1}{I} \right]$$

Given
Annuity = \$10
I = 12% (.12)
$N$ = 5 years

FUT WORTH = ANNUITY $*$ $(((1 + I) \wedge N - 1) / I)$

1 — $1 + .12 = 1.12$
2 — $1.12^5 = 1.762$
3 — $1.762 - 1 = .762$
4 — $\frac{.762}{.12} = 6.353$
5 — $10 \times 6.353 = 63.53$

Future worth of a \$10 annuity
for 5 years at 12% = \$63.53

## Control Instructions: Unconditional Transfer

GOTO.  The GOTO instruction causes an unconditional branch in the sequence of execution. The next statement to be executed is the statement at the line number specified in the GOTO instruction.

*Format*:  GOTO line number

*Example*:  GOTO 440

GOSUB/RETURN.  The driver program uses the GOSUB/RETURN combination of instructions to call and execute a module. The modules, also called **subroutines,** are a sequence of program instructions that are called and executed as needed.

Subroutines are used for the following reasons:

1. When a series of statements are to be executed several times throughout the program, or
2. To improve the logic of the program (i.e., structured programming).

The GOSUB/RETURN instruction pair gives us the capability to write structured programs.

*Format*:  GOSUB line number

      subroutine statement
          &#8942;
      subroutine statement
      RETURN [line number]

*Example*:  130 GOSUB 1000
             140 REM Call Module 1.2—Compute Total Sales
             150 GOSUB 2000
                &#8942;
             1000 REM ---- Module 1.1—Accept Sales Figures
             1010 INPUT S1, S2, S3
             1999 RETURN

The GOSUB instruction is a control instruction that causes an unconditional branch to the statement at the designated line number (1000 in the example above). Statement 1000 is the first statement for the subroutine of Module 1.1 of Example Program #1. The subroutine statements are executed in sequence through the RETURN instruction (1999). The RETURN instruction causes a branch to the instruction following the original GOSUB. In the example above, the next instruction is at statement 140. When the RETURN is followed by a line number (e.g., RETURN 100), the explicit line number overrides the default branch (instruction following GOSUB) and control of execution is passed to the statement at the line number. If your version of BASIC does not permit RETURNs to have a line number, *you will need to use alternative logic*, perhaps using GOTOs.

For now, the GOSUB/RETURN instruction pair is supported in the new ANS BASIC. However, GOSUB is designated for future removal from the standard as soon as the more sophisticated control structures (see Learning Module IX, "The 'New' ANS BASIC") have been implemented in most versions of BASIC. In many versions of BASIC, the GOSUB/RETURN combination is still the primary instruction for creating structured programs, but the GOTO is seldom needed. In keeping with the trend to *GOTO-less programming* (see Chapter 12, "Programming Concepts"), *we will use the GOTO instruction sparingly*. The GOTO is used only when its use is necessary to maintain structured logic.

END.   The purpose of the END instruction is to terminate program execution. Every program must have an END instruction. The END instruction can be placed anywhere in the program. Often the best place for it is at the end of the driver module. See Example Program #1, statement 180.

> *Example*:   999 END

## Control Instructions: Conditional Transfer

IF/THEN/ELSE.   An IF/THEN instruction is a conditional "branch" instruction. *If* a condition is evaluated to be true, *then* one of two things happens: (1) control of execution is transferred (a branch) to someplace else in the program, or (2) the instruction(s) following THEN is executed. *If* the condition is evaluated to be false, *then* the ELSE clause is executed.

> *Format*:   IF expression relational operator expression
> THEN line number or executable instruction(s)
> [ELSE line number or executable instruction(s)]

The **relational operators** shown in Figure B-5 are used to compare numeric or string expressions.

> *Example*:   IF CODE$ = "S" THEN 440 ELSE PRINT "Error"
>
>               IF AVERAGE >= 90 THEN PRINT "GRADE IS A"
>
>               COURSE$="DP101"
>               IF COURSE$ < "DP206" THEN 650

In the first example, if the value of CODE$ is equal to "S", then the statement at line number 440 is executed next. If the expressions are not equal, then the PRINT instruction following the *optional* ELSE clause is executed. In the second example, "GRADE IS A" is displayed only if the value of AVERAGE is greater than or equal to 90. Since

| COMPARISON | OPERATOR |
|---|---|
| Equal to | = |
| Less than | < |
| Greater than | > |
| Less than or equal to | < = |
| Greater than or equal to | > = |
| Not equal to | <> |

**FIGURE B-5**
**Relational Operators**

there is no ELSE clause, any other values of AVERAGE would cause the next sequential statement to be executed.

Inequality comparisons can also be made between string variables. The comparison is strictly alphabetic (e.g., SMITH before or less than SMYTH) for *alpha* comparisons. For *alphanumeric* comparisons, a number character is considered "less than" an alpha character (in the ASCII code, see Figure B-6), and the comparison is made from left to right, one character at a time. For example, "1" is less than "A"; that is, the decimal ASCII code for "1" is numerically less than the decimal code for "A" (i.e., 49 < 65). In the third example above, no action is taken until the third characters are compared and found to be not equal.

D = D = 68
P = P = 80
1 ≠ 2 (49, the ASCII code for 1, is less than 50, the ASCII code for 2)

**FIGURE B-6**
**ASCII Encoding System (Decimal)**

| ASCII code | Character | ASCII code | Character | ASCII code | Character | ASCII code | Character |
|---|---|---|---|---|---|---|---|
| 000 | Null | 032 | (space) | 064 | @ | 096 | ' |
| 001 | | 033 | ! | 065 | A | 097 | a |
| 002 | | 034 | " | 066 | B | 098 | b |
| 003 | | 035 | # | 067 | C | 099 | c |
| 004 | | 036 | $ | 068 | D | 100 | d |
| 005 | | 037 | % | 069 | E | 101 | e |
| 006 | | 038 | & | 070 | F | 102 | f |
| 007 | beep or bell | 039 | ' | 071 | G | 103 | g |
| 008 | | 040 | ( | 072 | H | 104 | h |
| 009 | tab | 041 | ) | 073 | I | 105 | i |
| 010 | line feed | 042 | * | 074 | J | 106 | j |
| 011 | | 043 | + | 075 | K | 107 | k |
| 012 | | 044 | , | 076 | L | 108 | l |
| 013 | carriage return | 045 | - | 077 | M | 109 | m |
| 014 | | 046 | . | 078 | N | 110 | n |
| 015 | | 047 | / | 079 | O | 111 | o |
| 016 | | 048 | 0 | 080 | P | 112 | p |
| 017 | | 049 | 1 | 081 | Q | 113 | q |
| 018 | | 050 | 2 | 082 | R | 114 | r |
| 019 | | 051 | 3 | 083 | S | 115 | s |
| 020 | | 052 | 4 | 084 | T | 116 | t |
| 021 | | 053 | 5 | 085 | U | 117 | u |
| 022 | | 054 | 6 | 086 | V | 118 | v |
| 023 | | 055 | 7 | 087 | W | 119 | w |
| 024 | | 056 | 8 | 088 | X | 120 | x |
| 025 | | 057 | 9 | 089 | Y | 121 | y |
| 026 | | 058 | : | 090 | Z | 122 | z |
| 027 | | 059 | ; | 091 | [ | 123 | { |
| 028 | right (cursor movement) | 060 | < | 092 | \ | 124 | \| |
| 029 | left (cursor movement) | 061 | = | 093 | ] | 125 | } |
| 030 | up (cursor movement) | 062 | > | 094 | ^ | 126 | ~ |
| 031 | down (cursor movement) | 063 | ? | 095 | _ | 127 | ⌂ |

Because 1 < 2, the comparison ("DP101" < "DP206") is true and the statement at 650 is executed next.

Notice in Figure B-6 that the ASCII code values of upper- and lower-case letters are different. In comparing "SMYTH" to "Smith", the comparison "SMYTH" < "Smith" would be true because the ASCII value of an uppercase "M" is less than that of a lowercase "m" (77 < 109).

In the example programs, most lines contain only one instruction. However, there are circumstances that call for combining several instructions in a single statement, usually on one line. To do this, simply end one instruction with a *colon* (:) [a *backslash* (\) on some systems] and begin another instruction on the same line. In the example below, the line number 3030 refers to both an IF and a GOSUB instruction. If the expression in the following example is true, then both of the instructions that follow the THEN clause are executed.

    3030 IF AVERAGE >= 90 THEN PRINT "GRADE IS A": GOSUB 2000

Multiple instructions can also be included following an optional ELSE clause.

### Other Instructions

REM.   REM, or "remark," instructions are a programmer convenience. All comments prefaced by REM are ignored by the computer and can be placed anywhere in the program. Use REM instructions to document your programs (see any of the example programs).

---

*Format*:   REM remarks

---

*Example*:   REM ---- Module 1.1—Accept Sales Figures

Remarks can be added to the end of a statement by prefacing the remarks with a single quote (') or, in some BASIC dialects, an exclamation mark (!).

*Example*:   LET COUNT = 1 'Initialize counter to 1

## B-7   SYSTEM COMMANDS

We use *system commands* to communicate to the computer what we want done with our BASIC program. For example, with system commands we can store, retrieve, and execute BASIC programs. System commands are not part of the program and are therefore not assigned line numbers.

These "command-level" instructions are only partially standardized and vary considerably between computers. The following system commands are common to many computers.

RUN.   The RUN command causes the program currently in primary storage to be executed.

---

MEMORY BITS

**PROGRAM INSTRUCTION CLASSIFICATIONS**
- Input/Output
- Data transfer and assignment
- Computation
- Control
  Unconditional branch
  Conditional branch
- Format

NEW.   The NEW command clears primary storage and readies the computer to accept a new BASIC program.

LOAD.   The LOAD command causes the program identified by "program name" to be retrieved from secondary storage and loaded to primary storage.

> *Format*:   LOAD program name

> *Example*:   LOAD PROG1

Some versions of BASIC require system command references to a program name to be prefaced by or enclosed in quotes.

> *Example*:   LOAD "PROG1
>
>                      LOAD "PROG1"

SAVE.   With the SAVE command, the program currently in primary storage is saved on secondary storage, probably magnetic disk, for recall at a later time. The format is similar to the LOAD command.

KILL.   The KILL command deletes a named file, program, or data, from disk. The format is similar to the LOAD command.

LIST.   The LIST command causes all or part of the program currently in primary storage to be displayed on the workstation monitor.

> *Examples*:   LIST               (display the entire program)
>                        LIST 1000          (display statement 1000)
>                        LIST 1000–1999     (display statements from 1000 through 1999)
>                        LIST 2000–         (begin with 2000 and display the remainder of the program)

LLIST.   The LLIST command causes all or part of the program currently in primary storage to be printed on a printer.

AUTO.   The AUTO command causes line numbers to be generated automatically according to your specifications (e.g., start with 100 and increment by 10).

EDIT.   The EDIT command puts you in *edit mode*. In edit mode you can modify or edit portions of an instruction without having to reenter it.

DELETE.   The DELETE command deletes those lines in the program that you designate (e.g., 1000 or 3000–3500).

RENUM.   The RENUM command causes all or part of the program lines to be renumbered according to your specifications (e.g., beginning at existing line 140, renumber starting at 100 and incrementing by 10).

The command-level instructions above are only a subset of available system commands. Your instructor will point out any variations in the list above and explain other helpful commands for your computing environment.

# EXAMPLE PROGRAM #1

This program accepts three sales figures, then computes and displays the total.

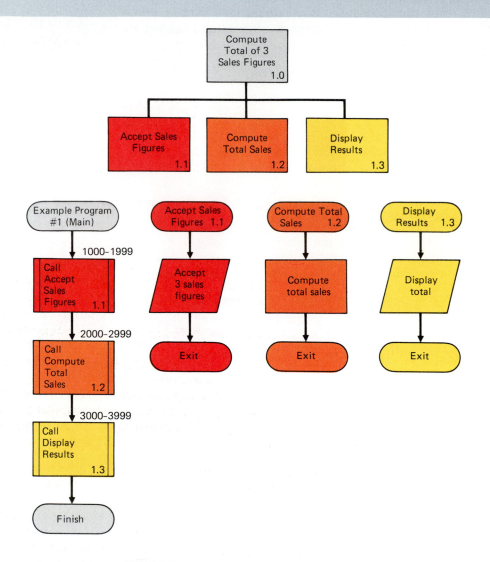

continued

## B-8 EXAMPLE PROGRAM #1: INPUT, PROCESSING, OUTPUT

The example programs are designed to illustrate the use of BASIC programming instructions and the structure of BASIC programs. Each example program introduces different BASIC features and general programming techniques. Example Program #1 accepts three sales figures (input), computes the total (processing), then displays the result (output).

This simple program is divided into three modules (see the structure chart): Module 1.1—Accept Sales Figures, Module 1.2—Compute Total Sales, and Module 1.3—Display Results. The first module is *input*, the

```
2    REM          **** Example Program #1 ****
4    REM  Description:
6    REM    This program accepts three sales figures, then computes and
8    REM    displays the total.
10   REM  Variables list:
12   REM    S1, S2, S3            - Sales figures (Stibs, Farkles, Teglers)
14   REM    TOTAL                 - Total sales
99   REM
100  REM  <<<< Start Main >>>>
110  REM
120  REM  Call Module 1.1 - Accept Sales Figures
130  GOSUB 1000
140  REM  Call Module 1.2 - Compute Total Sales
150  GOSUB 2000
160  REM  Call Module 1.3 - Display Results
170  GOSUB 3000
180  END
190  REM  <<<< End Main >>>>
999  REM
1000 REM  ==== Module 1.1 - Accept Sales Figures
1010 INPUT S1, S2, S3
1999 RETURN
2000 REM  ==== Module 1.2 - Compute Total Sales
2010 LET TOTAL = S1 + S2 + S3
2999 RETURN
3000 REM  ==== Module 1.3 - Display Results
3010 PRINT TOTAL
3999 RETURN
```

```
run
? 32000,28000,25000
 85000
ok
```

second is *processing*, and the third is *output*. This is a common modular structure for straightforward programs. The driver module (Main: 100–999) calls each of these modules in sequence (see flowchart) to produce the interactive session or RUN (execution) of the program. In the interactive session, three sales figures are entered and the resulting total is displayed.

Statement 130 GOSUB 1000, the first *executable instruction*, causes the execution of Module 1.1—Accept Sales Figures (1000–1999). An executable instruction causes some type of processing activity (e.g., I/O, assignment, computation, and so on) to occur. Control is transferred to statement 1000, and since REM is a *nonexecutable instruction*, control is passed on to statement 1010 INPUT S1, S2, S3. Once the three sales figures have been entered, the RETURN at 1999 causes control to be passed back to the driver module at statement 140, the statement following the original GOSUB at 130. The other two modules are called and executed in a similar manner. The END at 180 is encountered and execution is terminated.

**Inquiry and Response.** The interactive session of Example Program #1 is typical of the inquiry/response style of programming. In the interactive session, a question mark (?) is displayed to signal the user (inquiry) that the computer is ready to accept data (response). In Example Program #1 there are no prompts that tell the user what to enter, so the user must know that three sales figures are to be entered (the use of prompts is discussed in the next learning module). The user enters the three sales figures, separated by a comma (,) and the result is displayed on the next line. The program must be RUN again to compute the total of three more sales figures. Remember that input data are displayed in *white* characters so that you can distinguish between what is entered by the user and what is produced as a result of programming. Program-generated output is displayed in *yellow* characters.

**Developing Good Programming Habits.** The following BASIC statement produces exactly the same interactive session as Example Program #1.

```
10 INPUT A,B,C: PRINT A+B+C
```

So why do we need all the extraneous comments and instructions? The answer is simple: *to develop good programming habits from the very start*. The source code of Example Program #1 includes:

1. A program name (statement 2)
2. A program description (statements 4–8)
3. A list and description of all variable names (statements 10–14)
4. Internal comments (statements 120, 140, and others)
5. A structured design with a driver program (100–999) and subordinate modules (1000–3999)

All other example programs are organized in a similar manner. The above are considered to be the minimal *internal* documentation requirements for a program. The minimal *external* documentation requirements are the structure chart, a logic diagram (e.g., flowchart), and an interactive session. This amount of internal documentation may seem excessive for such a simple program, but it is important to practice good documentation and program design starting with your first program. You will not only learn to program more quickly, but you will be a better programmer, as well.

**Entering and Editing Programs.** To write a BASIC program, you must first inform the computer that you wish to enter a program. Do this by entering the word BASIC (or some variation, e.g., BASICA, GWBASIC) after the *operating system prompt* (e.g., A>, ], :) and pressing the carriage return. The BASIC software is loaded and an "Ok" prompt appears. This prompt means you are in *BASIC mode* and the system is ready to accept your program. Your instructor will provide the specifics for your hardware/software environment. The session might appears as follows:

```
A> BASIC
Ok
10 INPUT A, B, C
20 LET TOTAL = A+B+C
30 PRINT TOTAL
99 END
RUN
? 32000,28000,25000
 85000
Ok
```

Programs are entered one statement at a time. You can elect to number the statements yourself or request that the system do it automatically (i.e., use the AUTO system command). Editing procedures (modifying statements) vary widely between versions of BASIC, but the following are standard:

1. Backspace to delete the last character entered.

2. To replace a statement with another, key in the number of the statement to be replaced and the new statement.

3. To insert a statement in the program, key in a number that is numerically between the statement numbers adjacent to the desired location (e.g., key 15 to insert a statement between statements 10 and 20), then key in the statement.

4. To delete a statement from the program, key in the number of the statement, then press the carriage return.

## B-9  EXAMPLE PROGRAM #2: LOOP AND COUNTER

Example Programs #2, #3, and #4 are extensions of Example Program #1. Each of the three programs accomplishes the same task: *For any number of salespeople*, three sales figures are accepted, then the total is computed and displayed for *each salesperson*. The logic of each program varies slightly because different BASIC features are introduced in each program. Example Programs #2 and #3 produce the same interactive session. Input and output prompts are added in Example Program #4.

In Example Program #2, the process of computing and displaying the total for one salesperson (2000–4999, essentially Example Program #1) is included in a *loop* and repeated for each salesperson. Module 1.1—Accept Number accepts the number of salespeople to be processed. The loop is controlled by Module 1.5—Loop Control.

The loop is created by a *counter* (5020) and an IF instruction (5030). The loop (140–210) is repeated until the value of NUMBER (the number of salespeople entered in Module 1.1) is equal to the value of COUNT (the counter). Since the test-on-condition is at the end of the loop, the loop is a DOUNTIL loop structure (see Chapter 12, "Programming Concepts"). The DOWHILE loop structure is demonstrated in Example Program #4.

In BASIC, all numeric variables are set to zero at the start of program execution, so the value of COUNT is zero until the first execution of statement 5020. After the first time through the loop, the value of COUNT is 1. Thereafter, statement 5020 increments COUNT by 1 for each repetition of the loop (another salesperson processed). The THEN clause of the IF instruction at 5030 is ignored until COUNT equals NUMBER. In these cases, the RETURN at 5999 returns control of execution to the driver program and the loop is repeated. When the NUMBER equals COUNT, the THEN clause is taken and the END instruction is executed causing program execution to be terminated.

# EXAMPLE PROGRAM #2

This program accepts three sales figures for each of any number of salespeople.  The total is computed and displayed for each salesperson.

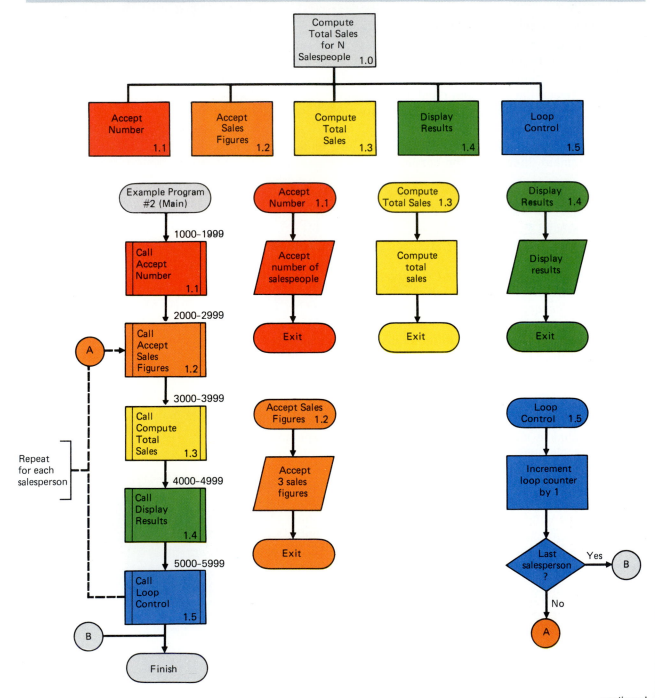

continued

Example Program 2 continued

```
2     REM              **** Example Program #2 ****
4     REM   Description:
6     REM     This program accepts three sales figures for each of any number
8     REM     of salespeople.  The total is computed and displayed for each
10    REM     salesperson.
12    REM   Variables list:
14    REM     NUMBER              - Number of salespeople
16    REM     S1, S2, S3          - Sales figures (Stibs, Farkles, Teglers)
18    REM     TOTAL               - Total sales
20    REM     COUNT               - Loop counter
99    REM
100   REM   <<<< Start Main >>>>
110   REM
120   REM   Call Module 1.1 - Accept Number
130   GOSUB 1000
140   REM   Call Module 1.2 - Accept Sales Figures
150   GOSUB 2000
160   REM   Call Module 1.3 - Compute Total Sales
170   GOSUB 3000
180   REM   Call Module 1.4 - Display Results
190   GOSUB 4000
200   REM   Call Module 1.5 - Loop Control
210   GOSUB 5000
220   END
230   REM   <<<< End Main >>>>
999   REM
1000  REM   ==== Module 1.1 - Accept Number
1010  INPUT NUMBER
1999  RETURN
2000  REM   ==== Module 1.2 - Accept Sales Figures
2010  INPUT S1, S2, S3
2999  RETURN
3000  REM   ==== Module 1.3 - Compute Average
3010  LET TOTAL = S1 + S2 + S3
3999  RETURN
4000  REM   ==== Module 1.4 - Display Results
4010  PRINT TOTAL
4999  RETURN
5000  REM   ==== Module 1.5 - Loop Control
5010  REM   Increment loop counter & test if last salesperson
5020  LET COUNT = COUNT + 1
5030  IF NUMBER = COUNT THEN RETURN 220
5999  RETURN 140
```

```
run
? 3
? 32000,28000,25000
 85000
? 50000,35000,20000
 105000
? 25000,30000,15000
 70000
ok
```

No more bugs! Every programmer has a sense of relief and accomplishment when the program finally runs. Some just lean back in their chair and grin—others explode with emotion.
(Photo supplied courtesy of Epson America)

## B-10   GETTING THE BUGS OUT: DEBUGGING

Once you have entered a program into the system, you may need to do a little **debugging** before the program works properly. A **bug** is a name given to an error in program syntax or logic.

**Syntax Errors.**   Debugging a program is a repetitive process, whereby each successive attempt gets you one step closer to a working program. The first step is to eliminate *syntax errors*. You get a syntax error when you violate one of the rules for writing instructions (e.g., placement of parentheses, spelling of commands, and so on). For example, you will get an error message if you enter PRNT rather than PRINT in statement 4010 of Example Program #2.

**Logic and I/O Errors.**   Once all the syntax errors have been removed, the program can be executed, but that does not always mean that you have a working program. You now have to debug the *logic of the program* and the *input/output formats*. To do this, you need to create *test data* and, perhaps, a *test data base* so that you know what to expect as output. In Example Program #2, you would expect the total to be 85000 if the test data for first salesperson are 32000, 28000, and 25000. If this is not the case, there is a bug in the program logic. A program whose logic is sound might have input or output formats that need to be "cleaned up" (e.g., columns properly aligned, heading centered, and so on). Do this after you have eliminated all the syntax and logic errors.

**Debugging Aids.**   Among the most helpful debugging aids, especially for finding logic errors, are the *trace* commands. These debugging aids permit a "trace" of the execution sequence of the program statements. When you ask for a trace, you get a sequential log of the order in which statements or sections of the program are executed. The trace also shows you which branches were taken during execution. By comparing the *actual* sequence of execution against the *expected* sequence of execution, you can usually isolate the error. The trace commands are:

```
TRACE ON      (or TRON on some versions of BASIC)
TRACE OFF     (or TROFF)
```

The TRACE ON command enables the display of each line number as the associated statement is executed. The TRACE OFF command disables the trace. Figure B-7 illustrates a trace of an execution of Example Program #2.

Programmers often add "extra" PRINT instructions to display the values of selected variables during the execution of a program. This technique helps you determine whether or not your program is doing what it is supposed to, when it is supposed to. Of course, once the program is working properly, the "extra" instructions are deleted.

Chapter 12, "Programming Concepts," contains a detailed discussion of the program development process and debugging concepts.

```
TRON
Ok
run
[2][4][6][8][10][12][14][16][18][20][99][100][110][120][130][1000][1010]? 3
[1999][140][150][2000][2010]? 32000,28000,25000
[2999][160][170][3000][3010][3999][180][190][4000][4010] 85000
[4999][200][210][5000][5010][5020][5030][5999][140][150][2000][2010]? 50000,35000,20000
[2999][160][170][3000][3010][3999][180][190][4000][4010] 105000
[4999][200][210][5000][5010][5020][5030][5999][140][150][2000][2010]? 25000,30000,15000
[2999][160][170][3000][3010][3999][180][190][4000][4010] 70000
[4999][200][210][5000][5010][5020][5030][220]
Ok
```

**FIGURE B-7**
**Interactive Session of Example Program #2 with the Trace "On"**
The trace is an excellent debugging aid that enables you to monitor the logic
of your program while it is being executed. The bracketed numbers list the
sequence in which the statements are executed.

## REVIEW EXERCISES (LEARNING MODULE II)

### BASIC Instructions and Concepts

1. What is the general function of system commands? Describe
   the specific function of LIST, LLIST, SAVE, LOAD, RUN, and
   NEW.

2. Associate each of the following BASIC instructions with an
   instruction category.
   (a) PRINT
   (b) IF/THEN
   (c) LET (two categories)
   (d) GOSUB/RETURN

3. "Trace" the execution of the following program by listing the
   line numbers in the order in which they are executed.

   ```
   100 GOSUB 400
   200 PRINT "The sum is ", X
   300 GOTO 700
   400 INPUT A, B
   500 LET X = A + B
   600 RETURN
   700 END
   ```

4. Identify the syntax error(s) in each of the following instructions.
   (a) 10 PRINT "          STATUS REPORT,

(b)  10 INPUT "Enter starting month and day": MONTH, DAY
(c)  10 LET X$ = Y+ Z
(d)  10 GOSUB 400 THEN 500
(e)  10 IF NAME = "Jones" THEN PRINT NAME

5. Use your hand calculator to determine what value of $X$ would be printed.

```
100 LET A=1
200 LET B=3
300 LET C=−4
400 LET X=(A/B+C)*B
500 PRINT X
600 END
```

6. Refer to Exercise 5. Use your hand calculator to determine what value of $X$ would be printed if statement 400 were replaced with the following statement.

```
400 LET X=(−B+(B^2−4*A*C)^.5)/(2*A)
```

7. In which of the IF instructions below is the comparison true?

```
100 LET A$="LESS"
200 LET B=5
300 IF "MORE" > A$ THEN 950
400 IF "LESS" <= A$ THEN 960
500 IF B^2 <= 28 THEN 970
600 IF C >= B THEN 980
700 LET DP$="DP101"
800 IF DP$ < "DP100" THEN 990
```

8. Which of the following statements will result in a program error? Describe the cause of each error.

```
100 REM PRINT "GRADE IS", A$
200 GOTO 10
300 LET A=4
351 LET C=0
500 LET X=(X*A)/2)
600 LET X$="(X*A)/2)"
700 PRINT "X=, X
800 LET Y=A/C
```

9. Write the print instructions that would produce the following output.

(a)

```
ZONE 1-------------- ZONE 2-------------- ZONE 3-------------- ZONE 4-------------- ZONE 5-------------
                              INVENTORY STATUS REPORT

PART NAME        PART NUMBER  ON HAND        USED-TO-DATE  ON ORDER
```

(b)

```
ZONE 1-------------- ZONE 2-------------- ZONE 3

QUANTITY ON HAND IS           S99999
QUANTITY ON HAND IS S99999
```

where S = sign, 9 = number

## Example Program #1

**10.** Follow the logic for the program, and manually perform the operations for sales figures 14356, 32091, and 22191. For 55486, 31075, and 11283.

**11.** How would you modify the program to total five sales figures?

**12.** How would you modify the program to route the output to the printer?

## Example Program #2

**13.** What is the fundamental difference in the logic of Example Programs #1 and #2?

**14.** What is the value of COUNT before any values have been entered? Why?

**15.** Follow the logic for the program, and manually perform the operations for two salespeople with sales figures of $46000, $30000, $22000 and $53000, $27000, and $12000. What are the values of the variables NUMBER, S1, S2, S3, TOTAL, and COUNT after the second execution of statements 3010 and 5020?

**16.** Fill in the blanks below to achieve the same objectives as the original statements 5030 and 5999.

```
5030 IF NUMBER > COUNT THEN RETURN ____
5999 RETURN ____
```

**17.** What is the purpose of statement 5020, the "counter"?

**18.** What statements in the Main driver program are within the "loop"?

**19.** How would you modify the program to eliminate Module 1.5?

## BASIC PROGRAMMING ASSIGNMENTS

**1.** Get acquainted with the computer and BASIC by entering and executing Example Program #1. Using the computer access procedures discussed in class, prepare to enter Example Program #1. Enter and execute this program and check your interactive session with that of the text.

**2.** Perform the following system-level operations on Example Program #1: name and SAVE the program; return to SYSTEM mode; return to BASIC mode; LOAD the program; EDIT S1, S2, and S3 to be F1, F2, and F3; RUN the program; LIST Module 1.3; KILL, or delete, the program file; and finally, SAVE the file again using the same name.

**3.** Revise Example Program #1 to be like Example Program #2. Execute, then save it for later recall. RENUMber the lines starting with 100 and incrementing by 10. Now RENUMber lines 200 and after in increments of 5.

**4.** Execute Example Program #2 with the trace command on. Compare your results with Figure B-7.

**5.** The number of widgets sold during each of the five days this last week is 71, 46, 92, 27, and 104. Write a program to enter the sales data and compute the total sales for the week, and to figure the average sold per day. The output (total sales and average) should appear as shown below.

340
68

**6.** Prepare a table converting centigrade temperatures from 0–31 degrees to Fahrenheit temperatures. The conversion formula is

F=(9/5)*C+32

The output should appear in columns in the first two print zones as shown below.

```
0          32
1          33.8
2          35.6
:          :
31         87.8
```

# Adding to Your Foundation

## B-11 BASIC INSTRUCTION SET: LEARNING MODULE III GROUP _____

In this learning module, two more control instructions are introduced. Both the FOR/NEXT and the WHILE/WEND instruction pairs make it easier to create loops. The three types of control instructions are *unconditional transfer* (e.g., GOSUB), *conditional transfer* (e.g., IF/THEN/ELSE), and *loop* (e.g., FOR/NEXT and WHILE/WEND, both described below).

| PROGRAMMING CONCEPTS |
|---|
| Conditional/Unconditional Transfers |
| Test-On-Condition |
| DOUNTIL and DOWHILE Loops |
| Infinite Loops |
| Nested Loops |
| Input Prompts |
| Output Descriptions |

### Control Instructions: Loop

FOR/NEXT. The FOR/NEXT combination of statements creates a loop in which the statements between a FOR instruction and a NEXT instruction are executed repeatedly. The FOR instruction specifies the number of times the sequence of statements is executed.

The FOR/NEXT combination is a programmer convenience for creating loops. We could do the same thing with an IF/THEN instruction and a counter (see Example Program #2), but the FOR/NEXT instruction just makes it easier to program and understand. The FOR/NEXT loop alternative is illustrated in Example Program #3.

> *Format*:  FOR variable = initial value TO limit value [STEP increment value]
>   statements
>       ⋮
>   NEXT [index variable]

*Examples:*

```
1.  FOR I=1 TO N
      statements
          ⋮
    NEXT I
2.  FOR I=2 TO 10 STEP 3
      statements
          ⋮
    NEXT I
3.  FOR I=2 TO −2 STEP −1
      statements
          ⋮
    NEXT I
```

In the examples above, the *variable* I takes on the value of the *initial value*. I is then incremented by the *incremental value*, which is determined by the STEP clause, after each execution of the loop. When the STEP clause is omitted (as in example 1 above), the incremental value is 1. Once the value of I passes the value of *limit value* (either positive or negative), the looping process is terminated and the statement following NEXT is executed. The initial value, limit value, and increment value can be either variables or constants.

For the three examples above, the values of I for each time through the loop are:

> ***Example 1***:   1, 2, 3, 4, 5, 6, 7 (for N = 7)
> ***Example 2***:   2, 5, 8
> ***Example 3***:   2, 1, 0, −1, −2

The two variations of the loop structure are *DOUNTIL* and *DO-WHILE* (see Chapter 12, "Programming Concepts," for details). The net effect of a FOR/NEXT loop is a DOUNTIL loop. The loop designated by the FOR/NEXT instructions is repeated *until* the limit value is equal to or exceeded by the value of the variable. When this happens, the statement following the NEXT is executed. Each execution of the NEXT instruction causes the variable to be incremented by the value in the STEP clause.

The loop in Example Program #2 is also a DOUNTIL structure. Notice that in a DOUNTIL loop, the statements in the loop are executed at least once.

**WHILE/WEND.** The WHILE/WEND instruction pair permits DO-WHILE looping. That is, the statements in a loop are executed repeat-

Because programmers may spend four or more hours each day at a workstation, vendors are paying more attention to the ergonomics (efficiency of the person-machine interface) of the programmer workstation. Features of these ergonomic workstations include a high resolution and non-glare display, tilt and swivel adjustments for the display, tilt adjustment for the keyboard, and noise level adjustments for prompting alarms.
(Sperry Corporation)

edly *while* the test-on-condition in the *WHILE* instruction is true. The use of the WHILE/WEND instruction pair is illustrated in Example Program #4.

---

*Format*:   WHILE expression   relational operator   expression
             statements
                  ⋮
             WEND

---

*Example*:   WHILE COUNT <= 50
              statements
                   ⋮
              WEND

In the example above, the statements between the WHILE and WEND are executed repeatedly "WHILE" the condition (COUNT <= 50) is true. The value of COUNT is in some way altered during processing so that eventually the condition is false (e.g., COUNT = 63). If a WHILE/WEND condition can never become false, your program will enter an *infinite loop* when executed. That is, the loop is repeated until you either cause a "break" in the program execution or turn off the computer. Later, we will learn that infinite loops have their uses.

In a WHILE/WEND loop, the condition is examined just prior to each *pass* (the execution of the instructions within the loop). If the condition is true, the loop is repeated. If the condition is false, the loop is bypassed and the statement following the WEND is executed. In the DOWHILE structure, if the condition is false when the WHILE is first encountered, the loop statements are bypassed completely and not executed.

Both the WHILE and FOR instructions must always be accompanied by their counterparts, WEND and NEXT—and vice versa. Of course, when you forget a WEND or a NEXT, you will soon be reminded of the omission when your program run is terminated prematurely and you get an error message. If you branch into the middle of a WHILE/WEND or FOR/NEXT loop and a WEND or a NEXT instruction is encountered without an accompanying WHILE or FOR, you will also get an error message.

**Nested Loops: Loops within Loops.**   When a *complete* loop is entirely within another loop, then the pair are referred to as **nested loops**. You can create all kinds of nested loops. You can program loops within loops, within loops, and so on. You can have several loops within a single loop. You will probably not run into any trouble as long as you follow one simple rule: *Do not overlap loops*. That is, don't nest the FOR or WHILE instructions inside one loop and the corresponding NEXT or WEND inside another loop.

Figure B-8 shows how a FOR/NEXT loop can be nested within another FOR/NEXT loop. Figure B-9 shows how two WHILE/WEND loops can be nested within a FOR/NEXT loop.

**FIGURE B-8**
**Nested Loops**
The flowchart logic, the corresponding BASIC code, and the results are shown for a FOR/NEXT loop that is nested within another FOR/NEXT loop.

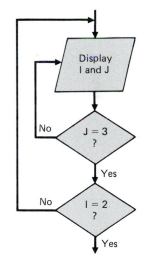

```
FOR I = 1 TO 2
   FOR J = 1 TO 3
      PRINT "I = "; I, "J = "; J
   NEXT J
NEXT I
```

| Results: | |
|---|---|
| I = 1 | J = 1 |
| I = 1 | J = 2 |
| I = 1 | J = 3 |
| I = 2 | J = 1 |
| I = 2 | J = 2 |
| I = 2 | J = 3 |

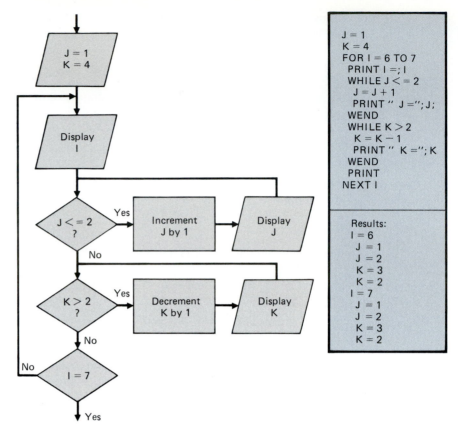

**FIGURE B-9**
**Nested Loops**
The flowchart logic, the corresponding BASIC code, and the results are shown
when a couple of WHILE/WEND loops are nested within a FOR/NEXT loop.

## B-12 EXAMPLE PROGRAM #3: AN EASIER WAY TO CREATE A LOOP

Example Program #3 performs exactly the same function as Example
Program #2. The difference is that the FOR/NEXT instruction combination creates the loop rather than the IF-counter combination. The interactive session is also the same.

The counter is embedded in the FOR/NEXT combination. The variable COUNT is incremented by 1 each time the loop in the Main program module (150–220) is executed. Therefore, the loop is repeated
until the value of COUNT becomes greater than the value of NUMBER.
In our example, the loop is executed three times with the variable
COUNT taking on values of 1, 2, and 3. After the third loop
(COUNT=NUMBER=3), processing "drops through" to the END instruction and execution is terminated.

# EXAMPLE PROGRAM #3

This program accepts three sales figures for each of any number of salespeople. The total is computed and displayed for each salesperson. It is the same as Example Program #2 with FOR/NEXT statements used to create the loop.

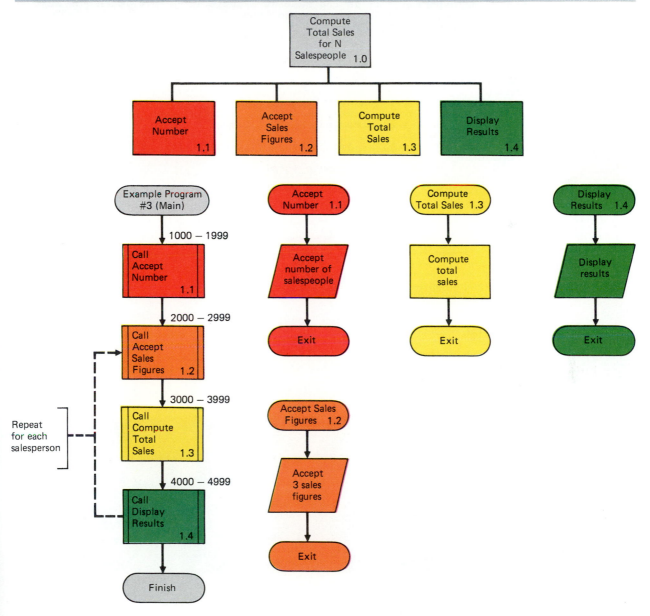

continued

```
2     REM            **** Example Program #3 ****
4     REM  Description:
6     REM    This program accepts three sales figures for each of any number of
8     REM    salespeople.  The total is computed and displayed for each
10    REM    salesperson.  It is the same as Example Program #2 with FOR/NEXT
12    REM    statements used to create the loop.
14    REM  Variables list:
16    REM    NUMBER                  - Number of salespeople
18    REM    S1, S2, S3              - Sales figures (Stibs, Farkles, Teglers)
20    REM    TOTAL                   - Total sales
99    REM
100   REM  <<<< Start Main >>>>
110   REM
120   REM  Call Module 1.1 - Accept Number
130   GOSUB 1000
140   REM  Begin loop to be executed 'NUMBER' times
150   FOR I=1 TO NUMBER
160     REM  Call Module 1.2 - Accept Sales Figures
170     GOSUB 2000
180     REM  Call Mcdule 1.3 - Compute Total Sales
190     GOSUB 3000
200     REM  Call Module 1.4 - Display Results
210     GOSUB 4000
220   NEXT I
230   END
240   REM  <<<< End Main >>>>
999   REM
1000  REM  ==== Module 1.1 - Accept Number
1010  INPUT NUMBER
1999  RETURN
2000  REM  ==== Module 1.2 - Accept Sales Figures
2010  INPUT S1, S2, S3
2999  RETURN
3000  REM  ==== Module 1.3 - Compute Total Sales
3010  LET TOTAL = S1 + S2 + S3
3999  RETURN
4000  REM  ==== Module 1.4 - Display Results
4010  PRINT TOTAL
4999  RETURN
```

```
run
? 3
? 32000,28000,25000
 85000
? 50000,35000,20000
 105000
? 25000,30000,15000
 70000
ok
```

## B-13  EXAMPLE PROGRAM #4: BEING "USER FRIENDLY"

Example Program #4 is another variation of Example Programs #2 and #3, except that this time the WHILE/WEND instruction pair creates the loop and the program input/output is made more "user friendly."

# EXAMPLE PROGRAM #4

This program accepts three sales figures for each of any number of salespeople. The total is computed and displayed for each salesperson. It is the same as Example Program #3 with input prompts and a WHILE/WEND loop replacing the FOR/NEXT loop.

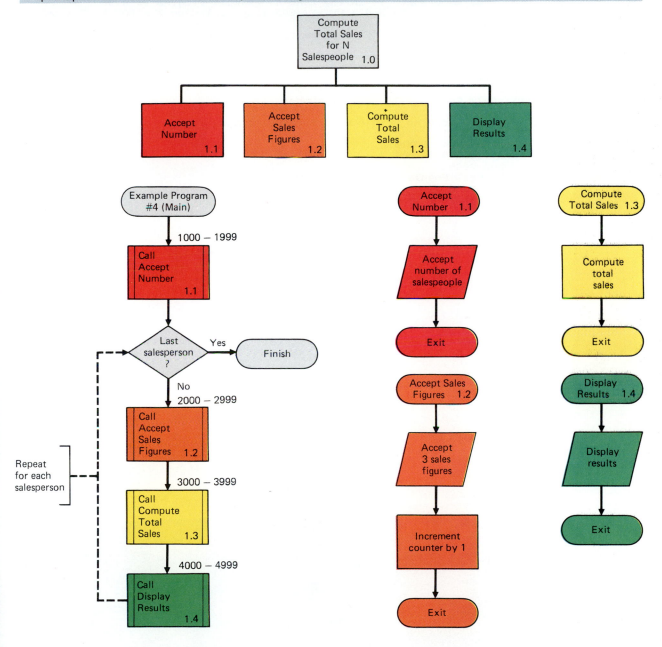

continued

Example Program 4 continued

```
2     REM           **** Example Program #4 ****
4     REM    Description:
6     REM      This program accepts three sales figures for each of any number of
8     REM      salespeople.  The total is computed and displayed for each
10    REM      salesperson.  It is the same as Example Program #3 with
12    REM      input prompts and a WHILE/WEND loop replacing the FOR/NEXT loop.
14    REM    Variables list:
16    REM      NUMBER                    - Number of salespeople
18    REM      S1, S2, S3                - Sales figures (Stibs, Farkles, Teglers)
20    REM      TOTAL                     - Total sales
99    REM
100   REM   <<<< Start Main >>>>
110   REM
120   REM   Call Module 1.1 - Accept Number
130   GOSUB 1000
140   REM   Begin loop to be executed 'NUMBER' times
150   LET COUNT = 1
160   WHILE COUNT <= NUMBER
170      REM   Call Module 1.2 - Accept Sales Figures
180      GOSUB 2000
190      REM   Call Module 1.3 - Compute Total Sales
200      GOSUB 3000
210      REM   Call Module 1.4 - Display Results
220      GOSUB 4000
230   WEND
240   END
250   REM   <<<< End Main >>>>
999   REM
1000  REM   ==== Module 1.1 - Accept Number
1010  PRINT "Enter total number of salespeople";
1020  INPUT NUMBER
1030  PRINT
1999  RETURN
2000  REM   ==== Module 1.2 - Accept Sales Figures
2010  REM   Input sales figures and add one to loop counter 'COUNT'
2020  PRINT "Enter gross sales for Stibs, Farkles, and Teglers"
2030  PRINT "  (separate by commas)";
2040  INPUT S1, S2, S3
2050  REM   Increment loop counter
2060  LET COUNT = COUNT + 1
2999  RETURN
3000  REM   ==== Module 1.3 - Compute Total Sales
3010  LET TOTAL = S1 + S2 + S3
3999  RETURN
4000  REM   ==== Module 1.4 - Display Results
4010  PRINT "The total sales amount is "; TOTAL
4020  PRINT
4999  RETURN
```

```
run
Enter total number of salespeople? 3

Enter gross sales for Stibs, Farkles, and Teglers
  (separate by commas)? 32000,28000,25000
The total sales amount is  85000

Enter gross sales for Stibs, Farkles, and Teglers
  (separate by commas)? 50000,35000,20000
The total sales amount is  105000

Enter gross sales for Stibs, Farkles, and Teglers
  (separate by commas)? 25000,30000,15000
The total sales amount is  70000

Ok
```

As long as the condition in the WHILE instruction is met (COUNT <= NUMBER), the loop is repeated and another salesperson is processed. COUNT is initially set to 1 (150), then incremented by 1 (2060) after each salesperson's sales figures are entered (Module 1.2). COUNT could just as well have been incremented in Modules 1.3 or 1.4. The condition is true during the first three passes through the loop, but after the third salesperson's sales figures have been processed, the value of COUNT is 4. When COUNT = 4, the condition becomes false and the statement following WEND (240 END) is executed and program execution is terminated.

The input/output is made more user friendly by adding *input prompts* (1010, 2020–2030) and *output descriptions* (4010). In the previous examples, the only signal given the user to enter data is a question mark. Nothing is displayed to tell the user what to enter. The result is simply a number with no description. A user executing Example Program #3 would have to know what, and how many, data items to enter, as well as how to interpret the results. We make programs more user friendly by requesting input data through prompts and by describing the output.

Besides the input prompts and output description, blank lines (1030, 4020) are inserted in the interactive session to improve readability. Also, the semicolons (;) at the end of the PRINT instructions for the input prompts (e.g., 1010) cause the cursor to remain positioned at the ends of the prompts. This permits data to be entered on the same line and adjacent to the prompts. The semicolon in the PRINT for the output description causes the result to be displayed adjacent to the description (4010). In the interactive session, notice that the numerical output begins in the second space of the display zone. The extra space is always reserved for an implied plus sign or an actual minus sign.

Numerous input prompts and output descriptions were added to an office directory program to make it more "user friendly" and, therefore, easier to use.
(Computer Consoles Inc.)

## REVIEW EXERCISES (LEARNING MODULE III)

### BASIC Instructions and Concepts

1. Identify the syntax error(s) in each of the following instructions.
   (a) 10 FOR COUNT$ = 1 TO 10 STEP 3
   (b) 10 WEND NUMBER <> 10
   (c) 10 WHILE COUNT$ <=−1
   (d) 10 FOR J = I UP TO J
2. Write instructions to produce the following interaction with the user.

   Enter quantity of part used today
   ? **4**
   Enter quantity of part received today
   ? **8**

**3.** What values of X and I are displayed?
  (a)  100 LET X=5
       200 FOR I=1 TO 8 STEP 3
       300 LET X=X + 1
       400 PRINT X,I
       500 NEXT I
       600 END
  (b)  100 LET X=2
       200 WHILE X <= 8
       300 LET X=X + 2
       400 PRINT X
       500 WEND
       600 END

**4.** Use a FOR/NEXT combination and write the sequence of instructions needed to produce the following output.

| zone 1-------- | zone 2-------- | zone 3-------- |
|---|---|---|
| X | X SQUARED | X CUBED |
| 1 | 1 | 1 |
| 2 | 4 | 8 |
| 3 | 9 | 27 |
| 4 | 16 | 64 |

**5.** Use a WHILE/WEND combination and write the sequence of instructions needed to produce the output described in Exercise 3.

**6.** How many times is the PRINT instruction executed? What values of $X$, $I$, and $J$ are displayed? Remember, all undefined variables are initially set to zero.

```
100   FOR I=1 TO 5
200     FOR J=2 TO 7
300       LET X=X + 1
400       PRINT X, I, J
500     NEXT
600   NEXT
700   END
```

## Example Program #3

**7.** The FOR/NEXT combination effectively replaces statements 5020 and 5030 of Example Program #2. What are the advantages of this substitution?

**8.** What is the purpose of the index variable I? Could it just as well have been called COUNT?

## Example Program #4

**9.** What makes Example Program #3 a DOUNTIL structure and Example Program #4 a DOWHILE structure?

**10.** What is the purpose of the PRINT instruction at 4020?

**11.** If the semicolon in 4010 were replaced with a comma, in what zones would the string constant and the value of TOTAL be displayed?

12. If the value of COUNT were set to 100 rather than 1 in statement 150, how would you revise the WHILE instruction to keep the same logic?

## BASIC PROGRAMMING ASSIGNMENTS —————————

1. Load Example Program #2 to memory and revise it to be like Example Program #3, then execute and save the revised program. If you did not have Example Program #2 saved, enter Example Program #3 and save it. Revise Example Program #3 to be like Example Program #4, then execute and save it. Now load, list (on the monitor and printer), and execute these programs again.

2. Combine instructions in Example Program #4 when possible to eliminate two unnecessary instructions. Execute the program again and verify its accuracy. [*Hint*: Integrate input prompts in INPUT instructions.]

3. Write a centigrade-to-Fahrenheit conversion program to list the output in four columns as shown below. The conversion formula is: $F=(9/5)*C+32$.

| CENTIGRADE | FAHRENHEIT | CENTIGRADE | FAHRENHEIT |
|---|---|---|---|
| 0 | 32 | 16 | 60.8 |
| 1 | 33.8 | 17 | 62.6 |
| 2 | 35.6 | 18 | 64.4 |
| : | : | : | : |
| 15 | 59 | 31 | 87.8 |

4. Write a program to accept the course data shown below (no more than three different courses). No course has more than two sections, and the data for multiple-section courses are to be entered consecutively.

| COURSE NUMBER | SECTION | # OF STUDENTS ENROLLED |
|---|---|---|
| CIS 11 | 1 | 30 |
| CIS 11 | 2 | 21 |
| CIS 41 | 1 | 72 |
| CIS 88 | 1 | 25 |
| CIS 88 | 2 | 23 |

Through comparisons and calculations, produce the following output.

| COURSE NUMBER | NUMBER OF SECTIONS | TOTAL STUDENTS |
|---|---|---|
| CIS 11 | 2 | 51 |
| CIS 41 | 1 | 72 |
| CIS 88 | 2 | 48 |

5. Write a program to compute an electric utility bill that is based

on time-of-day usage. The utility company charges $0.03/kilo-watt-hour from 8:00 P.M. until 6:00 A.M. The charge during the remainder of the day is $0.07/kilowatt-hour. Use the following data:

| Customer # | Prime Time Usage | Non-Prime-Time Usage |
|---|---|---|
| 44561 | 620 | 409 |
| 62178 | 780 | 165 |
| 55612 | 410 | 650 |

Produce the following interactive session and output for the first customer and similar I/O for the other two customers:

Enter number of customers to be processed? **3**

Enter customer #? **44561**
Enter prime time usage? **620**
Enter non-prime-time usage? **409**

Charges for customer #44561 are $55.67

6. Prepare an interactive program to illustrate to the novice BASIC programmer the use of the separators (comma and semicolon) and zones in the PRINT instructions. The instructive interactive session should illustrate the PRINT instruction features presented in Figure B-2.

# Generating Reports

## B-14 BASIC INSTRUCTION SET: LEARNING MODULE IV GROUP _____

PROGRAMMING
CONCEPTS

Formatting Output Fields
Arrays/Subscripted Variables
Initialization Routines
Logical Operators
Index Variables
End-of-File Entry
Report Formatting

Several more instructions are introduced in this learning module. The PRINT USING instruction, which is both an I/O and a format instruction, offers enhancements over the PRINT instruction. The READ/ DATA/RESTORE is a data transfer and assignment instruction combination that provides an alternative to the LET assignment instruction. Also introduced is the DIM statement, which does not fall into any of the major instruction categories.

### Input/Output Instructions and Format Instructions

PRINT USING.  The PRINT USING instruction differs from the PRINT instruction in that it ignores the print zones and lets you display print list items in a specified format.

> **Format**:  PRINT USING format string; list of variables and/or expressions

**Examples**:  PRINT USING "# # #.# #"; PAY, DEDUCT, NET

FORMAT$="\                                          \"
PRINT USING FORMAT$; NAME$

PRINT USING "**$# # #.# #"; PAY, NET

PRINT USING "# #−"; CREDIT, DEBIT

PRINT USING "# # # # #,.# # #"; 32850.789, TOTAL

In the examples, notice that the format string can be either a string variable (e.g., FORMAT$) or a string constant (e.g., "**$###.##"). Some versions of BASIC permit only one format field per PRINT USING instruction (as shown in the examples), and all of the similar print-list items (numeric or string) are displayed according to the specifications in the format string. Other versions of BASIC permit several format fields to be specified in a single format string. In the following discussion, we'll focus on PRINT USING instructions with a single format string.

The format string is made up of special *formatting characters*. Commonly used formatting characters are described and illustrated below: + − . , * $ and ˄ for numeric formats; and ! \ and & for string formats.

## Numeric Format Fields

\#

The number sign represents a digit position. A number is right justified in the print field and preceded by spaces as applicable.

```
10 LET A=12: LET B=123: LET C=123.45
20 PRINT USING "#####"; A,B,C
RUN
      12 123   123
```

The decimal point defines the location of the decimal in the format field. Numbers are rounded when the number of decimal places in the format is fewer than in the value of the number to be displayed.

```
10 LET A=12: LET B=345.67: LET C=−.8
20 PRINT USING "####.#"; A,B,C
RUN
   12.0  345.7   −0.8
```

Zeros are displayed to fill print positions for A and C. Only one zero is printed to the left of the decimal point. The value of B was rounded to one decimal point.

+ and −

A plus sign placed at the beginning or end of the format field causes the sign of the number (i.e., + or −) to be displayed just before or after the number. A minus sign placed at the end of the format field causes negative numbers to be displayed with a trailing minus sign.

```
10 LET A=12.34: LET B=−123: LET C=−12.34: LET D=−0.1
20 PRINT USING "+####.##"; A,B
30 PRINT USING "####.##−"; C,D
RUN
   +12.34 −123.00
   12.34−    0.01−
```

**

The double asterisk at the beginning of the format field causes leading spaces in the number to be filled with asterisks.

```
10 LET A=12: LET B=1234
20 PRINT USING "**#####"; A,B
RUN
*****12***1234
```

The asterisk fill is often used to make printed output more difficult to alter (e.g., net pay on a payroll check).

$$

A double dollar sign placed at the beginning of the format field causes a dollar sign to be displayed immediately to the left of the leftmost digit in the displayed number. The $$ adds two more positions, one of which is the dollar sign, to the format field.

```
10 LET A=1.23: LET B=12.00: LET C=1234.56
20 PRINT USING "$$# # # #.# #"; A,B,C
RUN
     $1.23 $12.00 $1234.56
```

**$       An asterisk/dollar sign combination (**$) placed at the beginning of the format field causes a dollar sign to be displayed immediately to the left of the leftmost digit in the displayed number and any remaining leading spaces to be filled with asterisks. The **$ adds three more positions, one of which is the dollar sign, to the format field.

```
10 LET A=1.23: LET B=12.0: LET C=1234.56
20 PRINT USING "**$# # #.# #"; A,B,C
RUN
****$1.23***$12.00*$1234.56
```

,       A comma to the left of the decimal point in the format field causes three-digit groups to the left of the decimal point to be separated by a comma.

```
10 LET A=1234.56: LET B=1234567.89
20 PRINT USING "# # # # # # # # #,.# #"; A,B
RUN
     1,234.56 1,234,567.89
```

On a few systems, the comma has to be inserted in the format field (i.e., "##,###,###.##").

~~~~       Four carets to the right of the digit positions in the format field cause the number to be displayed in exponential format. The four positions added to the field are needed to allow space for the exponential notation. The significant digits are left justified in the digit format and the exponent is adjusted accordingly.

```
10 LET A=−.12: LET B=12.345: LET C=123.45
20 PRINT USING "# # #.#~~~"; A,B,C
RUN
−12.0E−02 12.3E+00 12.3E+01
```

If you wish to align columns of numeric data evenly, simply pad the format field with extra digit positions (#). For example, the following PRINT USING instruction creates columns that are 15 positions in width.

```
10 LET A=12.34: LET B=345.67: LET C=7.89: LET D=56789.1
20 PRINT USING "# # # # # # # # # # # #.# #"; A,B,C,D
RUN
     12.34          345.67          7.89          56789.10
```

## String Format Fields

!                The exclamation point causes only the first character in the string to be displayed.

```
10 LET A$="Linda": LET B$="Bell"
20 PRINT USING "!"; A$, B$
RUN
LB
```

\n spaces\     The format beginning and ending with back slashes specifies that the string is to be left justified in a field that is 2 + n positions in length. The two backslashes in the format string represent two display positions. In the following examples, "Linda" and "Bell" are displayed in adjacent five-position fields in statement 20 and in adjacent six-position fields in statement 30.

```
10 A$="Linda":B$="Bell"
20 PRINT USING "\     \"; A$, B$
30 PRINT USING "\      \"; A$, B$
RUN
LindaBell
Linda Bell
```

&              An "and" sign in the format field causes the string to be displayed as it is defined.

```
10 LET A$="Linda": LET B$=" E. ": LET C$="Bell"
20 PRINT USING "&"; A$, B$, C$
RUN
Linda E. Bell
```

**FIGURE B-10**
**The PRINT USING Instruction**
Example PRINT USING format fields and their resulting displays are shown for a variety of numeric (N) and string (A$) constants.

Figure B-10 illustrates example format fields and the resulting display for various numeric (N) and string (A$) constants.

**LPRINT USING.** The LPRINT USING works like the PRINT USING except that the output line is routed to a printer instead of the monitor.

```
              PRINT USING FORMAT$; N                           PRINT USING FORMAT$; A$

FORMAT$=        N=          Displayed          FORMAT$=        A$=          Displayed
"#####"        12345            12345          "\ \"          "ONE"        ONE
"###.###"      23.45          23.450           "\ \"          "Two (2)"    Two
"**###.##"     23.45        ***23.45           "!"            "Three"      T
"$$###.##"     23.45          $23.45           "&"            " 4-Four"     4-Four
"**$##.##"     23.45         **$23.45          "\     \"      "FIVE SIX"   FIVE S
"##.###^^^^-"  -1234.56     12.346E+02-
"+##"          12               +12
"###"          -12              -12
"##-"          -12              12-
```

---

## MEMORY BITS

### SPECIAL CHARACTERS FOR PRINT USING FORMAT FIELDS

**Numeric Format Characters**

| | |
|---|---|
| # | Digit position. |
| . | Decimal point alignment. |
| + and − | Display + or − with number. |
| ** | Asterisk fill. |
| $$ | Leading dollar signs. |
| **$ | Asterisk fill with leading dollar sign. |
| , | Insert comma. |
| ^^^ | Exponential notation. |

**String Format Characters**

| | |
|---|---|
| ! | Display first character. |
| \\$n$ spaces\\ | Display in field of $2 + n$ length. |
| & | Display as defined. |

## Data Transfer and Assignment Instructions

**READ/DATA/RESTORE.** The *values* in a DATA statement(s) are assigned to the corresponding *variables* in a READ statement(s). Numeric variables must be matched with numeric constants, and string variables must be matched with string constants. A mismatch of variables and constants will result in a program error. If there are more variables than data, you will also get an error.

> *Format*: READ list of variables
> DATA constant values

> *Example*: READ COURSE$, NUMBER
> DATA "Government", 101
> DATA "French III", 206
> DATA "Management", 320

The DATA statements have no effect on program execution and can appear any place in the program. The first time the READ statement above is executed, it has the same effect as

COURSE$ = "Government"
NUMBER = 101

A "software" *pointer* monitors which data values have been assigned and is continually moved to "point" to the value to be assigned next. In the example, each time the READ statement is executed, two values in the DATA statements are assigned to COURSE$ and NUMBER. The first READ assigns the value of the string constant "Government" to the variable COURSE$ and the value of the numeric constant 101 to the variable NUMBER. With the assignment of the first two values, the pointer is moved and "points" to the next value to be assigned ("French III"). The next time the READ statement is executed, COURSE$ and NUMBER are assigned new values ("French III" and 206) and the pointer is moved to the next value ("Management").

The RESTORE statement causes the pointer to be repositioned at the first value in the *first* DATA statement ("Government"). The values in the data statements can then be reread.

BASIC is not only the most widely available language, it is also the most widely taught language. For the majority of students, their first programming language is BASIC.
(The DeVry Institutes)

The six values in the three DATA statements in the example above could just as well have been included in one DATA statement or six DATA statements. The computer assumes the values in the DATA statements to be one continuous list of values. The following DATA statements are equivalent to the DATA statements in the example above.

```
DATA "Government", 101, "French III"
DATA 206, "Management", 320
```

The READ instruction in the example above alternately "reads" a string constant and a numeric constant. The values in the DATA statements must match variable types in the READ statement. If the first two values in the DATA statement above were "Government" and "French III", you would get a type mismatch error (the second must be numeric), and program execution would be terminated.

## Other Instructions

DIM.    The DIM or dimension statement permits you to specify and allocate storage for **array** variables. In one dimension (one subscript), an array is the same as a list of similar data elements (e.g., employee names). In two dimensions (two subscripts), an array is the same as a table (e.g., table of employee names and pay rates). *Subscripts* [(1), (2), etc.] provide each storage location in the array with a unique name.

> *Format*:   DIM list of array variables with subscript maximums

> *Examples*:   DIM EMPLOYEE$(50), PAY(50)
>              DIM EMPLOYEE$(50,2)

The first example DIM statement sets aside 50 primary storage locations for string constants and 50 primary storage locations for numeric values. The string constant locations are referenced by the variable names EMPLOYEE$(1), EMPLOYEE$(2), EMPLOYEE$(3), . . . , EMPLOYEE$(50), and the numeric locations are referenced by the variable names PAY(1), PAY(2), . . . , PAY(50). The DIM statement, which is usually included in an initialization subroutine, can define any number of array variables. The use of one-dimensional array variables is discussed and illustrated in Example Programs #6 and #7.

The second example DIM sets up a *two-dimensional* array, or a table. In this way the employee's first name and last name can be referenced separately. The first subscript designates a particular employee and the second subscript designates whether the array variable refers to the first or last name. For example, consider the following table:

|   | 1 | 2 |
|---|---|---|
| 1 | Joyce | Cass |
| 2 | Harry | Jones |
| 3 | Mike | Green |
| 4 | Sally | Ackers |

EMPLOYEE\$(1,1) refers to "Joyce" and EMPLOYEE\$(1,2) refers to "Cass"; EMPLOYEE\$(3,1) refers to "Mike" and EMPLOYEE\$(3,2) refers to "Green"; and so on.

## B-15  EXAMPLE PROGRAM #5: LOGICAL OPERATORS AND MULTIPLE CONDITIONAL STATEMENTS

Example Program #5 is a logical extension of the previous example programs. The program logic is shown in the structure chart and flowchart. This program does much more than simply computing the sales totals for any number of salespeople (Example Programs #2 through #4). Besides the sales figures, the program accepts salesperson identification data (name and ID), commission rates for each of the three products (as a percent of sales), and an amount that represents the sales quota for the current month. Information computed for each salesperson includes total sales (for all products), commission earned, and quota category ("Below Quota", "Satisfactory", or "Outstanding").

This portable computer fits neatly into a briefcase. Nevertheless, it has the same kinds of BASIC programming instructions as mainframe computers.
(Courtesy of Apple Computer, Inc.)

Initialization.    Most programs require that certain variables be set, or *initialized*, to particular values prior to processing. In Example Program #5, the quota category names are assigned string variable names in Module 1.1—Assign Constants. In future example programs we will initialize the dimensions (DIM) for lists and tables. In this example the READ/DATA statements (1020–1030) are used to assign quota category values to string variables. These two statements are equivalent to

```
1020 LET BELOW$="Below Quota": LET SATIS$="Satisfactory": LET
       OUTST$="Outstanding"
```

The Loop.    The DOUNTIL loop (for each salesperson) is created in a slightly different manner from previous example programs. The user does not have to know the number of salespeople for which commissions are to be computed. Instead, after each salesperson is processed, the user is asked if there are more salespeople to be processed (6020). If the user responds with "Y" or "y" (yes), the loop (Modules 1.2 through 1.6) is repeated so that another salesperson can be processed.

You can see from the flowchart that each salesperson is completely processed (input, processing, output) before the next. Within the loop, quota categories are assigned in a series of conditional IF/THEN statements (4050–4060).

Embedded Input Prompts.    In Example Program #4, the input prompts are displayed with PRINT instructions. Using the PRINT/INPUT combination, an alternative to statement 3020 of Example Program #5 would have been

```
3020 PRINT "Salesperson name: ";
3025 INPUT SPNAME$
```

In Example Program #5, a prompt is embedded in the INPUT instructions before the variables list (see statements 3020, 3030, and 3050).

# EXAMPLE PROGRAM #5

This program computes the total sales and commission and assigns a quota category for any number of salespeople. The sales manager assisgns a commission rate to each of three products and enters a dollar amount representing this month's sales quota.

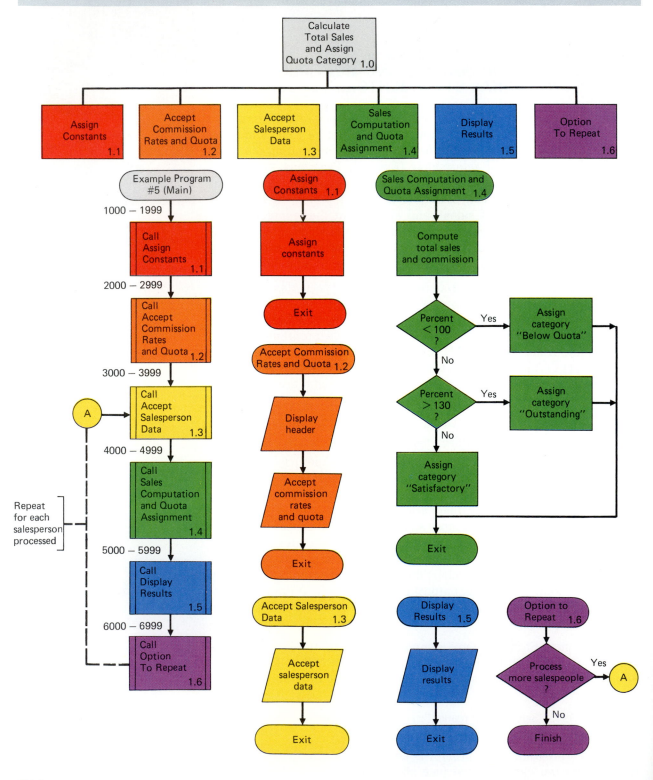

```
2    REM          **** Example Program #5 ****
4    REM   Description:
6    REM     This program computes the total sales and commission and assigns
8    REM     a quota category for any number of salespeople. The sales manager
10   REM     assigns a commission rate to each of three products and enters a
12   REM     dollar amount representing this month's sales quota.
14   REM   Variables list:
16   REM     BELOW$, SATIS$,
18   REM     OUTST$                  - Quota categories
20   REM     SPNAME$                 - Salesperson name
22   REM     C1, C2, C3              - Commission rates (Stibs, Farkles, Teglers)
24   REM     QUOTA                   - Sales quota
26   REM     ID                      - Salesperson ID
28   REM     S1, S2, S3              - Sales figures (Stibs, Farkles, Teglers)
30   REM     TOTAL                   - Total sales
32   REM     COMMISSION              - Total commission earned
34   REM     PERCENT                 - Percent of quota achieved
36   REM     CATEGORY$               - Quota category
38   REM     ANSWER$                 - Y or N response to inquiry
40   REM     F1$, F2$, F3$           - Strings for PRINT USING statements
99   REM
100  REM   <<<< Start Main >>>>
110  REM
120  REM   Call Module 1.1 - Assign Constants
130  GOSUB 1000
140  REM   Call Module 1.2 - Accept Commission Rates and Quota
150  GOSUB 2000
160  REM   Call Module 1.3 - Accept Salesperson Data
170  GOSUB 3000
180  REM   Call Module 1.4 - Sales Computation and Quota Assignment
190  GOSUB 4000
200  REM   Call Module 1.5 - Display Results
210  GOSUB 5000
220  REM   Call Module 1.6 - Option to Repeat
230  GOSUB 6000
240  END
250  REM   <<<< End Main >>>>
999  REM
1000 REM   ==== Module 1.1 - Assign Constants
1010 REM   Assign quota category constants to string variables
1020 READ BELOW$, SATIS$, OUTST$
1030 DATA "Below quota","Satisfactory","Outstanding"
1999 RETURN
2000 REM   ==== Module 1.2 - Accept Commission Rates and Quota
2010 PRINT "    --------- Sales Summary Report ---------"
2020 PRINT "Separate multiple entries by commas."
2030 PRINT
2040 PRINT "Enter commission rates (as a %)"
2050 INPUT "  for Stibs, Farkles, and Teglers: ", C1, C2, C3
2060 LET C1 = C1/100
2070 LET C2 = C2/100
2080 LET C3 = C3/100
2090 PRINT
2100 INPUT "Enter this month's sales quota (in dollars): ", QUOTA
2999 RETURN
3000 REM   ==== Module 1.3 - Accept Salesperson Data
3010 PRINT
3020 INPUT "Salesperson name: ", SPNAME$
3030 INPUT "Salesperson ID: ", ID
3040 PRINT "Enter gross sales for Stibs, Farkles, and Teglers"
3050 INPUT "  (separate by commas): ", S1, S2, S3
3999 RETURN
4000 REM   ==== Module 1.4 - Sales Computation and Quota Assignment
4010 REM   Compute total sales and commission and assign quota category
4020 LET TOTAL = S1 + S2 + S3
4030 LET COMMISSION = S1*C1 + S2*C2 + S3*C3
4040 LET PERCENT = TOTAL/QUOTA * 100
4050 IF PERCENT < 100 THEN LET CATEGORY$ = BELOW$ : RETURN
4060    IF PERCENT > 130 THEN LET CATEGORY$ = OUTST$ : RETURN
4070       LET CATEGORY$ = SATIS$
4999 RETURN
```

continued

```
5000 REM  ==== Module 1.5 - Display Results
5010 LET F1$="########      "
5020 LET F2$="########.##    "
5030 LET F3$="    \                    \"
5040 PRINT
5050 PRINT "Salesperson","ID Number","Total Sales","Commission",
5060 PRINT "Quota Category"
5070 PRINT SPNAME$,:PRINT USING F1$; ID,:PRINT USING F2$; TOTAL,
5080 PRINT USING F2$; COMMISSION,:PRINT USING F3$; CATEGORY$
5090 PRINT
5999 RETURN
6000 REM  ==== Module 1.6 - Option to Repeat
6010 REM  Give the user the option to process another salesperson
6020 INPUT "More salespeople? (Y or N) ",ANSWER$
6030 IF ANSWER$ = "Y" OR ANSWER$ = "y" THEN RETURN 160
6999 RETURN 240
```

```
run
   --------- Sales Summary Report ---------
Separate multiple entries by commas.

Enter commission rates (as a %)
  for Stibs, Farkles, and Teglers: 4,3,5

Enter this month's sales quota (in dollars): 80000

Salesperson name: Charles Roth
Salesperson ID: 46912
Enter gross sales for Stibs, Farkles, and Teglers
  (separate by commas): 32000, 28000,25000

Salesperson   ID Number   Total Sales   Commission   Quota Category
Charles Roth    46912       85000.00      3370.00      Satisfactory

More salespeople? (Y or N) y
```

```
Salesperson name: Lucy Cook
Salesperson ID? 77878
Enter gross sales for Stibs, Farkles, and Teglers
  (separate by commas): 50000,35000,20000

Salesperson   ID Number   Total Sales   Commission   Quota Category
Lucy Cook       77878      105000.00      4050.00      Outstanding

More salespeople? (Y or N) y

Salesperson name: Wayne Evans
Salesperson ID: 66941
Enter gross sales for Stibs, Farkles, and Teglers
  (separate by commas): 25000,30000,15000

Salesperson   ID Number   Total Sales   Commission   Quota Category
Wayne Evans     66941       70000.00      2650.00      Below quota

More salespeople? (Y or N) n
Ok
```

516

This consolidates the PRINT/INPUT combination illustrated in Example Program #4 into a single instruction.

When the descriptive prompt in an INPUT instruction is followed by a semicolon, a question mark prompt (?) is displayed immediately following and on the same line as the descriptive prompt. The instruction

    INPUT "Salesperson name: "; SPNAME$

results in the following prompt being displayed:

    Salesperson name: ?

A question mark is not needed here. To suppress the generic input prompt (?) in the INPUT instruction, follow the descriptive prompt ("Salesperson name: ") by a *comma* rather than a semicolon. The following version of the example above eliminates the "?" when the descriptive prompt is displayed:

    INPUT "Salesperson name: ", SPNAME$

The prompt is displayed as follows:

    Salesperson name:

The INPUT instructions in Example Program #5 employ a comma to suppress the "?" (see the interactive session).

**Assigning Quota Category.** The total commission (COMMISSION) earned by each salesperson is computed in statement 4030. Because the multiplication (*) arithmetic operator has a higher priority in the hierarchy of operations than the addition (+) arithmetic operator (see Figure B-3), the commission rates (entered in Module 1.2) are first multiplied by the sales amounts and the products are then added. To avoid confusion, you might prefer to insert parentheses.

    4030 COMMISSION = (S1*C1) + (S2*C2) + (S3*C3)

Statement 4040 computes PERCENT, the percent of the monthly sales quota achieved by a particular salesperson (TOTAL as a percent of QUOTA).

In statements 4050–4070, a quota category ("Below quota", "Outstanding", or "Satisfactory") is assigned to each salesperson based on a his or her performance for the month. Performance is evaluated by comparing a salesperson's total sales for the month (TOTAL) against a preset sales quota (QUOTA). IF the value of PERCENT (the percent of the monthly sales quota) is less than 100 percent, THEN the quota category (CATEGORY$) assigned is "Below quota" (4050). IF the value of PERCENT is greater than 130 percent, THEN the quota category assigned is "Outstanding" (4060). If neither of these conditions apply, processing "drops through" to statement 4070 and the quota category assigned that salesperson is "Satisfactory". Once a quota category is assigned, control is RETURNed to the driver module.

**Logical Operators.** We have already discussed arithmetic operators (Figure B-3) and relational operators (Figure B-5) in Learning Module II: Getting Started with BASIC. **Logical operators**, such as AND and OR (see Figure B-11), are placed between conditional expressions in an IF or WHILE instruction. In effect, logical operators enable us to

| OPERATION | OPERATOR |
|---|---|
| For the condition to be true: | |
| Both subconditions must be true | AND |
| At least one subcondition must be true | OR |

combine conditional expressions. When the OR operator is used, the condition is considered true if *at least one* subcondition is true. For example, at statement 6030, the THEN clause is taken and the loop is repeated IF the first OR the second expression is true. In this instance, the user can enter either "Y" or "y" to process another salesperson.

Without the logical operator, statement 6030 would be written as two IF instructions:

```
6030 IF ANSWER$ = "Y" THEN RETURN 160
6035 IF ANSWER$ = "y" THEN RETURN 160
```

When the AND operator is used, *both* conditions must be true for the THEN clause to be executed. An alternative way to write statements 6030 and 6999 in Example Program #5 is

```
6030 IF ANSWER$ <> "Y" AND ANSWER$ <> "y" THEN RETURN 240
6999 RETURN 160
```

In the case above, for the THEN clause to be taken, the character entered cannot be a "Y" AND it cannot be a "y". If both of these conditions are met, control is RETURNed to the driver module at the END instruction (240) and program execution is terminated.

The NOT operator reverses the logic of the expression it precedes. When the NOT operator is placed before a conditional expression, the condition must be false for the instruction following THEN to be executed. For example, the following instructions are equivalent to the example above:

```
6030 IF NOT ANSWER$ = "Y" AND NOT ANSWER$ = "y" THEN RETURN 240
6040 RETURN 160
```

**Display of Results.** In statements 5070 and 5080, the PRINT and PRINT USING instructions are combined in a single statement to create a better display of the results. The comma at the end of the end of each instruction causes the cursor to remain on the same display line. In this way, the numeric values of ID and COMMISSION can be displayed in formatted fields with PRINT USING instructions. For most versions of BASIC, two PRINT USING instructions would be necessary since two different formats are desired.

## B-16 EXAMPLE PROGRAM #6: ARRAYS AND REPORT FORMATTING

The input, processing, and output of Example Program #6 are similar to that of Example Program #5 except that *all salesperson data are entered and processed prior to being displayed*. Once entered, the data are processed and displayed in the form of a "Sales Summary" report.

# EXAMPLE PROGRAM #6

This program computes the total sales and commission and assigns a quota category for any number of salespeople. The sales manager assigns a commission rate to each of three products and enters a dollar amount representing this month's sales quota. Same as Example Program #5, but the results are printed in a report format.

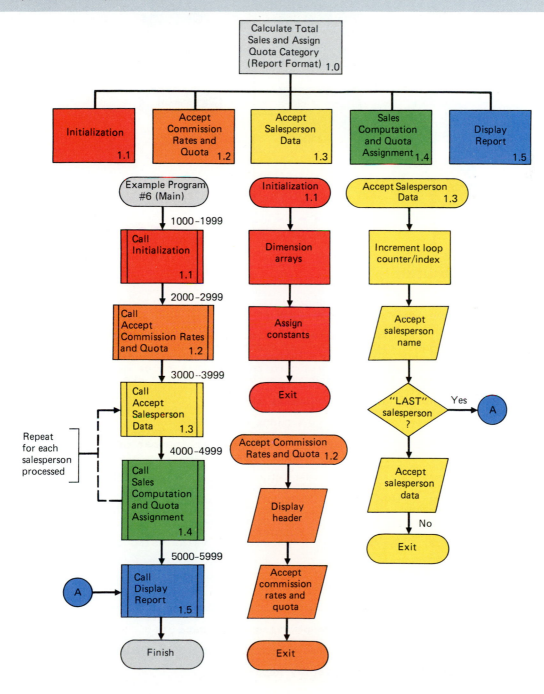

continued

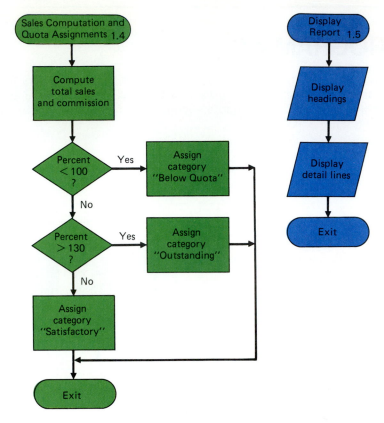

```
2    REM              **** Example Program #6 ****
4    REM   Description:
6    REM      This program computes the total sales and commission and assigns
8    REM      a quota category for any number of salespeople.  The sales manager
10   REM      assigns a commission rate to each of three products and enters a
12   REM      dollar amount representing this month's sales quota.
14   REM      Same as Example Program #5, but the results are printed in a
16   REM      report format.
18   REM   Variables list: () indicates array
20   REM      BELOW$, SATIS$,
22   REM      OUTST$                 - Quota categories
24   REM      C1, C2, CF             - Commission rates (Stibs, Farkles, Teglers)
26   REM      COUNT                  - Counter for the number of salespeople
28   REM      SPNAME$()              - Salesperson name
30   REM      ID()                   - Salesperson ID
32   REM      S1(), S2(), S3()       - Sales figures (Stibs, Farkles, Teglers)
34   REM      TOTAL()                - Total sales
36   REM      COMMISSION()           - Total commission earned
38   REM      PERCENT                - Percent of quota achieved
40   REM      CATEGORY$()            - Quota category
42   REM      I                      - Index for display loop
44   REM      F1$, F2$, F3$          - Strings for PRINT USING statements
99   REM
100  REM   <<<< Start Main >>>>
110  REM
120  REM   Call Module 1.1 - Initialization
130  GOSUB 1000
140  REM   Call Module 1.2 - Accept Commission Rates and Quota
150  GOSUB 2000
160  REM   Call Module 1.3 - Accept Salesperson Data
170  GOSUB 3000
180  REM   Call Module 1.4 - Sales Computation and Quota Assignment
190  GOSUB 4000
200  REM   Call Module 1.5 - Display Report
210  GOSUB 5000
```

Example Program 6 continued

```
220   END
230   REM   <<<< End Main >>>>
999   REM
1000  REM   ==== Module 1.1 - Initialization
1010  REM   Dimension arrays
1020  DIM SPNAME$(50),ID(50),S1(50),S2(50),S3(50),TOTAL(50)
1030  DIM COMMISSION(50), CATEGORY$(50)
1040  REM   Assign quota category constants to string variables
1050  READ BELOW$, SATIS$, OUTST$
1060  DATA "Below Quota","Satisfactory","Outstanding"
1999  RETURN
2000  REM   ==== Module 1.2 - Accept Commission Rates and Quota
2010  PRINT "    -------- Sales Summary Report --------"
2020  PRINT "Separate multiple entries by commas."
2030  PRINT
2040  PRINT "Enter commission rates (as a %)"
2050  INPUT "  for Stibs, Farkles, and Teglers: ", C1, C2, C3
2060  LET C1 = C1/100
2070  LET C2 = C2/100
2080  LET C3 = C3/100
2090  PRINT
2100  INPUT "Enter this month's sales quota (in dollars): ", QUOTA
2999  RETURN
3000  REM   ==== Module 1.3 - Accept Salesperson Data
3010  REM   Increment loop counter/index
3020  LET COUNT = COUNT + 1
3030  INPUT "Salesperson name (Enter LAST when complete): ", SPNAME$(COUNT)
3040  IF SPNAME$(COUNT) = "LAST" OR SPNAME$(COUNT) = "last" THEN RETURN 200
3050  INPUT "Salesperson ID: ", ID(COUNT)
3060  PRINT "Enter gross sales for Stibs, Farkles, and Teglers"
3070  PRINT "  (separate by commas): ";
3080  INPUT "", S1(COUNT), S2(COUNT), S3(COUNT)
3999  RETURN
4000  REM   ==== Module 1.4 - Sales Computation and Quota Assignment
4010  REM   Compute total sales and commission and assign quota category
4020  LET TOTAL(COUNT) = S1(COUNT) + S2(COUNT) + S3(COUNT)
4030  LET COMMISSION(COUNT) = S1(COUNT)*C1 + S2(COUNT)*C2 + S3(COUNT)*C3
4040  LET PERCENT = TOTAL(COUNT)/QUOTA * 100
4050  IF PERCENT < 100 THEN LET CATEGORY$(COUNT) = BELOW$ : RETURN 160
4060    IF PERCENT > 130 THEN LET CATEGORY$(COUNT) = OUTST$ : RETURN 160
4070      LET CATEGORY$(COUNT) = SATIS$
4999  RETURN 160
5000  REM   ==== Module 1.5 - Display Report
5010  LET F1$="########    "
5020  LET F2$="#######.##    "
5030  LET F3$="   \              \"
5040  REM   Display header
5050  PRINT
5060  PRINT TAB(30);"Sales Summary"
5070  PRINT
5080  PRINT "Salesperson","ID Number","Total Sales","Commission",
5090  PRINT "Quota Category"
5100  PRINT "-----------","---------","-----------","----------",
5110  PRINT "-------------"
5120  PRINT
5130  REM   Generate report
5140  LET COUNT = COUNT - 1
5150  REM   Begin loop to display detail lines - execute 'COUNT' times
5160  FOR I=1 TO COUNT
5170    PRINT SPNAME$(I),:PRINT USING F1$; ID(I),:PRINT USING F2$; TOTAL(I),
5180    PRINT USING F2$; COMMISSION(I),:PRINT USING F3$; CATEGORY$(I)
5190  NEXT I
5999  RETURN
```

continued

521

```
run
        -------- Sales Summary Report ---------
Separate multiple entries by commas.

Enter commission rates (as a %)
   for Stibs, Farkles, and Teglers: 4,3,5

Enter this month's sales quota (in dollars): 80000
Salesperson name (Enter LAST when complete): Charles Roth
Salesperson ID: 46912
Enter gross sales for Stibs, Farkles, and Teglers
   (separate by commas): 32000,28000,25000
Salesperson name (Enter LAST when complete): Lucy Cook
Salesperson ID: 77878
Enter gross sales for Stibs, Farkles, and Teglers
   (separate by commas): 50000,35000,20000
Salesperson name (Enter LAST when complete): Wayne Evans
Salesperson ID: 66941
Enter gross sales for Stibs, Farkles, and Teglers
   (separate by commas): 25000,30000,15000
Salesperson name (Enter LAST when complete): last
```

```
                        Sales Summary

Salesperson    ID Number   Total Sales   Commission   Quota Category
-----------    ---------   -----------   ----------   --------------

Charles Roth     46912      85000.00      3370.00     Satisfactory
Lucy Cook        77878     105000.00      4050.00     Outstanding
Wayne Evans      66941      70000.00      2650.00     Below Quota
Ok
```

**Arrays.** To present the results in a report format, the data for each salesperson must be kept in memory. In Example Program #5, when the sales figures of the second salesperson are entered, a new value is computed for COMMISSION, thereby erasing the commission of the first salesperson. We can use *arrays* (see DIM in the Learning Module IV instruction set) to retain data in primary storage so that they can be displayed together in a report format. To do this, a one-dimensional array, or list, is created for each salesperson data element (e.g., SPNAME$, ID, S1, S2, S3, etc.). It is not necessary to dimension S1, S2, and S3 to generate the report shown in the interactive session. These variables are dimensioned now so that the data are available if more sophisticated reporting is desired (see Example Program #7). This approach is common practice.

The DIM instructions in Module 1.1—Initialization (1020–1030) set aside, or "declare," 50 memory positions for each of eight array variables. The first five variables contain salesperson data entered by the user. The last three array variables, TOTAL(50), COMMISSION(50), and CATEGORY$(50), are determined and filled during processing.

In an array, values are stored and retrieved from a particular location by a *subscripted variable name*. All variables in a particular array have the same variable name (i.e., SPNAME$), but each has a subscript to make it unique. The value of the subscript determines which of the 50 locations is referenced. For example, SPNAME$(1) and ID(1) refer to the first items in the respective one-dimensional arrays. In the example programs, all subscripted variables with the subscript of (1) reference the data for the first salesperson. Those with the subscript of (2) reference the data for the second salesperson, and so on.

In Example Program #6, COUNT is the **index variable**. An array index can be a *constant*, a *variable*, or even an *expression*. The value of COUNT is the subscript for the array variables and designates which data are for which salesperson. The value of COUNT is incremented by 1 (3020) with each repetition of the loop (Modules 1.3 and 1.4). During the first time through the loop, COUNT is set to 1. Data that are entered, calculated, and processed are loaded to the first location in their respective arrays: SPNAME$(1), ID(1), and so on. During the second pass through loop, or second *iteration*, the value of COUNT is equal to 2, and data are loaded to the second location in their respective arrays: SPNAME$(2), ID(2), and so on. Because only 50 positions have been set aside in memory (1020), the maximum number of salespeople that can be processed is 50.

**The End-of-File Entry.** Example Program #6 illustrates how an *end-of-file* entry can be used to signal the program that data entry is complete. The INPUT instruction (3030) prompts the user to enter "LAST" instead of a salesperson's name when all data entry is complete. "LAST" is the end-of-file entry. The IF instruction at 3040 checks each name entered to see if it equals "LAST" or "last". When "LAST" is entered, statement 3040 causes a RETURN to the driver module at Module 1.5—Display Report for the printing of the Sales Summary report.

The end-of-file entry gives the user greater flexibility in entering data than in the previous example programs. In Example Programs #2, #3, and #4, the user had to count and enter the number of salespeople to be processed. This approach provides too much of an opportunity for human error. In Example Program #5, the user has to respond to a "More salespeople?" inquiry for each salesperson processed. This approach demands excessive user interaction.

**Report Formatting.** Module 1.5—Display Report causes the report *header* to be displayed. A header normally consists of a report title (5060) and column headings (5080–5110). Blank lines are inserted to make the report easier to read. Notice that TAB(30) is used in the PRINT instruction at 5060. The TAB(30) causes the report title to be displayed 30 spaces from the left margin. The **TAB** function is a handy tool for report generation.

The *detail lines* for each salesperson are displayed in a FOR/NEXT loop (5160–5190). For the data of the example interactive session, the index variable I is incremented from 1 to the value of COUNT (the number of salespeople to be processed, or 3 in the example) so that data for each salesperson are displayed.

The column headings are displayed in *zones*, since commas are used to separate the display list (5080–5110). The detail line is displayed using a combination of PRINT and PRINT USING instructions (see the discussion of Example Program #5).

Obtaining a Hard Copy.   The PRINT and PRINT USING instructions in Module 1.5—Display Report generate output for the workstation display screen. If a hard copy of the "Sales Summary" report is preferred, simply change the PRINT and PRINT USING instructions in Module 1.5 to LPRINT and LPRINT USING. This modification would result in a hard-copy report being produced on a printer.


## REVIEW EXERCISES (LEARNING MODULE IV) _____

### BASIC Instructions and Concepts

1. Identify the syntax error(s) in each of the following instructions.
   - (a)   10 DIMENSION DESCRIPTION$(100)
   - (b)   10 LPRINT USING "*$$##.##", AMOUNT
   - (c)   10 READ A: DATUM 345
   - (d)   10 LET X(1,-1)=0

2. What PRINT USING format fields would produce the following numeric and string displays?

   PRINT USING FORMAT$; 45.6789

   | | | | |
   |---|---|---|---|
   | (a)   45.679 | (c)   4.6E+01 | (e)   C | (g)   Computers |
   | (b)   **45.7 | (d)   $45.68 | (f)   Compute | (h)   Co |

   PRINT USING FORMAT$; "Computers"

3. What are the problems in the following instruction sequence?

   ```
   100 READ A,A$,B,C
   200 DATA 8,4,"BOLT"
   ```

4. What values of A, B, and C are displayed?

   ```
   100 READ A
   200 RESTORE
   300 READ C, B
   400 READ A
   500 DATA 1, 2, 3, 4
   600 PRINT A, B, C
   700 END
   ```

**5.** Combine the following statements into two statements without the use of a colon:

```
100 PRINT "Enter hours worked and rate"
200 INPUT HRSWORK, RATE
300 LET SALARY=HRSWORK*RATE
400 PRINT "Salary is", SALARY
```

**6.** Modify the PRINT instruction in the program segment above to an LPRINT USING/LPRINT combination of instructions that produce the following hard-copy output. [*Hint*: Put several instructions on the same line.]

SALARY IS $350.00 FOR   40 HOURS AT   $8.75 PER HOUR

**7.** Name an dimension arrays that will hold data for the following circumstances:
   (a)   quarterly sales figures for 18 regional offices
   (b)   the location (city) for 18 regional offices
   (c)   the first name, middle initial, and last name of at least 300 customers
   (d)   the identification number for at least 300 customers

**8.** Six letters are accepted and loaded to a three-row by two-column array, called LETTER$. The letters are entered in this order: A, E, I, O, U, and Y. Row 1 is filled first, then rows 2 and 3. What is the value of the following?
   (a)   LETTER$(2,1)      (c)   LETTER$(1,2)
   (b)   LETTER$(3,1)      (d)   LETTER$(2,2)

**9.** Which of the following conditional expressions are true?

```
100 LET X=10
200 LET Y=20
300 IF X<>Y AND Y<21 THEN PRINT "True"
400 IF Y=X+10 OR X=Y+10 THEN PRINT "True"
500 IF X<>Y OR NOT Y=20 THEN PRINT "True"
```

## Example Program #5

**10.** What do the PRINT USING instructions do in this program that cannot be done with PRINT instructions?

**11.** How would you modify the program to eliminate completely the need for Module 1.1—Assign Constants?

**12.** Describe in words what you would do to revise the program so that a user can enter and assign commission rates for four products.

**13.** How would the program logic change if the user were permitted to enter *up to* three sales figures and commission rates?

**14.** What happens if you enter a "Z" rather than a "Y" or "N" in response to the "More salespeople?" prompt in Module 1.6—Option to Repeat?

## Example Program #6

**15.** Compare the logic of Example Programs #5 and #6. Could #5 have been modified to produce a report without the use of arrays? Why or why not?

**16.** How many primary storage locations are declared in the DIM statements at lines 1020 and 1030 for numeric values and string values?

**17.** What must be done to modify the program to accommodate 60 salespeople?

**18.** Compared to entering the number of salespeople to be processed (Example Program #4) or asking the user after each entry if more salespeople are to be processed (Example Program #5), what are the advantages to using an EOF entry (i.e., "LAST")?

## BASIC PROGRAMMING ASSIGNMENTS

**1.** To optimize inventory, companies calculate the economic order quantity (EOQ) that would meet the company's demand for a particular item, yet minimize the cost of buying and holding the inventory. This is a trade-off between the number of times that a particular item must be ordered and the holding cost. Write a program to calculate the economic order quantity.

EOQ=(2*P*R/C)^.5
where   P = preparation cost per order
        R = annual requirement for an inventory item
        C = storage cost per item per year

Make the program interactive so that any number of EOQs can be computed until the operator enters −999.

**2.** Write an interactive program (without arrays) to compute gross pay and net pay for salaried, hourly, and commissioned employees. Assume that deductions are 20 percent of gross pay. For salaried employees, gross pay is entered directly. For hourly employees, the gross pay is equal to the number of hours worked times the pay rate. For commissioned employees, gross pay is equal to the rate of commission times total sales.

Present the following menu to the operator:

TYPE PAY
1 Salaried
2 Hourly
3 Commissioned
Select pay type?

Use the following prompts to enter pay data:

Enter salary:
Enter hours worked and pay rate:
Enter total sales and percent commission:

The output line for each employee should be

| EMPLOYEE NAME | PAY TYPE | GROSS PAY | NET PAY |
|---|---|---|---|
| T. Jones | Salaried | $3000.00 | $2400.00 |

Note that the heading would be printed for each calculation.

3.  Modify the program above to use arrays so that a payroll register can be produced that lists all the names and results consecutively rather than individually. The program should accommodate up to 20 employees.

PAYROLL REGISTER

| EMPLOYEE NAME | PAY TYPE | GROSS PAY | NET PAY |
|---|---|---|---|
| T. Jones | Salaried | $3000.00 | $2400.00 |
| D. Mattis | Hourly | $2100.00 | $1680.00 |
| D. Guyer | Commission | $3800.00 | $3040.00 |
|  | TOTAL | $8900.00 | $7120.00 |

# Writing Interactive Inquiry Programs

**B-17**  **BASIC INSTRUCTION SET: LEARNING MODULE V GROUP**_____

Four instructions are introduced in this group. One rather straightforward I/O instruction will give us the flexibility to substantially improve the appearance of the output displays. Two others are variations on the GOSUB and GOTO (see the Learning Module II instruction set). The fourth is a variation on the INPUT instruction.

## Input/Output Instructions

CLS.    The "clear screen" instruction removes any output on the display screen and positions the cursor to the "home" position, normally the upper left corner of the screen.

| |
|---|
| *Format*:   CLS |

In Example Program #6, the CLS instruction could have been inserted at the start of Module 1.5—Display Report to clear the input data from the screen so that the "Sales Summary" report could be positioned at the top of the screen.

The clear screen command is CLEAR or HOME on some versions of BASIC.

LINE INPUT.    The LINE INPUT instruction accepts whatever is entered, including delimiters such as commas, into a single string variable.

| |
|---|
| *Format*:   LINE INPUT "prompt"; string variable |
| |
| **Example:**   LINE INPUT "Enter comments"; COMMENTS$ |

In the instruction above, all characters (including spaces, commas, semicolons, etc.) entered prior to pressing the carriage return become a string constant and are assigned to the string variable COMMENT$.

## Control Instructions: Conditional and Unconditional Transfer

ON GOSUB/RETURN.    An optional form of the GOSUB instruction is used to direct processing to branch to a specified line number based on the value of a numeric expression. Processing is RETURNed to the statement following the ON GOSUB.

For the last several years, this product manager spent one hour each week tallying the regional sales figures. He finally spent five hours writing a BASIC program to help with this task. Now, his weekly sales reports take only 15 minutes and they are more accurate. In every office, there are many tasks for which a single BASIC program can be a real timesaver.
(Courtesy of Apple Computer, Inc.)

> ***Format***:   ON numeric expression GOSUB line number,
>                  line number, . . .

***Example***:   100  ON I GOSUB 2000, 3000, 4000
                 2000 INPUT A, B
                 2999 RETURN
                 3000 INPUT A$
                 3999 RETURN
                 4000 INPUT C, D$
                 4999 RETURN

In the example, control of execution is transferred to one of three line numbers depending on the value of I. If I = 1, control passes to the instruction at 2000, the first line number in the list; if I = 2, control passes to the instruction at 3000, the second line number; and so on. The value of the numeric expression is rounded to an integer, if needed. When the resultant value is negative, zero, or greater than the number of line numbers in the list, control is passed to the statement following the ON GOSUB. A RETURN instruction must be associated with each line number so that control can be returned to the statement following the ON GOSUB instruction.

ON GOTO.   The ON GOTO counterpart of ON GOSUB causes an unconditional branch to a specified line number.

> ***Format***:   ON numeric expression GOTO line number,
>                  line number, . . .

***Example***:   100 ON I GOTO 2000, 3000, 4000

## The "Bread and Butter" BASIC Instructions

You now have an arsenal of programming tools at your disposal. With the few BASIC instructions presented and explained in the instruction set groups in Learning Modules II through V, you should be able to model almost any business or scientific procedure. These "bread and butter" instructions comprise about 20 percent of the total number of BASIC instructions, yet they account for about 80 percent of the instructions in a typical program. In the remaining learning modules you will learn instructions that permit more sophisticated programming activities, such as disk file manipulation and graphics.

## B-18  EXAMPLE PROGRAM #7: INTERACTIVE INQUIRY

Example Program #7 is Example Program #6 with an add-on *Inquiry* module (Module 1.6). We will focus our attention on this inquiry module.

These programmers routinely use word processing software to prepare and maintain program documentation. This company's documentation policy calls for a detailed written description and a flowchart for each program.
(AT&T Information Systems)

# EXAMPLE PROGRAM #7

This program computes the total sales and commission and assigns a quota category for any number of salespeople. The sales manager assigns a commission rate to each of three products and enters a dollar amount representing this month's sales quota. The report of Example Program #6 is generated. An inquiry module allows the manager to interactively make inquiries with regard to:

1. Total sales by product
2. Breakdown by quota category
3. Salespeople with highest and lowest total sales

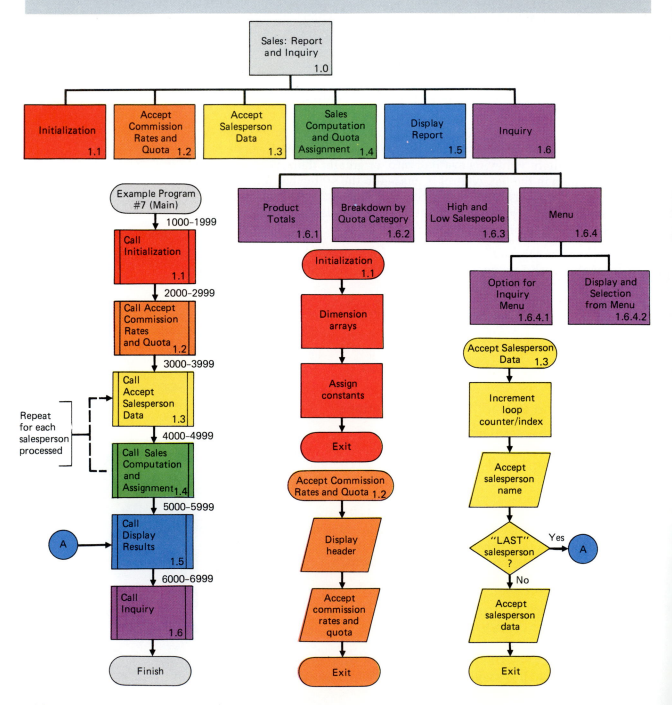

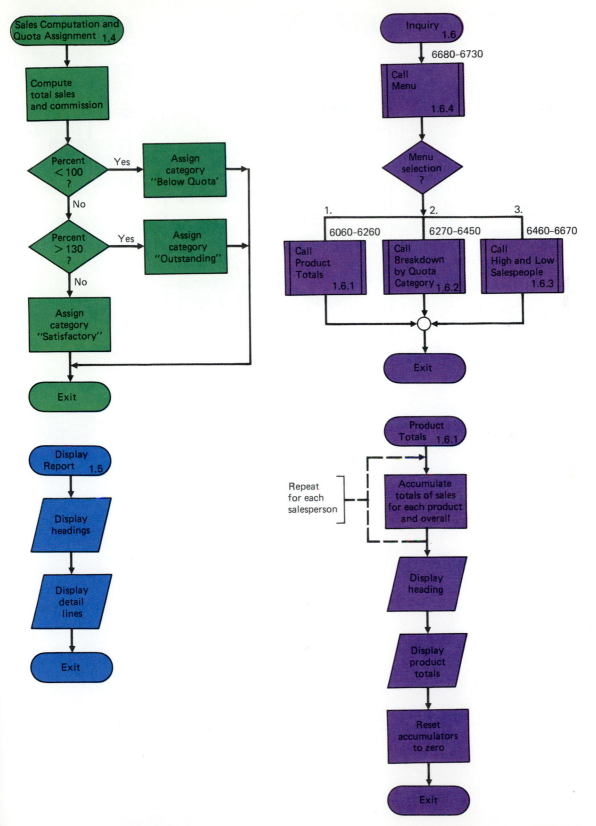

continued

Example Program 7 continued

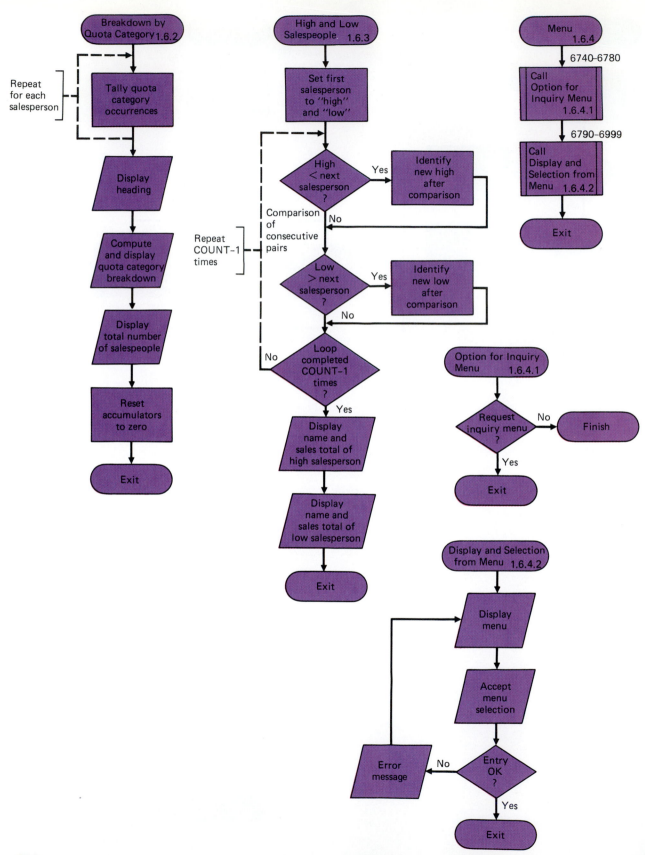

```
2    REM            **** Example Program #7 ****
4    REM   Description:
6    REM      This program computes the total sales and commission and assigns
8    REM      a quota category for any number of salespeople. The sales manager
10   REM      assigns a commission rate to each of three products and enters a
12   REM      dollar amount representing this month's sales quota. The report of
14   REM      Example Program #6 is generated. An inquiry module allows the
16   REM      manager to interactively make inquiries with regard to:
18   REM              1. Total sales by product
20   REM              2. Breakdown by quota category
22   REM              3. Salespeople with highest and lowest total sales
24   REM   Variables list:
26   REM      BELOW$, SATIS$,
28   REM      OUTST$                 - Quota categories
30   REM      C1, C2, C3             - Commission rates (Stibs, Farkles, Teglers)
32   REM      COUNT                  - Counter for the number of salespeople
34   REM      SPNAME$()              - Salesperson name
36   REM      ID()                   - Salesperson ID
38   REM      S1(), S2(), S3()       - Sales figures (Stibs, Farkles, Teglers)
40   REM      TOTAL()                - Total sales
42   REM      COMMISSION()           - Total commission earned
44   REM      PERCENT                - Percent of quota achieved
46   REM      CATEGORY$()            - Quota category
48   REM      I                      - Index for display loop
50   REM      F1$, F2$, F3$          - Strings for PRINT USING statements
52   REM      MENU                   - Menu item selected
54   REM      T1, T2, T3,            - Accumulators to compute sales totals
56   REM      BCAT, SCAT, OCAT       - Accumulators for each quota category
58   REM      HIGH, LOW              - Indices for high and low salespeople
99   REM
100  REM   <<<< Start Main >>>>
110  REM
120  REM   Call Module 1.1 - Initialization
130  GOSUB 1000
140  REM   Call Module 1.2 - Accept Commission Rates and Quota
150  GOSUB 2000
160  REM   Call Module 1.3 - Accept Salesperson Data
170  GOSUB 3000
180  REM   Call Module 1.4 - Sales Computation and Quota Assignment
190  GOSUB 4000
200  REM   Call Module 1.5 - Display Report
210  GOSUB 5000
220  REM   Call Module 1.6 - Inquiry
230  GOSUB 6000
240  REM
250  REM   <<<< End Main >>>>
999  REM
1000 REM   ==== Module 1.1 - Initialization
1010 REM   Dimension Arrays
1020 DIM SPNAME$(50),ID(50),S1(50),S2(50),S3(50),TOTAL(50)
1030 DIM COMMISSION(50), CATEGORY$(50)
1040 REM   Assign quota category constants to string variables
1050 READ BELOW$, SATIS$, OUTST$
1060 DATA "Below Quota","Satisfactory","Outstanding"
1999 RETURN
2000 REM   ==== Module 1.2 - Accept Commission Rates and Quota
2010 PRINT "    -------- Sales Summary Report --------"
2020 PRINT "Separate multiple entries by commas."
2030 PRINT
2040 PRINT "Enter commission rates (as a %)"
2050 INPUT "  for Stibs, Farkles, and Teglers: ", C1, C2, C3
2060 LET C1 = C1/100
2070 LET C2 = C2/100
2080 LET C3 = C3/100
2090 PRINT
2100 INPUT "Enter this month's sales quota (in dollars): ", QUOTA
2999 RETURN
3000 REM   ==== Module 1.3 - Accept Salesperson Data
3010 REM   Increment loop counter/index
3020 LET COUNT = COUNT + 1
3030 INPUT "Salesperson name (Enter LAST when complete): ", SPNAME$(COUNT)
3040 IF SPNAME$(COUNT) = "LAST" OR SPNAME$(COUNT) = "last" THEN RETURN 200
3050 INPUT "Salesperson ID: ", ID(COUNT)
```

continued

```
3060 PRINT "Enter gross sales for Stibs, Farkles, and Teglers"
3070 PRINT "   (separate by commas): ";
3080 INPUT "", S1(COUNT), S2(COUNT), S3(COUNT)
3999 RETURN
4000 REM   ==== Module 1.4 - Sales Computation and Quota Assignment
4010 REM   Compute total sales and commission and assign quota category
4020 LET TOTAL(COUNT) = S1(COUNT) + S2(COUNT) + S3(COUNT)
4030 LET COMMISSION(COUNT) = S1(COUNT)*C1 + S2(COUNT)*C2 + S3(COUNT)*C3
4040 LET PERCENT = TOTAL(COUNT)/QUOTA * 100
4050 IF PERCENT < 100 THEN LET CATEGORY$(COUNT) = BELOW$ : RETURN 160
4060    IF PERCENT > 130 THEN LET CATEGORY$(COUNT) = OUTST$ : RETURN 160
4070      LET CATEGORY$(COUNT) = SATIS$
4999 RETURN 160
5000 REM   ==== Module 1.5 - Display Report
5010 LET F1$="########        "
5020 LET F2$="#######.##    "
5030 LET F3$="    \                \"
5040 CLS
5050 REM   Display header
5060 PRINT
5070 PRINT TAB(30);"Sales Summary"
5080 PRINT
5090 PRINT "Salesperson","ID Number","Total Sales","Commission",
5100 PRINT "Quota Category"
5110 PRINT "-----------","---------","-----------","----------",
5120 PRINT "--------------"
5130 PRINT
5140 REM   Generate report
5150 LET COUNT = COUNT - 1
5160 REM   Begin loop to display detail lines - execute 'COUNT' times
5170 FOR I=1 TO COUNT
5180    PRINT SPNAME$(I),:PRINT USING F1$; ID(I),:PRINT USING F2$; TOTAL(I),
5190    PRINT USING F2$; COMMISSION(I),:PRINT USING F3$; CATEGORY$(I)
5200 NEXT
5999 RETURN
6000 REM   ==== Module 1.6 - Inquiry
6010 REM   Call Module 1.6.4 - Menu
6020 GOSUB 6680
6030 REM   Call appropriate inquiry module
6040 ON MENU GOSUB 6060, 6270, 6460
6050 GOTO 6010
6060 REM   ==== Module 1.6.1 - Product Totals
6070 REM   Compute sales totals for each product and display them
6080 REM
6090 REM   Accumulate totals for each product
6100 FOR I=1 TO COUNT
6110    LET T1 = T1 + S1(I)
6120    LET T2 = T2 + S2(I)
6130    LET T3 = T3 + S3(I)
6140 NEXT I
6150 PRINT
6160 REM   Display product totals
6170 PRINT "Product","Total Sales"
6180 PRINT
6190 PRINT "Stibs", "$";T1
6200 PRINT "Farkles", "$";T2
6210 PRINT "Teglers", "$";T3
6220 PRINT
6230 PRINT "Total sales", "$";T1+T2+T3
6240 REM   Reset accumulators to zero
6250 LET T1 = 0 : LET T2 = 0 : LET T3 = 0
6260 RETURN
6270 REM   ==== Module 1.6.2 - Breakdown By Quota Category
6280 REM   Tally quota category occurrences
6290 FOR I=1 TO COUNT
6300    IF CATEGORY$(I) = BELOW$ THEN LET BCAT = BCAT + 1
6310    IF CATEGORY$(I) = SATIS$ THEN LET SCAT = SCAT + 1
6320    IF CATEGORY$(I) = OUTST$ THEN LET OCAT = OCAT + 1
6330 NEXT I
6340 REM   Display quota category breakdown
6350 PRINT "Quota Categrory","Number of Salespeople","Percent"
6360 LET F3$ = "###.##"
6370 PRINT
```

```
6380 PRINT BELOW$,, BCAT,,:PRINT USING F3$; (BCAT/COUNT) * 100
6390 PRINT SATIS$,, SCAT,,:PRINT USING F3$; (SCAT/COUNT) * 100
6400 PRINT OUTST$,, OCAT,,:PRINT USING F3$; (OCAT/COUNT) * 100
6410 PRINT
6420 PRINT "Total number of salespeople:"; COUNT
6430 REM   Reset category counters to zero
6440 LET BCAT = 0 : LET SCAT = 0 : LET OCAT = 0
6450 RETURN
6460 REM   ==== Module 1.6.3 - High And Low Salespeople
6470 REM   Find and display salespeople with highest and lowest total sales
6480 REM
6490 REM   Set both HIGH and LOW to first salesperson
6500 LET HIGH = 1 : LET LOW = 1
6510 REM   Compare salesperson pairs to identify
6520 REM   salesperson with highest and lowest total sales
6530 FOR I=2 TO COUNT
6540    IF TOTAL(HIGH) < TOTAL(I) THEN LET HIGH = I
6550    IF TOTAL(LOW) > TOTAL(I) THEN LET LOW = I
6560 NEXT I
6570 REM   Display high and low salespeople
6580 PRINT "The salesperson with the highest total sales is "; SPNAME$(HIGH);
6590 PRINT " with a"
6600 PRINT "total sales amount of $"; TOTAL(HIGH); "and a commission of $";
6610 PRINT USING "#####.##"; COMMISSION(HIGH)
6620 PRINT
6630 PRINT "The salesperson with the lowest total sales is "; SPNAME$(LOW);
6640 PRINT " with a"
6650 PRINT "total sales amount of $"; TOTAL(LOW); "and a commission of $";
6660 PRINT USING "#####.##"; COMMISSION(LOW)
6670 RETURN
6680 REM   ==== Module 1.6.4 - Menu
6690 REM   Call Module 1.6.4.1 - Option for Inquiry Menu
6700 GOSUB 6740
6710 REM   Call Module 1.6.4.2 - Display and Selection from Menu
6720 GOSUB 6790
6730 RETURN
6740 REM   ==== Module 1.6.4.1 - Option for Inquiry Menu
6750 PRINT
6760 INPUT "Would you like to see the inquiry menu? (Enter Y or N) ",ANSWER$
6770 IF ANSWER$ = "N" OR ANSWER$ = "n" THEN RETURN 6999
6780 RETURN
6790 REM   ==== Module 1.6.4.2 - Display and Selection from Menu
6800 PRINT
6810 PRINT "    ---- INQUIRY MENU ----"
6820 PRINT "1. Total sales by product"
6830 PRINT "2. Breakdown by quota category"
6840 PRINT "3. Salespeople with highest and lowest total sales"
6850 PRINT
6860 REM   Accept menu selection
6870 INPUT "Make a selection from the menu: ", MENU
6880 CLS
6890 IF MENU > 0 AND MENU < 4 THEN RETURN
6900 REM   Error message
6910 PRINT "That was not a valid response, try again."
6920 GOTO 6790
6999 END
```

continued

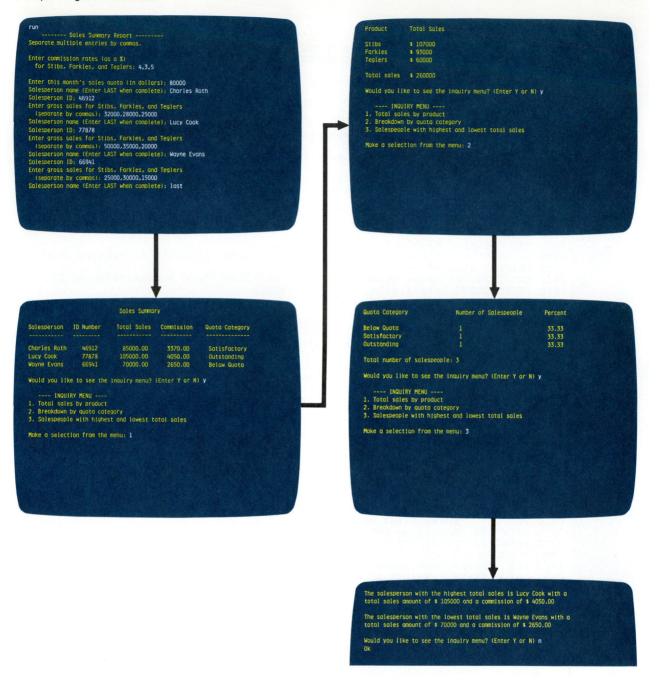

```
run
        -------- Sales Summary Report ---------
Separate multiple entries by commas.

Enter commission rates (as a %)
  for Stibs, Farkles, and Teglers: 4,3,5

Enter this month's sales quota (in dollars): 80000
Salesperson name (Enter LAST when complete): Charles Roth
Salesperson ID: 46912
Enter gross sales for Stibs, Farkles, and Teglers
  (separate by commas): 32000,28000,25000
Salesperson name (Enter LAST when complete): Lucy Cook
Salesperson ID: 77878
Enter gross sales for Stibs, Farkles, and Teglers
  (separate by commas): 50000,35000,20000
Salesperson name (Enter LAST when complete): Wayne Evans
Salesperson ID: 66941
Enter gross sales for Stibs, Farkles, and Teglers
  (separate by commas): 25000,30000,15000
Salesperson name (Enter LAST when complete): last
```

```
Product      Total Sales

Stibs        $ 107000
Farkles      $ 93000
Teglers      $ 60000

Total sales  $ 260000

Would you like to see the Inquiry menu? (Enter Y or N) y

    ---- INQUIRY MENU ----
1. Total sales by product
2. Breakdown by quota category
3. Salespeople with highest and lowest total sales

Make a selection from the menu: 2
```

```
                   Sales Summary

Salesperson  ID Number   Total Sales  Commission  Quota Category
-----------  ---------   -----------  ----------  --------------

Charles Roth   46912      85000.00     3370.00     Satisfactory
Lucy Cook      77878     105000.00     4050.00     Outstanding
Wayne Evans    66941      70000.00     2650.00     Below Quota

Would you like to see the Inquiry menu? (Enter Y or N) y

    ---- INQUIRY MENU ----
1. Total sales by product
2. Breakdown by quota category
3. Salespeople with highest and lowest total sales

Make a selection from the menu: 1
```

```
Quota Category          Number of Salespeople      Percent

Below Quota                   1                      33.33
Satisfactory                  1                      33.33
Outstanding                   1                      33.33

Total number of salespeople: 3

Would you like to see the Inquiry menu? (Enter Y or N) y

    ---- INQUIRY MENU ----
1. Total sales by product
2. Breakdown by quota category
3. Salespeople with highest and lowest total sales

Make a selection from the menu: 3
```

```
The salesperson with the highest total sales is Lucy Cook with a
total sales amount of $ 105000 and a commission of $ 4050.00

The salesperson with the lowest total sales is Wayne Evans with a
total sales amount of $ 70000 and a commission of $ 2650.00

Would you like to see the Inquiry menu? (Enter Y or N) n
Ok
```

The inquiry module permits the user to make inquiries about the salesperson data. For example, the user can ask for a breakdown by quota category. These inquiries are possible because any salesperson data entered and generated in Modules 1.1 through 1.5 (essentially Example Program #6) are still available in primary storage in the salesperson data arrays (see 1020).

This is the first example program for which the logic of the program dictates a third level in the structure chart. At the third level are the three types of inquiries (Modules 1.6.1, 1.6.2, and 1.6.3) and the menu module (1.6.4), all of which are subordinate to Module 1.6—Inquiry. For illustrative purposes, Module 1.6.4 is subdivided into a fourth level (Module 1.6.4.1—Option for Inquiry Menu, and Module 1.6.4.2—Display and Selection from Menu). In practice, a program of this level of complexity would not require a fourth-level breakdown. However, the level of detail in the program structure chart and flowchart is a matter of personal preference and logic complexity.

**The Program.** Don't let the 202 statements in Example Program #7 overwhelm you. Keep in mind that this program was compiled from several well-defined logical modules. When you consider that we have already discussed Modules 1.1 through 1.5 (Example Program #6) and the REM statements are nonexecutable, 67 statements are left. Now let's see how these statements are generated.

From the structure chart for Example Program #7 we know that Module 1.6—Inquiry is made up of the three inquiry options and the menu routine. A list of options presented to an operator is commonly referred to as a **menu**. The use of menus is an important facet of on-line interactive programs. The inquiry options, or menu items, are:

1. Total sales by product (Module 1.6.1)
2. Breakdown by quota category (Module 1.6.2)
3. Salespeople with highest and lowest total sales (Module 1.6.3)

The interactive session of Example Program #7 demonstrates the outcome for inquiries to each menu item.

**Module 1.6.4—Menu.** The first processing activity of the Module 1.6—Inquiry is to call Module 1.6.4—Menu (6020). Module 1.6.4 is further subdivided into Module 1.6.4.1—Option for Inquiry Menu and Module 1.6.4.2—Display and Selection from Menu. The purpose of Module 1.6.4.1 is to determine whether or not the user would like to see the inquiry menu (see the interactive session).

Compare the IF instructions in Example Program #5 (6030) and Example Program #7 (6770). Both evaluate the user's request, but in different ways. In Example Program #5, the THEN clause is taken (process another salesperson) if the character entered is "Y" or "y". In Example Program #7, the THEN clause is taken (end program execution) if the character is an "N" or "n". The menu is displayed when any character but an "N" or an "n" is entered.

Module 1.6.4.2 displays the menu on the screen and permits the user to make a selection from the list of items in the menu. As a programmer you must assume that if anything can go wrong, it will. You cannot assume that the user will always select one of the available menu items. If the user selects other than 1, 2, or 3, the error routine (6890–6920) displays an error message, then asks the user to "try again".

Once the user has made a valid menu selection, control is RETURNed (6890) to Module 1.6—Inquiry, where the ON GOSUB instruction (6040) is used to direct processing to the appropriate module. At statement 6040, control is passed to a subroutine statement (6060, 6270, or 6460) *depending on* the value of MENU (menu item selected). If menu item 1 is selected (MENU = 1), then Module 1.6.1—Product Totals is executed. If menu item 2 (MENU = 2) is selected, then Module 1.6.2—Breakdown by Quota Category is executed, and so on.

**Module 1.6.1—Product Totals.**   To compute the total sales amount for each of the three products (Stibs, Farkles, and Teglers), the sales figures of all products must be totaled. This is done in a FOR/NEXT loop containing four *accumulators* (6100–6140), one for each product (T1, T2, and T3). An accumulator format has the assignment variable on both sides of the equation. In this way, the current value of the accumulator is added to other values on the right side to obtain a new accumulator value. The process is repeated, as illustrated below, until all product sales figures (three each in our example) are accumulated.

$$6110 \qquad T1 = \qquad T1 + S1(I)$$

|  |  |
|---|---|
| For:$I = 1$ | $32000 = \quad 0 + 32000$ |
| $I = 2$ | $82000 = 32000 + 50000$ |
| $I = 3$ | $107000 = 82000 + 25000$ |

The total of all Stibs sales figures, now in T1, is 107000.

An arithmetic expression is embedded in the PRINT statement at 6230 to save programming time and simplify the program logic.

It is unlikely that the user will request menu item 1 again, but just in case, the accumulators must be reset to zero (6250). If this is not done, the accumulation of sales figures would begin, not with T1 = 0, but with T1 = 107000.

**Module 1.6.2—Breakdown by Quota Category.**   To achieve a breakdown by quota category (menu option 2), a series of IF statements is embedded in a loop (6290–6330). In the loop, each salesperson's quota category is compared in successive IF statements to string constant values of "Below Quota", "Satisfactory", or "Outstanding" that are stored in the variables BELOW$, SATIS$, and OUTST$. Only one of the three conditions will be met for any given salesperson. Each THEN clause contains a counter (BCAT, SCAT, OCAT) which is incremented by 1 when a condition is met. In this way, quota category occurrences are tallied. In the example interactive session of Example Program #7, Lucy Cook earned an "Outstanding" quota rating [CATEGORY$(1)="Outstanding"]. Since CATEGORY$(1)=OUTST$, OCAT is incremented from 0 to 1.

Again, in case the user selects menu item 2 a second time, the counters must be reset to zero (6440).

**Module 1.6.3—High and Low Salespeople.**   Of the menu options, the logic of Module 1.6.3—High and Low Salespeople is the most challenging. In this module the salespeople with the highest and lowest total sales are displayed. The approach illustrated in the flowchart of Example Program #7 compares consecutive total sales in the array TOTAL. TOTAL(1) is compared to TOTAL(2); TOTAL(2) is compared to TOTAL(3), and so on through the array.

The comparison is made in a loop which is repeated COUNT−1 (from 2 to COUNT) times, so that all pairs of total sales figures can be compared. In our example, the loop is repeated twice (3−1=2, see Figure B-12). The first salesperson (Charles Roth in the example) is arbitrarily identified as being both the high and the low salesperson at the start of the pairs comparisons. That is, HIGH=LOW=1 (6500). On the first pass through the loop, the total sales of the first salesperson (85000) is compared to the total sales of the second salesperson (105000). Since the condition in statement 6540 is met [TOTAL(1) < TOTAL(2) or 85000 < 105000], the index HIGH takes on the current value of I, which in the first loop is 2. With HIGH equal to 2, the second salesperson has the highest total sales so far in the comparison.

The same procedure is followed for the determination of the low salesperson. Since the condition in statement 6550 is not met [TOTAL(1) > TOTAL(2) or 85000 > 105000], the value of the index LOW is unchanged. The first salesperson continues to have the lowest total sales so far in the comparison.

Once the loop has been repeated the required number of times (twice in our example), the index of the high and low salespeople is contained in the variables HIGH and LOW (see Figure B-12). These values then become the subscripts for the SPNAME$ and TOTAL arrays when the high and low salespeople are displayed (6570–6660).

**FIGURE B-12**
**Index Values for Module 1.6.3—High and Low Salespeople**
This figure shows how the index values of HIGH and LOW change as Module 1.6.3 of Example Program #7 is executed with the data from the example interactive session.

| | | HIGH | LOW | COUNT |
|---|---|---|---|---|
| Initialize { | 6500 | 1 | 1 | |
| First pass of loop { | 6540 | 2 | 1 | 2 |
| | 6550 | 2 | 1 | 2 |
| Second pass of loop { | 6540 | 2 | 1 | 3 |
| | 6550 | 2 | 3 | 3 |

## B-19 EXAMPLE PROGRAM #8: TWO-DIMENSIONAL ARRAYS AND INPUT VALIDATION

**Working with Tables: Two-Dimensional Arrays.** In Example Program #7, the sales figures and the resultant total sales and earned commission were stored in lists (one-dimensional arrays). Each of these lists required a unique name: S1, S2, and so on. In Example Program #8, these like data (sales figures) are entered and processed in a single table, or two-dimensional array, called SALES. SALES is DIMensioned in statement 1020 to have up to 50 rows and five columns. The lists of Example Program #7 are equated to their Example Program #8 table equivalent next and in Figure B-13.

| *Example Program #7* | *Example Program #8* |
|---|---|
| S1(COUNT) | SALES(COUNT,1) |
| S2(COUNT | SALES(COUNT,2) |
| S3(COUNT) | SALES(COUNT,3) |
| TOTAL(COUNT) | SALES(COUNT,4) |
| COMMISSION(COUNT) | SALES(COUNT,5) |

In a two-dimensional array, the first subscript is conceptualized as the row number and the second as the column (see Figure B-13). In effect, the first subscript refers to a particular salesperson and the second subscript depicts which sales figure is being referenced. For example, SALES(3,2) references the third salesperson's sales for Farkles (the second product for which data are entered).

### FIGURE B-13
**Combining Related Lists into a Table**
The one-dimensional lists of Example Program #7 are combined into a two-dimensional table in Example Program #8.

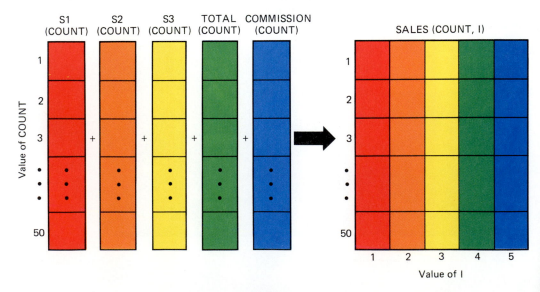

# EXAMPLE PROGRAM #8

This program computes the total sales and commission and assigns a quota category for any number of salespeople. The sales manager assigns a commission rate to each of three products and enters a dollar amount representing this month's sales quota. The report of Example Program #7 is generated. An inquiry module allows the instructor to interactively make inquiries with regard to:

1. Total sales by product
2. Breakdown by quota category
3. Salespeople with highest and lowest total sales

It is the same as Example Program #7 except that two-dimensional arrays are used for sales data and some simple input validation routines are added.

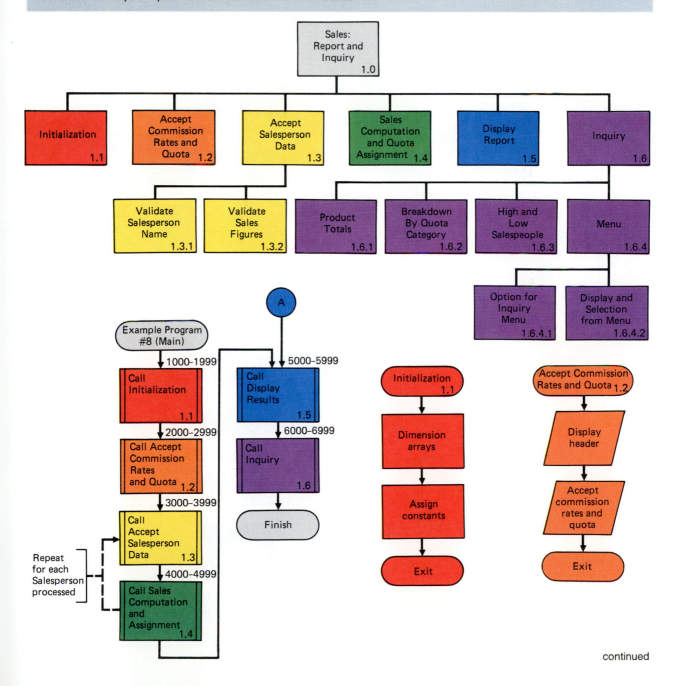

continued

Example Program 8 continued

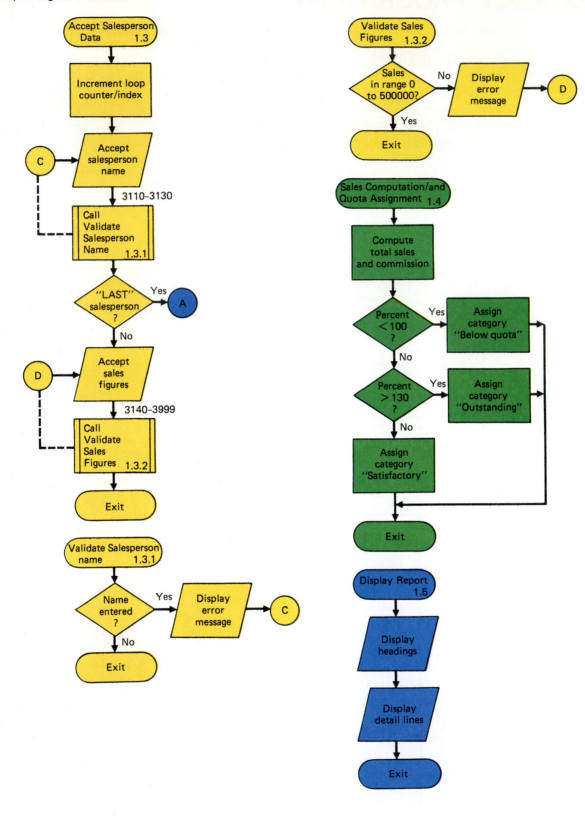

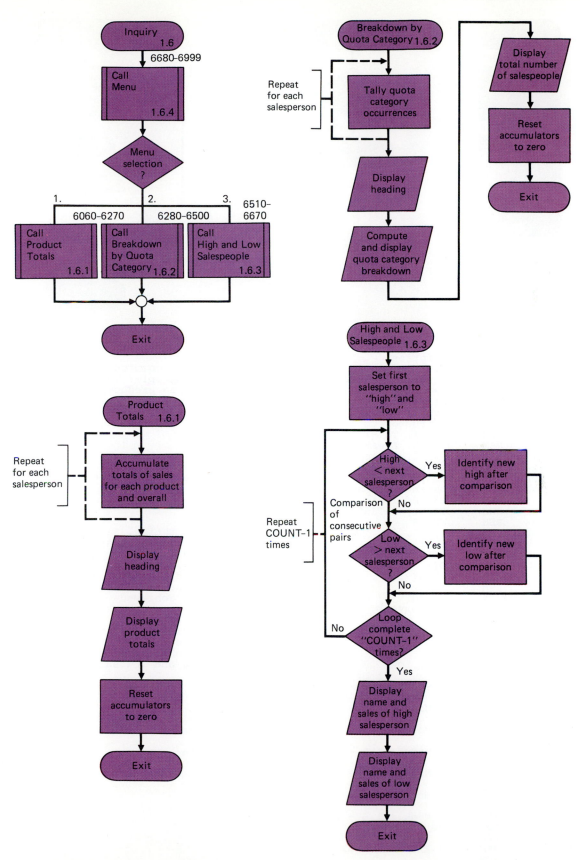

continued

Example Program 8 continued

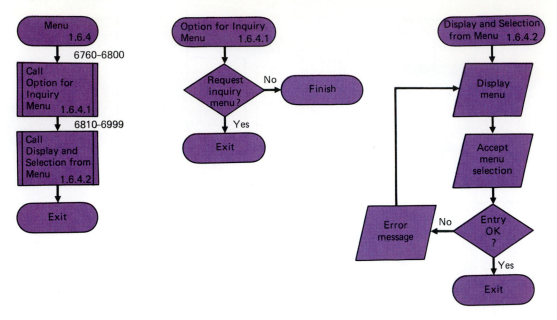

```
2    REM                    **** Example Program #8 ****
4    REM   Description:
6    REM      This program computes the total sales and commission and assigns
8    REM      a quota category for any number of salespeople. The sales manager
10   REM      assigns a commission rate to each of three products and enters a
12   REM      dollar amount representing this month's sales quota. The report of
14   REM      Example Program #7 is generated. An inquiry module allows the
16   REM      instructor to interactively make inquiries with regard to:
18   REM                 1. Total sales by product
20   REM                 2. Breakdown by quota category
22   REM                 3. Salespeople with hightest and lowest total sales
24   REM      It is the same as Example Program #7 except that two-dimensional
26   REM      arrays are used for sales data and some simple input validation
28   REM      routines are added.
30   REM   Variables list:
32   REM      BELOW$, SATIS$,
34   REM      OUTST$                - Quota categories
36   REM      C1, C2, C3            - Commission rates (Stibs, Farkles, Teglers)
38   REM      COUNT                 - Counter for the number of salespeople
40   REM      SPNAME$()             - Salesperson name
42   REM      ID()                  - Salesperson ID
44   REM      SALES( , )            - Sales figures, total sales, and commission
46   REM                              earned for each salesperson
48   REM      PERCENT               - Percent of quota achieved
50   REM      CATEGORY$()           - Quota category
52   REM      I                     - Index for display loop
54   REM      F1$, F2$, F3$         - Strings for PRINT USING statements
56   REM      MENU                  - Menu item selected
58   REM      TOT()                 - Accumulator to compute sales totals
60   REM      HIGH, LOW             - Indices for high and low salespeople
99   REM
100  REM   <<<< Start Main >>>>
110  REM
120  REM   Call Module 1.1 - Initialization
130  GOSUB 1000
140  REM   Call Module 1.2 - Accept Commission Rates and Quota
150  GOSUB 2000
160  REM   Call Module 1.3 - Accept Salesperson Data
170  GOSUB 3000
180  REM   Call Module 1.4 - Sales Computation and Quota Assignment
190  GOSUB 4000
200  REM   Call Module 1.5 - Display Report
210  GOSUB 5000
220  REM   Call Module 1.6 - Inquiry
230  GOSUB 6000
240  REM
250  REM   <<<< End Main >>>>
999  REM
```

```
1000 REM  ==== Module 1.1 - Initialization
1010 REM   Dimension Arrays
1020 DIM SPNAME$(50),ID(50),SALES(50,5),CATEGORY$(50), TOT(4)
1030 REM   Assign quota category constants to string variables
1040 READ BELOW$, SATIS$, OUTST$
1050 DATA "Below Quota","Satisfactory","Outstanding"
1999 RETURN
2000 REM  ==== Module 1.2 - Accept Commission Rates and Quota
2010 PRINT "     -------- Sales Summary Report --------"
2020 PRINT "Separate multiple entries by commas."
2030 PRINT
2040 PRINT "Enter commission rates (as a %)"
2050 INPUT "  for Stibs, Farkles, and Teglers: ", C1, C2, C3
2060 LET C1 = C1/100
2070 LET C2 = C2/100
2080 LET C3 = C3/100
2090 PRINT
2100 INPUT "Enter this month's sales quota (in dollars): ", QUOTA
2999 RETURN
3000 REM  ==== Module 1.3 - Accept Salesperson Data
3010 LET COUNT = COUNT + 1
3020 INPUT "Salesperson name (Enter LAST when complete): ", SPNAME$(COUNT)
3030 REM  Call Module 1.3.1 - Validate Salesperson Name
3040 GOSUB 3120
3050 IF SPNAME$(COUNT) = "LAST" OR SPNAME$(COUNT) = "last" THEN RETURN 200
3060 INPUT "Salesperson ID: ",ID(COUNT)
3070 PRINT "Enter gross sales for Stibs, Farkles, and Teglers"
3075 PRINT "  (separate by commas): ";
3080 INPUT "", SALES(COUNT,1),SALES(COUNT,2),SALES(COUNT,3)
3090 REM  Call Module 1.3.2 - Validate Sales Figures
3100 GOSUB 3150
3110 RETURN
3120 REM  ==== Module 1.3.1 - Validate Salesperson Name
3130 IF SPNAME$(COUNT) = "" THEN PRINT "Null salesperson name not allowed":
       PRINT:RETURN 3020
3140 RETURN
3150 REM  ==== Module 1.3.2 - Validate Sales Figures
3160 FOR I = 1 TO 3
3170  IF SALES(COUNT,I) < 0 OR SALES(COUNT,I) > 500000! THEN PRINT
       "Sales must be in the range 0 to 500000":PRINT:RETURN 3070
3180 NEXT I
3999 RETURN
4000 REM  ==== Module 1.4 - Sales Computation and Quota Assignment
4010 REM   Compute total sales and commission and assign quota category
4020 REM
4030 LET SALES(COUNT,4) = SALES(COUNT,1) + SALES(COUNT,2) + SALES(COUNT,3)
4040 LET SALES(COUNT,5) = SALES(COUNT,1)*C1 + SALES(COUNT,2)*C2 +
       SALES(COUNT,3)*C3
4050 LET PERCENT = SALES(COUNT,4)/QUOTA * 100
4060 IF PERCENT < 100 THEN LET CATEGORY$(COUNT) = BELOW$ : RETURN 160
4070   IF PERCENT > 130 THEN LET CATEGORY$(COUNT) = OUTST$ :RETURN 160
4080     LET CATEGORY$(COUNT) = SATIS$
4999 RETURN 160
5000 REM  ==== Module 1.5 - Display Report
5010 LET F1$="########     "
5020 LET F2$="#######.##    "
5030 LET F3$="   \          \"
5040 CLS
5050 REM   Display header
5060 PRINT
5070 PRINT TAB(30);"Sales Summary"
5080 PRINT
5090 PRINT "Salesperson","ID Number","Total Sales","Commission",
5100 PRINT "Quota Category"
5110 PRINT "-----------","---------","-----------","----------",
5120 PRINT "-------------"
5130 PRINT
5140 REM   Generate Report
5150 LET COUNT = COUNT - 1
5160 REM   Begin loop to display detail lines - execute 'COUNT' times
5170 FOR I=1 TO COUNT
5180   PRINT SPNAME$(I),:PRINT USING F1$; ID(I);:PRINT USING F2$; SALES(I,4),
5190   PRINT USING F2$; SALES(I,5),:PRINT USING F3$; CATEGORY$(I)
5200 NEXT
5999 RETURN
```

continued

```
6000 REM   ==== Module 1.6 - Inquiry
6010 REM   Call Module 1.6.4 - Menu
6020 GOSUB 6700
6030 REM   Call appropriate inquiry module
6040 ON MENU GOSUB 6060, 6290, 6480
6050 GOTO 6010
6060 REM   ==== Module 1.6.1 - Product Totals
6070 REM   Compute sales totals for each product and display them
6080 REM
6090 REM   Accumulate totals for each product
6100 FOR I = 1 TO COUNT
6110    FOR J = 1 TO 4
6120       LET TOT(J) = TOT(J) + SALES(I,J)
6130    NEXT J
6140 NEXT I
6150 PRINT
6160 REM   Display product totals
6170 PRINT "Product","Total Sales"
6180 PRINT
6190 PRINT "Stibs", "$";TOT(1)
6200 PRINT "Farkles", "$";TOT(2)
6210 PRINT "Teglers", "$";TOT(3)
6220 PRINT
6230 PRINT "Total sales", "$";TOT(4)
6240 REM   Reset accumulators to zero
6250 FOR J = 1 TO 4
6260    LET TOT(J) = 0
6270 NEXT J
6280 RETURN
6290 REM   ==== Module 1.6.2 - Breakdown By Quota Category
6300 REM   Tally quota category occurences
6310 FOR I=1 TO COUNT
6320    IF CATEGORY$(I) = BELOW$ THEN LET BCAT = BCAT + 1
6330    IF CATEGORY$(I) = SATIS$ THEN LET SCAT = SCAT + 1
6340    IF CATEGORY$(I) = OUTST$ THEN LET OCAT = OCAT + 1
6350 NEXT I
6360 REM   Display quota category breakdown
6370 PRINT "Quota Category","Number of Salespeople","Percent"
6380 LET F3$ = "###.##"
6390 PRINT
6400 PRINT BELOW$,, BCAT,,:PRINT USING F3$; (BCAT/COUNT) * 100
6410 PRINT SATIS$,, SCAT,,:PRINT USING F3$; (SCAT/COUNT) * 100
6420 PRINT OUTST$,, OCAT,,:PRINT USING F3$; (OCAT/COUNT) * 100
6430 PRINT
6440 PRINT "Total number of salespeople: "; COUNT
6450 REM    Reset category counters to zero
6460 LET ACAT = 0 : LET BCAT = 0 : LET CCAT = 0
6470 RETURN
6480 REM   ==== Module 1.6.3 - High And Low Salespeople
6490 REM   Find and display salespeople with highest and lowest total sales
6500 REM
6510 REM   Set both HIGH and LOW to first salesperson
6520 LET HIGH = 1 : LET LOW = 1
6530 REM   Compare salesperson pairs to identify
6540 REM   salesperson with highest and lowest total sales
6550 FOR I=2 TO COUNT
6560    IF SALES(HIGH,4) < SALES(I,4) THEN LET HIGH = I
6570    IF SALES(LOW,4) > SALES(I,4) THEN LET LOW = I
6580 NEXT I
6590 REM   Display high and low salespeople
6600 PRINT "The salesperson with the highest total sales is "; SPNAME$(HIGH);
6610 PRINT " with a"
6620 PRINT "total sales amount of $"; SALES(HIGH,4); "and a commission of $";
6630 PRINT USING "#####.##"; SALES(HIGH,5)
6640 PRINT
6650 PRINT "The salesperson with the lowest total sales is "; SPNAME$(LOW);
6660 PRINT " with a"
6670 PRINT "total sales amount of $"; SALES(LOW,4); "and a commission of $";
6680 PRINT USING "#####.##"; SALES(LOW,5)
6690 RETURN
6700 REM   ==== Module 1.6.4 - Menu
6710 REM   Call Module 1.6.4.1 - Option for Inquiry Menu
6720 GOSUB 6760
```

```
6730 REM   Call Module 1.6.4.2 - Display and Selection from Menu
6740 GOSUB 6810
6750 RETURN
6760 REM   ==== Module 1.6.4.1 - Option for Inquiry Menu
6770 PRINT
6780 INPUT "Would you like to see the inquiry menu? (Enter Y or N) ",ANSWER$
6790 IF ANSWER$ = "N" OR ANSWER$ = "n" THEN RETURN 6999
6800 RETURN
6810 REM   ==== Module 1.6.4.2 - Display and Selection from Menu
6820 PRINT
6830 PRINT "    ---- INQUIRY MENU ----"
6840 PRINT "1. Total sales by product"
6850 PRINT "2. Breakdown by quota category"
6860 PRINT "3. Salespeople with highest and lowest total sales"
6870 PRINT
6880 REM   Accept menu selection
6890 INPUT "Make a selection from the menu: ",MENU
6900 CLS
6910 IF MENU > 0 AND MENU < 4 THEN RETURN
6920 REM   Error message
6930 PRINT "That was not a valid response. Try again."
6940 GOTO 6820
6999 END
```

```
run
        -------- Sales Summary Report --------
Separate multiple entries by commas.

Enter commission rates (as a %)
   for Stibs, Farkles, and Teglers: 4,3,5

Enter this month's sales quota (in dollars): 80000
Salesperson name (Enter LAST when complete): Charles Roth
Salesperson ID: 46912
Enter gross sales for Stibs, Farkles, and Teglers
   (separate by commas): 32000,28000,25000
Salesperson name (Enter LAST when complete): Lucy Cook
Salesperson ID: 77878
Enter gross sales for Stibs, Farkles, and Teglers
   (separate by commas): 1000000,30000,40000
Sales must be in the range 0 to 500000


Enter gross sales for Stibs, Farkles, and Teglers
   (separate by commas): 50000,35000,20000
```

continued

547

```
Salesperson name (Enter LAST when complete):
Null salesperson name not allowed

Salesperson name (Enter LAST when complete): Wayne Evans
Salesperson ID: 66941
Enter gross sales for Stibs, Farkles, and Teglers
  (separate by commas): 25000,30000,15000
Salesperson name (Enter LAST when complete): last

                          Sales Summary

Salesperson   ID Number   Total Sales   Commission   Quota Category
-----------   ---------   -----------   ----------   --------------

Charles Roth    46912       85000.00      3370.00      Satisfactory
Lucy Cook       77878      105000.00      4050.00      Outstanding
Wayne Evans     66941       70000.00      2650.00      Below Quota

Would you like to see the inquiry menu? (Enter Y or N) n
Ok
```

See the interactive session of Example Program #7 for other input/output.

By using arrays, you don't have to worry about creating slightly different names for like data. For example, consider the accumulators in Module 1.6.1—Product Totals of Example Programs #7 and #8. Compare the accumulators in Example Program #7 (6110–6130) to the accumulators in Example Program #8 (6110–6130). In Example Program #7, it was necessary to assign a unique variable name to each accumulator (e.g., T1, T2, T3). In Example Program #8, all sales figures, including total sales and commission, are stored in the two-dimensional array SALES. This permits the totals of the three product sales figures and the overall totals to be accumulated in nested loops and stored in the array TOT [e.g., TOT(1), TOT(2), TOT(3), and TOT(4)]. With only three products, this approach is only marginally more efficient, but what if each salesperson had 23 products? In Example Program #7, you would need to identify 20 more accumulators and add 20 more accumulator instructions. With the nested loop logic of Example Program #8 (6100–6140), you would need only to change the limit value for the internal loop from 4 to 24, and redimension the sales figures array from SALES(50,5) to SALES(50,25).

Input Validation and Control Techniques. A good programmer assumes that the user will not always enter the correct data. In Example Program #7, the menu item selection was validated on input. The same routine

548

is also included in Example Program #8 (6910–6940). Example Program #8 demonstrates several other ways in which we can use programming techniques to validate the accuracy of the input. We build validation procedures into a program to alert users that their input is inconsistent with that expected. Of course, there are limits to what types of errors can be detected using programming techniques. For example, a validation routine will not detect when a sales figure of 32000 is incorrectly entered as 23000.

*Check for No Entry*.   In Example Program #8, the first piece of salesperson data accepted is the salesperson name [SPNAME$(COUNT)]. In Example Program #7, if the carriage return key is unintentionally pressed before a name is entered, a null is entered to a field in the SPNAME$ array. A null ("") is a characterless string constant. To avoid this possibility, Module 1.3.1—Validate Salesperson Name (3120–3140) was inserted in Example Program #8. When the user does not make any entry for salesperson name, a warning appears on the screen, and the user is given another opportunity to enter a salesperson's name. The use of these validation procedures is demonstrated in the interactive session.

*Limits Check*.   A limits check assesses whether the value of an entry is out of line with that expected. In our example, the sales figures for each product must be in the range 0 to 500000, inclusive. To ensure that negative values or sales figures in excess of 500000 are not entered, Module 1.3.2—Validate Sales Figures (3150–3999) alerts the user when a sales figure entered is not within the limits and requests that the sales figures be reentered. Since SALES is an array, each sales figure can be examined separately by incrementing the second subscript in a FOR/NEXT loop.

Another example of a limits check is the input validation routine in Module 1.6.4.2—Display and Selection from Menu (6910–6940). If the user does not select one of the available menu options, an error message is displayed and the user is asked to "try again".

*Other Input Control Techniques*.   When writing a program that may be used often by a number of people, it is a good idea to check input data as thoroughly as you can during the course of the interactive session. In our example, besides checking the limits of the sales figures entered, you could also use a *reasonableness check*. For example, you could compare the average of the Stibs and Teglers sales figures to the Farkles sales figure. If they differ by more than some arbitrary amount, say $12,000, a message is displayed and the user is given an opportunity to reenter the data.

For the salesperson name entry, you could also use a *character-type check*. The more advanced features of BASIC permit you to check each character of a name to ensure that it is a letter. The check would ensure that numbers are not accidentally keyed in the name field (e.g., Cha4les).

# REVIEW EXERCISES (LEARNING MODULE V)_____

## BASIC Instructions and Concepts

1. Identify the syntax error(s) in each of the following instructions.
   - (a)   10 ON I>3 GOSUB 40
   - (b)   10 CLS: "CLEAR THE SCREEN"
   - (c)   10 ON COUNT GOTO 40; 50; 60
   - (d)   10 LINT INPUT ALPHA

2. In what order are the animal names displayed in the following program?

   ```
   100 ON COUNT GOSUB 400, 500, 600
   200 PRINT "Cat"
   300 LET COUNT = COUNT +1: GOTO 100
   400 PRINT "Dog": RETURN
   500 PRINT "Horse": RETURN
   600 END
   ```

3. Explain the use of a menu in interactive inquiry programming.

4. Under what circumstances would you use the LINE INPUT instruction in lieu of the INPUT instruction?

## Example Program #7

5. Why is it necessary to subtract 1 from COUNT at statement 5150?

6. List the beginning and ending statement numbers of all the loops in Modules 1.6.1, 1.6.2, and 1.6.3.

7. What is the general name applied to statements like 6110–6130?

8. Why is it necessary to initialize certain variables to zero in statements 6250 and 6440?

9. How would you modify the program to include a menu item option 4 that permits the user to request a hard copy of the "Sales Summary" report?

## Example Program #8

10. What are the advantages of storing sales figure data in a single two-dimensional array (as in Example Program #8), as opposed to the several one-dimensional arrays in Example Program #7?

11. Write the code for a data entry reasonableness check that warns the user if the average of the Stibs and Teglers sales figures differs by more than $12,000 from the Farkles sales figure.

12. Describe other input validation routines that could be employed in Example Program #8.

# BASIC PROGRAMMING ASSIGNMENTS _____

1. Write a program to compile a sales report listing salespeople by sales (most sales first). Use the following input data.

| Salesperson | Monthly Sales |
|---|---|
| Monro | 28672 |
| Wilson | 14006 |
| Plebani | 22871 |
| Kane | 38222 |
| Groover | 76800 |

The output should appear as shown below.

```
           SALES REPORT
SALESPERSON   MONTHLY SALES
Groover          $76800
Kane             $38222
Monro            $28672
Plebani          $22871
Wilson           $14006
```

Sort the sales data in arrays to prepare the sales report.

Once the program has been debugged and can be executed to produce the output above, modify it to accumulate and display total sales at the bottom of the report as shown below.

_____

```
TOTAL SALES       $180571
```

2. Write a program that accepts an individual's birth date in the MM, DD, YY format, then translates the date to display the following:

The birth date of T. Jones is December 18, 1947

3. Companies "age" their accounts receivable records so that accounting can concentrate collection efforts on those companies that are most delinquent in their payments. Periodically, a report is prepared listing those accounts that are 30 days, 60 days, and 90 days overdue (to simplify the program, assume that each month has 30 days). Write a program to produce such a report. The program should accept the current date, then load customers in arrears to one of three arrays, depending on whether they are 30, 60, or 90 days in arrears. Use the following input format.

Enter current date (MM, DD, YY):
Enter customer name:
Enter amount due:
Enter date due (MM, DD, YY):

Include appropriate heading for output.

**4.** Prepare a program that generates a bar chart showing the schedules for four projects: A, B, C, and D. The start and completion days (if before day 30) are entered for each project. Use the following input format.

Enter data for Project A
Start day (1–30): 3
Completion day (1–30): 15

An example bar chart appears below.

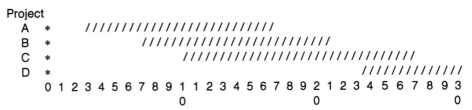

```
Project
  A  *        /////////////////////////
  B  *              /////////////////////////
  C  *                  ////////////////////////////////
  D  *                                        /////////////
       0 1 2 3 4 5 6 7 8 9 1 1 2 3 4 5 6 7 8 9 2 1 2 3 4 5 6 7 8 9 3
                           0                   0                   0
```

# Using Predefined Functions

## B-20 INTRINSIC FUNCTIONS: LET THE COMPUTER DO IT _____

Certain **intrinsic functions** are provided with a BASIC interpreter. Intrinsic functions save us a lot of time by performing routine processing tasks that would otherwise need to be programmed (e.g., take a square root or count the number of characters in a string constant).

A function consists of the *function name* and *argument*. The function names are signals to the BASIC interpreter to "call" a system-supplied BASIC program segment. The argument may contain one or several elements, depending on the function. The argument elements may be the variable or expression that is to be acted on or specification data for the function. A function with its argument can appear in any place in the program that a constant can appear. *The occurrence of a function and argument represents the result of a function acting on the argument*. That is, when the function SQR(4), the square root of 4, appears in a program, it actually represents the resultant value or 2.

Intrinsic functions are discussed in two parts. Those that deal primarily with *string operations* are discussed first, then those that deal primarily with *arithmetic operations*. The material in Section B-21 describes how you can define your own *user-defined functions*.

### String Operations

String operations are performed by those BASIC functions that allow us to manipulate alphanumeric character strings. Word processing is a good example of string manipulation. For example, to center a heading on a line, it is necessary to know how many characters are in the heading string constant. Or suppose that you wanted to display only the first name of a salesperson from a field (e.g., SPNAME$) that contained both the first and last names. The following functions enable you to perform these and other types of string operations.

CHR$. The CHR$ (character string) function converts the decimal value of a specified ASCII code to its character equivalent (see Figure B-6).

*Format*: CHR$ (decimal value of ASCII code)

*Example*: 
```
FOR N = 48 TO 57
    IF RESPONSE$ = CHR$ (N) THEN PRINT CHR$ (7)
NEXT N
```

In the example above, if RESPONSE$ equals "0" (ASCII code of 48),

"1" (ASCII code of 49), and so on to "9", then a tone is sounded (ASCII code of 7) on the workstation's speaker.

**LEN.** The LEN (length) function takes on the value of the number of characters in the string specified in the argument.

*Format*: LEN(string variable or constant)

*Example*: LET FIRSTNAME$ = "Carl"
LET TOTAL = LEN(FIRSTNAME$) + LEN("Brooks")

The value of TOTAL is 10: 4 (number of characters in "Carl") plus 6 (number of characters in "Brooks").

**VAL.** The VAL (value) function takes on the numerical value of the string specified in the argument.

*Format*: VAL(string variable or constant)

*Example*: LET BALANCE$="$ 42.55 CR"
LET BALANCE = VAL(BALANCE$)

Any characters that are not numeric are stripped from the character string, and the value of BALANCE becomes 42.55. The VAL is handy for obtaining the numeric portion of an alphanumeric character string, such as a street address.

**STR$.** The STR$ (string) function is the reverse of the VAL function. It takes on the string value of the number specified in the argument.

*Format*: STR$(numeric variable or constant)

*Example*: LET BALANCE = 42.55
LET BALANCE$ = "$" + STR$(42.55) + " CR"

In this example, 42.55 is made a string constant so that it can be joined together with a $ and CR. The plus sign in the example above permits character strings to be "added" together, or *concatenated*. After the concatenation, BALANCE$="$ 42.55 CR". Notice that the STR$ function and its argument result in a string value that includes a space for the implied plus sign.

**LEFT$.** The LEFT$ function takes on the value of the *n* leftmost characters of the string specified in the argument.

*Format*:   LEFT$(string variable or constant, *n*)
            *n* is a numeric variable or constant.

*Example*:   LET FIRSTNAME$ = LEFT$("Barbara L. Shaw", 7)

The first seven characters of the argument string are selected, and the value of FIRSTNAME$ becomes "Barbara".

RIGHT$.   The RIGHT$ function takes on the value of the *n* rightmost characters of the string specified in the argument.

*Format*:   RIGHT$(string variable or constant, *n*)
            *n* is a numeric variable or constant.

*Example*:   LET LASTNAME$ = RIGHT$("Barbara L. Shaw", 4)

The last four characters of the argument string are selected, and the value of LASTNAME$ becomes "Shaw".

MID$.   Use the MID$ function to:

1. Extract a portion of a string, or
2. Replace a portion of a string with another string.

In the first instance, the MID$ function takes on the value of the *m* characters in the string specified in the argument, beginning at the *n*th character from the left. In the second instance, MID$ is used as an instruction. Remember, all characters, including spaces, are counted. The *m* value is optional. If omitted, all of the rightmost characters are extracted beginning at the *n*th character.

*Format*:   MID$(string variable or constant, *n*[,*m*])
            *m* and *n* are numeric variables or constants.

*Examples*:   LET INITIAL$ = MID$("Barbara L. Shaw",9,2)
              LET STREET$ = MID$("317 High St.",5)

In the first example above, the value of INITIAL$ becomes "L." In the second example, STREET$ becomes "High St.".
    In the following example, MID$ is used as an instruction.

*Example*:   LET NAME$ = "Barbara L. Shaw"
             LET MID$(NAME$,12,4) = "Harrison"

In the example, the four characters starting with the twelfth character in NAME$ ("Shaw") are replaced with "Harrison". The value of NAME$ is now "Barbara L. Harrison".

Because computer processing at this newspaper office often involves text manipulation, programmers routinely take advantage of the available string functions.
(RCA)

INSTR.   The INSTR (in string) function permits you to search for the first occurrence of a particular character string in another character string. The value of the function becomes the starting character position of the first occurrence of the search string.

> **Format:**   INSTR(string variable or constant 1,
>                                string variable or constant 2)
>                                Where string 1 is the string to be searched
>                                and string 2 is the search string.

*Example*:   LET NAME$ = "Barbara L. Shaw"
                        LET PERIOD$ = "."
                        LET POSITION = INSTR(NAME$,PERIOD$)−1
                        LET INITIAL$ = MID$(POSITION,1)

The series of instructions above assigns the value of INITIAL$ to be the middle initial of a name. The INSTR function first locates the period in NAME$ and returns a 10 as the character position of the ".". One is subtracted from the location of the "." to identify the location of the initial (POSITION = 9). The MID$ function is then used to extract the initial from the NAME$ character string so that it can be assigned the variable name INITIAL$. In the example above, INITIAL$ becomes "L".

## Arithmetic Operations

Intrinsic functions are provided for many common arithmetic operations. As an example, consider the formula to compute the economic order quantity or EOQ. A company calculates the EOQ that would meet the company's demand for a particular item, yet minimize the cost of buying and holding the inventory. The EOQ formula is

$$EOQ = \sqrt{\frac{2 * P * R}{C}}$$

where P = preparation cost per order
          R = annual requirement for an inventory item
          C = storage cost per item per year

Instead of raising (2∗P∗R/C) to the 0.5 power, we can use the *square root function (SQR)*. The statement then becomes

    LET EOQ=SQR(2∗P∗R/C)

The *integer function (INT)* returns the largest whole number that is not greater than the value of the argument. For example,

    LET X=INT(14.7)
    LET Y=INT(−14.7)

After execution of the statements above, X=14 and Y=−15.

Other intrinsic arithmetic functions are listed and defined in Figure B-14.

```
ABS(X)          Absolute value
COS(X)          Cosine of X in radians
EXP(X)          e(2.71828) to power of X
FIX(X)          Integer part of X
INT(X)          Largest integer not greater than X
LOG(X)          Natural logarithm of X
RND(X)          Generates a random number between zero and one
                   (use RANDOMIZE instruction to seed RND function)
SGN(X)          Value of 1, 0, or −1 if X is positive, zero or negative,
                   respectively
SIN(X)          Sine of X in radians
SQR(X)          Square root of X
TAN(X)          Tangent of X in radians
```

**FIGURE B-14**
**BASIC Intrinsic Arithmetic Functions**

## B-21 USER-DEFINED FUNCTIONS

The intrinsic functions do not always cover the circumstances for which we want a function. For these cases, BASIC permits us to define our own *user-defined functions*.

*Format*:   DEF FN function name (parameter list) = definition of function

The function name follows the same naming rules as variable identifiers (see Learning Module I, Section B-4). The parameter list contains those variable names used in the definition of the function. The variables in the calling function are replaced *one for one* in the parameter list.

A user-defined function could be DEFined, named (PER), and used in the following statements in Example Program #8 to calculate the percent of salespeople in a particular sales quota category.

### Examples:

*Without FN*:

```
6400 PRINT BELOW$,,BCAT,,: PRINT USING F3$; (BCAT/COUNT)*100
6410 PRINT SATIS$,,SCAT,,: PRINT USING F3$; (SCAT/COUNT)*100
```

*With FN*:

```
6395 DEF FN PER(A,B)=(A/B)*100
6400 PRINT BELOW$,,BCAT,,: PRINT USING F3$; FN PER(BCAT, COUNT)
6410 PRINT SATIS$,,SCAT,,: PRINT USING F3$; FN PER(SCAT, COUNT)
```

The values of BCAT and COUNT are substituted, respectively, for A and B in the definition of the function. The result (percent of salespeople in a sales quota category) is returned and printed in statements 6400 and 6410. A function must be defined before it can be called.

## B-22 EXAMPLE PROGRAM #9: STRING PROCESSING

Example Program #9 illustrates the use of several functions in the manipulation of text data. The program permits the user to enter a person's name and address data. The data are then merged with a form letter to produce a "personalized" letter, such as the one shown in the interactive session. The program must be run again to produce another letter.

# EXAMPLE PROGRAM #9

This program merges user–entered name and address data with the text of a form letter and prints the results.

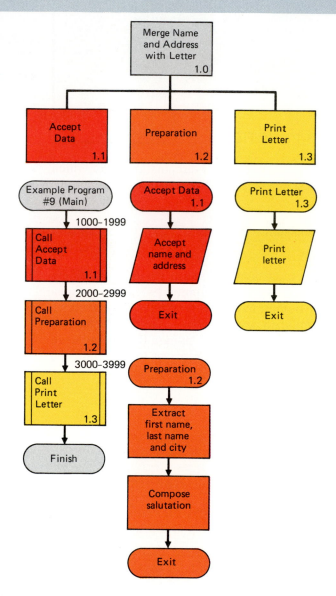

```
2     REM           **** Example Program #9 ****
4     REM   Description:
6     REM      This program merges user-entered name and address data with
8     REM      the text of a form letter and prints the results.
10    REM   Variables list:
12    REM      FULLNAME$                  - Full name including middle initial
14    REM      STREET$                    - Street address
16    REM      CITYSTATEZIP$              - City, state, and ZIP code
18    REM      FBLANK                     - Location of first blank in FULLNAME$ string
20    REM      FIRSTNAME$                 - First name
22    REM      COMMAPOSITION              - Location of first comma in CITYSTATEZIP$
24    REM      CITY$                      - City
26    REM      SALUTATION$                - Salutation
99    REM
100   REM   <<<< Start Main >>>>
110   REM
120   REM   Call Module 1.1 - Accept Data
130   GOSUB 1000
140   REM   Call Module 1.2 - Preparation
150   GOSUB 2000
160   REM   Call Module 1.3 - Print Letter
170   GOSUB 3000
180   END
190   REM   <<<< End Main >>>>
999   REM
1000  REM   ==== Module 1.1 - Accept Data
1010  INPUT "Enter full name ( FIRST MI. LAST ): ",FULLNAME$
1020  LINE INPUT "Enter street address: ",STREET$
1030  LINE INPUT "Enter city, state, and ZIP code: ",CITYSTATEZIP$
1999  RETURN
2000  REM   ==== Module 1.2 - Preparation
2010  LET FBLANK = INSTR(FULLNAME$," ")
2020  LET FIRSTNAME$ = LEFT$(FULLNAME$,FBLANK-1)
2030  LET COMMAPOSITION = INSTR(CITYSTATEZIP$,",")
2040  LET CITY$=LEFT$(CITYSTATEZIP$,COMMAPOSITION-1)
2050  LET SALUTATION$ = "Dear " + FIRSTNAME$ + ":"
2999  RETURN
3000  REM   ==== Module 1.3 - Print Letter
3010  CLS
3020  LPRINT
3030  LPRINT
3040  LPRINT FULLNAME$
3050  LPRINT STREET$
3060  LPRINT CITYSTATEZIP$
3070  LPRINT
3080  LPRINT SALUTATION$
3090  LPRINT
3100  LPRINT "      I would like to congratulate you on the fine job you are"
3110  LPRINT "doing with our retail sales department.  Your performance"
3120  LPRINT "has earned you quality points toward the Zimco end-of-year
3130  LPRINT "bonus.  Your 'Outstanding' rating qualifies you for Zimco's"
3140  LPRINT "salesperson of the year award for the ";CITY$;" area."
3150  LPRINT "      Again, ";FIRSTNAME$;", I congratulate you on your excellent"
3160  LPRINT "record."
3170  LPRINT
3180  LPRINT "                                    Sincerely,"
3190  LPRINT : LPRINT
3200  LPRINT "                                    George Brooks,"
3210  LPRINT "                                    Regional Director of Sales"
3999  RETURN
```

```
run
Enter full name ( FIRST MI. LAST): Lucy K. Cook
Enter street address: 820 Center Street
Enter city, state, and ZIP code: Green Bay, WI 54304
```

continued

```
                    Zimco Enterprises              Zimco
                       PO Box 723
                     Becker, MN 55308

    Lucy K. Cook
    820 Center Street
    Green Bay, WI 54304

    Dear Lucy:

        I would like to congratulate you on the fine job you are
    doing with our retail sales department.  Your performance
    has earned you quality points toward the Zimco end-of-year
    bonus.  Your 'Outstanding' rating qualifies you for Zimco's
    salesperson of the year award for the Green Bay area.
        Again, Lucy, I congratulate you on your excellent
    record.

                              Sincerely,


                              George Brooks,
                              Regional Director of Sales
```

**Module 1.1—Accept Data.** The name and address data are enterd in three lines: name, street address, and city-state-zip. The LINE INPUT instruction, introduced in Learning Module V, is often used when the program is designed to accept textual data. This is because it will accept whatever characters are entered, including commas. Notice in the interactive session that city, state, and zip are entered to a single character string (CITYSTATEZIP$) with a comma between city and state. In contrast, when the INPUT instruction is used, a comma serves as a delimiter between the data items entered and cannot be part of an input character string.

**Module 1.2—Preparation.** This module prepares appropriate character strings so that they can be merged with the text of the letter. The name and address data are inserted at several locations within the text of the letter: the inside address, the first name in the salutation and in the last sentence, and the city in the third sentence. The inside address is not a problem; the input strings are simply output to the printer. However, the first name and city must be extracted from the input strings. We do this with the string functions.

Several steps are needed to extract the person's first name. The INSTR function is used (2010) to determine the position of the first blank in the name string. Presumably, the first name would precede the first blank. The LEFT$ function in statement 2020 extracts the characters to the left of the first blank, or the first name (FIRSTNAME$). The city is extracted from the CITYSTATEZIP$ field in a similar manner.

The salutation is a concatenation of three strings: "Dear", FIRST-NAME$, and ":". The plus signs (+) in statement 2050 cause the three strings to be concatenated. The resultant string is stored in SALUTA-TION$.

**Module 1.3—Print Letter.** The letter, with appropriate character strings inserted, is routed to a printer for output.

## REVIEW EXERCISES (LEARNING MODULE VI)

### BASIC Instructions and Concepts

1. Identify the error(s) in each of the following instructions.
   (a) 10 PRINT CHR$(265)

(b)  10 LET ANSWER = 4/LEN("")
(c)  10 VALUE = VAL(ANSWER)
(d)  10 INT = FIX(NUMBER)
(e)  10 DEF FN ADDLIST (SUM) = A+B+C+D
(f)  10 CHARPOS = CHARPOS + INSTR(DESCRIP$,HYPHEN)

2.  Which of the following statements has the intrinsic function
    and which has the user-defined function? Identify the function
    names of each.

    300 LET SR=SQR(Y*Z)
    400 LET X=FN DP(Y,Z)

3.  Define a function for the following arithmetic expression and
    call it FUTVAL. The expression represents the future value
    of a uniform series of $1 investments for $n$ periods at $i$ interest.

    $$\frac{(1+i)^n - 1}{i}$$

4.  What values are displayed as a result of the following string
    operations?

    100 LET ADDRESS$ = "135 New Street"
    200 LET N$="N"
    300 PRINT VAL(ADDRESS$)
    400 PRINT INSTR(ADDRESS$,N$)
    500 PRINT MID$(ADDRESS$,5,3)
    600 PRINT RIGHT$(ADDRESS$,10)
    700 PRINT STR$(VAL(ADDRESS$))
    800 PRINT LEN(ADDRESS$)

## Example Program #9

5.  How would you modify the program to accept data and print
    the letter for any number of salespeople?

6.  From a data entry operator's viewpoint, would it be easier to
    enter city, state, and zip together (as in the program) or sepa-
    rately? Explain.

7.  How would you modify the program to eliminate the semicolons
    in statement 3140?

8.  Assume that each name is entered with a middle initial. Write
    the instructions needed to extract the last name from FULL-
    NAME$.

## BASIC PROGRAMMING ASSIGNMENTS

1.  The director of the residence operations at the college would
    like to send a personalized welcome memo to all students living
    on campus. One memo is to be sent to each room. All rooms
    are doubles. An example memo follows.

To: Harry Barnes and Jack Noble, Room 205

I would like to take this opportunity, Harry and Jack, to welcome you back to campus and the pursuit of knowledge. Good luck! If I or my staff can be of service, please call.

Mike Phillips, Director

Write a program that accepts student name, last name first (e.g., Barnes, Harry), and room number (e.g., 205) for up to 100 students and in any order. The program should match roommates and produce a memo for each room. Notice the insertion of the students' first names in the text of the memo. [*Hint*: Consider sorting an array of room numbers by comparing consecutive values, then switching array positions as needed. Continue comparing and switching pairs until the room numbers are in an array in ascending order. Be sure to keep the names matched with the proper room numbers.]

2. Enhance the program above so that the director has the option of producing an alphabetical listing of students (see below) and/or the memos. The report should have the following format.

| STUDENT NAME | ROOM NUMBER |
|--------------|-------------|
| Barnes, Harry | 205 |
| Cole, Sally | 106 |
| Lupus, Janet | 312 |
| Noble, Jack | 205 |

3. By using both intrinsic and user-defined functions, write a program to produce the following table;

| X | X SQUARED | X CUBED | SQUARE ROOT OF X |
|---|-----------|---------|------------------|
| 1 | 1 | 1 | 1 |
| 2 | 4 | 8 | 1.414212 |
| 3 | 9 | 27 | 1.732051 |
| ⋮ | ⋮ | ⋮ | ⋮ |
| 20 | 400 | 8000 | 4.472136 |

4. Use the trigonometric functions of sine (SIN), cosine (COS), and tangent (TAN) to complete the following table. Remember that the argument must be expressed in radians. The 360 degrees of the circle have 2 pi (pi = 3.141592) radians. Each 45-degree increment is 1/8 (45/360) of 2 pi radians. [*Hint*: Use the STEP clause in the FOR/NEXT statement.]

TRIGONOMETRIC TABLE

| DEGREES | SINE | COSINE | TANGENT |
|---------|------|--------|---------|
| 0 | | | |
| 45 | | | |
| 90 | | | |
| 135 | | | |
| ⋮ | | | |
| 315 | | | |
| 360 | | | |

# Disk Data Management

### B-23 DATA MANAGEMENT AND FILE PROCESSING

This learning module presents the BASIC instructions and programming techniques for storing and retrieving data from disk storage. By now you will already have stored and retrieved many files from disk storage. These, however, were *program files*. You used the SAVE system command to store program files on disk storage for later recall with the LOAD command. Now we are ready to learn how to store and retrieve *data files*. When you store and retrieve a program file, it is relatively easy, because you store the entire file and retrieve the entire file. Manipulation of data files is more challenging than program files, because you may want to work with only a portion of the file.

**The Hierarchy of Data Organization.** We can use the *hierarchy of data organization* to illustrate how data are stored on disk. At the lowest level of the hierarchy is the *bit* (0 or 1). A series of *bits* are configured to represent a *character* or *byte*. For example, an ASCII byte 1000001 represents the character A inside the computer and on disk. At the next level of the hierarchy, characters are combined to represent the value of a *data element*, or *field*. In our example programs, salesperson name (SPNAME$) and the Stibs sales figure (S1) are fields. Related data elements are grouped to form *records*. In the example programs, a salesperson record would consist of salesperson name, identification number, and the Stibs, Farkles, and Teglers sales figures.

At the fourth level of the hierarchy, records with the same data elements are combined to form a *file*. Figure B-15 shows a salesperson file with three records. This permanent source of salesperson data is called a *master file*. In traditional file processing, files are sorted, merged, and processed by a *key data element*. In the example programs that follow, we'll use salesperson identification number (ID) as the key data element. The key could just as well have been salesperson name.

## FIGURE B-15
**Salesperson File with Three Records**

|  | SPNAME$ | ID | S1 | S2 | S3 |  |
|---|---|---|---|---|---|---|
| Record 1 | Charles Roth | 46912 | 32000 | 28000 | 25000 | Sales-person file |
| Record 2 | Lucy Cook | 77878 | 50000 | 35000 | 20000 | |
| Record 3 | Wayne Evans | 66941 | 25000 | 30000 | 15000 | |

Sequential and Random Processing.   In BASIC, data are manipulated and retrieved using *sequential processing* or *random processing*. In sequential processing, records are written to the disk in sequence and they are accessed in that same sequence. If a particular salesperson's record is desired, each record, beginning with the first, is retrieved and loaded to memory one at a time until the value of that record's salesperson ID (the key) matches that of the desired salesperson.

A sequential file is processed from start to finish. Records can be added, or *appended*, to the end of the file, but if you wish to change an existing record, you would use the existing file to create a new file that includes the changed record. Sequential processing is demonstrated in Example Program #10.

A random file is a collection of records that can be processed randomly (in any order). This is called random processing. To do this in BASIC, however, you must know the *absolute location of the record within the file*. That is, you must know that a particular salesperson is the third record on the file. Some languages (and the more advanced versions of BASIC) permit you to use the key data element to retrieve a record, but for most versions of BASIC, a record is randomly retrieved by its absolute location in the file. But with a little programming ingenuity, we can create fairly sophisticated file access capabilities in BASIC.

The instruction set presented in this module covers only those instructions needed to create and manipulate sequential files. Random processing is beyond the scope of this book.

## B-24   BASIC INSTRUCTION SET: LEARNING MODULE VII GROUP

There are over 100 slightly different versions of BASIC. We are beginning to discuss the more advanced features of the BASIC language. As we do, there is a higher probability that there will be differences in the BASIC presented and that which you use. For example, the format of an instruction presented in the text may have a semicolon (;), but your BASIC may use a comma (,). You should be able to grasp the concepts and use of the instructions presented in this and subsequent learning modules, but check the *BASIC Reference Manual* for your system to get the exact syntax of these more advanced instructions.

### Input/Output Instructions

OPEN.   A disk file must be OPENed before you can do anything with it, and it must be CLOSEd when you are finished with it. The OPEN instruction permits input/output to a disk file.

*Format*:   OPEN filename$ [FOR mode] AS #filenumber

*Examples*:   OPEN "INVENTORY" FOR OUTPUT AS #1

SEQFILE$ = "INVENTORY"
OPEN SEQFILE$ FOR INPUT AS #1

The two examples open a sequential file named "INVENTORY". Sequential files are opened FOR INPUT, OUTPUT, or APPEND. For the modes of INPUT and OUTPUT, processing is begun with the first record. The APPEND mode, a special case of the OUTPUT mode, causes processing to begin after the last record.

CLOSE.    The CLOSE instruction signals the completion of input/output to a file.

*Format*:   CLOSE [#filenumber[, #filenumber. . .]]

*Examples*:   CLOSE #1

CLOSE

The first example closes the file that was OPENed as file number 1. The second example closes all files. To read a sequential file that has been opened as OUTPUT, the file must be closed and opened as INPUT, and vice versa.

WRITE #.    The WRITE instruction causes a record to be written to a sequential file.

*Format*:   WRITE #filenumber, list of data elements

*Example*:   WRITE #1, PARTNO, DESCRIP$, PRICE, QUANTITY

In the example, the values of the four data elements are written to the file opened as number 1. Some versions of BASIC employ a deriva-

Each of these Winchester disks (a standard and a half-height), a name given to disk drives containing a small fixed disk, has two read/write heads for each surface. Data are "written" to a spinning magnetic disk as "on" and "off" signals called bits. On input, several bits are combined to represent a character. On output, a bit string is interpreted by the computer system and translated to a character so that we can understand it.
(Seagate Technology)

tion on the PRINT statement (e.g., PRINT #1, PARTNO, DESCRIP$, PRICE, QUANTITY) to write to a disk file. Some versions have both. In these versions, the PRINT # instruction writes the image to disk as if it were to be displayed on a screen. This means that there are no delimiters to distinguish between the fields unless you put them there.

The system software maintains a file *pointer* for WRITE # (and INPUT #) instructions. The pointer "points" to where the next record is to be written (or from where the next record is to be read). Each execution of a WRITE # instruction causes the pointer to be positioned to write the next sequential record on the file.

INPUT #. The INPUT # instruction reads a record from a sequential file and assigns the values in the data elements to variable names.

> *Format*:   INPUT #filenumber, list of data elements

> *Example*:   INPUT #1, PARTNO, DESCRIP$, PRICE, QUANTITY

The instruction above reads four data elements from the file opened as number 1. The file must have been opened as INPUT. The type of the data read, numeric or string, must match up with the types in the list of data elements or an error will result. In the example, the second data element read must be a string constant.

## Other Instructions

KILL. The appropriately named KILL instruction deletes the specified file from disk storage.

> *Format*:   KILL filename$

> *Example*:   KILL "INVNTORY"

The example deletes, or "erases," the file named "INVNTORY" from disk storage. KILL is also a system command on some versions of BASIC.

EOF. The EOF (end-of-file) function is used to signal the end of a sequential file.

> *Format*:   EOF(filenumber)

> *Example*:   IF EOF(1) THEN END

The value of the EOF function becomes −1 when the end-of-file for file number 1 is reached. In the IF instruction example, the THEN clause is taken when the test on condition is false or the end-of-file is detected (value of the expression is −1).

## B-25 EXAMPLE PROGRAM #10: SEQUENTIAL FILE PROCESSING

Example Program #10 illustrates how the salesperson data used in previous example programs can be stored permanently in a sequential disk file. The program is a menu-driven program that permits a user to *create the file*, *add salesperson records*, *list salesperson records*, and *delete the entire file*. In a sequential file, records are stored in the order in which they are written to disk and are retrieved in the same order. Sequential processing concepts are discussed in Section B-23.

The Example Program #10 structure chart shows the hierarchical organization of the program. The three modules called from the driver module, and their subordinate modules, are discussed individually below.

**Driver Module.** Subroutines are called from the driver module in a DOWHILE loop. Loop processing continues while the value of MENU is not equal to 5 (entered in Module 1.1).

**Module 1.1—Menu Display and Item Selection.** In this module, the user is asked to make a selection from a menu of possible processing activities (see interactive session).

**Module 1.2—Process File.** The value of MENU obtained from Module 1.1 causes processing to be directed to one of several file activities. Each of these activities is handled in a subroutine that is subordinate to Module 1.2 (see the structure chart).

**Module 1.2.1—Create File and Add Records.** The same set of program instructions can be used to create the file and add records to the file. Notice that statement 2010 in Module 1.2 directs processing to Module 1.2.1 when MENU=1 (create file) or MENU=2 (add records).

In statement 2090, the SALESPER file is opened for APPENDing records. The APPEND mode positions the pointer at the next available record position. When creating the file, the pointer is at the start of the file. When adding to an existing file, the pointer is at the end of the file.

Data are entered and written to the sequential file in a loop. Once the data have been entered for a single salesperson, a WRITE # instruction (2160) writes a salesperson record to disk. The loop is repeated until the user enters "LAST" or "last" for salesperson name. Control of processing is then passed to Module 1.1—Menu Display and Item Selection to permit further file processing.

**Module 1.2.2—List Records.** The instruction sequence in Module 1.2.2 causes all records on the SALESPER file (#1) to be read and listed (see interactive session). The file is OPENed for INPUT in statement 2210. A heading is displayed; then for each pass of a loop, a record is read (INPUT # at statement 2270), then displayed until the end-of-file (EOF) is reached. When the EOF is detected (2260), control of execution is returned to Module 1.2, the calling module.

# EXAMPLE PROGRAM #10

This program permits the creation or deletion of a sequential file and the addition or listing of salesperson records.

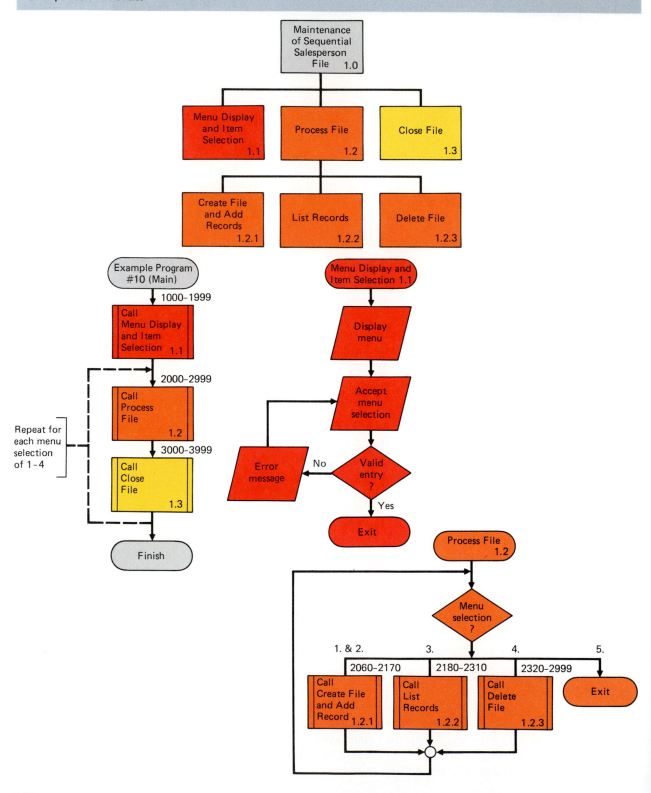

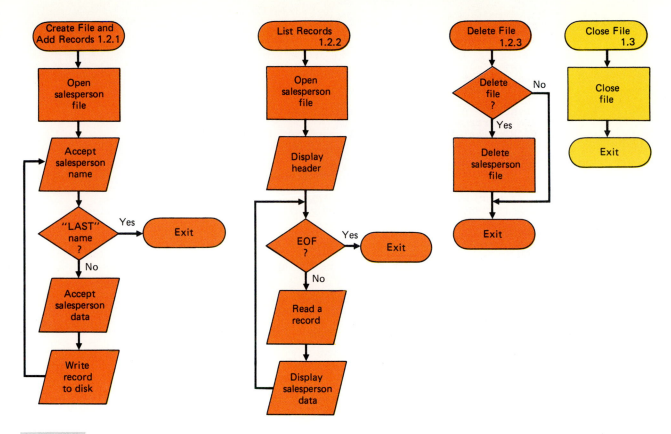

```
2      REM            **** Example Program #10 ****
4      REM   Description:
6      REM     This program permits the creation or deletion of a sequential
8      REM     file and the addition or listing of salesperson records.
10     REM   Variables list:
12     REM     SPNAME$                - Salesperson name
14     REM     S1, S2, S3             - Sales figures (Stibs, Farkles, Teglers)
16     REM     ID                     - Salesperson ID
18     REM     ANSWER$                - Y or N response to inquiry
20     REM     MENU                   - Menu item selected
99     REM
100    REM   <<<< Start Main >>>>
110    REM
120    WHILE MENU <> 5
130       REM  Call Module 1.1 - Menu Display and Item Selection
140       GOSUB 1000
150       CLS
160       REM  Call Module 1.2 - Process File
170       GOSUB 2000
180       REM  Call Module 1.3 - Close File
190       GOSUB 3000
200    WEND
210    END
220    REM  <<<< End Main >>>>
999    REM
1000   REM  ==== Module 1.1 - Menu Display and Item Selection
1010   REM  Display menu
1020   PRINT
1030   PRINT "      ****** Sequential Salesperson File Program ******"
1040   PRINT
1050   PRINT "              1. Create salesperson data file"
1060   PRINT "              2. Add salesperson records"
1070   PRINT "              3. List salesperson records"
1080   PRINT "              4. Delete salesperson data file"
1090   PRINT "              5. Exit Program"
```

continued

```
1100 PRINT
1110 REM   Accept menu selection
1120 INPUT "Make a selection from the menu: ",MENU
1130 PRINT
1140 IF MENU > 0 AND MENU < 6 THEN RETURN
1150 REM   Error message
1160 PRINT "That was not a valid response. Try again."
1170 PRINT
1999 GOTO 1120
2000 REM   ==== Module 1.2 - Process File
2010 IF MENU = 1 OR MENU = 2 THEN GOSUB 2060 'Call Module 1.2.1 - Create File
        and Add Records
2020    IF MENU = 3 THEN GOSUB 2180 'Call Module 1.2.2 - List Records
2030      IF MENU = 4 THEN GOSUB 2320 'Call Module 1.2.3 - Delete File
2040        IF MENU = 5 THEN RETURN
2050 RETURN
2060 REM   ==== Module 1.2.1 - Create File and Add Records
2070 REM
2080 REM   Open salesperson data file for appending records
2090 OPEN "SALESPER" FOR APPEND AS #1
2100 PRINT
2110 INPUT "Salesperson name (Enter LAST when complete): ",SPNAME$
2120 IF SPNAME$ = "LAST" OR SPNAME$ = "last" THEN RETURN
2130 INPUT "Salesperson ID: ",ID
2140 PRINT "Enter gross sales for Stibs, Farkles, and Teglers"
2150 INPUT "  (separate by commas): ", S1, S2, S3
2160 WRITE #1,SPNAME$, ID, S1, S2, S3
2170 GOTO 2100
2180 REM   ==== Module 1.2.2 - List Records
2190 REM
2200 REM   Open salesperson data file for input
2210 OPEN "SALESPER" FOR INPUT AS #1
2220 PRINT
2230 PRINT "Salesperson"; TAB(24);"ID"; TAB(33);"Stibs"; TAB(44);"Farkles";
2240 PRINT TAB(55);"Teglers"
2250 PRINT
2260 WHILE NOT EOF(1)
2270 INPUT #1, SPNAME$, ID, S1, S2, S3
2280 PRINT SPNAME$; TAB(22);ID; TAB(32);S1; TAB(43);S2; TAB(54);S3
2290 WEND
2300 PRINT
2310 RETURN
2320 REM   ==== Module 1.2.3 - Delete File
2330 PRINT
2340 INPUT "Do you wish to delete the file? (Enter Y or N) ",ANSWER$
2350 IF ANSWER$ <> "Y" AND ANSWER$ <> "y" THEN 2370
2360 KILL "SALESPER"
2999 RETURN
3000 REM   ==== Module 1.3 - Close File
3010 CLOSE #1
3999 RETURN
```

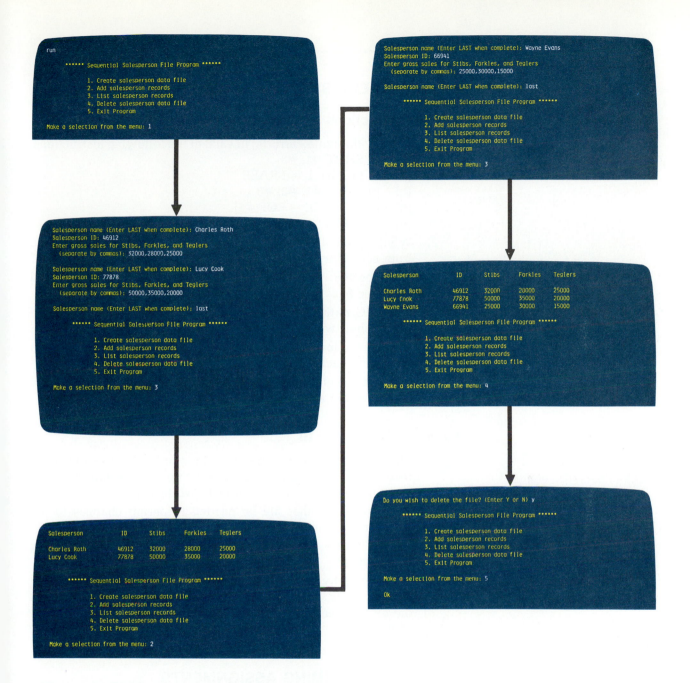

```
run

      ****** Sequential Salesperson File Program ******

            1. Create salesperson data file
            2. Add salesperson records
            3. List salesperson records
            4. Delete salesperson data file
            5. Exit Program

Make a selection from the menu: 1
```

```
Salesperson name (Enter LAST when complete): Charles Roth
Salesperson ID: 46912
Enter gross sales for Stibs, Farkles, and Teglers
  (separate by commas): 32000,28000,25000

Salesperson name (Enter LAST when complete): Lucy Cook
Salesperson ID: 77878
Enter gross sales for Stibs, Farkles, and Teglers
  (separate by commas): 50000,35000,20000

Salesperson name (Enter LAST when complete): last

      ****** Sequential Salesperson File Program ******

            1. Create salesperson data file
            2. Add salesperson records
            3. List salesperson records
            4. Delete salesperson data file
            5. Exit Program

Make a selection from the menu: 3
```

```
Salesperson name (Enter LAST when complete): Wayne Evans
Salesperson ID: 66941
Enter gross sales for Stibs, Farkles, and Teglers
  (separate by commas): 25000,30000,15000

Salesperson name (Enter LAST when complete): last

      ****** Sequential Salesperson File Program ******

            1. Create salesperson data file
            2. Add salesperson records
            3. List salesperson records
            4. Delete salesperson data file
            5. Exit Program

Make a selection from the menu: 3
```

```
Salesperson          ID       Stibs      Farkles    Teglers

Charles Roth         46912    32000      20000      25000
Lucy Cook            77878    50000      35000      20000
Wayne Evans          66941    25000      30000      15000

      ****** Sequential Salesperson File Program ******

            1. Create salesperson data file
            2. Add salesperson records
            3. List salesperson records
            4. Delete salesperson data file
            5. Exit Program

Make a selection from the menu: 4
```

```
Salesperson          ID       Stibs      Farkles    Teglers

Charles Roth         46912    32000      28000      25000
Lucy Cook            77878    50000      35000      20000

      ****** Sequential Salesperson File Program ******

            1. Create salesperson data file
            2. Add salesperson records
            3. List salesperson records
            4. Delete salesperson data file
            5. Exit Program

Make a selection from the menu: 2
```

```
Do you wish to delete the file? (Enter Y or N) y

      ****** Sequential Salesperson File Program ******

            1. Create salesperson data file
            2. Add salesperson records
            3. List salesperson records
            4. Delete salesperson data file
            5. Exit Program

Make a selection from the menu: 5

Ok
```

**Module 1.2.3—Delete File.**  The execution of this module results in the SALESPER file being deleted from disk storage. The KILL instruction (2360) performs the delete operation. It is good programming practice to force a user to make two separate requests before deleting an entire file. In Example Program #10, the user must select menu item 4 *and* enter an affirmative answer to a follow-up request (see interactive session) before the file is deleted.

**Module 1.3—Close File.**  The SALESPER file (#1) is CLOSEd in statement 3010. The file can now be reopened to service other user selections from the menu.

571

## REVIEW EXERCISES (LEARNING MODULE VII)

### BASIC Instructions and Concepts

1. Identify the syntax error(s) in each of the following instructions.
   (a)  10 SHUT #1, #3
   (b)  10 LET KILL = ERASE
   (c)  10 OPEN #1, #2, #3
   (d)  10 LET SIZE = EOF(#1)
   (e)  10 INPUT #3 A,B,C

2. What are the differences in the way program files are retrieved from secondary storage and the way data files are retrieved?

3. Describe the relationship between the key data element and a master file.

4. In BASIC, data are manipulated and retrieved from disk storage using what two types of processing?

5. Start at the lowest level of the hierarchy of data organization and name each level.

6. What is meant by a reference to the absolute location of a record within a file?

### Example Program #10

7. Module 1.2.1 is called when the file is to be created and when records are to be added to an existing file. Explain how the same instructions can accomplish two tasks.

8. Why would another file be needed to permit changes to the data for a particular record?

9. Why is it necessary to close a newly created file before listing the records?

10. Suppose that you selected menu item 1 and created a file with three records, then selected menu item 5. Suppose that you did exactly the same thing again. What would be the contents of the file?

## BASIC PROGRAMMING ASSIGNMENTS

1. The state highway patrol has asked you to write an interactive file processing program that would permit the creation of a sequential file of all licensed operators of vehicles. Each record would contain the following: an seven-digit operator ID (OPERATORID), the key; the full name of the operator (FULLNAME$); the street address (STREET$); the city (CITY$); the state (STATE$); and the zip (ZIP).

   Once the file has been created, permit the user to add records, list the records, or delete the entire file.

2. Modify the program above to add another user option. Permit the user of the program to select an option that would produce a report listing the operator ID and name of all licensed drivers in a particular city. The user would enter the name of the city (e.g., New Mayberry) and the following report would be produced.

Driver Summary—New Mayberry

============================

| OPERATOR ID | NAME |
|---|---|
| 5672978 | Mary Metler |
| 3497843 | Mark Bass |
| ⋮ | ⋮ |

# LEARNING MODULE VIII Graphics and Sound

<table>
<tr><td>
PROGRAMMING
CONCEPTS

Graphics
Pixels
Resolution
Screen Coordinates
Relative Coordinates
Bar Charts
Nassi-Shneiderman Charts
Sound
</td></tr>
</table>

## B-26 BASIC INSTRUCTIONS SET: LEARNING MODULE VIII GROUP_____

The BASIC instructions presented in this group let you present numeric results graphically, create elementary pictorial images, and output sound. It is important to reemphasize that the syntax of these more advanced BASIC instructions may vary considerably between versions of BASIC. Check the *BASIC Reference Manual* for your system for the exact instruction syntax and for other related instructions.

### Input/Output Instructions

LINE.    The LINE instruction causes a *line* or a *box* of specified dimensions to be drawn on the screen.

> **Format**:   LINE [$(x_1, y_1)$]—$(x_2, y_2)$ [,[color][,B[F]]]
>
> Where $x_1$, $y_1$, $x_2$, $y_2$ (the graphics coordinates)
> and "color" are numeric constants or expressions

*Examples*:

```
10    LINE (X1,Y1)—(X2,Y2)
20    LINE (20,20)—(280,20),1           'horizontal line of color 1
30    LINE (20,20)—(20,100),2           'vertical line of color 2
40    LINE (20,20)—(280,100),3          'diagonal line of color 3
50    LINE—(280,20),3                   'vertical line of color 3
60    LINE (10,10)—(290,110),2,B        'box of color 2
70    LINE (10,120)—(290,140),3,BF      'filled-in box of color 1
80    FOR X = 10 TO 250 STEP 40
90       LINE (X,150)—STEP(35,—35),2,B  'square boxes of color 2
100   NEXT X
```

*Pixels and Resolution*.   When doing programming in *graphics mode*, as opposed to *text mode*, you work with the screen as a *grid* of *picture elements*, or **pixels**. A pixel is a rectangular point on the screen to which light can be directed under program control. The number of pixels on the screen determines the **resolution** of the display. The resolution of a graphics display can vary from about 65,000 pixels for low-resolution screens to about 16 million pixels for very high-resolution screens.

*Coordinates*.   A particular pixel is identified by its coordinate location on the screen's grid. For our examples, we will assume a low-resolution screen with a 320 by 200 grid (see Figure B-16). That is, the grid is divided into 320 horizontal positions (across) and 200 vertical positions (up and down).

BASIC's graphics capabilities can be used to produce graphic images for a wide variety of business applications.
(Sperry Corporation)

574

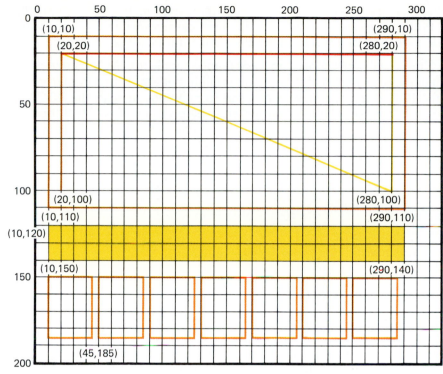

**FIGURE B-16**
**Graphics-Mode Grid and Layout**
The figure shows the output layout for the example LINE instructions in the text material.

A pixel coordinate is its horizontal and vertical position on the screen. The horizontal, or *x*, coordinate is first and the vertical, or *y*, coordinate is second. The coordinates of the *origin* of the grid, the upper left corner of the screen, are 0,0. On some systems the origin is the lower left corner of the screen.

*Creating Lines and Boxes.* The coordinates in a LINE instruction specify the end points, or *range*, of a line or box. The range of a box is the coordinates of any two opposite corners. The lines and boxes resulting from example statements 20–70 above are illustrated in Figure B-16. Statements 20–40 cause horizontal, vertical, and diagonal lines to be drawn between the coordinates specified in the color specified: 1 = red, 2 = orange, and 3 = yellow. Statement 50 causes a line to be drawn from the current position of the cursor (280,100) to the coordinates specified (280,20). Since the *x* coordinate is unchanged, the result is a vertical line.

The "B" option at the end of the LINE statement at 60 causes a box to be drawn in the range specified (see Figure B-16). The "BF" option at the end of the LINE statement at 70 causes a box filled with color 1 to be drawn in the range specified (see Figure B-16).

*Relative Coordinates.* The concept of relative coordinates is illustrated in example statements 80–100. When coordinates are prefaced by STEP, the position depicted is *relative* to the last coordinate position referenced. In statement 90 above, the second endpoint is relative to the first; that is, it is always 35 positions to the right and 35 positions down (a negative *y* coordinate signifies down) from the first endpoint.

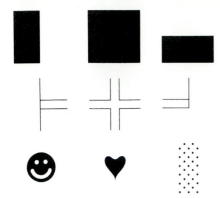

**FIGURE B-17**
**Example Special Characters**
Many special characters and symbols can be displayed by designating the decimal ASCII code in a PRINT CHR$() instruction.

For the first execution of the loop, the range of the box is (10,150)–(45,185). Repeated execution of the loop causes seven equal-size boxes of color 2 to be created along the horizontal (see Figure B-16).

PRINT.    We, of course, are very familiar with the PRINT instruction, but we have not used it to create graphic images. When in *text mode*, the PRINT instruction can be used in conjunction with the LOCATE instruction (see "Other Instructions" below) and the CHR$ function to produce any of a variety of special characters on the screen. The special characters associated with ASCII codes vary between computers. A few of the possible characters are illustrated in Figure B-17.

*Format*:   PRINT CHR$(ASCII code)

*Example*:   FOR I = 10 TO 60
                 LOCATE 20,I
                 PRINT CHR$(219)
             NEXT I

The loop above causes the ASCII character of decimal value 219 (■) to be displayed across row 20. The result is a thick solid line starting at column 10 and ending after column 60 (see explanation of LOCATE instruction). With a little imagination, you can be very creative with these special characters.

SOUND.    The SOUND statement generates a tone of a particular *frequency* and *duration*.

*Format*:   SOUND frequency, duration

*Example*:   LET FREQ = 440
             LET DURATION = 100
             SOUND FREQ, DURATION

A tone of 440 cycles per second (the A above middle C on a piano) is sounded for 100 time units. A time unit is a fraction of a second and could vary from one computer to the next.

INKEY$.    INKEY$ is both an instruction and a variable. INKEY$ accepts a single character from the keyboard into the variable INKEY$.

*Format*:   INKEY$

*Example*:   10 PRINT "Press any key to clear the graph and continue."
             20 IF INKEY$ = "" THEN 20

INKEY$ is automatically set to the null character ("") initially. Because INKEY$ = "", statement 20 above is itself a loop until a character is entered from the keyboard to give INKEY$ a value other than null. Upon encountering statement 20, the program enters an "infinite loop." This is a good way to pause processing or hold a graph on the screen until the user is ready to continue.

## Other Instructions

LOCATE. The LOCATE instruction positions the cursor on the *text-mode* screen at the display row and column specified.

> ***Format***:    LOCATE row, column

> ***Example***:   LOCATE 22,30

The LOCATE instruction deals with the rows and columns in which characters are displayed, not with pixels and coordinates, as in graphics mode. A typical screen has 24 or 25 rows and 80 columns. The LOCATE instruction positions the *text cursor*, as opposed to the *graphics cursor*, at one of the 24 or 25 rows (its vertical position) and one of the 80 columns (its horizontal position). The example LOCATE instruction positions the cursor at row 22 (from the top) and column 30 (from the left). Notice that the vertical designator (row) is first in the LOCATE instruction. In the LINE instruction, the horizontal designator (x coordinate) is first.

The LOCATE instruction is handy for displaying titles and labels on graphs that are produced in graphics mode.

SCREEN. A complete explanation of the SCREEN instruction is beyond the scope of this book. The SCREEN instruction statement sets a variety of screen attributes, including setting the computer to text or graphics mode. The fundamental use of the SCREEN instruction is illustrated in Example Program #11.

## B-27    EXAMPLE PROGRAM #11: GRAPHICS _____

Graphics adds another dimension to the presentation of data and information. The graphic images that you produce on the screen are not only visually stimulating, but they can convey information very effectively. It is much easier to detect trends and proportions from a bar or pie chart than it is from data that are in tabular form (rows and columns).

Graphics, however, is the most *machine-dependent* processing activity. What you can and cannot do depends very much on what kind of hardware you have. For example, most mainframe computers support graphics, but if you do not have a graphics workstation, you are limited in what you can do. To get graphics capability on some microcomputers, you may need to purchase an optional circuit board. Options for monitors include color and high resolution. Because there are so many hardware variables, the syntax for BASIC graphics instructions has evolved to using the capabilities of a particular hardware environment. This means that the BASIC graphics instructions vary a lot; therefore, we'll confine our discussion to fundamental graphics operations.

In Example Program #11, a *bar chart* is produced that graphically illustrates the sales averages for each of three sales managers. The average sales figure for any number of salespeople can be entered for each sales manager (see the interactive session). By now you are already familiar with the concepts illustrated in Modules 1.1—Initialization, 1.2—Accept Manager Data, and 1.3—Accept Salesperson Data, so we'll focus on Module 1.4—Draw Graph.

**Module 1.4—Draw Graph.**   This module calls six subroutines that process the data and draw the bar chart (see the interactive session).

**Module 1.4.1—Initialize Graphics Screen.**   The SCREEN instruction (4170) selects medium-resolution graphics as the processing mode. Other options are text mode and high-resolution graphics mode.

**Module 1.4.2—Draw Border.**   The LINE instruction at 4200 creates a box that serves as the border for the bar chart. The $x, y$ coordinates identify the range, which is any two opposite corners of the box.

**Module 1.4.3—Title and Axes Labels.**   The LOCATE instructions position the text cursor at a particular row and column. The title is printed beginning at row 1, column 4 (statement 4230–4240). The LOCATE/ PRINT combination is also used to display the labels for both axes.

**Module 1.4.4.—Tick Marks.**   In this module, tick marks are added to the $y$ axis at \$10,000 increments (every 15 pixels). It is sometimes necessary to make an adjustment to the value of the data to be graphed in order to make use of available screen space. The maximum allowable manager sales is \$100,000, but the bar is to be extended over 150 vertical coordinate positions (from 20 to 170, or 150 positions); therefore, a scaling factor of 0.0015 (150/100000) is used (statement 4420).

Eleven tick marks, which are actually short horizontal lines, are drawn on the $y$ axis in a FOR/NEXT loop (4430–4460). On the first pass through the loop, a line is drawn from coordinate positions 15,170 to 20,170 (bottom tick mark). On the next pass, a line is drawn from 15,155 to 20,155, and so on.

**Module 1.4.5—Calculate Averages.**   In this module, the average sales for the salespeople of each of three sales managers are calculated in nested FOR/NEXT loops. The outer loop (4500–4560) is repeated for each sales manager, or three times. The inner loop (4520–4540) is repeated a variable number of times, depending on the number of salespeople (NUMSALESP) under a particular manager. In the inner loop, a summation instruction (4530) calculates the sum of all sales figures for a particular manager. The manager average is calculated in the outer loop and stored in the array AVERAGE (4550).

# EXAMPLE PROGRAM #11

This program accepts salesperson sales data for three sales managers, then prepares and displays a bar chart showing averages for the salespeople of each sales manager.

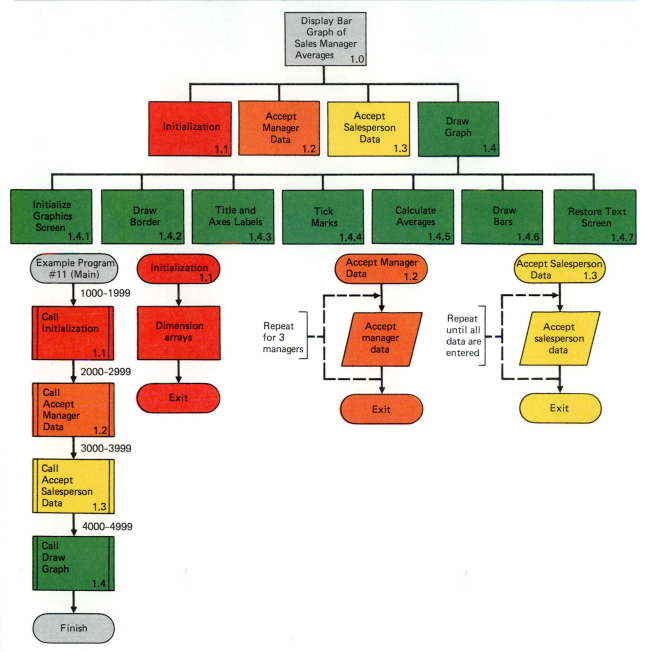

continued

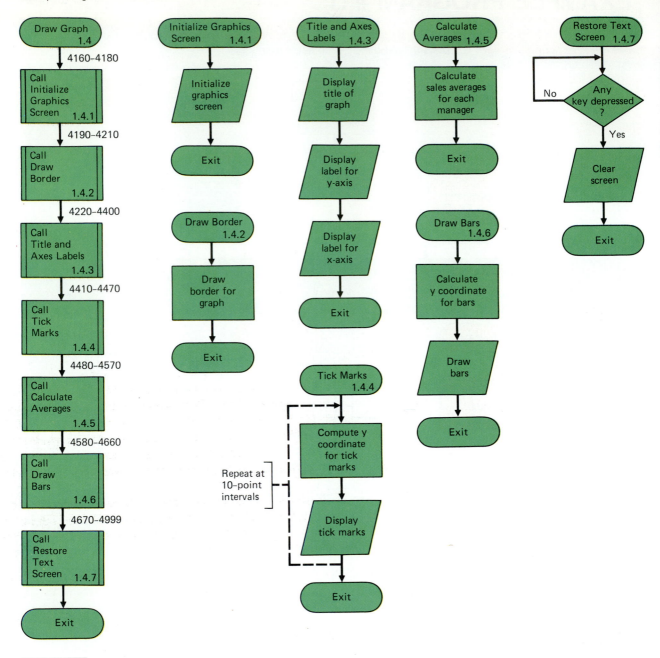

```
2    REM          **** Example Program #11 ****
4    REM   Description:
6    REM      This program accepts salesperson sales data for three sales
8    REM      managers, then prepares and displays a bar chart showing averages
10   REM      for the salespeople of each sales manager.
12   REM   Variables list:
14   REM      SALES( , )              - Sales array (manager,salesperson)
16   REM      MNAME$()                - Manager name array
18   REM      NUMSALESP()             - Number of salespeople under each manager
20   REM      AVERAGE()               - Array for sales averages
22   REM      COUNT                   - Index for loop control
24   REM      SALESP                  - Salesperson index
26   REM      MANAGER                 - Manager index
28   REM      YPOINT                  - Y coordinate of tick marks
30   REM      SCALE                   - Scaling factor
32   REM      Y1, Y2, Y3              - Y coordinates of upper-left corner of bars
```

```
99    REM
100   REM   <<<< Start Main >>>>
110   REM
120   REM   Call Module 1.1 - Initialization
130   GOSUB 1000
140   REM   Call Module 1.2 - Accept Manager Data
150   GOSUB 2000
160   REM   Call Module 1.3 - Accept Salesperson Data
170   GOSUB 3000
180   REM   Call Module 1.4 - Draw Graph
190   GOSUB 4000
200   END
210   REM   <<<< End Main >>>>
999   REM
1000  REM   ==== Module 1.1 - Initialization
1010  DIM SALES(3,50), MNAME$(3), NUMSALESP(3), AVERAGE(3)
1999  RETURN
2000  REM   ==== Module 1.2 - Accept Manager Data
2010  FOR COUNT = 1 TO 3
2020    PRINT "Enter last name of manager #";COUNT;": ";
2030    INPUT "", MNAME$(COUNT)
2040    INPUT "How many salespeople report to this manager";NUMSALESP(COUNT)
2050    PRINT
2060  NEXT COUNT
2070  INPUT "Enter name of sales region: ",REGION$
2080  PRINT
2999  RETURN
3000  REM   ==== Module 1.3 - Accept Salesperson Data
3010  FOR MANAGER = 1 TO 3
3020    PRINT
3030    PRINT "Enter sales figures for ";MNAME$(MANAGER);"'s salespeople."
3040    FOR SALESP = 1 TO NUMSALESP(MANAGER)
3050      PRINT "Enter sales for salesperson #";SALESP;": ";
3060      INPUT "", SALES(MANAGER,SALESP)
3070    NEXT SALESP
3080  NEXT MANAGER
3999  RETURN
4000  REM   ==== Module 1.4 - Draw Graph
4010  REM   Call Module 1.4.1 - Initialize Graphics Screen
4020  GOSUB 4160
4030  REM   Call Module 1.4.2 - Draw Border
4040  GOSUB 4190
4050  REM   Call Module 1.4.3 - Title and Axes Labels
4060  GOSUB 4220
4070  REM   Call Module 1.4.4 - Tick Marks
4080  GOSUB 4410
4090  REM   Call Module 1.4.5 - Calculate Averages
4100  GOSUB 4480
4110  REM   Call Module 1.4.6 - Draw Bars
4120  GOSUB 4580
4130  REM   Call Module 1.4.7 - Restore Text Screen
4140  GOSUB 4670
4150  RETURN
4160  REM   ==== Module 1.4.1 - Initialize Graphics Screen
4170  SCREEN 1   ' Medium resolution
4180  RETURN
4190  REM   ==== Module 1.4.2 - Draw Border
4200  LINE (20,20) - (299,170),3,B
4210  RETURN
4220  REM   ==== Module 1.4.3 - Title and Axes Labels
4230  LOCATE 1,4
4240  PRINT REGION$;" - Sales Manager Summary"
4250  LOCATE 5,1:PRINT "A"
4260  LOCATE 6,1:PRINT "v"
4270  LOCATE 7,1:PRINT "e"
4280  LOCATE 8,1:PRINT "r"
4290  LOCATE 9,1:PRINT "a"
4300  LOCATE 10,1:PRINT "g"
4310  LOCATE 11,1:PRINT "e"
4320  LOCATE 13,1:PRINT "S"
4330  LOCATE 14,1:PRINT "a"
4340  LOCATE 15,1:PRINT "l"
4350  LOCATE 16,1:PRINT "e"
4360  LOCATE 17,1:PRINT "s"
```

continued

```
4370 LOCATE 23,7:PRINT MNAME$(1);
4380 LOCATE 23,18:PRINT MNAME$(2);
4390 LOCATE 23,29:PRINT MNAME$(3);
4400 RETURN
4410 REM  ==== Module 1.4.4 - Tick Marks
4420 LET SCALE = .0015
4430 FOR G = 0 TO 100000! STEP 10000
4440    LET YPOINT = 170 - SCALE * G
4450    LINE (15,YPOINT) - (20,YPOINT)
4460 NEXT G
4470 RETURN
4480 REM  ==== Module 1.4.5 - Calculate Averages
4490 REM
4500 FOR MANAGER = 1 TO 3
4510    LET MANAGERSUM = 0
4520    FOR SALESP = 1 TO NUMSALESP(MANAGER)
4530       LET MANAGERSUM = MANAGERSUM + SALES(MANAGER,SALESP)
4540    NEXT SALESP
4550    LET AVERAGE(MANAGER) = MANAGERSUM / NUMSALESP(MANAGER)
4560 NEXT MANAGER
4570 RETURN
4580 REM  ==== Module 1.4.6 - Draw Bars
4590 REM  Calculate Y coordinates for bars
4600 LET Y1 = 170 - SCALE * AVERAGE(1)
4610 LET Y2 = 170 - SCALE * AVERAGE(2)
4620 LET Y3 = 170 - SCALE * AVERAGE(3)
4630 LINE (43,Y1) - (89,170),1,BF
4640 LINE (133,Y2) - (179,170),2,BF
4650 LINE (223,Y3) - (269,170),3,BF
4660 RETURN
4670 REM  ==== Module 1.4.7 - Restore Text Screen
4680 REM  Wait until a key is pressed to clear graph
4690 IF INKEY$ = "" THEN 4690
4700 CLS
4999 RETURN
```

```
run
Enter last name of manager # 1 : Shaw
How many salespeople report to this manager? 3

Enter last name of manager # 2 : Dow
How many salespeople report to this manager? 2

Enter last name of manager # 3 : Lee
How many salespeople report to this manager? 2

Enter name of sales region: Northern

Enter sales figures for Shaw's salespeople.
Enter sales for salesperson # 1 : 85000
Enter sales for salesperson # 2 : 105000
Enter sales for salesperson # 3 : 70000

Enter sales figures for Dow's salespeople.
Enter sales for salesperson # 1 : 75000
Enter sales for salesperson # 2 : 58000

Enter sales figures for Lee's salespeople.
Enter sales for salesperson # 1 : 88000
Enter sales for salesperson # 2 : 72000
```

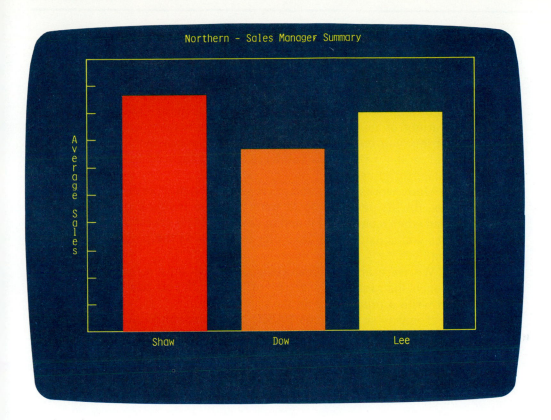

The **Nassi-Shneiderman chart** in Figure B-18 is provided to illustrate an alternative method for depicting the logic of the nested loop structures in Module 1.4.5. Compare the Nassi-Shneiderman chart of Figure B-18 with the flowchart for Module 1.4.5.

**Module 1.4.6—Draw Bars.**   Now for the fun part. All drawing and calculating thus far are done in preparation for this module. First, the $y$ coordinates, which designate the height of the bars, are determined (4600–4620). These values define the upper left corner of the boxes that create the bars. The opposite corner is to the right and on the $x$ axis. The LINE instructions (4630–4650) draw the boxes and fill them with three different colors (see the interactive session).

**Module 1.4.7—Restore Text Screen.**   The statement loop at 4690 causes the bar chart to stay on the screen until the user presses any key on the keyboard (see INKEY$ explanation in the instruction set for this module). The CLS at 4700 clears the screen in preparation for further text-mode processing.

## B-28   BUILDING ON A BASIC FOUNDATION

After studying and practicing BASIC, you should have acquired a solid foundation in BASIC and become a pretty good programmer. BASIC is a powerful and dynamic language, and we have covered only part of it.

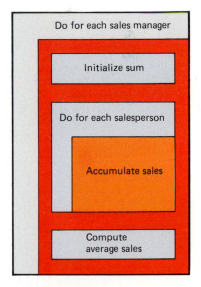

**FIGURE B-18**
**Nassi-Shneiderman Chart**
Nassi-Shneiderman charts are handy for depicting the logic of nested loop structures. This figure illustrates the logic of the loop structures in Module 1.4.5 of Example Program #11.

There are half again as many instructions that we did not cover. Depending on the version of BASIC you are using, you may have: instructions that permit input from light pens, joysticks, and the mouse; a family of instructions, called MAT instructions, that permit manipulation of matrices; a family of graphics instructions that lets you create a variety of images (e.g., ellipses) on the screen; an instruction set that lets you create and play music, and much more. You can even build on the instructions you have learned by investigating their more sophisticated uses.

Many workstations and micros have function keys, or "soft"(ware) keys. BASIC permits you to write program instructions that are activated when a particular function key (e.g., F1) is pressed. This capability gives you considerable flexibility in designing the program to be "user friendly."

We were able to illustrate and discuss only a few example uses of each instruction. As a rule of thumb: If you can imagine it, you can write a program to do it.

If you wish to pursue BASIC in greater depth on your own, you now have the background necessary to go directly to the *BASIC Reference Manual*. Each version of BASIC has such a guide. Several reference copies are usually made available for student use in the computer center or computer laboratory. Of course, if you have your own computer, chances are it comes with BASIC and a *BASIC Reference Manual*.

## REVIEW EXERCISES (Learning Module VIII)

### BASIC Instructions and Concepts

1. Identify the syntax error(s) in each of the following instructions.
   (a)   10 LINE (20,40)—(40,60)—(60,80)
   (b)   10 FOR I=1 TO 50: PRINT CHR$(0101010);: NEXT I
   (c)   10 LOCATE(24,270)
   (d)   10 SOUND 0, 85

2. Write the instructions that would draw a border around the screen that is 25 pixels wide and of color 2.

3. What is the relationship between pixels and screen resolution?

4. The following instructions create the "board" for what game?

   ```
   100 LINE (50,70)—(230,70)
   200 LINE (50,130)—(230,130)
   300 LINE (110,10)—(110,190)
   400 LINE (170,10)—(170,190)
   ```

5. What characters are displayed by the following instructions?

   ```
   100 FOR I=65 TO 90
   200 PRINT CHR$(I);
   300 NEXT I
   ```

6. What single instruction would hold a graph on the screen until the user entered a "C"?

## Example Program #11

7. Assume that the characters in the $y$-axis label (Average Sales) were individually defined in DATA statements in Module 1.1— Initialization.

   ```
   1020 DATA "A", "V", "E", "R", "A", "G", "E", " "
   1030 DATA "S", "A", "L", "E", "S"
   ```

   How would you modify the program to print the $y$-axis label with only one LOCATE instruction? Write the code that would replace statements 4250–4360.

8. What is the purpose of statement 4690?

9. What is accomplished in the inner loop in Module 1.4.5?

10. How would you modify the program to include numerical labels on the $y$-axis?

## BASIC PROGRAMMING ASSIGNMENTS _____

1. Repeat Programming Assignment 4 in Learning Module V, except this time use graphics capabilities to produce a more sophisticated bar chart. The bar chart should be tilted and have borders, labels for the axes, and solid horizontal bars to represent project schedules.

2. Write a program that permits the user to define the frequency and duration for each of three successive sounds. The user should select from these menu options: (a) listen to the sounds, (b) change the frequency and duration of the three sounds, and (c) exit the program. Give the sounds these initial frequencies and durations: 1800,2; 800,1; and 2500,3.

3. Use the SOUND instruction in conjunction with several loop structures to create a siren-type sound. Within a main loop, raise and lower the frequencies of the sounds such that when the main loop is executed repeatedly, the frequencies oscillate and the result is a siren-type sound. You may need to experiment with different frequencies and durations to get the sound you want.

# LEARNING MODULE IX

# The "New" ANS BASIC

Dr. Thomas Kurtz (left) and Dr. John Kemeny created the BASIC programming language over 20 years ago. Kurtz, Kemeny, and other computer scientists recently joined forces to create a modern version of BASIC. They call this version, which is based on the new BASIC standard, True BASIC. Example Program #12 in this learning module is written in True BASIC.
(True BASIC Inc.)

## B-29   A COMPARISON

An American National Standard (ANS) for Minimal BASIC was established in 1978. In 1985 a "new" standard for ANS BASIC was introduced. The original standard describes what is now a relatively primitive form of BASIC. Without any standards for the advanced BASIC features, over a hundred slightly different versions, or dialects, of BASIC evolved. As a result, a BASIC program written for one computer may need to be revised before it can be run on another computer.

The 1985 standard describes a modern BASIC. The existence of an up-to-date standard will encourage developers of future BASICs to conform to ANS BASIC. In a few years, we won't be so concerned about the differences between BASIC dialects. If you write a program using a BASIC that conforms to the new standard, the program will be mostly machine independent; that is, a single BASIC program can be run on a variety of different computers.

ANS BASIC is more an extension of the BASIC presented in this book than a revision. Most of the BASIC that you have learned to date is the same as, or very similar to, the new standard. The following points summarize the major differences.

1. The new standard contains sophisticated instructions that facilitate the development of structured programs.
2. The new standard discourages the use of statement numbers in favor of named subroutines. This, of course, makes the GOTO and GOSUB series of statements obsolete.
3. The new standard permits subroutines to be internal or external. External subroutines are defined, called, and stored as separate program units. In most current versions of BASIC, the subroutines are internal; that is, they are included in the same program as the main calling module.

The new standard also offers numerous enhancements to the individual instructions. New standards are defined for the precision of numeric constants and the maximum lengths of string constants. Graphics capabilities are substantially enhanced. There is greater flexibility in identifying variables, functions, subroutines, and so on. For example, all characters in an identifier are significant and the underscore (_) is a valid character (e.g., Average_ Sales).

## B-30   BASIC INSTRUCTION SET: LEARNING MODULE IX GROUP

Those ANS BASIC instructions that help facilitate the writing of structured programs are presented below. These instructions are especially formulated for the efficient handling of loop and decision structures (see Chapter 12, "Programming Concepts") and subroutines.

## Control Instructions

**DO/LOOP.**   The DO/LOOP permits both DO WHILE and DO UNTIL
loop structures.

*Format*:   DO WHILE expression  relational operator  expression
      statements
        ⋮
  LOOP

  DO
      statements
        ⋮
  LOOP UNTIL expression  relational operator  expression

*Examples*:   DO WHILE Count <= 50
      statements
        ⋮
  LOOP

  DO
      statements
        ⋮
  LOOP UNTIL Count > 50

The DO WHILE structure is similar to the WHILE/WEND instruction
pair introduced in Learning Module III: Adding to Your Foundation.
The LOOP UNTIL structure places the test-on-condition at the end of
the loop.

**SELECT CASE.**   The SELECT CASE permits you to define a series
of instruction blocks that are to be executed based on a test-on-condition. Each "case" is evaluated against the expression defined to the
right of SELECT CASE.

*Format*:   SELECT CASE expression
     CASE case-item
       statements
         ⋮
     CASE case-item
       statements
         ⋮
     CASE ELSE
       statements

     END SELECT

*Example*:  SELECT CASE Type_Employee$
              CASE "H"
                PRINT "Employee is hourly"
              CASE "C"
                PRINT "Employee is on commission"
              CASE ELSE
                PRINT "Employee is salaried"
            END SELECT

In the example above, the block (in this instance, only one instruction) following the first "case" is executed if Type_ Employee$ = "H". A block is executed only if a case test is positive. After the tests, processing continues after the END SELECT.

SUB/END SUB and CALL.   The SUB/END SUB instruction pair defines an internal subroutine. The subroutine is called by a CALL instruction.

*Format*:  SUB subroutine identifier
             statements
           END SUB
           CALL subroutine identifier

*Example*:  SUB Get_Message
              INPUT Message$
            END SUB
            SUB Display_Message
              PRINT "The message is: "; Message$
            END SUB
            REM----Main Program----
            CALL Get_Message
            CALL Display_Message
            END

The example above is a program unit with two internal subroutines and a main calling module (at bottom). *Processing skips over the subroutines and begins with the first CALL.*

## B-31  EXAMPLE PROGRAM #12: STRUCTURED PROGRAMMING WITHOUT GOSUBS AND LINE NUMBERS

Example Program #12 accomplishes the same processing activities as Example Program #5 in Learning Module IV. Both programs compute the total sales, commission, and assign a quota category for any number of sales people. Portions of Example Program #12 that illustrate instructions presented in Section B-30 are discussed below.

# EXAMPLE PROGRAM #12

This program computes the total sales and commission and assigns a quota category for any number of salespeople. The sales manager assigns a commission rate to each of three products and enters a dollar amount representing this month's sales quota. This program, which is functionally the same as Example Program #5, is written using True BASIC, an ANS BASIC.

Note: See Example Program #5 for the Structure Chart, Driver Module, Module Flowcharts, and Interactive Session.

```
!                  **** Example Program #12 ****
!   Descprription:
!     This program computes the total sales and commission and assigns
!     a quota category for any number of salespeople.  The sales manager
!     assigns a commission rate to each of three products and enters a
!     dollar amount representing this month's sales quota. This program,
!     which is functionally the same as Example Program #5, is
!     written using True BASIC, an ANS BASIC.
!   Variables list:
!     Below$, Satis$,
!     Outst$                - Quota categories
!     Spname$               - Salesperson name
!     C1, C2, C3            - Commission rates (Stibs, Farkles, Teglers)
!     Quota                 - Sales quota
!     Id                    - Salesperson ID
!     S1, S2, S3            - Sales figures (Stibs, Farkles, Teglers)
!     Total                 - Total sales
!     Commission            - Total commission earned
!     Percent               - Precent of quota achieved
!     Category$             - Quota category
!     Answer$               - Y or N response to inquiry
!     Format$               - String for PRINT USING statement
!
SUB Assign_Constants
!    Subroutine to assign quota category constants to variables
READ Below$,Satis$,Outst$
DATA "Below Quota","Satsifactory","Outstanding"
END SUB

SUB Accept_Commission_Rates_and_Quota
!    Subroutine for accepting commission rates and sales quota
PRINT "   ---------- Sales Summary Report ----------"
PRINT "Separate multiple entries by commas."
PRINT
PRINT "Enter commission rates (as a %)"
INPUT PROMPT "  for Stibs, Farkles, and Teglers: ":C1,C2,C3
LET C1 = C1/100
LET C2 = C2/100
LET C3 = C3/100
PRINT
INPUT PROMPT "Enter this month's sales quota (in dollars): ":Quota
END SUB

SUB Accept_Salesperson_Data
!    Subroutine for accepting individual salesperson data
PRINT
INPUT PROMPT "Salesperson name: ":Spname$
INPUT PROMPT "Salesperson ID: ":ID
PRINT "Enter gross sales for Stibs, Farkles, and Teglers"
INPUT PROMPT "  (separate by commas): ":S1,S2,S3
END SUB

SUB Sales_Computation_and_Quota_Assignment
!    Subroutine to compute commission and assign a quota category
!          for the salesperson
LET Total = S1 + S2 + S3
LET Commission = S1*C1 + S2*C2 + S3*C3
LET Percent = Total/Quota * 100
LET Percent = INT(Percent*100)/100
SELECT CASE Percent
   CASE 0 TO 99.99
      LET Category$=Below$
```

continued

```
      CASE 100 TO 130
         LET Category$=Satis$
      CASE ELSE
         LET Category$=Outst$
END SELECT
END SUB

SUB Display_Results
!    Subroutine to display salesperson information
LET Format$="<##########  ########    #######.##  #######.##   <##########"
PRINT
PRINT "Salesperson   ID Number   Total Sales  Commission  Quota Category"
PRINT USING Format$: Spname$,ID,Total,Commission,Category$
PRINT
END SUB

SUB Option_To_Repeat
!    Subroutine to ask if there are more salespeopl
INPUT PROMPT "More salespeople? (Y or N) " : Answer$
END SUB

!  <<<< Start Main >>>>
CALL Assign_Constants
CALL Accept_Commission_Rates_and_Quota
!  Do while there are more salespeople to be processed
DO WHILE Answer$ <> "N" AND Answer$ <> "n"
 CALL Accept_Salesperson_Data
 CALL Sales_Computation_and_Quota_Assignment
 CALL Display_Results
 CALL Option_To_Repeat
LOOP
END
```

**Driver Program.**   In ANS BASIC, subroutines must be defined before they are called; therefore, the Main program is placed at the end. Each salesperson is processed in a DO WHILE loop. The loop is repeated while Answer$ (to an option-to-repeat inquiry) equals anything but "N" or "n".

**SUB Compute_Commission.**   The SELECT CASE instruction is a natural for assigning quota categories. Each of the three "cases" is compared to Percent. In the first case, if Percent is between 0 and 99.99, inclusive, then Category$ is assigned Below$, or "Below Quota". If the test is false, then the block of instructions (only the LET in our example) following the first case is bypassed. Each case is tested against Percent in a similar manner.

**SUB Display_Results.**   Notice the Format$ for the PRINT USING instruction. Five format fields, both numeric and string, are defined in a single format string. The "<" in the first and last format fields causes the salesperson name and quota category to be left-justified when they are displayed.

**ANS BASIC Summary.**   Several ANS versions of BASIC were available even before the 1985 standard became official! But historically, widespread implementation of a new programming standard will take from three to five years. If history repeats itself, ANS BASIC will be the norm toward the end of the decade.

# REVIEW EXERCISES (LEARNING MODULE IX) _____

## BASIC Instructions and Concepts

1. Identify the syntax error(s) in each of the following.
   (a) DO UNTIL I=1 TO N
   (b) SELECT CASE Total
           CASE 0–1000
   (c) SUB Procedure Routine
2. What is the difference between an internal subroutine and an external subroutine?
3. What instructions permit you to define a series of instruction blocks that are to be executed based on a test-on-condition?

## Example Program #12

4. Why do you suppose the program does not have any line numbers?
5. Compare Example Program #5 and this program. Point out major differences between the two programs.
6. Rewrite the Sales_Computation_and_Quota_Assignment module and replace the usage of the SELECT CASE with an IF/THEN/ELSE series of instructions. The syntax for ANS IF/THEN/ELSE is similar to that of the IF/THEN/ELSE instruction presented in Learning Module II.

# BASIC PROGRAMMING ASSIGNMENTS _____

1. Do Programming Assignment 2 in Learning Module IV in ANS BASIC.
2. Do Programming Assignment 2 in Learning Module V in ANS BASIC.
3. Do Programming Assignment 4 in Learning Module V in ANS BASIC.
4. Do Programming Assignment 3 in Learning Module IV in ANS BASIC.

# GLOSSARY

**Access arm** The disk drive mechanism used to position the read/write heads over the appropriate track.

**Access time** The time interval between the instant a computer makes a request for a transfer of data from a secondary storage device and the instant this operation is completed.

**Accumulator** The computer register in which the result of an arithmetic or logic operation is formed.

**Acoustical coupler** A device in which a telephone handset is mounted for the purpose of transmitting data over telephone lines. Used with a modem.

**Ada** A multipurpose, procedure-oriented language.

**Address** (1) A name, numeral, or label that designates a particular location in primary or secondary storage. (2) A location identifier for terminals in a computer network.

**Alpha** A reference to the letters of the alphabet.

**Alphanumeric** Pertaining to a character set that contains letters, digits, punctuation, and special symbols (related to *alpha* and *numeric*).

**APL [A Programming Language]** An interactive symbolic programming language used primarily for mathematical applications.

**Application** A problem or task to which the computer can be applied.

**Application generators** Fifth generation of programming languages in which programmers specify, through an interactive dialog with the system, which processing tasks are to be performed.

**Applications software** Software that is designed and written for a specific personal, business, or processing task.

**Arithmetic and logic unit** That portion of the computer that performs arithmetic and logic operations (related to *accumulator*).

**Array** A programming concept that permits access to a list or table of values by the use of a single variable name.

**Artificial Intelligence [AI]** The ability of the computer to reason, to learn, to strive for self-improvement, and to simulate human sensory capabilities.

**ASCII** [American Standard Code for Information Interchange] An encoding system.

**Assembler language** A low-level symbolic language with an instruction set that is essentially one-to-one with machine language.

**Asynchronous transmission** Data transmission at irregular intervals that is synchronized with start/stop bits (contrast with *synchronous transmission*).

**Automatic teller machine** [ATM] An automated deposit/withdrawal device used in banking.

**Auxillary storage** Same as *secondary storage*.

**Back-end processor** A host-subordinate processor that handles administrative tasks associated with retrieval and manipulation of data (same as *data base machine*).

**Backup** Pertaining to equipment, procedures, or data bases that can be used to restart the system in the event of system failure.

**Backup file** Duplicate of an existing production file.

**Badge reader** An input device that reads data on badges and cards (related to *magnetic stripe*).

**Bar code** A graphic encoding technique in which vertical bars of varying widths are used to represent data.

**BASIC** A multipurpose programming language that is popular on small computer systems.

**Batch processing** A technique in which transactions and/or jobs are collected into groups (batched) and processed together.

**Binary notation** Using the binary (base two) numbering system (0, 1) for internal representation of alphanumeric data.

**Bit** A binary digit (0 or 1).

**Block** A group of data that is either read from or written to an I/O device in one operation.

**Blocking** Combining two or more records into one block.

**Boot** The procedure for loading the operating system to primary storage and readying a computer system for use.

**BPI** [Bytes per inch] A measure of data-recording density on secondary storage.

**Bug** A logic or syntax error in a program, a logic error in the design of a computer system, or a hardware fault.

**Byte** A group of adjacent bits configured to represent a character.

**C** A transportable programming language that can be used to develop both systems and applications software.

**CAD** [Computer-aided design] Use of computer graphics capabilities to aid in design, drafting, and documentation in product and manufacturing engineering.

**CAI** [Computer-assisted instruction] Use of the computer as an aid in the educational process.

**CAM** [Computer-aided manufacturing] A term coined to highlight the use of computers in the manufacturing process.

**Carrier, common** [in data communications] A company that furnishes data communications services to the general public.

**Cathode ray tube** *See CRT*.

**Cell** The intersection of a particular row and column in an electronic spreadsheet.

**Cell address** The location, column and row, of a cell in an electronic spreadsheet.

**Central processing unit** [CPU] Same as *processor*.

**Channel** The facility by which data are transmitted between locations in a computer network (e.g., workstation to host, host to printer).

**Character** A unit of alphanumeric datum.

**CIM** [Computer-integrated manufacturing] Using the computer at every stage of the manufacturing process, from the time a part is conceived until it is shipped.

**COBOL** [COmmon Business Oriented Language] A programming language used primarily for administrative information systems.

**Code** (1) The rules used to translate a bit configuration to alphanumeric characters. (2) The process of compiling computer instructions in the form of a computer program. (3) The actual computer program.

**Collate** To combine two or more files for processing.

**COM** [Computer Output Microfilm/Microfiche] A device that produces a microform image of a computer output on microfilm or microfiche.

**Common carrier** (in data communications) See *carrier*, *common*.

**Communications** See *data communications*.

**Compatibility** (1) Pertaining to the ability of one computer to execute programs of, access the data base of, and communicate with, another computer. (2) Pertaining to the ability of a particular hardware device to interface with a particular computer.

**Compile** To translate a high-level programming language, such as COBOL, to machine language in preparation for execution (compare with *interpreter*).

**Compiler** Systems software that performs the compilation process.

**Computer** Same as *processor*.

**Computer console** That unit of a computer system that allows operator and computer to communicate.

**Computer network** An integration of computer systems, workstations, and communications links.

**Computer system** A collective reference to all interconnected computing hardware, including processors, storage devices, input/output devices, and communications equipment.

**Computerese** A slang term that refers to the terms and phrases associated with computers and information processing.

**Concentrator** Same as *down-line processor*.

**Configuration** The computer and its peripheral devices.

**Contention** A line control procedure in which each workstation "contends" with other workstations for service by sending requests for service to the host processor.

**Contingency plan** A plan that details what to do in case an event drastically disrupts the operation of a computer center.

**Control clerk** A person who accounts for all input to and output from a computer center.

**Control field** Same as *key data element*.

**Control total** An accumulated number that is checked against a known value for the purpose of output control.

**Control unit** That portion of the processor that interprets program instructions.

**Conversion** The transition process from one system (manual or computer-based) to a computer-based information system.

**Cottage industry** People using computer technology to do work-for-profit from their homes.

**Counter** One or several programming instructions used to tally processing events.

**CRT** [Cathode Ray Tube] The video monitor component of a workstation.

**Cryptography** A communications crime-prevention technology that uses methods of data encryption and decryption to scramble codes sent over communications channels.

**Cursor** A blinking character that indicates the location of the next input on the display screen.

**Cyberphobia** The irrational fear of, and aversion to, computers.

**Cylinder** A disk storage concept. A cylinder is that portion of the disk that can be read in any given position of the access arm (contrast with *sector*).

**Daisy-wheel printer** A letter-quality serial printer, whose interchangeable character set is located on a spoked print wheel.

**DASD** [Direct-Access Storage Device] A random-access secondary storage device.

**Data** A representation of fact. raw material for information.

**Database** An alternative terminology for microcomputer-based data management software.

**Data base** An organization's data resource for all computer-based information processing in which the data are integrated and related such that data redundancy is minimized.

**Data base administrator** [DBA] The individual responsible for the physical and logical maintenance of the data base.

**Data base machine** See *back-end processor*.

**Data base management system** [DBMS] A systems software package for the creation, manipulation, and maintenance of the data base.

**Data base record** Related data that are read from, or written to, the data base as a unit.

**Data communications** The collection and/or distribution of data from and/or to a remote facility.

**Data communications specialist** A person who designs and implements computer networks.

**Data dictionary** A listing and description of all data elements in the data base.

**Data element** The smallest logical unit of data. Examples are employee number, first name, and price (same as *field*; compare with *data item*).

**Data entry** The transcription of source data into machine-readable format.

**Data entry operator** A person who uses key entry devices to transcribe data into a machine-readable format.

**Data flow diagram** [DFD] A design technique that permits documentation of a system or program at several levels of generality.

**Data item** The value of a data element (compare with *data element*).

**Data PBX** A computer that electronically connects computers and workstations for the purpose of data communication.

**Data processing** [DP] Using the computer to perform operations on data.

**Debug** To eliminate "bugs" in a program or system (related to *bug*).

**Decimal** The base-10 numbering system.

**Decision support system** [DSS] A sophisticated information system that uses available data, computer technology, models, and query languages to support the decision-making process.

**Decision table** A graphic technique used to illustrate possible occurrences and appropriate actions within a system.

**Decode** The reverse of the encoding process (contrast with *encode*).

**Density** The number of bytes per linear length of track of a recording media. Usually measured in bytes per inch (bpi) and applied to magnetic tapes and disks.

**Desktop computer** Any computer that can be placed conveniently on the top of a desk (e.g., *microcomputer*, *personal computer*).

**Diagnostic** The isolation and/or explanation of a program error.

**Digitize** To translate an image into a form that computers can interpret.

**Direct access** Same as *random access*.

**Direct-access file** Same as *random file*.

**Direct-access processing** Same as *random processing*.

**Direct-access storage device** See *DASD*.

**Director of information services** The person who has responsibility for computer and information systems activity in an organization.

**Disk, magnetic** A secondary storage medium for random-access data storage. Available as microdisk, diskette, disk cartridge, or disk pack.

**Disk drive** A magnetic storage device that records data on flat rotating disks (compare with *tape drive*).

**Diskette** A thin flexible disk for secondary random-access data storage (same as *floppy disk* and *flexible disk*).

**Distributed processing** Both a technological and an organizational concept based on the premise that information systems can be made more responsive to users by moving computer hardware and personnel physically closer to the people who use them.

**Distributed processor** The nucleus of a small computer system that is linked to the host computer and physically located in the functional area departments.

**Documentation** Permanent and continuously updated written and graphic descriptions of information systems and programs.

**Down-line processor** A computer that collects data from a number of low-speed devices, then transmits "concentrated" data over a single communications channel. Also called a multiplexor or concentrator.

**Download** The transmission of data from a mainframe computer to a workstation.

**Downtime** The time during which a computer system is not operational.

**Driver module** The program module that calls other subordinate program modules to be executed as they are needed.

**Dump** The duplication of the contents of a storage device to another storage device or to a printer.

**EBCDIC** [Extended Binary Coded Decimal Interchange Code] An encoding system.

**Education coordinator** The person who coordinates all computer-related educational activities within an organization.

**EFT** [Electronic Funds Transfer] A computer-based system allowing electronic transfer of money from one account to another.

**Electronic bulletin board** A computer-based "bulletin board" that permits external users access to the system via data communications for the purpose of reading and sending messages.

**Electronic funds transfer** See *EFT*.

**Electronic mail** A computer application whereby messages are transmitted via data communications to "electronic mailboxes." Also called E-mail.

**Electronic spreadsheet** See *spreadsheet*.

**Encode** To apply the rules of a code (contrast with *decode*).

**Encoding system** A system that permits alphanumeric characters to be coded in terms of bits.

**End user** The individual providing input to the computer or using computer output. Same as *user*.

**End-of-file** [EOF] **marker** A marker placed at the end of a sequential file.

**EPROM** Erasable PROM [programmable read-only memory] (related to *PROM*).

**Exception report** A report that has been filtered to highlight critical information.

**Expert system** An interactive computer-based system that responds to questions, asks for clarification, makes recommendations, and generally aids in the decision-making process (related to *knowledge base*).

**Feasibility study** A study performed to determine the economic and procedural feasibility of a proposed information system.

**Feedback loop**  In a process control environment, the output of the process being controlled is input to the system.

**Field**  Same as *data element*.

**File**  A collection of related records.

**Firmware**  "Hard-wired" logic for performing certain computer functions; built into a particular computer, often in the form of ROM or PROM.

**Flat files**  A traditional file structure in which records are related to no other files.

**Flexible disk**  Same as *diskette*.

**Floppy disk**  Same as *diskette*.

**Flowchart**  A diagram that illustrates data, information, and work flow via specialized symbols which, when connected by flow lines, portray the logic of a system or program.

**FORTRAN**  [FORmula TRANslator] A high-level programming language designed primarily for scientific applications.

**Front-end processor**  A processor used to offload certain data communications tasks from the host processor.

**Full-screen editing**  This word processing feature permits the user to move the cursor to any position in the document to insert or replace text.

**Gateway**  Software that permits computers of different design architectures to communicate with one another.

**General-purpose computer**  Those computer systems that are designed with the flexibility to do a variety of tasks, such as CAI, payroll processing, climate control, and so on (contrast with *special-purpose computer*).

**Gigabyte**  [G] Referring to one billion bytes of storage.

**Grandfather-father-son method**  A secondary storage backup procedure that results in the master file having two generations of backup.

**Hacker**  A computer enthusiast who uses the computer as a source of enjoyment.

**Handshaking**  The process of establishing a communications link between the source and destination.

**Hard copy**  A readable printed copy of computer output.

**Hardware**  The physical devices that comprise a computer system (contrast with *software*).

**Hashing**  A method of random access in which the address is arithmetically calculated from the key data element.

**Hexadecimal**  A base-16 numbering system that is used in information processing as a programmer convenience to condense binary output and make it more easily readable.

**High-level programming language**  A language with instructions that combine several machine-level instructions into one (compare with *machine language* or *low-level programming language*).

**HIPO**  [Hierarchical Plus Input-Processing-Output]  A design technique that encourages the top-down approach, dividing the system into easily manageable modules.

**Host processor**  The processor responsible for the overall control of a computer system. The host processor is the focal point of a communications-based system.

**Icons**  Pictographs that are used in place of words or phrases on screen displays.

**Idea processor**  A software productivity tool, also called an outliner, that allows the user to organize and document thoughts and ideas.

**Identifier**  A name used in computer programs to recall a value, an array, a program, or a function from storage.

**I/O**  [Input/Output] Input or output, or both.

**Index sequential-access method**  [ISAM] A direct-access data storage scheme that uses an index to locate and access data stored on magnetic disk.

**Information**  Data that have been collected and processed into a meaningful form.

**Information center**  A facility in

which computing resources are made available to various user groups.

**Information center specialist**  Someone who works with users in an information center.

**Information resource management**  [IRM] A concept advocating that information should be treated as a corporate resource.

**Information services department**  The organizational entity or entities that develop and maintain computer-based information systems.

**Information system**  A computer-based system that provides both data processing capability and information for managerial decision making (same as *management information system* and *MIS*).

**Input**  Data to be processed by a computer system.

**Inquiry**  An on-line request for information.

**Instruction**  A programming language statement that specifies a particular computer operation to be performed.

**Integrated software**  The integration of data management, electronic spreadsheet, graphics, word processing, and communications software.

**Intelligent**  Computer aided.

**Intelligent terminal**  A terminal with a build-in microprocessor.

**Interactive**  Pertaining to on-line and immediate communication between the end user and computer.

**Interblock gap**  [IBG] A physical space between record blocks on magnetic tapes.

**Interpreter**  Systems software that translates and executes each program instruction before translating and executing the next (compare with *compiler*).

**ISAM**  See indexed sequential access method.

**Job**  A unit of work for the computer system.

**K**  (1) An abbreviation for "kilo," meaning 1,000. (2) A computerese abbreviation for 2 to the 10th power or 1,024.

**Key data element**  The data element in a record that is used as an identifier for accessing, sorting, and collating records (same as *control field*).

**Keyboard**   A device used for key data entry.

**Knowledge base**   The foundation of a computer-based expert system (related to *expert system*).

**Layout**   A detailed output and/or input specification that graphically illustrates exactly where information should be placed/entered on a VDT display screen or placed on a printed output.

**Leased line**   A permanent or semipermanent communications channel leased through a common carrier.

**Lexicon**   The dictionary of words that can be interpreted by a particular natural language.

**Librarian**   A person who functions to catalogue, monitor, and control the distribution of disks, tapes, system documentation, and computer-related literature.

**Linkage editor**   An operating system program that assigns a primary storage address to each byte of an object program.

**Load**   To transfer programs or data from secondary to primary storage.

**Local area network**   [LAN or local net] A system of hardware, software, and communications channels that connects devices on the local premises.

**Loop**   A sequence of program instructions that are executed repeatedly until a particular condition is met.

**Low-level programming language**   A language comprised of the fundamental instruction set of a particular computer (compare with *high-level programming language*).

**Machine cycle**   The time it takes to retrieve, interpret, and execute a program instruction.

**Machine language**   The programming language in which a computer executes all programs, without regard to the language of the original code.

**Macro**   A sequence of frequently used operations or keystrokes that can be recalled and invoked to help

speed user interaction with microcomputer productivity software.

**Magnetic disk**   *See disk, magnetic.*

**Magnetic ink character recognition**   [MICR] A data entry technique used primarily in banking. Magnetic characters are imprinted on checks and deposits, then "scanned" to retrieve the data.

**Magnetic stripes**   A magnetic storage medium for low-volume storage of data on badges and cards (related to *badge reader*).

**Magnetic tape**   *See tape, magnetic.*

**Main memory**   Same as *primary storage*.

**Mainframe**   Same as *host processor*.

**Maintenance**   The ongoing process by which information systems (and software) are updated and enhanced to keep up with changing requirements.

**Management Information System**   [MIS] Same as *information system*.

**Master file**   The permanent source of data for a particular computer application area.

**Megabyte**   [M] Referring to one million bytes of primary or secondary storage capacity.

**Memory**   Same as *primary storage*.

**Menu**   A workstation display with a list of processing choices from which an end user may select.

**Message**   A series of bits sent from a workstation to a computer or vice versa.

**Methodology**   A set of standardized procedures, including technical methods, management techniques, and documentation, that provides the framework to accomplish a particular function (e.g., system development methodology).

**Micro/mainframe link**   Linking microcomputers and mainframes for the purpose of data communication.

**Microcomputer**   [or micro] A small computer.

**Microcomputer specialist**   A specialist in the use and application of microcomputer hardware and software.

**Microdisk**   A rigid $3\frac{1}{4}$- or $3\frac{1}{2}$-inch disk used for data storage.

**Microprocessor**   A computer on a single chip. The processing component of a microcomputer.

**Milestone**   A significant point in the development of a system or program.

**Minicomputer [or mini]**   Computers with slightly more power and capacity than a microcomputer.

**MIPS**   Millions of instructions per second.

**MIS**   [Management Information System] Same as *information system*.

**Mnemonics**   Symbols that represent instructions in assembler languages.

**Modem**   [Modulator-Demodulator] A device used to convert computer-compatible signals to signals suitable for transmission facilities and vice versa.

**Monitor**   A televisionlike display for soft copy output in a computer system.

**Motherboard**   A microcomputer circuit board that contains the microprocessor, electronic circuitry for handling such tasks as input/output signals from peripheral devices, and "memory chips."

**Multidrop**   The connection of more than one terminal to a single communications channel.

**Multiplexor**   Same as *down-line processor*.

**Multiprocessing**   Using two or more processors in the same computer system in the simultaneous execution of two or more programs.

**Multiprogramming**   Pertaining to the concurrent execution of two or more programs by a single computer.

**Natural language**   Sixth-generation language in which the programmer writes specifications without regard to instruction format or syntax.

**Nested loop**   A programming situation where at least one loop is entirely within another loop.

**Network, computer**   See *computer network*.

**Node**   An endpoint in a computer network.

**Numeric**   A reference to any of the digits 0–9 (compare with *alpha* and *alphanumeric*).

**Object program**   A machine-level program that results from the compilation of a source program.

**Octal**   A base-8 numbering system used in information processing as a programmer convenience to condense binary output and make it easier to read.

**Off-line**   Pertaining to data that are not accessible by, or hardware devices that are not connected to, a computer system (contrast with *on-line*).

**Office automation**   [OA] Pertaining collectively to those computer-based applications associated with general office work.

**Office automation specialist**   A person who specializes in the use and application of office automation hardware and software (see *office automation*).

**On-line**   Pertaining to data and/or hardware devices that are accessible to and under the control of a computer system (contrast with *off-line*).

**Operating system**   The software that controls the execution of all applications and systems software programs.

**Operator**   The person who performs those hardware-based activities necessary to keep information systems operational.

**Operator console**   The machine room operator's workstation.

**Optical character recognition**   [OCR] A data entry technique that permits original-source data entry. Coded symbols or characters are "scanned" to retrieve the data.

**Optical laser disk**   A read-only secondary storage medium that uses laser technology.

**Output**   Data transferred from primary storage to an output device.

**Packaged software**   Software that is generalized and "packaged" to be used, with little or no modification, in a variety of environments (compare with *proprietary software*).

**Page**   A program segment that is loaded to primary storage only if it is needed for execution (related to *virtual memory*).

**Parallel host processor**   A redundant host processor used for back-up and supplemental processing.

**Parity bit**   A bit appended to a bit configuration (byte) that is used to check the accuracy of data transmission from one hardware device to another (related to *parity checking* and *parity error*).

**Parity checking**   A built-in checking procedure in a computer system to help ensure that the transmission of data is complete and accurate (related to *parity bit* and *parity error*).

**Parity error**   Occurs when a bit is "dropped" in the transmission of data from one hardware device to another (related to *parity bit* and *parity checking*).

**Pascal**   A multipurpose procedure-oriented programming language.

**Password**   A word or phrase known only to the end user. When entered, it permits the end user to gain access to the system.

**Patch**   A modification to a program or information system.

**Peripheral equipment**   Any hardware device other than the processor.

**Personal computer**   [PC] Same as *microcomputer*.

**Personal computing**   A category of computer usage that includes individual uses of the computer for both domestic and business applications.

**PL/I**   A multipurpose procedure-oriented programming language.

**Plotter**   A device that produces hard copy graphic output.

**Point-of-sale [POS] terminal**   A cash-register-like terminal designed for key and/or scanner data entry.

**Polling**   A line control procedure in which each workstation is "polled" in rotation to determine whether a message is ready to be sent.

**Port**   An access point in a computer system that permits communication between the computer and a peripheral device.

**Post-implementation evaluation**   A critical examination of a computer-based system after it has been put into production.

**Primary storage**   The memory area in which all programs and data must reside before programs can be executed or data manipulated (same as *main memory*, *memory*, and *RAM*; compare with *secondary storage*).

**Printer**   A device used to prepare hard copy output.

**Private line**   A dedicated communications channel between any two points in a computer network.

**Problem-oriented language**   A high-level language whose instruction set is designed to address a specific problem (e.g., process control of machine tools, simulation).

**Procedure-oriented language**   A high-level language whose general-purpose instruction set can be used to model scientific and business procedures.

**Process control**   Using the computer to control an ongoing process in a continuous feedback loop.

**Processor**   The logical component of a computer system that interprets and executes program instructions [same as *computer*, *central processing unit* (*CPU*)].

**Program**   (1) Computer instructions structured and ordered in a manner that, when executed, cause a computer to perform a particular function. (2) The act of producing computer software (related to *software*).

**Programmer**   One who writes computer programs.

**Programmer/analyst**   A position title of one who performs both the programming and systems analysis function.

**Programming**   The act of writing a computer program.

**Programming language**   A language in which programmers communicate instructions to a computer.

**Project leader**   The person in charge of organizing the efforts of a project team.

**PROM**   [Programmable Read-Only Memory] ROM in which the user can load read-only programs and data.

**Prompt**   A program-generated message describing what should be entered by the end user operator at a workstation.

**Proprietary software** Vendor-developed software that is marketed to the public (related to *packaged software*).

**Protocols** Rules estabilshed to govern the way that data are transmitted in a computer network.

**Prototype system** A model of a full-scale system.

**Pseudocode** Nonexecutable program code used as an aid to develop and document structured programs.

**Pull-down menu** A menu that is superimposed in a window over whatever is currently being displayed on a monitor.

**Query language** A fourth-generation programming language with Englishlike commands used primarily for inquiry and reporting.

**RAM** [Random Access Memory] Same as *primary storage*.

**Random access** Direct access to records, regardless of their physical location on the storage medium (contrast with *sequential access*).

**Random file** A collection of records that can be processed randomly.

**Random processing** Processing of data and records randomly (same as *direct-access processing*; contrast with *sequential processing*).

**Read** The process by which a record or a portion of a record is accessed from the magnetic storage medium (tape or disk) of a secondary storage device and transferred to primary storage for processing (contrast with *write*).

**Read/write head** That component of a disk drive or tape drive that reads from and writes to its respective magnetic storage medium.

**Record** A collection of related data elements (e.g., an employee record).

**Register** A small, high-speed storage area in which data pertaining to the execution of a particular instruction are stored. Data stored in a specific register have a special meaning to the logic of the computer.

**Reserved word** A word that has a special meaning to a compiler or interpreter.

**Resolution** Referring to the number of addressable points on a monitor's screen. The greater the number of points, the higher the resolution.

**Response time** The elapsed time between when a data communications message is sent and a response is received (compare with *turnaround time*).

**Reusable code** Modules of programming code that can be called and used as needed.

**Reverse video** Characters on a video display terminal presented as black on a light background; used for highlighting.

**Robot** A computer-controlled manipulator capable of moving items through a variety of spacial motions.

**Robotics** The integration of computers and industrial robots.

**ROM** [Read-Only Memory] RAM that can only be read, not written to.

**RPG** A programming language in which the programmer communicates instructions interactively by entering appropriate specifications in prompting formats.

**Run** The continuous execution of one or more logically related programs (e.g., print payroll checks).

**Schema** A graphical representation of the logical structure of a CODASYL data base.

**Secondary storage** Permanent data storage on magnetic disk and tape (same as *auxillary storage*; compare with *primary storage*).

**Sector** A disk storage concept. A pie-shaped portion of a disk or diskette in which records are stored and subsequently retrieved (contrast with *cylinder*).

**Sequential access** Accessing records in the order in which they are stored (contrast with *random access*).

**Sequential files** Files that contain records that are ordered according to a key data element.

**Sequential processing** Processing of files that are ordered numerically or alphabetically by a key data element (contrast with *direct-access processing* or *random processing*).

**Set** A CODASYL data base concept that serves to define the relationship between two records.

**Smart card** A card or badge with an embedded microprocessor.

**Soft copy** Temporary output that can be interpreted visually as on a workstation monitor (contrast with *hard copy*).

**Software** The programs used to direct the functions of a computer system (contrast with *hardware*).

**Software package** Same as *proprietary software*.

**Sort** The rearrangement of data elements or records in an ordered sequence by a key data element.

**Source document** The original hard copy from which data are entered.

**Source program** The code of the original program (compare with *object program*).

**Special-purpose computer** Computers that are designed for a specific application, such as CAD, video games, robots (contrast with *general-purpose computer*).

**Spooling** The process by which output (or input) is loaded temporarily to secondary storage. It is then output (or input) as appropriate devices become avaiable.

**Spreadsheet** (electronic) Refers to software that permits users to work with rows and columns of data.

**Statement** Same as *instruction* (for a computer program).

**Structured programming** A design technique by which the logic of a program is addressed hierarchically in logical modules.

**Structured walkthrough** A peer evaluation procedure for programs and systems under development. It is used to minimize the possibility of something being overlooked or done incorrectly.

**Subroutine** A sequence of program instructions that are called and executed as needed.

**Supervisor** The operating system program that loads programs to primary storage as they are needed.

**Switched line**  A telephone line used as a regular data communications channel. Also called dial-up line.

**Synchronous transmission**  Terminals and/or computers transmit data at timed intervals (contrast with *asynchronous transmission*).

**Syntax error**  An invalid format for a program instruction.

**System development methodology**  Written standardized procedures that depict the activities in the systems development process and define individual and group responsibilities.

**System life cycle**  A reference to the four stages of a computer-based information system—birth, development, production, and death.

**Systems analysis**  The analysis, design, development, and implementation of computer-based information systems.

**Systems analyst**  A person who does systems analysis.

**Systems software**  Software that is independent of any specific applications area.

**Tape, magnetic**  A secondary storage medium for sequential data storage. Available as a reel or a cassette.

**Tape drive**  The secondary storage device that contains the read/write mechanism for magnetic tape.

**Task**  The basic unit of work for a processor.

**Technology transfer**  The application of existing technology to a current problem or situation.

**Telecommunications**  Communication between remote devices.

**Teleprocessing**  A term coined to represent the merging of telecommunications and data processing.

**Template**  A model of a particular application of an electronic spreadsheet.

**Terminal**  Any device capable of sending and/or receiving data over a communications channel.

**Throughput**  A measure of computer system efficiency; the rate at which work can be performed by a computer system.

**Timesharing**  Multiple end users sharing time on a single computer

system in an on-line environment.

**Top-down design**  An approach to system and program design that begins at the highest level of generalization; design strategies are then developed at successive levels of decreasing generalization, until the detailed specifications are achieved.

**Trace**  A procedure used to debug programs whereby all processing events are recorded and related to the steps in the program. The objective of a trace is to isolate program logic errors.

**Track, disk**  That portion of a magnetic disk face surface that can be accessed in any given setting of a single read/write head. Tracks are configured in concentric circles.

**Track, tape**  That portion of a magnetic tape that can be accessed by any one of the nine read/write heads. A track runs the length of the tape.

**Transaction**  A procedural event in a system that prompts manual or computer-based activity.

**Transaction file**  A file containing records of data activity (transactions); used to update the master file.

**Transaction-oriented processing**  Transactions are recorded and entered as they occur.

**Transcribe**  To convert source data to machine-readable format.

**Transmission rate**  The number of characters per second that can be transmitted to/from primary storage from/to a peripheral device.

**Transparent**  A reference to a procedure or activity that occurs automatically and does not have to be considered in the use or design of a program or an information system.

**Turnaround document**  A computer-produced output that is ultimately returned to a computer system as a machine-readable input.

**Turnaround time**  Elapsed time between the submission of a job and the distribution of the results.

**Uninterruptible power source** [UPS]  A buffer between an external power source and a computer system that supplies clean and continuous power.

**Universal product code** [UPC]  A 10-digit machine-readable bar code placed on consumer products.

**Upload**  The transmission of data from a workstation to the mainframe computer.

**User**  Same as *end user*.

**User friendly**  Pertaining to an on-line system that permits a person with relatively little experience to interact successfully with the system.

**User liaison**  A person who serves as the technical interface between the information services department and the user group.

**Utility program**  An often-used service routine (e.g., a program to sort records).

**Value added network** [VAN]  A specialized common carrier that "adds value" over and above the standard services of common carriers.

**Variable**  A primary storage location that can assume different numeric or alphanumeric values.

**Variable name**  An identifier in a program that represents the actual value of a storage location.

**VDT** [Video Display Terminal]  A terminal on which printed and graphic information is displayed on a televisionlike monitor and data are entered on a typewriterlike keyboard.

**Video display terminal**  See *VDT*.

**Videodisk**  A secondary storage medium that permits storage and random access to "video" or pictorial information.

**Videotext**  The merging of text and graphics in an interactive communications-based information network.

**Virtual machine**  The processing capabilities of one computer system created through software (and sometimes hardware) in a different computer system.

**Virtual memory**  The use of secondary storage devices and primary storage to effectively expand a computer system's primary storage.

**Walthrough, structured**  See *structured walkthrough*.

**Window** (1) A rectangular section of a display screen that is dedicated to a specific activity or application. (2) In integrated software, a "view" of a designated area of a worksheet, such as a spreadsheet or word processing text.

**Window panes** Simultaneous display of subareas of a particular window (*see window*).

**Word** For a given computer, an established number of bits that are handled as a unit.

**Word processing** Using the computer to enter, store, manipulate, and print text.

**Workstation** The hardware that permits interaction with a computer system, be it a mainframe or a multiuser micro. A VDT and a microcomputer can be workstations.

**Write** To record data on the output medium of a particular I/O device (e.g., tape, hard copy, workstation display; contrast to *read*).

**Zoom** An integrated software command that expands a window to fill the entire screen.

# INDEX

Note: When several page references are noted for a single entry, boldface denotes the page(s) on which the term is defined or discussed in some depth. Page references refer not only to the text material, but also to the photo captions and figure captions.

# BASIC INSTRUCTIONS

| FORMAT | DESCRIPTION |
|---|---|

## Input/Output Instructions

| FORMAT | DESCRIPTION |
|---|---|
| **CLOSE** [#filenumber[, #filenumber . . .]] | Signals the completion of input/output to a file. |
| **CLS** | Clears the display screen. |
| **GET** #filenumber[, record number] | Retrieves a record from a random file. |
| **INKEY$** | Accepts a single character from the keyboard into the variable INKEY$. |
| **INPUT** ["prompt";] list of variables | Accepts data from the keyboard. |
| **INPUT** #filenumber, list of data elements | Reads a record from a sequential file and assigns the data items to variable names. |
| **LINE** [$(x_1,y_1)$]—$(x_2,y_2)$ [,[color][,B[F]]]  where $x_1$, $y_1$, $x_2$, and $y_2$ are graphics coordinates | Displays a line or box of specified dimensions and color on the monitor. |
| **LINE INPUT** "prompt"; string variable | Accepts data into a single string variable. |
| **LPRINT** list of variables and/or expressions | Displays output line on a printer. |
| **LPRINT USING** format string; list of variables and/or expressions | Displays formatted output line on a printer. |
| **OPEN** filename$ [**FOR** mode] **AS** #filenumber [**LEN** = record length] | Permits input/output to a disk file. |
| **PLAY** string variable or constant | Plays musical notes as specified in a coded string value. |
| **PRINT** list of variables and/or expressions | Displays output line on the monitor. |
| **PRINT USING** format string; list of variables and/or expressions | Displays formatted output line on the monitor. |
| **SOUND** frequency, duration | Generates a tone of a specified frequency and duration. |
| **WRITE** #filenumber, list of data elements | Writes a record to a sequential file. |

## Data Transfer and Assignment Instructions

| FORMAT | DESCRIPTION |
|---|---|
| **LET** variable = variable or constant value | Assigns a value to variable (see also *Computation Instructions*). |
| **READ** list of variables  **DATA** constant values  **RESTORE** | Assigns the values in DATA statements to corresponding variables in READ statements; repositions pointer to first value in first DATA statement. |

## Computation Instructions

| FORMAT | DESCRIPTION |
|---|---|
| **LET** variable = expression | Performs computations (^, *, /, +, −). |

## Control Instructions

| FORMAT | DESCRIPTION |
|---|---|
| **END** | Terminates program execution. |
| **FOR** variable = initial value **TO** limit value [**STEP** increment value]  statements  **NEXT** [index variable] | Statements between FOR and NEXT are executed repeatedly a specified number of times. |
| **GOSUB** line number  subroutine statement  **RETURN** [line number] | Branches unconditionally to specified line number, then returns to the line following the GOSUB. |

# BASIC INSTRUCTIONS

## FORMAT                          DESCRIPTION

### Control Instructions

| FORMAT | DESCRIPTION |
|---|---|
| **GOTO** line number | Branches unconditionally to specified line. |
| **IF** expression relational operator expression **THEN** line number or executable instruction(s)   **ELSE** line number or executable instructions | If a condition is true, then a branch is taken to a specified line number or the instruction(s) following THEN is executed. If false, the ELSE clause is executed. |
| **ON** numeric expression **GOSUB** line number, line number, . . . | Branches to a specified line number based on the value of a numeric expression. Processing is returned to the statement following the ON GOSUB. |
| **ON** numeric expression **GOTO** line number, line number, . . . | Branch unconditionally to a specified line number based on the value of a numeric expression. |
| **WHILE** expression relational operator expression   statements | Statements between the WHILE and WEND are executed while the test-on-condition is true. |
| **WEND** | |

### Other Instructions

| FORMAT | DESCRIPTION |
|---|---|
| **DIM** list of array variables with subscript maximums | Specifies and allocates storage for array variables. |
| **KILL** filename$ | Deletes a file from disk storage. |
| **LOCATE** row, column | Positions cursor on text-mode screen at specified row and column. |
| **REM** remarks | Remarks for internal documentation (ignored by computer). |

### User-defined Functions

| FORMAT | DESCRIPTION |
|---|---|
| **DEF FN** function name (parameter list) = definition of function | Defines a function. |

### ANS BASIC Instruction

| FORMAT | DESCRIPTION |
|---|---|
| **DO**     statements<br>**LOOP UNTIL** expression relational operator expression<br>**DO WHILE** expression relational operator expression statements<br>**LOOP** | Permits both DOUNTIL and DOWHILE loop structures. |
| **SELECT CASE** expression<br>  **CASE** case-item<br>    statements<br>  **CASE** case-item<br>    statements<br>  **CASE ELSE**<br>**END SELECT** | Defines a series of instruction blocks to be executed based on a test-on-condition. |
| **SUB** subroutine identifier<br>    statements<br>**END SUB**<br>**CALL** subroutine identifier | The SUB/END SUB instruction pair defines an internal subroutine. The subroutine is called by a CALL instruction. |